THE VAN NOSTRAND SERIES IN SOCIOLOGY

Edited by
WILBERT E. MOORE

Professor of Sociology, Princeton University

MARTIN H. NEUMEYER—Social Problems and the Changing Society

M. BERGER, T. ABEL AND C. H. PAGE—Freedom and Control in Modern Society

MARTIN H. NEUMEYER—Juvenile Delinquency in Modern Society, 2nd Ed.

OLIVER M. BUTTERFIELD—Planning for Marriage

MELVIN J. VINCENT AND JACKSON MAYERS—New Foundations for Industrial Sociology

DON MARTINDALE—American Society

ROSE K. GOLDSEN, MORRIS ROSENBERG, ROBIN M. WILLIAMS, JR., AND EDWARD A. SUCHMAN—What College Students Think

CHARLES P. LOOMIS—Social Systems: Essays on Their Persistence and Change

CHARLES P. LOOMIS AND ZONA K. LOOMIS—Modern Social Theories

JACK P. GIBBS—Urban Research Methods

Additional titles will be listed and announced as published.

URBAN

Edited by
JACK P. GIBBS
The University of Texas
Austin, Texas

RESEARCH METHODS

D. VAN NOSTRAND COMPANY, INC.
PRINCETON, NEW JERSEY
TORONTO   LONDON
NEW YORK

D. VAN NOSTRAND COMPANY, INC.
120 Alexander St., Princeton, New Jersey (*Principal office*)
24 West 40 Street, New York 18, New York

D. VAN NOSTRAND COMPANY, LTD.
358, Kensington High Street, London, W. 14, England

D. VAN NOSTRAND COMPANY (Canada), LTD.
25 Hollinger Road, Toronto 16, Canada

Published simultaneously in Canada by
D. VAN NOSTRAND COMPANY (Canada), LTD.

PRINTED IN THE UNITED STATES OF AMERICA

PREFACE

Urban Research Methods comprises readings selected to acquaint beginning students with methods for the study of demographic and ecological aspects of cities and urbanization. As originally planned, the readings were to be a collection of papers devoted exclusively to research techniques and procedures. It was felt, in the early stages of preparation, that all methods could be explained to the novice without including reports of substantive research, but it soon became evident that this was not the case. The reasons why this is so are discussed in the introduction. It will suffice to say that where it was either not possible or not desirable to describe a particular method in universal terms (i.e., such that it could be applied without modification in the study of any city or any country), a report of substantive research has been included to provide an illustration of the method as applied to a special case. Such reports at least provide the beginning student with some basis for formulating research procedures suited to the conditions peculiar to his investigation.

Although some of the readings were written especially for this volume, most of them are reprinted from articles in professional journals. My gratitude to the authors and publishers for their permission to reprint these papers is very great.

This book represents one of a series of projects sponsored by International Urban Research (University of California, Berkeley) to further the investigation of cities and urbanization throughout the world. My indebtedness to IUR is very real indeed, since it made possible the allocation of time to the preparation of the manuscript. It also extends to the individual members of IUR's staff. Harley L. Browning and Richard L. Forstall offered many

v

86589

constructive suggestions; and comments on the manuscript by Kingsley Davis, Director of International Urban Research, were particularly helpful. Eleanor Langlois and Mrs. Barbara Ledger provided excellent research and secretarial assistance. To all of these persons I wish to record my appreciation for their invaluable help and, at the same time, free them from any responsibility for the shortcomings.

JACK P. GIBBS

The University of Texas
Austin, Texas
February, 1960

Table Of Contents

PREFACE   v

FOREWORD *by* Kingsley Davis   xi

INTRODUCTION   1

Part I: URBAN UNITS, THEIR NATURE AND BOUNDARIES

Introduction   14

CHAPTER 1: ILLUSTRATIONS OF THE PROBLEM OF URBAN BOUNDARIES   21

  A. "The Influence of the Definition of the Urban Place on the Size of the Urban Population" *by* Miloš Macura   21

  B. "Some Notes on the Concepts of 'City' and 'Agglomeration'" *by* G. Goudswaard   31

CHAPTER 2: SOME NATIONAL APPROACHES TO DELIMITING URBAN BOUNDARIES   41

  A. "The Delimitation of Urban Areas" *by* Olaf Boustedt   41

  B. "Urbanized Areas" *by* THE U.S. Bureau of the Census   45

  C. "The Growth and Study of Conurbations" *by* THE General Register Office   47

  D. "Standard Metropolitan Statistical Areas" *by* THE U.S. Bureau of the Census   53

CHAPTER 3: INTERNATIONAL METHODS OF DELIMITATION   57

  A. "Methods and Problems in the Delimitation of Urban Units" *by* Jack P. Gibbs   57

Part II: SOME BASIC CHARACTERISTICS OF URBAN UNITS

Introduction   80

CHAPTER 4: DEFINITIVE CHARACTERISTICS   86

A. "Measurement and Control of Population Densities" *by* WILLIAM H. LUDLOW   86

B. "A Method for Comparing the Spatial Shapes of Urban Units" *by* JACK P. GIBBS   99

CHAPTER 5: POPULATION GROWTH AND COMPOSITION   107
A. "The Measurement of Change in the Population Size of an Urban Unit" *by* JACK P. GIBBS   107
B. "Components of Population Change in Suburban and Central City Populations of Standard Metropolitan Areas: 1940 to 1950" *by* DONALD J. BOGUE AND EMERSON SEIM   114
C. "Methods for Describing the Age-Sex Structure of Cities" *by* HARLEY L. BROWNING   129

PART III: THE SPATIAL STRUCTURE OF URBAN UNITS
Introduction   142

CHAPTER 6: ON THE USE OF SPATIAL DIVISIONS FOR STATISTICAL PURPOSES   148
A. "The City Block as a Unit for Recording and Analyzing Urban Data" *by* EDWARD B. OLDS   148
B. "The Theory and Practice of Planning Census Tracts" *by* CALVIN F. SCHMID   166

CHAPTER 7: URBAN SUB-AREAS   176
A. "The Compatability of Alternative Approaches to the Delimitation of Urban Sub-Areas" *by* WILLIAM H. FORM *et al.*   176
B. "Delimiting the CBD" *by* RAYMOND E. MURPHY AND J. E. VANCE, JR.   187
C. "The Use of Local Facilities in a Metropolis" *by* DONALD L. FOLEY   220

CHAPTER 8: SPATIAL DISTRIBUTION   235
A. "Some Measures of the Spatial Distribution and Redistribution of Urban Phenomena" *by* JACK P. GIBBS   235

PART IV: URBAN HINTERLANDS AND FUNCTIONAL TYPES OF CITIES
Introduction   254

CHAPTER 9: FUNCTIONAL LINKAGE WITH SURROUNDING TERRITORY   263
A. "Urban Hinterlands in England and Wales: An Analysis of Bus Services" *by* F. H. W. GREEN   263

B. "Hinterland Boundaries of New York City and Boston in
    Southern New England" *by* HOWARD L. GREEN   286
C. "Differentiation in Metropolitan Areas" *by* LESLIE KISH   309

CHAPTER 10: URBAN UNITS AS FUNCTIONAL ENTITIES   329
A. "The Measurement of the Economic Base of the Metro-
    politan Area" *by* JOHN M. MATTILA AND WILBUR R.
    THOMPSON   329
B. "The Functions of New Zealand Towns" *by* L. L.
    POWNALL   349
C. "A Service Classification of American Cities" *by* HOWARD
    J. NELSON   353
D. "Economic Structural Interrelations of Metropolitan
    Regions" *by* WALTER ISARD AND ROBERT KAVESH   374

PART V: CHARACTERISTICS OF URBANIZATION
Introduction   392

CHAPTER 11: ON DEMOGRAPHIC ATTRIBUTES OF URBANIZATION   401
A. "Some Demographic Characteristics of Urbanization" *by*
    JACK P. GIBBS   401
B. "Conventional Versus Metropolitan Data in the Interna-
    tional Study of Urbanization" *by* JACK P. GIBBS AND
    KINGSLEY DAVIS   419

CHAPTER 12: SYSTEMS OF CITIES   436
A. "Some Measures of Demographic and Spatial Relation-
    ships Among Cities" *by* HARLEY L. BROWNING AND JACK
    P. GIBBS   436

PART VI: RURAL-URBAN DIFFERENCES
Introduction   462

CHAPTER 13: ON THE DISTINCTION BETWEEN RURAL AND URBAN   472
A. "On the Distinction Between Urban and Rural: National
    Practices and Recommendations" *by* THE UNITED NA-
    TIONS   472
B. "Community Size and the Rural-Urban Continuum" *by*
    OTIS DUDLEY DUNCAN   490

CHAPTER 14: RESEARCH ON SOME RURAL-URBAN CONTRASTS   505
A. "Traits of the Urban and Rural Populations of Latin
    America" *by* ANA CASIS AND KINGSLEY DAVIS   505
B. "Trends in Rural and Urban Fertility Rates" *by* T. J.
    WOOFTER, JR.   526

C. "Regional Comparisons Standardized for Urbanization"
    by OTIS DUDLEY DUNCAN   534

PART VII: RURAL-URBAN INTERRELATIONS
Introduction   542

CHAPTER 15:   URBAN INFLUENCE ON RURAL AREAS   550
    A. "Gradients of Urban Influence on the Rural Population"
        by OTIS DUDLEY DUNCAN   550
    B. "Note on Farm Tenancy and Urbanization" *by* OTIS
        DUDLEY DUNCAN   556

CHAPTER 16:   RURAL-URBAN MIGRATION   562
    A. "On the Estimation of Rural-Urban Migration" *by* JACK
        P. GIBBS   562

SUBJECT INDEX TO THE BIBLIOGRAPHY   577
BIBLIOGRAPHY   581
INDEX   623

FOREWORD: URBAN RESEARCH AND ITS SIGNIFICANCE

Urbanization is an extremely new phenomenon in human history, so recent that its rapid growth and full potentialities are not yet thoroughly understood or realized. The first small urban centers appeared only some five to six thousands years ago, a fact which demonstrates how recent were the faint beginnings in the long course of socio-cultural evolution. True urbanization, however, is much more recent than that. The earliest urban centers are called "cities" mainly by courtesy of the archeologists, for they had at the maximum only a few thousand inhabitants and would be barely classed as towns today. Even the later and larger cities of the ancient world—Memphis, Thebes, Babylon, Athens, Carthage, Rome—did not include more than a minute proportion of the total population inhabiting the region that supported them. They were mere urban islands in a vast sea of rurality. In fact, it has been only in the last century (the latest moment in history) that the urban population has come to comprise a substantial fraction of the inhabitants of a whole country, and only in the last few decades that the fraction has risen above fifty per cent in some countries. This increase in the proportion in cities is what we mean by urbanization, and its recency is greater than most people suppose.

Since most of us who read, write, and think about such matters live in a highly urbanized country or at least in one or another of the world's urban agglomerations, we tend to overlook the historical peculiarity of genuine urbanization. We take for granted the heavy concentration of people in cities without examining its underlying conditions or its revolutionary social impact. Yet a solid comprehension of the great transformation now taking place in human society requires that the process of urbanization, an essential part of the transformation, be thoroughly understood —especially since urbanization is now occurring on a scale and in a manner never before experienced.

The importance of cities has of course been abundantly recognized. But reflection on their nature and their effects has often been more moralistic than scientific, more offhand than rigorous.

The abundance of the moralistic and reformist urban literature attests both the newness and the significance of cities. Otherwise it is hard to understand the strength and the ambivalence of the emotions toward them. Often condemned as abnormal seed-beds of sin, scepticism, greed, crime, misery, filth, and congestion, cities have also been praised as sources of civilization and progress where innovation, science, education, art, and commerce thrive and diffuse to the rural hinterland. In either case, whether in condemnation or in praise, tribute is implicitly paid to the human significance of the city. Although a more detached point of view is emerging, the flow of reformist literature has not yet been matched by an equally voluminous scientific literature on cities. The tendency has been to blame cities, to decry and try to correct their evils, to plan the ideal city; or else to defend cities, to satirize their foibles, or to describe and perhaps eulogize the idiosyncrasies of particular cities. As one would expect, the task of learning what gives rise to cities in general, of seeing how they operate and what their trends are, has been undertaken less frequently.

By now, however, there is a substantial body of relatively impartial social science literature on cities—literature which has grown out of the effort to cope with practical problems. Since cities embrace in one way or another nearly everything in life, this literature is extremely diverse. It may deal with urban traffic or urban housing, with municipal government or finance, with fire protection or park maintenance, with juvenile delinquency or commercialized vice. It seeks, through systematic knowledge, to find ways of solving some of the difficulties, nuisances, dangers, and derelictions to which urban agglomerations supposedly give rise. The emphasis on problems is natural and necessary, because the close-packing of thousands and millions of people in small space inevitably creates conditions universally regarded as unfortunate. Some of these conditions, furthermore, are so new that there are no traditional modes of handling them. They can be dealt with only by taking thought, by investigating, by inventing new institutional arrangements. The use of social science under these conditions can only be commended.

THE NATURE OF URBAN RESEARCH

As one would expect, the now voluminous urban literature is overwhelmingly substantive. It deals with the history or ecology or government of particular cities, with municipal affairs in general or in a particular country, with rural-urban contrasts in demographic behavior or in social structure, etc. All of the social science textbooks on cities seem to be substantive in character, dealing with economic, political, or sociological aspects. However, scattered here and there in the mass of publications, are methodological pieces—articles or chapters which explain how scientific information on urban phenomena can be obtained and analyzed. The emergence of such technical material indicates a growing maturity in the science of cities. Since exact knowledge depends on exact methods, a systematic understanding of cities and urbanization can be achieved only when the approach to such understanding is self-consciously explicit and critical in regard to its research techniques.

The aim of the present volume is to fill a gap in the current array of urban textbooks by dealing purely with methods and techniques of scientific work in this field. It sets out to collect in one place, convenient for all who are concerned with cities in any professional or scholarly way, the most relevant writings on the ways of obtaining and utilizing basic data on cities. In addition, whenever it seems that a certain methodological problem can be handled better by a new treatment, an article written expressly for the present book is included. Approximately one-fifth of the material printed here has never been published before.

The assembly of these methodological contributions, including the writing of original articles and of introductions to the various sections, was done under the auspices of International

Population and Urban Research, (formerly International Urban Research), University of California, at Berkeley. Professor Jack P. Gibbs, who was on the staff of IPUR for two years prior to joining the faculty of the University of Texas, was in charge of this project. He had the assistance of other members of the staff, in particular Harley L. Browning, Richard Forstall, and Eleanor Langlois, as well as the present writer.

The ultimate purpose of our research office in sponsoring this work was to advance the study of urban problems as fast as possible. With urbanization proceeding at a rapid pace throughout the world, especially in the still relatively nonindustrial countries, with new forms and by-products of urban agglomeration emerging even in the older industrialized countries, there is an increasing need for urban research to help solve difficulties that have already arisen and to help forestall difficulties that may arise in the future. Our original intention was to utilize principally illustrations of method as applied in the less industrialized countries, on the ground that such countries will be experiencing the greatest need for increased urban research and yet will have the fewest experts trained in this field. As might have been anticipated, however, especially with editors primarily attuned to American and European scholarship, the most concise and up-to-date methodological contributions seem mainly to come from and to be applied in the industrially advanced countries. Actually, this circumstance represents no serious damage to our principal purpose, because the main thing is the quality of the contributions rather than the particular locale from which they come or to which they refer.

It should be made clear that the phrase "urban research" as used in the present book has a specific meaning which can be grasped only by realizing what it does not as well as what it does include. To begin with, it does not refer to research which happens to be done *in* cities. By their very character, cities are places within which virtually all aspects of life can be lived. There are consequently very few topics that cannot be studied in an urban milieu. Although something like "farm practices" could not conveniently be studied there, an array of other subjects could be, from divorce and prostitution to corporation management, leadership selection, juvenile delinquency, and religious belief. The truth is, however, that "the city," from a scientific point of view, is not a concrete entity. It is not Cincinnati, Bangkok, or New Delhi; it is not Liverpool, Lima, or Cebu. It is, rather, all of these places looked at from a particular point of view. What is relevant to this point of view is determined by the point of view itself, not by what is physically present or absent in such places. Thus, the fact that cities have people in them does not mean that this is a defining characteristic, for all countries have people in them too. Since something like juvenile delinquency can occur in cities or outside of them, it is not, in and of itself, an urban topic even when it is studied in a city. Any topic, to be relevant to urban science, must somehow be studied from the standpoint of how it affects or is affected by that set of variables, or factors, which we abstract out of total reality and call "the city." In a moment I shall try to make clear what these components are taken to be in the present work, but let us finish the list of excluded elements first.

Largely as a consequence of its criteria of relevance, but also for other reasons, the present book makes no attempt to cover the techniques of what has come to be called survey research. The reader will not find here any exposition of how to formulate questionnaires, how to interview people, how to take a sample of persons or households for interview, or how to code and tabulate the results. These topics are omitted, not because they are considered unimportant for social science in general (quite the contrary), but because they have no necessary connection with strictly urban questions. Survey research is applicable to a great variety of questions concerning human conduct and motivation, and it is thus not specific to urban problems or limited to the urban milieu. The techniques of survey research form an independent subject matter which has been well treated in separate manuals and textbooks.[1] Such techniques necessarily can be used *in* urban research, but they are not a distinguishing feature of that subject.

What, then do we consider to be peculiarly relevant, methodologically speaking, to urban research? The answer is complicated

[1] See, for example, Claire Selltiz *et al.*, *Research Methods in Social Relations* (New York: Henry Holt and Co., 1959); C. A. Moser, *Survey Methods in Social Investigation* (New York: The Macmillan Co., 1958); Herbert Hyman, *Survey Design and Analysis* (Glencoe, Ill.: The Free Press, 1955).

by the fact that, as in many other aspects of human science, there are two different levels being dealt with at once. Terms like "urban," "the city," and "urbanization" are used to refer, on the one hand, to certain physical and geographical features of human life, and, on the other hand, to social and attitudinal characteristics. Just how these two sides of urban reality are interrelated is an interesting scientific problem. Are cities in the physical sense, for example, conducive to "anomie," social heterogeneity, individualism, etc.? Unfortunately, there has been a tendency to try to settle this scientific problem by definition rather than by investigation. One of the most explicit instances is Louis Wirth's famous definition of a city as "a relatively large, dense, and permanent settlement of socially heterogeneous individuals." [2] Not only is such a definition indeterminate, since it does not say how "large" and "dense" the settlement must be or define the key term *settlement* itself (would all of Belgium be a city?), but it is also premature. It closes the question of how and to what degree, empirically speaking, social heterogeneity and density are related. The same tendency, in less explicit but in much more flagrant form, is found in the works of those who attempt to distinguish societal types and interpret social change in terms of the so-called folk-urban continuum.[3]

Our preference is to define the city in demographic and spatial terms. In this way a consistent conception can be stated which is not only close to usage but also leaves open the question of the socio-economic causes and consequences of urbanization. It furnishes, moreover, a fairly clear criterion of relevance for judging whether or not research methods fall into the category of urban research. Those techniques are relevant to our purpose which enable investigators to delimit the actual boundaries of cities, to determine the rate and sources of growth in the urban population

---

[2] "Urbanism as a Way of Life," *American Journal of Sociology*, Vol. 44 (July, 1938), p. 5.

[3] This particular dichotomy was popularized by Robert Redfield. See, for example, his article, "The Folk Society," *American Journal of Sociology*, Vol. 52 (January, 1947), pp. 293-308, and his book, *The Folk Culture of Yucatan* (Chicago: University of Chicago Press, 1941), esp. Ch. 12. His views have been widely discussed. One of the most penetrating criticisms was that of Oscar Lewis in *Life in a Mexican Village* (Urbana: University of Illinois Press, 1951) and a spirited defense was offered by Horace Miner in "The Folk-Urban Continuum," *American Sociological Review*, Vol. 17 (October, 1952), pp. 529-537.

and area, to study the changing structure of the urban population, to determine the functional or ecological subareas within the city, to examine the linkages between the city and its hinterland, and to analyze the interrelations between spatial and demographic change on the one hand and economic and social change on the other. The basis of selection will become clearer if we now set forth our definition more explicitly.

When we think of a town or city we ordinarily have in mind a sizable number of people, at least a thousand or more, permanently or durably settled together in a limited area and separated from other centers of close settlement by a much greater area of relatively open or thinly settled land. Obviously one of the factors involved is density of settlement, but this is not the sole factor. A hundred people may happen to live very close together, separated by open country from other dense settlements, but the place would ordinarily be called a "hamlet" or "village" rather than a town or city. To qualify as an urban place in the eyes of most observers, a settlement would have to embrace a more substantial population and a larger area. In other words, we implicitly recognize not only the factor of density (the ratio between population and the settled area) but also the absolute population and the absolute area. We think of a place as more urban the larger and more closely packed is its population. In the back of our minds, too, is some feeling for the sheer territory included: if the territory is too big to be contiguously and closely settled (like the entire state of New Jersey), it is not thought of as a single city; but if it meets the criteria of urban continuousness and density of settlement, the extent of territory becomes a factor in our assessment of the "size" of the city. Thus Reno, Nevada, having in 1950 a population of only 32,500, an area of only 7.0 square miles, and a resulting density of 4,642 persons per square mile, is felt to be less urban, less of a city, than Indianapolis, where the figures for the same date were 427,200 people, 55.2 square miles, and 7,739 persons per square mile.

Of course, as the absolute number of people living close together rises, the possibility of a majority practicing agriculture becomes remote. Although nearly everybody in a town of 10,000 could travel out to the fields and earn a living from cultivation, this is more difficult for people in a city of 100,000 and becomes out of the question in a place of 500,000 or more. Since land is the chief factor in agricultural production, this type of activity necessarily requires that people spread out over the land, either in scattered homesteads or in villages or small towns. Most other economic activities, however, use land simply as a site and can therefore facilitate the division of labor by close spatial proximity, thus giving rise to cities. Consequently, we normally think of city people as practicing "urban"—that is, nonagricultural—occupations.

Whether one includes the occupational element in a definition of the city is a matter of preference. The present writer prefers to exclude it from the theoretical definition, because he has an interest in the empirical question of the extent to which agriculture is actually practiced by people living in towns and cities and the extent to whch "urban" occupations are practiced by people living in the country. This sort of question tends to be shunted aside if a city is defined to begin with as a place where people are not farmers. There is some hazard, on the theoretical level, in using compound definitions which mix different universes of discourse. We can put so many elements into the definition of a city (e.g., sophistication, cultural heterogeneity, common government, feeling of community) that very few of what are actually called cities will qualify. Indeed, it is possible to construct an "ideal type" definition of a city—that is, a theoretical class having no actual representatives. The conception of a city in terms of people and space has the advantage of leaving open the question of the causes of concentration and deconcentration. It allows us to ask how social and economic conditions such as the occupational structure are in fact related to the spatial patterning of human settlement. Why is it, for example, that in the United States in 1950 less than one per cent of the employed labor force in urban places was engaged in agriculture, whereas in India in 1951 there were cities such as Patna and Shajahanpur with 11 to 17 per cent in agriculture? Why is it that even in rural areas in the United States in 1950 only 36 per cent of the employed labor force was in agriculture, whereas the percentage is 80 to 90 per cent in some underdeveloped countries?

Needless to say, the suitability of a definition depends upon the point of view. Cities can be studied and analyzed from any number of standpoints—governmental, economic, architectural, technological, etc. The present volume is primarily concerned with cities from an ecological and demographic point of view, and therefore defines them in this context. Operationally, governments and research workers are faced with the necessity of actually delimiting the boundaries of cities for over-all, or administrative, purposes. Accordingly, the criteria employed usually include information on one or more socio-economic indicators such as occupations, commuting, or utilities. Since the present volume deals with the need for and ways of obtaining practical information about cities, it frequently includes socio-economic criteria in the operational definition of urban units.

THE RISING NEED FOR URBAN RESEARCH

Our feeling is that the concentration of greater and greater proportions of people in urban aggregations is a process so fundamental that it necessarily has close connections with the whole economic and social order. To focus on the phenomenon of urbanization, on the ecological and demographic aspects of human spatial distribution, is therefore not to manifest a narrow interest but rather to pursue a sharply defined and highly important and ramified interest.

The implications of the continuing growth of urbanization in the world deserve careful consideration. They are not necessarily obvious, and when they are made clear they give some idea of the importance of the various research tasks described in the present book. For one thing, the most rapid rate of urbanization tends to occur when countries are in the early stages of industrialization. In the United States, for example, the fastest increase in the proportion living in cities occurred between 1830 and 1890; in England and Wales, between 1811 and 1851; and in Australia, between 1861 and 1891. Since most of the world's nations are currently still underdeveloped—that is, in the early stages of industrialization—the big rise in urbanization in the world as a whole is just commencing, despite the fact that the process long ago tapered off in the older industrial countries.

The future picture cannot be grasped fully, however, simply by pointing to the forthcoming rise in the *proportion* of the population urban. Even if the proportion did not rise at all, and certainly in some countries such as Britain where it may even decline, the *absolute size* of urban agglomerations will increase. The reason for this is to be found in the growth of the total population. If the urban proportion of the population remains constant, an inflation of the total population will mean an exactly corresponding increase in the urban population. Since the territory available to the population is fixed, as techniques of transport and communication improve a point is reached where the expansion of the urban population (still assuming its proportion to the total to be fixed) is not matched by a corresponding rise in the number of urban places. As a consequence, the absolute size of urban agglomerations expands almost as fast as the total urban population.

If both the proportion urban and the total population are rising, the absolute size of the metropolitan complexes will rise rapidly. Today this is the situation throughout most of the world, and it is likely to continue for some time. As is well known, the world's population is expanding at a dizzy pace unmatched in previous history. Projections made by the United Nations indicate that this pace may continue, or even be surpassed in the next forty years. Furthermore, the most rapid demographic increase is occurring, and will occur, in the countries in the early stages of industrialization where the rise in the proportion urban will be sharpest.[4] Consequently, we can expect that the number of great cities in the world will increase very rapidly, and that the absolute size of the largest of these will stagger the imagination. Already the New York agglomeration includes about 15 million people, who live at an average density of approximately 3,750 per square mile. Projections for India suggest that the largest city in that country may have between 36 and 66 million people

[4] For future estimates of population on a global basis, see United Nations, *Future Growth of World Population* (1958), *The Population of Asia and the Far East, 1950-1980* (1959), *The Population of South-East Asia, 1950-1980* (1958). For an analysis of the factors involved in the rising trend, see K. Davis, "The Unpredicted Pattern of Population Change," *Annals of the American Academy of Political and Social Science*, Vol. 305 (May, 1956), pp. 53-59; Philip M. Hauser, "Demographic Dimensions of World Politics," *Science*, Vol. 131 (June 3, 1960), pp. 1641-1647; K. Davis (ed.), *A Crowding Hemisphere: Population Change in the Americas*, Annals, Vol. 316 (March, 1958); Alfred Sauvy, *De Malthus à Mao Tsé Toung* (Paris: Denoël, 1958).

by the year 2,000, and the second city may have between 18 and 33 million.[5]

As the size of the total populations involved gets larger, the volume of internal migration entailed by the process of urbanization becomes enormous. In the case of India it is possible that there may be more than 150 million net migrants moving into cities of 20,000 or more during the period from 1950 to 2000.[6]

Clearly, the countries of the world seem destined to face urban problems which exceed in magnitude and variety those that have gone before. Even in the older industrial countries, where the urban proportion will cease to rise much, the growth in the sheer size of cities and the changes in their structure will occasion new difficulties; for instance, the outward spread of metropolitan areas arising from economic and technological gains, together with the by-products of high level of living, is causing traffic congestion, air pollution, agricultural retreat, water shortages, and waste of resources on a scale never envisioned by our ancestors. In the newly industrializing countries, the unprecedented rate of population growth, the fantastic rural overcrowding, the drastic steps necessary to bring economic development by forced-draft —all are bringing huge waves of rural-urban migration, millions of peasants landing in cities ill-equipped to handle them from an economic, sanitary, political, or any other point of view.

The speed of urban change and the relative recency of truly mass urbanization have left national and local governments without consistent policies for dealing with the resulting problems. At the moment, whether one looks at highly industrial or at agrarian regions, it appears that there is a growing awareness of urban problems but a great uncertainty as to the best methods of dealing with them. Although governments frequently express antipathy to the growth of cities, the whole process of urbanization is so massive and so intimately bound up with the coveted goal of economic development that it is probably impossible to stop. If

[5] K. Davis, "Urbanization in India: Past and Future," prepared for the Seminar on Urbanization in India, held at the University of California in Berkeley, June 26 to July 2, 1960. Mimeographed; to be published in the Proceedings of the conference by the University of California Press.

[6] *Ibid.* See also the writer's paper, "Internal Migration and Urbanization in Relation to Economic Development," in United Nations, *World Population Conference, 1954* (New York: United Nations, 1955), Vol. 2, pp. 783-801.

so, this means that the innumerable problems growing out of massive urbanization must somehow be solved without eliminating the basic cause which is urbanization or city growth itself. Yet, even on this piecemeal basis, policies as yet seem neither to be clear nor consistent.

Under the circumstances, scientific research in regard to urban phenomena is urgently needed. Such research cannot, of course, determine policy. It can, however, help to eliminate fatuous and wasteful measures and to suggest new alternatives; for it can bring into view a greater knowledge of the realities with which policies must deal. Not only an accurate grasp of current conditions, but a comprehension of the patterns of change and the factors responsible for the patterns, is necessary for the adoption of effective measures. Otherwise, the policies adopted tend to be mere reflections of anachronistic sentiments and pious wishful thinking. At their best, they tend to solve one problem while creating or exacerbating several others.

The present volume is an attempt to promote urban research around the world by dealing with some fundamental scientific questions concerning urban entities. It brings together expert discussions of the nature and logic of these questions, always from the standpoint of the research techniques required to answer the questions. The volume, as I have tried to make clear, does not encompass all aspects of urban phenomena, and above all it does not cover all kinds of research which could be conducted *in* cities. Instead, it has concentrated on those questions which most specifically concern cities and city-systems as demographic and ecological phenomena. Such considerations, we feel, are basic to all other contexts in which cities can be considered. If it stimulates more basic urban research, or if it improves the quality of either basic or applied research in this field, we shall feel that the venture (by no means an easy one) will have been worthwhile.

KINGSLEY DAVIS

University of California
Berkeley, California
November, 1960

INTRODUCTION

Despite the enormous growth of urban studies in this century, research methods for the analysis of cities and urbanization have developed in a rather haphazard way. On the whole, investigators have created methods appropriate to each particular situation, drawing on their own ingenuity, practical experience, and the techniques of other disciplines (demography, ecology, biology, sociology, and statistics, to mention a few). This procedure was necessary in the early stages of urban research, and it has worked fairly well up to now; however, a turning point appears to have been reached.

Future studies of cities and urbanization will be undertaken more and more by persons with little prior research experience. These persons, the beginning students, cannot be expected to create their own techniques or draw them from other disciplines, as professionals have done in the past; and they should have access to a systematic treatment of at least some of the fundamental research methods. These methods should not be set forth solely to stimulate a greater number of urban studies. The need is not so much for an increase in the volume of research but rather for investigations to move from a narrow provincialism to international and cross-cultural comparisons, for it is only in a comparative context of such a scope that our knowledge and explanations of urban phenomena may be judged adequate and valid.

With each decade witnessing greater opportunities for the study of cities and urbanization throughout the world, the possibility of achieving international and cross-cultural comparisons has become more and more real. But an increase in studies throughout the world will not alone achieve this level of compar-

1

ison. If the findings of studies in different countries are to be compared, they must be established by similar procedures, and this points to the necessity for the standardization of research methods. Such standardization is especially necessary in regard to the stimulation of research in underdeveloped countries, where cities and urbanization have been studied least of all. It is the beginning student in these countries who will especially profit by becoming familiar with research methods; but, unless the methods are standardized, the findings of his studies cannot be compared with those established in other countries, and this would defeat the essential purpose of research.

The above observations have led to the preparation of *Urban Research Methods,* which comprises a collection of readings intended to acquaint beginning students with methods for the investigation of cities and urbanization. It treats urban studies at two levels. Parts I-IV are concerned with research methods as they apply to individual cities. Beginning with Part V attention is shifted to the study of urbanization, wherein the cities of a country or region are considered together as the unit of observation.

PURPOSES

The desire to achieve a better understanding of cities and urbanization, as evidenced by the multiplication of investigations, raises two questions: How should the subjects be studied? and Where should they be studied? This volume is oriented toward these two inquiries.

With reference to the first question, it is clear that an adequate understanding of cities and urbanization, at least in a scientific sense, will not be achieved by simply increasing our knowledge of these phenomena. The ultimate goal of urban research is not an encyclopedic inventory of facts but rather a general and systematic theory which will enable us to explain why a particular city, or urbanization in a single country, has certain features and not others; and the adequacy of such a theory is judged by how well it applies to other cities and to urbanization in other countries. Comparisons among cities and countries are thus essential both in formulating explanations and evaluating their adequacy. But comparisons are meaningful only when they are based on scientific knowledge, and the findings of studies do not provide such knowledge unless they are systematic, verifiable, and additive.

With regard to the systematic quality of scientific knowledge, we should first note that there are a sufficient number of aspects of urbanization and cities to engage hundreds of investigations without any two of them considering the same subject. Clearly then, the first step toward scientific knowledge is selectivity in what will be studied, for it is only through the concentration of research on particular subjects that knowledge becomes additive. The most feasible way to secure this concentration is to direct the attention of the beginning student to certain features of cities and urbanization that call for further investigation, which is one of the purposes of this book.

The concentration of research on particular phenomena is of course only the first step toward scientific knowledge. For the findings of studies to be additive they must be systematic not only in that they relate to the same thing but also in that they can be compared (i.e., the difference between the findings of two or more studies can be assessed in objective terms). Consider, for example, the following statements as they might appear in research reports:

(1) The population of the city has increased enormously over the past few years.

(2) The average annual per cent increase of the population in the urban areas was 4.2 over the years 1949-1950.

(3) A large proportion of the total population of the country resides in cities.

(4) 52.5 per cent of the total population of the country resides in urban areas of over 5,000 inhabitants.

The first and third statements are all but useless as far as comparisons are concerned. This is so not only because they are couched in impressionistic terms and defy verification, but also because the term "city" is an inadequate identification of the units of observation. In contrast the second and fourth statements clearly indicate that the unit of observation is an urban area (which is different from either a political city or metropolitan area) and express a finding in quantitative terms, and thereby make verification and objective comparisons possible.

Reports of research and observations on cities and urbanization are replete with vague terms—socially heterogeneous, complex, extreme congestion, rational economy, uneven distribution of population, city dominance, technologically advanced, anonymity of social relations, marked spatial segregation, etc. These terms may convey a general meaning, but they are not suited for an objective description of the differences between individual cities or between urbanization in two countries. This is also true of maps and descriptions of cities and urbanization in terms familiar to the layman.

In the final analysis there is no satisfactory substitute in comparative urban research for a description of phenomena in quantitative terms. But quantitative description in itself is not enough. There are a variety of ways in which such descriptions can be achieved, and one essential element in the systematic quality of scientific activity is standardization. It is necessary, then, that the beginning student be encouraged not only to quantify his descriptions but also to use standard techniques for this purpose, so that the results of his studies can be readily and objectively compared with the findings of others.

Another consideration in relation to quantification is the nature of the units of observation. Characteristics of political cities in one country, urban areas in another, and metropolitan areas in still another should not be subjected to comparisons, regardless of the degree of quantification and standardization of techniques. These units are simply different entities, and their comparison is akin to grouping horses, camels, and cows. Progress in research is thus in part a matter of achieving a quantitative description of comparable units of observation, and this volume seeks to acquaint the students with methods to that end.

Up to this point we have considered the purpose of this book only with regard to how cities and urbanization should be studied. Let us now turn to the second orienting question: Where should they be studied? It might appear that the answer is obvious—anywhere and everywhere—but the question actually presents a complex problem in research strategy.

A consideration of this problem should begin with the recognition that extensive and systematic urban studies have on the whole, been restricted, to Europe, North America, and Oceania.

This limitation in the scope of research is far more serious than it might appear. For one thing, the countries in these three regions are highly urbanized and highly industrialized; consequently, our knowledge of urban phenomena is based on data that represent a biased global sample. Moreover, we have sufficient evidence to indicate that the characteristics of urbanization and cities in the other parts of the world—and especially the industrially underdeveloped countries—are different in several respects. On this basis alone there is ample reason to question the adequacy of existing theories, since their validity and limitations cannot be fully established without applying them to all parts of the world. Thus, the answer to the second question is given: cities and urbanization should be studied in the less industrialized countries and territories.

There are certain implications in this answer that warrant consideration. It is not proposed that a science of urbanization in unindustrialized countries be established, for such a notion is alien to the universal character of science and its subject matter. That the countries in question are unindustrialized is only secondary to the fact that they are the ones in which urbanization and cities have been least studied.

And what of urban research in the more urbanized countries? The answer to the question would suggest that it cease entirely. This is not intended, of course, as the research methods are aimed at all beginning students (which is another reason for not treating unindustrialized countries as though they constitute a unique universe of scientific inquiry). But it is suggested that both the novice and the professional researcher in highly urbanized societies shift the focus of their attention from the monotonous repetition of studies in their native countries to other parts of the world. There is already sufficient information to attempt comparative research on an international scale (for that matter, there are more studies of cities and urbanization in unindustrialized countries than is generally recognized), and there is likely to be a substantial increase in such information within a few years.

LIMITATIONS

There are several limitations of this book as far as furthering the cause of urban research is concerned, and most of them can be traced directly to its purposes. Concentration on standardized methods clearly limits the coverage in terms of the topics and types of empirical variables which are treated. Numerous urban phenomena do not currently lend themselves to systematic treatment, at least to the extent that it appears feasible to formulate universally applicable research methods.

This limitation in the coverage of *Urban Research Methods* has one ramification that is most undesirable. The danger is that the beginning student will select only those research problems that can be treated in terms of existing methods. Needless to say, such a course could lead to scientific sterility, and the novice should actually be encouraged to undertake problems that require him to formulate his own methods. Even here, however, the book may be of value in that it emphasizes objectivity and universal applicability as essential features of research methods.

Another limitation stems from the fact that it is intended primarily for persons with little experience in urban research. Accordingly, it was necessary to demand simplicity in the treatment of the various methods, in so far as this is possible, with the result that several papers on inherently complex subjects were not included. As a consequence, the professional researcher will find little here in the way of novelty, nor will he be likely to find methods that assist him in the analysis of the more complicated aspects of cities and urbanization.

The nature of the intended audience has also made it necessary to exercise a great deal of caution in selecting research methods to be treated. There are a number of techniques in urban research which produce valid results only under particular conditions, and judgments in this regard are difficult for the beginning student. Consequently, research methods that are prone to be misused by the inexperienced have been excluded from consideration. This applies particularly to techniques for making population estimates and projections. Some of these techniques are simple enough, but their use by the novice is likely to do more harm than good.

In view of the fact that this volume is intended particularly for the beginning student in unindustrialized countries, one might expect to find that it presents an elaborate program for research in those parts of the world. Such is not the case. The readings are not reports of studies in unindustrialized countries, and they are not meant to be models for research in any particular part of the world. Moreover, a review of urban studies in unindustrialized countries is not undertaken, and the *Bibliography* is not intended as a guide to the literature on the subject. Now all of this may appear to defeat one of the major purposes. However, the reader should not ignore one overriding consideration—the subject is standardized research methods for dealing with urban variables as universal phenomena and not the unique or particular properties of these variables in a special group of countries. To regard the subject in any other light would be the very negation of comparative research.

The task of providing the beginning student with uncomplicated and universally applicable research tools is a difficult one primarily because very few papers have been written on the subject of methods. On the whole the literature comprises reports of substantive research, in which methods are treated either incidentally or only in terms of a single country or locality. This is particularly true for studies of cities and urbanization in unindustrialized countries. In either case, the methods are not described in terms that make them universally applicable. Where no universally applicable method has been formulated, it has proven necessary to include readings in which research methods are stated in terms relative to particular cities and countries. This was done in the hope that the readings would provide the beginning student with at least a general idea of the type of method needed to treat the subject in question. For example, a paper dealing with the delimitation of an urban service area, or a metropolitan region, in a particular locality suggests what the research methods are intended to accomplish, even though they are stated in relative terms; and on this basis the student is in a better position to formulate his own approach to the problem.

The fact that several research methods are considered in relative rather than universal terms is not altogether undesirable. We should first note that there are only a few specific urban research procedures which can be recommended for universal application, since very little experimental work has been done to gauge the adequacy of existing methods under varying conditions. Moreover, in so far as research methods are stated in specific terms, they call for certain types of data that will rarely be available. As a consequence, one must be able to modify his methods to fit the types of data that are available. A description of the research procedure followed in a particular case is thus not without value, since it may illustrate modification of methods.

Perhaps the most serious limitation of this volume is the absence of an adequate treatment of theoretical considerations in urban studies. Research methods can be divorced from theory only in the abstract, and the dangers of such a separation are very real indeed. The beginning student must realize at the outset that scientific activity involves far more than the selection, or formulation, of an appropriate research method. We have already noted that scientific knowledge is additive in more than an encyclopedic sense; the accumulation of facts is oriented toward the goal of explanation, and the mastery of research methods is only a means to that end. More specifically, the description of the characteristics of cities and urbanization in objective and comparable terms is not to be undertaken for its own sake. We want to know why these characteristics vary from one place to another, and we also want to establish the consequences of this variability. Why are some cities much larger than others? What differences among cities can be traced to variation in their size? Why do countries differ sharply as to the per cent of the total population who are city residents? What influence does the concentration of the population in cities have on the level of fertility in a country? Such questions guide urban research, and the answers to them are anticipated, or at least should be, on a theoretical level, rather than determined through a blind trial and error research process.

A treatment of theory construction is not attempted here; however, the subject is not ignored entirely. Some attention is devoted to theoretical considerations in the introduction to each of the seven parts, but it extends neither to a review of past studies nor to a critical appraisal of existing hypotheses. The observations made on these subjects in the introductions are of a general nature, and they are intended only to give the beginning student a sense of direction in his investigations. In this regard, the fact that several of the readings are reports of substantive research is most desirable, since some of them provide a brief review of past studies and existing theories.

Not all the limitations of this book stem from its restricted purpose. A truly comprehensive treatment of the subject of urban research methods would embrace such diverse topics as the organization of research surveys, the use of standard statistical techniques, and the preparation of research reports. It would also extend to methods for the analysis of a wide variety of phenomena—social stratification, deviant behavior, voluntary associations, governmental institutions, to mention a few—in an urban setting. Such a comprehensive treatment would indeed be most desirable, but space limitations alone have made it impossible. Apart from considerations already mentioned, two general rules have governed the selection of topics to be covered:

(1) Consider only those topics that relate to essentially urban phenomena,

(2) Exclude from consideration those research methods that are treated in other monographs.

The first of these two rules is obviously not a very specific one, since all of the activities that are found in cities may in a sense be regarded as urban phenomena. This broad interpretation is not intended, however. The phenomena considered as essentially urban relate, for the most part, to variables that are explicit or implicit in definitions of cities and urbanization. This conception places emphasis on certain demographic and ecological features —the nature of urban boundaries, population size and density, shape and internal spatial structure, characteristics of cities as sustenance organizations, locational patterns, variation in the size of cities, the degree of urbanization—and change in these features. Concern with these morphological characteristics of cities and urbanization should not be interpreted to imply that other types of variables are unimportant. The broad range of phenomena designated as "urbanism" (i.e., the cultural, social, and psychological aspects of city life) is certainly a part of the subject matter of urban studies. Such phenomena are not treated here, however, because of space limitations and certain considerations regarding the best strategy for furthering urban research. It is felt that the mastery of methods for dealing with the basic demographic, ecological, and economic features of cities and urbanization is a necessary first step toward the analysis of social, cultural, and psychological aspects of urban life. Moreover, on the basis of the availability of research data alone, studies of these features are currently much more feasible and lend themselves more to international comparisons than is the case for investigations of other aspects of cities and urbanization.

The reader will find that one of the essential steps in research, the acquisition of data, receives only incidental treatment in this book. Most of the methods considered deal with the analysis of data and not the procedures by which data can be obtained. Certain types of urban research, particularly studies at the national level, must of necessity look to census reports and other publications of statistical gathering agencies as the only possible source of information. However, where data are not available in published form, they can be obtained only through a research survey; and a comprehensive treatment of research procedures would consider data gathering surveys as one of the methods of urban studies. Two considerations precluded treatment of the subject. First, an adequate treatment of the organization and execution of a research survey would call for a publication fully as long as this volume. And, secondly, in accordance with the general rules governing the selection of topics, the subject is excluded from consideration because it has already been treated in a number of prior publications.

What has been said of research surveys applies equally well to statistical and demographic techniques for the measurement of fertility and mortality. These techniques are frequently employed in urban research; however, since a vast number of publications provide the beginning student with an introduction to the subjects, they are not treated here.

Finally, a word should be said about the failure to consider urban planning and the governmental-administrative aspects of cities and urbanization. The failure is due not to a feeling that these subjects are unrelated to urban research but rather to the recognition that a number of recent publications provide a far better treatment of them than could have been accomplished in this book.

ADJUSTMENT TO THE LIMITATIONS

The limitations mentioned above make it necessary for the beginning student, in dealing with particular problems, to supplement this volume with other publications. The *Bibliography* and the *Index to the Bibliography* are intended to facilitate a search of the literature for treatments of particular problems. The *Index* is so organized that a number of references are provided for each of the topics not treated in the readings. For example, Sections 20, 21, 26, 16, 28, and 3 of the *Index* relate, respectively, to population estimates and projections, research surveys, statistical techniques, fertility and mortality rates, urban planning, and governmental-administrative aspects of cities and urbanization. Other sections pertain to particular types of urban variables (e.g., population growth in cities, functional types of cities, characteristics of urbanization), with the references encompassing theoretical considerations, reports of research, and further treatment of research methods. Publications that deal with subjects on a theoretical level are included to give the beginning student a sense of direction beyond that provided by this volume, and the reports of research offer further illustrations of the application of research methods.

As suggested earlier, the *Bibliography* is not intended as a guide to the literature on cities and urbanization in unindustrialized regions. Some of the references relate to the subject, but most of them pertain to studies in highly urbanized countries and the United States in particular. This is not altogether undesirable, however, since these studies set forth a variety of hypotheses that can be considered by persons studying unindustrialized countries; and tests of these hypotheses in those parts of the world would be a great step forward in comparative urban research.

PART I

URBAN UNITS, THEIR NATURE
AND BOUNDARIES

Introduction to Part I

Any analysis of urban phenomena must in one way or another come to grips with the problems of defining and delimiting cities. This concern goes beyond merely being systematic, that is, beyond a rigorous identification of the units of observation; for there is every reason to believe that the conclusions one reaches in an urban study depend, at least in part, on the way cities are defined and the methods used to establish their boundaries.

Part I is devoted exclusively to the problem of defining these units and demarcating their limits. Seven papers which bear directly on methods of delimitation are presented. Their contents will be described after consideration has been given to the definition of urban units, a problem which is logically prior to that of delimitation.

The definition of urban units. With increasing experience has come recognition that no single definition of a city is suitable for all research purposes. Rather than contribute to an endless debate on the subject, as so many have done in the past, it is more realistic to grant that there are numerous ways of viewing cities, all of which are relevant to urban research taken as a whole. We can define cities in terms of political status, demographic attributes (size and/or density), economic variables (the prevalence of nonagricultural occupations), socio-cultural patterns of behavior independent of sustenance activities, and even psychological characteristics. To be sure, some of the definitions pose particular problems (e.g., a vagueness in terminology), but none of them is intrinsically either "right" or "wrong."

The definitive attributes of cities applied in a study should be closely geared to the theory being pursued and the nature of the research derived from it. If the concern is with types of governmental structure, political boundaries are of course relevant; but they may not be relevant when we view cities as economic entities, points of population concentration, etc. This is not to suggest that only one attribute should be used to define cities for a

14

particular type of analysis. On the contrary, depending upon the nature of a given study, a configuration of attributes may be used. One can even concentrate on determining the extent of empirical correspondence between the attributes. Thus, for example, with what frequency are "demographic cities" also "economic cities"? This sort of question is implicit in much of urban research.

A relativistic approach to definition neither captures the essence of cities, if such can be said to exist, nor insures homogeneity in all of their characteristics. Cities defined in demographic terms, for example, may indeed manifest considerable political, economic, socio-cultural, and psychological diversity. However, this would be true for any definition of a city in terms of one attribute; in the final analysis, the matter of homogeneity is entirely relative to the problem at hand.

From the point of view set forth here the term city is a generic one, encompassing numerous types of population and territory which qualify under one definition or another. To underscore the generic nature of the term and avoid political connotations, we may simply refer to all of the different kinds of cities as *urban units*. This approach circumvents sterile debates over definition and places only two requirements on urban research. First, regardless of the purpose of the analysis, one must provide an explicit definition of the kind of urban unit studied. It is in part through fulfilling this requirement that the comparability of different pieces of research can be gauged. This is, of course, an essential element in the additive quality of scientific knowledge. At the same time the requirement serves as an antidote for pseudo propositions. All too often we find statements ascribing properties to cities that appear to be empirically contingent propositions, when in reality they are nothing more than ill-disguised definitions that are subject neither to proof nor disproof. It is pointless, for example, to define a city in terms of a certain socio-cultural pattern and then proclaim this pattern to be causally associated with city residence. Only when definitions are made explicit do such pseudo propositions become readily apparent.

A second requirement of research calls for a detailed description of the method of delimitation. It is one thing to provide a general definition of the kind of urban unit studied but a quite different thing to specify the way in which the boundaries of the individual units were established. Specification of methods of delimitation is perhaps even more important than general definitions in comparing the results of different pieces of urban research. For example, the fact that two studies have defined cities as "points of population concentration" means neither that the cities are identical in all respects nor that their boundaries were established in a similar way. Comparability in such a case depends on two specific characteristics—size and density—of the points of population concentration and the procedure followed in demarcating their limits.

The importance of delimitation in urban research. Three questions are posed with respect to the problem of delimitation. First, to what extent do the political boundaries of cities correspond with boundaries established on the basis of non-political criteria? Second, how can non-political boundaries of a city be established? And, third, how much correspondence do we find between two or more non-political boundaries of a city? Since each of the papers in this part of the book deals with one or more of these questions, some comments on the basic issues are in order.

Despite the prevalence of different conceptions of cities (i.e., how they should be defined), most urban research until quite recently was based on observations of only one type of unit, the incorporated municipality. This paradox can be attributed to the fact that most investigations have been dependent upon data published by governmental agencies, typically one responsible for conducting and reporting the results of a census of population. Such reports are virtually indispensable as sources of information for urban research; but, because the censuses are the affairs of the state, the data in them usually pertain to territorial units demarcated along administrative lines that may not be related to demographic, economic, and socio-cultural distinctions. Thus, until recently, the information on urban units offered by a census report was restricted for the most part to political cities. As a consequence, if urban units were conceived as anything other than governmental entities, census data could be used to study them only by assuming that their administrative boundaries are closely related to their economic, demographic, and/or socio-cultural limits. Such a correspondence may be true in certain cases (and perhaps more so for ancient cities than contemporary ones), but observations to date suggest that a close relation is not inevitable.

A recent study by International Urban Research of large urban units (*The World's Metropolitan Areas*. Berkeley and Los Angeles: University of California Press, 1959) has pointed to various cases where the administrative limits of a city bear little correspondence to its boundaries as a demographic and economic entity. This study has also described three ways in which such a lack of correspondence may be manifested. One of these is found in the case of an "underbounded" city. Here the governmental entity is completely or partially surrounded by a continuous or nearly continuous area containing a predominantly nonagricultural population. This type is frequently encountered in North America, Europe, and Oceania. For example, in 1950 some 110,-000 persons resided within the political limits of the city of Wilmington, Delaware, but this number represented only 41 per cent of the population of the Wilmington Metropolitan Area (268,-000), a much larger area containing a predominantly nonagricultural population. Even greater contrasts can be found in Australia. Sydney municipality, for example, had a population of about 96,000 in 1947, but in the same year the Sydney Metropolitan Area contained some 1,626,000 residents. Thus, both Wilmington and Sydney are "underbounded," though by no means to the same degree.

Illustrations of a second type of divergence between political and other cities are provided by several of the Chartered Cities in the Philippines. These units are typically "overbounded," meaning that their administrative limits extend far beyond any particular point of population concentration and encompass large strips of territory that are rural by virtually any standard. This is particularly striking in the case of Davao City. There, in 1948, the administrative limits contained approximately 111,000 residents; but the boundaries of an urban unit drawn along nonadministrative lines would have encompassed a population of somewhere between 47,000 and 82,000.

In those cases where administrative lines cross other types of boundaries at two or more points we have an instance of a third type of divergence. Cities of this type are not uncommon in all of the world's regions. Unlike the first two types ("underbounded" and "overbounded"), they illustrate the point that even when two or more different boundaries include about the same number of people, they may not closely coincide.

The importance of the divergence between political and other boundaries of a city is obvious. If we compare cities as administrative entities, the results may be very different from those obtained by a comparison made along non-political lines. Thus, as cities in a governmental sense, Davao had a larger population than Wilmington, and Wilmington had a larger population than Sydney. However, as demographic and economic urban units (i.e., as Metropolitan Areas), Sydney is larger than Wilmington and Wilmington is larger than Davao.

The character of administrative boundaries can lead to erroneous conclusions in comparisons both of city size and of population growth. This was noted by an early student of urban phenomena, Paul Meuriot.

. . . any truly scientific study of urban agglomerations thus presupposes the liaison between the city and its suburbs. If one rejects this postulate, one falls fatally into the grossest errors. A striking example of this is furnished us by the two metropolises of Central Europe, Berlin and Vienna. From 1900 to 1910 the population of the Austrian capital increased 356,000, growing from 1,674,000 to 2,030,000. During the same period the German capital increased from 1,888,000 to 2,070,000; it grew only 182,000. This suggests that Vienna grew twice as much as Berlin; but this is only the appearance. The territorial extent of Berlin is only 6,300 hectares; that of Vienna is 17,000, nearly three times as large. Thus Vienna, properly speaking, has no suburbs outside of its administrative boundaries; its growth takes place within the city limits, as does that of all cities with very extensive areas. In the case of Berlin, however, the equivalents to the suburbs of Vienna are outside the administrative limits of the city. If one adds to the territorial extent of Berlin that of the immediately adjoining suburbs, the total area equals that of Vienna. Now within these revised limits, the growth of the Berlin agglomeration is more than double that of Vienna. The population of this complex grew from 2,460,000 in 1900 to 3,215,000 in 1910, an increase of 755,000 as compared to

356,000 for Vienna. Berlin's increase in just the 1905-1910 period, 357,000 was just equal to that of Vienna for 1900-1910.[1]

Contents of the papers. The first paper in Chapter 1, "The Influence of the Definition of the Urban Place on the Size of the Urban Population" by Miloš Macura, serves an an introduction to the problems of delimitation by pointing to the variety of ways in which urban units can be defined. The author illustrates the importance of this by showing that each of several types of definitions yields a different picture of urbanization in Serbia. His study also shows that the identification of urban units in economic terms does not always produce the same results as identification on the basis of a purely demographic criterion. Furthermore, whether the units are identified in economic or demographic terms, the exact definition applied in either case makes an appreciable difference in the size of the urban population.

The second paper in Chapter 1, "Some Notes on the Concepts of 'City' and 'Agglomeration'" by G. Goudswaard, provides even more evidence of the divergence between political and other limits of urban units. His study clearly shows that the administrative boundaries of European cities commonly do not closely coincide with what is urbanized territory from a geographical point of view. This is also shown to be the case for some of the extra-administrative urban units (agglomerations which include cities and adjacent administrative divisions) that were established in Europe, a feature that makes Goudswaard's report useful as an introduction to the problems of delimitation. This study also indicates that a lack of correspondence between city and agglomeration boundaries may have consequences beyond a discrepancy in population size; it may also mean that the characteristics of the two populations are different. Goudswaard's data show that in certain cases a substantial difference exists between agglomerations and cities as to rates of fertility and mortality computed on the basis of *de facto* populations.

Along with the recognition that the different types of city boundaries may not closely correspond with each other, attempts have been made in several countries to delimit standard non-po-

[1] Paul Meuriot, "De la Mesure des Agglomérations Urbainese," *Bulletin de l'Institut International de Statistique,* Vol. 19, No. 1, Part 2 (1911), pp. 158-159.

litical or extra-administrative urban units. Although the methods and criteria vary from case to case, each approach represents the accumulation of a considerable amount of research experience. For this reason reports on the delimitation of urban units in three countries have been included in Chapter 2. These reports describe the practices and methods used in West Germany ("The Delimitation of Urban Areas" by Olaf Boustedt), England and Wales ("The Growth and Study of Conurbations" by the General Register Office), and the United States ("Urbanized Areas" and "Standard Metropolitan Statistical Areas" by the U.S. Bureau of the Census).

Since the various criteria for delimitation presented in Chapter 2 were designed for particular countries, they are not meant to be applied on a world-wide basis. The statement of methods which hold forth the promise of international applicability is left to Chapter 3.

In concluding we should note that the approaches to delimitation set forth in Chapters 2 and 3 do not characterize urban units in terms of only one attribute. Typically, both economic and demographic variables are incorporated in the criteria. The papers in Part I cover two of the more generally recognized types of urban units—the urban area and the metropolitan area. Finally, additional references on delimitation are provided in Sections 6, 18, and 27 of the *Subject Index to the Bibliography*.

Chapter 1

ILLUSTRATIONS OF THE PROBLEM
OF URBAN BOUNDARIES

THE INFLUENCE OF THE DEFINITION OF THE URBAN PLACE ON THE SIZE OF THE URBAN POPULATION *

MILOŠ MACURA

In spite of several decades of discussion and many recommendations, no general agreement has been reached on an international definition of urban population. Nor can the latest recommendation of the U.N. Population Commission be considered adequate in making international comparisons. Variations in national levels of economic and social development, differences in the social and political institutions of countries, and different historical and geographical conditions make international comparisons very difficult. The advantages of establishing an international standard make a new attempt worthwhile, however, even at the price of abandoning definitions which are convenient for study at the national level.

About thirty definitions of urban population are in current use, but none of them is really satisfactory for use in making international comparisons. The kind of definition of urban population most widely used is based on the size of the place. Thirty-five per cent of the countries for which any data are available

* Adapted from *Proceedings of the World Population Conference, 1954* (New York: United Nations, 1955), Vol. IV, pp. 741-756, with permission of author and publisher. Translated from French by Richard L. Forstall and Ward J. Barrett, members of the staff of International Urban Research.

apply this criterion, using a total of eight different lower limits of population, ranging from 300 to 20,000, above which a place is considered to be urban. This hardly seems to offer an objective and comparable criterion.

It seems to me that establishing a sufficiently elastic world-wide standard will not create any more problems in urban research than has the acceptance of the international classification of economic activities or the international definition of national income and its constituent elements. I would like to offer some ideas on the subject, using some data pertaining to the People's Republic of Serbia, which offer particularly apposite examples for discussion.

Serbia, the largest of the federal republics of Yugoslavia, occupies the central part of the Balkan Peninsula and extends into the southern section of the Pannonian Basin. It has experienced a wide range of social and cultural influences, and its population agglomerations offer a most varied picture. Eight of the ten types and varieties of villages that the geographer Cvijic has distinguished in the Balkans are found in Serbia, and it has four of his five varieties of cities. The demographic characteristics of the country similarly present a range of variations that may prove useful in a general discussion.

CRITERIA FOR THE DEFINITION OF URBAN PLACES

So far as I know, all attempts to define urban population have considered only the population living in urban places, thus making the concept of place central to the definition. For some decades, however, there has been no progress in determining what is an urban place. The criterion of an incorporated status, while often coming close to the real concept of urban place, seems unsatisfactory because it is determined arbitrarily and in the last analysis is subject to factitious changes.

The criterion of population density is of special interest for large cities, and has for a long time received attention principally because of rapid urbanization. As commonly defined, however, density is of little value because it depends on the administrative boundaries of the urban place. Giusti's concept of "densité foncière" (population/area of land under use) has certain advantages, but a serious disadvantage is that it is very difficult to apply in the study of a large number of cases. It may be justified in principle, but its use raises several practical problems.

Thus, two criteria remain: the population size of a place, and the industrial composition of its population. In actual practice these two criteria are applied independently of one another. The Bunle Committee has proposed using the second, but has advised use of the size of the principal nucleus of the commune when the second criterion cannot be applied.

APPLICATION OF DIFFERENT DEFINITIONS OF URBAN PLACE TO SERBIA

Comparison of these criteria with the aim of (1) establishing a definition of urban place and (2) determining the effect of the resulting definition on the absolute and relative size of the urban population may afford a basis for evaluating their worth. It is not possible to compare the criteria applied in different countries on the basis of their respective official figures, because it is impossible to separate changes in the urban population that are due to actual urbanization from those resulting from the method of definition. Table 1 shows the results of application of the above-mentioned criteria to the population of Serbia.

The variations in Table 1 show a considerable range, and without a prior examination it is difficult to say which of these criteria is more applicable than the others.

THE URBAN PLACE

It seems to me desirable to clarify the concept of place to which "urban" may or may not be applied, before considering an over-all definition. It is common practice in statistical and related work to use the commune or other basic administrative division as the unit in determining what is an urban place. In addition, for about fifty years it has been suggested that suburban areas should be included with the city whether or not they are legally part of the urban commune. Another conception starts, on the contrary, with a geographical view of the place, without taking account of its administrative status. According to this conception,

TABLE 1

APPLICATION OF DIFFERENT DEFINITIONS OF URBAN PLACE
TO THE POPULATION OF SERBIA

Definitions	Number of Urban Places	Urban Population		Average Population Size of the Urban Places
		Number	*Per Cent of Total Population*	
Administrative:				
1948	34	1,329,776	19.0	39,111
1952 (widest sense)	96	1,814,864	26.0	18,905
1952 (narrowest sense) ..	7	838,321	12.0	119,760
Iceland: 300 or more inhabitants				
9 countries: 2,000 or more inhabitants	572	3,310,541	47.4	5,787
Holland: 20,000 or more inhabitants	17	959,904	13.7	56,465
Bunle: 60 per cent or more of the population nonagricultural	202	1,467,541	21.0	7,265
Italy: 50 per cent or more of the population nonagricultural	289	1,682,182	24.1	5,820
Bunle: with a nucleus containing 2,000 or more inhabitants	487	3,139,701	45.0	6,447

communes that comprise several separate inhabited localities are not regarded as single units for study. In spite of technical difficulties that it may pose, the use of the latter concept appears more justifiable to me than does the use of the first, primarily because of the instability of the administrative divisions on which the first criterion depends. In Serbia, administrative changes are especially frequent, partly due to the social dynamism of the country. Just since the end of the war the apparatus for changing commune boundaries has been used 1,626 times, and the number of changes has varied from 3,816 in 1946 to 2,206 in 1952. The number of places legally defined as urban changed from 36 in 1951 to seven in 1952. Before the First World War, 9,166 boundary changes occurred within Serbia, which was smaller at that time. I have not studied commune boundary changes in other countries, but I am aware of the difficulties that changes in large or small scale administrative units may produce in statistics. Another theoretical support for the geographical criterion is the generally accepted conception of human agglomerations as consisting of contiguous sites of habitation. It is true that population density in administrative divisions increases in proportion to the development of modern means of communication, but it seems to me that "urban place" acquires conceptual importance only if it is limited by definition to one locality. The use of any other definition of this term will result in the paradox of an administrative unit being treated as urban even though it contains only scattered dwellings.

THE INDEPENDENT INHABITED LOCALITY

The difference between communes and independent inhabited localities depends on the population size of the latter and on the character and importance of the communes in the administrative system. Table 2 shows these differences for Serbia.

TABLE 2

COMMUNES AND INHABITED LOCALITIES BY POPULATION SIZE GROUPS IN SERBIA

Population Size Groups	Communes		Inhabited Localities	
	Number	Inhabitants	Number	Inhabitants
Less than 2,000	1,057	1,416,121	5,541	3,673,003
2,000 to 3,000	564	1,400,809	156	609,010
3,000 to 5,000	445	1,683,447	178	687,674
5,000 to 10,000	139	852,232	87	574,912
10,000 or more	55	1,630,935	51	1,438,945
Total	2,260	6,983,544	6,093	6,983,544

Many different factors, geographical, economic, historical, cultural, etc., determine the size of the population and the character of inhabited localities. These factors in turn are reflected in the character of the communes, whether they are made up of one or many localities. But one must recognize that the boundaries of communes may in addition reflect their function in the country's municipal organization.

Reducing the notion of an urban place to the concept of independent inhabited locality is open to serious objection. It destroys the unity of a city with its suburbs and breaks the continuity of their economic and demographic ties. Moreover, it reduces the urban population by excluding smaller suburban places that fall below the minimum size limit that establishes a place as urban. It introduces technical problems concerning the presentation of data on births, deaths, marriages, etc. that do not occur at the place of residence of the people involved. There are other objections based on administrative and planning considerations.

On the whole, however, the advantages of applying the criterion of the independent inhabited locality outweigh the disadvantages. The criterion eliminates the risk of including with the city any areas that lack the demographic, organizational, and social features commonly thought of as urban. Moreover, it permits a clearer examination of the process of urbanization, which gradually makes urban places larger, and excludes the possibility that a mere administrative change, by diminishing or extending administrative areas, will introduce artificial changes in statistics on the process. For these reasons I feel one may accept the criterion of independent inhabited locality.

URBAN CHARACTERISTICS

From the demographic point of view, the urban place is best determined in terms of the size of the inhabited locality and the structure of its population; density cannot be used as a criterion because of difficulties posed in its measurement. An urban place is distinguished from a rural agglomeration by having a larger population and a considerable degree of division of labor in both industrial production and services. The degree of the division of labor does not vary directly with the size of the population of a place in all cases, however. There are some fairly large places which have retained a primitive social organization and little division of labor; this is due to the inhibiting effects of their patriarchal system on the expansion of their productive forces. Only the differentiation of population through the development of industry can give an inhabited place an urban character. In addition to a well developed organization of production, such urban attributes as rapid communication, efficient transportation, higher education, the provision of adequate sanitary facilities, and the presence of other highly differentiated activities exist only in a milieu of a superior economic level. However, the development of the economic structure of the population cannot alone give urban character to a place, especially in cases where that development is uniform and oriented toward a single activity. For example, there are places with a very high percentage of non-agricultural population (particularly mines, isolated factories, etc.) which, nevertheless, lack the character and organization of urban places, as a result of having too few inhabitants or consumers. Thus, I feel that the urban character of a place depends upon the concurrence of these two factors, the size of the population and its type of economic development.

The two criteria that define urban population, the size of the population of a place and the percentage of nonagricultural population, should be applied concurrently to avoid the difficulties that might arise if either were used alone. By establishing a minimum population requirement for an urban place, we can eliminate small places that have few inhabitants, even though they have a complex economic structure. By requiring that a certain percentage of the population be nonagricultural, we can eliminate larger places qualifying as urban by reason of their size but lacking an urban economic structure.

The relative importance of these two criteria depends on the strength of their reciprocal relationship, which is determined by a graph whose coordinates are "size of place" and "percentage of population engaged in nonagricultural activity." It follows that for smaller places to be regarded as urban they should have a population with a high nonagricultural percentage, while this percentage may be low in larger places. The minimum limits of the two characteristics as denoting urban status will depend, at the national level, on specific analysis of localities, which should not be limited to demographic data alone. International comparability can be assured by an appropriate choice of international standards obtained from studying the solutions arrived at in different countries. These standards will differ to some extent from the national rules, but they will make better international comparisons possible. The following diagram presents the results of the concurrent application of the two criteria to the Serbian data shown in the Appendix Table.

Per Cent of the Population Nonagricultural	Number of Inhabitants			
	Below 3,000	3,000- 10,000	10,000- 15,000	15,000+
Less than 40	—	—	—	x
40 to 70	—	—	x	x
More than 70	—	x	x	x

The scheme outlined by this diagram is preliminary and does no more than illustrate the viewpoint developed in this paper. It excludes from the urban category: (1) all places of less than 3,000 population, no matter what their nonagricultural population; (2) all places of less than 10,000 unless their nonagricultural population is more than 70 per cent of the total population; and (3) all places of less than 15,000 unless their nonagricultural population is more than 40 per cent. Places having more than 15,000 are treated as urban without reference to their economic structure, but it may be noted that places of this size do in fact have a nonagricultural ratio greater than 40 per cent.

The application of this definition of urban place to the inhabited localities of the People's Republic of Serbia produces the following results:

Number of urban places	69
Urban population	1,492,576
Per cent of population urban	21.4
Per cent of inhabited localities considered urban	1.1
Average size of urban place	21,632

Certain additional comments should be made relative to the provision for eliminating places of under 3,000 and larger places with low nonagricultural proportions. After eliminating temporary localities (e.g., those near construction projects), the places of under 3,000 with more than 80 per cent nonagricultural had the following characteristics as to the dominance of a particular economic activity (i.e., the activity which accounts for more than 30 per cent of the total):

(1) Eleven places with 12,048 inhabitants were miner's colo-

nies with a high average proportion (⅔) of the population dependent on mining;

(2) Four places with 4,801 inhabitants were dominated by manufacturing;

(3) Fourteen places with 11,531 inhabitants were dependent principally on government;

(4) Eight places with 13,937 inhabitants were minor commercial and administrative centers.

Only in the last group do we encounter a relatively balanced distribution of the different economic activities. But the character and small population of these places make it difficult to class them as urban. To the extent that the number and size of these places justifies special treatment, it might be best to call them "mixed places" in a sense analogous to the "mixed communes" described in the recommendations of the Bunle Commission.

At the opposite extreme from these places, in the Pannonian Basin there are many large localities, often of more than 10,000 inhabitants, that so far remain rural in character. This is confirmed by the low percentage of their nonagricultural population. In spite of their size and population density these places are thoroughly rural and therefore should not be included in the urban category.

SOCIO-ECONOMIC CRITERIA OF URBAN CHARACTER

We may now test the 69 inhabited localities that have been classified as urban on the basis of population size and per cent nonagricultural to see whether they possess the socio-economic attributes commonly associated with urban status. We may consider the following elements: from the administrative viewpoint, (a) whether the place is legally a city or urban commune and (b) whether it is a district capital; as far as communications are concerned, (c) whether the place is on a railroad; from the economic viewpoint, whether the place has (d) manufacturing establishments, (e) wholesaling establishments, and (f) banking establishments; from the public health viewpoint, (g) whether the place has permanent sanitary facilities and installations; from the education viewpoint, (h) whether there is a technical or a complete secondary school; and from the cultural viewpoint,

TABLE 3

THE DISTRIBUTION OF LOCALITIES IN SERBIA BY POPULATION SIZE, PER CENT OF POPULATION NONAGRICULTURAL AND CERTAIN POLITICAL, ECOLOGICAL, ECONOMIC, AND CULTURAL CHARACTERISTICS

Localities According to		Total Numbers		Number of Localities With A Specified Characteristic*									
Number of Inhabitants	Per Cent of Population Nonagricultural	Localities	Population	a	b	c	d	e	f	g	h	i	j
3-10,000	70+	23	112,034	7	16	15	16	13	17	23	14	—	3
10-15,000	40-70	6	72,175	3	4	6	5	2	4	6	2	1	—
15,000	70+	10	126,714	10	10	9	10	10	10	10	9	4	4
	40-70	11	231,530	11	9	10	10	10	10	11	10	2	4
	70+	19	950,123	11	19	19	19	18	19	19	19	14	17
Total	—	69	1,492,576	42	58	59	60	53	60	69	54	21	28

* See text for description of the ten characteristics.

whether there is a (i) theater or (j) museum. Table 3 presents the answers to these questions for the places under discussion.

The next table (Table 4) presents data on the presence in the 69 inhabited localities of municipal and social conditions usually found in urban places; it shows the number of places with (1) electric lighting, (2) running water, (3) sewers, (4) public street-cleaning services, (5) hot-water public baths, (6) parks, (7) more than half their streets paved, (8) public transportation, (9) public fire protection, (10) public chimney-sweeping service, (11) social insurance, and (12) a labor employment office.

It appears to me that most of the places defined as urban by the two criteria have also most of the economic, social, sanitary, educational, cultural, and communal facilities common in the towns of this region, a fact of importance in the formulation of a definition of urban place. Although it is of value to define urban places in this way for demographic studies, it is true that the use of the definition may be less valuable in other research. But each scientific discipline has definitions which differ from those used in other disciplines. The definition given in this paper may have omitted certain categories of urban places or included some types of rural places, but this is a risk inherent in all definitions that use quantitative variables.

SOME NOTES ON THE CONCEPTS OF "CITY" AND "AGGLOMERATION" *

G. GOUDSWAARD **

With a view to the publication of a Statistical Yearbook of Great Cities, the International Statistical Institute has collected demographic data concerning all European cities with populations in excess of 100,000 inhabitants. The collected data concern 156 cities in Austria, Belgium, Denmark, Finland, France, West Germany, Greece, Italy, Netherlands, Norway, Portugal, Saarland, Spain, Sweden, Switzerland, Turkey, Yugoslavia, and Egypt.

* Adapted from *Proceedings of the World Population Conference, 1954* (New York: United Nations, 1955), Vol. IV, pp. 685-693, with permission of author and publisher. Translated from French by Suzanne Angelucci and Ward J. Barrett, members of the staff of International Urban Research.
** In collaboration with J. Schmitz.

TABLE 4

The Distribution of Localities in Serbia by Population Size, Per Cent of Population Nonagricultural, and Characteristics Relating to Municipal and Social Conditions

Localities According to		Total Number of Localities	Number of Localities With A Specified Characteristic [*]											
Number of Inhabitants	Per Cent of Population Nonagricultural		1	2	3	4	5	6	7	8	9	10	11	12
3-10,000	70+	23	23	11	6	13	16	15	12	—	22	8	16	14
10-15,000	40-70	6	6	—	2	5	4	6	—	—	6	6	4	4
15,000	70+	10	10	4	6	10	9	10	6	—	10	9	10	10
15,000	40-70	11	11	3	5	10	9	11	3	—	11	9	9	9
15,000	70+	19	19	10	12	19	18	19	12	4	19	16	19	19
Total	—	69	69	28	31	57	56	61	33	4	68	48	58	56

[*] See text for description of the 12 characteristics.

APPENDIX TABLE

LOCALITIES AND THE NUMBER OF THEIR INHABITANTS ACCORDING TO THE PER CENT OF THE POPULATION NONAGRICULTURAL

Per Cent of Population Nonagricultural		Number of Inhabitants									
		Less than 1,000	1-3,000	3-5,000	5-7,000	7-10,000	10-12,000	12-15,000	15-17,000	17-20,000	20,000+
0-10	a	2,777	760	46	3	1	—	—	—	—	—
	b	1,330,542	1,117,687	169,815	17,233	8,050	—	—	—	—	—
10-20	a	849	365	77	25	4	3	—	—	—	—
	b	421,283	588,775	302,140	144,927	32,044	33,139	—	—	—	—
20-30	a	351	133	20	8	8	1	1	—	—	—
	b	162,379	207,584	80,178	49,148	65,562	11,639	13,625	—	—	—
30-40	a	189	50	8	10	2	—	—	—	—	—
	b	88,051	85,612	32,261	57,741	15,791	—	—	—	—	—
40-50	a	91	23	4	3	5	3	1	1	—	2
	b	40,199	38,574	15,557	17,802	40,921	32,784	14,453	15,461	—	48,870
50-60	a	67	7	3	2	2	1	1	1	1	2
	b	30,326	29,355	11,659	11,398	18,381	11,297	13,641	15,120	17,079	56,385
60-70	a	39	15	7	1	3	—	—	1	1	2
	b	17,666	27,546	28,496	6,752	24,696	—	—	15,618	18,540	44,457
70-80	a	13	15	5	3	—	1	2	—	1	2
	b	6,311	27,765	18,384	18,849	—	11,339	26,368	—	18,539	86,534
80-90	a	9	6	1	2	2	2	3	1	1	2
	b	5,141	9,467	3,268	12,989	16,386	21,674	39,794	15,416	19,987	68,913
90-100	a	18	20	7	3	—	—	2	2	3	7
	b	10,365	35,850	25,916	16,242	—	—	27,539	32,655	53,334	654,745
Total	a	4,403	1,394	178	60	27	11	10	6	7	17
	b	2,112,263	2,168,215	687,674	353,081	221,831	121,872	135,420	94,270	127,479	959,904

a: Number of localities
b: Number of inhabitants

Topographic maps have also been collected for the purpose of indicating the boundaries of the cities and surrounding communes.

A primary problem encountered in work of this type stems from the use of administrative boundaries in census enumerations; as a result, economic, sociological, and other kinds of analyses must be based on census figures derived from purely governmental units.

This problem has been widely discussed. A variety of criteria have been proposed for use in defining an "agglomeration," each of which has its advantages and disadvantages; for example, the definition of "agglomeration" that is most useful to sociologists is not necessarily the one most useful to economists. Furthermore, the lack of statistical data limits the practical application of all these definitions, at least in making international comparisons. Even if one succeeds in delimiting an agglomeration "correctly" according to one of the definitions, the statistical data needed for a sociological or economic analysis of the delimited area may prove to be unavailable, sufficiently detailed figures being in general available only for the administrative city, if at all.

Data on the territorial extent and population of cities and their neighboring communes as of December 31, 1951, that were used in this study can best be described in terms of the following format:

A. Territory of the city [1]

	Territorial Extent in Hectares	
	Total	Of Which Water [3]
Territory		
Urbanized territory [2]		

[1] Excluding surrounding communes.

[2] The territory which forms a single built-up unit, including streets, squares, parks, etc.

[3] Shown only for cases with a total water area exceeding 25 hectares.

B. The name, area, and population of each of the neighboring communes which form, with the city, a continuous area

C. Territory of the agglomeration (the city and its neighboring communes)

	Territorial Extent in Hectares	
	Total	Of Which Water [2]
Territory		
Urbanized territory [1]		

[1] The territory which forms a single built-up unit, including streets, squares, parks, etc.

[2] Shown only for cases with a total water area exceeding 25 hectares.

An agglomeration in the case of "C" consists of a city and those surrounding communes which contain a part of the urbanized territory that extends beyond the city's limits. In this study the outer limits of the urbanized territory were established through the use of topographic maps. One of the principal advantages of this approach is that statistical data are available for agglomerations so defined, since they consist of governmental units (cities and communes). One disadvantage, however, is that these agglomerations may encompass some rural areas, since a commune needs only to contain some urbanized territory to be considered a part of the agglomeration. Also to be noted is that in some cases the boundaries of the agglomerations correspond with those of official agglomerations and that the latter were used in Yugoslavia.

Some of the data collected by ISI are presented below in five graphs and one table. It must be noted that variations in the number of cities and agglomerations from one graph to the next are due to the fact that in some cases the desired data were not available.

Graph I brings out the considerable discrepancy within the administrative boundaries of the cities between total area and urbanized territory. It is true that one must take into account the differences in the interpretation of the concept of urbanized territory, but topographic maps confirm that the variations are in great part real ones.

The cities shown in Graph I as having an urbanized territory

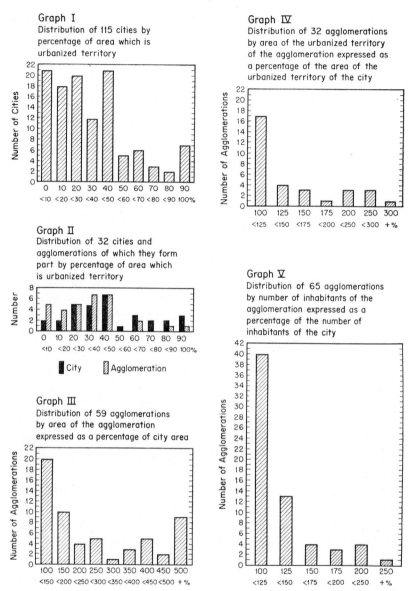

Graph I
Distribution of 115 cities by
percentage of area which is
urbanized territory

Graph IV
Distribution of 32 agglomerations
by area of the urbanized territory
of the agglomeration expressed as
a percentage of the area of the
urbanized territory of the city

Graph II
Distribution of 32 cities and
agglomerations of which they form
part by percentage of area which
is urbanized territory

■ City   ▨ Agglomeration

Graph V
Distribution of 65 agglomerations
by number of inhabitants of the
agglomeration expressed as a
percentage of the number of
inhabitants of the city

Graph III
Distribution of 59 agglomerations
by area of the agglomeration
expressed as a percentage of city area

of less than ten per cent of their total area are listed in Table 1.
Spanish and Italian cities predominate in the table, most of them
situated on narrow coastal plains. The total area of most of these
cities (see Table 1) is much larger than the average total area of
the 115 cities of Graph I, which is about 13,500 hectares. On the

TABLE 1

Cities	Number of Inhabitants	City Area in Hectares	Area of City's Urbanized Territory	
			In Hectares	As a % of Column 3
1	2	3	4	5
AUSTRIA				
Innsbruck	92,420	40,435	1,078	3
SPAIN				
Córdoba	165,403	124,461	810	1
Gijon	110,985	18,415	1,200	7
La Coruña	133,844	3,684	280	8
Málaga	276,222	40,546	747	2
Palma de Mallorca ...	136,814	19,939	601	3
San Sebastian	113,776	7,109	189	3
Santander	102,462	3,392	225	7
Valencia	503,886	13,465	668	5
Valladolid	124,212	19,423	1,520	8
Vigo	137,873	10,944	500	5
Zaragoza	235,444	108,455	900	1
ITALY				
Ferrara	138,330	40,435	1,078	3
Messina	230,626	21,155	1,548	7
Modena	117,269	18,363	992	5
Parma	123,986	20,562	1,195	6
Reggio di Calabria ...	143,489	24,354	840	3
Taranto	195,660	31,015	867	3
Venezia	322,762	45,635	841	2
NETHERLANDS				
Enschede	109,326	14,107	975	7

other hand, the urbanized territory of each of the cities in Table 1 is much smaller than the average urbanized territory of the 115 cities, which is about 4,700 hectares.

Graph II shows the distribution, according to the percentage of the total area which is urbanized territory, of (1) 32 agglomerations (i.e., the city and surrounding communes) and (2), for comparative purposes, the chief cities of these agglomerations. In general the percentage of urbanized territory is lower for the agglomerations than for the cities.

Graph III expresses the total areas of 59 agglomerations as a percentage of the total areas of their respective cities. The nine cases for which the ratio is above 500 per cent are Pôrto, Seville, Bergen, Stockholm, Aarhus, Copenhagen, Basel, Athens, and Piraeus.

Graph IV expresses the area of the urbanized territory in 32 agglomerations as a percentage of the area of the urbanized territory in their respective cities. The extreme cases where the agglomeration contains far more urbanized territory than does the city (above 200 per cent) are Aachen, Antwerp, Athens, Piraeus, Aarhus, Compenhagen, and Basel. Here the difference between the urbanized territory of the agglomeration on the one hand and the city on the other tends to be less than the difference between the total area of the agglomeration and the total area of the city (shown in Graph III).

The disparity between the agglomeration and the city is less when comparisons are made on the basis of the number of inhabitants in each (Graph V); in 40 of the 65 agglomerations which are included in Graph V the difference between the population of the agglomeration and that of the city is less than 25 per cent. The population of the agglomeration is more than twice that of the city in the cases of Antwerp, Brussels, Roubaix, Rouen, and Pôrto.

The topographic maps, which unfortunately cannot be reproduced here, show clearly the considerable differences in the interpretation of the concept "agglomeration" from country to country.

For example, a very loose interpretation of "agglomeration" is used in Yugoslavia, where the agglomeration is a purely administrative entity of which urbanized territory forms a relatively small part. Subotica, Yugoslavia, for example, a city of over 100,-000 inhabitants, does not have the urban character that one expects in a city of that size.

There are also cases where the agglomeration is considered as a regional economic entity, i.e., the city proper with the hinterland which supplies it with provisions (e.g., Copenhagen and Stockholm).

The concept of the total built-up entity has been often used in the delimitation of numerous official agglomerations that consist of a city and a certain number of suburbs, some of which have been annexed and some of which have not. There are cases where the annexation takes place rather easily, but there are also cases where the suburbs continue an independent administrative existence, sometimes being excluded from the agglomeration because of local politics. The opposite tendency also exists, notably in Greece, where a certain quarter of the city may be separated administratively from the city and continue its existence as a neighboring commune when it becomes developed. In any delimitation of built-up entities, one should ignore these sorts of administrative distinctions; however, the application of the criterion of the built-up entity in the delimitation of agglomerations takes diverse forms, and the criterion itself is at times very ambiguous.

Urbanized territory is also differently interpreted. Should territory that is not built-up but having an urban function be included? In addition to public gardens, squares, and highways, athletic fields, airports and in some cases even woods are often considered as urbanized territory.

From the point of view of international comparability, certain conclusions emerge from the material assembled by the ISI. In the majority of cases, one is obliged for purposes of statistical analysis, to take as a basis the city within its administrative boundaries because figures are seldom available for agglomerations. However, there is little reason for lament at this situation, because the variations presented by the agglomeration concept, and the practical impossibility of applying a uniform definition in different countries, would render the advantages of a substitution of agglomerations for cities in international comparisons more or less imaginary.

A lack of correspondence between the boundaries of a city and the associated agglomeration has consequences beyond a disparity in the size of their areas and population; it may also result in differences in the characteristics of their inhabitants. For example, in a comparison of birth and death rates of the *de facto* population, one must not lose sight of the possibility that hospitals and maternity homes may be concentrated in the city proper. As examples of variations in birth and death rates dependent on such concentrations, the different figures for the agglomerations and cities of Brussels, Antwerp, Ghent, and Liège are listed below. The figures are given for the *de facto* and *de jure* populations for comparison.

Type of Population	Brussels		Antwerp		Ghent		Liège	
	Aggl.	City	Aggl.	City	Aggl.	City	Aggl.	City
Live Births Per 1,000 of the Mean Population, 1950								
de facto pop.	12.5	9.8	11.4	14.1	19.2	24.7	17.3	16.5
de jure pop.	11.8	11.1	13.8	13.1	13.5	13.5	14.5	15.0
Deaths Per 1,000 of the Mean Population, 1950								
de facto pop.	12.8	17.3	10.8	12.9	15.8	16.2	15.7	18.5
de jure pop.	12.8	13.8	11.5	12.0	14.3	13.9	14.7	15.6

SOURCE: *Annuaire Statistique de la Belgique et du Congo Belge,* Tome 72, 1951.

The effect of the substitution of the agglomeration for the city depends on both the size of the city relative to that of the agglomeration and the type of phenomenon under analysis. Consequently, the results of the substitution can only be determined for each case separately.

Chapter 2

SOME NATIONAL APPROACHES TO DELIMITING URBAN BOUNDARIES

THE DELIMITATION OF URBAN AREAS *

OLAF BOUSTEDT

No less important than the precise definition of the term "urban population" is the geographic delimitation of the "urban area" *(Stadtgebiet).* Interest primarily concentrates on the administrative delimitation, for every administration has a restricted area of authority, and only collects the necessary statistical data for its own area. But even here it becomes evident that it is impossible to cover living reality by using the standards of administrative law. Urban agglomerations do not keep within governmental boundaries, but spread within a narrower or wider zone around administrative centers. Thus, whereas the problem in defining the concept of urban population is to find a lower limit for it, the task in demarcating "urban areas" geographically is to find the characteristics that fix their outer limits.

Attempts at statistical description of urban areas were made in Germany at the beginning of this century, particularly by Brückner, Hasse, and Schott. In their efforts to find comparable delimitations for different cities they defined the urban area as a geographic unit delimited by circles around the center of the city, using a radius of at first 10, later 15, and even 20 km. Such

* Adapted from "Urban Population, Urban Areas, and the Problem of Dominance in West-German Statistics," *Proceedings of the World Population Conference, 1954,* Vol. IV (New York: United Nations, 1955), pp. 491-503, with permission of author and publisher.

a schematic analysis, though advantageous for comparative studies, was not adapted to showing actual geographic inter-action because:

(1) areas were included which were not urban in character, and

(2) the method did not take into account the actual interaction between the central city and areas external to it; this probably was its decisive defect.

Use of this method gave way to monographic studies of in-dividual cities which used a wide range of characteristics suitable for determining the urban area. Excellent as many of these stud-ies have been, one great deficiency has remained. On such a basis official statistics did not include (despite their comprehensive character, especially the population censuses) the data for urban agglomerations in their regional tabulations, in addition to their purely administrative breakdown.

The development of the concepts *metropolitan area* in the United States and *conurbation* in the United Kingdom has revived discussion of the concept agglomeration in Germany. To begin with, various monographic studies have been undertaken, e.g., for Kiel, Darmstadt, and Cologne. A major investigation com-prising the whole state of Bavaria was implemented by the author. All these are at present being discussed in the *Stadtgeo-graphischer Arbeitskreis* (Municipal Geography Committee) of the *Bundesanstalt für Landeskunde* at Remagen. Some of the Committee's conclusions on terminology are shown in the follow-ing schematic representation of the "Stadtregion" (urban re-gion), as the whole of the agglomeration area has been called.

There is also agreement concerning certain basic character-istics of the region and its component parts. Always to be taken into account are:

(a) the share of the labor force engaged in agriculture, a ratio which characterizes population structure;

(b) the density of the population and, if possible, the type of buildings, as characterizations of the residential pattern;

(c) the number of persons commuting from the individual parts of the agglomeration area into the central city, as a characterization of interaction.

On the basis of these characteristics the author investigated

Schematic structure of the urban region

the urban regions of 18 Bavarian towns. In this study the "agglomeration area" signifies the area which by the economic structure of its population forms a more or less homogeneous, predominantly nonagricultural geographic unit, and whose population to a prevalent or at least considerable extent finds its livelihood directly in places of employment within the central city. The "agglomeration area" was deliberately demarcated in such a way as to indicate its *utmost* limits. The commercial, cultural and administrative aspects of the dominance of the central city, however, were not taken into account because they have nothing to do with the agglomeration as such; and, besides, these aspects are very difficult to describe statistically.

The criteria used for determining urban regions in this study are set forth in Table 1.

The minimum requirements for qualifying as an urban region were that the central city itself have at least 30,000 inhabitants, and the agglomeration area at least 50,000. The details of the investigation and its results have been published in the *Allgemeines Statistisches Archiv*.[1] The results of this study showed a

[1] Vol. 37 (1953), pp. 13-26.

TABLE 1

CHARACTERISTICS OF THE TERRITORIAL PARTS OF AN URBAN REGION

Zones	Residential Pattern		Economic Structure	Employment-Residence Ratio	
	Inhabitants Per km ^{2}	Prevalent Types of Residential Buildings *	Per Cent of Gainfully Employed Workers in Agriculture	Number of Persons Commuting into the Central Area as a Per Cent of:	
				Non-Agricultural Workers	Total of Out-Commutors
Central Area (A)	More than 500	ME, EM	less than 20		
Urbanized Zone (B)	no limit	EB	less than ·35	more than 30	
Border Zone (C)					more than 60
1 inner (C₁)	no limit	B	less than 50	more than 20	
2 outer (C₂)	no limit		50-65	more than 20	

* The prevalent types of residential buildings were determined as follows:
ME — Multi-family and single-family houses ⎫ more than 67 per cent
EM — Single-family and multi-family houses ⎪ of all residential
EB — Single-family houses and farm houses ⎬ buildings
B — Farm houses ⎭

very satisfactory picture for Bavaria, although in individual cases certain changes are still desirable for one community or another because of special local conditions beyond statistical coverage. It is true that conditions for delimitation are favorable in Bavaria, inasmuch as the major urban centers are rather far apart; there are no overlappings, and the separation of town and countryside is fairly well marked. In highly urbanized areas, particularly in the Ruhr, analysis is more difficult. The criteria need to be improved and additional characteristics must be included to achieve realistic delimitations within these very complex geographic groupings.

Finally, it is to be hoped that by carrying on these studies the concept of the agglomeration area can before long be introduced into German official statistics, not only for the large censuses but also for various periodic statistics. The need for this also results from the organization of a German sample census, which in the selection of its regional sampling units naturally cannot view the large cities apart from their surroundings but must take their agglomeration areas into account with them.

URBANIZED AREAS *

U.S. BUREAU OF THE CENSUS

The major objective of the Bureau of the Census in delineating urbanized areas was to provide a better separation of urban and rural population in the vicinity of the larger cities, but individual urbanized areas have proved to be useful statistical areas. They correspond to what are called "conurbations" in some other countries. An urbanized area contains at least one city of 50,000 inhabitants or more in 1960,[1] as well as the surrounding closely settled incorporated places and unincorporated areas that meet the criteria listed below. All persons residing in an urbanized area are included in the urban population.

It appeared desirable to delineate the urbanized areas in terms of the 1960 Census results rather than prior to the census as was done in 1950. For this purpose a peripheral zone around each 1950 urbanized area and around cities that were presumably approaching a population of 50,000 was recognized. Within the unincorporated parts of this zone small enumeration districts were planned,[2] usually including no more than one square mile of land area and no more than 75 housing units.

Arrangements were made to include within the urbanized area those enumeration districts meeting specified criteria of population density as well as adjacent incorporated places. Since the urbanized area outside of incorporated places was defined in terms of enumeration districts, the boundaries for the most part

* Reprinted from U.S. Bureau of the Census, *U.S. Census of the Population: 1960. Number of Inhabitants,* Final Report PC(1)-17A (Washington, D.C.: U.S. Government Printing Office, 1960), pp. vi-vii, with the permission of the publisher.

[1] There are a few urbanized areas where there are "twin central cities" that have a combined population of at least 50,000. See section on "Standard Metropolitan Statistical Areas" for further discussion of twin central cities, neither of which has a population of 50,000 or more.

[2] An enumeration district (ED) is a small area assigned to an enumerator which must be canvassed and reported separately. In most cases an ED contains approximately 250 housing units.

follow such features as roads, streets, railroads, streams, and other clearly defined lines which may be easily identified by census enumerators in the field and often do not conform to the boundaries of political units.

In addition to its central city or cities, an urbanized area also contains the following types of contiguous areas, which together constitute its urban fringe:

1. Incorporated places with 2,500 inhabitants or more

2. Incorporated places with less than 2,500 inhabitants, provided each has a closely settled area of 100 dwelling units or more

3. Towns in the New England States, townships in New Jersey and Pennsylvania, and counties elsewhere which are classified as urban

4. Enumeration districts in unincorporated territory with a population density of 1,000 inhabitants or more per square mile (The area of large nonresidential tracts devoted to such urban land uses as railroad yards, factories, and cemeteries, was excluded in computing the population density of an enumeration district.)

5. Other enumeration districts in unincorporated territory with lower population density provided that they served one of the following purposes:

    a. To eliminate enclaves

    b. To close indentations in the urbanized area of one mile or less across the open end

    c. To link outlying enumeration districts of qualifying density that were no more than 1½ miles from the main body of the urbanized area.

Contiguous urbanized areas with central cities in the same standard metropolitan statistical area are combined. Urbanized areas with central cities in different standard metropolitan statistical areas are not combined, except that a single urbanized area was established in the New York–Northeastern New Jersey Standard Consolidated Area, and in the Chicago–Northwestern Indiana Standard Consolidated Area.

The boundaries of the urbanized areas for 1960 will not conform to those for 1950, partly because of actual changes in land use and density of settlement, and partly because of relatively minor changes in the rules used to define the boundaries. The changes in the rules include the following:

1. The use of enumeration districts to construct the urbanized areas in 1960 resulted in a less precise definition than in 1950 when the limits were selected in the field using individual blocks as the unit of area added. On the other hand, the 1960 procedures produced an urbanized area based on the census results rather than an area defined about a year before the census, as in 1950.

2. Unincorporated territory was included in the 1950 urbanized area if it contained at least 500 dwelling units per square mile, which is somewhat different criterion than the 1,000 persons or more per square mile of the included 1960 unincorporated areas.

3. The 1960 areas include those entire towns in New England, townships in New Jersey and Pennsylvania, and counties that are classified as urban in accordance with the criteria listed in the section on urban-rural residence. The 1950 criteria permitted the exclusion of portions of these particular minor civil divisions.

In general, however, the urbanized areas of 1950 and 1960 are based on essentially the same concept, and the figures for a given urbanized area may be used to measure the population growth of that area.

An urbanized area may be thought of as divided into the central city, or cities, and the remainder of the area, or the urban fringe. Any city in an urbanized area which is a central city of a standard metropolitan statistical area is also a central city of the urbanized area. With but two exceptions, the names of the central cities appear in the titles of the areas. The central cities of the New York—Northeastern New Jersey Area are the central cities of the New York, Newark, Jersey City, and Paterson-Clifton-Passaic Standard Metropolitan Statistical Areas. Likewise, the central cities of the Chicago—Northwestern Indiana Area are the central cities of the Chicago and Gary-Hammond-East Chicago Standard Metropolitan Statistical Areas.

THE GROWTH AND STUDY OF CONURBATIONS *

GENERAL REGISTER OFFICE

Flourishing cities and towns quickly expand beyond their formal limits, which seldom move far enough or frequently

---

* Adapted from "Report on Greater London and Five Other Conurbations," *Census, 1951, England and Wales* (London: H.M.S.O., 1956), pp. xiii-xv, with the permission of the publisher.

enough to keep pace with the growth of the natural community. A recent historical development, associated with industrialization, has been the rapid massing of populations in a few giant urban centers or super-cities, which have enveloped whole neighbouring towns and settlements and so entirely over-run local government boundaries. These are described as "urban agglomerations" in the Demographic Yearbooks of the United Nations, as "metropolitan areas" in the United States and as "conurbations" in this country. In the 1952 *Demographic Yearbook* statistics are given for more than fifty urban agglomerations or cities with more than a million inhabitants, most of them comprising the capital cities of the countries concerned.

The growth of metropolitan London has been studied for a long time, and as long ago as the first census in 1801 it was remarked that the total population enumerated within eight miles of St. Paul's exceeded one million. The total population of England and Wales was then under nine million. In 1951 the population of the area known as Greater London was over eight million, almost a fifth of that of England and Wales (and incidentally larger than that of many countries in Europe), whereas in the United States at the 1950 Census the standard metropolitan area of New York, with over twelve million, exceeded every other state, apart from the state of New York, in population, but because of the greater number of large cities only accounted for a tenth of the total population of that country.

During the nineteenth century similar rapid urban growth could be observed in other industrial areas principally in the north and midlands of England, and by the close of the century major conurbations had developed in the regions of Manchester, Birmingham, Liverpool, Newcastle upon Tyne and the Leeds-Bradford area. In 1951 the population enumerated in the five conurbations centered on these cities accounted for a further fifth of the total for England and Wales.

The term "conurbation" appears to have been first used in the earlier part of this century by Professor P. Geddes, to refer to "city-regions" or "town-aggregates" such as Greater London.[1] During the inter-war years Professor C. B. Fawcett studied the subject in some detail, publishing two papers on conurbations,

[1] See, for example, *Cities in Evolution* (1915).

based respectively on the 1921 and 1931 census results [2] and a book in 1935.[3] The Royal Commission on the Distribution of the Industrial Population (the Barlow Commission), which reported in 1940, paid considerable attention to this phenomenon, and at their request the General Register Office compiled a considerable amount of statistical and other material on a conurbation basis as well as for the usual regions, county boroughs and counties. The conurbations dealt with in the memorandum of evidence submitted by the Registrar General under the title *Statistics of Mortality in Connection with Urbanisation and the Distribution of Industry,* (Minutes of Evidence, 28th Day) were those of over 100,000 population at the 1931 census, as defined by Professor Fawcett in his 1932 paper. There were 37 of these, five being in Scotland, but in several cases only one local authority area was involved, e.g., the city of Sheffield.

The growing interest in special qualities of conurbations made them a natural subject for further study at the subsequent census, which owing to the war did not take place until 1951. This was also in line with international recommendations. The United Nations Population Commission, at its fifth session in 1950, recommended that summary census tabulations should be made for "agglomerations or clusters of population living in built-up contiguous areas which, according to the definition adopted in each country, are considered as single localities or population centers." Article 6 of the Nomenclature Regulations adopted by the World Health Assembly, 1948, requires member countries to publish statistics of causes of death for "each town of 1,000,000 population and over, otherwise the largest town with a population of at least 100,000." The word "town" can obviously in this context be interpreted to mean a conurbation and not merely an urban area under the control of one administrative authority.

Greater London and the five major conurbations in England and Wales were accordingly identified for statistical purposes in the 1951 Census, as was the Central Clydeside conurbation in Scotland. Populations were given in the *Census 1951, England*

---

[2] "British Conurbations in 1921," *Sociological Review*, April, 1922, and "Distribution of the Urban Population in Great Britain, 1931," *Geographical Journal*, February, 1932.

[3] *Millionaire Cities.*

and Wales, Preliminary Report, and an extended range of data in the *Census 1951, Great Britain, One Per Cent Sample Tables.* The present report is entirely devoted to them, and further important data will be given in the *Occupation Tables* and *Industry Tables* volumes. Conurbations have also been identified in the *Registrar General's Annual Statistical Review* since 1950. Their definition is further discussed below.

PRINCIPLES OF DEFINITION

Professor Geddes did not define his concept of conurbation in any detail, but Professor Fawcett devoted much attention to it, in his 1932 paper giving the following definition:

"a conurbation is an area occupied by a continuous series of dwellings, factories and other buildings, harbour and docks, urban parks and playing fields, etc., which are not separated from each other by rural land; though in many cases in this country such an urban area includes enclosures of rural land which is still in agricultural occupation."

Professor Fawcett emphasized the difficulty of determining the precise boundaries even on the basis of his definition, and considered that it was only possible on the basis of acquaintance with the area and a careful study of large scale maps. The Barlow Commission [4] felt that Fawcett's definition placed too much emphasis on bricks and mortar as constituting the link and that, while in many cases it might be adequate, in others a better test would seem to be how far out from a given center industry or the industrial population looked to that center as essential to its life and as the focus of its business activities. It was recognized that a definition of any particular conurbation would require a statement of the administrative areas included as a result of applying the adopted criteria.

The conurbations as defined for the 1951 census are aggregates of local authority areas. Since the needs of both central and local government so require, demographic and other statistics have usually to be compiled on the basis of local administrative

---

[4] *Royal Commission on the Distribution of the Industrial Population, Report,* paragraph 12. Cmd. 6153. H.M.S.O., 1940.

areas. General convenience and ease of integration therefore suggest that the larger unit should be an aggregate of complete smaller units. This may lead to a certain amount of difficulty in delimiting the fringe—there is no intermediate position between wholly including or wholly excluding a smaller unit—but the general statistical picture is hardly affected. An important consequence of this type of definition is that statistics for conurbations can easily be aggregated either for earlier years or for any data given for local administrative units. It may be noted that conurbations are thus parallel to the "standard metropolitan areas" identified in the United States censuses.

No two conurbations are quite alike either in originating influences, geography or local government structure. There are general similarities, but each must be studied for itself. The definitions finally agreed for each represent the sum of informed local opinion rather than the expression of uniform scientific rules.

Finally it must be emphasized that these definitions have been formed to delimit areas for statistical analysis and are not at all concerned with the way in which the boundaries of individual urban areas or groupings of areas should be determined for general administrative or local government purposes.

DEFINITION OF MAJOR PROVINCIAL CONURBATIONS

In 1950 the standing Interdepartmental Committee on Social and Economic Research expressed the view that the major conurbations should be defined for use in statistical analyses. It was thought that there would be little difference of opinion over the smaller conurbations, but that differences might well arise over the precise constitution of the six major conurbations (other than Greater London) which Professor Fawcett called "millionaire cities," viz., Greater Birmingham, Greater Manchester, Merseyside, Tyneside, West Yorkshire and Greater Glasgow. Greater London, which had been identified as a unit for statistical purposes for some time, was excepted from immediate study, the unit being generally taken to cover the metropolitan community (although the boundary had in fact been over-run in some places by urban development, e.g. Romford, Hornchurch, Dartford).

Draft proposals were assembled for study by the Interdepartmental Committee, which were based on Professor Fawcett's proposals and the views of the Barlow Commission as well as a detailed examination of the areas. The further examination of the proposals was at the Committee's request carried through to a conclusion by the Central Statistical Office. Interested Departments were consulted, and detailed consideration of the proposals referred to regional committees convened by the Ministry of Town and Country Planning, representing the regional interests of departments and the local universities. Thus the proposals as finally agreed upon represented the largest common measure of agreement for an all purpose statistical unit, and included the consensus of expert local opinion. In the event they also satisfied the test, suggested by the Barlow Commission, of collecting together industrial areas which looked to the same center as a focal point for commercial and other activities.

The regional committees had the proposals and notes in front of them which had originally been considered by the Interdepartmental Committee on Social and Economic Research. The one over-riding condition under which they worked was that each conurbation should be an aggregate of local authority areas. Three other factors of varying importance were also to be taken into account; first, that the conurbation generally should be a continuously built-up area, but on the one hand this should not include ribbon development, and on the other it should not necessarily exclude a built-up area separated by a narrow strip of rural land from the main built-up area to which it was strongly attached for employment or other reasons; second, that a local area should be considered for inclusion in a conurbation to whose focal center it was strongly attached as a center for work, shopping, higher education, sports or entertainment; third, that some consideration should be given to population density.

Although differences in the circumstances of the five areas may have led to differences in the relative weight given to these three factors, the results of the regional meetings showed a remarkable degree of consistency in the general method of drawing boundaries and this consistency may be regarded as being enhanced by the fact that their recommendations were finally reviewed centrally from a common standpoint. There was also a general agreement that, where two definitions were possible, other things being equal, the larger area should be taken. This had the merit of promising a longer life to the constitutions so proposed before review and amendment were required, thus extending a longer period of continuity to the statistics so presented. The wider definition was in line with the adoption originally of the Metropolitan Police District as Greater London, though in the intervening years development had covered most of the area. In general it may be repeated that the criterion for inclusion or exclusion was community of interest, considered from many aspects, but taking into account mainly the degree of centripetal attraction exerted by the central areas, especially as regards employment, on those surrounding areas which prima facie would seem to form part of the continuous urbanized area.

STANDARD METROPOLITAN STATISTICAL AREAS *

U.S. BUREAU OF THE CENSUS

It has been long recognized that for many types of social and economic analysis it is necessary to consider as a unit the entire population in and around the city whose activities form an integrated social and economic system. Prior to the 1950 Census, areas of this type had been defined in somewhat different ways for different purposes and by various agencies. Leading examples were the metropolitan districts of the Census of Population, the industrial areas of the Census of Manufactures, and the labor market areas of the Bureau of Employment Security. To permit all Federal statistical agencies to utilize the same areas for the publication of general-purpose statistics, the Bureau of the Budget has established standard metropolitan statistical areas (SMSA's).[1]

Except in New England, an SMSA is a county or group of contiguous counties which contains at least one city of 50,000 inhabitants or more or "twin cities" with a combined population of

---

* Reprinted from U.S. Bureau of the Census, *U.S. Census of the Population: 1960. Number of Inhabitants*, Final Report PC(1)-17A (Washington, D.C.: U.S. Government Printing Office, 1960), pp. vii-viii, with the permission of the publisher.

[1] See also the Bureau of the Budget publication *Standard Metropolitan Statistical Areas*, U.S. Government Printing Office, Washington 25, D.C., 1959.

at least 50,000. In addition to the county, or counties, containing such a city or cities, contiguous counties are included in an SMSA if, according to certain criteria, they are essentially metropolitan in character and are socially and economically integrated with the central city. The criteria followed in the delineation of SMSA's relate to a city, or cities, of sufficient population size to constitute the central city and to the economic and social relationships with contiguous counties that are metropolitan in character.

1. Each SMSA must include at least:

a. One city with 50,000 inhabitants or more, or

b. Two cities having contiguous boundaries and constituting, for general economic and social purposes, a single community with a combined population of at least 50,000, the smaller of which must have a population of at least 15,000.

2. If two or more adjacent counties each have a city of 50,000 inhabitants or more and the cities are within 20 miles of each other (city limits to city limits), they will be included in the same area unless there is definite evidence that the two cities are not economically and socially integrated.

The criteria of metropolitan character relate primarily to the attributes of the outlying county as a place of work or as a home for a concentration of nonagricultural workers. Specifically, these criteria are:

3. At least 75 per cent of the labor force of the county must be in the nonagricultural labor force.

4. In addition to criterion 3, the county must meet at least one of the following conditions:

a. It must have 50 per cent or more of its population living in contiguous minor civil divisions with a density of at least 150 persons per square mile, in an unbroken chain of minor civil divisions with such density radiating from a central city in the area.

b. The number of nonagricultural workers employed in the county must equal at least 10 per cent of the number of nonagricultural workers employed in the county containing the largest city in the area, or the outlying county must be the place of employment of at least 10,000 nonagricultural workers.

c. The nonagricultural labor force living in the county must equal at least 10 per cent of the nonagricultural labor force living in the county containing the largest city in the area, or the outlying county must be the place of residence of a nonagricultural labor force of at least 10,000.

5. In New England, the city and town are administratively more important than the county, and data are compiled locally for such minor civil divisions. Here, towns and cities are the units used in defining SMSA's. In New England, because smaller units are used and more restricted areas result, a population density of at least 100 persons per square mile is used as the measure of metropolitan character.

The criteria of integration relate primarily to the extent of economic and social communication between the outlying counties and the central county.

6. A county is regarded as integrated with the county or counties containing the central cities of the area if either of the following criteria is met:

a. If 15 per cent of the workers living in the given outlying county work in the county or counties containing the central city or cities of the area, or

b. If 25 per cent of those working in the given outlying county live in the county or counties containing the central city or cities of the area. Only where data for criteria 6a and 6b are not conclusive are other related types of information used. This information includes such items as average telephone calls per subscriber per month from the county to the county containing central cities of the area; per cent of the population in the county located in the central city telephone exchange area; newspaper circulation reports prepared by the Audit Bureau of Circulation; analysis of charge accounts in retail stores of central cities to determine the extent of their use by residents of the contiguous county; delivery service practices of retail stores in central cities; official traffic counts; the extent of public transportation facilities in operation between central cities and communities in the contiguous county; and the extent to which local planning groups and other civic organizations operate jointly.

7. Although there may be several cities of 50,000 or more in an SMSA, not all are necessarily central cities. The following criteria are used for determining central cities:

a. The largest city in an SMSA is always a central city.

b. In addition, one or two additional cities may be second-

ary central cities on the basis and in the order of the following
criteria:

   (1) The additional city or cities have at least 250,000
inhabitants.

   (2) The additional city or cities have a population of
one-third or more of that of the largest city and a minimum population of 25,000, except that both cities are central cities in those
instances where cities qualify under criterion 1b. (A city which
qualified as a secondary central city in 1950 but which does not
qualify in 1960 has been temporarily retained as a central city.)

   8. The titles of the SMSA's consist of the names of the central
cities followed by the names of the States in which the areas are
located.

   In view of the special importance of the metropolitan complexes around New York and Chicago, the Nation's largest cities,
several contiguous SMSA's and additional counties that do not
appear to meet the formal integration criteria but do have strong
interrelationships of other kinds have been combined into the
New York–Northeastern New Jersey and the Chicago–Northwestern Indiana Standard Consolidated Areas, respectively. The
former is identical with the New York–Northeastern New Jersey
SMA of 1950, and the latter corresponds roughly to the Chicago
SMA (two more counties having been added).

Chapter 3

INTERNATIONAL METHODS OF DELIMITATION

METHODS AND PROBLEMS IN THE DELIMITATION OF URBAN UNITS *

JACK P. GIBBS **

Previous papers in Part I represent observations on the definition of urban units and procedures for their delimitation in particular countries. What is offered here is an explication of delimitation methods which can be applied throughout the world. In considering these methods the readers, and the newcomers to the field in particular, should realize that no hard and fast rules can be laid down with a guarantee of realistic results. Consequently, any method recommended for universal application must be treated with caution and, above all, applied with a liberal dosage of common sense.

ESTABLISHING THE BOUNDARIES OF AN URBAN AREA BY DIRECT EXAMINATION

The fact that cities have physical as well as political limits is not a scientific discovery; it is, rather, a matter of common experience. As one approaches a city there is a definite change in the pattern of settlement; buildings cease to be separated by farm land or forests, and the pattern becomes one of congestion and a

* Written especially for this volume.
** Member of the staff of International Urban Research.

somewhat regular spacing of dwelling places. The exact point at which this pattern begins is debatable in some cases, but the approximate limits of an urban area [1] are, as a rule, clearly apparent.

The fact of physical distinctness makes it possible to establish a boundary through the "walk-around" method. Armed with a map an observer can establish the approximate limits of an urban area by moving around it and noting surrounding landmarks. In this method the choice of landmarks is the foremost problem, for only those which can be located on the map are suitable as points of reference; and they must on the one hand enclose as much of the urban area as possible but on the other a minimum of rural territory.

Once the surrounding landmarks are located on a map, a continuous line connecting them demarcates the urban area. Some idea of the nature of the boundary so formed can be obtained by an inspection of Figure I, which depicts a hypothetical region.

The use of landmark lines is justified only when other types of reference points cannot be used. Actually, as Figure I suggests, a closer approximation can usually be achieved through the use of "line features"—such as railroads, rivers, and roads [2]—assuming that they can be located on a map. Delimitation in these terms proceeds in the same manner as in the case of landmark lines. A map which shows all of the major line features in the vicinity of an urban area is first secured. The second step is that of circling the urban area and noting those line features which bear the closest correspondence to its periphery. When these line features are located on the map, as shown in Figure I in the form of railroads, rivers, and roads; they indicate the approximate extent of continuous urban settlement. [3]

An alternative to the walk-around method of delimitation involves the use of aerial photographs. A picture taken over the center of an urban area at an altitude sufficient to provide a wide view of the surrounding territory reveals in a most dramatic fashion the physical reality of its boundaries. Although the technical

[1] The concept "urban area" is used to designate cities as demographic-ecological entities rather than political units.

[2] The term "line feature" is used here to designate any landscape characteristic which forms a part of the boundary of a territorial unit.

[3] The combination of landmark lines and line features may afford a better approximation of the urban area than either taken separately.

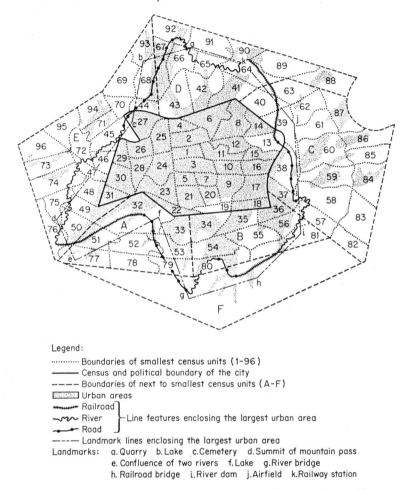

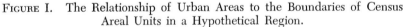

Legend:

.... Boundaries of smallest census units (1-96)
—————— Census and political boundary of the city
– – – – Boundaries of next to smallest census units (A-F)
▨▨▨ Urban areas
╫╫╫╫ Railroad ⎤
~~~~ River ⎬ Line features enclosing the largest urban area
•—•— Road ⎦
– · – · – Landmark lines enclosing the largest urban area
Landmarks: a. Quarry   b. Lake   c. Cemetery   d. Summit of mountain pass
             e. Confluence of two rivers   f. Lake   g. River bridge
             h. Railroad bridge   i. River dam   j. Airfield   k. Railway station

FIGURE I.   The Relationship of Urban Areas to the Boundaries of Census
Areal Units in a Hypothetical Region.

complexity and expenses entailed may often preclude the use of
aerial photography, it warrants consideration as providing what
is perhaps a superior means of delimitation.[4]

[4] For a treatment of aerial photography in general see: A. J. Eardley, *Aerial
Photographs: Their Use and Interpretation* (New York: Harper and Brothers,
1942); H. T. U. Smith, *Aerial Photographs and Their Application* (New York:
D. Appleton-Century Co., 1943); Lyle G. Trorey, *Handbook of Aerial Mapping
and Photogrammetry* (Cambridge, England: University Press, 1950). As intro-
ductions to the use of aerial photography in urban research see: Melville C.
Branch, Jr., *Aerial Photography in Urban Planning and Research* (Cambridge:
Harvard University Press, 1948); Norman Carls, *How to Read Aerial Photographs*

As an aid to delimitations an aerial photograph must meet two requirements. First, it must encompass not only the main built-up unit [5] but also its immediate environs. And, second, the photograph must be in detail sufficient to reveal differences in land use patterns and show those landmarks which locate the boundaries of census units within and around the urban area.[6]

All other things being equal, the crucial factor in the use of aerial photography is the size of the urban area being considered. Where it is large a single photograph will not meet the second requirement stated above. Because the picture must be taken at a very high altitude to meet the first requirement, it will not reveal those details which are needed in the different steps of delimitation. In a situation of this sort a composite picture of the urban area must be constructed on the basis of a series of photographs. Ordinarily, since no precise measurements are intended, this composite picture can take the form of an uncontrolled mosaic.[7]

Problems in delimitation by direct examination. A description of methods of delimitation inevitably represents an oversimplification. Each situation presents unique problems that cannot be resolved by appealing to universal rules. On the other hand, there are certain problems which can be anticipated and dealt with in a somewhat standardized way.

In the process of delimitation one often finds territory within the main built-up unit which is not settled in an urban fashion. Such territory is here designated as an *enclave;* and it typically appears in the form of a place for recreation, a body of water, or

---

for *Census Work* (Washington: U.S. Bureau of the Census, 1947), particularly pp. 14-29; Rene A. Huybens, *La Photographie Aérienne et l'Urbanisme* (Linkebeek, Belgium: A. Pinkers, 1955); N. A. Sokolova, *Aerofotosyemka Gorodov v Masshtabakh 1: 2000 i 1: 5000* (Moskva: Gosoodarstvennoye Izdatyelstvo, 1952).

[5] A built-up unit is a strip of land which is uniformily settled in an urban fashion. The territory thus appears to be completely covered by buildings (meaning in this case all types of structures—factories, stores, warehouses, hospitals, etc., in addition to dwelling places) and streets. The main built-up unit is the largest piece of land in an urban area which meets this description, with the remainder of the urban area consisting of smaller built-up units and intervening spaces that are not under agricultural occupation.

[6] A census unit is a territorial division which is used in reporting a census of population.

[7] See Branch, *op. cit.*, pp. 22-26.

a cemetery.[8] Regardless of its nature, however, in so far as the space is surrounded by the main built-up unit, the common practice is to consider it as a part of the urban area.

The truly difficult questions in establishing a boundary arise in the treatment of land on the periphery of the main built-up unit, for it is here that one often finds territory not characterized by uniform land use. The common practice, and the one recommended here, is to exclude from the urban area:

1) settled or unsettled land (with the distinction being dependent on the presence or absence of dwelling places) which is used to produce agricultural or forestry products,

2) unsettled land which is not used for any particular purpose, and

3) bodies of water not traversed by a bridge or a tunnel connecting the main built-up unit with other urban settlements

This practice assures the inclusion of parks, cemeteries, recreation places, and airfields which touch upon the main built-up unit. It also means that outlying urban settlements are included in the urban area if they are not separated from the main built-up unit by excluded territory.

Two boundary problems remain to be considered. With the growth of efficient transportation there is a tendency for a thin line of urban settlement to move out from the main built-up unit along highways, railroads, or watercourses. These patterns are designated here as *arterial urbanization*. Two guides are suggested for establishing the limits of an urban area along a line of arterial settlement. First, the two sides of the transportation course should be treated separately. And, second, if at any place along the transportation path we find one of the three types of territory which are to be excluded (these three having been described above), this marks the outer extent of the urban area.[9] The best general rule in dealing with arterial urbanization is to require a continuous built-up zone, with any appearance of land

[8] This use of the term *enclave* attaches to it a much broader meaning than is sometimes the case.

[9] There appears to be no common practice in dealing with arterial urbanization. Conurbations in England and Wales exclude "ribbon development," but it is not clear what is subsumed under this category. The U.S. Bureau of the Census allows for gaps up to 1½ miles between an urban settlement and the main part of an Urbanized Area.

under agricultural use marking the outer limits of the urban area. This is particularly true when a thin line of settlement connects two otherwise distinctly independent urban areas.

A final boundary problem is that of the treatment of bodies of water. Consistent with the basic idea underlying the urban area concept, in cases where urban settlements are separated by water there must be some constructed physical connection between them before they are considered as parts of one unit. This connection can take the form of either a bridge or a tunnel. Were we concerned with the broad class of phenomena termed "functional linkage" or "functional integration," the separation of urban settlements by bodies of water or certain types of land would be accorded an entirely different treatment. The idea of functional connection, however, is basic to the delimitation of metropolitan areas and not urban areas.

THE COORDINATION OF URBAN AREA BOUNDARIES WITH CENSUS UNITS

If research is dependent on census data for information, the boundaries of the urban area must correspond with territorial divisions recognized in census reports (i.e., census units).[10] Such a correspondence does not come about naturally; it is achieved only through a coordination of the physical boundary of the urban area with administrative lines.[11]

Steps in coordination. The first goal in delimitation has already been described—that of locating the boundaries of an urban area on a map, either in terms of landmark lines or line features.[12] The map shows nothing more than territorial extent, but it does provide a basis for seeking a correspondence between census boundaries and the urban area. This correspondence is established by first locating the boundaries of census units on the map which shows the landmark lines, or line features, that enclose the

[10] Such a correspondence may be said to hold only when the census units that contain the urban area can be specified.

[11] This assumes of course that there is no close relationship between the urban area and the political limits of the city. If there is a close relationship between the two, the city is treated as the equivalent to the urban area, since it is usually treated as a census unit in census reports.

[12] The treatment of an aerial photograph will be taken up in a later section.

urban area. Figure I provides an illustration of such boundaries. Inspection will reveal that neither the landmark lines nor the line features closely follow the boundaries of census units. Consequently, the second step is that of selecting those census boundaries which are the closest to the lines [13] that enclose the urban area. Since the census units wholly within the lines are automatically included, the only questionable cases are those on the periphery. As a rule the best policy in such cases is to include census units with one-half or more of their area within the line.[14]

The application of the above rule to the landmark lines in Figure I produces an Urban Area [15] bounded by the outer limits of the following census units: 50, 51, 32, 33, 54, 80, 81, 56, 37, 38, 39, 40, 64, 65, 66, 67, 68, 44, 27, 26, 29, 46, 30, 48, and 49. There are several discrepancies between this boundary and the actual extent of urban settlement. In some instances this is due to the unrealistic nature of the landmark lines (see census units 27, 13, and 65), and in other cases it is due to a lack of correspondence between the census boundaries and the landmark lines (see census unit 53). Despite these discrepancies, however, the units listed above form a far more realistic ecological entity than does the "city" in Figure I.[16]

In a few instances the coordination of census boundaries with line features in Figure I produces more realistic results than is the case for landmark lines. The coordination of the two creates an Urban Area bounded by the outer limits of these census units:

[13] These may be either landmark lines or line features, as they are treated in an identical manner.

[14] This applies only when the concern is with the territorial extent of the urban area. Another rule is called for with respect to population. If an inspection of the unit in question indicates that more than one-half of the dwelling places are within the line, the whole of the unit should be included in the urban area. Where the census units are small and the concern is with population, a more practical rule is to include the whole of a unit if any part of it is within the line. This rule is far more easy to apply, and it makes for a greater constancy in the boundary over time, since it includes territory into which the urban area is likely to expand.

[15] The capitalization of the term urban area (Urban Area) indicates that reference is made to an area with census boundaries. These boundaries should bear a close correspondence to the urban area as it appears on an aerial photograph or a map, but the correspondence between the two is only rarely a close one.

[16] If the end product, the Urban Area, bears a closer correspondence to the pattern of urban settlement than does the city as a political entity, the delimitation has at least improved on the existing situation.

50, 32, 53, 79, 80, 81, 56, 37, 38, 13, 14, 40, 64, 42, 66, 67, 44, 27, 26, 29, 46, 47, 48, and 49. Once again the boundary is not exactly what it should be, but it provides a fairly close approximation of the urban area.[17]

It is in the use of aerial photographs that one source of discrepancy between the urban area and its census boundary is eliminated. We have noted in Figure I how landmark lines and line features are far removed at certain points from the actual pattern of settlement.[18] In comparison, an aerial photograph more precisely shows the extent of an urban area; and, when the census units are drawn in, the photograph provides a better basis for coordinating boundaries.

The shaded sections of Figure I represent urban areas as they would appear on an aerial photograph. All census units which are entirely within the largest shaded part would automatically be included in the Urban Area.[19] The questionable cases are, once again, on the periphery.[20] The treatment of these units calls for two general rules. In so far as one is concerned with territorial extent, if over one-half of a census unit contains a part of the urban area, the whole of the unit should be included. A second rule should be applied when the concern is with urban population. If over one-half of the dwelling places appear to be in that part of the census unit which contains a section of the urban area, the whole of the unit should be included.

The application of the first rule (which relates to territory) in the case of Figure I results in an Urban Area bounded by the outer limits of census units 30, 31, 23, 22, 33, 54, 35, 56, 37, 16, 15, 12, 14, 8, 41, 6, 43, 67, 27, 26, and 29. This boundary fails to en-

---

[17] The reader is reminded that a somewhat different boundary would be taken if the concern were with urban population rather than territory.

[18] This is particularly true for the lines which run through or to the outside of census units 38, 39, 40, 64, 65, and 66.

[19] It is the largest urban area which is the concern here. The others are considered to be independent. Each urban area shown in Figure I consists of one or more built-up units and contiguous land under non-agricultural use. The unshaded areas in Figure I thus represent farms, forests, bodies of water, and land serving no particular purposes.

[20] For this reason, in actual practice only those census units on the approximate edge of an urban area need be drawn on an aerial photograph or a map. The inclusion of other census units can be determined on the basis of their location relative to those on the periphery.

compass all that it should, because the census lines have no close connection with the shape of the urban area.[21]

While the boundary given above is somewhat realistic as far as the spatial dimensions of the urban area is concerned, it is most unrealistic with regard to population. Several census units are excluded which, in an actual situation, would probably contain far more urban than rural residents. A more realistic population boundary (second rule) is formed by the outer limits of units 50, 51, 32, 53, 80, 55, 56, 37, 38, 15, 12, 14, 8, 41, 42, 66, 92, 93, 68, 44, 27, 26, 29, 30, 47, 48, and 49.

PROBLEMS IN THE COORDINATION OF BOUNDARIES

In actual practice the results achieved in the coordination of boundaries are contingent on the size of the census units. To understand this better let us assume that the small census units in Figure I (numbered 1-96) cannot be used in delimitation. Faced with this situation the researcher has no alternative but to use the political limits of the city and the larger census units (A-F). The most realistic delimitation in this case would be to consider the Urban Area as territorially consisting of the city and census unit B. From the viewpoint of urban population, it would have to be considered as encompassing the city and census units A, B, and D. The results in either case are not particularly good, but they do point to the fact that one has no choice in delimitation except to coordinate the boundaries of the urban area with those of the smallest census unit.

One major problem in delimitation by the method of direct examination remains to be considered. The purpose of coordinating an urban area with census units is to obtain information on the urban population. One must not lose sight of the fact, however, that data in census reports are always for a specific point in time; and if there is any appreciable lag between the date of the census and that of delimitation, information in census reports no longer applies to the Urban Area.

[21] If the exclusion of a census unit results in the division of what is actually a continuous urban area, it should be included. Census unit 43 in Figure I is thus included even though it does not meet the rule, because it contains a strip of the urban area leading to unit 67, which does meet the rule and is a part of the urban area.

THE DELIMITATION OF URBAN AREAS BY
INDIRECT EXAMINATION

Where it is not possible to delimit urban areas by direct examination, boundaries must be established through an inspection of data in census reports on territorial divisions. Basic to this method is the hypothesis that certain traits characterize urban populations and reflect the approximate spatial limits of urban settlements. In particular, there are reasons to believe that the occupational structure of a population and its density provide an adequate basis for a specification of the census units which contain an urban area.[22]

Prior to a statement of criteria and procedural steps for delimitation by indirect examination let us consider some of the problems entailed. Most of the major problems stem from variation in the characteristics of urban settlements and the nature of census units. With respect to the former, there is evidence that the relation between population density, occupational structure, and urban settlement varies from one country to the next. The nature of census units poses an even more serious obstacle. Their size varies from place to place, and the correspondence between their boundaries and the pattern of urban settlement cannot be assumed to be other than fortuitous.

The import of these "facts of delimitation" can best be appreciated when one fully understands what is involved in the method of indirect examination. Since the researcher cannot "see" the pattern of urban settlement, as he does in the case of direct examination, boundaries must be established through inference. This inference rests on the assumption that when population density and/or non-agricultural employment[23] reaches a certain point, a census unit may be considered as urban.

It is the determination of this "certain point" which poses the first major problem in setting forth delimitation criteria. Given variability in the correlates of urban settlement and the arbitrari-

---

[22] The method of indirect examination has been applied by International Urban Research in an attempt to delimit metropolitan areas throughout the world. See International Urban Research, *The World's Metropolitan Areas* (Berkeley and Los Angeles: University of California Press, 1959).

[23] Here, as elsewhere, non-agricultural employment is meant to exclude hunting, fishing, and forestry, as well as farming.

ness of census units, no perfect solution can be achieved. Certain agricultural regions in Asian countries, for example, have a population density equal to or exceeding that of some territory presently included in the Urbanized Areas of the United States. At a first glance, however, it would appear possible to arrive at a figure which provides a reliable basis for differentiation. Thus, a density of 2,000 persons per square mile in an area is normally the minimum found associated with a closely spaced street pattern in the United States,[24] a country with low urban densities, and this number is well beyond that of most agricultural areas. What this ignores, however, is the difference between census or administrative units and "areas," or "regions," as natural geographical entities. As an illustration, consider census unit "b" in Figure II.

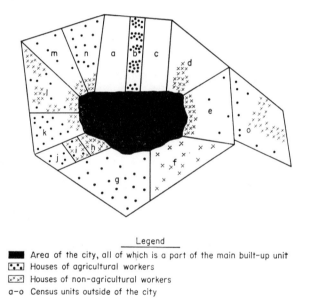

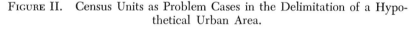

Legend

█ Area of the city, all of which is a part of the main built-up unit
▒ Houses of agricultural workers
▨ Houses of non-agricultural workers
a–o Census units outside of the city

FIGURE II. Census Units as Problem Cases in the Delimitation of a Hypothetical Urban Area.

Inspection will reveal that "b" comprises clusters of agricultural residences and is bounded on both sides by unsettled land. The "natural area" here comprises units "a," "b," and "c," since the

[24] U.S. Bureau of the Census, *U.S. Census of Population: 1950.* Vol. II, *Characteristics of the Population,* Part 1, "United States Summary" (Washington, D.C.: U.S. Government Printing Office, 1953), p. 22.

farm population and the land which supports it should be considered together. The combination of the three would result in a population density of less than 2,000 persons per square mile. But the method of indirect examinations makes no allowances for such combinations. Since the situation cannot be determined by direct examination, one must accept the density figure for "b" as it appears in a census report, and it could conceivably be over 2,000. The application of a density criterion would thus result in the inclusion of territory that would be excluded on the basis of direct examination.[25]

Undesirable results in the application of a density criterion can take the other direction. Consider, for example, census unit "e" in Figure II.[26] Here we have practically all of the inhabitants residing in an extension of the main built-up unit. However, because of the size of "e" and the lack of correspondence between its boundaries and land use pattern, its population density would probably be less than 2,000 per square mile. Thus, it is possible for a census unit to be excluded on the basis of a density criterion even though all or nearly all of its inhabitants reside in the main built-up unit.

What has been said of "e" applies equally well to "d" in Figure II. Taken together the two demonstrate that the shape of a census unit is no basis for judging the arbitrariness of boundaries. A realistic demographic unit in the case of "d" would be a narrow strip extending away from the city, while the same for "e" would closely follow the contour of the city limits.

Still another illustration of the inadequacy of a density criterion is offered in Figure II. An inspection of census units "m" and "n" reveals that an extension of the main built-up unit has been divided among the two, with "n" having far more agricultural workers than "m." Of the two, then, with respect to population, "m" more nearly deserves inclusion in the Urban Area, since far more of its residents are in the main built-up unit. If a density criterion is applied, however, it is "n" that is the more likely to be included.

[25] All, or practically all, of census unit "b" would be excluded because the clusters of houses are separated by strips of land not under urban settlement.

[26] It is highly improbable that all of the problem cases depicted in Figure II would ever be present in any real situation. They are considered here together (in an oversimplified form) only for purposes of illustration.

In each case described above the fault lies not so much with the density criterion *per se* but, rather, with the nature of the census boundaries. Where the census units are either uniformly small or bear a correspondence to the actual pattern of settlement,[27] a density requirement of 2,000 per square mile will usually achieve good results.

With respect to the population of an urban area, the application of a non-agricultural criterion to each of the census units cited above produces far more realistic results. If one requires that at least 65 per cent of the economically active residents be engaged in non-agricultural industries,[28] census units like "b" will be excluded, while those resembling "d" and "e" will be included.

Although the non-agricultural criterion appears to handle certain types of problem cases, there are dangers in its application. As examples in Figure II, both census units "f" and "l" would be included in the Urban Area, even though neither contains a part of the main built-up unit.[29]

At a first glance it might appear that the use of both a density and non-agricultural requirement would achieve success in treating problem cases such as "f" in Figure II. Nothing is gained by the combination of the two, however. It would in fact result in the exclusion of "f" cases, but it would do the same for "e," and the latter should be included. Furthermore, the combination of the two will not result in the exclusion of census units that resemble "l" in Figure II. This is a problem case for which there is no solution other than knowledge of the region, or a field investigation.[30]

[27] Only census units "f," "g," "h," "i," and "j" in Figure II meet these conditions.

[28] This particular criterion is suggested because it has been subjected to a trial on a world-wide basis. See International Urban Research, *op. cit.*

[29] In an actual situation census units resembling "f" or "l" would likely be considered part of the metropolitan area, because of the probability of a high level of commuting to the city. The concern here, however, is with Urban Areas, and census units like "f" or "l" should not be included.

[30] If the population clusters in "l" formed a continuous extension of the main built-up unit, its inclusion in the Urban Area would be desirable. In cases where this cannot be determined on the basis of maps, aerial photographs, or a field investigation, one can only apply the non-agricultural criterion. However, if a census report recognizes the existence of urban localities (towns, villages, municipalities, etc.) in a census unit, the localities should be treated separately. If the remainder of the census unit (i.e., excluding the population of the urban localities) meets the non-agricultural requirement, then the whole of the unit can be treated as part of the Urban Area.

The inclusion or exclusion of census units on the basis of both a non-agricultural and density criterion is feasible only when the concern is with territorial extent. Under a non-agricultural criterion alone the Urban Area in Figure II would include the city and units "d," "e," "f," "h," "i," and "l." This territory is well over twice as large as the actual area of urban settlement, even though its boundaries are somewhat realistic with respect to population. If one applies both a density and non-agricultural criterion, the territory is much more reasonable. Here it would comprise the city, unit "h," and possibly units "l" and "i." This points to the need to delimit two Urban Areas—one with regard to territory and the other with regard to population.

The tendency for a non-agricultural criterion to overextend the territory of an urban area has ramifications beyond spatial distortion. Since more land is included than should be, the greater is the possibility that the territory will contain urban localities that are in no way connected to the main built-up unit. For example, under the non-agricultural rule both "o" and "e" in Figure II would qualify for inclusion, even though the main built-up unit does not extend into "o."

The case of "o" illustrates how the uncritical application of a non-agricultural standard to large census units in highly industrialized countries could easily result in the creation of Urban Areas that are much too large, even from the viewpoint of population. In short, since delimitation proceeds through successive rings of census units, it could go almost indefinitely before a ring is encountered in which none of the units meets the non-agricultural criterion.

A particular kind of density criterion is one possible safeguard against overextended Urban Areas. Census units which immediately surround the main built-up unit and contain only small parts of it tend to have a low population density. These units should be included, providing that they meet the non-agricultural requirement, but their low density indicates that the main built-up unit does not extend across them and into the next outer ring. Consequently, before a census unit is considered part of the Urban Area, it should touch upon territory already included which has a density of 2,000 or more. Without this continuity in high density there is no assurance whatever that the boundaries encompass a continuous urban area and not a series of independent urban settlements.

One other reason for the tendency of Urban Areas to be over-extended under a non-agricultural criterion is not illustrated in Figure II. As in the case of population density, it is not an easy matter to arrive at a defensible cutting point for non-agricultural employment. The criterion of 65 per cent appears to work well in underdeveloped countries; but, when applied to an industrialized society, where the percentage is likely to be well above 65 for the country as a whole, the results are enormous Urban Areas which contain a mixture of rural territory and independent urban localities. In fact, it is possible for the Urban Area to have a greater proportion of agricultural workers than does the country as a whole, and the territory delimited has no more claim to being an urban area than does the entire nation. One improvement on the criterion is to require both an absolute level and one relative to the country. The standard recommended here is that a census unit have a level of non-agricultural employment which is higher than that for the country as a whole, as well as being beyond the point of 65 per cent.

In concluding it should be noted that the above modifications and combinations of criteria do not by any means provide a solution to all problems. We have seen this to be the case for "m" and "l" in Figure II, and it is even more so for "k." There, regardless of the criteria, a small extension of the main built-up unit is almost certain to be left out of the Urban Area; and this situation could be modified only by shifting census boundaries.

Summary of criteria and procedural steps in delimitation. With respect to delimiting population a census unit is included in the Urban Area if:

(a) it touches upon territory already included which has a population density of 2,000 or more persons per square mile *and*

(b) has 65 or more per cent of its economically active residents engaged in non-agricultural industries *and*

(c) the per cent of its economically active residents in non-agricultural industries is higher than that for the country as a whole, *or*

(d) it is surrounded by territory already included.

With respect to delimiting territory a census unit is included in the Urban Area if:

(a) it touches upon territory already included *and*

(b) 65 or more per cent of its economically active residents are engaged in non-agricultural industries *and*

(c) the per cent of its economically active residents engaged in non-agricultural industries is higher than that for the country as a whole *and*

(d) it has a population density of over 2,000 persons per square mile.

The territory designated as a city [31] in a census report is a point of departure for the first step in delimitation, which is the location of the approximate center of the main built-up unit. In seeking this point, one must bear in mind that the designation of territory as a city only suggests the possibility that the whole of the unit is under urban settlement. Consequently, whenever possible, delimitation should start with an inspection of census units within the city. [32] This inspection aims for the location of the census unit having the highest population density. Once selected this unit is considered to be the central district of the Urban Area. [33]

The next step in delimitation is the location of the census units which surround the central district. In Figure I, assuming that census unit 1 has the highest density, the surrounding units are 2, 11, 3, 24, and 25. The corresponding areas in Figure II (where the city is taken as the central district) are a, b, c, d, e, f, g, h, k, l, m, and n. Once these first ring units are established, the criteria for delimiting the population of the urban area is applied to each unit. The delimitation comes to an end when a ring is found in which none of the units qualify for inclusion.

One further comment is in order. In working with the Urban

[31] Other equivalent terms, such as municipality, borough, town, etc., may be used. In certain countries, Spain and Italy being examples, where urban localities are merged administratively with larger territorial units, those minor civil divisions (*communes, municipios,* etc.) with a high level of population density should be taken as city equivalents.

[32] The class name for such census units varies, of course, from country to country. They may be known as wards, *barrios,* precincts, census tracts, *ku, stadtteile,* to mention only a few designations.

[33] Where there are no census units within the city limits, the city itself must be treated as the central district.

Area the purpose of the research must be kept in mind. Where the concern is with the characteristics of the urban population, it is the central district and those units which qualify under the population criteria that are to be considered. However, if the research relates to territorial extent, areal shape, and/or population density, it is the central district and those units which meet the territorial criteria that make up the Urban Area. Only in cases where all of the units involved meet both sets of criteria can such a distinction be ignored.

THE DELIMITATION OF METROPOLITAN AREAS

It often happens in scientific activity that certain changes in the phenomenon under consideration necessitate the development of a new unit of observation and an associated concept. Such has been the case in the study of urbanization in the 20th century.

With the creation of efficient forms of transportation cities have come to take on another spatial dimension. Whereas the population directly participating in the economic life of a city had been closely identified with a compact urban area, the growth of a broad zone of commuting has created a new entity, the metropolitan area. In an early classic study McKenzie [34] pointed to its essential feature—functional integration of areal parts. Unlike an urban area, the boundaries of a metropolitan area are not necessarily physically distinct. It is, rather, the interdependence of component areal parts which underlies its unity.

Statement of criteria and procedural steps. Drawing on the experience of the U.S. Bureau of the Census and International Urban Research, the following method is recommended for the delimitation of a metropolitan area:

(1) As an initial step an Urban Area is established either through direct or indirect examination. [35]

(2) The smallest census units which surround the Urban Area are located on a map in a series of concentric rings.

[34] R. D. McKenzie, *The Metropolitan Community* (New York: McGraw-Hill Book Company, Inc., 1933).

[35] In cases where an Urban Area cannot be delimited, the city as a political unit can be treated as its equivalent in the different steps of delimitation.

(3) Each census unit, starting with the first ring, is included in the Metropolitan Area [36] if it:

   (a) touches upon the Urban Area or another unit already included in the Metropolitan Area (with separations by water being ignored) *and*

   (b) has at least 65 per cent of its economically active residents engaged in non-agricultural industries *and*

   (c) has a higher percentage of its economically active residents engaged in non-agricultural industries than does the country as a whole *and*

   (d) has at least 15 per cent of its economically active residents employed in the Urban Area *or* draws at least 20 per cent of its work force from the Urban Area's resident population *or* has a percentage of its residents employed in the Urban Area which is equal to or greater than the largest percentage of residents in any unit of the Urban Area who are employed outside the unit but within the Urban Area *or* draws a percentage of its work force from the Urban Area which is equal to or greater than the lowest percentage of the work force drawn by any unit within the Urban Area from the remainder of the Urban Area *and*

   (e) has more of its economically active residents commuting to work in the Urban Area in question than to any other Urban Area *or*

   (f) is surrounded by census units already included in the Metropolitan Area.

To understand the criteria better let us consider their application to census unit 71 in Figure I. With regard to criterion (3a) this means that one of the surrounding units (72, 45, 70, or 94) would have to be included in the Metropolitan Area before 71 could be considered. Criteria (3b) and (3c) have been explained in the section on the delimitation of Urban Areas and call for no further comment at this point.

The alternative requirements listed under (3d) hold the key to evidence of functional integration. Census unit 71 would not have to meet all four of the requirements. It would be excluded from the Metropolitan Area only if it failed to meet at least one of them. Thus, if 15 per cent of its economically active residents

[36] The capitalization of the term indicates territory demarcated by census boundaries.

are employed in the Urban Area or if 20 per cent of its work force reside in the Urban Area, unit 71 would meet the (3d) criterion. Let us suppose, however, that the figure is only 14 in the first case and 18 in the second case. Under this condition census unit 71 can be still considered for inclusion if either of these figures is equal to or higher than a corresponding percentage for any unit within the Urban Area. If, for example, only 14 per cent of the residents of unit 37 (which is within the Urban Area) commute to the remainder of the Urban Area, 71 would meet the third requirement under (3d). Similarly, it would meet the fourth requirement if any census unit in the urban area draws 18 per cent or less of its work force from the remainder of the Urban Area.

The rationale for the comparison of units within and outside of the Urban Area as to levels of commuting is tied up with the idea of integration. If one follows the commonly accepted practice of treating all of the Urban Area as part of the Metropolitan Area, this implicitly assumes the equation of physical with functional linkage. However, if a census unit outside the Urban Area is as closely linked in a functional sense to the Urban Area as any unit within it, there is no defensible basis for excluding the unit from the Metropolitan Area.

Criterion (3e) is an extension of the integration concept. Since a census unit cannot be assigned to different Metropolitan Areas, it can best be considered part of the one to which it sends the largest number of commuters.

The final criterion, (3f), is meant to insure the inclusion of *enclaves.* Any unit which is surrounded by territory already assigned to the Metropolitan Area is also included regardless of the other requirements. Those units which are not surrounded must meet each of the first five criteria—(3a) through (3e)—before they can be included.

A particular problem in the delimitation of metropolitan areas. An attempt at delimitation is rarely blessed with the commuting data called for by the above criteria. In their absence it may prove feasible to employ alternative indicators of functional integration. Some examples of alternatives are: number of telephone calls, volume of mail, amount of traffic, and the place of residence of the customers of business establishments.

Given data on one of these variables, the foremost problem

is that of establishing some defensible criterion for their treatment. The requirements listed under criterion (3d) cannot be used because the variables do not pertain to commuting *per se*. In this connection, however, the last two requirements under (3d) can be modified so as to be applicable to virtually any phenomenon deemed indicative of functional integration.

As an illustration of the modification of criteria let us suppose that commuting data are not available for the census units in Figure I. Suppose further, however, that it is possible to locate the residences (by census units) of the customers of a sample of establishments in census unit 1 (this being considered as the central business district). The number of customers in each census unit, when converted to a proportion of the resident population, serves as a gauge of the relative degree of integration between each unit and the economic center of the urban area. Because the meaning of the data is relative to the nature of the sample, the way in which the central business district has been delimited, and the economic characteristics of the region, it is not feasible to state an absolute level for the measure which is universally applicable as a criterion. However, it is feasible to modify the third requirement under (3d) to fit the measure. If, for example, it were known that the proportion of the residents in census unit 71 who are customers of an establishment in the central business district is equal to or greater than the corresponding proportion for any unit in the Urban Area, this would constitute a defensible basis for including 71 in the metropolitan area.

CONCLUDING OBSERVATIONS ON DELIMITATION

For various reasons any delimitation should not be regarded as anything other than an experiment. This point of view is a realistic one, because, in final analysis, the results can be interpreted only in the context of the methods and data employed. It is true, of course, that a delimitation aims to capture the reality of urban entities through the application of standardized criteria; however, the goal of research and the results achieved should never be confused. There are several factors which operate to create a discrepancy between the intent of delimitation and the end product.

For one thing, the central concepts which guide delimitation—metropolitan area or urban area—remain somewhat vague. Beyond this there is room for doubt as to what criteria offer the best results when applied universally. There are even reasons to believe that standards must be made relative to the characteristics of the region under consideration. In brief, no particular set of criteria advanced to date (including those recommended here) can lay claim to being definitive. In addition to the validity of different approaches to delimitation one must not lose sight of the fact that circumstances regarding the availability of data often dictate the choice of criteria.

All of the above comes to one essential point. Whatever criteria one applies in delimitation, whether selected by choice or dictated by circumstance, they must be clearly set forth in the report of research. For if the essential step in urban research is to be taken, that is, comparison of urban units, there must be some assurance that they have been delimited in comparable terms.

PART II

SOME BASIC CHARACTERISTICS
OF URBAN UNITS

Introduction to Part II

Urban and metropolitan areas possess certain basic characteristics which are involved in the definition of an urban unit. There may be disagreement as to the nature of these definitive traits, but, as far as the writer knows, everyone recognizes that a certain population size and level of population density are at least necessary conditions for urban status. Thus, these two characteristics are basic to the point that they determine what is and is not an urban unit. Equally basic to urban status is the notion of territoriality. The inhabitants of a city do not necessarily share something in common as a consequence of kinship or being members of a formal voluntary association. Such ties among people are non-spatial in nature, but it is precisely on the basis of a common habitat that we consider paupers and priests, bakers and bankers as members of one and the same population. In other words, urban status is accorded a territory as well as its population. This is immediately evident when we consider that, for example, should the residents of Mexico City disperse, this urban unit and its population would no longer exist. The fact of territoriality adds two basic characteristics to urban units—areal extent and spatial shape. Unlike population size and density, there is neither a particular areal size nor a particular shape which is a definitive trait of urban status; however, the territorial nature of urban units makes these two characteristics basic.

Apart from the logical connection between population size, density, areal extent, and spatial shape on the one hand and urban status on the other, each of the four variables may be considered of importance to both substantive theory and practical concerns. In the case of population size it has long been recognized that a certain minimum number of people is a necessary condition for the existence of some types of social and cultural phenomena, in particular a high degree of division of labor and all that goes with it. On the biological level it can also be seen that the size of a population determines its minimal sustenance needs and, at the same time, sets limits on the manpower resources which are available to satisfy these needs.

In terms of its influence on other characteristics of urban units, the exact nature of the consequences of the level of population density have yet to be established. However, disregarding its possible influence on the frequency and nature of social interaction, there are reasons to believe that high density is conducive to the development of certain ecological patterns of behavior. In particular it appears to make possible a greater use of establishments and facilities (stores, schools, places of recreation, etc.) by virtue of the fact that the members of the population have immediate access to them. The factor of immediate access probably plays a role in the creation of a larger number and variety of establishments and facilities, since, for economic reasons, some types of establishments and facilities cannot exist without the frequent use engendered by close proximity to members of the supporting population. Also to be considered is the fact that high density reduces the cost of establishing lines of communication and providing public utilities. In most general terms, then, all other things being equal, a high level of population density makes possible certain forms of social and ecological organization; and it is perhaps in this respect that the variable deserves recognition as having considerable theoretical significance.

The influence of areal extent and shape on other characteristics of urban units has not been extensively studied, and the two variables are perhaps not as important as population size and density; however, it appears probable that the two are closely linked on the one hand to certain patterns in the spatial distribution of population and establishments within urban units and on the other hand to particular modes of transportation and communication.

Turning from theoretical considerations, it is obvious that the four basic characteristics described above are at the root of man's practical concerns with the problems posed by an urban environment. Apart from the organizational effort required to secure sustenance for large numbers of people who do not grow their own food, a huge population presents an almost endless series of complications regarding the establishment and maintenance of social order and the protection of public welfare. The difficulties of maintaining a truly representative form of government, enforcing laws, safeguarding public health, providing municipal services, and securing consensus on social values are all magnified in the city with a large population. A variable related to population size, an increase in the number of urban residents, is one of the major concerns of those who deal with the problems posed by cities; for it multiplies existing problems and produces new ones, such as the demand for additional housing and the orderly absorption of in-migrants. Also of importance is the fact that the rapid growth of individual cities results in an increase in the level of urbanization for the country as a whole, which in turn creates serious problems on the national level, most of them stemming from an increase in inter-urban and inter-regional dependency.

Associated with an increase in the number of residents are the problems posed by an areal expansion of urban units. Such expansion makes existing political lines unrealistic, results in the depletion of agricultural land, and tends to create chaotic conditions of land use both within the city and on its expanding periphery.

With the advent of the automobile and rapid public transportation systems, the level of population density in cities has decreased considerably in the 20th century; however, congestion still remains one of the more undesirable aspects of an urban environment. Further, horizontal expansion and decentralization, the very factors which reduced urban densities, have created additional problems. City dwellers face the choice of living under congested conditions or the trials and tribulations involved in commuting, neither of which is regarded as a pleasant alternative.

Finally, even the spatial shape of a city may pose practical problems. It may either produce grotesque political boundaries or result in a situation which virtually defies a correspondence between the political and ecological limits of a city. There is also a possibility that a substantial change in the shape of a city may make certain forms of public transportation and systems of traffic control inadequate.

Contents of the papers. Beyond the establishment of boundaries and the definition of a resident, no special technique is required for the treatment of population size as a variable. However, unlike the treatment of the number of city residents, a consideration of population density may pose several technical problems, particularly when one seeks to employ more refined and meaningful measures than gross density (i.e., the number of persons per square mile of territory in the city limits). Such refined measures are the subject of William H. Ludlow's paper, "Measurement and Control of Population Densities," in Chapter 4. In addition to his treatment of the different ways in which population density can be gauged, Ludlow offers some observations that are relevant to the control of congestion as a problem confronting the urban planner.

The last paper in Chapter 4, "A Method for Comparing the Spatial Shapes of Urban Units," deals with a somewhat neglected characteristic of cities. We know very little of the causes and consequences of variation in the shapes of cities, urban areas, or metropolitan areas. This is due, at least in part, to the fact that past studies of individual cases have not described the characteristics of shape in such a way as to make objective comparisons possible. The application of a standard technique in future studies should prove to increase both an interest in and understanding of the causes and consequences of variation in the spatial shape of cities.

The papers included in Chapter 5 deal with variables that are of a different logical order from those designated as basic characteristics of urban units. These variables are change in population size, the components of change, and the age-sex structure of populations. None of them has the logical status of a basic characteristic, since they do not enter into any of the commonly accepted definitions of urban units; however, all of them are directly or indirectly linked to population size and for this reason are fundamental to urban research.

In a mathematical sense population growth can be measured in the same way for any type of territory, whether a nation, region, minor civil division, or an urban unit. Consequently, were it not for a particular problem, the subject of growth would not call for treatment beyond reference to standard demographic techniques. The problem which necessitates special treatment stems from the fact that the population of an urban unit can increase by an expansion of boundaries (horizontal growth) as well as by an increase in density. Since shifts in boundaries pose a problem peculiar to urban research, the population growth of a city, urban area, or metropolitan area is accorded special treatment in the first paper in Chapter 5, "The Measurement of Change in the Population Size of an Urban Unit."

Measures of change in population size, such as those described in the first paper, do not reveal the demographic processes which underlie an increase or decrease in numbers. In short, they do not indicate how much of the change in the population size of an urban unit over a period is due to an imbalance between births and deaths and between out-migration and in-migration, nor do they reveal how much of the change is due to a shift in boundaries. The determination of the amount of change which is due to these individual factors calls for techniques such as those described in the second paper of Chapter 5, "Components of Population Change in Surburban and Central City Populations of Standard Metropolitan Areas: 1940 to 1950" by Donald J. Bogue and Emerson Seim. The findings of the study reported in this paper relate only to particular types of urban units in the United States; but, in terms of its purpose and methods, the study can serve as a guide to an analysis of the components of population change in virtually any type of locality. It should prove to be particularly useful as a guide for research in cases where components of population growth cannot be obtained directly from census publications and must be derived through estimating procedures.

Age-sex structure is of importance to a consideration of population size in at least two respects. For one thing, the extent to which the number of inhabitants determines minimal sustenance needs and sets limits on the manpower available for satisfying these needs depends on the age-sex structure of the population. The sustenance needs of an elderly population appear to be different from the needs of a population characterized by a predominance of young adults, and it is equally evident that the two do not have the same amount of manpower. Sex composition affects the consequences of population size just as age structure does.

Another link between age-sex structure and population size is evidenced by the influence of the former on change in the latter. This influence is manifested through the effect that the age-sex distribution has on levels of mortality and fertility, factors which, along with net migration, determine the amount of increase or decrease in the size of populations. All other things being equal, an elderly population will have higher mortality and lower fertility than a young population and a consequent lower rate of increase.

For purposes of comparative research it is necessary to supplement the usual pictorial representations of age-sex structure with descriptions expressed in quantitative terms. Techniques which provide such descriptions are the subject of the last paper in Chapter 5, "Methods for Describing the Age-Sex Structure of Cities," by Harley L. Browning.

Numerous demographic techniques for the analysis of vital processes underlying population growth—mortality and fertility —are not considered in any part of this volume. These techniques have been excluded from consideration primarily because a number of existing publications provide the beginning student with an introduction to them. References to some of these publications are found in Section 16 of the *Index to the Bibliography*. Studies relating to population size, density, the shape of urban units, population growth, and age-sex structure are cited in Sections 1, 7, 8, 10, and 11.

Chapter 4

DEFINITIVE CHARACTERISTICS

MEASUREMENT AND CONTROL OF
POPULATION DENSITIES *

WILLIAM H. LUDLOW

The problem of urban population densities has long been a thorny one for city planners. Most cities have only very indirect controls through provisions in the zoning ordinances governing yards, courts, setbacks and height of buildings in apartment areas, and minimum lot sizes in one- or two-family districts. A number of municipalities, however, have regulations on the maximum number of families per acre, sometimes stated in terms of the minimum square feet of lot per family. For example, in Cleveland, the maximum number of families permitted in new or re-modelled dwellings in the highest density residential zone is 72 per acre; in Baltimore, 80 per acre; and in Pittsburgh, a minimum of 250 square feet of lot per family, which is equivalent to 174 families per acre.

In New York City, problems of population density are particularly acute. Recently a detailed research report was published by the Citizens' Housing Council of New York. Prepared under the direction of Henry S. Churchill, Chairman of the Council's Committee on City Planning and Zoning, by the author of this article, the report is available in mimeographed form.[1] Herein are summarized portions of the report generally applicable

* Reprinted from *Journal of the American Institute of Planners*, Vol. 11, No. 2 (April-June, 1945), pp. 17-25, with permission of author and publisher.
[1] Available from the Citizens' Housing Council, 470 Fourth Avenue, New York 16, New York. Price $1.

to most American cities, together with suggested methods of population density control and appropriate maximum limitations.

In dealing with the subject of population density, one of the greatest sources of confusion is the lack of clear definition of terms used. For example, Manhattan Island is sometimes said to have an average density of 240 persons per acre. This is true if parks and commercial and industrial sections are omitted. If, however, the total area of Manhattan is included, the average density is only 135 persons per acre. If occupied residential lots alone are considered, the density is 570 persons per acre. The need for standardized terms to indicate just what type of density is meant is very apparent, since, by the last measurement, the density is more than twice that of the first measurement, and more than four times greater than by the second measurement.

It has been proposed that all such measurements should be made in terms of acres per 1,000 population. For example, a hypothetical city might have an average of 10 acres per 1,000 population in residential lots on which dwellings had actually been constructed. In addition there might be, per 1,000 population: one acre of business property, one acre of private institutions and public-buildings, one acre of industrial property, two acres of park and playground, eight acres in streets and seven acres in vacant land, making a total of 30 acres of city area per 1,000 population. This method has much to recommend it for city planning studies, for comparing residential densities in different areas, and for measuring the amount of land in other than residential uses. There is little chance for ambiguity, and quick computation of different density measurements is facilitated. For example, whereas the density of the *total urban area* is 30 acres per 1,000 population, the density of the *developed urban area* (excluding seven acres per 1,000 population in vacant land) is 23 acres per 1,000 population. Similarly the *net area* of occupied dwelling lots is 10 acres per 1,000 population.

On the other hand, for general popular use and for real estate and building interests that will be most intimately concerned with conforming to density controls, the more usual "persons per

acre" is considered preferable. Not only is it more easily understood, but it also is easier to apply to a specific lot or site. For
example, on a site of a given size, it is more natural to think of
100 persons per acre than its equivalent, 10 acres per 1,000 population. It should be noted that one form is quickly converted
into the other by dividing the density figure into 1,000.

In connection with either "persons per acre" or "acres per
1,000 population," it is necessary to have strict definitions of
whatever terms are used. For purposes of simplicity and standardization, the number of terms in common use should be limited.
In all cases these terms consist of two parts, one describing the
area, the other, population (or bulk of building). The three major
headings apply to areas successively smaller in size, and the
variety of land uses included in each is successively limited.

URBAN AREA (OR METROPOLITAN AREA):

This term applies to a single municipality, a large subdivision
thereof, or a group of adjoining municipalities forming a metropolitan area.

Total Urban Area: includes all land area within designated
limits. Water area shall be excluded.

Developed Urban Area: includes all land area within designated limits except land undeveloped for urban purposes, such
as agricultural or unbuilt land, unopened streets, unbuildable or
unusable land.

RESIDENTIAL AREA:

Applies to residential sections of a metropolitan area, a single
municipality, or a portion thereof at least large enough to support
a school and a reasonably wide variety of business facilities and
public and private institutions.

Developed Residential Area: includes all land used for residence, local or incidental business, public and private institutions,
playgrounds, athletic fields and small parks. The following shall
be *excluded*:

1. Industrial, railroad and airport properties.

2. City-wide business districts (usually not applicable to cities
of less than 25,000 population).

3. Large parks and parkways, cemeteries, golf courses, and

other recreational or institutional uses large in area. Playgrounds in large parks, however, may be allocated to the residential areas they serve.

4. Vacant land or land undeveloped for urban use.

Predominantly Residential Area: includes the same uses as developed residential area, except that some mixture of the above excluded uses may be included to the extent that they occur as areas too small to be shown separately on the maps or by the survey procedure used.

NET OR GROSS AREA (OF DWELLING LOTS):

Applies to lots, blocks, or groups of blocks; may be used also for whole municipalities if complete detailed surveys are made.

Net Area: includes land used for dwellings and incidental service uses normally furnished on the dwelling lot, such as driveways, small storage garages, parking areas, heating plants for large projects, play space for small children. *Excluded* use shall be Nos. 1 to 4 above and:

5. Public streets.

6. Local business not directly beneath dwelling space.

7. Garage space for three or more cars not directly below dwelling space.

8. Public parks and playgrounds for older children.

9. Institutional facilities such as schools, churches, community buildings, unless located beneath or above dwelling space.

Gross Area: includes the same uses as net area other than that public streets shall be included up to the center line of bounding streets, except for the following qualifications. Where streets are more than 100 feet wide, or parcels abut on large permanent open spaces such as parks, bodies of water, spacious institutional grounds, etc., gross area shall be measured up to 50 feet from the property line. In case of street widenings as part of a proposed project, the line before widening determined by the above rules shall apply.

"GROSS" RATHER THAN "NET" AREA
FOR CONTROL PURPOSES [2]

Zoning ordinances have based density controls on the net area of the lot. This method is simple and in ordinary circumstances does not present the measurement problems encountered with gross area. However, the measurement of *net* area is controversial for large scale projects, particularly those containing private roads and parking areas that in effect take the place of public streets. By using the *gross* area measurements, the controversial aspect of relying on *net* area can be avoided.

The principal reason for recommending *gross* instead of *net* area for control purposes is that it more adequately satisfies the purposes of density regulation. Briefly stated, these are:

1. To provide adequate light, air, and general openness.

2. To prevent overcrowding of such local facilities as recreation areas, streets, and transit systems.

3. To encourage rational use of all land by preventing unwarranted concentration of population in some areas at the expense of other perhaps equally well located areas.

In providing adequate light and air, it makes little difference whether open space around buildings is on the lot or in adjacent street space. The use of gross area allows for the greater openness provided by wider streets or, in the case of corner lots, by more than one street frontage. (See Chart No. I.) In relation to the second purpose above, the use of gross rather than net area removes the advantage to developers to reduce excessively street or parking areas. It eliminates increasing the total density of a project when, for example, streets between adjacent blocks are closed. Thus the load on neighboring parks, streets and transit cannot be increased by this device. Furthermore, planning to achieve the third purpose above would be facilitated since a desirable over-all distribution of population can be more accurately worked out when differences are eliminated arising from varying proportions of the total area in streets.

[2] For a more detailed discussion of definitions, and other methods of street measurement in connection with gross area, applicable to large projects, see the Citizens' Housing Council report.

DUAL CONTROLS BASED ON "GROSS AREA"

Turning from terms pertaining to area to those relating to population (or bulk of building), careful consideration has been given to various types of measurement. For example, "persons per gross acre" is suitable to describe measuring the density of areas where people are already living, but for buildings in the planning stage it can be used as a measure for control only by assuming an arbitrary standard of occupancy related to the number of apartments or number of rooms.

In order to circumvent this difficulty, zoning ordinances attempting a direct limitation on density generally use "families per acre." More accurately, this should be stated as "families capacity per acre" or "dwelling units per acre." The number of persons living in a single dwelling unit, however, may vary from one to ten and more. Furthermore, the use of "families per acre" has prevented some very desirable changes in some cities. For purposes of illustration assume there is an old apartment house in a blighted district, which contains apartments of five and six rooms. Many of the tenants who live in the building take roomers to help pay the rent. This results in a high population density and an undesirable class of tenants. The owner of the building wishes to remodel, to produce a larger number of apartments, although smaller in size. Although the total number of people living in the building in this case probably would be reduced, and the class of tenant could be improved, the change is not allowed under the existing ordinance because the number of dwelling units per acre would then be higher than permitted. This is a familiar situation where there is a demand for remodelling arising from the current demand for quarters for small families. After the war, the expected formation of many new family units, consisting mostly of two or three persons, will greatly intensify the problem of regulation of remodelling operations, and "families per acre" requirements will multiply the difficulties.

Although many zoning ordinances do not have direct limitations on number of families per acre, nearly all have partial limitations on bulk of building through yard, coverage, height and setback provisions. As limitations on building bulk, and controls indirectly of population density, such regulations may be useful where lots are relatively small, but they are very often inadequate for control of bulk on large sites. Furthermore, they tend to place all buildings in the same mould, and result in stereotyped, unimaginative design.

Direct controls on building bulk in terms of cubage would leave architects freer in terms of design, but present problems in devising rules of measurement, and require complex computations.

To avoid the difficulties mentioned above, the following terms for control of densities are recommended, not because they are without disadvantages, but because they represent workable compromises to accomplish desired ends:

1. *Floor area ratio (gross)* to prevent overcrowding the land with *buildings,* accomplishing purpose No. 1 above.

2. *Rooms per gross acre* to prevent overcrowding the land with *people,* accomplishing purposes Nos. 2 and 3 above.

Whichever is the more restricted of these two measures should apply. The definitions are intended to be used only in connection with multi-family buildings. For one- and two-family dwellings, minimum lot areas are considered adequate. The meaning and application of these two terms are discussed below.

FLOOR AREA RATIO (GROSS)

Limitation on total bulk of buildings by the "floor area ratio" method is relatively new. Originally proposed for New York City, it has been included in the city's zoning resolution in a few minor places. It limits the sum of the gross area of all floors in a building in relation to the size of the lot on which it is built. For example, a floor area ratio (net) of 1.8 means that the combined area of all floors cannot be greater than 1.8 times the net site area. Incidentally, the New York City Planning Commission has set up this ratio as a guide for approval of public housing projects, although exceptions are allowed in certain cases. Assuming all floors of a building are of equal area, a floor area ratio (net) of 1.8 would allow a three-story building with 60 per cent coverage of the lot, a six-story building with 30 per cent coverage, a nine-story building with 20 per cent coverage, or any other combination of height and coverage whose mathematical product equalled 1.8. Or the architect could design varying floor areas and heights, providing the total area of all floors did not exceed 1.8 times the net site area. By this method bulk can be strictly limited, although variations in ceiling heights would result in some differences. They would be of little practical importance, however, except in the case of tall buildings.

For reasons previously explained, it is recommended in the full report that floor area ratio be applied to the gross rather than the net area. The accompanying Chart I, reprinted from the original report, illustrates the floor area ratio (gross) of 1.2 applied diagrammatically to typical interior and corner lots 100 by 100 feet. Incidentally, 1.2 floor area ratio (gross) is closely equivalent to 1.8 floor area ratio (net), assuming 33⅓ per cent of the gross area is in streets. The chart shows an easy method of converting floor area ratio (gross) into height and net coverage. The conversion factor from gross to net is simply the ratio of the gross area to the net area. As shown on the lower diagram, when the corner lot coverages are arranged on two street frontages, building depths are very close to those on interior lots. To explore the application of floor area ratio (gross) to superblock developments, a series of diagrams were prepared representing typical apartment buildings using the efficient cross-type plan. These demonstrations indicated the usefulness of density regulations in terms of floor area ratio (gross) to yield approximately the same light and air to at least the more usual types of well designed apartment buildings.

In addition to floor area ratio (gross), some regulations as to yards, setbacks, etc. would be needed if buildings were not to be so placed that they unnecessarily stole the light from each other. The density research report mentioned previously includes an extensive analysis of the relation of building spacing to adequate daylight and sunlight. Although considerable research is available on various phases of this problem, no ready-made standards for natural illumination in dwellings and their relationship to density could be found. An important contribution of the full-scale density report is that it brought together pertinent research, and

	STREET 100' WIDE					STREET 60' WIDE				
	Conversion factor*	Floor area ratio	Per Cent Coverage			Conversion factor"	Floor area ratio	Per Cent Coverage		
			3 stys.	4 stys.	6 stys.			3 stys.	4 stys.	6 stys.
Gross	1.00	1.20	40	30	20	1.00	1.20	40	30	20
NET Interior lot	1.50	1.80	60	45	30	1.30	1.56	52	39	26
Corner lot**	2.25	2.70	90	67.50	45	1.95	2.34	78	58.50	39

METHODS OF CALCULATING NET COVERAGE
FROM 1.2 FLOOR AREA RATIO (GROSS)

*From gross to net values. Relation of net area to gross area.
**Intersecting street 100' in width.

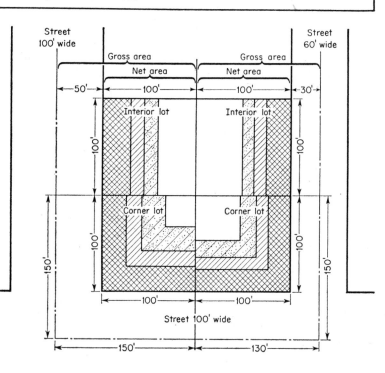

LEGEND

Area of lot covered by buildings of

6 stories   4 stories   3 stories

CHART I. Typical Interior and Corner Lots 100 x 100' with 3, 4 and 6
Story Buildings at 1.2 Floor Area Ratio (Gross).

resulted in a well-documented analysis, supporting the conclusion that for adequate daylight and sunlight at the latitude of New York City, the minimum distance between residence buildings should be equal to twice their height. This permits a light angle of 26½ degrees between buildings, which is the level of the sun at noon in New York City on December 21. This light angle would also provide, under average winter conditions, sufficient daylight for general illumination at the back of most rooms and for working areas within eight to ten feet of windows. This 26½-degree light angle could be assured by a setback to a 45-degree angle from the center of streets and from rear lot lines, provided buildings were of approximately equal height. Such a regulation limits building heights to five or six stories except where lot depth is substantially greater than 100 feet. Chart II illustrates the regulation graphically.

Some students of city planning and housing have maintained that ideally three, or at most four stories is the maximum story height for apartments. Higher apartments require elevators, which not only increase the cost of housing but also are much less satisfactory for families with children. Except in apartments renting at levels that support provision of elevator operators, young children too short to reach the push buttons of automatic elevators are prevented from having ready access to outdoor play, unless accompanied by an older person. Furthermore, children playing outdoors are difficult to control from a location higher than third or fourth story windows. For walk-up apartments, the Federal Housing Administration will generally not insure loans of a four-story apartment building, although in low-rent public housing there should be no health objections to fourth floor occupancy from a health standpoint, provided tenancy is confined to families in normal health and without small children. In general, an average height of not more than three stories is probably appropriate for most American cities. In very few cities is there any real need for crowding so many people on so little land that density regulation need envisage higher *average* heights, although taller buildings on occasion should not be forbidden.

When continuous lines of buildings having a typical thickness of thirty-five feet are placed at the recommended spacing

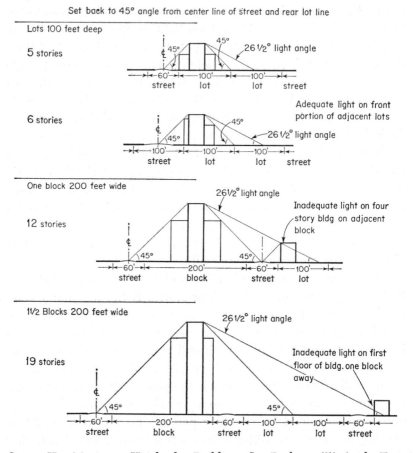

Set back to 45° angle from center line of street and rear lot line

Lots 100 feet deep

5 stories

45°   45°   26 ½° light angle

60' 100' 100'
street   lot   lot   street

6 stories

Adequate light on front
portion of adjacent lots

45°

45°   26 ½° light angle

100' 100' 100'
street   lot   lot   street

One block 200 feet wide

26½° light angle

12 stories

Inadequate light on four
story bldg on adjacent
block

45°   45°

60' 200' 60' 100'
street   block   street   lot

1½ Blocks 200 feet wide

26½° light angle

19 stories

Inadequate light on first
floor of bldg. one block
away

45°   45°

60' 200' 60' 100' 100' 60'
street   block   street   lot   lot   street

CHART II.   Maximum Height for Buildings Set Back to 45° Angle From
Center Line of Street and Rear Lot Line.

(namely at a distance equal to twice their height), the resulting
floor area ratios (gross) are 1.1 for three-story structures and 1.2
for four-story structures. These ratios remain substantially the
same, not only for the hypothetical continuous rows of buildings,
but also when these rows are broken up and wings are added to
form typical cross, or T-type, apartment plans. The conclusion
drawn is that, although no bulk controls can guarantee adequate
light, with good design it is possible to achieve adequate light in
most rooms of four-story buildings at a floor area ratio (gross) of
1.2. This bulk control is recommended for most of New York City,

except in Manhattan and a few other very crowded sections where extraordinarily high population density will require larger bulks, at least for some years.

Although the situation varies from city to city, and each case deserves special study, it is believed that in very few cases would it be necessary for a city to allow a floor area ratio (gross) of more than 1.2; in many cases only 1.1 or 1.0 is satisfactory. This would not prohibit high buildings, but would merely preserve adequate space around them. Moreover, for the outlying sections of many cities, lower bulk limitations would be appropriate.

ROOMS PER GROSS ACRE

Whereas bulk regulations may be used to mitigate overcrowding of the land with buildings, it is still possible to overcrowd the land with people by producing very small rooms and permitting a high occupancy in terms of persons. With moderate-size rooms (for example, 260 square feet of gross floor area per room, including public hall, stair wells, etc.) and occupancy similar to the average for New York City or three-fourths person per room, a building with floor area ratio (gross) of 1.2 would have 200 rooms and 150 persons per gross acre. On the other hand, with rooms as small as those in recent public projects in New York City (160 square feet of gross floor area per room) and the occupancy of one person per room characteristic of some public housing projects, a building of the same bulk would have over 300 rooms and 300 persons per gross acre. Thus the population density would be doubled, and playgrounds, transit, and schools would also have to be double in capacity to accommodate the population.

In the Citizens' Housing Council density report, therefore, as a complement to the floor area ratio (gross) of 1.2, a regulation of 200 rooms per gross acre is recommended. This would be a limiting factor only when units smaller than 260 square feet of gross floor area per room were proposed. In many cities where population pressure on parks, streets and transit is not acute, bulk limitations alone might be deemed adequate to keep population density within reasonable limits. In some cities, however, particularly in the larger ones where excessive densities are more likely, the additional regulation pertaining to rooms per gross acre is very desirable.

Since there are many methods of counting rooms, strict definition of what is to be considered a room is necessary. Briefly it is recommended that major rooms used for general living purposes should be counted, while bathrooms, halls, alcoves, closets or storage rooms should not be counted. Strip kitchens or kitchens in closets ought to be counted as full rooms to avoid a tendency to reduce room counts with this device. No half rooms should be recognized.

The relationship between persons and rooms should be investigated separately for the apartment districts of each city where regulation by room count is being considered. However, the figure probably would not vary greatly from the New York City average of three-fourths person per room. It is very curious and interesting to note that in the few single family areas in New York City, and in the very high rent Park Avenue area, occupancy approaches an average of one-half person per room. At the lower end of the rent scale, in public housing and in most limited dividend projects, occupancy was found to be very close to one person per room. But even in New York's worst slum areas, the average occupancy is very close to three-fourths person per room.

For subsidized public projects, and those receiving tax ememption as under urban redevelopment acts, special regulations are proposed. In return for public aid, and because the occupancy is likely to be close to one person per room, 150 rooms per gross acre is recommended for those sections of New York City where the maximum recommended floor area ratio (gross) is 1.2 for unaided private building. In addition, the floor area ratio (gross) of .9 is recommended for publicly-aided projects in these areas. However, because such projects may have a tendency to rather small rooms, the bulk limitation will rarely be a limiting factor. It is so only when room sizes are greater than 260 square feet of gross floor area per room.

In addition to the material summarized above, the full-scale research report has assembled much material on population trends, and present and probable future needs in various categories of land use in New York City. The total expected population of each borough has been studied in relation to the amount of land likely to be available for residence, after ample allowance is made for commerce, industry, parks and playgrounds, and other types of non-residential land use. Density recommendations are so drawn that there will be ample room for the expected population of each borough. Standards of acreage per 1,000 population for parks and playgrounds, local business and other non-residential functions considered suitable for New York City may be found in the full report.

Planners and housers who wish to carry further their investigations in density standards, and regulations appropriate to this subject, may therefore find it profitable to consult the more detailed research study, to which reference has been made in this article.

A METHOD FOR COMPARING THE SPATIAL SHAPES OF URBAN UNITS *

JACK P. GIBBS **

Numerous observations have been made on the spatial shapes of cities in relation to urban growth, urban planning, and technological developments in transportation.[1] To date research on

* Written especially for this volume.

** Member of the staff of International Urban Research.

[1] For examples of studies and observations on the subject see Hans Blumenfeld, "Theory of City Form, Past and Present," *Journal of the Society of Architectural Historians*, Vol. 8 (July-December, 1949), pp. 7-16; Ernest W. Burgess, "The Growth of the City" in Robert E. Park, Ernest W. Burgess, and Roderick D. McKenzie (eds.), *The City* (Chicago: University of Chicago Press, 1925), pp. 47-62; Ernest W. Burgess, "Urban Areas" in T. V. Smith and Leonard D. White (eds.), *Chicago, An Experiment in Social Science Research* (Chicago: University of Chicago Press, 1929), pp. 113-138; Maurice R. Davie, "The Pattern of Urban Growth," in George Peter Murdock (ed.), *Studies in the Science of Society* (New Haven, Conn.: Yale University Press, 1937), pp. 133-161; Federal Housing Administration, *The Structure and Growth of Residential Neighborhoods in American Cities* by Homer Hoyt (Washington, D.C.: Government Printing Office, 1939); Harry B. and Audrey E. Hawthorn, "The Shape of a City: Some Observations on Sucre, Bolivia," *Sociology and Social Research*, Vol. 33 (November-December, 1948), pp. 87-91; Kevin Lynch, "The Form of Cities," *Scientific American*, Vol. 190 (April, 1954), pp. 55-63; Lewis Mumford, *The Culture of Cities* (New York: Harcourt Brace and Co., 1938); William F. Ogburn, "Inventions of Local Transportation and the Patterns of Cities," *Social Forces*, Vol. 24 (May, 1946), pp. 373-379; and James A. Quinn, "The Burgess Zonal Hypothesis and Its Critics," *American Sociological Review*, Vol. 5 (April, 1940), pp. 210-218.

the subject has suffered from the absence of a method for making objective and systematic comparisons; studies have traditionally used only maps or photographs in an analysis of the shapes of cities. These materials are suited for demonstrating that some urban units have a spatial form radically different from others, and they can also be used to illustrate certain types—circular, rectangular, star shaped, and elongated, to mention only a few common patterns. Thus, for example, on the basis of an inspection of maps, it is obvious that the outlines of London and Stalingrad are quite dissimilar, with London resembling a star and Stalingrad having an elongated form.[2] However, neither maps nor photographs by themselves provide a basis for expressing the nature of spatial differences in a standardized way.

THE MEASUREMENT OF ONE ASPECT OF SHAPE

On the assumption that the boundaries of an urban area may resemble a circle and with the knowledge that such a figure has some relatively simple geometrical properties, a method has been devised to measure the degree to which the shape of a city has a circular form. The explication of the method can best begin with reference to Figure I, which shows the political boundaries [3] of four cities in the United States.

Although it would be possible to find more extreme cases, visual inspection indicates considerable variability among the four as to shape. Further, the cities resemble, to varying degrees, four of the basic types—circular, rectangular, star-shaped, and elongated.

If the boundary of any one of the cities formed a circle, it would be possible to deduce the amount of area contained within it from knowledge of the maximum distance between any two points on the periphery. In other words the distance would be the diameter of a circle, and the area contained could be determined by the familiar formula: $A = 3.1416 \ R^2$. Accordingly, the two most distant points on the periphery of a city establish the absolute maximum area that could be contained within its bound-

---

[2] Lynch, *op. cit.*, pp. 60-61.
[3] Other types of boundaries will be considered in a later section.

aries. In the case of Raleigh, North Carolina (see Figure I), given the distance of 4.5 miles between the two most distant points on its periphery, the area within the city limits could not be more than 15.9 square miles; and it would not equal that amount with-

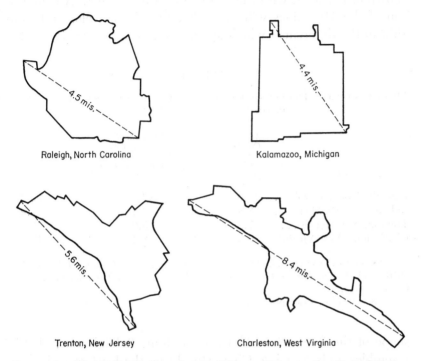

Raleigh, North Carolina

Kalamazoo, Michigan

Trenton, New Jersey

Charleston, West Virginia

FIGURE I. The Political Boundaries of Four Cities in the United States, 1950.

out the city having the shape of a circle. This being the case, the correspondence between the actual area and the maximum area is indicative of the degree to which a city has a circular shape. Raleigh's city limits enclose 11.0 square miles, which is 69.2 per cent of the maximum. This figure (69.2) thus indicates the degree to which the shape of Raleigh corresponds to that of a circle.

The formula for the measurement of this feature of the shape of urban units is:

$$Mc = \frac{100Aa}{(3.1416)\,(Dp/2)^2}$$

where *Mc* is the measure of circularity in shape, *Aa* is the actual area contained in the urban unit, and *Dp* the distance between the two most distant points on the boundary of the unit.

The above measure has been applied to each of the four cities shown in Figure I, with the results given in Table 1. A comparison of the *Mc* values will show that they bear a close relationship to the differences which appear in a visual inspection of the

TABLE 1

MEASURES OF THE DEGREE OF CIRCULARITY IN THE SHAPES OF FOUR CITIES
IN THE UNITED STATES, 1950 *

City	Area of City in Square Miles (Aa)	Distance in Miles Between Two Most Distant Points on City's Periphery (Dp)	Measure of Circularity (Mc) **
Raleigh, North Carolina.	11.0	4.5	69.2
Kalamazoo, Michigan ..	8.8	4.4	57.9
Trenton, New Jersey....	7.2	5.6	29.3
Charleston, West Virginia	9.6	8.4	17.3

* SOURCE OF DATA: U.S. Bureau of the Census. *U.S. Census of Population: 1950.* Vol. I, *Number of Inhabitants* (Washington, D.C.: Government Printing Office, 1952).
** See text for description of measure.

shape of the four cities. Thus, of the four, Raleigh most closely resembles a circle, while Charleston bears the least resemblance. Accordingly, their *Mc* measures are 69.2 and 17.3, and these represent the highest and lowest values among the four cities.

The technique offered here has certain characteristics which enhance its value as a research tool. For one thing the measure is easily computed and calls for nothing more than a map drawn to a specified scale and knowledge of the amount of area within the boundary of the urban unit. The *Mc* values are mathematically independent of the size of the entities; and comparisons are also facilitated by the fact that the measure has an absolute maximum value of 100 and, for all practical purposes, a fixed minimum of 0.0; consequently, its meaning is not a relative one.

A *Mc* value not only expresses the degree of circularity in shape but also provides a clue as to the type of geometrical figure which most closely resembles the city in question. Although no hard and fast rules can be applied, it appears that as the value decreases the city tends to resemble first a square, then a star, then a thin winding strip, and at the lowest values, a narrow rectangle.

One possible objection to the measure is that it may be influenced appreciably by one isolated projection of the urban unit. It should be noted, however, that such an extension is in fact a part of the unit (if one accepts its boundary), and it is virtually impossible to formulate any objective rule for the identification and exclusion of "eccentricities" in spatial form.[4]

THE MEASUREMENT OF SHAPE AND THE NATURE OF URBAN BOUNDARIES

The mathematical description of the spatial form of urban units presupposes the existence of boundaries. Consequently, the extent to which a given urban unit resembles a circle is in part, if not altogether, a matter of the way in which its outer limits have been established. This is true of course for the ascription of any sort of attribute to an urban area or its population; nevertheless, the problem warrants consideration.

To illustrate the importance of boundaries three Mc values have been computed for six urban localities in the U.S., with each value based on a different type of boundary. The results are shown in Table 2, and the magnitude of the differences among the values within each row of the table makes it abundantly clear that the spatial shape of an urban locality is to a large extent dependent upon the type of boundary employed.

Equally important is the fact that the nature of the difference by type of boundary varies from place to place. On the whole it appears that the shape of "political cities" tends to resemble that of a circle far more than do Urbanized Areas, but Mc values for Los Angeles show that this is not always the case. This incon-

---

[4] One alternative is to consider the mean or average distance between several points on the periphery. However, there is no standard for locating such points other than maximum distance. An almost infinite number of lines can be drawn through a city, and the shortest distance "across" is relative to the position of the observer.

TABLE 2

MEASURES OF THE DEGREE OF CIRCULARITY IN THE SHAPE OF SIX U.S.
URBAN LOCALITIES FOR THREE TYPES OF BOUNDARIES *

Urban Locality	Type of Boundary		
	Political	Urbanized Area	Urbanized Area Excluding Non-Contiguous Parts **
Salt Lake City, Utah	62.2	29.9	33.1
Wichita, Kansas	58.0	39.4	59.3
Lawrence, Massachusetts.	53.2	28.3	35.2
Trenton, N. J.	30.1	23.0	24.0
Los Angeles, California..	29.7	46.2	44.3
Charleston, West Virginia	17.3	6.4	6.4

* See Table 1 for source of data.
** Ignoring separations by water.

sistency in the nature of differences also applies to the two types of Urbanized Areas. All in all there would appear to be no mathematical necessity for Mc values to increase or decrease in any particular way from one type of boundary to the next.

A measure based on one kind of boundary is of course just as real in a sense as one based on another, but it would appear that a comparison of the shapes of urban units with different types of limits is not particularly meaningful. On the other hand, however, a lack of correspondence between two or more boundaries for the same urban locality may be of importance. Thus, to the student of local government, the differences between the form of a political city and that of its associated urban area is not only real but possibly of considerable significance.

THE USE OF THE MEASURE

The method of measurement proposed here is perhaps most relevant to the problems and concerns of urban planning, urban ecology, and urban geography. On the surface at least it would appear that the shape of an urban unit is linked to such problems as the organization of municipal transportation, the management of traffic, zoning, the location of urban sub-centers, and defense against aerial attack. These are all concerns of the urban planner, and it is not within the purview of this paper to discuss the solution of planning problems that are linked to the spatial shapes of cities; however, it is obvious that satisfactory answers can best be based on comparative research, and this requires techniques for measurement.

The spatial shape of urban units is a subject of interest for both urban geography and ecology, as well as planning. Variability in form is something which calls for explanation; but the influence of possible determinants (topographic and technological variables being those most frequently considered) cannot be established without a systematic means for describing the dependent variable—that is, the spatial form of units. Another use of the measure relates to one of the research practices of urban ecologists in their study of the influence of a city on surrounding territory. Such studies typically begin with a grouping of territorial divisions about the political limits of the city in a series of concentric zones. The characteristics of the population of these divisions are subsequently examined for the purpose of testing some hypothesis, with distance from the city usually serving as the independent variable. Implicit in this approach is the assumption that cities tend to grow and radiate influence orbicularly. On the surface this assumption appears to be most warranted when the urban area of the city resembles that of a circle. In other words, where one is dealing with a city which has an urban area that is non-circular in shape (a low Mc value), the position of a territorial division relative to the shape of the urban area should perhaps be taken into account, as well as its distance from the center of the city. This is something which only future research can determine, and the measure suggested here should prove useful in experimentation along these lines.

One additional use of the technique should be mentioned. Given certain types of data it is possible to specify the proportion of the population growth of an urban unit which is due to an extension of its boundaries. However, such a figure would indicate only the role of areal expansion in over-all growth, and would not tell us anything about the form of the expansion other than the fact that the urban unit is larger. However, given Mc values at two points in time (assuming that shifts in the boundary were not artificial), the difference between the values provides a description of the nature of the changes in the periphery. The significance of the use of the measure in this way is, of course, as in all other suggested applications, relative to the research problem at hand.

Chapter 5

POPULATION GROWTH AND COMPOSITION

THE MEASUREMENT OF CHANGE IN THE
POPULATION SIZE OF AN URBAN UNIT *

JACK P. GIBBS **

In view of the tremendous increase in the size of cities and world-wide urbanization during the past two centuries, it is not altogether surprising that the study of urban growth has received a great deal of attention. Basic to such study is an understanding of methods for the measurement of change in any population size and associated problems. The methods pertain to formulas for the mathematical expression of change, while the associated problems relate for the most part to the treatment of boundaries. This paper offers a brief treatment of these methods and problems as they apply to individual urban units, with the growth of population in the vicinity of Palermo, Italy, used for illustration.

MEASURES OF CHANGE IN POPULATION SIZE

Of the various formulas which can be used to express the amount of change in population size, the least complex one is:

$$r = \frac{(P_2 - P_1)/t}{(P_2 + P_1)/2} \times 100$$

r, the rate of change, is a function of the mathematical relationships among the population size at one point in time (P_1), popu-

* Written especially for this volume.
** Member of the staff of International Urban Research.

lation size at a later point in time (P_2), and the number of years over the period (t). This *average arithmetical* formula expresses change in numbers on an annual basis ($P_2 - P_1$)/t as a per cent of the average population size ($P_2 + P_1$)/2 over the period of time (t), and it is suited for comparing cities with respect to growth regardless of variation in their population size or the number of years in the growth periods. The formula yields results which are more realistic than those produced by the simple interest formula; furthermore, although easy to compute, values of r usually are very close to growth rates derived from the complex *exponential* and *compound interest* formulas.[1]

THE TREATMENT OF BOUNDARIES IN MEASURING CHANGE IN POPULATION SIZE

Since the *average arithmetical* formula can be applied to any type of population, its use in urban research poses no mathematical complications. The major problem posed in its application (or any other for that matter) is that the growth of an urban unit can be registered in either or both of two directions—*vertical* or *horizontal*.[2] In the former the boundary of the unit remains constant, while the number of residents increases; thus, *vertical* growth is always accompanied by an increase in the level of population density. In contrast, the basis for *horizontal* growth is an expanding rather than a fixed boundary. This areal expansion of an urban unit adds to its population the residents of territories which were outside the boundary at one point in time but within it at a later point in time.

The fact that the population of an urban unit may increase in these two ways makes it imperative that both of them be taken into account in measuring growth. If allowance is not made for the possibility that the boundary may have expanded over the years considered, the only way in which an increase in numbers can occur is by a rise in the level of population density. Under such a condition the people who reside in newly developed urban

---

[1] See Carl Hammer and Natalie Rogoff, "Relative Merits of Various Formulas for Rates of Growth" (unpublished monograph, Columbia University, Bureau of Applied Social Research).

[2] This holds true for a decrease as well as for growth.

territory would not be counted as additions to the population, and in certain cases, particularly in technologically advanced countries, the growth rate would actually show a loss of residents.

When one speaks of the horizontal expansion of an urban unit, it is generally understood that territory adjacent to the city has acquired an urban character according to a given set of criteria, such as particular levels of population density or nonagricultural employment. This is true, however, only when one is dealing with either urban areas or metropolitan areas and not cities in a governmental sense. The presence or absence of a change in the political boundary of a city cannot be taken to mean that horizontal growth has or has not taken place. In some cases the boundary may remain fixed during a period of years even though the associated urban area has expanded beyond it. On the other hand, the political limits may be shifted in such a way that they encompass rural territory far beyond the periphery of the urban area. In the first case, where the boundary remains fixed, a growth rate will indicate less of an increase than actually took place; while in the second case, where the boundary is pushed beyond the pattern of urban settlement, growth is exaggerated.

Even a realistic shift in political boundaries (i.e., one in which the administrative limits are moved in such a way as to correspond with the urban area) may create a distorted rate of growth. This happens when the shift is not synchronous with the period in which the growth actually took place. For example, let us consider the growth of a hypothetical city between the years 1940-1950 and 1950-1960. Suppose that in the first decade the urban area expanded far beyond the political limits, which remained fixed over the ten years and contained the same number of people in 1950 as in 1940. Under this condition a growth rate for the *city* would show no change in population size. Let us further suppose that in the second decade the population of the urban area expands neither *horizontally* nor *vertically,* and in the year 1959 the boundary of the city is enlarged to make it correspond to the limits of the urban area. As a consequence of the shift in the boundary, a growth rate for the city based on a census enumeration of the resident population in 1950 and in 1960 would be very high. Thus, while the rates of growth for the city would indicate no increase in population size during the first decade and a great increase in the second decade, exactly the opposite would apply to the associated urban area—its rate of growth would be high for the first decade and low for the second decade.

There remains one other way in which the nature of the boundaries may generate distorted rates of growth. The population size of an urban unit depends in part upon the way in which its limits have been established. For example, as a rule, the number of residents in a political city is either more or less (typically the latter) than the number in the associated urban area. This being the case, it is a questionable practice to use one type of boundary for an urban unit at the start of the growth period and another at the end of the growth period (e.g., to use a political boundary at the start of the growth period and a demographic-ecological one at the end of the period or vice versa). Such a practice may add territory that was already urban at the start of the growth period, add rural territory, or even reduce the size of the urban unit; and in any case the result will be a distorted rate of growth.

All of the above points to three salient facts concerning change in the population size of urban units. First, insofar as the concern is with urban areas and metropolitan areas, two delimitations of their boundaries are necessary for a valid measure of growth—one at the start of the growth period and one at the end of the period. Second, measures of growth based on political limits should be interpreted with the realization that they may either exaggerate or underestimate the actual change in the population size of the urban areas that are associated with the cities. And, third, a change in the type of boundary (i.e., from political to demographic-ecological limits or vice versa) over the growth period is particularly conducive to generating distorted rates of growth.

POPULATION GROWTH IN PALERMO, ITALY:
AN ILLUSTRATION OF PROBLEMS

The importance of the treatment of boundaries in measuring change in the population size of an urban unit can be illustrated by data pertaining to Palermo, Italy. The growth of population between 1936 and 1951 in the vicinity of the urban center can be gauged in terms of three territorial units. Two of them had a fixed boundary over the years 1936-1951—the commune of Palermo and the four administrative divisions designated as *mandamenti urbani*. The latter, taken together as a unit, are considered to be the central or nonsuburban part of the urban center; and they are treated here as the counterpart to an "underbounded" political city. The second territorial unit with a fixed boundary is the commune of Palermo. Since the commune encompasses all of the population in the vicinity of Palermo, it is considered here as a special type of territorial unit for the measurement of growth—one so large that it is certain to contain the *horizontal* as well as the *vertical* expansion of the urban center located within it.

The third territorial unit to be considered is the Palermo urban area, the boundaries of which were established both for 1936 and 1951 by applying a density criterion of 2,000 residents per square mile. Since the boundaries were established both at the start and end of the growth period, changes in population size reflect both *vertical* and *horizontal* expansion of the urban area. Consequently, the rate of growth for the urban area can be used as a standard to judge the adequacy of other rates based on different types of territorial units. These other rates, as well as the rate for the Palermo urban area, are shown in Table 1.

As computed on the basis of the *average arithmetical* formula, the population of the Palermo urban area grew at an annual rate of 1.5 per cent over the years 1936-1951. Several of the rates of growth shown in Table 1 differ markedly from that of the urban area. In two cases we find much lower rates (—0.5 and —1.3), and in two cases the rate is much higher (2.8 and 3.1). Without exception, each of these four rates is based on a type of boundary at the start of the growth period (1936) which is different from that at the end of the growth period (1951). These cases illustrate how a change in the type of boundary of an urban center can lead to erroneous conclusions regarding the rate of growth.

Even when the type of boundary at the start of the growth period corresponds to the type at the end of the period the rate of growth may give a misleading picture of change in the population size of the urban center. This is particularly true when

TABLE 1

POPULATION GROWTH IN THE VICINITY OF PALERMO, ITALY BETWEEN
1936 AND 1951 BY DIFFERENT SETS OF BOUNDARIES *

1951 Boundaries	1936 Boundaries		
	Urban Area **	Mandamenti Urbani ***	Palermo Commune ****
Urban Area **	1.5	2.8	0.8
Mandamenti Urbani ***	—0.5	0.7	—1.3
Palermo Commune ****	1.9	3.1	1.2

* SOURCE OF DATA: Palermo, Ufficio Statistica e Censimenti, *Panormus, Rassegna del Comune di Palermo e Bollettino di Statistica, 1956* (No. 50, New Series). Growth rates are based on the *average arithmetical* formula.

** Delimited on the basis of a density criterion of 2,000 persons per square mile.

*** Treated as the equivalent to an "underbounded" political city. Boundary constant between 1936 and 1951.

**** Administrative division which encompasses all of the other territorial units in the table. Boundary constant between 1936 and 1951.

the boundaries at the start of the growth period are purely administrative and remain fixed throughout the period, as was the case for the boundaries of the *mandamenti urbani* and commune of Palermo. The rate of growth of the *mandamenti urbani* (0.7) was less than one-half that of the urban area (1.5), which illustrates the consequence of ignoring the *horizontal* expansion of a "city" that was already "underbounded" at the start of the growth period. In the case of the Palermo commune we find a rate of growth (1.2) that is fairly close to the rate of the urban area (1.5). The fact that the former is lower than the latter is of particular significance. When a large administrative division is used to gauge the amount of increase in the population size of its urban center, it contains not only the urban area but rural territory as well. Since the number of rural inhabitants tends to increase at a lower rate than does the urban population, the rate of growth for the administrative division is likely to be lower than that of the urban area. As a general rule, a large administrative division should not be used to gauge growth if it contains either more than one urban center or a large number of rural inhabitants.

For one of several reasons, it often happens in research that a constant boundary is used as the basis for gauging the growth of an urban unit.[3] This practice should be avoided whenever possible, particularly in cases where the boundary is a purely administrative one; and when it is necessary to use a constant boundary, figures on change in population size should be interpreted with certain reservations as to their validity.

If the boundary of an urban unit at the start of a growth period is held constant, a possible increase in population through horizontal expansion cannot be taken into account, with the consequence that growth is underestimated. This is seen to be the case for the Palermo urban area when the 1936 boundary is held constant throughout the growth period. As shown in Table 2,

TABLE 2

RATES OF POPULATION GROWTH * IN THE PALERMO URBAN AREA BETWEEN 1936 AND 1951 BY CONSTANT AND VARIABLE BOUNDARIES **

Urban Area's Boundaries and Population	1951 Boundaries, 1951 Population, 464,390	1936 Boundaries, 1951 Population, 426,258
1936 Boundaries, 1936 Population, 367,692	1.5	1.0
1951 Boundaries, 1936 Population, 394,914	1.1	0.5

* Growth rates are based on the *average arithmetical* formula.
** See Table 1 for source of data.

the rate of growth on the basis of the 1936 boundary is 1.0, in contrast to 1.5 on the basis of a variable boundary. Thus, the difference between the two rates is due to the fact that *horizontal* expansion is taken into account in the latter.

If the 1951 boundary is used both for 1936 and 1951, the growth rate for the Palermo urban area is 1.1, which is slightly

[3] See, for example, Donald J. Bogue, *Population Growth in Standard Metropolitan Areas, 1900-1950* (Washington, D.C.: Housing and Home Finance Agency, 1953).

higher than that obtained by holding the 1936 boundary constant (1.0). The 1951 boundary, unlike the 1936 boundary, contained all of the *horizontal* expansion that took place during the growth period, but it encompassed some territory that was rural in 1936. The inclusion of rural territory lowered the growth rate because the rural residents did not increase at a rate equal to that of the urban residents. Nevertheless, despite the fact that rural territory may be included when only the boundary at the end of the growth period is used, it is less serious than excluding any possibility of *horizontal* growth, which is the inevitable consequence of using only the boundary at the start of the growth period. In either case, however, holding the boundary constant will result, as a rule, in an underestimation of the rate of growth.

In concluding it should be noted that what has been said with regard to individual urban units applies equally well to the total urban population of a country. This means that the *average arithmetical* formula yields a satisfactory measure of change in the size of the total urban population and that the boundaries of all of the urban units in the country should be treated in the manner recommended for an individual case.

COMPONENTS OF POPULATION CHANGE IN SUBURBAN AND CENTRAL CITY POPULATIONS OF STANDARD METROPOLITAN AREAS: 1940 to 1950 *

DONALD J. BOGUE AND EMERSON SEIM

The rapid growth of surburban areas during the last half-century has been documented in previous studies.[1] Demographers, ecologists, and sociologists are now at work gaining more detailed knowledge about a variety of aspects of the process. One contribution which demographers can make to progress in this area

* Reprinted from *Rural Sociology*, Vol. 21, Nos. 3-4 (September-December, 1956) pp. 267-275, with permission of authors and publisher.
[1] E.g., see Warren S. Thompson, *The Growth of Metropolitan Districts in the United States: 1900-1940* (Washington, D.C.: Government Printing Office, 1947), and Donald J. Bogue, *Population Growth in Standard Metropolitan Areas: 1900-1950, with an Explanatory Analysis of Urbanized Areas* (Washington, D.C.: Government Printing Office, 1953).

is to show the sources of population change and how rapidly suburban populations are growing as a result of the change contributed by each source. These changes are best understood by viewing them in comparison with the population changes occurring in the metropolitan area as a whole and in the central city. The present paper undertakes to make this contribution.

There are two ways in which a suburban area can gain population: by natural increase and by net in-migration. (Between 1940 and 1950 the in-migration could have been military as well as civilian.) There are three ways in which a suburban area can lose population: by natural decrease, by net out-migration, and by annexation of territory by the central city. Suburban populations are noted for being more fertile than the populations of central cities. The fast growth of suburbs is due, therefore, to a combination of higher-than-average birth rates and rapid in-migration. A question of central importance is, "How much growth is due to each of the possible sources?" In other words, "What are the components of population growth in suburban areas?" A similar question can be asked about the central city. A comparison of the components of growth for central cities and suburban areas is especially meaningful because of the supposition that much of the net migration to suburban areas comes directly from the central city. Migration to suburban areas which does not come from the central city is, in any case, an alternative to settlement in the central city.

The components of population growth cannot be obtained directly from census publications. They must be estimated by applying certain demographic techniques to census data and vital statistics data. As one of their joint projects in population distribution, the Scripps Foundation (Miami University) and the Population Research and Training Center (University of Chicago) are making estimates that will supply these components for each state economic area in the nation. The principal standard metropolitan areas are also designated as economic areas and, since the estimates were prepared separately for the central city and the suburban-ring portions of each standard metropolitan area, it is possible to report specific information about the components of suburban and central-city growth. The following pages describe briefly the procedure used in making the estimates and summarize the results that were obtained. The full detail for each area will be presented in a forthcoming monograph. The factors that seem to account for the variations in net migration among suburban and central city areas are being analyzed by Emerson Seim.

ESTIMATING PROCEDURE

Step 1. Estimate the natural increase for the central city and the suburban ring of each S.M.A.[2] The births that occurred in the central city and the ring portions of each S.M.A. (and in non-metropolitan areas) between April 1, 1940 and April 1, 1950 were determined by adding the registered births that occurred in each calendar year or fraction of a year during the decade. These figures were corrected for underregistration, taking account of the progressive improvement of birth registration during the decade. The totals for corrected births were adjusted to equal state totals that were prepared by the Bureau of the Census. The total number of deaths that occurred during the decade was similarly assembled and adjusted to census totals for each state, to which some adjustment for underregistration had been made. Natural increase (before correction for annexation) is equal to corrected births minus corrected deaths.

Step 2. Adjust the 1940 population for change in definition of college students. In 1940, the usual residence of most college students was defined by the census as the residence of their parents. In 1950, the usual residence of college students was defined as the place of attending school. Since in several instances a significant share of the population increase reported for an S.M.A., central city, or ring was due largely to this change, it was necessary to adjust 1940 allocation of college students to conform to the 1950 definition. This adjustment was made by following a slightly modified version of a procedure devised by Burton L. French.[3] Briefly, the procedure consists of estimating the number of persons reported for each area in 1940 who were actually attending college, subtracting this number from the total 1940

[2] "S.M.A." = standard metropolitan area.
[3] Burton L. French, "Procedure for Adjusting 1940 Census Data for College Students to be Comparable with 1950 Data," *Agricultural Economics Research*, VI:2 (Apr., 1954).

population, and then adding to the total 1940 population the number of person actually enrolled in colleges located in the area, as reported by the United States Office of Education.

Step 3. Estimate the increase in military and civilian population, 1940-50. After the 1940 population had been corrected for the changes in definition of college students, it was possible to obtain a revised statement of total population change for the 1940-50 period by subtracting the revised 1940 population from the census population for 1950. In many of the areas a substantial part of the change was due to the expansion of military establishments, as well as to the influx of civilian population. Accordingly, the total increase was divided into a military and a civilian component. The 1950 military population was obtained by subtracting the civilian labor force from the total labor force, the difference representing the military population in 1950. The military population in 1940 was comparatively small. Although data concerning its distribution are meager, only a comparatively minor error can result from assuming that it was proportionately distributed in 1940 as in 1950. This assumption was made to distribute the 1940 military population. The 1940-50 change in military population is obtained by subtraction, as for total population change. The 1940-50 change in civilian population was obtained by subtracting the 1940-50 change in military population from the total population change between 1940 and 1950, corrected for change in residence of college students.

Step 4. Estimate the population annexed to the central cities during the decade. There were large annexations of suburban territory to central cities in a few of the S.M.A.'s, and smaller annexations for a great many S.M.A.'s. In order to establish comparable components of change, it was necessary to fix the boundaries of central cities as they were in 1940 and to adjust the components to conform to these boundaries. The 1940 boundaries for each central city were compared with the 1950 boundaries, as drawn on the official census maps.[4] All boundary changes, whether of annexation to or separation from the central city, were noted. From records for enumeration districts, census tracts, and

---

[4] The authors are indebted to the Geography Division, U.S. Bureau of the Census, for permission to go to the Census Bureau and make the boundary comparisons from the official maps.

city wards, an estimate was made of the 1950 population contained in each parcel of land that was annexed to, or separated from, the central cities. The annexed population was adjusted for its estimated natural increase (allowing the average rate for the entire S.M.A.) between the time of the annexation and the 1950 census. Subtracting this natural increase yields the estimated population of the annexed territory at the time of annexation. This estimated population became the annexation component. It represents an increase for the central city and a loss for the suburban ring. The natural increase of the annexed population was added to the natural increase of the ring population. This yielded an estimate of what the natural increase of the suburban population would have been had there been no boundary change during the decade.

Step 5. Separate the total increase of the civilian population into its components of natural increase and net migration. The adjusted natural increase, obtained from Step 4, was subtracted from the total civilian increase, as established in Step 3, to obtain the net civilian migration. This completed the estimating procedure.

In summary, then, the total population change has been adjusted to make allowance for the change in definition of college students and then subdivided into the following four components:

   a. Natural increase of the civilian population
   b. Net civilian migration
   c. Increase in military population
   d. Change due to annexation

Rates of increase have been computed by basing the total change and components of change upon the 1940 population as revised for the change in college population. The estimates of net migration derived by this procedure are residuals that remain after all other components have been estimated. For this reason, they are subject to a great deal of error and should be interpreted as being only approximations of what must have been the true net migration.

RESULTS

The above procedure was applied individually to each S.M.A. in the United States. The components of change, for all S.M.A.'s combined, and for central cities and rings, are shown in Table 1. This table reveals the fact—which may be somewhat surprising —that, *between 1940 and 1950, central cities as a group lost population through net migration.* The moderate growth which they experienced was due to their own natural increase and to annexation. In fact, central cities grew only because their populations were fertile enough to more than make up for the net migration loss. Even though the central cities undoubtedly received many in-migrants from rural and smaller urban places, the pull of the suburban drift was more than enough to outweigh the migration gain. Since many cities were receiving large numbers of Negro in-migrants during this decade, this could only mean that the central cities were losing, by suburbanization, large numbers of white residents. The average loss of population for central cities through net migration was 1.8 per cent, while the average gain for the metropolitan suburban rings as a result of net migration was 26.4 per cent. The higher rate of natural increase in suburban areas than in central cities should not be interpreted as being due entirely to the difference in fertility. The method of estimating allocates all children born to in-migrating parents to the area of birth. Thus, areas that were growing rapidly by the influx of many young parents also experienced unusually large natural increases as a result of the fertility of the migrants. Since the base of the rate of natural increase is the 1940 population, it is possible to obtain rates of natural increase for suburban areas that are quite high.[5]

There was much variation among the S.M.A.'s in the components of their growth, however, and among the central city and suburban parts of the S.M.A.'s. This fact is demonstrated in

[5] In reviewing this paper at the time of its reading, C. Horace Hamilton made the excellent suggestion that an average rate of natural increase, derived by applying the compound interest formula, compounded quarterly or monthly, would eliminate this difficulty and would permit a direct comparison of rates of natural increase as well as rates of migration. This new rate would have a slightly different meaning from that desired here, namely, percentage change in initial population as a result of natural increase.

TABLE 1

Components of Population Change, 149 Standard Metropolitan Areas of the United States, 1940-50 [1]

Components of Population Change	Number			Per Cent Change, 1940-50		
	S.M.A. Total	Central Cities	Suburban Rings	S.M.A. Total	Central Cities	Suburban Rings
Adjusted 1940 population	69,622,757	43,066,301	26,556,456	—	—	—
Total change	15,134,766	5,716,091	9,418,675	21.7	13.3	35.5
Change in civilian population ...	14,684,348	4,139,758	10,544,590	21.1	9.6	39.7
Natural increase	8,421,083	4,897,295	3,523,788	12.1	11.4	13.3
Net migration	6,263,265	−757,537	7,020,802	9.0	−1.8	26.4
Change in military population	450,418	174,041	276,377	0.6	0.4	1.0
Annexation	—	1,402,292	−1,402,292	—	3.3	−5.3

[1] The standard metropolitan areas included are those that had a population of 100,000 or more in 1950, plus Phoenix, Arizona, and Hampton-Newport News-Warwick, Virginia, which were added since the 1950 census. The town-delimited New England areas have been approximated by their county equivalents.

TABLE 2

FREQUENCY DISTRIBUTION, BY PERCENTAGE CHANGE IN POPULATION AND COMPONENTS OF CHANGE, FOR STANDARD METROPOLITAN AREAS, CENTRAL CITIES, AND SUBURBAN RINGS, 1940-1950

Type of Place and Component of Population Change	All Areas	Decrease		Number of Places, by Per Cent Change, 1940-50 — Increase					
		10.0 or More	0.0 to 9.9	0.0 to 4.9	5.0 to 9.9	10.0 to 14.9	15.0 to 29.9	30.0 to 59.9	60.0 or More
Standard metropolitan areas, total	149	2	3	3	11	23	60	32	15
Natural increase	149	—	—	2	25	63	58	1	—
Civilian net migration	149	6	17	38	29	20	15	21	3
Military increase	149	—	11	130	4	3	1	—	—
Central cities, total	149	1	11	23	29	20	26	29	10
Natural increase	149	—	—	2	37	55	50	5	—
Civilian net migration	149	26	84	16	8	5	8	2	—
Military increase	149	—	11	135	—	2	1	—	—
Annexation	96	—	—	46	15	10	11	9	5
Suburban rings, total	* 148	4	9	1	6	13	29	50	36
Natural increase	148	—	1	3	23	53	60	8	—
Civilian net migration	148	6	6	8	14	10	36	32	36
Military increase	148	—	11	122	6	5	3	1	—
Annexation	96	48	48	—	—	—	—	—	—

* Hampton-Newport News-Warwick, Virginia, S.M.A. has no suburban ring.

Table 2, which is a frequency distribution by growth rates and components of growth. From this table it may be seen that the central cities of 110 S.M.A.'s (73.8 per cent of the S.M.A.'s) lost population through net migration, and that all but twelve suburban metropolitan rings gained population through net migration. The proportionate gains from net migration were very great in some cases. Increases of 30.0 per cent or more were experienced by 68 areas, and 36 suburban areas had increases of 60.0 per cent or more. The comparatively small over-all importance of the military population as a source of growth may be noted from Table 1, where it is shown that all S.M.A.'s grew by 0.6 per cent as a result of this component. However, it was quite important in a few areas. The following areas increased three per cent or more as a result of military expansion during the decade:

S.M.A.	Per Cent
Albuquerque, N. Mex.	7.7
Augusta, Ga.	3.3
Charleston, S. C.	4.2
Columbus, Ga.	9.8
Corpus Christi, Tex.	4.0
El Paso, Tex.	9.1
Hampton—Newport News—Warwick, Va.	10.7
Norfolk—Portsmouth, Va.	17.5
San Antonio, Tex.	6.8
San Diego, Calif.	13.8
San Francisco—Oakland, Calif.	3.0
Tucson, Ariz.	4.3
Washington, D.C.	3.2

The significance of annexation may be noted from Table 1. An average gain of 3.3 per cent to central cities, and an average loss of 5.3 per cent to suburban rings resulted from this source. The following areas had major annexation changes during the decade:

Area	1950 Population of Annexed Area	Per Cent Gain to Central City
Albuquerque, N. Mex.	29,190	78.7
Baton Rouge, La.	88,271	261.6
Beaumont—Port Arthur, Tex.	27,987	26.7
Birmingham, Ala.	28,482	10.7
Bridgeport—Stamford—Norwalk, Conn.	19,686	8.5
Charlotte, N. C.	19,127	19.0
Corpus Christi, Tex.	42,546	74.4
Dallas, Tex.	120,830	41.1

Area	1950 Population of Annexed Area	Per Cent Gain to Central City
Evansville, Ind.	26,371	27.3
Fort Worth, Tex.	41,457	23.3
Fresno, Calif.	26,680	41.7
Greenville, S. C.	23,687	66.7
Houston, Tex.	134,634	35.1
Jackson, Miss.	21,784	34.9
Kansas City, Mo.	24,163	6.1
Little Rock—North Little Rock, Ark. .	24,764	22.7
Lubbock, Tex.	31,099	87.9
Memphis, Tenn.	37,042	12.7
Mobile, Ala.	29,104	37.3
Phoenix, Ariz.	34,353	52.7
Richmond, Va.	35,180	18.0
Roanoke, Va.	23,474	34.3
San Antonio, Tex.	99,608	39.2
Wichita, Kan.	22,182	19.3

To illustrate the results obtained for individual areas, the components of growth are shown in Table 3 for the twenty-five largest S.M.A.'s.

Estimates of this type can be prepared for the 1930-40 decade or earlier decades as well as for 1940-50. Moreover, by applying the survival ratio technique of estimating net migration,[6] it is possible to subdivide the net migration as obtained by this vital statistics procedure into color, age, and sex components. Such a subdivision is now being made for the estimates for each S.M.A., central city, and ring, and will be published as a part of the final report. Table 4 shows the estimates for the Chicago S.M.A., central city, and suburban ring for both the 1930-40 and 1940-50 decades, by color, sex, and age. This table illustrates the vast amount of information about the sources of growth that can be accumulated by combining the two estimating procedures.

[6] C. Horace Hamilton and F. M. Henderson, "Use of the Survival Rate Method in Measuring Net Migration," *Journal of the American Statistical Association*, XXXIX: 226 (June, 1944).

TABLE 3

COMPONENTS OF POPULATION CHANGE FOR THE TWENTY-FIVE LARGEST STANDARD METROPOLITAN AREAS, 1940-50

Standard Metropolitan Area	Total Change	Population Change, 1940-50 — Civilian Population — Total	Natural Increase	Net Migration	Military Change	Annexation	Total Change	Per Cent Change, 1940-50 — Civilian Population — Total	Natural Increase	Net Migration	Military Change	Annexation
New York-Northeastern, N. J.	1,228,691	1,224,421	966,824	257,597	4,270	—	10.5	10.5	8.3	2.2	0.0	—
Central cities	385,436	383,778	707,395	-323,617	1,658	—	4.7	4.7	8.6	-3.9	0.0	—
Ring	843,255	840,643	259,429	581,214	2,612	—	24.5	24.4	7.5	16.9	0.1	—
Chicago, Ill.	654,862	644,048	485,910	158,138	10,814	—	13.5	13.3	10.0	3.3	0.2	—
Central city	212,709	210,766	312,172	-101,406	1,604	339	6.2	6.2	9.2	-3.0	0.0	0.0
Ring	442,153	433,282	173,738	259,544	9,210	-339	30.9	30.3	12.1	18.1	0.6	0.0
Los Angeles, Calif.	1,465,091	1,452,563	386,200	1,066,363	12,528	—	50.5	50.0	13.3	36.7	0.4	—
Central city	469,977	452,818	172,310	280,508	1,816	15,343	31.3	30.2	11.5	18.7	0.1	1.0
Ring	995,114	999,745	213,890	785,855	10,712	-15,343	71.0	71.3	15.3	56.0	0.8	-1.1
Philadelphia, Pa.	459,762	436,628	291,327	145,301	23,134	—	14.3	13.6	9.1	4.5	0.7	—
Central city	128,530	123,288	152,515	-29,227	5,242	—	6.6	6.3	7.8	-1.5	0.3	—
Ring	331,232	313,340	138,812	174,528	17,892	—	26.1	24.7	10.9	13.8	1.4	—
Detroit, Mich.	637,172	634,029	388,396	245,633	3,143	—	26.8	26.7	16.3	10.3	0.1	—
Central city	217,922	217,347	235,557	-18,210	575	—	13.4	13.3	14.4	-1.1	0.0	—
Ring	419,250	416,682	152,839	263,843	2,568	—	56.1	55.8	20.4	35.3	0.3	—
Boston-Lawrence-Lowell, Mass.	210,382	199,936	218,638	-18,702	10,446	—	7.9	7.5	8.2	-0.7	0.4	—
Central cities	12,900	6,937	65,358	-58,421	5,963	—	1.3	0.7	6.8	-6.0	0.6	—
Ring	197,482	192,999	153,280	39,719	4,483	—	11.6	11.4	9.0	2.3	0.3	—
San Francisco-Oakland, Calif.	763,425	718,761	218,892	499,869	44,664	—	51.7	48.7	14.8	33.8	3.0	—
Central cities	229,860	211,915	85,630	126,285	17,945	—	24.7	22.8	9.2	13.6	1.9	—
Ring	533,565	506,846	133,262	373,584	26,719	—	97.5	92.6	24.4	68.3	4.9	—
Pittsburgh, Pa.	127,948	126,974	221,889	-94,915	974	—	6.1	6.1	10.6	-4.6	0.0	—
Central city	-3,851	-4,314	73,524	-77,838	268	195	-0.6	-0.6	10.8	-11.4	0.0	0.0
Ring	131,799	131,288	148,365	-17,077	706	-195	9.4	9.3	10.6	-1.2	0.1	0.0

St. Louis, Mo.	249,890	242,308	146,419	95,889	7,582	—	17.5	16.9	10.2	6.7	0.5	—
Central city	35,837	35,099	65,784	−30,685	738	—	4.4	4.3	8.0	−3.7	0.1	—
Ring	214,053	207,209	80,635	126,574	6,844	—	35.1	33.9	13.2	20.7	1.1	—
Cleveland, Ohio	194,421	193,924	144,087	49,837	497	—	15.3	15.3	11.3	3.9	0.0	—
Central city	26,954	26,615	96,171	−69,556	339	—	3.0	3.0	10.8	−7.8	0.0	—
Ring	167,467	167,309	47,916	119,393	158	—	43.7	43.7	12.5	31.2	0.0	—
Washington, D. C.	484,432	452,909	185,010	267,899	31,523	—	49.4	46.2	18.9	27.3	3.2	—
Central city	129,266	119,944	90,000	29,944	9,322	—	19.2	17.8	13.4	4.4	1.4	—
Ring	355,166	332,965	95,010	237,955	22,201	—	115.8	108.5	31.0	77.6	7.2	—
Baltimore, Md.	254,569	243,150	140,207	102,943	11,419	—	23.5	22.5	12.9	9.5	1.1	—
Central city	89,368	87,856	95,718	−7,862	1,512	—	10.4	10.2	11.1	−0.9	0.2	—
Ring	165,201	155,294	44,489	110,805	9,907	—	74.3	69.8	20.0	49.8	4.5	—
Minneapolis—St. Paul, Minn.	169,301	169,380	127,969	41,411	−79	—	17.9	17.9	13.5	4.4	0.0	—
Central cities	44,775	44,816	97,897	−53,081	−41	—	5.7	5.7	12.4	−6.7	0.0	—
Ring	124,526	124,564	30,072	94,492	−38	—	78.4	78.4	18.9	59.5	0.0	—
Buffalo, N. Y.	136,046	135,995	102,697	33,298	51	—	14.3	14.3	10.8	3.5	0.0	—
Central city	2,089	2,064	49,172	−47,108	25	—	0.4	0.4	8.5	−8.1	0.0	—
Ring	133,957	133,931	53,525	80,406	26	—	35.7	35.7	14.3	21.4	0.0	—
Cincinnati, Ohio	110,738	110,512	78,018	32,494	226	—	14.0	13.9	9.8	4.1	0.0	—
Central city	39,673	29,570	36,776	−7,206	139	9,964	8.5	6.4	7.9	−1.6	0.0	2.1
Ring	71,065	80,942	41,242	39,700	87	−9,964	21.6	24.6	12.5	12.1	0.0	−3.0
Milwaukee, Wis.	106,131	105,232	85,819	19,413	899	—	13.9	13.8	11.2	2.5	0.1	—
Central city	50,496	33,813	60,402	−26,589	803	15,880	8.6	5.8	10.3	−4.5	0.1	2.7
Ring	55,635	71,419	25,417	46,002	96	−15,880	31.3	40.1	14.3	25.8	0.1	−8.9
Kansas City, Mo.	129,585	128,730	72,521	56,209	855	—	18.9	18.8	10.6	8.2	0.1	—
Central city	57,966	33,569	33,468	101	234	24,163	14.5	8.4	8.4	0.0	0.1	6.1
Ring	71,619	95,161	39,053	56,108	621	−24,163	25.0	33.3	13.6	19.6	0.2	−8.4
Houston, Tex.	277,146	274,969	109,757	165,212	2,177	—	52.3	51.9	20.7	31.2	0.4	—
Central city	212,167	76,981	76,733	248	552	134,634	55.3	20.0	20.0	0.1	0.1	35.1
Ring	64,979	197,988	33,024	164,964	1,625	−134,634	44.6	136.0	22.7	113.3	1.1	−92.5

TABLE 3—*Continued*

COMPONENTS OF POPULATION CHANGE FOR THE TWENTY-FIVE LARGEST STANDARD METROPOLITAN AREAS, 1940-50

Standard Metropolitan Area	Total Change	Population Change, 1940-50 Civilian Population			Military Change	Annexation	Per Cent Change, 1940-50 Total Change	Civilian Population			Military Change	Annexation
		Total	Natural Increase	Net Migration				Total	Natural Increase	Net Migration		
Seattle, Wash.	223,980	217,057	75,696	141,361	6,923	—	44.0	42.6	14.9	27.8	1.4	—
Central city	93,465	68,254	59,097	9,157	6,007	19,204	25.0	18.2	15.8	2.4	1.6	5.1
Ring	130,515	148,803	16,599	132,204	916	-19,204	96.8	110.3	12.3	98.0	0.7	-14.2
Portland, Ore.	206,856	206,196	67,630	138,566	660	—	41.5	41.4	13.6	27.8	0.1	—
Central city	70,285	68,902	38,488	30,414	289	1,094	23.2	22.7	12.7	10.0	0.1	0.4
Ring	136,571	137,294	29,142	108,152	371	-1,094	70.2	70.5	15.0	55.6	0.2	-0.6
New Orleans, La.	130,569	127,487	84,648	42,839	3,082	—	23.5	23.0	15.3	7.7	0.6	—
Central city	72,966	70,010	68,054	1,956	2,956	—	14.7	14.1	13.7	0.4	0.6	—
Ring	57,603	57,477	16,594	40,883	126	—	100.4	100.2	28.9	71.3	0.2	—
Providence, R. I.	49,240	48,579	56,827	-8,248	661	—	7.8	7.7	9.0	-1.3	0.1	—
Central city	-6,261	-6,441	20,637	-27,078	180	—	-2.5	-2.5	8.1	-10.6	0.1	—
Ring	55,501	55,020	36,190	18,830	481	—	14.7	14.6	9.6	5.0	0.1	—
Atlanta, Ga.	150,689	148,820	85,673	63,147	1,869	—	28.9	28.6	16.4	12.1	0.4	—
Central city	26,643	23,259	45,082	-21,823	382	3,002	8.7	7.6	14.8	-7.2	0.1	1.0
Ring	124,046	125,561	40,591	84,970	1,487	-3,002	57.3	58.0	18.8	39.3	0.7	-1.4
Dallas, Tex.	217,556	216,688	74,606	142,082	868	—	54.8	54.5	18.8	35.8	0.2	—
Central city	140,302	19,113	44,349	-25,236	359	120,830	47.7	6.5	15.1	-8.6	0.1	41.1
Ring	77,254	197,575	30,257	167,318	509	-120,830	74.9	191.7	29.4	162.3	0.5	-117.2
Louisville, Ky.	123,600	123,041	64,376	58,665	559	—	27.3	27.1	14.2	12.9	0.1	—
Central city	47,444	37,627	47,917	-10,290	425	9,392	14.7	11.7	14.9	-3.2	0.1	2.9
Ring	76,156	85,414	16,459	68,955	134	-9,392	57.9	64.9	12.5	52.4	0.1	-7.1

TABLE 4

COMPONENTS OF POPULATION CHANGE IN THE CHICAGO STANDARD METROPOLITAN AREA, 1930-40 AND 1940-50

Component, Color, Sex, and Age	1940-50 Decade			1930-40 Decade		
	S.M.A. Total	City of Chicago	Suburban	S.M.A. Total	City of Chicago	Suburban
Total population change during decade	654,862	212,709	442,153	149,650	20,370	129,280
White	385,097	−13,939	399,036	99,172	−22,529	121,701
Male	170,628	−21,534	192,162	8,986	−42,961	51,947
Female	214,469	7,595	206,874	90,186	20,432	69,754
Nonwhite	269,765	226,648	43,117	50,478	42,899	7,579
Male	131,882	110,207	21,675	16,907	13,963	2,944
Female	137,883	116,441	21,442	33,571	28,936	4,635
Natural increase, total	485,910	312,202	173,708	207,491	152,345	55,146
White	427,004	264,905	162,099	213,379	158,704	54,675
Male	188,119	116,632	71,487	106,553	81,700	24,833
Female	238,885	148,273	90,612	106,846	77,004	29,842
Nonwhite	58,906	47,297	11,609	−5,888	−6,359	471
Male	27,477	21,994	5,483	−1,930	−1,826	−104
Female	31,429	25,303	6,126	−3,958	−4,533	575
Increase in military population, total	10,814	1,604	9,210	—	—	—
White male	9,572	1,231	8,341	—	—	—
White female	760	240	520	—	—	—
Nonwhite male	410	70	340	—	—	—
Nonwhite female	72	63	9	—	—	—
Net civilian migration	158,138	−101,097	259,235	−57,841	−131,975	74,134
White	−52,239	−280,315	228,076	−114,207	−181,233	67,026
Male	−27,063	−139,397	112,334	−97,547	−124,661	27,114
Female	−25,176	−140,918	115,742	−16,660	−56,572	39,912
Nonwhite	210,377	179,218	31,159	56,366	49,258	7,108
Male	103,995	88,143	15,852	18,837	15,789	3,048
Female	106,382	91,075	15,307	37,529	33,469	4,060

TABLE 4—*Continued*

COMPONENTS OF POPULATION CHANGE IN THE CHICAGO STANDARD METROPOLITAN AREA, 1930-40 AND 1940-50

Component, Color, Sex, and Age	1940-50 Decade			1930-40 Decade		
	S.M.A. Total	City of Chicago	Suburban	S.M.A. Total	City of Chicago	Suburban
Net civilian migration, by age—white	−52,239	−280,315	228,076	−114,207	−181,233	67,026
0– 9 years	−28,079	−71,145	43,066	−9,352	−24,321	14,969
10-14 years	−7,486	−26,881	19,395	−17,222	−21,268	4,046
15-19 years	1,648	−12,347	13,995	2,034	−1,851	3,885
20-24 years	32,581	17,904	14,677	34,649	27,210	7,439
25-29 years	45,931	19,021	26,910	36,379	28,141	8,238
30-34 years	7,914	−21,197	29,111	−7,025	−17,704	10,679
35-39 years	−7,257	−36,566	29,309	−32,780	−41,448	8,668
40-44 years	−9,611	−31,129	21,518	−26,253	−31,696	5,443
45-49 years	−10,387	−23,790	13,403	−20,783	−26,070	5,287
50-54 years	−13,612	−20,474	6,862	−24,265	−20,847	−3,418
55-64 years	−29,292	−36,136	6,844	−29,389	−29,590	201
65-74 years	−25,820	−25,288	−532	−20,148	−19,496	−652
75 and over	−8,769	−12,287	3,518	−52	−2,293	2,241
Net civilian migration, by age—nonwhite	210,377	179,218	31,159	56,366	49,258	7,108
0– 9 years	15,079	13,011	2,068	3,692	3,004	688
10-14 years	14,652	11,911	2,741	4,018	3,631	387
15-19 years	13,674	11,005	2,669	6,129	5,232	897
20-24 years	30,112	25,673	4,439	10,759	9,306	1,453
25-29 years	41,318	35,944	5,374	17,184	15,028	2,156
30-34 years	32,997	28,816	4,181	9,819	8,381	1,438
35-39 years	23,406	20,246	3,160	1,265	1,277	−12
40-44 years	13,844	11,924	1,920	−522	−146	−376
45-49 years	9,359	7,737	1,622	−182	−638	456
50-54 years	5,157	4,220	937	−620	−185	−435
55-64 years	7,657	6,324	1,333	2,307	2,051	256
65-74 years	1,831	1,435	396	1,791	1,687	104
75 and over	1,291	972	319	726	630	96

METHODS FOR DESCRIBING THE AGE-SEX STRUCTURE OF CITIES *

HARLEY L. BROWNING **

Virtually any study of social groups may be enhanced by a consideration of the age and sex characteristics of their members, for few variables in social science find wider application. It is almost automatic procedure for many urban studies—whether an analysis of the labor force, the educational attainments of the population, or the reproductive behavior of a specified group, etc.—to introduce classifications in terms of age and sex.

The various techniques to be considered in this paper enable us to determine for any given city the concentration of the population in the early, middle or late years, and state the excess, if any, of females or males. Once this information has been obtained, however, we must be able to interpret it, and here a comparative approach is indispensable. Is the proportion of the population in a particular age category high or low? Does one sex outnumber the other to an unusual degree? We have little basis for answering such questions without some knowledge of the age-sex composition of other cities. And it is only through systematic comparisons along these lines that the determinants and consequences of the various age-sex patterns can be established. Therefore, wherever possible, studies should use standardized methods which express age-sex characteristics in comparable terms.

The utility of the comparative approach for the study of age-sex differences holds whatever the level of inquiry. The subdistricts of a city can be as readily compared with each other as world regions, and quite often the interplay in shifting from one level to another provides valuable interpretative suggestions. To illustrate this point let us consider India, beginning with the city of Agra. This city of more than 300,000 inhabitants has a sex ratio of 122, that is, there are one hundred and twenty-two men for every hundred women. Is this rather high sex ratio a characteristic of other cities in India, or is it an isolated case, account-

---

* Written especially for this volume.
** Member of the staff of International Urban Research.

able by special circumstances? A comparison with other large Indian cities indicates that Agra is not atypical; nearly all of them have high sex ratios. But we need not limit ourselves to sub-national comparisons. An examination of the large cities of other countries in Southern Asia would reveal a similar pattern of male predominance. However, in some world regions, Latin America being an outstanding example, there is a clear excess of females in the cities. Once these differences among world regions are es-tablished, we are ready to look for those aspects of the social and economic structures of countries which determine the age-sex characteristics of their cities.

Another broad area of fruitful inquiry is found in the consider-ation of the actual and potential consequences of different age-sex distribution with respect to the growth of cities and their economic characteristics. A particular age-sex distribution in effect sets certain limits on the levels of fertility and mortality in a population, and by extension the growth or decline of a city. For example, a city with a substantial share of its population over forty is likely to have a lower rate of natural increase than a city with proportionately many more people in the young adult ages. Similarly, a city with an extreme imbalance of the sexes would not be expected to have the same reproductive performance as a city with a more even distribution. In like manner, the age-sex composition establishes certain limits on the manpower resources of a city. In all of these cases, it must be pointed out, knowl-edge of the age-sex distribution is insufficient in itself to predict the actual performance of the population in terms of births, deaths, and employment. All we can know, in a general way, are certain limits which the age-sex distribution sets for the popula-tion. Finally, with respect to economic characteristics, it has been noted that the functional specialization of cities (i.e., manufac-turing, commercial, and resort centers) tends to be reflected in their age-sex composition.[1]

It should be clear by now that the fundamental objective of most work in this field is the attempt to establish the causes and consequences of variation in the age-sex structure of cities. This

[1] Albert J. Reiss, Jr., "Functional Specialization of Cities," in Paul K. Hatt and Albert J. Reiss, Jr. (eds.), *Cities and Society* (Glencoe, Ill.: The Free Press, 1957), pp. 562-575.

paper is necessarily limited to an exposition of the various ways of describing age-sex data rather than in setting forth an analytic method for the interpretation of differences. This is so both in view of space limitations as well as in the fact that the variety of investigations making use of age-sex data is so broad as to create problems in formulating specific rules appropriate for every situation. Nevertheless it must be repeatedly stressed that the proper selection and use of age and sex indices is but one part of an investigation.[2]

AVAILABILITY AND ADEQUACY OF DATA

One reason why age and sex variables are included in so many studies is simply because the data are so often available. Virtually all census reports, for instance, provide some information on age and sex. They are not always presented in a way to satisfy best the needs of the researcher, but compared with other census items, such as occupation, these two variables are more likely to be provided, and they also present fewer difficulties in classification.

The availability of the data does not mean there are no problems involving defective data. Even sex data, the most unambiguous of all demographic categories, are subject to a certain amount of error. The accurate reporting of age by single year intervals is difficult in all countries, but it is notoriously difficult in many of the less developed countries, where large numbers of people simply do not know this information. Since all population data are faulty to some degree it is not a question of throwing out the data if errors are found but rather of ascertaining whether adjustments can be made or, failing this, in deciding whether the

---

[2] The reader may refer to the following studies which make age-sex differences central to their discussion. Robert E. Chaddock, "Age and Sex in Population Analysis," in Joseph J. Spengler and Otis D. Duncan (eds.), *Demographic Analysis* (Glencoe, Ill.: The Free Press, 1956), pp. 443-54; Joseph Greenburg, *Numerical Sex Disproportion* (Boulder, Colo.: University of Colorado Press, 1950); Charles Newcomb, "Graphic Presentation of Age and Sex Distribution of Population in the City," in Paul K. Hatt and Albert J. Reiss, Jr. (eds.), *Cities and Society* (Glencoe, Ill.: The Free Press, 1957), pp. 382-92; S. H. Franklin, "The Age Structure of New Zealand's North Island Communities," *Economic Geography*, Vol. 34 (January, 1958), pp. 64-79; S. H. Franklin, "Patterns of Sex Ratios in New Zealand," *Economic Geography*, Vol. 32 (April, 1956), pp. 162-176.

error is great enough to invalidate one's conclusions.[3] Generally speaking, the imperfect nature of the data is sufficient reason not to overload the analysis with conclusions based on very small differences.

A REVIEW OF SPECIFIC TECHNIQUES

The investigator who wishes to introduce age and sex categories into his analysis has at his disposal a variety of simple but effective indices of the age-sex distribution. No one index, of course, can describe every detail of the distribution and it is likely that the investigator will wish to use several indices, depending upon the nature of his particular problem.

Let us begin our review of techniques by considering some of the graphic means of presentation. Undoubtedly the most familiar of these is the *age-sex pyramid,* sometimes called the "population pyramid" (see Figure I). Its construction is not difficult. Each of the horizontal bars which make up the pyramid (usually given in five-year intervals) are expressed either as a per cent of the total population or in absolute numbers. Males are placed to the left and females to the right of the axis.

The virtue of the age-sex pyramid, as of all graphic techniques, lies in our ability to absorb a great deal of information in a glance. Not only can we "see" a young or an old population, but important historical events, such as wars and famines and baby booms, are clearly revealed in the "sculpturing" of the sides of the pyramids. Our illustrations are the very different age-sex pyramids of three ethnic groups in metropolitan Johannesburg, Union of South Africa. Most striking is the unbalanced Native pyramid which reflects the heavy migration of young adult males into the area to work in mines and factories.

---

[3] There are a number of useful manuals which offer guides to the evaluation of age and sex data. See, for example, George W. Barclay, *Techniques of Population Analysis* (New York: John Wiley and Sons, 1958); A. J. Jaffee, *A Handbook of Statistical Methods for Demographers* (Washington, D.C.: U.S. Department of Commerce, 1951); United Nations, Population Division, "Accuracy Tests for Census Age Distribution Tabulated in Five-Year and Ten-Year Groups," *Population Bulletin,* No. 2 (October 1952), pp. 59-79. A word of caution is advisable in the use of those tests which try to make an evaluation, on the basis of internal checks, of the adequacy of the age data, because they are based on the assumption that migration is negligible. While this may be a valid assumption in dealing with countries, it is, as a rule, not appropriate for cities, which are likely to be greatly affected by migration.

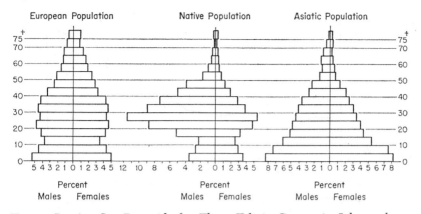

FIGURE I. Age-Sex Pyramids for Three Ethnic Groups in Johannesburg, Union of South Africa, 1946.*

* Source: Union of South Africa, Office of Census and Statistics, *Eighth Census of the Population of the Union of South Africa, 7th May, 1946,* Vol. 2 (Pretoria, 1950.)

Other forms of visual display are charts or graphs. The data can be plotted directly onto the chart or graph, or they can be converted into index numbers and then plotted. Essentially index numbers are used to highlight the variations of subgroups within the larger population by comparing each of the subgroups to the total population. The illustration is provided by Costa Rica (Figure II). The per cent of the population in each five-year interval for both the urban and rural residents is divided by that of the nation as a whole to produce index numbers, which are then plotted on a graph.[4] By this means we can easily compare the divergent experience of the urban and rural populations.

Graphic displays are very useful but they are all subject to the same important limitations. First, they do not make it possible to compare a large number of cases; we can readily inspect two age-sex pyramids, but not two hundred. Second, they do not enable us to express the difference between two or more cases in quantitative terms. Therefore, while graphic techniques are ideal for illustrative purposes, especially for emphasizing certain points, it is recommended that whenever they are used the data should also be made available in tabular form.

[4] For example, the per cent in the 20-24 category of the urban population is 10.37. Dividing this by the comparable figure for the total population, 9.62, and multiplying by 100 we get an index number of 108.

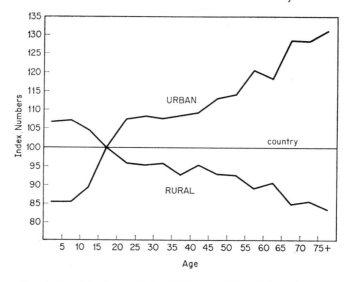

FIGURE II.   Index Numbers of the Urban and Rural Populations of Costa
Rica (1950).*

* See text for description of index numbers. Source of data: 1950 census report of Costa Rica.

In handling the age distribution in tabular form and constructing indices, one often combines the five-year intervals [5] into three
broad categories: the young ages, 0-14; the adult period, 15-64;
and the older years, 65+. There is nothing fixed about these
groupings; they are presented because they represent the most
frequent contemporary usage. Essentially the same results would
obtain from 15-19, or 20-59, or 20-64. Nevertheless, the researcher should remember that if he adopts unusual cutting points
in establishing his main groupings it will be difficult, if not impossible, to compare his results with those of studies using more
conventional groupings.[6]

Table 1 provides age breakdowns for four cities: Guayaquil,
Ecuador; Geneva, Switzerland; San Salvador, El Salvador; and

[5] Single year intervals are rarely used; this would be too cumbersome. It is
customary to take five-year intervals, although there are frequent exceptions involving longer periods.

[6] Frequently investigators are forced to use different age groupings because
they are the only ones obtainable from census and official reports It would be
a considerable service if census bureaus could be persuaded to report their age
distributions by five-year intervals wherever possible.

TABLE 1

AGE AND SEX INDICES OF FOUR SELECTED CITIES *

| | CITIES | | | |
INDICES	Guayaquil 1950	Geneva 1950	San Salvador 1950	Colombo 1953
Per Cent of Total Population in Each Age Group				
0-14	37.6	12.9	30.8	30.5
15-64	59.8	69.1	65.9	66.7
65+	2.6	18.0	3.3	2.8
Dependency Ratio ..	67.2	44.7	51.7	49.9
Index of Aging				
Male	5.4	105.4	8.1	8.9
Female	8.6	172.4	13.7	9.3
Total	6.9	139.5	10.7	9.2
Median Age	20.7	41.9	23.1	24.5
Sex Ratio				
Total	92.9	80.6	84.2	154.8
0-14	100.8	102.4	98.8	105.6
15-64	89.6	82.1	79.5	189.6
65+	64.6	62.7	59.1	101.2
Per Cent Male				
Total	48.1	44.6	45.7	60.8
15-64	47.3	45.1	44.3	65.5

* The populations of these cities for the census dates given are: Guayaquil 258,966; Geneva 156,900; San Salvador 161,951; Colombo 426,127.
SOURCES: Latest census reports of each country.

Colombo, Ceylon.[7] These cities were especially selected for illustrative purposes because they provide a good idea of the considerable variation in the age-sex structure of urban populations. Guayaquil and Geneva represent young and old extremes in city populations. Proportionately, Guayaquil has nearly three times as many young people (0-14) as Geneva, while the latter has six times as many older persons (65+).

The *dependency ratio* is a well-known index which provides a rough but serviceable measure of the number of people in the

[7] All future references to these cities will be in terms of this table.

so-called "active" ages (15-64) as compared to those in the "dependent" age groups (0-14 and 65+):

$$\text{Dr} = \frac{(0\text{-}14) + (65+)}{(15\text{-}64)} \times 100$$

Because dependency relationships take place in family environments, male and female ratios are not often computed separately. The lower the ratio, presumably the more "productive" the population because of a lower dependency load. In Geneva there are more than two people in the working ages for every one outside of it, while in Guayaquil the relationship is one-and-one-half to one. With rare exceptions, urban populations have lower dependency ratios than rural populations, but this difference is partially offset by the greater opportunity for both young and old to contribute in some way to the economic goals of the rural family.

The dependency ratio combines the young and the old into one total. We know, however, that the actual physical and social requirements of these two groups are quite different. Therefore, we need an index which will express the relationship of the young to the old in a given population; that is, an *index of aging:*[8]

$$\text{Ia} = \frac{(65+)}{(0\text{-}14)} \times 100$$

This index has a much greater range than the dependency ratio, as indicated by the cases of Colombo and Geneva. Their dependency ratios do not differ greatly (49.8 and 44.7) but the index of aging (total population) is very low for Colombo (9.2) and very high for Geneva (139.3).

One final index of the age structure is a summary measure, *median age.* This may be defined as the age of that person at the midpoint of the age distribution. In the population there are as many persons older than he as there are persons younger. To estimate the median age from grouped data, we first find the interval of the age distribution that contains the midpoint. We then interpolate within this interval to estimate the age of that

---

[8] See Vasilios Valaoras, "Young and Aged Populations," *Annals of the American Academy of Political and Social Science,* Vol. 316 (March, 1958), pp. 69-83.

person at the midpoint of the entire age distribution.[9] Median age is an effective over-all way of expressing the young or old character of a population, although it cannot tell us whether the population is concentrated or dispersed about the median. Again the contrast between Guayaquil and Geneva is very great; the median age of Geneva is more than double that of Guayaquil.

SEX DIFFERENCES

The most commonly used technique for expressing the sex distribution has already been mentioned, the *sex ratio:* $Sr = \frac{Males}{Females} \times 100$. Occasionally this is expressed in reverse manner (the number of females per 100 males), but in the interest of comparability the more customary usage is urged. One cannot infer the sex structure from an examination of the age distribution of the total population. San Salvador and Colombo, for example, are virtually identical in terms of per cent in the three main age groups, but there is a striking difference, if we inspect the sex ratios for these two cities. Colombo is an exceptionally masculine city with almost two men for every woman in the active (15-64) ages.

There is another way of expressing sex differences which has certain advantages not possessed by the sex ratio. This is the per cent male index: $Pm = \frac{Males}{Total\ Population} \times 100$. It is computed by simply expressing the male population as a per cent of the total population. This index can be substituted for the sex ratio in cases where it is desirable to use a measure which has absolute minimum and maximum values. As constituted, the sex ratio and the per cent male index both can approach zero, but the latter can never be greater than 100 while the former has no absolute upper limit.

[9] There are a number of interpolating procedures (available in most statistical texts) which vary greatly in complexity. The simplest one, the "linear" method, assumes the population to be evenly distributed throughout the interval. The margin of error is apt to be smaller when using one year periods; the method is more dubious when applied to five or ten year intervals.

TABLE 2

AGE-SEX INDICES FOR GUAYAQUIL, GENEVA, SAN SALVADOR AND COLOMBO EXPRESSED AS CITY-COUNTRY RATIOS

INDICES	Guayaquil, Ecuador (1950)			Geneva, Switzerland (1950)			San Salvador, El Salvador (1950)			Colombo, Ceylon (1953)		
	City (a)	Country (b)	Ratio (a/b)100	City (a)	Country (b)	Ratio (a/b)100	City (a)	Country (b)	Ratio (a/b)100	City (a)	Country (b)	Ratio (a/b)100
Per Cent by Age Groups												
0-14	37.6	42.5	88	12.9	23.6	55	30.8	41.1	75	30.5	39.7	77
15-64	59.8	54.0	111	69.1	66.8	103	65.9	55.9	118	66.7	56.8	117
65+	2.6	3.5	74	18.0	9.6	186	3.3	3.0	110	2.8	3.5	80
Per Cent Male												
Total Pop. ...	48.1	49.8	97	44.6	48.2	93	45.7	49.5	92	60.8	52.7	115
15-64	47.2	49.1	96	45.1	48.0	94	44.3	48.5	91	65.5	54.0	121

SOURCES: Latest census reports of each country.

MIGRATION AND AGE-SEX DIFFERENCES

If the sex ratios and per cent male indices in Table 1 are again examined we may note that in all four of our cities there is a fairly close balance of the sexes in the young (0-14) ages. With the exception of Colombo, there is also a distinct excess of females in the aged group (65+), due principally to differential mortality. It is in the active ages (15-64) where we find the greatest variation among our cities. This variation is due in large measure to differential migration, for the most mobile of age groups are the adult groups, particularly the young adults. Therefore, sex differences for such age categories as 15-29 or 20-39 offer good clues as to the presence or absence of migration. These differences are not so helpful in estimating either the total amount of migration or the current rate of migration. We must examine the age distribution for further leads and here the age-sex pyramid of the native population of Johannesburg (see Figure I) presents a most interesting situation. Heavy in-migration of both males and females in the adult years is clearly indicated because the base of the pyramid is so narrow that it could not possibly supply the upper part. Note also that the age-sex pyramid for the Asiatic population (especially in the ages above 50) indicates that at an earlier time migration was almost wholly male.

Another means of indicating the volume of migration is provided by a comparison of the age structure of a nation with that of its cities. In Table 2 a number of such comparisons are set forth in the form of city-country ratios. In all cases the cities have relatively a greater proportion of their populations in the 15-64 category than the country as a whole. Other comparisons, such as urban-rural or city-rural, may provide a better indication of the amount of migration. These ratios are admittedly a crude measure of migration but they are of help in those situations where no migration statistics are available.

This completes our review of the more familiar indices of age and sex distributions. All are of an uncomplicated nature, easy to compute and to use. The challenge of age-sex research does not lie in the problems of expressing differences by means of various techniques. The challenge lies, rather, in asking the right kind of questions about the meaning of these differences.

Part III

THE SPATIAL STRUCTURE
OF URBAN UNITS

Introduction to Part III

The study of urban spatial structure deals with a wide range of topics which encompasses patterns in the location of such diverse phenomena as places of residence, commercial establishments, transportation lines, ethnic or racial groups, places of worship, manufacturing plants, vacant land, hospitals, public parks, and areas demarcated along social class lines. Much more is entailed in the study of the subject than merely isolating and describing location patterns. There is always a temptation to count and map things just because it is easy to do so, and the danger in spatial studies is that description will be pursued for its own sake. Spatial structure and the spatial distribution of urban phenomena deserve study only insofar as they are related to other aspects of cities and to urban problems. In this area of research, the novice must particularly bear in mind that a mastery of methods is not an end in itself; for it is in this area that research is often undertaken without sufficient concern for the significance of the subject.

Unfortunately, a discussion of the theoretical aspects of spatial structure and their significance cannot be pursued at length here, but a few remarks can be made. Space is something which confronts all groups and populations and sets certain limits on the ways in which their social relations and interaction with the physical environment can be patterned. Accordingly, certain relations hold between the spatial structure of a city and some of its basic characteristics as described in Part II. For example, it has been repeatedly found that business establishments tend to be concentrated in a central position relative to places of residence. The position of this "central business district" may shift in time, but the concentration of business establishments and the centripetal orientation of the population, taken together, represent one of the ways in which people organize themselves to cope with the friction of space (i.e., the fact that movement through space necessarily entails an expenditure of time and energy). The central location reduces the average distance between the establishments and the residences of the persons who make use of them; and this is often taken to be an explanation of the existence of the pattern, on the grounds that the cost and time involved in travel preclude a peripheral location of the main business district. In a small urban unit, however, where movement from any one point to another requires little time or energy, the population is not confronted with the locational imperatives that operate in a large metropolis. In the case of small urban places, although business establishments may be concentrated in a central position, there is reason to believe that their location relative to the population is more subject to the influence of non-spatial factors than is the case in huge cities. In other words, with increasing areal extent, the main concentration of business establishments in urban units tends more and more to occupy a central position. This, of course, is only a hypothesis; but it serves to illustrate a possible relation between patterns in spatial structure and one of the basic characteristics of urban units described in Part II.

Our understanding of the variety, causes, and consequences of spatial patterns in cities is meagre, mainly because the subject has been investigated in relatively few cultures. The literature abounds with data on the spatial structure of North American and European cities; but, because there are so few studies on the subject in other regions, we are not able to speak with any degree of certainty as to either the causes or consequences of these patterns. A notable case is that of the location of better residential areas. In some North American cities the pattern is one of increasing residential quality from the city center outward. This is consistent with the theory that land use tends to change with distance from the central business district in the form of fairly distinct concentric zones, but other observations have been made to the contrary. In certain cases, notably in Latin America, the better residential areas appear to be located near the heart of the city; and it is generally recognized that land use patterns in some cities, even in North America, do not change uniformly with increasing distance from the central business district. These examples suggest that the spatial structure of cities varies tremendously, and it is only through broadening the scope of urban research beyond local studies to systematic international comparisons that the various patterns can be adequately explained.

A concern with spatial structure, far from being only of theoretical interest, is central to the field of urban planning. Most of the major problems confronting man in his new habitat—the problems of traffic, residential congestion, blighted areas and urban sprawl—are part and parcel of spatial structure. A consideration of urban planning is beyond the scope of this book, but it is worth noting that a mastery of research methods is just as essential to that subject as it is to more theoretical interests.

Contents of the papers. The first requisite of spatial analysis in an urban or metropolitan area is the establishment of spatial statistical divisions within the larger boundary. The next step is to obtain data on the population and land use characteristics of each of the parts. In many cases such data are provided in census reports. However, one may not wish to accept the statistical divisions employed for census purposes. Accordingly, research on the subject of spatial structure can best begin with three questions as they relate to the urban unit under consideration. First, what are the different types of spatial divisions that can be used for statistical purposes? Second, what are the characteristics of the different types, particularly in regard to size, homogeneity, and boundaries? And, third, what potentialities for research are offered by each type with regard to the availability of data on population and land use characteristics? These questions are central to the two papers in Chapter 6—"The City Block as a Unit for Recording and Analyzing Urban Data" by Edward B. Olds and "The Theory and Practice of Planning Census Tracts" by Calvin F. Schmid.

As a rule a study of spatial structure should employ the smallest statistical divisions in existence, since such divisions more finely indicate variations in land use and population characteristics. This being the case, the observations by Olds on the city block in U.S. urban places are particularly relevant. He notes the different kinds of statistics which are available for this type of spatial division, describes methods for the systematic organization of such statistics, and illustrates some of their possible applications.

Although Olds deals only with cities in the U.S. (and St. Louis in particular), his observations are relevant for research conducted elsewhere. In the first place he deals with a basic urban statistical division, the city block. If this division is defined as an area surrounded on all sides by streets, it is present in every urban place, even though it may vary greatly as to size and shape. Consequently, regardless of the locale, Olds' paper suggests uses of one of the smallest types of statistical divisions which can be used in research on spatial structure. Further, his discussion of the treatment of block statistics is relevant to the planning of field investigations designed to secure information not already in existence.

It often happens that the compilation and publication of data for city blocks is too expensive. Hence larger territorial divisions have often been established for use in individual studies or as standard units for regularly gathering and reporting mass statistics. One such division in U.S. cities, the *census tract*, is the subject of Schmid's paper. The observations offered there should prove useful to persons confronted with the task of establishing statistical divisions, either by a field investigation or through the combination of small divisions (such as the city block) for which data are available.

A study of internal structure calls for a distinction between spatial divisions that are simply statistical units and those that are delimited in accordance with some concept. The former merely divide up the city (often in a somewhat arbitrary manner), while each of the latter has distinctive characteristics which set it off from the remainder of the city. For example, it is commonly recognized that the individuals comprising an ethnic or racial group tend to cluster in a particular part of a city. Given the per cent of the population in each statistical division (preferably the city block) who are members of a particular ethnic group, one can isolate those parts of an urban unit which are residentially characterized by a predominance of the group. Similar delimitations involving other ethnic categories can be made, with the result that the whole of the urban unit is divided into a number of ethnic "neighborhoods." The boundaries of other types of urban sub-areas can be established along the lines of occupational composition, age-sex structure, land use, etc.

Urban sub-areas demarcated by combining lesser contiguous

divisions are, however, no more "real" or "natural" than the criteria used in establishing their boundaries. Such combinations are always made on the basis of an explicit or implicit set of rules, the nature of which varies according to the character of the data and the purpose of the research. It is neither possible nor advisable to set forth specific and universally applicable criteria for the delimitation of all of the different types of urban sub-areas. Until such time as standardization becomes more feasible, each investigation must formulate its own set of rules for demarcating sub-areas. One is nevertheless obliged to make his rules explicit in the report on his research.

Naturally, the boundaries of different types of sub-areas may not coincide. For example, territorial divisions established on the basis of occupational differences would not necessarily correspond with divisions made on the basis of racial differences.

Such considerations are well illustrated in Chapter 7 in the paper, "The Compatability of Alternative Approaches to the Delimitation of Urban Sub-Areas." Since the authors deal with only one city (Lansing, Michigan), their findings are not necessarily applicable to all other urban places, but the study provides a methodological guide to research on sub-areas and considers the central issues and problems involved.

Certain types of urban sub-areas are common to all cities, while others are not. Thus, in each instance we may expect to find upper-class residential areas (even though their specific character varies from city to city), but a particular ethnic or racial neighborhood may not be present in a given case. Of the various types of universal urban sub-areas, the main or central business district is of outstanding importance, largely because of the functions which it performs for all of the city. The second paper in Chapter 7, "Delimiting the CBD" by Raymond E. Murphy and J. E. Vance, Jr., sets forth criteria for the delimitation of business districts and reports the results of applying the criteria to cities in the U.S. As the authors suggest, their methods lay no claim to universal validity, but their paper is an excellent introduction to the subject.

The final paper in Chapter 7, Foley's "The Use of Local Facilities in a Metropolis," goes beyond a static picture of spatial structure and analyzes factors involving location. The fact that an establishment occupies a fixed point in space does not tell us who makes use of it, and yet it is this use that explains the location of different establishments with respect to one another and with respect to the population. Foley's paper, although restricted to a study of a sub-area of St. Louis, sets forth some methods for research on the use of urban facilities which are applicable to cities outside of North America.

Chapter 8 deals with methods for the study of the spatial distribution of urban phenomena. It is concerned with methods that are not restricted in application to a particular locale and which provide a standardization of areal analysis sufficient to make possible comparative studies among cities, whether they are located in the same or different countries.

It would be misleading to imply that an abundance of standardized research methods for the study of urban spatial structure is at the disposal of the novice. Quite the opposite is true, largely because of the diversity of the phenomena encompassed by the subject and because of the variability of conditions (notably the nature of available data) which confront research. For this reason the beginning student must undertake his investigation with imagination and exercise more than a little common sense. The nature of his task makes frequent reference to the literature mandatory. Section 14 of the *Subject Index to the Bibliography* provides several references to the treatment of urban sub-areas, spatial structure, and spatial distribution.

Chapter 6

ON THE USE OF SPATIAL DIVISIONS FOR STATISTICAL PURPOSES

THE CITY BLOCK AS A UNIT FOR RECORDING AND ANALYZING URBAN DATA *

EDWARD B. OLDS

The need for some type of standard unit geographic area for recording data about a city is apparent to many research workers and administrators faced with the problem of drawing conclusions from statistics about the city. The census tract, popularized by Dr. Walter Laidlaw and later by Howard Whipple Green, has served as the most generally accepted statistical unit area for American cities. It was developed as a compromise device to facilitate the analysis of population trends and characteristics in sections of cities. Honest attempts have been made to define census tract boundaries so that they include territory with reasonably homogeneous characteristics and with a population of from 3,000 to 6,000 persons. Unfortunately, characteristics change and what were once good boundary lines in terms of economic or ethnic indicators are not always good boundary lines. To preserve comparability from one census to another, it is necessary to keep census tract boundaries intact except for changes in city limits. However, within limits, the census tract served to reveal

* Reprinted from the *Journal of the American Statistical Association*, Vol. 44, No. 248 (December, 1949), pp. 485-500, with permission of author and publisher.

gross average differences between major sections of cities, as well as trends from one census to another. The census tract has admittedly an important place in the analysis of urban data, since it is small enough to show up differences between major sections of cities, and yet large enough to be easily manipulated without considerable expense. In large cities, such as New York and Chicago, it has been found necessary to combine census tracts into statistical or community areas providing more adequate bases for the computation of death rates and simplifying the mechanics of presenting and interpreting data about sections of the city.

Just as the magnifying glass is not completely replaced in usefulness by the microscope, so the usefulness of the census tract is not displaced by a more minute and precise unit area. But there are many uses of spatially ordered data about the city which can be made when they are available by a smaller unit area than the census tract. If it is conceded that a smaller unit area is desirable, the question comes up as to how much smaller the area should be and how it should be defined. Should it be something like a precinct used in organizing elections, a "beat" in police circles, or some other arbitrary grouping of city blocks? No matter what grouping is adopted, there will always be districts which cannot be made to fit the established boundaries. Does this mean that the problem is insoluble? It can be easily answered by the adoption of the city block as a unit area. Nearly all of the following types of districts are composed of city blocks.

School districts	Campaign solicitation unit areas
Water districts	Diocese and parishes
Sewer districts	Census tracts
Health districts	Neighborhood areas
Precincts and wards	Improvement districts
Police precincts and beats	Zoning districts
Meter reading districts	Fire districts
Telephone exchange districts	Library districts
Power districts	Welfare administration districts

TAX ASSESSMENT DISTRICTS

Data compiled by blocks with totals recorded in punch cards can be economically summarized by almost any of the above districts for any city. On the other hand, it is only rarely that data tabulated by census tracts or even enumeration districts can be accurately compiled according to the above types of districts. Even though an attempt is made in establishing census tracts to follow the boundaries of various administrative districts, the problem is practically insoluble without shifting the boundaries of the districts.

The proponents of census tracts sometimes argue that if administrators will not take the trouble to change the boundaries of their districts to conform to census tract boundaries, they can do without statistical information. Such an attitude fails to take cognizance of some of the very real difficulties preventing administrative districts from being brought into congruity with the boundaries of census tracts. For example, boundaries of school districts may have to be altered as there is movement of population, to maintain the proper balance of school enrollees in each school. If one district is growing in population while its neighbor is declining, it is obviously simpler to move the boundary of the district to correct the unbalanced enrollment situation, rather than to change the capacity of the school. Moreover, for many purposes, it is necessary to have some unit smaller than a census tract to serve as an administrative area. For example, police beats, precincts, or campaign solicitation areas must be considerably smaller than the census tract with a population usually between 3,000 and 6,000. The investment of sizeable funds in capital equipment such as telephone exchanges, power lines, sewer mains or water pipes may make it impractical to change boundaries of control areas merely to make them conform with artificial statistical areas. Unless accurate summaries can be made of the expensively compiled census information, many valuable uses are lost. Of course, in some instances it is possible to make estimates and approximations by prorating census tract data or by using overlay maps. But as business and government become more scientific, there is increasing demand for *accurate* information on which to base future plans and policies. By use of the block summary punch cards, accurate summaries can be obtained economically without excessive cost beyond the cost of coding the original data in terms of blocks. In relation to the total cost of training enumerators, conducting the canvass, designating areas, coding and tabulating, the preparation of block summary punch cards is not excessive. If a five or ten per cent increase in cost makes possible a many-fold increase in the uses of urban data, such additional costs should be justified.

THE ST. LOUIS BLOCK STATISTICS PROJECT

Some indication of the possibilities in the use of block statistics may be gained by examining the St. Louis experience. In the fall of 1945, the local committee on census enumeration areas, called the Metropolitan St. Louis Census Committee, obtained the cooperation of 21 business, government, welfare and educational establishments in sponsoring a local block statistics project. This involved purchasing a deck of block summary cards for St. Louis from the U.S. Census Bureau, converting the census block numbers to those used locally for over 60 years, and publishing a Block-Street Address Directory and Map. The cost of this work was largely covered by the sale of directories, maps, and sustaining memberships. The form of the directory and map, which was published by the offset reproduction of machine listings, is indicated in Figure I. The map location code facilitates locating a specific block on the block map. It is also used to sort and list cards in geographic sequence to improve the efficiency of mapping. The neighborhood district name symbol and water district code were included in the directory to satisfy two agencies which assisted considerably in its compilation, the City Plan Commission and the St. Louis City Water Department.

The use of locally established block numbers facilitates obtaining and compiling current local information. The chief data compiled regularly are:

1. Number of dwelling units in new homes for which building permits have been issued.

2. Number of dwelling units in homes for which demolition permits have been issued.

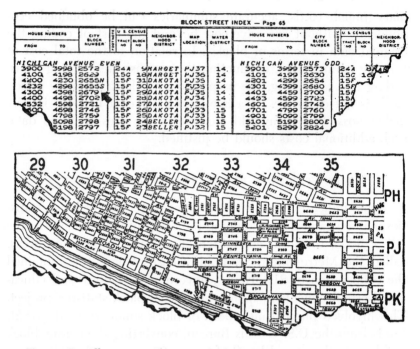

FIGURE I.   Illustration of Form of Block-Street Directory and Map.

3. Number of white and Negro children enrolled in public elementary schools.

These data are useful locally to provide some indication of marked increases or decreases in population in particular neighborhoods. The school enrollment data are particularly useful in revealing annual shifts in the location of the Negro population of St. Louis. Since the city and school authorities routinely code their records by city block numbers, the cost of making block tabulations using punch card machines is comparatively small. Summaries are tabulated by census tracts, neighborhood districts, census districts, precincts, and wards. The preparation of these summaries is facilitated by the use of a master deck of cards containing a series of code punchings signifying to which census tract, neighborhood district, etc., the particular block belongs.

For recording summary statistics about blocks, use is made of a specially printed card illustrated in Figure II. The fields lettered from A to Q are used for quantities, such as the number

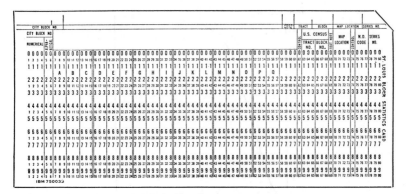

FIGURE II. Punch Card Form Used for Recording Various Types of Statistical Data for City Blocks.

of dwelling units, white school children, or dwelling units constructed in 1944. The fields printed with city block number, U.S. census tract number, block number, etc. are used for standard area codes. Reproduced decks of cards in the master file can be prepared for use by members having their own machine facilities.

ECONOMIC RATING OF BLOCKS

To provide a convenient means of classifying addresses by economic status, a block economic rating on the basis of 1940 rents was prepared. The block summary cards from the 1940 census contained information on the average rent in each block. These cards were sorted by this average rent, listed, and at the same time the number of dwelling units in each block was cumulated. Those blocks with the lowest rents which included one per cent of the dwelling units in the city, were given a code of "01." The blocks with slightly higher rents, which included another one per cent of the homes, were given a code of "02." This process was continued until the blocks with the highest rents, which included one per cent of the homes, were given a code of "100." Addresses coded in terms of this block economic index can be conveniently grouped into economic tenths, fifths, thirds, etc. Figure III illustrates the relationship between the block economic code and average rents.

Some of the uses which have been made of the block eco-

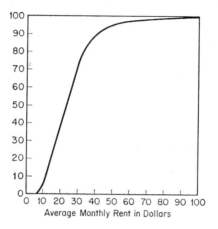

FIGURE III.   Cumulative Per Cent of Homes in St. Louis Blocks with Less
Than Specified Average Rents, 1940.

nomic code may be of interest. In a public opinion survey, a random area sample was selected, using blocks as primary sampling
units. Since it was not practical to make follow-up calls on every
family in the sample, the possible biasing effect of differences in
the percentage responding from low and high income areas was
controlled by means of the block economic code. Tabulations
were made of the number of families in the sample from five
groups of economic areas classified by means of the block economic code. The distribution of usable questionnaires from these
five groups of economic areas was also determined. Any significant differences in the distribution of questionnaires and the
distribution of the families in the sample were corrected by obtaining more interviews. In this way, the economic composition
of the families represented by the questionnaires analyzed was
kept close to the composition of the population.

In a study of subscriptions to the Community Chest obtained
through neighborhood solicitation, the block economic code was
used to provide an index of economic status for each solicitation
area. A comparison between this economic index and subscriptions per family, indicated a marked association as illustrated in
Figure IV. This information was helpful in determining the areas
where neighborhood solicitation produced insufficient returns to
justify the costs involved.

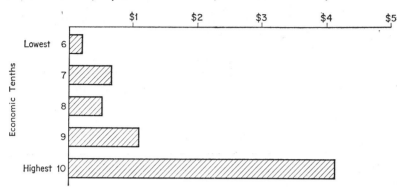

FIGURE IV.   Average 1947 Community Chest Gift per Family in Neighborhood Solicitation of Part of St. Louis Classified by Economic Tenths.

In a study of dwelling units constructed during the period 1940 to 1946, the economic status of the blocks in which the construction took place was determined by the block economic code. A tabulation of the units constructed and demolished according to economic tenths (each tenth containing one-tenth of the 1940 dwelling units) indicated a highly skewed distribution as shown in Figure V. The areas with the highest economic status had the

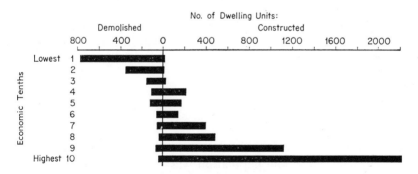

FIGURE V.   Dwelling Units Constructed and/or Demolished Under Private Auspices in St. Louis Economic Tenths During the Period 1940-46.

most building, and the areas with the lowest economic status had the least building going on. On the other hand, the high economic areas had the least demolition of homes while the low economic areas had the most demolition taking place.

Several applications of the block economic code have been

made in classifying addresses in St. Louis City according to economic status. Although considerable error can result through such a method for estimating the income status of an individual, it is believed that for groups of persons or families, this method provides a fairly reliable index. Figure VI illustrates the rela-

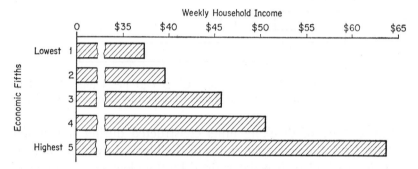

FIGURE VI.   Median Weekly Household Income Reported in July 1947 by Families in Each Economic Fifth of St. Louis.

tionship that was found between average income reported by families in a sample survey and the block economic code based on 1940 rents. The interviews with the families were conducted in July 1947, and each family was asked to indicate in which one of the following classes their household income would fall:

Under $25 per week
$25 to $49 per week
$50 to $99 per week
$100 or more per week

A study of the economic status of the blocks in which more than 40 per cent of the population was Negro, indicated a heavy concentration of Negro blocks in the lower economic brackets. As shown in Figure VII, none of the Negro blocks were in the highest economic tenth, while 20.3 per cent of the Negro homes were in the lowest economic tenth.

Although no analysis of vital statistics data has been made, using the economic code, it is believed that highly significant differences would be found from a comparison of life expectancy, infant deaths, etc., in low and high income areas. Such analysis

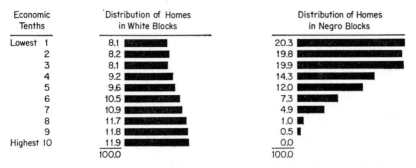

Economic Tenths	Distribution of Homes in White Blocks	Distribution of Homes in Negro Blocks
Lowest 1	8.1	20.3
2	8.2	19.8
3	8.1	19.9
4	9.2	14.3
5	9.6	12.0
6	10.5	7.3
7	10.9	4.9
8	11.7	1.0
9	11.8	0.5
Highest 10	11.9	0.0
	100.0	100.0

FIGURE VII. Comparison of Distribution of Homes in White and Negro Areas of St. Louis According to Economic Tenths. Note: Each economic tenth included 10 per cent of the homes in St. Louis in 1940.

require the coding of births and deaths by blocks, as well as the tabulation of population census data by blocks.

COMPILATIONS FOR SPECIAL AREAS

The block data on punch cards have been used to obtain summary tabulations of housing, school enrollment, and building permit statistics for such areas as neighborhood districts, precincts, and wards. The City Plan Commission has divided the city into 99 neighborhood and industrial districts, basing the determination of boundaries upon such factors as major streets, railroads, proximity to parks and playgrounds, land use, etc. Until block statistics were available, it was not possible to obtain accurate housing statistics for these basic planning units. As part of the St. Louis block statistics project, summary tabulations of the 1940 housing census block statistics were obtained. These included the following data:

Residential structures
Dwelling units (homes)
Owner occupied homes
Tenant occupied homes
Homes built 1930 to 1939
Homes built 1920 to 1929
Homes built 1900 to 1919
Homes built before 1900
Negro families

Homes with more than 1.5 persons per room
Homes needing major repairs
Homes without private bath
Average monthly rent of homes
Total rent
Number reporting rent

VOTING BEHAVIOR STUDY

Summaries of housing data have been made for the precincts and wards of St. Louis. The summarized data were then used to compute octile ratings for each precinct in each of four housing factors. This was done by computing percentages for each precinct, ranking the percentages, and then grouping the ranked precincts into eight groups. The four factors were as follows:

1. Per cent of homes owner occupied.
2. Per cent of homes built before 1900.
3. Per cent of public schools enrollees who were Negro in Nov. 1946.
4. Average rents.

The block data were also used to prepare estimates of the population 21 and over in each precinct as of January 1, 1948. These estimates were based upon the current estimated number of families, using the 1940 count of dwelling units, plus units represented in building permits issued since 1940, and less the dwelling units represented in permits for demolitions since 1940. The estimated number of families was multiplied by the 1940 ratio of population 21 and over, to families in the nearest census tract. The sum of these products for the city was compared with the estimated population 21 and over in the city. The provisional estimate for each precinct was then multiplied by a correction factor so that the figures finally used add up to the estimated population 21 and over in the city. While this method is subject to considerable error, it was considered more reliable than any other available method for obtaining a current estimate of population 21 and over. Percentages and octile ratings were then computed for the proportion of the voting population registered to vote. A series of 28 other octile ratings was computed from the election statistics on civic issues, as well as for political parties in eight elections held since Nov. 1944. Comparisons were not made prior to this time because of non-comparable precinct boundaries. The data prior to 1948 for each precinct were summarized on one specially printed tabulating card. Other punched cards were used to list the statistical data onto the printed card. Complete sets of 784 precinct data cards were turned over to the sponsors of the project. Other sets can be prepared economically from the master cards. The top line of each card contains a series of 23 octile ratings. The percentages upon which these ratings were based are specified by small numbers printed below each rating and in the lower left corner of each percentage cell. A set of punched cards containing the octile ratings was used for an intercorrelation analysis, using the tetrachoric correlation method. This analysis indicated the following significant relations between the housing and voting indexes:

1. Democratic precincts tended to remain Democratic and Republican precincts tended to remain Republican.
2. Precincts with a large proportion of the population registered tended to have a large proportion of the registrants voting in each election.
3. Areas with high home ownership had a larger proportion of the population registered than areas with low home ownership.
4. High rent areas were more inclined to vote Republican than low rent areas.
5. Areas with many old homes opposed daylight saving time and a new state constitution.

TABULATION OF SCHOOL ENROLLEES

Each year in November, the Board of Education asks each elementary school to prepare a report listing the block numbers in which their pupils reside and the number of pupils in each block. The Block-Street Address Directory is used in coding addresses by blocks. Since St. Louis has a completely segregated school system, it is possible to make tabulations of these data to show the number of white and Negro school enrollees in each block. Such tabulations have been made for each of the following years:—1941, 1945, 1946, 1947. From these data by block, it has been possible to prepare a map which shows the trend of movement of the Negro areas in St. Louis during the period 1941 to 1947. Figure VIII illustrates the *Post Dispatch* map [1] drawn from the more precise block map published in two colors by the

---

[1] The *St. Louis Post Dispatch* carried a feature article by Richard G. Baumhoff on this study in the Sunday issue, August 15, 1948.

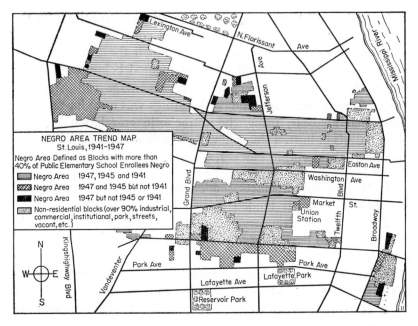

FIGURE VIII.   Negro Area Trend Map.

The author wishes to acknowledge with thanks the permission granted by the
St. Louis Post Dispatch to publish this map.

Social Planning Council and the Urban League. The housing
statistics and land use data by blocks were used to compute differences in dwelling units per residential area between white
and Negro areas.

ESTABLISHING CAMPAIGN DISTRICTS

Uses of the Block-Street Address Directory can be shown by
describing a project involving the grouping of addresses of campaign prospects into convenient solicitation control areas. Cards
were punched alphabetically giving the names and addresses of
about 20,000 prospects. The punching of names and addresses
was needed for the preparation of prospect lists, pledge cards,
and mailing strips. In punching the addresses, house numbers
were punched in one field while street names were punched in
another field. Accordingly, it was possible to mechanically sort
the cards by street and house number, keeping the odd house

numbers separate from the even house numbers. The use of the Block-Street Address Directory, together with a listing of these sorted address cards, provided a highly efficient means of establishing the block codes. In marking the list with the block code, it was found that usually from five to 20 adjacent listings would be in the same block. The punching of the block code into the cards was accomplished by manually filing the cards behind prepunched block master cards and then intersperse gang punching the cards. The cards were then sorted down and tabulated by block. Work maps were posted with the number of prospects in each block and area boundaries were drawn to include the proper number of prospects in each area.

MAKING SPOT MAPS

In St. Louis, the city block numbers consist of four numerical digits and two alphabetical suffixes. Although this makes a rather cumbersome number, it is useful because many city records and maps are referenced with these official city block numbers. However, to locate any given block efficiently, it is necessary to have what is called a supplementary "map location" number. This number consists of two letters followed by two numbers, like "PQ42" which defines a particular square of land in the city with sides one-fourth mile long. Every block is assigned to one specific square on the basis of where the majority of its area is located. Cards punched with city block number or census tract and block number can be automatically gang punched with this map location number and other area codes at one operation. They can then be sorted and listed in geographic columns and rows which greatly facilitates the spotting of block maps to show the accurate distribution of addresses.

POTENTIAL USES OF BLOCK DATA

The foregoing examples represent only a few of the possible uses of population and housing statistics by blocks. A consideration of these uses should suggest many others which would be made if data were available uniformly for every metropolitan area including the suburbs as well as the central city. The fact that accurate summaries can be made economically for a wide variety of administrative and study areas opens up uses which cannot be made of census tract statistics.

Some of the uses which could be made through a more general availability of block statistics are indicated in the following list:

Determination of fire, theft, and life insurance risks in different types of neighborhoods.

Studies of land values as related to population, sales, etc.

Determination of business areas of the Metropolitan District.

Planning changes in the location of transportation and utility lines.

Appraisal of property for loans or taxation.

Determination of cost of governmental and philanthropic services in each section of the city as compared to tax income obtained.

Planning optimum location of public, private or commercial facilities for recreation, education, sales, health or welfare service, etc.

Estimates of sales or consumption using block statistics in the design of the sampling plan.

Indexing detail real estate or land use maps.

Determination of optimum districts for neighborhood improvement, police beats, meter readers, relief investigators.

SUGGESTED NEW CENSUS BLOCK DATA

One of the limitations upon the use of block statistics is the paucity of information generally available by blocks. It is believed that there could be a considerable increase in the variety of data tabulated from the decennial census without greatly increasing costs. If territory is assigned enumerators by blocks (as was done in the 1940 housing census) the punching of a block designation in all punch cards made from the schedules would be comparatively simple. Then special tabulations could be run by blocks or groupings of blocks for any desired detail. Routinely, it is believed that certain summary information could be tabulated by blocks recording the totals in summary cards. The following items could be recorded in three decks of such cards:

Housing data (in order of importance):
   Number of dwelling units.
   Contract or estimated monthly rent.
   Owner occupied dwelling units.

Dwelling units occupied by non-white persons.
Dwelling units built before 1900.
Dwelling units with no private bath.
Number of dwelling structures.
Dwelling units according to type of structure (three groups).
Dwelling units without private flush toilet.
Dwelling units without running water.
Dwelling units without mechanical refrigeration.
Dwelling units without central heating.

Population data (in order of importance):
Number of persons.
Age distribution (five groups).
Sex and color (four groups).
Population 25 and over by years of school completed (six groups).
Population 14 and over by employment status and sex (twelve groups).
Employed persons 14 and over by major occupation groups (nine groups).

These data could be economically published by listing them on plastic offset plates and reproducing several hundred copies for sale to users at a charge set to write off the publication cost. Users would be encouraged to purchase decks of cards on printed card forms clearly indicating the information punched in the cards. Users could also be supplied at cost with block maps of adequate scale for work purposes, reproduced through a blue print process from masters kept in the Census Bureau. Such maps should be in sections that would be small enough to be handled easily on normal size desks and drafting tables, and yet so made that they could be easily assembled to make up a one-piece map for a Metropolitan District. A certain amount of skilled consultation service should be made available by the Census Bureau to help users in making the best possible use of the block data.

SUGGESTED LOCAL BLOCK TABULATIONS

The preparation of block statistics as outlined above would require local committees in each community to help in making the best uses, as well as in promoting the compilation of local material. One of the first projects for each city committee would be the purchase of decks of the summary cards and sets of block maps in the form of negative blue print masters. Another project would involve the compilation of a local block-street address directory to facilitate the compilation of local data by blocks. The promotion of local tabulations should include consideration for obtaining the following types of information:

Building erections and demolitions.
School census or school enrollment data.
Land use statistics.
Police arrests.
Juvenile delinquency cases.
Births and deaths.
Persons receiving welfare services (chronically ill, tubercular, mentally ill, general hospitalization, foster home placement, etc.).
Old age assistance, aid to dependent children, and general relief cases.
Tax assessments and collections.
Fire losses.

The financing of local projects can be handled in various ways, depending upon the community. Generally, it is possible for each administrative agency to include in its budget, small amounts sufficient to cover the processing of statistics, falling within its jurisdiction. Sales of directories can be used to cover the cost of their compilation and publication. Contributions from utilities, banks, chambers of commerce, universities, foundations, real estate firms, etc., can be used to write off the cost of local projects. However, it is necessary to have interested and competent leadership for local committees. Such persons may be found in a local city plan commission, council of social agencies, university, chamber of commerce, utility, board of education, etc. If interest warrants, it may be possible in certain communities to establish agencies equipped with staff and machinery for the most efficient processing of statistical data having general community-wide significance. Block statistics would be one of the kingpins in such a community research agency.

National agencies and concerns should find considerable uses for block statistics when they become uniformly available together with adequate maps and street address directories. Survey and polling organizations should be able to effect economies and improvements in their work through the use of block statistics. With adequate materials and interpretation, it should be possible to cover some of the added census cost of block statistics through the sale of cards, maps, and listings.

COMPARATIVE ADVANTAGES OF CENSUS TRACT
AND BLOCK DATA

From the St. Louis experience, we find that block statistics are essential for the following types of analyses:

1. Compilation of census statistics for administrative areas which are not multiples of census tracts or enumeration districts.
2. Compilation of census statistics for areas within a specified distance or travel time of a particular geographic location (half mile or mile).
3. Classification of addresses according to economic status based upon economic index computed for blocks.
4. Appraisal of neighborhood characteristics in immediate vicinity of a specified address.
5. Determination of exact boundaries of areas inhabited predominantly by a particular ethnic group.
6. Design and selection of area samples for use in factual, attitude, and opinion surveys.

Census tract data are inadequate, although better than no data, for analyses such as the above. However, census tract data are preferable to block data for analyses such as the following:

1. Community studies of districts or sections within an urban area when the population of the district is over 20,000.
2. Computation of ratios such as tuberculosis death rates for sections of a city.
3. Presentation of a general view of the variation from community to community within a city in significant population or housing characteristics.

In large cities even census tracts are too small for use in analyses such as the above.

In conclusion, statistical tabulations of selected types of data by city blocks supplement, rather than displace tabulations by census tracts. Wherever possible, administrative districts within a metropolitan area should be established as multiples of census tracts. Block statistics should be used only for analyses which require greater geographic detail than can be provided by census tract data. The judicious use of block and census tract statistics can make a noteworthy contribution to the more scientific administration of business and governmental services.

THE THEORY AND PRACTICE OF PLANNING CENSUS TRACTS *

CALVIN F. SCHMID

When the present writer was requested to lay out census tracts for the three major cities of Minnesota, Minneapolis, St. Paul, and Duluth, he was confronted with a number of very practical problems, chief among which were technique and method. Since no satisfactory published data were available to answer adequately even the most fundamental questions relating to procedure, inquiries were sent to a number of people who either had practical experience in laying out census tracts or were especially interested in census tracts as a research tool.[1]

Although the basic data [2] contained in this note were gathered

* Reprinted from *Sociology and Social Research*, Vol. 22, No. 3 (January-February, 1938), pp. 228-238, with permission of author and publisher.

[1] The following comprise the list of correspondents to whom grateful acknowledgement is made: Mr. C. E. Batschelet, Professor William J. Blackburn, Jr., Professor R. E. Chaddock, Mr. Howard Whipple Green, Professor E. T. Krueger, Dr. Walter Laidlaw, Dr. Charles S. Newcomb, Mr. Frederick F. Stephan, Dr. Leon E. Truesdell, Professor W. Wallace Weaver, and Professor R. Clyde White. In addition, valuable assistance was obtained from the writings of Ernest W. Burgess, C. E. Gehlke, George A. Lundberg, R. D. McKenzie, Jerry A. Neprash, Robert E. Park, C. C. Peters, Frank A. Ross, Samuel A. Stouffer, and Harvey W. Zorbaugh. Only two studies which directly relate to methods and procedure of constructing census tracts have been published: Calvin F. Schmid, *Memorandum on Census Tracts for Minneapolis and St. Paul*, University of Minnesota Committee on Census Tracts (24 pp. mimeographed), and Howard Whipple Green and Leon E. Truesdell, *Census Tracts in American Cities*, United States Bureau of the Census (14 pp. mimeographed). These studies were published in the spring and fall of 1934, respectively.

[2] It was through the urgent suggestion of Professor Read Bain that these data were organized and interpreted for publication in this form. Special credit is also due Professor Bain for reading the manuscript and contributing many helpful suggestions.

originally for a definitely practical reason, as a guide in laying out census tracts in the three Minnesota cities, the purpose of the present paper is twofold: (1) to discuss in some detail the techniques and procedures used in planning census tracts, and (2) to examine briefly the adequacy and limitation of census tract data in the light of certain generally accepted theoretical assumptions.

At the time the inquiries were sent out the following questions appeared foremost in mind: (1) What criterion or criteria should be used in delimiting census tracts? (2) How large should the population of census tracts be? (3) Should census tracts be of uniform size? (4) Should adjustments be made in the size of census tracts for population growth or decline in various parts of the city? (5) To what extent should census tracts be made to conform to wards or other administrative districts? (6) What kind of boundaries are most satisfactory for census tracts? (7) What kind of numbering system is most logical and efficient? Let us consider each question separately.

1. *What criterion or criteria should be used in delimiting census tracts?* The deficiencies of wards and other administrative areas for research purposes have long been recognized. Besides being relatively impermanent, areas of this kind are usually districted for political and administrative convenience and without reference to geographic, social, or demographic homogeneity. Facts in order to be really significant for studies in human ecology should conform to natural areas—units that are actual factors in the processes under examination. In addition, since census tracts are manipulated as statistical units in many types of analyses, they should be comparable and homogeneous.[3]

In actual practice, however, the theoretical requirements of homogeneity and comparability can, at best, only be approximated. The availability of truly diagnostic and measurable criteria, the necessity of adhering to a certain size of population, the desirability of conforming to certain administrative districts, as well as the requirements of following definitely defined bound-

[3] Cf. Frederick F. Stephan, "Sampling Errors and Interpretations of Social Data Ordered in Time and Space," *Journal of the American Statistical Association*, Papers and Proceedings (March, 1934, Supplement), Vol. XXIX, N.S., No. 185A, pp. 165-66; Jerry A. Neprash, "Some Problems in the Correlation of Spatially Distributed Variables," *ibid.*, pp. 167-68.

aries, preferably streets, are perhaps some of the more important restricting considerations. Besides, even though a district may be homogeneous, the ravages of time may radically change the picture of a district in a relatively short time.

It was the general belief of the informants that census tracts should be made as homogeneous as possible, but at the same time the difficulties of actually attaining anything like complete homogeneity were clearly recognized. As far as specific criteria are concerned, economic characteristics were considered most significant, although geographic, cultural, social, and demographic characteristics were ranked as very important.

It is interesting to note in this connection that when New York was originally divided into census tracts—the first city in the United States to be districted in this way—the basic criterion was one of area, although other factors were taken into consideration.[4]

A fundamental criterion for the size of the tracts in all five boroughs was equalized acreage. . . . My original quantum for tracts was 160 acres, one-quarter of a square mile, because I feared I could not induce the Census Bureau to agree to tabulate smaller units.

At that time, however, the Tenement House Department was seeking, if possible, to induce the Bureau to tabulate the whole area of New York by blocks—nearly 50,000 of them.

Resisting this because the trees would hide the forest, I eagerly accepted the suggestion of Professor William B. Bailey of Yale, then assisting the Population Division of the Census Bureau, to divide my 160 acre units by four, and our city's area is patterned permanently into a few more than 3,400 census tracts averaging a little over 40 acres each, but with park areas of course unbroken, except in the case of Central Park. . . .

It was the equalized acreage idea which captured the conviction of Mr. William C. Hunt, chief statistician for population in the Census Bureau, when I first propounded the idea of the tract system to him.— Walter C. Laidlaw.

Although equalized areas may be a satisfactory criterion for

[4] Cf. Godias J. Drolet and William H. Guilfoy, "Organization of Local Health Area Statistics in New York City," *American Journal of Public Health,* 20: 381-386, April, 1930.

densely and relatively evenly populated sections, it would seem that for cities as a whole with diverse topographical and social characteristics and uneven distribution of population such a criterion would be very unsatisfactory.

In planning the census tracts for the three major cities of Minnesota every effort was made to attain as high a degree of homogeneity as possible. During the early stages of the work the following types of data were superimposed upon large-scale street maps for each city with a view to delimiting as far as practicable the more significant and distinctive natural areas: (1) physiographic characteristics; (2) land use; (3) demographic characteristics; (4) indices of socioeconomic status; and (5) indices of social disorganization.[5] The middle sector of each of the three cities, which includes the central business district, hobohemia, and main apartment house and rooming house districts, and one or more slums, was studied in minute detail. After the tracts were tentatively laid out in the laboratory and preliminary field checks had been made, the writer with the assistance of the city planning engineers in the respective cities made complete field checks of every tract. Before the maps were submitted to more than 25 interested local organizations for examination, additional field and laboratory checks were made. After the maps had been endorsed locally they were forwarded to the United States Bureau of the Census for final checking and approval.

2. *How large should the population of census tracts be?* Even from a purely methodological standpoint, there seems to be no consensus concerning the optimum size of the population of census tracts, although it is generally agreed that the population should be relatively small. As stated in actual numbers the range of the optimum population varied according to the correspondents from 1,000 to 6,000. Existing census tracts are frequently over 10,000 in population and sometimes less than 1,000. Of the 42 census tract cities in the United States at the present time, the mean population of census tracts varies from approximately 1,700 in Yonkers, New York, to almost 14,000 in Berkeley, California.[6]

[5] Cf. Calvin F. Schmid, "Criteria for Judging Community Organization and Disorganization," *Publications of the Sociological Society of America*, 27: 116-122, May, 1933.

[6] For discussions of some of the theoretical problems relating to size of census tracts see: Robert E. Chaddock, "Significance of Infant Mortality Rates for Small

By making the population of census tracts relatively small it is possible to regroup the tracts for any desired purpose.

It would seem that *a size appropriate for one purpose is not so for another purpose;* for example, the general death rate as contrasted with the infant mortality rate or the rate for a single cause; or a delinquency rate for boys of Jewish or Irish extraction.

All of this leads me to a conclusion that, after all, relatively small "census tracts" are desirable, so that they may be combined, the population being available in tabulations of small "tracts," into a size appropriate for such analysis as any one proposes according to his research needs. . . . I used to think we had many too many "census tracts" in New York but now I am not so sure.—R. E. Chaddock.

In determining the size of census tracts statistical and other methodological factors are not the only ones to be taken into consideration. The very practical problem of obtaining sufficient funds for special tabulations has been of considerable importance in determining the size of census tracts in many cities since the cost of tabulation is in more or less direct proportion to the number of tracts.[7] The following quotation relative to the city of Nashville clearly illustrates this point.

Our first plan was to create rather small tracts, in order to manipulate them by combination into any larger tract system we might desire. An estimate of costs for census data by small tracts soon taught us that the cost would be prohibitive. We were then requested to combine our 160 small tracts into forty large tracts. Roughly for Nashville this would give us an average tract population of 4,000. We find this too large for the most fluid use of tract data. . . .—E. T. Krueger.

Geographic Areas," *Journal of the American Statistical Association,* 29:243-49, September, 1934; Frank Alexander Ross, "Ecology and the Statistical Method," *The American Journal of Sociology,* 38: pp. 507-522, January, 1933; C. E. Gehlke and Katherine Biehl, "Certain Effects of Grouping Upon the Size of the Correlation Coefficient in Census Tract Material," *Journal of the American Statistical Association,* Papers and Proceedings (March, 1934, Supplement), Vol. XXIX, N.S., No. 185A, pp. 169-70; and Sophia Moses Robison, *Can Delinquency be Measured?* (New York: Columbia University Press, 1936), pp. 190-203.

[7] Dr. Leon E. Truesdell writes, "I find on inspecting the record of costs for the 1930 tract cities which ordered the entire series of tables that the cost is around $1,500 per 100 tracts. It would seem likely to vary almost directly in proportion to the number of tracts, so that the cost for tracts of 3,000 would be one-third greater than the cost for tracts of 4,000."

The smallest numbers of tracts consistent with (a) homogeneity, (b) comparability, (c) potential growth or decline of population, and (d) conformity to natural or otherwise logical boundaries should be desired. And, of course, the cost of tabulation should not be overlooked. In planning the size of the census tracts for Minneapolis, St. Paul, and Duluth these considerations were clearly kept in mind. The question of cost, however, was generally secondary to homogeneity and the other criteria listed above. The approximate mean sizes of the 121 tracts in Minneapolis, the 76 in St. Paul, and the 38 in Duluth are 3,900, 3,600, and 2,700, respectively. The range is from approximately 1,000 to 6,000 with about 75 per cent 3,000 and over in population.

3. *Should census tracts be of uniform size?* It is very apparent that census tracts of uniform size, shape, and area would be not only undesirable but virtually impossible. Differences in population density, the potential growth or decline of population in certain sections, the criterion of homogeneity, topographical characteristics, and the necessity of following distinct and logical boundaries are some practical considerations which would preclude anything like uniformity of census tracts.

4. *Should adjustments be made in the size of census tracts for population growth or decline in various parts of the city?* In laying out census tracts probable ultimate populations should be taken into consideration. For example, in view of the outward flow of population in recent decades census tracts toward the center of the city should be made large because of their tendency to diminish in population, whereas tracts toward the periphery should be made relatively small because of their tendency to increase. Although it is very difficult and sometimes hazardous to predict future trends in population, every effort should be made to determine population movements over a period of time as well as to analyze the more important factors influencing the potential growth or decline of population in different parts of the city.

Since our tracts (in the city of Columbus) were first laid out in 1930, we did not have a problem of re-adjustments from previous census figures. We did, however, take account of population and industrial trends that might be expected to influence developments materially within the next decade or more. Where population was sparse but increasing we made the boundaries wide to allow for future subdivisions.—William J. Blackburn, Jr.

Of course, unforeseen factors may require census tracts to be divided or combined in future censuses because of a pronounced growth or decline of population. If division becomes necessary, the original boundaries should be retained for purposes of comparison. To illustrate how rapidly population changes occur in many of our large cities, a few facts for the city of Cleveland might be cited.

Census tract T-8 was created in 1920 as a part of a large area used in the 1910 and 1920 census. If it had been created in 1910 it would have been a census tract with but 59 persons. In 1920 this census tract had 1,557 persons, in 1930 it had 10,577 persons. It is too large at the present time. However, I feel sure that the 1940 census will show a smaller population for this tract. If indications do not point this way we shall probably have to divide it in two, creating two tracts in the place of one.

As an illustration of how the population of a tract may disappear I would like to call your attention to census tract J-1. In 1910 there were 6,114 persons living in this tract. In 1920 there were 493, and in 1930, but 49. . . .—Howard W. Green.

5. *To what extent should census tracts be made to conform to wards or other administrative districts?* Before any tract boundaries were actually laid out in the three major cities of Minnesota a detailed and systematic analysis was made of the more important and representative administrative areas in order to ascertain to what extent it would be possible to have the census tracts conform to existing administrative areas. The main value of this analysis was to emphasize the illogicality and complete lack of uniformity of most so-called administrative districts. Any attempt to make census tracts conform to existing systems of administrative areas was virtually abandoned. Even the enumeration districts of 1930 which were used for both the population and housing enumerations had to be largely disregarded in planning the census tracts since they were not well districted for permanent use. The only administrative areas that were closely adhered to were the 1930 ward boundaries of Minneapolis and St. Paul so that the forty-year record of population compiled on

the basis of these wards could be preserved and extended into the future.

In most cities census tracts have been laid out without attempting to make them conform to administrative districts with the exception of wards and in one instance, at least, of school districts.[8] For example:

All of our census tracts (in the city of Pittsburgh) are subdivisions of wards and are designated by the ward number and a letter to separate tracts within the same ward. We conformed to ward boundaries because a good deal of material was available by wards, because we wanted governmental agencies to use the tract system, and because the ward boundaries have not changed, except by annexation, since 1907. We also tried to conform as much as possible to a set of tracts originally laid out in 1910 as subdivisions of wards.—Frederick F. Stephan.

The following quotation illustrates very clearly why wards and other administrative districts are usually not recognized in planning census tracts:

Tracts are permanent areas and, while they are almost invariably smaller than wards, it is not necessary to follow ward boundaries in establishing the tracts, as ward boundaries change from time to time and the tract areas are held from census to census. In establishing the enumeration districts, the Bureau will follow the tract boundaries and ward boundaries, so that figures can be secured for each of these units. In this way, we are able to compile total figures by wards, which are necessary, and also census data by tracts, so essential for demographic studies.—C. E. Batschelet.

6. *What kind of boundaries are most satisfactory for census tracts?* The United States Bureau of the Census requires that all tract boundaries be relatively permanent and clearly defined, since they must also form the limits of enumeration districts. Enumeration districts are followed in the field canvass where any uncertainties or confusion concerning boundaries might result in omissions, duplications, and other serious errors. No matter how desirable a boundary may be from an ecological point of view, if it does not meet the very practical requirements of the

[8] Cf. Ernest W. Burgess, "Basic Social Data" in *Chicago: An Experiment in Social Science Research* (Chicago: The University of Chicago Press, 1929), pp. 54-55, edited by T. V. Smith and Leonard D. White.

Census Bureau it will not be approved. Certain physiographic features such as hills or valleys and arbitrary political and legal limits as townships and section lines, the projection of streets, and "paper" thoroughfares are generally not acceptable. The most commonly used boundaries for census tracts are streets, although streams and railroads are sometimes used. The center of the street is always taken as the division line, and where a railroad is used as a tract limit, the center of the railroad track is considered the boundary rather than the right of way. The Census Bureau does not require a written description of the boundaries of each tract but it does require a large-scale map showing the tract outlines.

7. *What kind of numbering system is most logical and efficient?* In order to facilitate easy reference to census tract maps, street coding guides, and tabular and other data, some kind of numbering system for the census tracts is indispensable. At the present time there are several numbering systems in use. Seemingly, all possess certain advantages as well as disadvantages. However, it would be very difficult to state definitely which system is most satisfactory since the purpose at hand in devising a numbering system as well as local conditions would preclude absolute uniformity. For example,

In designating the tract numbers, the system which we use is one which would be applicable only to Philadelphia because our ward lines in Philadelphia are permanent and the tracts are drawn in such a way that no tract overlaps the ward line. Consequently, we used the numeral for the ward and lettered the tracts alphabetically by wards.—W. Wallace Weaver.

Or again, in the city of Indianapolis,

We simply numbered our tracts with arabic symbols to 108. The numbering has no particular logic in it because the whole system of numbering the school census districts seems to have developed rather haphazardly and we attempted to use numbers which corresponded as closely as possible to their system. . . .—R. Clyde White.

Another type of letter-number system based on broad geographical divisions rather than wards is used in several cities. In Cleveland,

We use a numbering system including letters and numbers, the first tract being A-1, the next A-2, etc., to A-9, and then B-1, B-2, etc., to B-9 etc., through the alphabet. These could just as well have been numbered from one to two hundred-and-five, but I have always felt that it was easier to remember where F-1 was located, which of course, would be around the F's, in the southwest section of the city, rather than remembering where census tract 45 was located.

I still think the letter and number combinations are preferable although there is a serious objection to their use when it comes to putting census tract data on punch cards, for then each letter must be translated into a number, which really requires coding. We, of course, have used 01 for A, 02 for B, etc., making the highest number in the city proper 261, indicating Z-1.—Howard W. Green.

Perhaps the most common system is simply to number the tracts consecutively from left to right beginning at the northwest corner of the map. This method of numbering was used for all three of the Minnesota cities.

Chapter 7

URBAN SUB-AREAS

THE COMPATIBILITY OF ALTERNATIVE APPROACHES TO THE DELIMITATION OF URBAN SUB-AREAS *

WILLIAM H. FORM, JOEL SMITH, GREGORY P. STONE, AND JAMES COWHIG

Locating the boundaries of urban sub-areas has been an emerging controversial issue among sociologists over the past decade. Before that time, traditional ecologists dominated the scene by presenting rather simple and direct means of isolating sub-areas or census tracts. More recently some urban sociologists have contended that the distribution of social phenomena may not be directly dependent on variations in land use, natural barriers, and other ecological factors. They contend that the social integration of areas should be considered as important in this regard as ecological criteria. Demographers have also suggested that population indices are very sensitive to differences among the social sub-areas of cities. Other interested students have adopted a synthetic approach—suggesting that ecological, demographic, and social criteria are equally important in deriving a set of urban sub-areas useful for sociological investigations.[1] Yet, almost no research has attempted to show the relations among these criteria.[2]

* Reprinted from the *American Sociological Review*, Vol. 19, No. 4 (August, 1954), pp. 434-440, with permission of authors and publisher.

[1] Calvin F. Schmid, "The Theory and Practice of Planning Census Tracts," *Sociology and Social Research*, 22 (1938), pp. 228-238; *Census Tract Manual*, U.S. Department of Commerce, Bureau of the Census, January, 1947.

[2] Some exceptions are: Trenton W. Wann, "Objective Determination of Urban

During the past two years a research team at Michigan State College has attempted to attack this problem as part of a long range study in Lansing, Michigan.[3] In the process of setting up a census tract plan, ecological, demographic, and social indices were used to derive separate sub-areas for the city. The question this study posed is, "What are the various implications for sociological research of subdividing a city according to one or the other of the sets of indices used?" The resolution of this question has consequences both theoretical and methodological for urban sociology, ecology, and deriving census tracts in urban areas.

Answering this question involved the amassing of a great amount of data, most of which had to be obtained from unpublished sources and extensive interviewing. Ecological data were made available from the Lansing City Plan Commission, demographic data from the U.S. Bureau of the Census, social data from about 550 interviews with residents of the city and 200 interviews with local businessmen. These data were supplemented by continuous field study. Because the analysis is still in its preliminary stage, the observations made here are restricted to selected methodological problems in deriving a sub-area plan.

ECOLOGICAL SUB-AREAS [4]

The preparation of an ecologically drawn map of sub-areas was achieved on the basis of traditional criteria. Specifically, they were:

(1) Natural boundaries or barriers, such as rivers, parks, playgrounds, topographic features, railroads, main streets, factories, and highways.
(2) Prevailing land use and zoning plans.
(3) Value of dwelling units.
(4) Racial segregation.

Sub-Culture Areas" (unpublished Ph.D. dissertation, Department of Psychology, University of California [Berkeley], 1949); Eshref Shevky and Marilyn Williams, *The Social Areas of Los Angeles, Analysis and Typology,* Berkeley and Los Angeles: University of California Press, 1949.

[3] Lansing, Michigan, contains roughly 100,000 people. It is the capital of the state and its main industries are automobile and metal manufacturing.

[4] The authors are indebted to Jack DeLora for preparing the ecological map.

Data for determining boundaries according to the last three criteria were available by blocks. Other data, such as monthly rental and number of dwelling units, were also available but were not useful. The clear-cut distribution of rivers, railroads, industry, public property, and main streets facilitated the task of locating sub-areas in Lansing by the ecological approach. The resultant 35 natural ecological areas appear in Figure I.

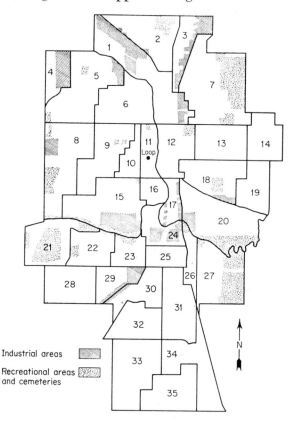

FIGURE I.   Areas of Lansing Based on Ecological Criteria.

DEMOGRAPHIC SUB-AREAS [5]

The task here was to see whether Lansing could be sub-

[5] See Joel Smith, "A Method for the Classification of Areas on the Basis of Demographically Homogeneous Populations," *American Sociological Review*, 19 (April, 1954), pp. 201-207. Most of the material in this section is taken from the above paper.

divided by the criterion of homogeneity applied to demographic data. These were made available by the U.S. Census Bureau for all of the 139 enumeration districts of Lansing. These data were computed to establish for each district the percentages of population non-white, foreign-born, male, under 21 years, over 55 years, and the ratio of population under 21 to population 55 and over, and the fertility ratio.

Two operations were involved—(1) the development of a technique to describe the demographic characteristics of each district that would make its position *on each of the seven sets of data comparable,* and (2) the development of a technique to group districts with similar profiles.

(1) It was decided to shift from a classification of districts based on raw data to a classification *based on deviations from city ratios.* Thus a chi-square test of goodness of fit was computed for each enumeration district on all seven demographic indices, making it possible to describe the probability that each enumeration district departed from the city distribution for each demographic characteristic. Then districts were grouped in classes according to a prearranged set of seven probability limits [6] and were mapped.

(2) In order to develop a technique to group districts with similar profiles, it was decided to subject the enumeration district probability data in (1) above to a Guttman scale analysis. The

[6] These limits are presented in the following table:

CLASS INTERVALS USED FOR COMPARABLE DESCRIPTIONS OF ENUMERATION
DISTRICTS ON DIFFERENT TYPES OF DATA

Probability Limits	Sign	Meaning Based on Assumption that Sub-Area Not Different from City
.01 and below	—	Very significantly less than expected
.01—.20	—	Significantly less than expected
.20—.70	—	Less than expected
.70—.70	±	As expected
.70—.20	+	More than expected
.20—.01	+	Significantly more than expected
.01 and below	+	Very significantly more than expected

steps in this process are reported elsewhere.[7] Only the results
need to be reviewed here. The 66 enumeration districts with a
surplus of foreign-born formed a scale with 90 per cent reproducibility on the items of "under 21 years," "race," and "sex." This
yielded five scale types. The 63 districts with surpluses of native-
born residents were found to form a scale with 85.2 per cent
reproducibility on the items of "age ratio," "fertility ratio," and
"sex." This yielded five scale types.

These areas of demographic homogeneity were then mapped
as in Figure II by combining contiguous enumeration districts
of like scale types. About 60 per cent of the area and population
of the city were included in these contiguous areas. It would
have been possible to include another twenty per cent of the
districts and population in the demographic map by admitting
a wider range of scale types. The substantive interpretation of
Figure II, which cannot be done here, involves an analysis of the
composition, relative size, and distribution of each scale type.
Suffice it to say that the size and shape of these demographic
areas vary considerably. Some areas stretch across almost half
of the city, while others are smaller and more compact. The
boundaries of these demographic areas do not follow ecological
barriers in any consistent way. Confusion in interpreting Figure
II is heightened by the arbitrary character of the boundaries of
the enumeration districts. However this method of spatial demographic analysis is useful and will be explored further when
population data are made available for more meaningfully drawn
sub-areas of the city.

SOCIAL SUB-AREAS

Deriving the pattern of social areas for Lansing proved to be
the most difficult step. Initially, the research committee decided
to give the social criterion primacy in determining the final sub-
area plan. The central hypothesis was that the city may be divided into areas which may vary in a range from high integration
to either disintegration or non-integration. The criteria selected
to determine the state of integration of a sub-area were: (1)
consensus on local boundaries, (2) consensus on community soli-

[7] Joel Smith, *op. cit., passim.*

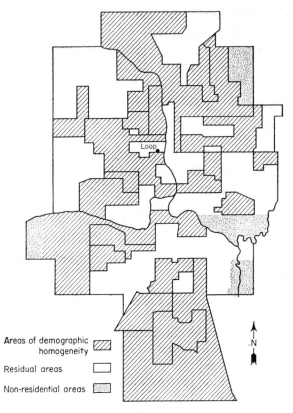

FIGURE II.   Demographic Areas of Lansing.

darity, (3) identification with the local area, (4) locality con-
sciousness, (5) use of local facilities, and (6) development of
local formal and informal organization.   Information on all of
these factors was available from over 500 interviews with Lansing residents.   These interviews represented at least one family
in slightly more than one-half of the blocks in the city.   Thus a
relatively large spatial sample was available.   However, using
each of these factors separately or together to locate the social
areas presented an almost insurmountable problem.

To orient ourselves, overlay spot maps were made of many of
the above social items in the hope that clusterings of traits in
different sections of the city would be apparent.   Extreme responses which reflected differences in neighborhood intimacy,
estimates of types of neighborhood change, shopping patterns

inside the neighborhood, and social activities (such as visiting friends and relatives, and playing cards with neighbors) were plotted on separate overlays. This disclosed that different indices of social integration and intimacy had different territorial distributions. Some of them pointed to integration on the neighborhood level, some to the sub-community, and others to the city as a whole. Some indices of economic and social integration, such as grocery shopping and visiting friends, had only a slight locality concentration, and were discarded for the purposes at hand. Other activity indices of social integration were eliminated because only a minority of the population engaged in these activities. These included bowling, watching TV at a neighbor's home, and going to movies, parks, taverns, and restaurants.

Six social attributes which clustered consistently on spot maps pointed to some aspects of neighborhood intimacy and identification. These questions were.

(1) How well do you think the people in the neighborhood know each other?

(2) About how many of them would you say you know by name?

(3) About how many do you spend a whole afternoon or evening with every now and then?

(4) If you had your choice would you continue living in this neighborhood?

(5) How many families in your neighborhood do you come in contact with for a few minutes every day or so?

(6) Do you think this neighborhood is getting better or getting worse?

The responses to these six items were then trichotomized and subjected to a Guttman scale analysis. Ultimately, the first four of them (one trichotomous and three dichotomous) were found to scale, with a coefficient of reproducibility of .894. The resulting six scale types for degree of social intimacy [8] in the neighborhood appear in Table 1.

The 566 blocks in which interviews were secured were then designated as exhibiting either high or low social intimacy according to whether they fell into the upper or lower three scale types.

[8] It is recognized that the scale items used connote both intimacy and identification. For purposes of simplicity, however, we refer to the items as a scale of social intimacy.

TABLE 1

NEIGHBORHOOD SOCIAL INTIMACY SCALE

Question	Intimate (+)	Intermediate (0)	Non-Intimate (−)
1	quite well, very well	fairly well	not at all, not so well
2	one or more		none
3	about half or more		none, a few
4	yes		no, don't know

Ideal Scale Types	Pattern of Responses to Items				Number of Cases *
	1	2	3	4	
I	+	+	+	+	34
II	0	+	+	+	19
III	0	−	+	+	12
IV	0	−	−	+	16
V	−	−	−	+	14
VI	−	−	−	−	21

$$\frac{\text{Coefficient of}}{\text{Reproducibility}} = 1 - \frac{49}{4 \times 116} = .894 *$$

* This scale was developed on the basis of a randomly selected 20 per cent sample of the block interviews. Previous experience of the authors with scales based upon samples of this magnitude shows that coefficients of reproducibility can be expected to vary only within a small range of one per cent. The coefficient is computed after the formula presented in Samuel A. Stouffer, Louis Guttman, et al., *Studies in Social Psychology in World War II: Volume IV, Measurement and Prediction*, Princeton: Princeton University Press, 1950, p. 117.

These intimacy extremes were then plotted on a map of the city, and areas having adjacent blocks falling into the same categories were demarcated. Perhaps the most impressive characteristic of Figure III is the very small area in which there are wide variations in social intimacy from block to block ("mixed" in Figure III). In general, Lansing is characterized by broad areal bands in which social intimacy is consistently high or low.

It must be emphasized that the areas which were homogeneous in intimacy were not necessarily neighborhoods, but contiguous areas with similar intimacy scores. The high and low intimacy areas of Lansing were about equally distributed, each accounting for almost one-half of the city as a whole, with a very small residual area of mixed social intimacy. High and low intimacy areas were found in sections with both high and low property values. However, high intimacy areas seemed to be more

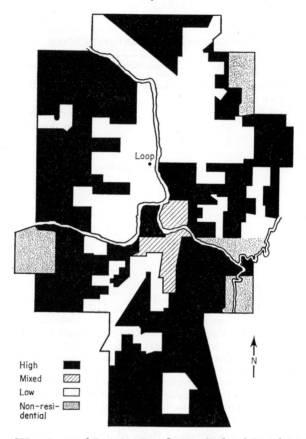

FIGURE III.   Areas of Lansing Based on a Scale of Social Intimacy.

frequently associated with areas exhibiting a high degree of home ownership. The area of highest intimacy was an ecologically segregated middle income area of high home ownership containing families with children of grammar school age and below. There appeared to be no consistent association between social intimacy and the presence of local shopping and other facilities. A more detailed evaluation of the spatial distribution of these scale types awaits further analysis.

COMPARISON OF SUB-AREA PLANS

A systematic and detailed comparison of the maps based on the ecological, demographic, and social criteria cannot be made here. Some of the outstanding convergences and dissimilarities among them may be noted, as well as some of the problems involved in such a comparative analysis.

(1) There is no direct, simple, or unilinear relationship among areas drawn according to ecological, demographic, or social indices. Indeed, it is possible, using each approach, to derive separate plans roughly alike in the number of sub-areas and the size of population contained in them.

(2) Every type of ecological barrier, including rivers, railroads, main streets, and factory districts was violated when demographic and social indices were used to locate boundaries.

(3) The problem of finding to what degree ecological boundaries also constitute boundaries for demographic areas is complicated by the areal basis of collecting demographic data. Boundaries used by the Census Bureau for enumeration districts are apparently not determined by any systematic procedure. In addition, the districts are generally so large that they hide considerable internal demographic variation. Ideally, data for residential units are needed to test the question of demographic sensitivity to ecological boundaries.

(4) Only in a very general sense, with some important exceptions, areas in the periphery of the city tend to exhibit high social intimacy, while internal areas tend to exhibit low or mixed social intimacy. Lowest intimacy sections were found in the oldest section of the city and along some thoroughfares.

(5) Very generally speaking, internal areas of the city which fell into demographic scale types tended to be in areas characterized by low social intimacy. Extensive analysis of the *composition* of the scale types is needed to make the above generalization more meaningful. Probably these areas are demographically homogeneous in the sense that they contain inhabitants whose characteristics deviate from those of middle size, middle status group, native-born families in similar directions.

(6) Exceptions to the generalizations in (4) and (5) above are found in the southern and east south central sections of the city. Apart from isolating areas for intensive sociological field work, these non-convergences suggest a variant relationship between social intimacy and some types of demographic char-

acteristics, such as particular nationality concentrations, age-groupings, and family structures.

(7) All three maps in one manner or another isolate areas which are populated mostly by Negroes. However, this convergence is only of the grossest type. The area is by no means internally homogeneous either in its demographic composition or in the degree of social intimacy. This internal heterogeneity reflects internal social stratification as well as the dynamics of the ecological process of invasion outward from a central core.

(8) The ecological approach yielded areas of rather equal size because some kinds of barriers were generally available for purposes of delimitation. The odd-shaped areas provided in the

Ecological boundaries   ———

Demographic boundaries   — — —

Social intimacy boundaries ··············

FIGURE IV.   Boundary Divergences in a Small Area of Lansing.

demographic and social plans are useful to locate territorial divisions which demand intensive sociological study.

(9) Several boundary agreements were found by all three approaches. All of them isolated certain heavy industry areas, a few residential neighborhoods, and some large outlying sectors.

(10) The social and demographic techniques also singled out small, highly homogeneous, and distinctive areas of the city which were concealed by the ecological approach. For example, Figure IV shows a segment of the city which is completely enclosed by rivers, railroads, factories, and main thoroughfares. The boundaries indicated by the demographic and social indices do not correspond to the ecological ones. Further, this area is not internally homogeneous from other points of view. Two types of demographic areas have boundaries which at places coincide, fall within, and extend beyond the ecological boundaries. The same applies for two types of social intimacy which lie across the area in question.

Obviously compromises among the boundaries were necessary to arrive at a satisfactory general sub-area plan for the city. Since no one of the three plans was satisfactory in every way to meet census tract requirements, they were all used in making the eventual plan. How the compromises were made will be reported elsewhere.

DELIMITING THE CBD *

RAYMOND E. MURPHY AND J. E. VANCE, JR.

The Central Business District, frequently referred to as the CBD,[1] is the heart of the American city. Here one finds the greatest concentration of offices and retail stores reflected in the city's highest land values and its tallest buildings. Here, too, is the chief focus of pedestrian and automobile traffic. By way of

---

* Adapted from *Economic Geography*, Vol. 30, No. 3 (July, 1954), pp. 189-222, with permission of authors and publisher. The technique of delimitation described by the authors was established through observations on nine cities, each of which is treated in detail in the original version of the paper.

[1] Among alternative names by which the CBD is known are Central Traffic District, Central Commercial District, Downtown Business District, and, more popularly, Downtown.

the transportation net the remainder of the city and an area of decreasing intensity extending far beyond the city's corporate limits are oriented toward the CBD.

Interest in the district has been increasing rapidly in recent years. Studies have been made of its theoretical shape and of the daily movements to and from this critical area. Planners, with more immediate, practical aims, are working on the problems of routing through traffic in such a way as to avoid this congested district, and, at the same time, of providing parking space for the many who work in the CBD or who seek the goods and services it has to offer. And business men, who have seen their large investments in the district threatened by the growth of outlying shopping centers, are striving mightily to maintain the supremacy of this central area.

In view of these impinging interests it is surprising that so far no uniform method of delimiting the district has been used, that for each city the limits of the CBD have been largely a matter of local agreement. This is all very well for a planner in an individual city, working on local problems, but it is only through the use of a standardized method of delimitation that significant comparisons of CBD's are possible. And it is only through such comparisons that a real knowledge of the content and functioning of this critical area can be attained. The development of a practical technique for delimiting the CBD, essentially a geographic problem, is the central theme of this paper.

VARIATIONS WITHIN THE CBD

Even a cursory examination of the area we are proposing to delimit brings out the fact that it is far from homogeneous. First of all is a variation in what might be called commercial intensity. This is reflected in the tendency of some writers to use the designation "commercial core" for the more highly concentrated central portion of the CBD. In similar fashion the term "hard core" has been used to distinguish this central area from the remainder of the district, and others have spoken of a "primary area" and a "secondary area."

It should not be inferred, however, that sharply defined intensity areas are normal. Generally, there is a point of maximum intensity which is well known locally: the street intersection around which the average front-foot lot value is highest. This *peak land value intersection*, as it is here called, is likely to be the locality with the maximum pedestrian concentration, and, not infrequently, the point of greatest vehicular congestion. From this center, various measures of intensity ordinarily decline toward the edges of the city, though more sharply in some directions than in others.

This does not mean that there is no observable regionalization within the CBD. Financial, theater, night club, and intensive shopping districts may often be differentiated; and there may be areas devoted to those industrial types that characterize the CBD or to the single-company office buildings of insurance companies and oil companies. Such regionalization varies greatly with individual cities and generally is more striking the larger the city. In addition there is a vertical zonation, retail stores tending to occupy the choice ground floor positions and offices or sometimes merchandise storage, the higher floors. In smaller cities the upper floor space may be shared with dwelling units. But over all is the tendency for intensity to decline with distance from the peak value point.

NATURE OF THE CBD EDGE

It follows from the fact that intensity values decline with distance from a point of maximum concentration that the edge of the district is itself gradational. As Bartholomew says, "It (the CBD) is a somewhat vague area with no definite boundaries." [2] Such obstacles to expansion as a park, or, in the case of a state capital, a group of government buildings, may give the CBD some line boundaries, but such sharp edges are exceptional. Much more often the edge is a belt or zone.

This zonal character of the CBD border has been recognized by various students of the city, partly because the zone is in several respects a problem area. As Dickinson puts it, ". . . the combination of high land values and obsolescent buildings, ripe

[2] Harland Bartholomew: "Urban Land Uses: Amounts of Land Used and Needed for Various Purposes by Typical American Cities, An Aid to Scientific Zoning Practice," Harvard City Planning Studies IV, Cambridge, 1932, p. 12.

for demolition, accounts for the dingy-looking 'zone of deterioration' that surrounds the business centre of almost every city."[3] Firey refers to the border area as, ". . . the blighted zone which generally lies between a city's central business district and the surrounding residential districts . . ."[4] The blighted condition of the zone has been attributed to ". . . slackening in the expansion of commercial and industrial uses near central business districts . . ."[5] Not infrequently it is this zone that has furnished the sites for the redevelopment projects that have been planned in so many cities.

THE CBD AS A REGION

What we have been saying is, essentially, that the CBD is a region with the normal qualities of a region. It has a core area in which the definitive qualities reach their greatest intensity; it has zonal boundaries, and these boundaries, for the most part, are impermanent.

THE PROBLEM RESTATED

Though the boundaries of the CBD may be impermanent and zonal, for any particular time it should be possible to draw a line that would approximate this zonal edge. The problem undertaken by the writers of this paper was the development of a practicable method for drawing such a line. If a defensible method could be developed and were widely accepted, it could result in the delimitation of comparable CBD's in various cities. This, the writers believed, was a necessary step to gaining a deeper understanding of the nature and functioning of the CBD.

DELIMITATION METHODS USED BY PLANNING AGENCIES

Since local determinations so often have been relied upon, it was decided, as an early step in the boundary study, to investi-

[3] Robert E. Dickinson: "City Region and Regionalism," London, 1947, p. 96.
[4] Walter Firey: "Ecological Considerations in Planning for Rurban Fringes," *Amer. Soc. Rev.*, Vol. 11, 1946, p. 411.
[5] Homer Hoyt: "Structure and Growth of Residential Neighborhoods in American Cities," Federal Housing Administration, Washington, 1939, p. 108.

gate methods used locally throughout the United States. Accordingly, letters were written to the head planning officials of some 25 or 30 medium-sized cities asking, in each case, for a map showing the extent of the area regarded as the CBD in their city and for a statement of the methods used in arriving at the CBD boundaries.

Most of those queried sent maps outlining their respective CBD's, but there was little uniformity in methods of arriving at the boundaries. In several instances the planner said that for his city no single answer was attempted; instead the zoning ordinance might give one CBD delimitation and the traffic ordinance a different one, and the fire department might use still a third. For most cities, however, a single delimiting line was used, in nearly all instances following block boundaries. The area shown was "generally understood locally" to be the CBD; in one instance it was arrived at "intuitively." Barriers such as rivers or railroad tracks were mentioned as forming parts of the boundaries of some CBD's. In general, a knowledge of local land use lay back of the judgments, but in most instances no specific or exact delimiting techniques were used.

In cases of only two of the cities queried were any definite techniques reported. One of these was in use in Worcester. Charles M. Downe, Director of the Worcester Department of Planning and now Director, Division of Planning, The Massachusetts Department of Commerce, based his delimitation upon land values. He used assessed land values by lots reduced to value per front-foot at a uniform 100-foot depth, drawing his CBD boundary line at the outer limit of the lots with front-foot land valuations of $300 or more (Figure I). In similiar fashion he used the area enclosing lots with front-foot land values of $2000 or more to delimit an inner area that he called the "hard core."

This was a very satisfactory delimitation for one city, but since valuation methods differ markedly from city to city the direct use of land values can hardly be expected to yield comparable CBD's for different cities. The whole matter of the use of valuation data will be considered more fully in later pages of this study.

The second technique reported was used in Denver. The following paragraphs describe the method in detail:

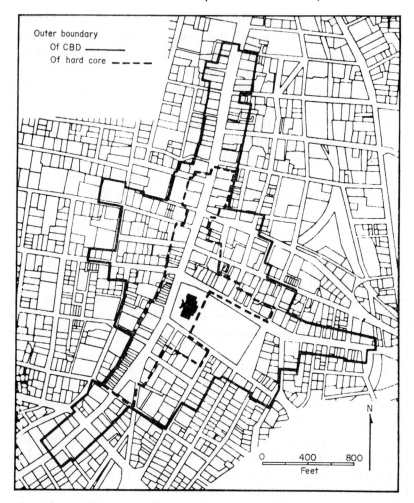

FIGURE I. Worcester's CBD and hard core as delimited by Charles M. Downe. He worked with lots, basing his boundaries on front-foot land values reduced to uniform 100-foot depth. The black area near the center of the hard core is the City Hall.

This method requires only the use of an ordinary land use map. It presumes that you want a brief method which takes account of the characteristics of land use.

1. Base—land use map.

2. Land use to be included in CBD:—business, commercial and industrial.

3. An "analysis unit" comprising a group of blocks should be selected to serve the following purpose: the group should be wider in radius than the width of a typical business ribbon along a transit street. A diameter of four blocks is suggested.

4. *Procedure:*

   A. Cut a circle in a sheet of paper, the diameter of which is four blocks at the scale of the land use map. This template represents the size of the "analysis unit."
   B. Lay tracing paper over the land use map. Draw a perimeter around the obvious core of the CBD.
   C. Place the center of the template at any point along this perimeter and slide it outward, radially away from the CBD unit until half of the included land uses become residential. At this point business and residential use will be interspersed but a fairly objective determination can be made of the relative proportion of nonbusiness uses.
   D. Place a dot on the tracing paper in the center of the template. Return the template to the CBD core line, one diameter away from the previous starting point. Repeat the process of sliding the template radially to a point where half of the uses become residential.
   E. After completing the process around the entire CBD, a number of points representing the *margin* of the CBD will encircle the CBD core. Simply connect these points by a line. It may be adjusted to coincide with the nearest streets or other cultural boundaries.[6]

The chief objection to this method is that too much is included in the CBD. Using this technique, areas of solid manufacturing development, of wholesaling, and of railroad yards are included—in fact everything out to the point where half or more of the land is used for residences. This, it seems to the writers of this article, is too liberal a definition of the CBD. And the very fact that one city may delimit its CBD on the basis of land values and another on the basis of non-residential land use shows why some standardization of delimitation techniques is necessary if comparative studies of the district are to mean anything.

[6] Quoted from a letter from W. F. Henniger, Director, Department of Planning, City and County of Denver, July 9, 1952.

THE LITERATURE OF DELIMITATION

A search of the literature dealing with the CBD revealed little that was pertinent to the present problem. Most geographers, sociologists, and other writers who have focussed upon the CBD or dealt with it incidentally have relied, in the case of each city, upon local judgment as to the extent of the district.[7] The inadequacy of such locally-determined boundaries for any work involving city comparisons is obvious. As Foley and Breese put it, "The areal definition of the CBD has not yet been standardized . . . eventually technicians and scholars may be able to construct a workable definition of the CBD that could be applied to all cities." [8]

Some work done in Sweden and Norway, however, and one study carried on in this country bear sufficiently upon the problem of delimitation to be considered more fully here. First, let us note the work of William-Olsson on Stockholm.[9] In studying retail trade, which he defined as trade not only in goods but also in meals, amusements, and lodgings, he used a *shop rent index*

[7] See A. E. Parkins: "Profiles of the Retail Business Section of Nashville, Tennessee, and their Interpretation," *Annals of Assn. of Amer. Geogrs.*, Vol. 20, 1931, pp. 164-176; Earl S. Johnson: "The Natural History of the Central Business District with Particular Reference to Chicago," Univ. of Chicago Ph.D. Dissertation, Chicago, 1941; Gerald W. Breese: "The Daytime Population of the Central Business District of Chicago," Univ. of Chicago Press, Chicago, 1949; George W. Hartman: "Central Business District, A Study in Urban Geography," *Econ. Geog.*, Vol. 26, 1950, pp. 237-244; Donald L. Foley: "The Daily Movements of Population into Central Business Districts," *Amer. Soc. Rev.*, Vol. 17, 1952, pp. 538-543; and Richard U. Ratcliff: "The Madison Central Business Area, A Case Study of Functional Change," Wisconsin Commerce Papers, Vol. I, No. 5, Bureau of Business Research and Service, University of Wisconsin, Madison, 1953. See, also, such more general studies as Harland Bartholomew, *op. cit.*; Homer Hoyt, *op. cit.*, especially pp. 107-109; Malcolm J. Proudfoot, "City Retail Structure," *Econ. Geog.*, Vol. 13, 1937, pp. 424-428; and Richard U. Ratcliff: "The Problem of Retail Site Selection," *Mich. Bus. Studies*, Vol. IX, No. 1, Bur. of Bus. Research, School of Bus. Admin., Univ. of Mich., Ann Arbor, 1939. There are, in addition, numerous studies of individual cities which show the CBD delimited along with other areas of the city. Such delimitations are based on local opinion or upon the author's subjective judgment. In no case that has come to the writers' attention is any systematic delimitation technique used.

[8] Donald L. Foley and Gerald Breese: "The Standardization of Data showing Daily Population Movement into Central Business Districts," *Land Econs.*, Vol. 27, 1951, pp. 348-353, ref. on pp. 349-350.

[9] See W. William-Olsson: "Stockholm: Its Structure and Development," *Geogr. Rev.*, Vol. 30, 1940, pp. 420-438. See also William-Olsson's "Huvuddragen av Stockholms geografiska utveckling 1850-1930." Stockholm 1937. Stadskollegiets Utlåtanden och Memorial, Bihang Nr. 11 (1937).

(butikshyrestal) which he described as the total of shop rents of a building divided by the length of its frontage. This was indicated graphically on William-Olsson's maps by rectangles, the base of each being a building frontage, and the vertical, reaching away from the street, the shop rent index in kroner.[10]

Sund and Isachsen in a study of dwelling and working places in Oslo [11] point out that they were unable to obtain shop rent data for Oslo and hence used the total turnover or trade instead. Their *trade index* (omsetningsverdi) is plotted on a map in much the same manner as William-Olsson's index except that in this case the vertical dimension of the rectangle (that at a right angle to the street frontage) is proportional to total trade.

It might appear, at first glance, that some minimum shop rent index or trade index value could be used to delimit the CBD. However, both methods require data that would be difficult if not impossible to assemble for the average American city.

Volume of trade was used in an interesting study of Philadelphia supervised by Malcolm J. Proudfoot.[12] In setting up "intra-city business areas" "block-frontage-volume-of-sales" was used. This term refers to the total annual volume of sales, for each side of a block, of all stores whose addresses indicate that they front on that side. Thus any block would have four such totals though the figure might be "0" for one or more sides if no establishments fronted on those sides. "For the outer zone of the central business district . . . a block frontage lower limit of $75,000 was used . . ." [13] An inner zone of the central business district also was delimited; this had a block frontage lower limit $500,000.

In Proudfoot's study only volume of retail sales was used. This works better for delimiting outlying shopping centers than for the CBD, since in the outlying shopping centers retail trade is more predominant. But much is carried on in the CBD besides retail trade. It would be possible in the case of any city to have the Census prepare at cost a map showing total volume not only

---

[10] William-Olsson, *op. cit.*, Figures VII and VIII, p. 426.

[11] Tore Sund and Fridtjov Isachsen: "Bosteder og arbeidssteder i Oslo," Oslo, 1942.

[12] United States Census Bureau: "Intra-City Business Census Statistics for Philadelphia, Pa." (prepared under supervision of Malcolm J. Proudfoot, Research Geographer) May, 1937.

[13] *Ibid.*, p. 7. See, also, the business areas map, Figure II in the same report.

of retail trade but of services and wholesale trade as well for each side of each block in the central portion of a city, and these data could even be totaled by blocks if one preferred to work with blocks. But, aside from the time and cost involved, such a method would still fail to take account of offices (such as the central office of a large oil company), of banks, and of certain other activities that are important in the CBD.

NUMEROUS POSSIBILITIES

Of course from the very conception of the current project the authors had certain ideas as to possible means of delimiting the CBD. The correspondence with planning agencies added to this growing list of possibilities and so, too, did the literature survey and conversations with countless individuals. All of these possibilities were listed, and each that appeared to have promise was considered, in an attempt to develop a delimitation system that was practicable and, at the same time, could be defended on philosophical grounds. The first several months of research time were spent at Worcester, Massachusetts, home base for the project, and were devoted to this preliminary trying out of various possibilities and to laying of plans for further work.

Shop rent index, trade index, and block-frontage-volume-of-sales have been discussed, and it has been pointed out that their use would be impracticable for work on the average American city. There appeared to be three other principal groups of possibilities: (1) population distribution and related phenomena; (2) valuation of land or of land and buildings; and (3) land use.

POPULATION AND RELATED DATA

Several delimitation possibilities are based directly upon man. These deal in turn with distribution of population, pattern of employment, movements of pedestrians, and traffic flow.

Distribution of Population Use of population data, either directly as such or through the location of dwelling units, is based on the fact that the CBD is essentially lacking in permanent residents.

One might visualize a map of population per unit of area,

with the CBD appearing as essentially empty and a certain density ratio marking its edge. Unfortunately, however, the smallest unit for which direct population data are available, the Census Enumeration District, is too large to permit any reasonable approximation of the CBD edge. Moreover, the blank area at the center is not necessarily central business; it is merely non-residential. Blocks of factories or public schools might well be responsible for sections of the blank area and yet obviously are non-CBD in character.

Population distribution may be presented indirectly by a map of dwelling units per unit of area based on block housing data from the census. This has an advantage over the population map since data are by blocks. Nevertheless, the dwelling unit density map is subject to the same criticism as the population map: though the blank central area is non-residential it may include blocks of non-central business use.

We must conclude that neither the population density map nor the dwelling unit density map is of much help in precise delimitation of the district. In each case it would have to be supplemented by a land use map.

Pattern of Employment If it were possible to obtain, and to localize on a map, data on the number of persons employed in offices and retail stores, this might form the basis for a delimitation technique. Sund and Isachsen were able to obtain statistics on the number of persons who worked in each building in Oslo and to break these data down on the basis of general types of employment.[14] But such data are difficult to obtain. Though they might be assembled for any city the time and effort involved would be entirely too great for employment to be used as the basis for a standardized delimitation technique.

Pedestrian Counts and Traffic Flow Pedestrian counts and traffic flow, reflecting as they do the activity on the streets, form other possible approaches to CBD delimitation and are used in some cities in establishing land values for commercial property. The edge of the district on each street leading away from the peak intersection might, conceivably, be fixed where certain minimum counts were reached.

[14] Sund and Isachsen, *op. cit.*, pp. 95-101. See also, Tore Sund: "Bergens byområde og dets geografiske utvikling 1900-1940," Bergen, 1947.

Traffic flow may be briefly dismissed since it has some very obvious flaws as a possible basis for delimitation. For instance, in some cities all through traffic passes through the peak intersection; in others, fortunately an increasing number, the modern tendency is to route traffic so as to avoid the peak point. Moreover, many cities prohibit downtown parking during the busier hours of the day; hence traffic bears little relation to volume of business. Since cities have different policies in these respects it is hard to see how traffic flow could furnish a basis for delimiting districts that would be at all comparable.

Pedestrian counts are somewhat more promising, since movement of people on the streets is essential to the central functions of the CBD. But techniques based on pedestrian counts suffer from the same handicap as those based on population density and dwelling unit density (or on traffic flow, either, for that matter): pedestrians may include factory workers, and students on their way home from a downtown high school. This difficulty may be partially offset by proper timing of the counts. Another problem is that the same limiting pedestrian count could hardly be expected to prevail in one city as in another. However, if all counts in a city were expressed as percentages of the count for the peak point, a limiting percentage might be found that would be reasonably consistent from city to city.

The possibilities of pedestrian counts were not investigated in the current project. Up-to-date counts are not available for the average city or at least not in a form that could be used for CBD delimitation, and to make such a count requires a considerable force of experienced workers.[15] Nevertheless, the use of pedestrian counts remains a possibility that might be worth investigating.

But it must be pointed out that there is another obvious flaw in the use either of pedestrian counts or traffic flow: they would at best result only in a point on each street. How could these points be connected in a sufficiently objective manner so that the resulting area in one city would be comparable with that in another?

---

[15] The use of properly timed air photos of a large scale as a basis for such counts is an intriguing possibility.

LAND VALUES AND CBD DELIMITATION

Valuation data are of considerable interest in connection with delimiting the CBD,[16] but unfortunately their use presents many problems to the research worker. For example, the valuation data for a city may be established on either of two bases: appraisal or assessment. *Appraisal* is intended to be a close approximation of the market value of the property, in contrast to *assessment,* which represents the legal valuation of a property for tax purposes.

Basis for assessment is the percentage of the market value at which the property is appraised. It often is fixed by law, and differs from city to city and also regionally. Thus New England and other areas of eastern United States tend to have a higher basis for assessment than do Middle Western or Far Western areas or the South.

Since the assessed value is often a stated percentage of the appraised value it is possible by simple calculation to convert assessed values into appraised values. But the situation is complicated by the fact that the basis of assessment in some areas differs with the major type of land use. This requires further adjustments in converting assessed values to appraised values.

For most cities, data by lots are collected both for land value and for the value of land plus buildings. It can be assembled from the Assessor's records, but this is a time-consuming operation. Fortunately for anyone interested in comparing CBD's, the data on land values for the central section of the city frequently have been brought together on maps that are available locally. Less commonly, land and building values have been so assembled.

Frequently the data on land values (not including buildings) are expressed as front-foot values. These data are based on the fact that for commercial property the frontage on the street is of considerably greater value than the land farther to the rear of the lot. For this reason the relative values of lots are more dependent upon their frontages on the business street than upon their sizes. To correct for unevenness in lot sizes, front-foot values

---

[16] Sund and Isachsen used tax data in differentiating central Oslo but did not attempt to draw a line boundary, *op. cit.,* Figure 46 and pp. 104-105.

may be adjusted to a standard depth. Where land values have been assembled for the central area of a city they usually have been adjusted in this way, ordinarily to a 100-foot depth.

As part of the current project, valuation data were collected and their potentialities for CBD delimitation were investigated.

Techniques Based on Valuation Data Land values, it was decided, furnished a more promising basis for delimitation than land and building values. Building values vary essentially in proportion to the size and age of buildings and do not grade regularly from any peak point. Moreover, a large, new apartment house or a factory at the edge of the CBD would result in a marked area of high land and building values, though the uses were obviously not central business uses in type. There was the added practical point that, though most city planning agencies had assembled land values, land and building values were not so readily available.

The bases for land values differ so much from city to city that direct city comparisons are unreliable. But it may be assumed that the data for any one city are derived in a reasonably consistent manner. Therefore, as far as reliability of data is concerned, land values could form an adequate basis for a CBD delimitation for that city. This was the basis on which Downe delimited the Worcester CBD. But the same limiting values that he applied in Worcester would mean little in another city.

Another possibility would be to use lot land values (not front-foot values) in order to arrive at an average value per unit of block area. By selecting a limiting value a CBD boundary could be drawn on a block basis. Like the method mentioned in the last paragraph, however, there would be no basis for comparability from city to city.

The authors experimented with a method that seems to be more broadly applicable. This involves the use of a system of index numbers. Thus the front-foot land value at 100-foot depth for the highest-valued lot was represented by the number 100; the value of each other lot was shown by the number corresponding to its percentage of the value of the peak value lot. The line enclosing those lots with indexes of five or higher seemed best to represent the edge of the CBD. Since this technique is based on the percentage that each lot value makes up of the highest lot

value, it makes no difference whether the land value data are
given as assessed values or as appraised values. Moreover, such
an index system allows comparability from city to city. Figure
II shows the delimitation of Worcester's CBD that results from
the use of the five per cent land value line.

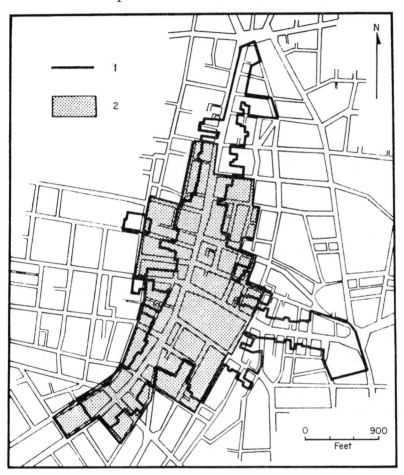

FIGURE II. The area in Worcester outlined by the 5 per cent land value
line (1 on map) does not correspond very closely with the CBD based on
land use (area 2 on map), the delimitation of which is discussed later in
this study. In part this difference results from lots forming the basis for the
land value line and blocks for the CBD based on land use. But there is the
added fact that land values do not discriminate among uses. Apartment
houses and factories may occur in areas of high land values, and, conversely,
stores or other central business uses may extend beyond the 5 per cent land
value line.

The land valuation technique just described requires no field work. Also, since land values are on a lot basis, the delimitation is a fine-textured one.[17] But balanced against these advantages are a number of objections to any method based on land values. In some cities the data, though on the Assessor's books, have not been assembled. In others, though the data have been brought together, local authorities, for one reason or another, are unwilling to make the information public. When the data are obtained it must be remembered that they represent subjective judgments. Another difficulty is that tax free property (schools, churches, public buildings) are commonly not assigned a valuation. As a result the actual drawing of a boundary based on land values is sufficiently subjective so that the districts delimited by two different individuals might vary considerably.

But two other objections to any land value technique are even more serious. One of these is that if the valuation is properly done it does not reflect the height of buildings; yet surely the vertical dimension needs to be considered. The second is a shortcoming that the land value technique shares with the delimitation methods mentioned earlier: it does not discriminate among land uses. It is entirely possible for a factory block or a block of apartment houses to occur in an area of high land values and hence to be included in the CBD even though not central business in type. This problem is not so likely to arise near the center of the CBD; it is near its edge that these other uses may compete successfully with central business for the land. It is equally true that along the edge of the CBD central business uses may extend into areas of lower land values. And it is at the edge that the problem of drawing the boundary is localized.

LAND USE AND CBD DELIMITATION

Land values are, after all, only a reflection of the use to which land can be put. It would appear, therefore, that land use should furnish a more direct and realistic approach to delimitation of the CBD than land values. There are several possible delimitation methods which, though based on land use, do not require a

---

[17] Although the technique was tried out only with lot values, there is no reason why it could not be applied to the land values per unit of block area described in an earlier paragraph.

complete job of land use mapping. These will be considered first.

Break in Continuity The first and most obvious technique of this sort and the one most likely to be used by the casual observer is a simple break in continuity of central business uses. This generally is thought of in connection with ground floor use. At some point on every street leading away from the peak land value intersection the shops and office buildings that characterize the CBD will give way to residences or factories or to some other non-central business use.

But break in continuity has decided limitations as a basis for locating a CBD boundary. For instance, there is the question: How much of a break must there be in order for it to be significant? Moreover, the method results at best in a point along each street. How should the points be connected on the map? Any resulting delimitation must be a highly subjective one, and workers in various cities could hardly be expected by such means to arrive at comparable CBD's.

Types of Establishments at CBD Edge Another possible method of determining the approximate position of the CBD boundary is based on the hypothesis that certain types of establishments tend to be concentrated at or near the boundary. Supermarkets, automobile sales rooms, filling stations, furniture stores, rooming houses, and several other types of land use have this reputation. To what degree do these establishments coincide with the boundary? Are they really concentrated at the CBD edge or is the CBD merely a relatively blank area on a map showing distribution of any one of them?

A graduate student, working under the senior author's direction, attempted to answer these questions [18] for one city: Worcester, Mass. For each type of establishment suspected of marking the edge, a separate map of central Worcester was used and each occurrence was spotted on through field work. On each of these maps lines were drawn at regular distance intervals parallel to the CBD edge as determined later in this study. These zones were used to measure degrees of concentration.

It was decided that there were two general types of establishments that might show concentration along the CBD border.

[18] Lane J. Johnson: "The Coincidence of Certain Types of Establishments with the Edge of the CBD," unpublished M.A. thesis, Clark University, 1954.

One type might be expected to concentrate in a more or less continuous belt. Rooming houses formed the best example of this type. The work in Worcester brought out a very definite concentration of rooming houses along the CBD border.

The second type consisted of such establishments as supermarkets and filling stations that obviously tended to occur chiefly along important streets leading away from the CBD. In Worcester, establishments of this second type showed less concentration along the CBD edge than was expected, though filling stations and automobile sales agencies showed a slight concentration at the edge. The general conclusion regarding the second type was that, though such establishments were rare within the CBD, they showed no marked concentration at its edge. However, there was a definite tendency for the CBD to be a relatively blank area on the map showing any one of these distributions. Though they showed little edge concentration, the beginning of their occurrence along any street leading away from the CBD might serve to mark the edge. Some combination of these establishments—for example, a supermarket and a filling station, or a supermarket, a filling station, and automobile sales rooms—would appear to be a more effective telltale of the edge than any one of them alone.

This study of edge establishments would need to be carried further and applied to a number of cities in order to arrive at any worthwhile generalizations. From the standpoint of CBD delimitation, however, it appears that this line of work could be of value only for a preliminary, rough spotting of the boundary of the district on the principal streets leading away from the center.

LAND USE MAPPING BASIC TO CURRENT PROJECT

As various techniques were tested, the authors became increasingly convinced that detailed land use mapping furnished the most practical common denominator for the determination of comparable CBD's. The district is best thought of as an assemblage of land uses, some of which are especially distinctive. Moreover, land use maps are relatively easy to construct since they do not depend upon the availability of any unusual data.

Hence, it was decided to carry out land use mapping in a number of cities, at the same time collecting all other available information that might prove useful in CBD delimitation. The resulting detailed field mapping in nine cities and more limited observations in many others form the chief bases for this study.[19]

Choice of Cities for Study The nine cities in which detailed field mapping was done were chosen with certain definite considerations in mind. In the first place it was decided that restriction of the cities to the same general size group would simplify the problem, since it would rule out great differences due to size alone. Moderate-sized cities rather than very large or very small ones seemed best fitted for the study. Very large cities, such as New York or Philadelphia, have so much individuality as to make generalizations mean little; and in very small cities the CBD is not strikingly enough developed to show all of the features that people have come to associate with the district. With this background of thinking it was decided to use cities whose urbanized areas [20] were in the 150,000 to 250,000 population class (Table 1).[21] This size had the further advantage that there were enough such cities to permit some selectivity. Moreover, the sort of mapping contemplated was more practicable for these than for larger cities.

In addition to the factor of size there were other considerations in selecting the nine cities. In order to avoid local regional peculiarities, cities widely scattered in location were chosen. Also, it was considered desirable to select cities that varied in their basic support. Finally, a few cities were ruled out because preliminary correspondence showed that the maps and data available were so limited as seriously to handicap the proposed field work.

Through application of the criteria that have been described, the nine cities were selected for study. They may be briefly

[19] The field mapping and other field observations, except in the case of Roanoke, were carried on by the junior author between October 1, 1952, and June, 1953. The Roanoke mapping was done by graduate students as one of the field exercises in the 1953 fall field camp of the Graduate School of Geography, Clark University.

[20] As defined by the 1950 United States Census.

[21] Roanoke, though it has a somewhat smaller population total than the others, was studied because of adjacency to the Clark University fall field camp.

characterized as follows.[22] Worcester is an old manufacturing city of New England. Grand Rapids is a younger, Midwest, manufacturing center. Salt Lake City is primarily a wholesale center, but is also the state capital and a religious center. Tacoma is a diversified city with manufacturing predominant. Sacramento is primarily a state capital. Phoenix, a relatively new city, is more predominantly a retail center than any of the others, but is also a state capital and winter resort. Tulsa, like Phoenix a young city, is diversified, though retail trade is outstanding. Mobile is a port, but like Tulsa is a diversified city where retail trade is predominant. And Roanoke, a city created by a railroad, is likewise a diversified city where retail trade is outstanding.

Only Central Areas Mapped It was obviously unnecessary as well as impracticable to map the entire area of each city. There is in every city a central section where department stores, banks, offices, and the like are concentrated to a greater degree than anywhere else. This is unquestionably part of the CBD. The field mapping in each of the nine cities covered this obvious area and extended far enough beyond to encompass any land that could possibly be thought of as included in the CBD. Even this, in the size group of cities dealt with, meant the mapping, in the average city, of a total area of somewhat less than one square mile.

TABLE 1

Population Data, April 1, 1950, for the Nine Cities Studied
(U. S. Census of Population)

	Incorporated City	Urbanized Area
Worcester, Mass.	203,486	219,330
Grand Rapids, Mich.	176,515	226,817
Salt Lake City, Utah	182,121	227,368
Tacoma, Wash.	143,673	167,667
Sacramento, Calif.	137,572	211,777
Phoenix, Ariz.	106,818	216,038
Tulsa, Okla.	182,740	206,311
Mobile, Ala.	129,009	182,963
Roanoke, Va.	91,921	106,682

[22] The following characterizations are based in part on Victor Jones: "Economic Classification of Cities and Metropolitan Areas," The Municipal Year Book, 1953, pp. 49-54 and 69, and Table IV.

Central Business Uses It early became apparent to the writers that not all the land uses represented in the CBD were equally at home. There is a considerable difference in this respect between a church, engulfed by CBD development, and a department store, which depends upon the advantages that a CBD location has to offer. A decision as to what were and were not typical central business uses was a necessary preliminary to delimitation.

The really essential central business functions appeared to be the retailing of goods and services for a profit and the performing of various office functions. Stores of all sorts that retail merchandise, shops that offer services, and the whole miscellany of offices so often found near the center of a city—all appear to represent characteristic central business uses. Similar stores and shops and offices occur elsewhere in the city, but their area of maximum concentration is the CBD, where they are oriented around the peak land value intersection and where they serve the city as a whole rather than any one section or any one group of people. These establishments, it was decided, were the ones upon which any delimitation of the CBD should be based.

In accordance with this decision, various types of land use, though found in the CBD, were considered not to represent real central business uses. Wholesaling is one of these. It is not a central business function since it is localized more by the presence of railroads or other transportation media than by the pull of centrality. Even more obviously, factories and residential units (private dwellings, apartment houses, and rooming houses),[23] though represented in the CBD, are not characteristic elements.

Absence of the normal profit motive excludes from the characteristic CBD list municipal and other governmental buildings and parks, churches and other religious establishments and land, public and other non-profit making schools, organizational establishments such as the quarters of fraternal orders, and several other types of space occupance. The establishments included in this group perform necessary functions, and they add to the

---

[23] The residential sequence extends from private dwellings to hotels, and the line between non-central business and central business in this sequence is difficult to draw. In this study the break was considered as coming between rooming houses and obviously transient hotels.

crowding, and hence to the problems, of the CBD. But it is the contention of the writers that these are not the central businesses that give the area its essential character.

It may be argued that certain forms of retailing are non-central business in character, and it is undoubtedly true that super-markets, filling stations, and automobile sales agencies are rare within the CBD. But if these specific types of retailing are non-central business there are others that are only a little less so; and, although wholesaling is considered non-central business, there are certain specific types of wholesaling that profit considerably from a central location. In short a whole series of centrality judgments are involved that are unnecessary and beyond the scope of this study. In view of these considerations the writers decided not to attempt to split the retailing group.

An exception to the general rule regarding factories may be made in the case of the city newspaper. To a considerable degree getting out a newspaper is a manufacturing operation. Yet the same concern sells newspapers and sells advertising in the newspapers, and is so closely identified with central business activities that the authors have considered the whole operation as part of the CBD assemblage along with stores retailing merchandise, shops offering services, and the miscellany of offices.

A problem is presented, too, by large specialized office buildings such as the home office of an insurance company or the home or regional office of an oil company, a telephone company, a steamship line, or a railroad. In some respects these do not fit into the group of characteristic CBD establishments since some of them might equally well be located almost anywhere in the city. Still, they derive benefits from the association with banks, lawyers' offices, restaurants, and the like in the CBD. Because of this and because they are so much like other CBD establishments in type they are included in the group of characteristic establishments.

In line with the foregoing, it was decided that, for the purposes of this study, certain uses would be considered as non-central business in character. These are listed in Table 2. All of them are found to some degree in the CBD, but they are considered to be either antagonistic to true central business uses, as in the case of permanent residences or industrial establishments, or neutral, as in the case of government establishments.

With this background we are in a position to consider in detail the mapping method that was used and the techniques that were based on the mapping.

TABLE 2

GENERAL TYPES OF LAND OCCUPANCE CONSIDERED TO BE NON-CENTRAL BUSINESS IN CHARACTER

Permanent residences (including apartment houses and rooming houses)
Governmental and public (including parks and public schools as well as establishments carrying out city, county, state, and federal governmental functions)
Organizational establishments (churches, fraternal orders, colleges, etc.)
Industrial establishments (except newspapers)
Wholesaling
Vacant buildings or stores
Vacant lots
Commercial storage

The Mapping Procedure For the central area of the average American city a lot line map on a scale of 1 inch to 200 feet is available. This was the normal map equipment for the CBD mapping described in this paper.[24] The desired results were three maps: one for the ground floor, one for the second floor, and a third that generalized the remaining floors.

In the land use mapping of the nine cities due cognizance had to be taken of the upper stories. Most planning agency land use maps show ground floor uses only, but the CBD involves three dimensions. Any measures of intensity of land use in the district must take the vertical dimension into account; in addition, the land use of upper stories is a part of the CBD picture just as is that of the ground floor.

Though maps for each floor can be constructed directly in the field, the profile method was found to be more efficient for recording the desired information. The profiles are made on ordi-

[24] Though the scale of one inch to 200 feet is recommended, a larger scale can be used. For two of the nine cities lot line maps at one inch to 200 feet were not available so maps at one inch to 100 feet were used instead. With larger scales mapping can be done in great detail but the time required to do the work increases correspondingly.

nary lined tablets. The horizontal scale is the same as the scale of the base map, and the space between each two lines on the tablet is considered as one story. On these profiles each non-central business unit on each floor (as shown in Table 2) is indicated by an "X." Each other space unit is marked with the letter "C," which indicates the presence of any central business use. To discriminate between the individual central business or non-central business uses requires much more mapping time and is unnecessary if the purpose is merely one of delimitation.[25] Every floor of use is thought of as one story in vertical dimension. A parking lot is mapped as one story of "C," and a vacant lot as one story of "X." Moreover, each building is mapped as if occupying its entire lot, unless the deviation from this situation is extreme. In general throughout the CBD such deviations are slight, and to map separately the small scraps of land that may be left over around buildings would require more time than the slightly increased accuracy of result would justify. The completed profiles show at a glance the number of floors for each space unit as well as indicating the use.

In order to make the method clear, the details of profiling for one block in downtown Tulsa are shown in Figure III. Section I shows a plan view of the block as it would appear on a typical lot line map of the downtown area of any city. Section II shows the profiles of the four sides of the block, and Section III shows the three resulting land use maps of the block. Note that even the ground floor map departs considerably from the original lot lines. The lot at the corner of Fourth Street and Detroit Avenue, for example, is divided into seven establishments.

The third map, the "upper floors" map, is a generalized representation of the third and higher floors. Floors above the second normally are so uniform in use that such a generalization is practicable. On this upper floors map the letters represent third floor use only, unless a number is given. If there are more than three stories then a number is shown. This tells the number of floors of the particular use above the second. Thus, on this map

[25] The research project on which this paper is based went far beyond delimitation. Therefore, in the basic field work, land use, in both the "X" and in the "C" categories, was broken down in considerable detail. The resulting information regarding the several cities will be discussed in later articles.

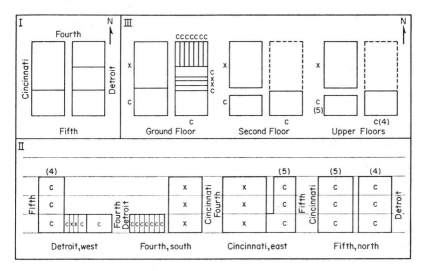

FIGURE III. A block of downtown Tulsa on a scale of 1 inch to 200 feet. A plan view of the block showing lot lines (I) is followed by profiles (II) and the three resulting land use maps (III). Each profile is drawn from left to right as the observer faces the block. "DETROIT, west" refers to the west side of Detroit Avenue; "FOURTH, south" to the south side of Fourth Street, and so on around the block.

the letter "X" standing alone shows that the building is three stories in height with the upper floor in non-central business use. And the letter "C" accompanied by the number "5" indicates that central business use prevails, or at least predominates, on the third to seventh floors of a seven story building.

Of course it is possible for sharp differences in land use to exist above the third floor. If these are substantial and obvious they should be taken into account. Suppose, for example, that a department store occupies the lower three floors of a five-story building and that the upper two floors of the building are occupied by some fraternal organization. The simplest way to take care of the situation would be to show, on the upper floors map, one-third of the space as C(3) and two-thirds as X(3). In this connection it must be remembered that the three maps are not made to show exact distribution of central business and non-central business establishments on each floor but merely to form the basis for calculations leading to delimitation of the CBD.

Although a single block is used here in order to make the

method of profiling and map construction clear, in practice the profile may be made for the same side of a street for a series of blocks. And the end product is not a number of maps of individual blocks but three maps (ground floor, second floor, and upper floors) for the entire central section of the city.[26]

More detail is shown regarding one group of non-central business uses—governmental establishments. Though shown with the X designation just as are other non-central business establishments, they are also labeled in some manner on the maps. This is done because, in the delimitation method recommended later in this paper, a special rule is applied to such structures.

It would be possible to make more exact profiles of the upper floors so that detailed maps of the third, fourth, or any number of floors could be made, but this more exact profiling would require an inordinate amount of field time. In the present study the three maps were considered adequate and the profiling was done accordingly.

Blocks vs. Streets At this stage a decision had to be made—whether to base calculations upon street frontage or upon blocks. Frontage is admittedly more realistic, since the tendency for land use to differ by streets rather than by blocks is a matter of common observation.

But there were obvious difficulties. Using street frontage would result in certain sides of blocks falling within the CBD and others not. To obtain a continuous CBD area, which seemed desirable from a practical standpoint, it would then be necessary to decide how to split the blocks. Blocks vary so much in shape (see, e.g., the map of Worcester, Figure IV) as to make such an operation decidedly difficult. At best, subjective judgments would be involved, and the writers were seeking a method that would be sufficiently objective and standardized so that it could be widely used with comparable results. Any division smaller than blocks would imply, too, a precision of mapping which it was felt would be impractical. Working with street frontage had the further disadvantage that it did not lend itself to calculations of the contents of the CBD. After considering the pros and cons at length the authors decided to work with block units. Even this

---

[26] Of course for a city substantially larger than the ones worked with in this study each map might have to be presented in several sections.

did not completely solve the problem, as it is sometimes hard to decide what constitutes a block. In general the practice was followed of considering that a block ended only where a named street occurred.

Office Calculations The three land use maps are by no means end products. The office calculations that follow involve, first of all, finding the area of all floor space units. For this purpose a pattern of squares .1 inch on a side and ruled on transparent paper was used. All measurements are based on floor areas, but, since an assumption of equal height is made for all floors, the relationships between areas is unaltered if the height factor is omitted from calculations. A vacant lot or a parking lot is considered to be one floor in height just as is a one-story building, so that the total ground floor space in the block is the total of all ground floor area minus alleys. Streets are left out of the calculations; so, too, are railroad tracks or yards. Second floor space is the total floor area at the second floor level of all buildings that are two stories or greater in height; and upper floor space is the total of all floor areas above the second floor. The system of tabulating the data resulting from the area calculations will be clear from a comparison of Table 3 with Figure III. To simplify later checking, all measurements begin at the southeast corner of the block and proceed clockwise around the block.

We are now in a position to calculate some interesting ratios for each block.

The first of these is the *Total Height Index* or height in floors if all of the space were spread uniformly over the block. It is obtained by dividing the total floor space (at all levels) by the total ground floor space (Table 3). (THI = total floor space ÷ total ground floor space.)

The *Central Business Height Index* is the number of floors of central business uses if these are thought of as spread evenly over the block. It is obtained by dividing the total floor area of all central business uses by the total ground floor area of the block. (CBHI = central business space ÷ total ground floor space.)

The *Central Business Intensity Index* is the proportion of all floor space in central business uses. It is the percentage that total floor area of central business uses makes up of the total

TABLE 3

MEASUREMENTS AND CALCULATIONS FOR TULSA BLOCK SHOWN IN
FIGURE III

(All measurements are in square inches at a scale of 1 inch to
200 feet. Measurements begin with the first land use at the
southeast corner of the block and proceed clockwise around
the block)

First Floor		Second Floor		Upper Floors			Block Inventory	
Use	Space	Use	Space	Use	Space	Adjusted Value	Use	Space
C	0.350	C	0.350	C	0.350 x 4	1.400	C	4.935
C	0.385	C	0.315	C	0.315 x 5	1.575	X	2.135
X	0.665	X	0.665	X	0.665	0.665		
C	0.050						Total	7.070
C	0.050							
C	0.050							
C	0.050							
C	0.050							
C	0.050							
C	0.140							
X	0.070							
X	0.070							
C	0.070							
Total 2.100		1.330				3.640	Total Space = 7.070	

Total Height Index = Total Space ÷ Ground Floor Area = 7.070 ÷ 2.100 = 3.4.

Central Business Intensity Index = ("C" space ÷ Total Space) × 100 = 2.100 = 2.4.

Central Business Intensity Index = ("C" space ÷ Total Space) × 100 = (4.935 ÷ 7.070) × 100 = 69.8%.

floor space at all levels. (CBII = [central business space ÷ total floor space] × 100).

In summary, note that the block shown in Figure III has a Total Height Index of 3.4, a Central Business Height Index of 2.4, and a Central Business Intensity Index of 69.8 per cent.

DELIMITATION TECHNIQUES BASED ON
THE LAND USE MAP

Having described the method of land use mapping, the construction of the maps, and the measurements and calculations based on these maps, we can now consider techniques of delimitation which the maps make possible.

Building Heights Building heights furnish a simple, approximate method of delimiting the CBD. The district is likely to stand out on an air photo as the area of taller than average buildings. For more exact work a map of building heights can easily be constructed from the land use maps earlier described, since they show the number of floors for each building. Or, a building height map on a block basis may be constructed using the Total Height Index described above. In either case a limiting value must be decided upon to mark the edge of the CBD.

In a general way such maps show the location of the CBD. But building heights have the obvious disadvantage that they take no account of use. Apartment houses, government buildings, factories, and other non-central business uses may rank with office buildings or department stores in terms of height. At best, then, the building height map can furnish only a rough indication of the extent of the CBD.

Central Business Height Index Floors of central business uses is a much better basis for delimiting the CBD than building height. Just as in the case of the building heights maps, a map of floors of central business use can be made on a building basis, the height shown for each building being the total height minus the floors of non-central business uses. But the resulting map presents a very uneven pattern and is difficult to work with.

Use of the Central Business Height Index by blocks gives a more valuable picture since many of the irregularities are ironed out. In the present study it was decided that the Central Business Height Index of one (the equivalent of a one-story building devoted to central business uses and covering the entire block) gave a good limiting value. Figure IV shows which blocks met this requirement in Worcester. This technique has a great advantage over the use of building height since it rules out non-central business. But it has one serious limitation: it fails to show the proportion of space in central business uses. Though central business uses might average two stories for a given block, these two stories might be overlain by three stories of apartments or three stories of manufacturing.

Central Business Intensity Index The proportion of space

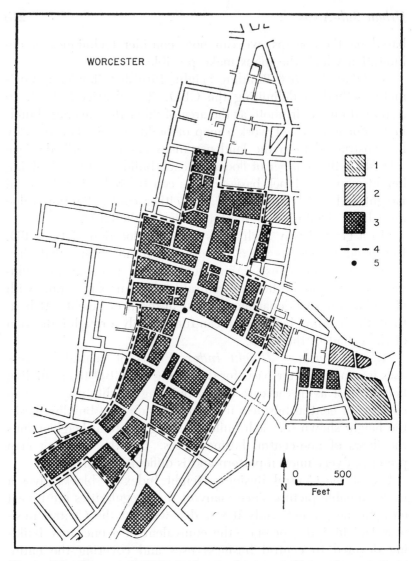

FIGURE IV. Worcester's CBD is elongated in a roughly north-south direction along its axis, Main Street. Relatively steep slopes to the west, particularly north of the center, and the presence of railroad tracks to the east help to account for this shape. The peak land value intersection is at the point where Pleasant Street reaches Main from the west and continues southeastward as Front Street. In Worcester as in Grand Rapids the delimitation problem is complicated by a great range of block sizes. Compare this map with Figures I and II.

Key to legend: 1. Central Business Height Index of 1 or more; 2. Central Business Intensity Index of 50 or more; 3. Central Business Height Index of 1 or more and Central Business Intensity Index of 50 or more; 4. CBD boundary; 5. Peak land value intersection.

devoted to central business uses can be shown on a block basis by means of the Central Business Intensity Index. A limiting value of 50 per cent was decided upon, since it was felt that unless at least half of the available space were devoted to central business uses a block should hardly be considered as belonging in the CBD. Figure IV shows the extent in Worcester of blocks that met this intensity requirement.

A delimitation based on the Central Business Intensity Index by itself has this fault: it takes no account of the gross amount of central business floor space. A block might have a Central Business Intensity Index of 50 per cent, which would place it within the CBD, but this might be achieved by a one-story building which, though entirely devoted to central business uses, occupied only half of an otherwise vacant block.

THE CENTRAL BUSINESS INDEX METHOD

If both the Central Business Height Index and the Central Business Intensity Index are considered, a more realistic delimitation is achieved. In this combination of techniques a block, to be considered CBD in character, must have a Central Business Height Index of one or more and a Central Business Intensity Index of 50 per cent or more. In Figure IV the crosshatched blocks are those that met both criteria.

Although the group of crosshatched blocks around the peak value intersection of any one of the cities is a close approximation of our final CBD, some decisions still have to be made in drawing the exact line. There are crosshatched blocks separated from the main cluster; there are blocks which fail to "make the grade" on one or both indexes but are surrounded by blocks that do; and there are still other irregular cases that have to be taken care of.

To meet the special problems just mentioned the following special rules were set up:

(1) To be considered part of the CBD a block must be part of a contiguous group surrounding the peak value intersection. Even though a block touches the others only at one corner it is considered contiguous.

(2) A block that does not reach the required index values but is surrounded by blocks that do is considered part of the CBD.

(3) A block completely occupied by the buildings and grounds of a city hall or other municipal office building, a municipal auditorium, city police or fire department headquarters, or a central post office is included within the CBD if it is adjacent to blocks meeting the standard requirements. In some cities it will be necessary to add to the list the buildings and grounds of certain other government buildings: the courthouse in a county seat; the state capitol building of a state capital; and occasionally certain federal buildings in addition to the post office, e.g., a federal court building or other federal office building the activities of which are closely integrated with those of the city and the region. In no instance should such government buildings as those described in this paragraph result in the extension of the CBD for more than one block beyond normal CBD blocks. Thus where there is a group of state buildings occupying several blocks that border the CBD, as in some state capitals, the whole group is considered non-CBD.

(4) If the structures mentioned in Rule 3 occupy only part of a block which is contiguous to other CBD blocks and if the inclusion of these establishments as central business would bring the two indexes of the block to the required totals then the block is considered part of the CBD.

The *Central Business Index Method,* which we are here suggesting, involves the application of the two indexes and the special rules just described. Using this method, boundaries were drawn for Worcester.[27]

[27] Would it be possible to achieve the same or a close approximation of the same CBD boundaries through air photograph interpretation? If so there would be certain obvious advantages, the chief of which is that it would then be unnecessary to visit a city in order to delimit its CBD.

A definite answer to this question would require complete air coverage for each of the nine cities, and the carrying out the inquiry in detail would be a major project in itself. It appears to the writers, however, that the chief possibilities lie in a building-height map from which various non-central business uses have been eliminated. It should be possible in most instances to identify private homes, rooming houses, and apartment houses; parks, public schools, churches, and some governmental structures such as a post office, city hall, or courthouse; the buildings and grounds of a college or university; most factories, where they occupy independent buildings; and vacant lots. On the other hand certain types of land occupance which were listed as non-central business in character appear essentially impossible to identify from air photographs. In this group are upper floor residential use; wholesale establishments; commercial storage; vacant building space; factories when not in a separate building; some governmental establishments; and such organizational space use as the quarters of fraternal orders.

THE BOUNDARY ANALYZED

A more careful analysis of the boundary in Figure IV will show how application of the indexes and special rules work out.

In Worcester a block far to the south and a cluster of three small blocks to the east were omitted from the CBD because of noncontiguity. Special cases of included blocks are the post office block, near the southern end of the district; the block occupied by the city hall and Common just southeast of the peak value intersection; and, farther north, two blocks that reflect in turn Rule 1 and Rule 4. A county courthouse and a municipal building at the northern edge of the mapped area were excluded because they are separated from the main CBD area by several blocks that do not meet the required index values.

EVALUATION OF THE CENTRAL BUSINESS INDEX METHOD

The Central Business Index Method is not presented as an absolute and final answer to the problem of delimiting the CBD, but rather as a first step in that direction.

It should be re-emphasized, first of all, that the boundary drawn on any one of the maps is not *the* boundary of the CBD for that city. To think that it is would be naïve indeed since the edge of the CBD is a zone or belt of transition. But the area delimited in each case does include the major part of the CBD for that city, and the boundary is believed to be as fair an approximation of the zone as a single line can be. Moreover, since each of the boundaries is drawn according to the same indexes and rules the areas delimited in the various cities are comparable for analysis purposes.

There are certain shortcomings of the method of which the authors are well aware. For instance, delimitation is by block units, and block size varies greatly from city to city and even within cities. Also, the indexes are based on a subjective classification of certain establishments as "central business" and others as "non-central business." The authors realize, too, that there is a factor of quality which the method fails to take into account. There may be two blocks with identical indexes but one block may represent a much lower grade or quality of establishments than the other.

Finally, the method was applied only to cities of a limited size range. Will it work for cities of 25,000 population? For very large cities? The authors believe that the use of the block unit may result in too great a percentage error in very small cities, but that the method should be applicable to large cities where it may well serve to bring out secondary business districts as well as the CBD. The only way really to answer these questions is by trying out the method on cities of varying sizes.

Balanced against the shortcomings of the method is the fact that it works and can be carried out rapidly. In fact, after some experience, it is possible for the field man to determine almost at a glance the blocks that are unquestionably CBD and those that are unquestionably not, leaving only a fringe of doubtful blocks to be mapped. And the method is sufficiently objective so that the resulting areas obtained by workers in different cities should be reasonably comparable.

THE USE OF LOCAL FACILITIES IN A METROPOLIS *

DONALD L. FOLEY

The rise of metropolitan centers has undoubtedly been accompanied by significant changes in social pattern. Few urban studies have directly investigated the place of neighborhood or local community life within the larger metropolis. It is not yet known, for example, to what extent individual metropolitan residents carry out their various out-of-the-home activities locally, as in a rural village or in a small community, or, conversely, to what extent they carry out these activities on the metropolitan scale.

Previous research has demonstrated a decline in the primary-group type of urban neighborhood.[1] Such concepts as "com-

* Reprinted from the *American Journal of Sociology*, Vol. 56, No. 3 (November, 1950), pp. 238-246, with permission of author and publisher.

[1] Roderick D. McKenzie, *The Neighborhood: A Study of Local Life in the City of Columbus, Ohio* (Chicago: University of Chicago Press, 1923); M. Wesley Roper, "The City and the Primary Group" (unpublished Ph.D. dissertation, Department of Sociology, University of Chicago, 1935); Bessie A. McClenahan,

munality" and "personal neighborhood," for example, have been suggested as more accurately descriptive of current urban life.[2] The implication is that an individualistic type of social bond, such as that of the voluntary association, has extensively displaced traditional neighborhood ties. The dearth of neighborhood or local-community sentiments and association patterns has been included as an integral feature of the "urban society" when conceived as an ideal type.[3] In certain of these previous studies it has been inferred that, paralleling the decline of the urban neighborhood as a social entity, urban residents were becoming less locally self-sufficient in their use of facilities,[4] coming rather to depend upon facilities located throughout the city.

This article reports a study made in 1947 of facility use by residents of a district in northwest St. Louis.[5] Questions were asked to discover the relative extent of the residents' use of local facilities in contrast to their use of nonlocal facilities; what proportion of their facility use could be classified as local; what proportion as nonlocal or metropolitan; with what factors local- or nonlocal-facility use was associated; which facility uses were the most local; which the least local; what types of residents tended to be locally oriented in their use of facilities; which nonlocally.

To answer these questions required an examination of day-to-day, away-from-the-home activities of the urban dweller. Has he lost touch with local activities? Or does there still remain a vestige of the local community, in the sense of a service center at

---

The Changing Urban Neighborhood (Los Angeles: University of Southern California, 1929).

[2] McClenahan, *op. cit.,* and "The Communality: The Urban Substitute for the Traditional Community," *Sociology and Social Research,* XXX (March–April, 1946), 264-74. Frank L. Sweetser, Jr., "A New Emphasis for Neighborhood Research," *American Sociological Review,* VII (August, 1942), 525-533.

[3] Cf. Louis Wirth, "Urbanism as a Way of Life," *American Journal of Sociology,* XLIV (July, 1938), 1-24.

[4] "Use of facilities" and "facility use" are used synonymously as generic terms meaning the functional dependence by residents on such organized, specifically located meeting places or service centers as stores, places of employment, schools, churches, doctors' offices, and movie theaters. Whereas the "primary-group type of neighborhood" involves informal social relations of "neighboring," the "use of facilities" is conceived of as being more formal and as involving specific, organized "facilities."

[5] More completely reported as the writer's "Urban Neighborhood Facilities: A Study of a Residential District in Northwest St. Louis" (unpublished Ph.D. dissertation, Department of Sociology-Anthropology, Washington University, 1948), esp. chap. iii.

least, within the larger metropolitan area? It was the writer's hypothesis (using the term in a general or guiding sense) that metropolitan residents make relatively little use of local facilities.[6]

That the approach in this research is ecological is admitted; and, if this study were to be considered in isolation, it might be appraised as peripheral to sociology. But the study of as complex a phenomenon as metropolitan social life presents an unusual challenge to the researcher to utilize an assortment of complementary research techniques. The present study, then, is most logical if its findings are treated as but one segment of a more comprehensive framework of urban analysis.[7]

A five-square mile residential district in northwest St. Louis was selected for the study. (See accompanying map.) The district is located between 4.5 and 6.5 miles from downtown St. Louis and is just within the political limits of the central city. The characteristics of the district and its residents are generally intermediate between those of the more central portions of the city and of the suburbs beyond; it could probably be termed middle class, shading toward lower middle class. That the population of the area is generally representative of St. Louis is shown in Table 1.

In a number of ways this district is more homogeneous than is St. Louis as a whole. For example, the range of 1940 average-block rentals for the district is from $15.00 to $83.00; for the city as a whole (not known for the county) it was from $1.00 to

[6] Literally to test this hypothesis was difficult, for the hypothesis assumed that one could determine with some finality just where the line was to be drawn between "local" and "nonlocal" facilities and what in a metropolitan setting would constitute "relatively little use" of local facilities. Lacking previous definitions, an attempt to force a strict test of the hypothesis would have involved a certain arbitrariness, unwarranted at this stage of the research, in selection of appropriate criteria. Consequently the findings are offered in such form as to be relevant to the hypothesis, without definitely upholding or rejecting it. The findings as they are reported are, then, largely descriptive, with certain tentative classifications suggested upon which further research could draw.

[7] An exploratory attempt to use this general approach in studying social organizational and social psychological aspects is being undertaken in the sociology department of the University of Rochester. Under way is an attempt to translate the idea of a "local-community" to "metropolitan" continuum into workable terms. Pilot research in Rochester has included such aspects as neighborliness and sense of local identification as well as use of facilities. The goals of such an undertaking include the possibility of stating where, along this continuum, various activities and/or attitudes of urban residents seem to belong.

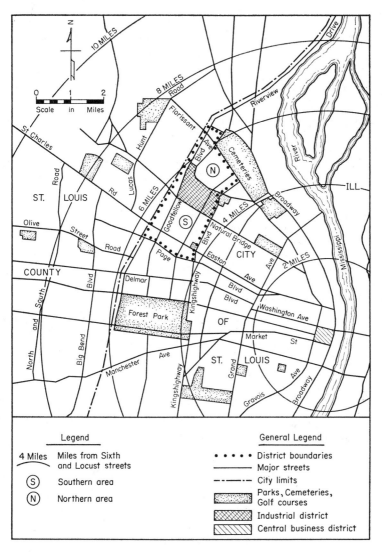

Residential District in Northwest St. Louis in Its Metropolitan Setting.

$293.00. In one important respect, intentionally a part of the research design, the district differs from the larger St. Louis community: it contains practically no Negroes—although Negroes constituted eleven per cent of the total population of St. Louis City and County in 1940—and was selected because such complications as segregation were thereby avoided. The leading foreign-born

TABLE 1

SELECTED CHARACTERISTICS FOR THE RESIDENTIAL DISTRICT
STUDIED AND FOR ST. LOUIS CITY AND COUNTY

Characteristics (from the 1940 Census Unless Otherwise Stated)	District Studied	City of St. Louis and St. Louis County *
Percentage of population under 14 years of age	19.8	18.7
Percentage of population 65 years of age and over	6.6	7.3
Percentage of population foreign-born	11.6	6.7
Percentage of population 25 years and over with 6 years or less schooling	18.8	21.4
Percentage of employed population 14 years old and over classified as "operatives and kindred workers" or as "laborers"	29.0	28.1
Average monthly dwelling-unit rental	$27.53	$29.24
Percentage of dwelling units owner-occupied.	37.4	34.4
Ratio of dwelling units to residential structures	1.5	1.7
Ratio of population per passenger automobile †	5.6	5.2
Total population	71,899	1,090,278

* These two units represent roughly the Missouri portion of the St. Louis metropolitan district as defined in 1940. The Illinois segment of the district (with about 268,000 population) was not included, because certain needed statistics were not available.

† Estimated as of 1946 by the writer.

nationality represented in the district is Russian, presumably Jewish, on the whole, while the nationality in the city is German. The southern portion of the district is generally the older and the more densely developed (35 persons per gross acre) and is better served by commercial facilities. The largest single outlying shopping center in metropolitan St. Louis—Wellston, with nearly four hundred retail stores—lies at the southwest corner of this southern segment, and other commercial centers and clusters are also readily accessible. The northern portion of the district, with its single-family-home type of development, is somewhat suburban in character, with a lower density (20 persons per gross acre). Many of its residents are a considerable distance from any shopping center.

Schools, churches, movie theaters, and other facilities are generally available. There is probably more than typical opportunity for employment, particularly in the industrial area within the district. Not available in the district, although accessible in varying degrees, are public high schools; large parks (of which St. Louis has several); and facilities, other than movie theaters, providing professional entertainment such as major-league baseball or the outdoor municipal opera.

To obtain a representative sample of the estimated 20,000 families living in the district, an areal sampling technique was used and an optimum sample size of about 400 families was set. A panel of addresses was selected by drawing every nth dwelling unit from the most recent Polk city directory, using only street addresses falling within the district. After twelve addresses were dropped as nonresidential and 36 addresses were substituted (from certain predesignated extras) for a similar number of nonresponses, the final sample numbered 401 families. At least one member of each family was interviewed on the use made by the various family members of selected facilities. Each address was revisited, if necessary, as many as five or six times, in an effort to locate some family member. Straight refusals to answer were given in ten families; illness, summer vacationing, and odd working hours accounted for the remaining cases where substitution was necessary.

Each respondent was asked to tell where every family member (over five years of age) went for the following: (1) employment, (2) food, (3) clothing, (4) furniture or household equipment, (5) school, (6) church, (7) medical care, (8) outdoor recreation, (9) miscellaneous indoor activities. Each member's use of a specific facility was treated as a "report." (For example, the use of two different food stores by a housewife was treated as two reports; the use of a church by all four members of a family was treated as four reports.) On this basis, there was an average of sixteen reports per family—6,216 reports in all. Each report included background information about the family member involved, location of home, type and location of the facility, type of transportation used, and the distance from home to facility. The interviewing was carried out from June to August, 1947, and reflects summertime uses of the facilities.

The major variable was the airline distance from home to facility, and this served as the primary index of local use.[8] The

---

[8] This use of distance as an index excluded trip time and cost and did not measure either frequency or intensity of facility use. Methodological research

frequency distribution of this major variable provided a primary answer in itself. In addition, the distribution of facility's uses as falling within, adjacent to, or away from the district was examined. Also analyzed were the relations between the major variable—distance—and the following: (1) type of facility use, (2) type of transportation, and (3) certain other variables pertaining to family or personal background.

One could undoubtedly interpret the findings in a number of ways. One could point to very considerable evidence that the residents made relatively great use of facilities located well outside the district and often several miles from the users' homes, thus indirectly supporting the writer's hypothesis. Or, one could find strong supporting evidence that the use of facilities located near home and within the immediate district was surprisingly extensive considering the fact that the district is in a metropolis. A third interpretation—and one that tends to take both of the former ones into account—is that large-city living involves an intricate balance between the relative use of local and nonlocal facilities. The writer was impressed by the different "levels" of facility use that were observed and the wide distribution of facility uses among the levels.

The study revealed that 47 per cent of the reported facility uses were within one mile of the user's home, 20 per cent were between one and three miles from home, and 33 per cent were at least three miles away. About 30 per cent were within 0.5 mile; ten per cent were at least six miles away. The median distance from home was 1.2 miles, while the arithmetic mean was estimated as about 2.4 miles. (See Table 2.) It is thus apparent that a little over half of all the reports involved the use of facilities located in or near the residential district.

The transportation, as facility-use reports showed, was: walking from home, 36 per cent; public transit from home, 31 per

---

considered beyond the scope of this particular study was called for. In the writer's pilot study of 50 families he used travel time as an index and ascertained the frequency of each facility's use. The final decision simply to use distance was based on these considerations: Distance provides a clear-cut, reliable measure along a single continuum; it reduces the time and complexity of interviewing and analysis operations; and for the purposes of this study (for the question of transportation economics was not being raised) it provides a generally valid measure of local versus nonlocal facility use.

TABLE 2

Location of Facility Use		Percentage Distribution of Reports Analyzed
Within or adjacent to district		53
Within the district	41	
Adjacent to the district *	12	
Away from district		47
In central business district †	14	
Other "away" location	33	
Total of all facility uses		100

* Included as "adjacent" were facilities that were within about a quarter-mile of the district. For the commercial facilities, the bulk of those classed as adjacent were located in four outlying shopping centers—Wellston, Pine Lawn, Jennings, and Easton and Kingshighway (including a Sears, Roebuck store)—on the periphery of the district.
† The 84-block area bounded by Franklin Avenue, Third Street, Market Street, and Twelfth Boulevard.

cent; and automobile from home, 30 per cent.[9] (Three per cent were classed in a miscellaneous category including "from other than home," such as shopping from place of work.)

Thus between one-third and one-half of the reported facility uses could be classified as "local." Table 3 gives alternative per-

TABLE 3

Facilities	Per Cent
Within ½ mile from home	30
To which walked from home	36
Within the district	41
Within 1 mile from home	47
Within or adjacent to the district	53

tinent measures and corresponding percentages, 100 per cent in each case equaling the total of all the facility-use reports. There could be two possible interpretations here of "nonlocal": (1) Local and nonlocal might be dichotomous, nonlocal including all

[9] Of the families sampled, 48 per cent had no automobile; 37 per cent had an automobile, but, because it was used as transportation to and from work, it was not available during the day; 15 per cent had an automobile available for family use during the day, although not necessarily driven then.

those facilities not classed as local. In such a case, obviously, between two-thirds and one-half of the reports of facility uses were nonlocal. (2) Local and nonlocal might be conceived of as extreme positions on the continuum with a middle or intermediate classification as well. Nonlocal would include only facilities three miles or more (three miles representing a little over halfway downtown), in which case one-third of the facility-use reports would be included.

It is to be expected that children in attending school will go a shorter distance than will adults in shopping for items that are mainly carried in downtown department stores. How various types of facility uses were arrayed according to their average distance from the user's home is shown in Table 4. Whether

TABLE 4

SELECTED FACILITY USES RANKED ACCORDING TO LOCALIZATION

Facility Uses *	Avail-ability of Facility †	No. of Reports Analyzed	Mileage from User's Home to Facility Median	Standard Error
Food shopping, at small stores	A	351	0.23	.06
Attendance at Orthodox Jewish synagogues	L	67	0.23	.04
Elementary-school attendance	L	148	0.35	.05
Children's use of playgrounds	L	58	0.49	.06
Catholic church attendance	L	395	0.50	.03
Food shopping, at large stores	A	222	0.55	.09
Movie attendance, at small theaters. .	A	1,081‡	0.57	.05
Protestant church attendance	A	342	0.66	.09
Clothing, household-equipment, or furniture shopping, at small stores§	A	241	0.82	.18
Bowling	A	60	1.39	.23
Attendance at Reformed Jewish temples	N-L	27	1.55	.21
Playing organized ball	A	24	2.01	.70
High-school attendance	A	51	2.02	.26
Visiting doctors' offices	A	556	2.17	.09
Part-time employment	A	21	2.40	.75
Municipal-opera attendance	N-L	93	2.56	.12
Going to ball games (mostly major league)	N-L	164	2.70	.08
Meetings of fraternal or military organizations	MN-L	51	2.74	.49
College or trade-school attendance. . .	N-L	24	2.86	.66

Facility Uses *	Avail-ability of Facility †	No. of Reports Analyzed	Mileage from User's Home to Facility	
			Median	Standard Error
Meetings of business or professional organizations	MN-L	16	3.53	.64
Full-time employment	MN-L	427	3.87	.14
Outdoor swimming	N-L	86	3.93	.31
Meetings of labor organizations	MN-L	40	3.96	.35
Movie attendance, at large theaters..	N-L	204‡	4.42	.10
Playing golf	N-L	25	5.12	.79
Clothing, household-equipment, or furniture shopping, at large stores§	MN-L	633	5.39	.07
Going on picnics and outings	N-L	241	6.81	.28
Hunting and fishing	N-L	44	‖	...
Total	...	5,999#	1.21	.04

* Since interviewing was done in the summer, facility uses and amounts of participation are valid for summer.

† A, available both locally and nonlocally; L, available (either physically or for administrative or practical reasons) only locally; MN-L, available mainly only nonlocally; N-L, available only nonlocally.

‡ In most cases involves reports on two different theaters per person; hence the large number of reports.

§ Reports were secured only on purchases of clothing of $5.00 or more and of furniture or household equipment of $10.00 or more.

‖ Indeterminate from data, but over 7 miles.

Grand total of 6,216 reports less 217 for which distance was indeterminate.

the particular distance involved choice as between local and nonlocal facilities or whether the distance reflected merely a particular situation as to local or nonlocal availability is indicated in the second column. (A in the column indicates more choice on the part of the user as between a local and a nonlocal facility than does L, MN-L or N-L [see table footnotes].)

An over-all summary of the distribution of facility-use groupings as within or away from the residential district studied is provided in Table 5. The groupings are arranged so as to rank the percentage located away from the district. Rather different types of facilities, such as elementary and secondary schools and colleges, small local stores, and large downtown department stores, are in some instances here grouped intentionally in order to summarize major functions.

From the data presented in Table 5 it is evident that the four general types of facilities that are used preponderantly within or

TABLE 5

LOCATION OF FACILITY-USE REPORTS IN RELATION TO STUDY DISTRICT

Major Groupings of Facility Uses *	No. of Reports Analyzed	Percentage Distribution by Location			
		Within District	Adjacent to District †	Away from District	Total
Food shopping	573	69.3	26.5	4.2	100.0
Church attendance	831	77.1	5.2	17.7	100.0
School attendance	223	68.2	9.0	22.8	100.0
Movie attendance	1,285‡	58.4	15.6	26.0	100.0
Miscellaneous indoor activities (association meetings, sports, etc.).	380	35.5	9.7	54.8	100.0
Visiting doctors' offices	563	29.7	8.5	61.8	100.0
Clothing, household-equipment, or furniture shopping §	874	5.1	19.7	75.2	100.0
Employment	434	17.5	5.3	77.2	100.0
Miscellaneous outdoor activities (sports, outings, etc.)	795	10.1	0.4	89.5	100.0
Total	5,958	41.0	11.7	47.3	100.0

* Since interviewing was done in the summer, facility uses and amounts of participation are valid for summer.

† Included as "adjacent" were facilities that were within about a quarter-mile of the district. For the commercial facilities, the bulk of those classed as adjacent were located in four outlying shopping centers—Wellston, Pine Lawn, Jennings, and Easton and Kingshighway (including a Sears, Roebuck store)—on the periphery of the district.

‡ In most cases involves reports on two different theaters per person; hence the large number of reports.

§ Reports were secured only on purchases of clothing of $5.00 or more and of furniture or household equipment of $10.00 or more.

adjacent to the residential district studied are food stores, churches, schools, and movie theaters. A more detailed breakdown of these major groupings shows certain exceptions. For example, while the attendance at Orthodox Jewish synagogues is 100 per cent within the district, that at Reformed Jewish services is completely away from the district, because there is no local Reformed temple. While movie attendance is heavily concentrated within the area, there is also considerable attendance at the large theaters in or near the central business district. Elementary-school attendance is 98 per cent within or adjacent to the district, and high-school attendance is 49 per cent; attendance at college or trade school is only eight per cent.

The summertime participation in outdoor activities is completely nonlocal except for the children's use of playground facilities. Practically 100 per cent out of the district are major-league ball games, the municipal opera, the zoo or large parks, outdoor swimming, golf, hunting and fishing, and picnics and outings. Attendance at union meetings and at business and professional meetings is about 90 per cent out of the district. Employment is preponderantly nonlocal, although there are firms that hire large numbers of employees within or adjacent to the district.

Further general findings are as follows:

1. The distance from home to facility varies directly with the mode of transportation employed, as is shown in Table 6. The shorter median distance for automobile use was interpreted as being due partly to the many short trips which one would take with an automobile but which one might not care or be able to take by public transit and partly to the extensive use of good public transportation for the five- or six-mile trip downtown.

TABLE 6

User's Transportation	Median Mileage, Home to Facility
Walking from home	0.35
Automobile from home	2.70
Public transit from home	3.50

2. Family nonownership of automobiles is associated with a proportionately greater use of local facilities (Table 7). This

TABLE 7

Family Ownership of Automobile	Median Mileage, Home to Facility
Ownership	1.68
Nonownership	0.82

held true in spite of the fact that the automobile trips per se were of shorter median distance than were trips by public conveyance.

3. Young persons, especially those under twelve years of age, and persons over 65 make relatively the most extensive use of local facilities. Young adults, aged 18 to 34, make the least (see Table 8).

TABLE 8

User's Age in Years	Median Mileage, Home to Facility
5-12	0.70
13-17	0.99
18-24	2.29
25-34	2.28
35-49	1.51
50-64	1.18
65 and over	0.68

4. Table 9 shows that the less the user's formal education, the more use he makes of local facilities. In this statement of relationship, however, age and other factors were not held constant.

TABLE 9

Education of Users 18 Years of Age and Over	Median Mileage, Home to Facility
3 Years' high school or more	2.05
2 Years' high school or less	1.23

5. Females use local facilities more than males do (Table 10). In contrast to that of the adult male, the adult-female average is kept closer to home by nonemployment, by the need to do extensive shopping, and by considerable participation in local leisure activities.

TABLE 10

User's Sex	Median Mileage, Home to Facility
Male	1.77
Female	1.15

6. On the surface there appears to be a direct relation between lower economic status and greater use of local facilities, but when automobile-ownership is held constant, the economic status factor loses most of its significant association with the major variable.

7. Residential density appears to be of greater significance than homeownership in its association with local-facility use. Thus, within the district the older and more densely built-up section, with greater relative tenancy, shows somewhat more extensive use of local facilities than does the sparser, single-family section where homeownership rates are high.

CONCLUSIONS

For the student of urban social organization this study should demonstrate the variety of "levels" at which facilities in a metropolis are used.

A number of facilities are extensively used at the local level. Food and certain other types of shopping, children's attendance at elementary schools and use of play facilities, attendance at certain churches, and patronage of certain small movie theaters take place to a great degree within a neighborhood or local-community sphere. It would be unrealistic to neglect this important local phase of urban social life either as a basis for understanding the present organization or for future planning. Inasmuch as this important condition of city life exists, it appears that the thoroughgoing, ideal-type urban pattern falls short of applicability *in toto*. Our large cities, for all their urbanity, seem to contain an impressive degree of local community life within their metropolitan limits.

But urban life involves more than this local level; many lines of functional interdependency extend out from any designated residential district. In spite of the fact that the area studied was approximately a half-hour or more from St. Louis' central business district, the dependence by residents on that business district was striking—especially for employment, for shopping, and for miscellaneous services. With adequate transportation urban residents will and do go far out of their local districts to make use of many types of facilities. It is apparent that most residents accept the longer trip as a counterpart of the specialization that is so intrinsically a part of metropolitan growth. Thus, trips to the large department stores downtown, to the large theaters, and to doctors' offices in established medical-office buildings are widely and casually reported.

The study—although not specifically carried out with this in mind—suggests striking differences in uses of facilities, even within the same family, and indicates the divisive influences and interests not atypical, it would seem, of the urban family. This phase of the picture deserves further study. One possible classification of facility-use patterns or complexes at a family level might distinguish (1) employment and related facility uses, (2) keeping house and related facility uses, (3) children's use of facilities, and (4) various adult leisure uses of facilities.

The relations between urban-facility-use patterns and users' attitudes were only briefly explored in the present study. Further research is needed so that the association between the level of facility use and the degree to which a resident may or may not be characterized as holding metropolitan (or urban) attitudes can be stated with some degree of certainty. To date there is little research literature on any special operational definition of "metropolitan" (or "urban") attitudes. Is there one continuum along which attitudes may be measured as more, or less, urban? Or are there many continua involved? This, in turn, raises the whole question of the rural-urban dichotomy: Are there degrees of what we call "urban," and are there shades that can be termed "metropolitan"?

Chapter 8

SPATIAL DISTRIBUTION

SOME MEASURES OF THE SPATIAL DISTRIBU-
TION AND REDISTRIBUTION OF
URBAN PHENOMENA *

JACK P. GIBBS **

Most studies of the internal spatial structure of urban areas are concerned with one of three topics:

(1) the nature of the distribution of a given phenomenon in the area,

(2) the association between the distributions of two or more classes of phenomena, or

(3) changes in (1) or (2).

The purpose and subject of the research may vary, of course, but all studies of this kind, insofar as they are concerned with comparisons, are confronted with the same question: how can a distributional pattern be described in a systematic, standardized way? This question poses a problem in measurement, and it will be considered here in relation to four concepts—concentration, deconcentration, centralization, and decentralization.

These concepts ordinarily relate to population; however, they apply to the distribution of any type of unit which can be assigned a fixed point in space. Thus, the locational pattern of business establishments, different types of land use, and non-economic institutions within a city may be described in much the same terms as that of population.

* Written especially for this volume.
** Member of the staff of International Urban Research.

A *concentrated* distribution refers to the clustering of units within the boundaries of a given area. Put most simply this means that a minimum distance separates each unit from all others. The process of *concentration* takes place when the units change position in such a way that the average distance between them decreases. Contrasting terms are *deconcentrated* and *deconcentration;* with the former describing an even spatial distribution of units and the latter applying to distributional changes in which the average distance between units increases. The difference between a concentrated and deconcentrated population is of course one of degree. Concentration and deconcentration as processes are also reckoned in quantitative terms, but they indicate distributional changes in opposite directions.

Centralization, decentralization, centralized, and decentralized signify distributional patterns which are special cases of concentration and related terms. They describe distribution relative to a point taken to be the center of the area. The degree to which units are centralized depends on their average distance from this point, and to the extent this distance increases or decreases, centralization or decentralization has taken place. In a sense centralization and concentration are synonymous; however, a highly concentrated distribution is not a highly centralized one unless the units cluster at the point taken to be the center of the area, while all highly centralized distributions are by definition also highly concentrated.

Although definitions of the basic distributional concepts have been set forth in terms of the distance separating individual units, the measures corresponding to them are typically based on territorial divisions of the area under consideration. This is due, primarily, to the practice of reporting the results of a census enumeration by territorial divisions. As a consequence, when dealing with spatial distribution in an urban area, city, or metropolitan area, the units of observation are located relative to the boundaries of territorial divisions of the area rather than at fixed points in space. A second reason for this, and one independent of census practices, is the amount of labor involved in the measurement of distance between individual units.

Where the analysis of spatial distribution is based on territorial divisions rather than points in space, measures of concentration describe the degree of correspondence between units and area. If the units are distributed evenly throughout the urban area, each territorial division will contain a proportion of all units equal to the proportion of the total area enclosed by its boundaries. For example, if under such a condition a division accounts for eight per cent of the total area, then it contains an identical per cent of the total number of units.

An illustration of spatial distribution is provided by Table 1, which shows the number of residents and hectares in each *mandamenti urbani* and *frazioni suburbane* of the urban area of Palermo, Italy.[1]

An inspection of Table 1 reveals that neither population nor area is divided equally among the Palermo divisions and that the per cent of the total population located in a division bears little relation to the per cent of the total area enclosed by its boundaries. There is, in short, an uneven distribution of residents. This much can be seen at a glance; however, a quantitative expression of the degree to which the population is concentrated calls for the application of a mathematical formula.[2]

Since the uneven distribution of population in the Palermo urban area is reflected in a discrepancy between a division's share of the total population and its share of the total area (see the third column of figures in Table 1), the degree to which the residents are concentrated may be gauged by determining the per cent of the total population who would have to move out of one division and into another to bring about a uniform population density throughout the urban area. Thus, seven per cent of the total population would have to move out of the Tribunali

[1] To be included in Palermo's urban area a territorial division had to have a population density of eight or more per hectare (about 2,000 per square mile) and touch upon a division already included.

[2] Although various techniques for measurement can be applied in the study of spatial distribution, the present analysis will be restricted to techniques which offer the greatest simplicity and ease of computation. For observations on other types of measures see Otis Dudley Duncan, "The Measurement of Population Distribution," *Population Studies,* Vol. 11 (July, 1957), pp. 27-45.

TABLE 1

AREA AND POPULATION OF THE TERRITORIAL DIVISIONS OF THE
PALERMO URBAN AREA, 1951 *

Territorial Division **	Area in Hectares	Area as Per Cent of Total (X)	|(X)-(Y)|	Population as Per Cent of Total (Y)	Popula- tion
Tribunali	71	0.6	7.0	7.6	35,413
Palazzo Reale	58	0.5	7.1	7.6	35,363
Monte Pieta	56	0.5	6.3	6.8	31,765
Castellammare ...	54	0.5	4.4	4.9	22,730
Molo	315	2.8	10.2	13.0	60,406
Zisa	313	2.7	17.7	20.4	94,965
Cuba	408	3.6	6.2	9.8	45,631
Oreto	131	1.2	1.7	2.9	13,681
Settecannoli	699	6.1	2.1	4.0	18,363
Brancaccio	1,074	9.4	7.0	2.4	11,197
Mezzomonreale ...	915	8.0	5.3	2.7	12,376
Altarello	1,886	16.6	12.7	3.9	18,191
Uditore	1,897	16.7	10.7	6.0	27,832
Resuttana	1,557	13.7	10.1	3.6	16,536
Pallavicino	584	5.1	4.1	1.0	4,755
Falde	1,367	12.0	8.7	3.3	15,186
Total	11,385	100.0	121.3	99.9	464,390

* SOURCE OF DATA: Palermo, Ufficio Statistica e Censimenti, *Panormus, Rassegna del Comune di Palerno e Bollettino di Statistica, 1956* (No. 50, New Series).
** *Mandamenti urbani* or *frazioni suburbane.*

division (see the third column of figures in Table 1) to equalize residents and area in that division. In contrast, 12.7 per cent of the urban area's population would have to move into Altarello division. When the figures in the third column of Table 1 are added the total is 121.3. Since all residents who move out of a division also move into one, each movement is counted twice in arriving at the total of 121.3; consequently, dividing this number by two gives the per cent of the total population who would have had to change their place of residence from one division to another to bring about an even distribution of population. The per cent in this case is 60.7.

The formula for computing a measure of the degree to which a population is concentrated (C) is:

$$C = \Sigma \, |X - Y| \, /2$$

where X is the per cent of the total urban area in a territorial division, and Y is the per cent of the total population located within its boundaries. The difference between each pair of percentage figures is treated as positive numbers in the process of summation.

The values of C may vary from a fixed minimum of 0.0 to a maximum very near 100.0 (specifically, 100.0 minus the per cent of the total area contained in the smallest division), and they are mathematically independent of the number of divisions, the areal size of the urban area, and the number of inhabitants. A high value of C is indicative of an uneven distribution of population, which is manifested in a considerable amount of variability among the territorial divisions as to population density, but it does not provide a basis for any inferences about the absolute level of density in either the divisions or the urban area as a whole.

The measure is always based on a particular set of boundaries which divide up a given area, and any C value is subject to change when a different set is used. There is no way to determine the probable influence of a modification in boundaries beyond noting that the combination of territorial divisions into a set of larger divisions cannot produce an increase in a C value. Thus, if the 16 divisions in the Palermo urban area were grouped into four, C could not be greater than 60.7. Accordingly, the creation of sub-divisions within each of the 16 divisions, or within any one of them, would not result in a value of less than 60.7. On the other hand, boundaries of the divisions could be changed in such a way as to increase or decrease the measure without changing the number of divisions. The fact that different results may be obtained with different boundaries is a serious defect of the measure, but this limitation applies to all measures of spatial distribution which are based on territorial divisions.[3]

THE MEASUREMENT OF DECONCENTRATION

As explained earlier, the term deconcentration refers to a process in which the units of observation become more evenly

[3] For further observations on the measure set forth here see Duncan, *op, cit.,* pp. 30-32, and Edgar M. Hoover, Jr., "Interstate Redistribution of Population, 1850-1940," *Journal of Economic History,* Vol. 1 (November, 1941), pp. 199-205.

distributed in space. Given two C values deconcentration (D) may be expressed as: $D = C_1 - C_2$, with C_1 representing the degree to which the population was concentrated at one time and C_2 representing the condition at a later time. This formula expresses the amount of deconcentration in absolute terms, but it may be modified to express C_1 as a ratio to C_2: $D = C_1/C_2$.

To illustrate the measurement of deconcentration C values have been computed for the Palermo urban area at two points in time, 1936 (C_1) and 1951 (C_2).[4] C_1 proved to be 64.1 and C_2, as we have already seen, is 60.7. When these values are inserted in the formula $(D = C_1 - C_2)$, D is +3.4 in absolute terms and 1.06 when expressed as the ratio of C_1 to C_2.

The absolute values for D range between — 100.0 and + 100.0, with those above 0.0 (positive numbers) indicating deconcentration and those below 0.0 (negative numbers) indicating concentration. When D is expressed as a ratio of C_1 to C_2, values above 1.00 reflect deconcentration and those less than 1.00 reflect concentration.

Deconcentration, boundary changes, and differential growth. In the examination of shifts in the distribution of population within an urban area it is imperative that attention be given to boundary changes. As we shall come to see, a measure of deconcentration may be based on either a constant or a variable boundary, and its magnitude may be quite different in the one case from the other.

The above figures relating to Palermo are based on two delimitations of the urban area—one for 1936 and the other for 1951. Successive delimitations take into account the horizontal growth of the urban area, a dimension of expansion which would be ignored in applying the 1936 boundary to the 1951 population. Had the earlier boundary been held constant, we would have found ourselves comparing all of the urban area at one date with only part of it at a later date. On the other hand, had the 1951 boundary been applied to the 1936 population, a considerable amount of rural territory would have been treated as part of the urban area in 1936.

The consequences of failing to make allowances for boundary

[4] The boundary of Palermo's urban area in 1936 was established by criteria identical with those applied in 1951.

changes in the measurement of deconcentration can be illustrated
by considering the results obtained when the limits of the Palermo urban area are held constant over the years 1936-1951.

	1936 Population	1951 Population	$D = C_1 - C_2$
1936 boundaries	$C_1 = 64.1$	$C_2 = 61.2$	2.9
1951 boundaries	$C_1 = 64.6$	$C_2 = 60.7$	3.9

It can be seen from the above that the amount of deconcentration which took place in Palermo is relative to the boundary employed in measurement. If the 1936 boundary is projected, the
value of D is lower than it is if the 1951 boundary is retrojected
to 1936. Moreover, in both cases the value of D is different from
that obtained when the boundaries are allowed to vary between
1936 and 1951. Although a measure of deconcentration based
on a constant boundary may have some special uses, it should be
employed with the realization that the limits may either encompass only a part of the urban area at one point in time or include
rural territory at another.

The question of boundary changes assumes additional importance when considered in the light of the practice of researchers
to associate differential growth (a higher rate of population increase in peripheral zones of an urban area than in the central
zones) with deconcentration or decentralization. This pattern of
growth is often taken as evidence on the one hand that residents
are moving from the center to its periphery and on the other that
the population is becoming more evenly distributed. However,
differential growth can actually take place in a wide variety of
ways without centrifugal movement, and deconcentration is a
consequence of differential growth only if the urban boundary is
held constant.

As a means of demonstrating how the influence of differential
growth is contingent upon constant boundaries, Table 2 provides
data on the territorial divisions of a hypothetical urban area at
the beginning and end of a 20 year period. It shows an extreme
case of differential growth, with the central divisions of the urban area actually losing population during the period. When a
deconcentration measure is computed, however, it becomes obvious that differential growth does not necessarily produce a

TABLE 2

Population and Area for the Territorial Divisions of a Hypothetical
Urban Area at Two Points in Time

Territorial Divisions Grouped by Zones	Year Included As a Part of the Urban Area *	Area in Square Miles	1938 Population	1958 Population	Per Cent Growth 1938-58
Central	1938	14	301,000	290,000	—3.7
A	1938	2	84,000	80,000	—4.8
B	1938	4	64,000	61,000	—4.7
C	1938	3	60,000	59,000	—1.7
D	1938	2	45,000	44,000	—2.2
E	1938	2	48,000	46,000	—4.2
Peripheral, 1938		23	152,000	152,000	0.0
F	1938	4	24,000	24,000	0.0
G	1938	5	25,000	25,000	0.0
H	1938	5	35,000	35,000	0.0
I	1938	5	40,000	40,000	0.0
J	1938	4	28,000	28,000	0.0
Peripheral, 1958		46	72,000	100,000	38.9
K	1958	7	12,000	15,000	25.0
L	1958	9	14,000	18,000	28.6
M	1958	8	13,000	17,000	30.8
N	1958	6	9,000	13,000	44.4
O	1958	4	7,000	10,000	42.9
P	1958	6	8,000	14,000	75.0
Q	1958	6	9,000	13,000	44.4

* On the basis of a density criterion of 2,000 or more residents per square mile.

more even distribution of population when the urban boundaries
expand. The C value for the hypothetical urban area in 1938 is
28.6, and it is 38.9 for 1958. The measure of deconcentration is
thus —10.3 ($D = C_1 — C_2 = 28.6 — 38.9 = —10.3$), which indicates that a more even distribution of population did not take
place; in fact, the change was toward concentration. Only when
the limits of the hypothetical urban area are held constant over
the period is deconcentration the consequence of differential
growth. This is shown below.

	1938 Population	*1958 Population*	$D = C_1 — C_2$
1938 boundaries	$C_1 = 28.6$	$C_2 = 27.8$	0.8
1958 boundaries	$C_1 = 43.9$	$C_2 = 38.9$	5.0

These figures also demonstrate once again how relative C and D values are to the nature of the boundaries.

THE MEASUREMENT OF CENTRALIZATION

As noted earlier, the term centralization designates a process in which the distribution of units in an area changes in such a way as to reduce the average distance between each unit and the point taken to be the center of the area. This process differs from concentration in that a highly concentrated population is not necessarily a highly centralized one, since the units may cluster on the periphery or at places other than the center. This is particularly true of the location of certain types of institutions or establishments such as industrial plants.

A variety of points may be considered to be the "center" of an urban unit, depending on the research problem at hand. In addition to central points determined by the more abstract centrographic concepts,[5] such locations as the point of highest population density, the conjunction of major transportation lines, and the central business district may be treated as centers of an urban area. Regardless of the type of point considered, however, the manner in which it was located must be carefully specified in a report of research, if we are to determine the degree of comparability between measures of centralization for different urban areas.

Since a centralized population is one in which the units are clustered around a particular point, measurement must be based on the distance which separates the individual units from the point and not the correspondence between the area and population contained in territorial divisions. However, where only the number of units of observation in the divisions is known, distance must be reckoned from the approximate geographical center of each division. This practice rests on the assumption that the individual units are evenly distributed within each territorial division; this is often not the case, but when the divisions are small, the errors introduced by an uneven distribution are negligible. For this reason, all measures of population distribution

[5] See Duncan, *op. cit.*, pp. 34-37.

should be based on the smallest type of territorial division in the urban area.

If the number of units in each division (P) is multiplied by the distance (D) separating the approximate geographical center of the division from a central point [6] and the sum of the products is divided by the total number of units (N), the resulting quotient is the approximate average distance between the individual units and the point. This number indicates the degree to which the population is centralized (Ce), and it is derived from the formula:

$$Ce = \Sigma\, D \cdot P/N$$

To illustrate the application of the above formula, data are presented in Table 3 for the territorial divisions of George Town municipality (Malaya). As shown by the figures in the second and third columns of Table 3, the 188,586 residents (N) of George Town would have to travel a total of 181,095 miles ($\Sigma D \cdot P$) for each person to move from his place of residence to the point taken to be the center of the municipality. When these numbers are inserted in the formula, Ce for George Town is .96. As a measure of the degree to which the population is centralized, this value indicates that the residents live on the average about one mile from the center of the municipality.

In contrast to the measures of distribution heretofore considered, there is no constant upper limit of Ce values; they must be interpreted in terms of distance and not the degree to which they approach an absolute limit. A limit does exist, of course, but it varies from case to case, depending upon the distance from the center to the most distant point on the periphery of the area.

Although it is possible for a large urban area to have a lower Ce value than a smaller one, if two areas have similar shapes and similar population distributions, the larger one will have a higher Ce value. In short, other things being equal, the measure varies directly with areal size. The fact that differences among Ce values may reflect variation in areal size rather than patterns of population distribution makes it necessary to control the influ-

[6] In cases where the geographical center of a division is also taken to be the center of the urban area, D is one-half of the approximate distance between the center of the division and its periphery.

TABLE 3

Territorial Divisions of George Town Municipality, Malaya:
Their Population and Distance from the Center *
of the Municipality, 1947 **

Division	Distance in Miles from Center of Munici- pality (D)	Population (P)	D·P	Population Under a Condition of an Even Distribution (Pe)	D·Pe
1	0.56	22,631	12,673	7,826	4,383
2	0.24	18,804	4,513	3,206	769
3	0.29	22,553	6,540	5,620	1,630
4	0.66	19,828	13,086	10,636	7,020
5	0.75	20,024	15,018	7,827	5,870
6	0.75	21,368	16,026	9,429	7,072
7	1.50	21,808	32,712	17,652	26,478
8	2.06	11,705	24,112	30,098	62,002
9	1.50	7,935	11,903	14,482	22,263
10	1.88	16,067	30,206	27,288	51,301
11	2.44	5,863	14,306	54,162	132,155
All Divisions	—	188,586	181,095	188,586	320,943

* Center of municipality taken to be at the intersection of Maxwell Road and Pitt Street, a point adjacent to the three divisions having the highest levels of population density.
** Source of data: M. V. del Tufo, *Malaya: A Report on the 1947 Census of Population* (London: Crown Agents for the Colonies).

ence of size. This is accomplished by determining how much the actual distribution of the population reduces the average distance between the center and residents from what would be the case were the residents evenly distributed (i.e., each territorial division containing a population in proportion to its area).

If the residents of George Town had been distributed evenly throughout the municipality in 1947, Ce would have been 1.70.[7] The ratio of this hypothetical value (designated as Ch) to Ce gives us a second measure (Cr) which indicates how much the average distance has been reduced as a consequence of the clustering of the population about the center. This measure for George Town is: Cr = Ce/Ch = .96/1.70 = .44. Thus, the spatial distribution of the population of George Town is such that the average distance separating residents from the center is less

[7] This figure is derived through an application of the formula to the numbers shown in the last two columns of Table 3.

than one-half of what would result from an even distribution throughout the city's area.

One of the major advantages of the Cr measure is that it is not influenced by the areal size of an urban unit. Equally important is the fact that although it has no constant upper limit, the measure can be interpreted in terms of a set standard. To the extent that it is less than 1.00 the individual units are more *centralized* than would be the case for an even distribution, and to the extent that it is greater than 1.00 the units are more *decentralized*. Thus, the higher a Cr value the more the average distance between the individual units and the center has been maximized.

Shifts in the degree to which a population is centralized (that is, shifts toward either centralization or decentralization) can be expressed mathematically as the difference between two Ce values, or between two Cr values. If Ce_1 is a measure of the degree to which a population was centralized at one time and Ce_2 is the measure at a later time, then the degree of decentralization (D_z) is: $D_z = Ce_2 - Ce_1$, with negative numbers indicating that the distribution has become more centralized during the period. An alternative formula $(D_z = Ce_2/Ce_1)$ expresses the amount of decentralization relative to the original Ce value, with values less than 1.00 indicating centralization.

The difference between Ce_1 and Ce_2 in any given case may be a function of an expanding boundary and not an actual change in the pattern of distribution. For this reason Cr values should be used to express shifts in population distribution independently of an increase in the areal size of the urban area. This measure (Dr) may be computed in two ways: $Dr = Cr_2 - Cr_1$ or $Dr = Cr_2/Cr_1$. The first formula expresses the change in distribution in absolute terms (with negative numbers indicating centralization), while the second formula expresses change relative to the original level (here values less than 1.00 indicate centralization).

THE MEASUREMENT OF ASSOCIATION IN SPATIAL DISTRIBUTION

Up to this point attention has been focused on methods suited for a quantitative description of the way in which a given set of units are distributed in space. We shall now turn to the problem of describing the association between the spatial distribution of two or more different types of phenomena. It is generally recognized that the residents and institutions in an urban area do not locate in a purely random fashion. For a variety of reasons [8] separate nuclei and differentiated districts come into being, and this reflects differences and similarities in the locational requirements of various activities which go on in an urban area. A desire for pleasant surroundings, for example, is said to motivate people to live apart from industrial plants. On the other hand, a common need, such as easy access to transportation facilities, may create a clustering of institutions. Locational associations of this sort are often a matter of common knowledge. An awareness of the phenomena, however, is not a substitute for a standardized measure of the degree to which certain types of institutions, or classes of population (such as ethnic or racial groups), are spatially associated.

Although the following method for the measurement of locational association can be applied to virtually any phenomena, we shall concern ourselves, for purposes of illustration, with the distribution of manufacturing and retail establishments in the San Francisco-Oakland Standard Metropolitan Area (S.M.A.).

Given the per cent of the total number of establishments located in each major territorial division (county) of the S.M.A., as shown in Table 4, the degree of locational association (La) between the distribution of retail stores and manufacturing plants can be expressed mathematically as:

$$La = 100.0 - [\Sigma \, |X - Y|/2]$$

where X and Y are the per cent of each of the two types of establishments located in each county.

The application of the above formula to the data in Table 4 yields a La value of 89.8 for the distribution of manufacturing and retail establishments. This suggests a high degree of association, since the minimum La value is 0.0 and the maximum is 100.0, and it indicates that in 1954 only 10.2 per cent of either type of establishment would have had to move from one county

[8] See Chauncy D. Harris and Edward L. Ullman, "The Nature of Cities," *Annals of the American Academy of Political and Social Science*, Vol. 242 (November, 1945), pp. 7-17.

TABLE 4

THE DISTRIBUTION OF MANUFACTURING AND RETAIL ESTABLISHMENTS
AMONG THE COUNTIES CONSTITUTING THE SAN FRANCISCO-OAKLAND,
CALIFORNIA, STANDARD METROPOLITAN AREA, 1954 *

Counties	Number of Manufacturing Establishments	Manufacturing Establishments As Per Cent of Total (X)	|(X)-(Y)|	Retailing As Per Cent of Total (Y)	Retail Establishments
Alameda	1,404	34.2	1.8	32.4	8,579
Contra Costa ..	233	5.7	5.7	11.4	3,011
Marin	92	2.2	1.5	3.7	978
San Francisco ..	1,901	46.3	8.4	37.9	10,045
San Mateo	413	10.1	0.5	10.6	2,812
Solano	63	1.5	2.6	4.1	1,093
All counties ...	4,106	100.0	20.5	100.1	26,518

* SOURCE OF DATA: U.S. Bureau of the Census, *County and City Data Book, 1956* (U.S. Government Printing Office, Washington, D.C., 1957), pp. 29-30.

to another to bring about an equal per cent of the two in any given county. The degree of correspondence is, however, always relative to the nature of the territorial divisions employed. The La value cannot be taken to mean that manufacturing plants tend to be located adjacent to retail stores; it does indicate that marked territorial segregation of manufacturing and retailing has yet to appear on the county level.[9]

The measure of locational association described above may also be used to express a temporal change in the spatial association of units. Thus, as can be determined from Table 5, the degree of association between the distribution of manufacturing and retail establishments among the counties in the San Francisco-Oakland S.M.A. was 86.6 in the years 1947-1948. It was 89.8 in 1954, as we have seen. Although some questions may exist regarding the comparability of the two sets of data, it appears that a slight increase (3.2 or 89.8-86.6) in the degree of association was registered over the years 1947 to 1954.

Measure of locational association may also be applied to shifts in the spatial distribution of the same units or type of units. The

[9] For an application of a similar measure of association to the residential distribution of persons in different occupations see Otis Dudley Duncan and Beverly Duncan, "Residential Distribution and Occupational Stratification," *American Journal of Sociology*, Vol. 60 (March, 1955), pp. 493-503.

TABLE 5

THE DISTRIBUTION OF MANUFACTURING ESTABLISHMENTS, 1947, AND RETAIL
ESTABLISHMENTS, 1948, AMONG THE COUNTIES CONSTITUTING THE
SAN FRANCISCO-OAKLAND, CALIFORNIA, STANDARD
METROPOLITAN AREA *

Counties	Number of Manufacturing Establishments 1947	Manufacturing Establishments As Per Cent of Total (X)	|(X)-(Y)|	Retail Establishments As Per Cent of Total (Y)	Retail Establishments 1948
Alameda	1,186	32.3	1.8	34.1	8,537
Contra Costa ..	168	4.6	5.9	10.5	2,632
Marin	57	1.6	1.5	3.1	778
San Francisco ..	1,990	54.2	13.4	40.8	10,225
San Mateo	228	6.2	1.5	7.7	1,922
Solano	42	1.1	2.8	3.9	975
All counties ...	3,671	100.0	26.9	100.1	25,069

* SOURCE OF DATA: U.S. Bureau of the Census, *County and City Data Book,*
1952 (U.S. Government Printing Office, Washington, D.C., 1953), pp. 110-111.

findings reported above, for example, suggest that there were
some changes in the distribution of manufacturing and/or retail
establishments between 1947 and 1954. The magnitude of the
change can be determined for each type of establishment through
an application of the formula to the appropriate figures in Tables
4 and 5. The measure of association between the second column
of figures in Table 4 and the second column in Table 5 is 92.1,
and for the next to the last columns in the two tables it is 95.4,
which indicates a slightly greater shift in the locational patterns
of manufacturing over the years 1947-1954 than for retailing
during the period 1948-1954.

COMPARISONS WITHIN AN URBAN UNIT

Up to this point the different measures of spatial distribution
and redistribution have been considered as applied to the urban
area as a whole. They may also be used, however, to compare
locational patterns in any part of the urban area with those in
another, insofar as the parts are clusters of territorial divisions.

Although territorial divisions can be grouped in a variety of
ways, a common practice is to arrange them according to their

proximity to the center of the urban area. This may be accomplished either by an actual measurement of the distance separating each division from the center or by grouping the divisions in a series of concentric zones about the center of the city. Each such zone may thus be characterized as being nearer or farther from the center than another zone. This concentric arrangement makes it possible to gauge the relation between distance from the center and such characteristics as land use, demographic traits of the population, and the incidence of certain forms of behavior (crime, psychoses, etc.). In North American cities, for example, it is often found that spatial patterns exhibit a gradient effect, meaning that the presence of certain phenomena tends to increase or decrease somewhat regularly with distance from the center of the city.

A gradient effect is only one of several patterns which may appear when territorial divisions are grouped. Each of the different measures of spatial distribution described previously can be applied to any cluster of divisions, whether the divisions are grouped into a concentric zone or otherwise. All that is required is that each cluster be treated as though it were an urban area rather than a part of one. Thus, if the territorial divisions are grouped into concentric zones, measures of concentration, centralization, and locational association can be computed for each zone in exactly the same way as they are for the urban area as a whole. These measures make it possible to determine if distance from the center of the city is related to patterns of spatial distribution and redistribution within each of the zones.

CONCLUDING OBSERVATIONS

Since the techniques for the measurement of spatial distribution and redistribution do not have to be modified to fit the characteristics of the phenomenon being studied, they are particularly useful in making comparisons. For any given urban area they provide answers to such questions as: Is the distribution of industrial plants more concentrated than places of residence? Have commercial establishments become more decentralized than noneconomic institutions? Is the association between the distribution of land devoted to recreational uses and the distribution of population greater than is the case for vacant land and population? Answers to these and other similar questions are possible because the various measures have a standard meaning regardless of the units of observation.

Just as comparisons within urban areas are facilitated by standardization, so are they among urban areas. Here, though, because each measure is relative to a given set of territorial divisions, a great deal of caution must be exercised in an evaluation of differences. It is possible that a higher value for one urban area as opposed to another reflects nothing more than a difference in the nature of the boundaries of their territorial divisions.[10]

As the size of the territorial divisions decreases, the results are closer to measurements based on individual units. Consequently, given a choice among different types of territorial divisions, a study of spatial distribution should always make use of the smallest type. A report of research should in turn indicate the number of the territorial divisions, their average size, and the amount of variation in size. This practice provides a basis (though not an entirely adequate one) for assessing the comparability of measures for different urban areas. In general, the smaller the territorial divisions and the more uniform their size the more meaningful are the comparisons.

[10] This is even true for a comparison within an urban area, since the nature of territorial divisions may influence a measure for one type of phenomenon more than another.

PART IV

URBAN HINTERLANDS AND
FUNCTIONAL TYPES OF CITIES

Introduction to Part IV

It has been suggested that the *sine qua non* of urban existence is the concentration of people who do not grow their own food. This observation suggests a fundamental question for theory and research. One may well ask: If the majority of urban residents do not grow their own food, how do they survive? Only cursory observation is needed to provide the answer. The residents of a city survive by virtue of the fact that a large portion of them provide some type of service for either the rural population or the inhabitants of other cities, and it is this fact which is the essential feature of a city as an ecological entity. These *urban exchange services* comprise a wide variety of activities—commercial, governmental, manufacturing, transportation, religious, artistic, to mention only a few—and they are the basis for the system of exchange that provides the urban residents with indispensable material goods.

There are two essential features of urban exchange services (sometimes designated as "basic" services). We should first note that while the services may involve objects, as in the case of manufacturing, they are not usually oriented toward the production of raw materials. Thus, with regard to material goods, the urban worker typically stands between the primary producer and the consumer. He may transport objects, process them in one way or another, combine them in their original form, but he does not "produce" them (the exceptions are persons engaged in certain extractive industries, such as coal mining).

The second feature of exchange services is that they clearly do not involve all of the labor force. In any given urban unit a proportion of the labor force renders services for their fellow residents rather than for persons who live outside the urban unit. These *non-exchange services* are important, because a sizeable proportion of the labor force is engaged in them and because some of them are closely linked to exchange services.

Beyond the connection between the existence of cities and the

254

services which they provide, two fundamental questions are posed for research. First, for any given case, what territory contains the persons who are dependent on the services provided by the urban unit? And, second, what is the nature of the services? These two questions lead to a consideration of three major concepts in research—*urban service area* and *metropolitan region* in the case of the first question, and *functional type* in the case of the second.

With reference to the first question, it is generally recognized that persons may be dependent on urban services in either of two ways. They may be *directly* dependent in that they must travel to the urban unit to obtain the service, or obtain it by mechanical means, as in the case of public utilities; in either case, the person does not rely on an intermediary.

Examples of *direct* dependence are common—the farmer who transacts business in person with a bank located in a city near his farm, the housewife who resides in a small town but buys clothes for the family in a nearby metropolis, and the rural resident who makes use of medical facilities located in the nearest urban center. As a rule, all persons who are directly dependent upon the same services share at least one thing in common—they reside in the immediate vicinity of the urban unit. This means that persons do not usually avail themselves of urban services located a great distance from their place of residence. Exactly how far they travel for this purpose varies of course from place to place, depending for the most part on the efficiency of transportation, but it is generally agreed that persons who make direct use of urban services live in close proximity to the urban unit. Such territory is considered to be an *urban service area,* and it extends as far as it contains a predominance of people who are directly dependent on the services provided by the urban unit.

For purposes of discussion an urban unit has often been treated as though it has one service area, i.e., as if all its direct services extended out to precisely the same limit. In reality, however, each urban unit has not one but several service areas, with each activity having a different boundary. Some of the more universal service areas are related to retail trade, public utilities, transportation, medical facilities, education, recreation, and religion. Although the limits of these individual areas may not correspond, the same general method can be used to delimit them. In close proximity to the periphery of an urban unit there is always a composite service area, which contains at least a part of each individual service area.

The dependence of persons on an urban unit extends beyond the periphery of service areas. Each large city is surrounded by territory containing people who are *indirectly* dependent on its services. This form of dependence is characterized by the existence of an intermediary between the recipients of the service and the urban residents who provide it, and the most common such intermediary is the retail establishment. Even when a community is far removed from an urban center, its retail establishments may depend on wholesale outlets in the center, and this places the inhabitants of the community in a condition of *indirect* dependence. Such a relation between a community and an urban unit may be said to place the former under the dominance of the latter; and the total of all such dominated communities constitutes the metropolitan region of the urban center.

While the boundaries of service areas and metropolitan regions represent particular kinds of territorial limits, they do not reveal the relative importance of each type of service to the overall economy of a city, which is a necessary consideration in seeking a full understanding of a city as an economic organization. If all cities provided the same types and amounts of services, they would differ very little as far as their essential economic characteristics were concerned. However, from ancient times to the present, and particularly since the Industrial Revolution, cities have differed in the special services they provide for their hinterlands.

With the growth of urbanization and the increased efficiency of transportation and communication, cities have become not only more specialized but specialized over larger regions. Detroit and New York City, the automotive and financial capitals of the United States, are outstanding examples. In recognition of this increase in specialization, persons concerned with the study of urbanization have come to speak of cities in terms of functional types. Although this concept may be defined to encompass a wide range of variables, more than anything else it has to do with the nature of a city's services—either as to what they are or the degree to which one of them is predominant.

Urban service areas, metropolitan regions, and functional types are relevant to an explanation of the existence of cities and to understanding differences among cities with regard to the characteristics described in Part II. The influence of service areas and metropolitan regions on the associated urban units has yet to be determined. Nevertheless, it appears that a direct relation holds between the population size of an urban unit and that of its service areas and metropolitan region, particularly when the urban units considered are not highly specialized (i.e., when they offer several exchange services rather than a few). It is also possible that changes in the characteristics of service areas and metropolitan regions (e.g., an increase in the number of their inhabitants) are closely linked to changes in the population size of urban units. Consequently, on the basis of such possibilities as these, the two types of territorial units are fundamental in urban research.

Much remains to be known regarding the relationship between the functional type of an urban unit and its other characteristics, but theoretical considerations and research findings suggest that the former is at least linked to population size and age-sex structure. At least two factors operate to produce this relationship. First, a city's functional type sets certain limits on the population size and age-sex structure which its exchange services will support. And, second, each functional type calls for a certain amount of manpower resources, and these resources are in turn dependent on population size and age-sex structure.

Contents of the papers. As a study of the literature cited in Sections 19 and 29 of the *Index to the Bibliography* will show, during recent years very little research has been devoted to the development of methods for delimiting urban service areas and metropolitan regions. This is perhaps due to the fact that, on the whole, governmental agencies responsible for gathering and publishing such data have yet to concern themselves with the delimitation of these two territorial units.

The absence of standardized methods for delimiting metropolitan regions and service areas, and the paucity of data on them, are most unfortunate for urban research. For one thing, although the importance of the two types of territorial units is generally recognized, they are rarely considered in comparisons of cities. Furthermore, the beginning student is discouraged from conducting an investigation of the two not only because of the problem of obtaining relevant data, but also because his seniors currently have little to offer him in the way of specific methods for delimitation.

The first two papers in Chapter 9 provide an illustration of the delimitation of territorial units that are functionally linked to cities. These territorial units are referred to in both papers as "hinterlands," but the authors actually deal with two distinctly different types of units. F. H. W. Green's paper, "Urban Hinterlands in England and Wales: An Analysis of Bus Services," reports a study which was concerned for the most part with delimiting hinterlands that represent service areas; while Howard L. Green's paper, "Hinterland Boundaries of New York City and Boston in Southern New England," is devoted to what has been designated here as a metropolitan region.

Neither of the two papers sets forth precise and universally applicable methods for delimiting the types of areas concerned. The formulation of such methods is virtually impossible under the conditions that presently confront urban research, and this will probably be the case for some time to come. In the first place, the two concepts—service area and metropolitan region—remain somewhat vague. Moreover, since there has been relatively little experimentation on the subject in different countries, we do not have a sufficient basis for evaluating the validity of particular delimitation methods. And, finally, since methods must fit the data that can be utilized in research and the nature of such data varies from case to case (even within a single country), any set of specific rules for delimiting service areas and metropolitan regions can be applied in only a few isolated instances. Faced with this situation, the beginning student must formulate his own approach to the problem and treat particular studies, such as those reported in the first two papers of Chapter 9, as providing only general guides.

The third paper, "Differentiation in Metropolitan Areas" by Leslie Kish, undertakes an analysis of an assumed consequence of the dependence of service areas and metropolitan regions on urban units. It deals not so much with establishing the fact of such dependence as with demonstrating a particular spatial pattern that appears to be associated with the relationship. The findings indicate that as distance from an urban unit increases there is less territorial differentiation (i.e., the characteristics of the territorial units and their populations come to resemble each other more and more). This suggests that along with dependence the spatial structure of service areas and metropolitan regions is influenced by the urban unit. Much remains to be known regarding this aspect of dominance. The findings of Kish's study describe the situation only in the United States, and it may well be that the relation between territorial differentiation and distance from an urban unit is quite different in other countries; however, the methods employed in the study are applicable to virtually any place where the requisite data are available. Similar studies in other countries may throw new light on the assumed connection between the levels of urbanization and territorial interdependence, since the latter presupposes differentiation.

One of the principal obstacles to analyzing cities in terms of functional types is the fact that neither official nor unofficial statistics are likely to distinguish between exchange and nonexchange services, a distinction, it should be added, that is very difficult to make. As a rule, available data relate only to the per cent of the labor force engaged in certain industrial or occupational categories, and it is on the basis of a "surplus" of persons in particular categories that inferences about the exchange services of an urban unit are made. It is the determination of this "surplus" and the related assumptions that are central to methods for constructing a functional typology of cities.

Both the mathematical basis for computing the "surplus" described above and the nature of the assumptions associated with it are treated in the first paper in Chapter 10, "The Measurement of the Economic Base of the Metropolitan Area." While the authors do not construct an elaborate functional typology of cities, they set forth some methods for measuring variables that form the basis for such a typology; and in this regard their paper serves as an excellent introduction to the subject.

Techniques for classifying cities in terms of functional types are the subjects of the second and third papers in Chapter 10—

"The Functions of New Zealand Towns" by L. L. Pownall and "A Service Classification of American Cities" by Howard J. Nelson. Both of the classificatory schemes considered assign cities to functional types on the basis of a "surplus" of the labor force engaged in the different industries (i.e., manufacturing, commerce, etc.). This is accomplished in each of the two schemes by the "ratio method," in which a "surplus" is determined through a comparison of the proportion of a city's labor force in a given industry with the corresponding proportion in other cities. For example, if the proportion of the labor force engaged in manufacturing exceeds that of the other cities to some particular degree, this is considered to be one of the attributes of the city's functional type.

The classificatory schemes advanced by Pownall and Nelson thus share certain things in common. They differ, however, in two important respects. Pownall's method involves a comparison of a city with all others of approximately the same size, a possibility noted by Nelson but not incorporated in his typology. The two classificatory schemes also differ as to the statistical values that are used to determine individual types.

Differences in the approaches to the problem taken by Pownall and Nelson should neither be a cause for confusion nor taken to mean that one of the methods is superior to the other. The adequacy of a functional typology depends in final analysis on the purposes for which it is utilized. If one is concerned with accounting for variation in the growth of cities, a particular classificatory scheme may have more utility than do others; on the other hand, it may prove to be clearly inadequate in a consideration of difference in the age-sex structure of cities. In short, no classificatory scheme is intrinsically right or wrong, provided that it is empirically applicable and based on exhaustive but mutually exclusive categories. Consequently, the beginning student should not feel obliged to use either of the two classificatory schemes, but rather look on them as providing guides in the construction of a functional typology to fit the problem at hand.

The belief that the growth of urbanization is associated with an increase in territorial interdependence has implications beyond the relationship between urban units and their service areas, or metropolitan regions. A consideration of equal importance in attempting to demonstrate territorial interdependence is that of inter-urban relations. With their functional specialization cities have come to render services not only for the rural population but also for each other. We know even less of the latter relationship than the former, but the observations made in technologically advanced countries leave little doubt as to its importance. The long and short of the matter is that cities are becoming less and less self-contained; the orbit of their exchange services is expanding far beyond adjacent territory. This means more than an increase in territorial interdependence; for the expansion also affects the basic characteristics of urban units, particularly population size. Thus, from virtually any point of view, a concern with inter-urban relations in a study of an individual city is not only warranted but also perhaps necessary to explain fully why it possesses certain characteristics and not others.

As one might expect, our meager knowledge concerning the nature of inter-urban relations is matched by the absence of standardized methods for conducting research on the subject. One of the few papers that deals with such methods, "Economic Structural Interrelations of Metropolitan Regions" by Isard and Kavesh, appears in Chapter 10. In presenting a model of inter-industry and inter-regional economic relations, the authors provide the beginning student with a frame of reference for analyzing any type of spatial flow within and between cities, urban areas, metropolitan areas, service areas, and metropolitan regions.

It is true that particular, and perhaps unique, assumptions are made by Isard and Kavesh in applying their model to economic variables as they relate to metropolitan regions, but the principles underlying their methods of organizing and analyzing data may be applied to other variables and all types of territorial units. Furthermore, the fact that they consider the model only in an economic context is far from undesirable, since economic variables are of crucial importance in a study of inter-urban relationships.

It is recognized that Isard and Kavesh's paper may appear to be of questionable value to the novice. For one thing, the type of data needed to apply the method, whether to economic or to non-economic variables, are not available in the form of published statistics. Also, in contrast to most of those heretofore considered, the method is by no means a simple one, a fact that may cause the beginning student some difficulty, particularly if he attempts to modify the method and apply it to other phenomena. Despite these two problems, however, the novice should become acquainted with at least one view of inter-urban relations if only because the concept appears destined to play an important role in future research.

Only in rare instances will the reader find it possible to apply the methods described in Chapters 9 and 10 without modifying them in one way or another. Because of a lack of experimentation and the complex nature of the subjects, there are few standardized methods in this sphere of research; consequently, one will often find that he must create methods to fit his particular needs and the nature of his data. The papers in Chapters 9 and 10 may prove to be of value as guides in formulating methods, but the task may also require a search of the literature for additional assistance. Accordingly, four sections of the *Index to the Bibliography* are devoted to the subjects considered here—Section 29, urban service areas; Section 19, metropolitan regions; Section 13, functional types; and Section 17, functional relations among cities.

Chapter 9

FUNCTIONAL LINKAGE WITH SURROUNDING TERRITORY

URBAN HINTERLANDS IN ENGLAND AND WALES: AN ANALYSIS OF BUS SERVICES *

F. H. W. GREEN

The main purpose of this paper is to demonstrate the application of an objective method of determining the approximate boundaries of urban spheres of influence or hinterlands, for the conception of rural-urban communities of interest is not only of sociological significance in the scientific sense but of practical value in planning. The method, namely an analysis of country bus services, is of value not only in studying specific cases, but in providing a sufficient number of examples for some tentative statistical conclusions to be reached. A study of this kind moreover enables one to pose in tangible form questions which hitherto were perhaps not always easily defined. Hinterlands of peculiar shape or unexpected size, hinterlands in which the urban focus is eccentrically placed, boundaries which are very irregular, all call for explanation. No two cases will prove to be identical, but useful points of analogy will be found so that the history of change in one place may be used by town and country planners to forecast the probable results of developments proposed in another.

The work of defining the boundaries of the urban hinterlands

* Reprinted from *Geographical Journal*, Vol. 116, Nos. 1-3 (July-September, 1950), pp. 64-81, with permission of author and publisher.

described in this paper and of making the statistical analyses was not completed without the willing assistance of the staff in the Maps Office of the Ministry of Town and Country Planning, in particular of Mrs. K. M. Knight and Miss U. M. E. Rodd. Most of the detailed records, only summarized in this article, are available for inspection and study in the Ministry's Map Library and in the Regional Offices.[1]

The definition of urban centres. It is important to introduce at the start the conception of centres of different orders of significance. Five such orders are postulated.

First Order	Metropolitan Centre
Second Order	Provincial Centre
Third Order	Major Regional Centre
Fourth Order	Ordinary Regional Centre
Fifth Order	Service Village

London, as the metropolis of England and Wales, stands on its own as a centre of the First Order, having functions which are performed nowhere else in the country. At the other end of the scale are what are sometimes now described as "service villages," which provide facilities lacking in their immediate neighbours. Between the two extremes there is no clear-cut gradation, but three main types can be recognized; the Provincial Capital, exemplified by Birmingham or Bristol; the typical major regional centre or country town exemplified by Ipswich or Exeter; and the ordinary small town with minimum urban functions. It is also clear that a town of any order performs, in a greater or less degree, the functions proper to lower orders as well. Certain specialized towns may have almost no Fourth Order function at all, serving a very wide area for a specific purpose only. Torquay and Bournemouth are examples.

The use of bus services in defining urban hinterlands. The analysis of country bus services affords a useful means of defining centres of the Fourth Order and delimiting their hinterlands. During the two inter-war decades services spread all over the country to such an extent that it is now difficult to find a hamlet of any size in England and Wales that is not on a bus route.

---

[1] Mr. Green, formerly lecturer in Geography at University College, Southampton, is now Maps Officer at the Ministry of Town and Country Planning.

The process was accompanied by intense competition and it is safe to assert that, in most areas, the most economic routes were discovered by a process of trial and error. The operators had in effect carried out an elaborate questionnaire to discover what was the potential demand. They had discovered where the majority of persons wished to make the majority of journeys. In the United Kingdom buses are also the cheapest form of public transport except where, in a few anomalous cases, the route taken by the road vehicle is necessarily so much more circuitous than that taken by another means of transport that the alternative means is cheaper as well as quicker. But it is quite easy to pick out the very few cases in England and Wales where this anomaly is significant. Barmouth in Merioneth is a good example; it is the railway bridge over the Mawddach estuary which brings the settlements of Arthog and Fairbourne into cheaper and quicker communication with Barmouth than with any other centre.

It is true, on the other hand, that in providing a new form of transport the bus services were creating a demand, and perhaps altering the natural spheres of influence of towns. It is possible, for example, that in areas of static or decreasing population the development of bus services encouraged the growth, relative or absolute, of major centres at the expense of minor ones. Be that as it may, a study of services existing in 1939 would have indicated not only what opportunities for travel existed, but also the extent to which they were utilized. An inspection of time-tables also shows that, in spite of the present shortage of vehicles, services in 1947 were generally speaking similar to those of 1939, though there had been some significant changes; duplicate buses were more frequently run, and double-deckers had often taken the place of single-deckers in areas showing an increase of population and daily movement. Winter time-tables for 1947-48 were therefore used.

There are a number of points that must be taken into consideration if time-tables are to be used for defining the limits of urban hinterlands. It is essential that all stage carriage services are taken into account, and all express services, and special services (e.g. factory services) eliminated. Most of the larger companies issue time-tables, but many of the smaller operators do not do so, and it was therefore necessary to consult the Regional

Traffic Commissioners, who were able to extract the approved timings for the latter class from their records of licences issued. Their ready cooperation greatly reduced the labour of the inquiry.

In many areas the full network of services is developed only on certain days in the week; services operating on Sunday only were, for fairly obvious reasons, neglected. Those operating on Saturdays only presented a problem, but experience in drawing the diagrams soon revealed that the Saturday services very rarely covered an area different from that defined by market day services. Eventually the method adopted was to plot market day services, (see Fig. I), and to add in a different symbol services which operated only on certain other specified days. But this refinement was in fact scarcely necessary.

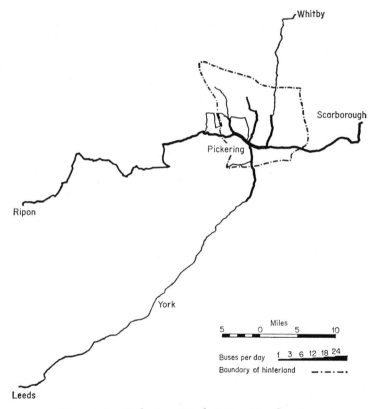

FIGURE I.   Pickering: Market Day Bus Services.

Method and results of the analysis. Whereas a questionnaire automatically reveals which places the local population regards as centres, this is not the case with time-tables. For the purpose of the inquiry, towns were deemed to qualify as centres if there operated from them any bus services which served no places larger than themselves. With certain obvious limitations this proved a workable definition. It meant that if a place was served only by through routes (to and from larger towns) it did not appear as an "independent" centre. Provided there was at least one local route, serving perhaps only a neighbouring village, the place could qualify as a centre.

Having obtained records of all bus services, the method then consisted in drawing diagrams of the services radiating from each centre and superimposing them upon those of their neighbours. Figure II illustrates this in respect of Reading and Newbury, and the pecked line shows how the boundary between the two towns was drawn. There can be little argument that this line does define the boundary between the area where the bus travel facilities are better to Reading, and the area where they are better to Newbury. In most cases there was little difficulty in drawing the boundary lines.

Efforts were made to avoid "island outliers" of the hinterland of one town within the territory of another. This difficulty did not arise as often as might have been expected and was averted, with one single exception, either by providing a narrow neck of territory within that of a neighbouring centre, or between the territories of two other centres (see Fig. II); or by recognizing the existence in certain cases of "subsidiary" centres, a subsidiary centre being one where the bus routes radiating from a larger neighbouring town are so inter-digitated with its own as to indicate an area in which the two towns compete on about equal terms (see Fig. III). About eighty such subsidiary centres were recognized.

The drawing of a single line as the boundary may be criticized on the grounds that hinterlands normally overlap. But on the analogy of watersheds, these boundaries may sometimes have sharp crestlines and sometimes resemble the Great Divide of the Canadian Prairie, both of which can be represented by a single line. It would have been possible, as it is indeed desirable, to

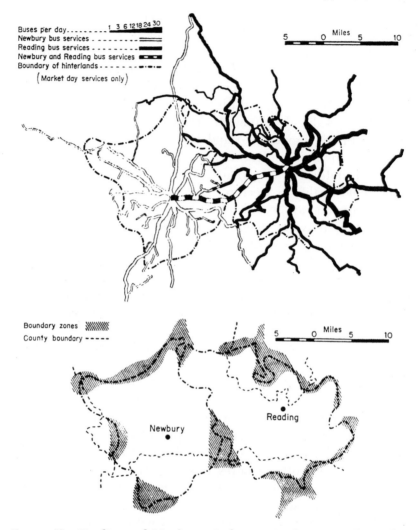

FIGURE II.   Reading and Newbury: Radiating Bus-Services and Overlapping Hinterlands.

give some indication on the map of this kind of variation, but this would require a good deal more investigation. Even by the present method some idea of the sharpness of the divisions may be obtained. (Fig. II.)

The total number of centres, including subsidiary centres, which resulted from the application of this method was approxi-

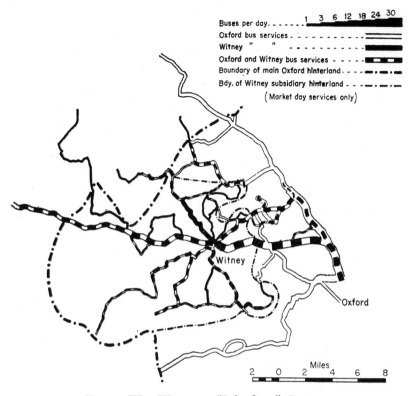

FIGURE III.   Witney, a "Subsidiary" Centre.

mately 700. This agrees well with the total of 708 adduced by Smailes on an entirely different line of approach, based on facilities offered.[2] The lists of places qualifying by the two different criteria are however not coincident. In a number of sparsely inhabited rural areas places appear to function as Fourth Order centres though they do not possess what Smailes considers the minimum number of urban facilities. Allendale Town and Bellingham in Northumberland, and St. Columb Major in Cornwall, are examples. Conversely, a number of sizeable industrial towns and seaside resorts possess adequate facilities but command little or no allegiance over the surrounding countryside. Such for instance are Lyme Regis, Flint, and places like Eccles or Bacup in Lancashire. A comparison of the present map with a map con-

[2] A. E. Smailes, "The urban hierarchy in England and Wales," *Geography* 29 (1944), 41-51.

structed to show the distribution of cinemas throughout the country reveals that only twelve towns which qualify as bus centres are without provision for this form of entertainment; the majority of the twelve are in rural Wales. Such a high degree of correlation indicates the great significance which the cinema has now attained in rural as well as urban life. Access to cinemas must be taken into account in any kind of rural planning. Another comparison which has been made concerns provincial weekly newspapers. Here the factors are very complicated, and the degree of correlation is not so high, but it is of considerable interest to observe that the total number of towns where weekly newspapers are published is about the same as the number of bus centres (excluding subsidiary centres), and about 75 per cent are common to both lists.

The areas and populations of urban hinterlands. The areas of the hinterlands have all been measured and tabulated; the average, including subsidiary centres, works out at 81 square miles, the median being approximately 61 square miles. Estimates have also been made of the mid-1939 population of each urban centre and its hinterland. A map was prepared from these estimates, part of which is shown in Figure IV, and the table given below is a summary of the compilation.

TABLE—Distribution of Hinterlands by Area and Population

Population (thousands)	Areas in Square Miles						Totals
	0-25	25-50	50-100	100-200	200-400	over 400	
0-5	65	56	34	16	4	—	175
5-10	30	35	52(1)	25	4	—	146(1)
10-20	12(2)	16(1)	30(1)	52(3)	16(6)	1	127(13)
20-50	9	9	24	35(8)	20(5)	5(5)	102(18)
50-100	—	5(3)	10(9)	13(7)	9(9)	3(6)	40(34)
100-200	—	2	5(7)	3	3(2)	2(4)	15(13)
over 200	—	—	—	2	2(2)	1(2)	5(4)
Totals	116(2)	123(4)	155(18)	146(18)	58(24)	12(17)	610(83)

(Figures in brackets indicate the number of subsidiary centres associated with the centres in each category.)

A few words of caution are necessary with respect to these figures. In the first place the functions of the centres themselves

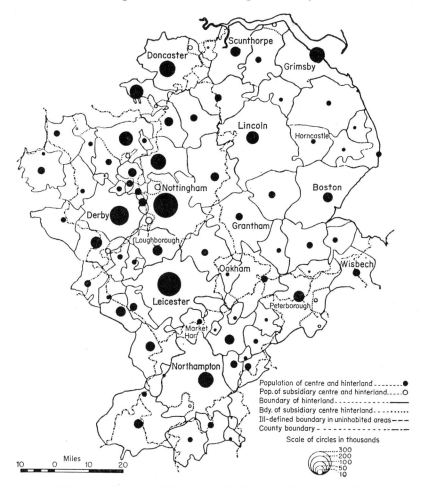

FIGURE IV. Populations of Towns and Hinterlands; the North Midland
Region.

are varied, some being purely market towns, others primarily self-
contained industrial towns in which the major part of the population is in occupations not directly connected with the economy
of the immediate hinterland. Such towns are often made up of
more than one administrative unit. Care must also be taken to
include the right units to determine the total population of the
centre itself and in towns where much recent expansion has taken
place there is commonly a sprawl of population into neighbouring
rural districts. To avoid subjective error, the latter factor has not

been taken into account. Again, since towns may have several functions in addition to that of being Fourth Order centres for the surrounding countryside, it is more suitable for many purposes of comparison to make use of the population estimates of the hinterlands alone. When this is done, we find that the average population for the latter is about 16,500 and the median about 8500.

A survey made on an exactly similar basis for Northern Ireland [3] gives corresponding figures of 17,800 as the average, and 9700 as the median.[4] In Denmark a survey,[5] also on a transport basis with bus services as the main criterion, produced figures of 17,300 and 14,200; this similarity is a fact of considerable sociological significance. A preliminary survey of Eire gives a rather strikingly different result, the average being 55,700 and the median 27,000.[3] The implication is that the population of Eire uses the bus only for more significant journeys than in England, Wales, Northern Ireland and Denmark, and that there the bus centres are not necessarily Fourth Order centres. The matter would obviously repay further study.

Considering area and population together, we find that 60 towns had a population in the hinterland of over 50,000, and 70 towns served an area of over 200 square miles. In only 20 instances was both the hinterland population over 50,000 and the area served over 200 square miles. Five of these are remarkable in serving over 400 square miles. Ipswich and Exeter serve something over 50,000 people each, and Bristol and Norwich each serves over 100,000. The hinterland of Norwich is the largest in the country (over 600 square miles), which helps to justify the oft-remarked suggestion that Norwich has more provincial individuality than any other town in the country. The hinterland of Newcastle-on-Tyne exceeds 400 square miles by reason of its extension into Redesdale. At the other end of the scale there were 37 towns in which the total population served, town as well as hinterland, was less than 5000. Only 86 had an area of less than

---

[3] F. H. W. Green, "Town and country in Northern Ireland," *Geography* 34 (1949), 89-96.

[4] In all these statements, subsidiary centres are considered as though they were independent.

[5] H. Hinz, 'Oplandet og dets Behydning for Køpstaedernes Erhvervsliv,' Dansk Byplanslaboratorium, 1941.

20 square miles. Such an area is, of course, less than that of many large towns themselves. In only nine cases was both the population served less than 5000 and the area less than 20 square miles.

These densities must be particularly borne in mind when correlations are sought between populations in urban hinterlands and services provided (shops, cinemas, hospitals and the like). By studying a sufficiently large number of examples some useful generalizations may however be made. The numbers of the shops have been counted for the centres in south-west England, and from the tables thus constructed it appears that there is an average of about 110 persons (in town and hinterland) for each shop in the centre; the average for a town alone is about 60 persons per shop. This matter needs much closer study and analysis, but it is at least a quick pointer to anomalies which need investigation, and it can have certain immediate applications. One example may be given. A certain town in southern England which had suffered considerable bomb damage sought a Compulsory Purchase Order for the reconstruction of its central area and claimed what appeared to be an unduly large acreage as a shopping centre. It was readily shown that the number of sites thereby provided would, when added to the existing shops, so greatly exceed the admittedly tentative figures quoted above that one could be safe in asserting that the shopping precinct was too large.

Population structure in the hinterlands. Centres of the Fifth Order present many points of interest, but this is not the place to enter into the controversy about "key villages." It is however worth recalling the relationship between what Professor Stamp has, with reference to rural areas, called the primary, secondary and adventitious elements in the population. My colleague S. W. E. Vince has observed that, in a Rural District the population of which is known to be almost exclusively devoted to agriculture, the proportion of primary agricultural workers to secondary workers (those mainly employed in providing services for the former) is in the ratio of two to one. He studied Marshland, a Fenland Rural District in Norfolk; it may be found that where the agriculture is of a different type the proportion is a little different, but the divergence is not likely to be great. The secondary population in such a rural area will be found mainly in nucleated villages in Anglo-Saxon England, or in the specialized hamlets of the Celtic west—in other words in the Fifth Order centres. Difficulties arise where, as in East Anglia, many places are doubtfully classified as between the Fourth and Fifth Order; and bus services have themselves played some part in the rise and fall between the two categories. But it is clear that certain functions are normally not carried out in Fifth Order settlements, and that for them the rural dwellers frequently travel (commonly once a week) to the nearest accessible market town.

If, in a purely agricultural area, our estimates of population in centres and hinterlands are correct we should, by studying instances which are not too complex, be able to obtain an idea of the ratio between the urban, mainly secondary, population and the rural population within which, as we have seen, the ratio is about two to one. Several small towns in eastern England may be said to have very few families who are not associated with agriculture, and Wisbech may be taken as a typical example. Here, and in such characteristic market towns in purely rural areas as Horncastle (Lincolnshire), Launceston (Cornwall), Ledbury (Herefordshire), Northallerton (Yorkshire), Kirkby Stephen (Westmoreland), Market Weighton (East Riding), or Llanidloes or Ruthin in Wales, the population ratio between town and hinterland is found to be fairly constant at three to five. Since one-third of the hinterland population is assumed to be secondary, the ratio between secondary and primary in the town and hinterland together emerges as $[3 + (\frac{1}{3} \times 5)] : [(\frac{2}{3} \times 5)]$; i.e. 7 to 5.

In spite of the perverseness of administrative boundaries and the existence of subsidiary, moribund, or growing centres within the hinterlands themselves, with the consequent difficulty of estimating populations, divergences from these ratios are a valuable guide in the study of rural facilities. If for example the ratio of town population to hinterland population is much lower than three to five, it must mean one of four things; agriculture is either more backward, less mechanized, less intensive, or of such a nature that marketing is less complicated than normal; or the town is deficient in urban facilities; or there is an unusually high proportion of secondary population in villages or hamlets within the hinterlands; or there is an excess of adventitious population in the hinterland and not in the town itself (which is unlikely). These are questions which those engaged in rural planning must attempt to answer. One may mention a few towns without attempting to explain the low ratio they exhibit; Holsworthy (ratio 1 to 4 instead of 3 to 5), Lampeter (1 to 9), Llangefni (1 to 3), Leyburn (1 to 4).

If on the other hand a town in a mainly agricultural area has a comparatively large population in comparison with its hinterland, it may mean that it has either Third Order functions as well as Fourth Order, or that it has a large adventitious population. It is probable that the latter is usually the main reason. It is indeed not easy to find a Third Order town without a considerable adventitious population; Boston (Lincs.) and Bury St. Edmunds are probably as good examples as can be found, and examination shows that the ratio of population in the town to that in its Fourth Order hinterland is here only slightly greater than three to five. This would suggest that the Third Order function does not always involve a much larger secondary population than does the Fourth Order. Many parts of the country are indeed without direct access by bus, or easy access by any means of transport, to a Third Order centre; presumably the local residents save up for infrequent visits to the Second Order town, the Provincial Capital, or even to London. The study of the hinterlands of these major cities is however beyond the scope of the present inquiry.

In modern England and in much of modern Wales the great majority of Third Order towns, and probably even the majority of Fourth Order towns, have an adventitious population (industrial, commercial, administrative or retired) and discrepancies from the three to five ratio are in the main due to this. Occasionally one finds a fortuitous three to five ratio hiding a similar proportion of adventitious population in the town and in its hinterland. Such is certainly the case with such strange bed-fellows as Neath and Ystalyfera in Glamorgan, and Tunbridge Wells, Barnsley and Haywards Heath.

Different types of urban hinterland. The fact that hinterlands overlap need not worry us greatly if we remember the conception of a low or high watershed. An average hinterland is however made up of many components. Every single commercial, industrial, professional and administrative undertaking has a territory of its own, and these territories cannot exactly coincide. To take an average of the boundaries between different types of hinterland would involve assessing subjectively the amount of significance to attach to each; hence the merit of tackling the problem indirectly, by studying transport facilities provided and used. Nevertheless it is apparent that in some urban hinterlands the average is a mean between almost coincident individual functional hinterlands, whereas in others there is so much difference that the average is of somewhat reduced value. It is therefore important to consider significant types of functional hinterland. Hinterlands defined by the daily journey to work and by retail shopping and distribution are perhaps the two most significant, and it can indeed be argued that all others tend eventually to conform to them. It may further be argued that the journey-to-work hinterland ultimately reveals itself as the dominant factor.

In the North Midland Region, surveys, organized by the Regional Office of the Ministry of Town and Country Planning, have been made of these two types of functional hinterland. Both surveys are imperfect; the journey-to-work survey was by means of a questionnaire sent to employers of more than 20 insured workers and not all of these replied; the shopping survey was a village-to-village questionnaire. But there is no reason to suppose that there is any great inaccuracy in the general picture. Figure V shows for Grantham and Scunthorpe the "watershed" lines of (a) the Journey-to-Work Survey, (b) the Weekly Shopping Survey, and (c) the "average" hinterland obtained by the present method of study. One would conclude, and rightly, that Grantham and its surrounding territory have a well-integrated community of interest. At Scunthorpe, on the other hand, the journey-to-work and shopping hinterlands are not coincident to the same degree. The bus service hinterland derived from market day services does coincide more closely with the weekly shopping hinterland, but it may well be expected that the better daily services to Scunthorpe (by train as well as road) will lead to the shopping "watershed" of the latter extending eastwards as the journey-to-work has done. Corby in Northamptonshire well illustrates the tendency for a newly developed work centre to become also a shopping and entertainment centre, and the decision

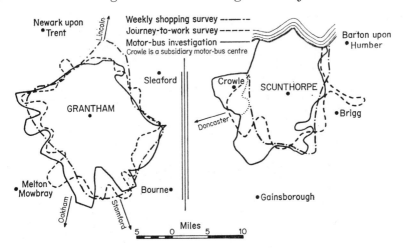

F<small>IGURE</small> V. Grantham and Scunthorpe: "Watershed" Lines for Different Functions.

to apply the New Towns legislation here will, one hopes, lead to better planning than would otherwise have been the case.

If one examines 20 towns in the North Midland region which emerged as centres in the shopping survey but which failed to qualify as bus centres, one finds that 14 of them "exported" more workers daily than they "imported." There is every reason to suppose therefore that, if recent tendencies continue, they will go on losing ground as shopping centres. Of the six exceptions, Sandiacre, Kirkby-in-Ashfield, and Beeston are part of the South Nottinghamshire industrial area and either directly adjoin, or are virtually part of, larger urban centres. There remain three, Caistor, Immingham and Raunds, each of which is worthy of closer examination for there must be, or must recently have been, a growth of population here. Is it still continuing?

A fairly detailed survey of functional hinterlands is to be found in Bracey's survey of Wiltshire.[6] In that county of nucleated villages it was relatively easy to conduct a reliable survey by questionnaire. In a comparison between the results of the present investigation and the answers to his question concerning weekly shopping the agreement is good. Figure VI summarizes the results of a survey of the boundaries of six voluntary county

---

[6] H. E. Bracey, 'Wiltshire: rural realities,' Methuen (in press).

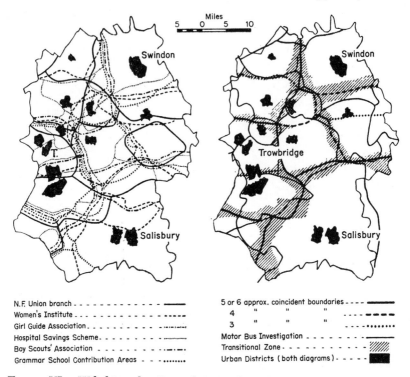

N.F. Union branch - - - - - - - - - - - - - - ——
Women's Institute - - - - - - - - - - - - - - - - - -
Girl Guide Association - - - - - - - - - - - - -·-·-·-·-
Hospital Savings Scheme - - - - - - - - - -···········
Boy Scouts' Association - - - - - - - - - - -·—·—·
Grammar School Contribution Areas - - -·········

5 or 6 approx. coincident boundaries - - - - ——
4   "   "   "   - - - - — — —
3   "   "   "   - - - -·········
Motor Bus Investigation - - - - - - - - -·——·
Transitional Zone - - - - - - - - - - - ▨
Urban Districts (both diagrams) - - - - - ██

FIGURE VI.   Wiltshire; the General Coincidence of Areas of Voluntary Associations and of Bus Service Hinterlands.

associations and the approximate coincidence of the areas so defined and the bus hinterlands. Except near the county boundary which, in these activities, imposes an obligatory limit it will again be seen that the comparison with the boundaries of the hinterlands of bus centres is very close. It must not be supposed that such a close coincidence always exists; in Somerset, for example, the corresponding boundaries show far less coincidence either with each other or with the bus service hinterlands. This is certainly related to the difficulty evidently experienced by operators in the south-east of that county in finding economic routes for their bus services; for their successive time-tables show more frequent changes than are usual.

The boundaries of food delivery areas have been ascertained in certain cases and the divergences from the bus hinterlands are of interest. In the new 'North Staffordshire plan' Eccleshall appears as a centre for food delivery, but its failure to qualify as a bus centre is to be correlated with its not being a centre to which any appreciable number of persons travel daily to work and it has no cinema. Regular journeys to work account for the extent of Stone's hinterland northwards of its present food delivery area and of Leek's hinterland to the south-west.

A very large conurbation presents certain special problems in that its different functional centres and their hinterlands are often very far from coincident. In Greater London for example the places where men work and where their wives shop and where both go for recreation and entertainment may be entirely different. With the assistance of the London Transport Executive an attempt was made to determine the main shopping foci of London's suburbia, and to define their hinterlands by the method described in this paper. It is hoped to describe the results in detail elsewhere. The most distinguishing feature of life in the suburbs of a very large town is this lack of cohesion between the different aspects of daily life. It presents a fundamental problem in modern urban communities and the internal social structure of conurbations merits much further attention.

Where a change is taking place and the direction of change is not frequently altering, it would seem that the different types of functional hinterland tend to coincide. To revert to the "watershed" analogy, there are however certain areas of stagnation which may be likened to areas of inland drainage. There are small hinterlands which, according to the criterion adopted, either just appear or just fail to appear on a map. If it were possible to obtain sufficient data to construct it, a three-dimensional model would illustrate this, and other points, exceedingly well. Failing such a model, a series of sections could be used instead. An imaginary section drawn along a line between Norwich and Bury St. Edmunds might resemble Figure VII. The most dominant place is Norwich, a city which is a major centre for so many

FIGURE VII.   An Analogy of "Watersheds."

different functions that it may, to preserve the physical analogy, be said to represent a low base-level which enables its converging transport services to cut back into its neighbours' territory. By most counts, Wymondham has been "engulfed"; its catchment area is represented but as a step on the road leading into Norwich. Attleborough, farther away, appears by some criteria as an area of independent drainage; by other counts it has been engulfed by Norwich. Thetford retains independence, with a catchment area of some 110 square miles lying between those of Norwich and of Bury St. Edmunds. The latter has not such a large tributary area as Norwich, but is nearer to Thetford and probably therefore the more dangerous competitor. One may say here that the one "gradient" is steeper than the other.

Implicit in these remarks is the conception of centres of different orders of significance. Norwich and Bury St. Edmunds are towns with a Third Order function; Thetford is not. Norwich is perhaps the most important Third Order town in the country which does not qualify for the additional function of Provincial Capital. It is possible to map, by methods similar to those here employed, the approximate hinterlands of Third Order towns as such, if one accepts Smailes' definition of minor cities and major towns in identifying the centres. A portion of the map so constructed is shown in Figure VIII.

Physical factors affecting types of urban hinterland. The most obvious type of topographical control is illustrated by a more or less self-contained valley hinterland. Good examples are provided by Machynlleth and Llanidloes in Wales, and by Alston (Cumberland), Allendale Town, Rothbury and Bellingham (Northumberland), in the north of England. The last two illustrate another point of interest in that a valley which is a through route may appear to lack a centre; for Rothbury and Bellingham, serving the valleys of the Coquet and the North Tyne, qualify as centres while no centre is revealed in Redesdale, a valley lying between them. Redesdale appears to be a prolongation of Newcastle's hinterland. One may fairly safely assert that this is related to the fact that Redesdale carries the main road traffic from Newcastle to Edinburgh across Carter Bar. It is not likely that the local agricultural community pays very frequent visits to Newcastle but it is likely that, because of the facilities available,

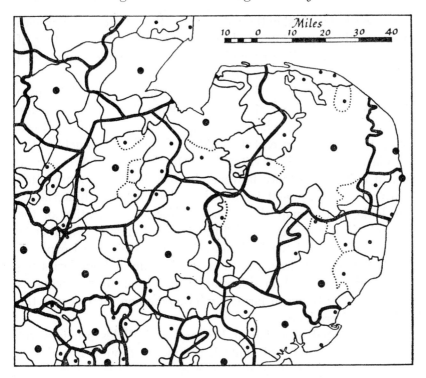

FIGURE VIII.   Hinterlands of Third Order Centres.

it pays more frequent visits there than the population of the neighbouring dales, and that there is in Redesdale a larger non-farming population which has a community of interest along the main road.

In lowland England there are of course many instances of lines of old market centres along valleys, though they are not usually so distinct since they are not separated from one another by unpopulated watersheds. Other factors come into play in delineating the hinterlands of such valley towns as Bedford, St. Neots, Huntingdon and St. Ives on the river Ouse, and Warwick, Stratford and Evesham on Shakespeare's Avon. Where a river flows in an entrenched valley which is topographically difficult for through communication it has taken little to divert the traffic in another direction. For example, though Whitby serves Lower Eskdale the middle and upper parts of that valley appear to fall within the hinterlands of Loftus and Middlesbrough respectively, though each lies outside the valley altogether. Often a town with an unusually large hinterland is a route center at a meeting of several valleys. Salisbury and Exeter are examples and, on a rather smaller scale, Launceston and Monmouth.

Dorchester is situated near the southern edge of its own hinterland with comparatively gentle slopes down to it from the valleys to the north, whereas a mile or two south of the town comes the upstanding east-west ridge of chalk which acts as the boundary between the territories of Dorchester and Weymouth. Such a coincidence may however be fortuitous for, more often than not, an escarpment is not a boundary between hinterlands. One looks at the map almost in vain for any indication of the lines of the Cretaceous and Jurassic escarpments which cross South England and the Midlands. The usual historical explanation is that market towns commonly grew up at boundaries between areas engaged in different types of farming, serving as meeting points between farmers whose common interest was the exchange of produce.

The indented coastline of England and Wales provides yet another type of physical control, commonly though not always exercised indirectly. The small average size, and irregular shape, of the hinterlands in Cornwall is due in part to the indented peninsular character of the county. But, apart from seaport towns which like Bristol and Hull have long since developed into centres of more than local significance, the hinterlands of coastal towns tend to be smaller than the average. The most obvious reason is that only about half as much territory can lie within the same radial distance from the centre. In medieval times seaport towns were frequently situated as far as possible up-river; not merely for shelter, but because such a site is central to a more extensive hinterland than one at the river mouth. This is perhaps rather more revealing than merely to state that the lowest bridging point of a river or estuary commonly coincides with the highest navigable point. Exeter and Ipswich are two characteristic examples. Some seaside towns are very specialized and, as with mining towns, the physical factor acts indirectly.

Economic and social factors. Hinterlands of small area characteristically occur in densely populated industrial districts, but each district has characteristics of its own. In South Wales topographical units coincide in general with social and industrial areas and cause the valley hinterlands to be sharply defined. In the upland parts of the West Riding there are several hinterlands (e.g. of Sheffield and Barnsley) where the dominant factors are seen to be topographical in the west and social and industrial in the east. In the West Riding generally, and in Lancashire, a close analysis of the effects of the various factors would be well repaid.

An interesting point is well illustrated in the Black Country, where six centres have been identified. Two, Dudley and West Bromwich, in the "industrial core," have almost exclusively urban hinterlands. Around them lie, in order of importance, Birmingham, Wolverhampton, Walsall and Stourbridge, three of which reveal very clearly the tendency of rural hinterlands to be developed eccentrically on the side opposite to the nearest conurbation. In Lancashire and Yorkshire this tendency can be seen not only in the small centres immediately around the Manchester-Salford conurbation, but also in the larger towns just outside the whole industrial area; the large hinterland of York, for example, being less extensive to the south-west than in any other direction.

County Durham is a complex area in which a considerable lack of coherence is evinced. Spennymoor is an extreme example which illustrates the tendency. The area of greatest lack of unity of outlook in this county is that near Easington which has been selected as the site of the New Town of Peterlee. This draws attention to a point of general interest, examples of which can be seen all over the map. Some hinterlands are a neatly shaped approach to the theoretical hexagon of the honeycomb, whereas in others straight line boundaries alternate with irregular interdigitating lines. It must not be supposed that these latter are an entirely accurate representation of the irregular boundaries of the neighbouring hinterlands, but they are of some significance and indicate that in such a border area there is competition between one town and another. Where three or four hinterlands meet under such confused conditions one might well say that there is a *prima facie* case for a New Town. For example, a New Town sited near Charing or Lenham in Kent, where the hinterlands of Canterbury, Maidstone, Faversham and Ashford converge, could reasonably be planned as a focal point for a group of persons who have now no ties with any one particular town.

The community of interest focusing on a line of communication has already been illustrated by the Newcastle–Edinburgh road and examples may be seen around London. The line of the Great North Road can be detected in the elongated hinterland of Hatfield, and to some extent at Hitchin. The partial severance of the hinterland of Leighton Buzzard is seen to be due to the influence of the Holyhead road, which has created a community of interest of its own; the influence of the Folkestone road can be seen in the alignment of the hinterlands of Wrotham and Swanley Junction, two places which qualify as centres only by reason of local bus routes running along this road. The "streakiness" of several hinterlands to the south-west of the metropolis can be related to the lines of roads across the heath country, and also to the railways. Here towns such as Woking have sprung up around railway stations, as dormitories for London workers.

Hinterlands whose orientation, and even existence, is due to railway communications are revealed by the survey, which stresses the fact that in general bus services reflect tendencies already initiated by other forms of transport. Thus the eastward extension of the hinterland of Romford (part of the undifferentiated hinterland of the London conurbation) was due to facilities early provided by the electrified District Railway. This is faithfully reflected in the local bus network.

Industry is not confined to the great industrial areas; there are a number of industrial towns of various ages set down in rural England which have carved out hinterlands for themselves. Eastleigh (Hants) where the L.S.W.R. set up its main railway works in the middle of the last century qualifies as a small but growing centre. A reverse tendency can be seen in some of the little industrial towns of earlier ages. Higham Ferrers, Burton Latimer, and Rothwell in central Northamptonshire are, by contrast with neighbouring Corby, no longer centres; Desborough qualifies by little more than an academic margin. In several parts of the country small medieval wool towns no longer function as centres. On the other hand Swindon, which until the nineteenth century was a very small market town, has now become a railway and general engineering centre; it has increased its hinterland greatly, at the expense of its neighbours including

Marlborough, and has engulfed several smaller areas such as Wooton Bassett and Highworth.

Mineral extraction often leads directly to industrial development and thus to the growth of a town, as can be seen for example in South Wales, Lancashire, Yorkshire, and County Durham. The growth and decay of towns can sometimes be traced as mining activities shift from exposed to concealed coalfields. In the latter, new centres can be seen developing at the present day. Thus Dinnington, which has no urban history, appears as a subsidiary centre at the eastern extremity of the Sheffield hinterland and Bolsover, a little farther south, now qualifies as an independent centre.

A geological control acting through the social history of mining communities is illustrated by the two very unusually shaped hinterlands of Ammanford in South Wales and Spennymoor in County Durham. The Ammanford hinterland extends in a long arm down the Gwendraeth valley between the hinterlands of Carmarthen and Llanelly. This can only be explained by the tendency of residents in the old anthracite collieries in the valley to maintain a common interest with the "anthracitopolis" of Ammanford. Spennymoor is the only case where the hinterland had to be shown on the map in two parts, the main one round the town itself and the other near the coast, completely surrounded by an area in which Sunderland holds the major interest, and separated also by a territory primarily tributary to Durham city. The explanation would seem to be a community of interest between mining families in the newer colliery area near the coast and their connections in the older area near Spennymoor. Coal mining is not the only activity which has led to this result. Ironworks set up where the ore is extracted afford a good example, as in the village which within the last twenty years has grown into the town of Corby (Northants). Corby has already carved itself out a hinterland from the territories of Stamford and Kettering.

HINTERLAND BOUNDARIES OF NEW YORK CITY AND BOSTON IN SOUTHERN NEW ENGLAND *

HOWARD L. GREEN

The concept of the metropolitan community upon which this study is based holds that a large city tends to organize the region surrounding it, that such cities enter into a relationship with their hinterlands.[1] The city is the focal point of regional activity, with the hinterland carrying on functions that are necessary to the metropolitan community as a whole. The purpose of this paper is to define and analyze the hinterland boundaries in southern New England between two such large cities, New York and Boston.

THE NEW ENGLAND REGION

The traditional concept of New England as a homogeneous metropolitan region focusing upon Boston has been increasingly questioned during the last quarter century. As early as 1930, Kent Hubbard, President of the Connecticut Manufacturers Association, suggested that Connecticut should leave New England because the state was farther advanced than the rest of New England.[2] A few months later, Frederick G. Fasset wrote, "If there was a New England as revealed by a common outlook, it has ceased to exist." [3]

In 1950, John H. Fenton stated that New England "appears actually to have been subdividing for the last twenty years" into

---

* Reprinted from *Economic Geography*, Vol. 31, No. 4 (October, 1955), pp. 283-300, with permission of author and publisher.

[1] McKenzie defined the territorial differentiation of functions in the metropolitan community as follows: "communications, finance, management and the more specialized commercial and professional services, are becoming more highly concentrated in or near the center of the dominant city; while other activities, such as manufacturing, the less specialized forms of merchandising, and institutions catering to leisure time activities, are becoming more generally dispersed throughout the region, in accordance with local conditions of topography, transportation and population pattern." R. D. McKenzie: *The Metropolitan Community*, New York, 1933, pp. 70-71. See also, N. S. B. Gras: *Introduction to Economic History*, New York, 1922, pp. 187-269.

[2] *Boston Evening Transcript*, November 12, 1930, p. 8.

[3] F. G. Fasset, *Boston Evening Transcript*, January 26, 1931, p. 15.

three parts—Maine, New Hampshire, and Vermont forming one area; Massachusetts and Rhode Island another. Connecticut, however, "because of its geographical position relative to the metropolitan New York area, might be considered a third sub-division, possibly even embodying the best of the old New England tradition." [4] Fenton's informants based their opinions on "intangibles" and were "unsupported by statistics." Thus, despite widespread obituaries on the demise of New England, there has been little quantitative corroboration.

PREVIOUS DELIMITATIONS

Three earlier studies of metropolitan regions are examined here as aids to defining the hinterland boundary between New York City and Boston (Fig. I).

Park and Newcomb. In "Newspaper Circulation and Metro-

[4] J. H. Fenton, *The New York Times,* July 23, 1950, p. 40.

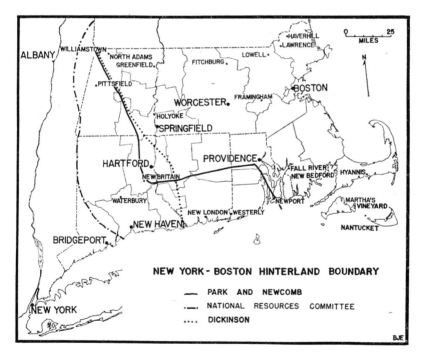

FIGURE I.

politan Regions," Park and Newcomb claim that the distribution of newspapers is related to the distribution of economic and social features; therefore, a map of newspaper regions measures social and economic regions.[5] To illustrate, they note a correlation between newspaper circulation and wholesale trade, and a further correlation between Chicago newspaper distribution and the sale of train passenger tickets to and from Chicago.

Park and Newcomb selected 41 cities as metropolitan centers (Federal Reserve cities and six others), picked the dominant morning newspaper as representative of the community, and mapped the newspaper's distribution. The boundary line lay at a point where one metropolitan paper replaced another as the dominant one. Audit Bureau of Circulations figures were utilized to give a common source of information.

For southern New England, *The Boston Globe* and the *New York Times* were chosen for study. The boundary between their areas of domination appears to run on a line from Williamstown, in northwestern Massachusetts, to Westfield, near the Massachusetts-Connecticut state line. From there the boundary proceeds to a point south of Providence. Then the boundary curves seaward to the vicinity of Newport.

Questions arise: How representative is a single criterion—newspaper circulation—as a measure of the extent of a metropolitan region? Shall we assume that one function is so constituted that it can speak for the others? The author of this article believes that metropolitan newspaper circulation tells us about metropolitan newspaper circulation. It may be a clue, but only a clue, to other functions.

National Resources Committee. A second source of metropolitan regional delimitation is a study published in *Regional Factors in National Planning and Development.*[6] This report contains a map showing "Possible Planning Regions Based upon Metropolitan Influence." The boundary between the respective hinterlands of New York City and Boston runs along the edge of Fairfield County in southwestern Connecticut, coincides with the western Connecticut and Massachusetts borders, and includes a

---

[5] R. E. Park and C. Newcomb, Chapter VIII, pp. 98-110, in McKenzie's *The Metropolitan Community*, 1933.

[6] National Resources Committee, Washington, 1935, pp. 158-159.

small part of eastern New York State opposite Williamstown as part of the Boston region.

The map, according to the report, is based upon studies of 96 metropolitan areas (1930 census definition) and 43 areas of newspaper circulation from metropolitan cities. However, it is difficult to see the relation between these criteria and the resulting regions. A study of the location of those metropolitan areas that lie in southern New England does not give the facts upon which to draw such boundaries, nor does the Park and Newcomb study of newspaper circulation yield results congruent with the map presented. The more important considerations, it appears, were the limits of the Federal Reserve districts and state boundaries.

Dickinson. Dickinson defined hinterland boundaries by analyzing and mapping various kinds of service areas.[7] The resulting boundary in New England places eastern Connecticut—Tolland, Windham, and New London Counties—in Boston's zone of influence, and continues toward the northwest, running between Hartford and Springfield and on across Berkshire County to the corner of Massachusetts.

That these three studies do not agree on the location of the boundary zone between New York City and Boston is obvious. In Massachusetts, the boundary may fall either east or west of Berkshire County; in Connecticut, boundary variations cover most of the State. One study includes part of Rhode Island in the New York area; the others do not. There is need, therefore, to define a usable boundary girdle.

THE APPROACH

In this paper, the boundary between the New York City and the Boston metropolitan hinterlands is determined from a study of the respective metropolitan functions of the two cities. Ideally, the most important metropolitan functions should be chosen as measures. In practice, however, this is impossible because of lack of data. Nevertheless, a variety of functional indicators can be measured that will provide a sample wide enough to establish the extent and importance of the two hinterlands. Measures of

[7] R. E. Dickinson: "The Metropolitan Regions of the United States," *Geogr. Rev.*, Vol. 24, 1934, pp. 278-291.

each of the following functions will be presented: transportation (truck, railroad, ship); communications (newspaper circulation, telephone calls); agriculture; recreation; manufacturing; and finance.

TRANSPORTATION

The revolution in transportation during the last century has altered both the size and shape of metropolitan regions. Formerly, ships from numerous coastal cities distributed products from small, circumscribed hinterlands to other coastal centers and to foreign ports. Then railroads, focusing upon any given center, spread the axial range of its metropolitan influence. Finally, motor transport, free from the confines of either a waterfront location or rails, diffused metropolitan influences into every hamlet.

To define the boundary of transportation flow, available data for three prime movers of persons and goods—railroads, ships, and motor trucks—are examined here.

Rail freight. Because trucking is cheaper than rail transport for short-haul freight, little rail tonnage is carried between either New York City or Boston and intermediate points. Of almost two million tons of freight analyzed by the New Haven Railroad in one sample period, only two and one half per cent of the total was conveyed between New York City and southern New England points and about the same percentage between Boston and towns in this same three-state region. Since more than half of this small percentage of traffic is between New York and Boston themselves, rail freight movements between hinterland cities and either metropolis are of little importance.[8]

Rail passengers. Passenger traffic, however, is more important. Data on point-to-point ticket sales have been compiled by the railroads of the region, although not all this information is gathered for the same period. In those places where information is recorded by different years, however, there appear to be few discrepancies.

Two factors limit the utility of the information. First, rail routes cover only specific points along the tracks. Isopleths of passenger traffic, therefore, are interpolations connecting known

[8] Conversation with Mr. John Ramsey, Research Department, New Haven Railroad.

stations and passing through many points set at some distance from the tracks. A second limiting characteristic is the lack of direct connection at every station with both New York and Boston. Stockbridge, Massachusetts, for example, enjoys direct connections with New York City via the New Haven Railroad; in order to reach Boston, it is necessary to change at Pittsfield to a Boston and Albany train. Despite these limitations, the data offer a realistic picture of rail passenger traffic flow.

Both metropolises have well-developed zones beyond their built-up areas from which people commute daily. Major commuter zones are, of course, areas with which a metropolis has a tightly knit community of interest. Places with 100 or more daily commuters lie largely within one and a half hours' travel time from each city (Fig. II). From New York City, places with 100 or more commuters reach as far north as Danbury and New Haven, including the entire Connecticut panhandle. For commuters to Boston, the zone extends in an arc with a 40-mile

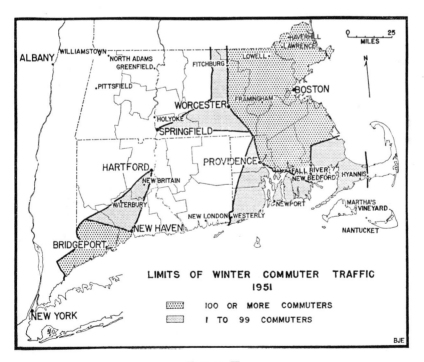

Figure II.

radius including Fitchburg, Worcester, Providence, Fall River, New Bedford, and Plymouth. During the summer the belt is extended south of Plymouth to nearer portions of Cape Cod.

Beyond these limits are extremes set by a few hardy commuters: the extreme distance to New York extends northward in the Connecticut Valley to Hartford, a trip of over 100 miles each way; the extremes to Boston are almost as great. On the three rail lines leading into Boston from southern New England, the following are absolute points: Gardner, Massachusetts, on the Boston and Maine route (65 miles); Springfield, Massachusetts, on the Boston and Albany line (98 miles); and Westerly, Rhode Island, on the New Haven road (88 miles). Because time-distance accessibility is a prime consideration, it is not surprising that commuter traffic actually crosses the hinterland boundaries as determined by other measures.

For rail coach passengers, the boundary nearly bisects southern New England (Fig. III). However, along the coastal route of the New Haven Railroad, the New York 90 per cent isopleth

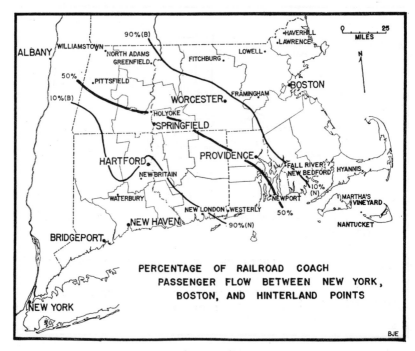

PERCENTAGE OF RAILROAD COACH
PASSENGER FLOW BETWEEN NEW YORK,
BOSTON, AND HINTERLAND POINTS

FIGURE III.

(of the total movement to New York and Boston combined) extends to New London, half the total distance to Boston, whereas the 50 per cent isopleth reaches almost to Providence. Along the inland route, via the Connecticut Valley, the 90 per cent isopleth for New York extends to Hartford, again half the total distance to Boston. Springfield lies within the New York zone, although eastward in Massachusetts, Boston rapidly becomes dominant. Boston's 90 per cent isopleth encompasses all of eastern Massachusetts. In the western interior the hilly country is largely oriented to New York with the breaking point near Pittsfield. Northward the territory is linked primarily with Boston.

Shipping. The dominant trend in shipping is an increased use of New York by New England shippers and a consequent decline of the port of Boston as an outlet. Actually, it is incorrect to speak of a hinterland for Boston, because there is no part of New England (with the possible exception of metropolitan Boston) that does not ship most of its exports via New York. In 1928, an extensive survey indicated that 65 per cent of New England's exports were shipped through New York and only 14 per cent through Boston.[9] Twenty years later, a study by the Federal Reserve Bank corroborated the earlier results: 81 per cent of the manufacturers queried shipped through New York, and only twelve per cent said that they shipped by way of Boston.[10]

The decline of Boston as exporter for New England, and especially that part of New England in which Boston enjoys freight rate advantages, is well known. The reason: a lack of bulk exports available for shipment through Boston. Most northeastern overseas shipments are composed of high-value manufactured goods, usually shipped in small amounts to any one specific destination. The Boston area is particularly deficient in bulk cargo; hence infrequent sailings are made from the port of Boston. Shippers, seeking full cargoes, use ports offering sufficient heavy cargo to fill out the load. This need is satisfied by New York, and New England manufacturers use the superior services of the larger port.

[9] C. E. Artman and S. H. Reed: *Foreign Trade Survey of New England,* Bureau of Foreign and Domestic Commerce, Dom. Commerce Series No. 40, Washington, 1931.

[10] A. P. Sullivan: "The Port of Boston," *Monthly Review,* Federal Reserve Bank of Boston, Vol. 32, No. 2, Feb. 1950, pp. 1-7.

Among others, one further interesting factor contributes to the choice of New York: the unexcelled development of metropolitan functions. Many firms maintain export agents or departments in the city of New York. Often, also, marketing and administrative offices are centralized here. The sum of the banking, marketing, distribution, and transportation facilities located in New York City is a major attraction for shippers. Even with more favorable freight rates, it is doubtful that Boston could regain much of its lost tonnage.

It is impossible to delimit the import boundaries between New York and Boston. New York imports for the entire nation; it is the national terminal port *par excellence.* Though the port of Boston is a major foreign and inter-coastal importer of such items as petroleum, sugar, and lumber, few of these supplies are destined for hinterland communities. Almost all of Boston's imports are utilized within the immediate environs of the city.[11] Eighteen other New England ports receive cargo for use in their local areas.

Truck transportation. Statistical data relating to point-to-point motor freight movement are scant. Gathering accurate information is difficult, since over 300 independent motor carriers operate in southern New England and few operate between all points in the three-state region. These findings, therefore, gathered from trucking industry spokesmen, are informed estimates.[12] The resulting pattern gives Boston dominance within 35 miles. The remainder of the southern New England area has greater interchange with New York City. Providence, though near the boundary line, moves more tonnage to and from New York. Worcester and Fitchburg are the western limits of Boston's dominance of metropolitan freight interchange.

COMMUNICATIONS

Rapid and efficient communications have spread the influence of the metropolis over wide areas. The daily metropolitan press

[11] War Department and U.S. Maritime Commission: *The Port of Boston, Mass.,* Port Series No. 3 (Revised 1946), Washington, D.C., pp. 301-306.

[12] From discussions with Mr. R. Woodbury for the New England Motor Rate Bureau, Inc., Boston, and Mr. H. Wagner of Malkin Motor Freight Co., Cambridge.

has become a powerful force in the acceptance of urban ideals and ideas throughout the larger community. The ability to talk person-to-person, provided by the telephone, has further extended commercial and social links with the central city.

Newspapers. Metropolitan newspaper circulation frequently is used to measure metropolitan influence. The choice of one or two newspapers from each of the two cities as a basis for measuring the extent of metropolitan influence would merely repeat the incompleteness of earlier studies. However, Audit Bureau of Circulations figures, published annually, afford a comparable measure of New York and Boston distribution. Such figures are tallied for each hinterland community for all newspapers.[13]

The information available in A.B.C. statements offers several problems of tabulation. First, Boston and New York papers are audited at different seasons of the year. Boston figures used are for the twelve months ending March 31, 1949, whereas the New York figures represent the year ending September 30, 1949. The variation introduced by this difference appears minor. A second difficulty of tabulation arises from the lack of uniformity of community names; the destination of New York papers in New England is listed by post office address, the destination of Boston papers in New England, by town names. For purposes of clarity, the data were reclassified by town names.

A final problem is posed by towns that are an integral part of a larger metropolitan area such as bedroom communities. To eliminate variations, data for each metropolitan area (as defined by the census) are gathered into a composite figure for the entire area.[14]

The resulting map indicates that the spatial transition between areas that lie distinctly within the New York readership zone and those that lie in Boston's are narrow and clearly marked (Fig. IV). At some points, the New York circulation drops from 90 per cent of the combined New York and Boston circulation to less than ten per cent within the short space of 30 miles. The 50 per cent boundary lies slightly east of Williamstown in northwest-

[13] Included are, for Boston, *The Herald-Traveler, Globe, Post,* and *Record-American;* for New York, *The Times, Herald-Tribune, Journal-American, World-Telegram, Post, Sun, Daily News,* and *Mirror.*
[14] For instance, the Brockton, Massachusetts, metropolitan area includes eleven towns, whose circulations have been totaled into one area figure.

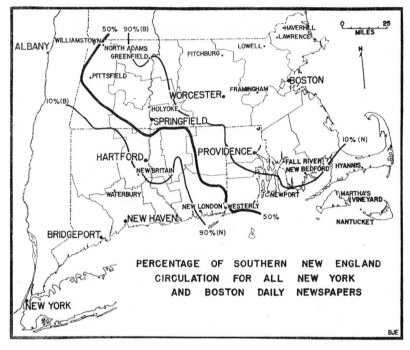

FIGURE IV.

ern Massachusetts, veers westward to the New York border and recurves eastward to the Massachusetts-Connecticut boundary south of Springfield, continues across eastern Connecticut to the Rhode Island border and arches northward some ten miles along the immediate coastal fringe.

Areas of almost complete dominance by one metropolis or the other are large. New York circulation is over 90 per cent of the combined New York City and Boston circulation in all of western Connecticut and even the southwestern corner of Massachusetts. The Boston 90 per cent isopleth of metropolitan circulation also encompasses a wide area. It extends south from Greenfield in northwestern Massachusetts, runs along the eastern border of the Connecticut Valley in Massachusetts, and finally curves southeastward to the Providence area. Cape Cod, a popular New York vacation area, is not within the 90 per cent Boston influence zone.

The extent of intermixture of metropolitan papers in the Connecticut Valley is noteworthy. From Middletown and Meridan on the south to Greenfield on the north—a distance of more than 70 miles—neither New York nor Boston has 90 per cent of the metropolitan readership. Perhaps because of the large hinterland cities of Hartford and Springfield, roughly equi-distant from New York City and Boston, the region looks to both of the larger cities with some degree of interest yet maintains a semi-independent attitude.

The comparatively large circulation of New York papers in Boston's territory causes a less sharp transition on the northern side of the boundary. The national character of New York's papers, transcending regional bounds, may be one cause of this feature; the higher editorial quality of New York papers in comparison with the Boston dailies is another.

Telephone calls. Though newspapers have been widely used as a measure of metropolitan influence, long distance telephone calls are an equally valid measure.[15] The excellence of telephone data lies in their comprehensive nature; they record both the economic and the social links of people separated by distance. In addition, they have three specific advantages over newspaper circulation: (1) Most newspapers make little attempt to push circulation beyond the trading area of their advertisers, whereas people make necessary telephone calls without consideration of trading area boundaries; (2) The telephone time-distance factor is reduced because telephone calls cover great distance with little elapsed time; (3) There is no problem of differences in quality (as with newspapers) affecting comparability. There is, however, one weakness in telephone call data: costs rise with increased call distances.

Two characteristics of the data affect the results. First, telephone call surveys are normally made during the summer, when long-distance calls are at a peak. The influx of New York City residents into southern New England during this vacation period increases New York City's proportion of the total in vacation areas, particularly in western Massachusetts, southern Rhode Island, and Cape Cod. Second, the two Bell Telephone Com-

[15] Use of telephone calls as measures of the centrality of specific communities was suggested by E. Ullman, "A Theory of Location for Cities," *Amer. Journ. of Soc.*, Vol. 46, 1941, p. 858.

panies operating in New England gather data differently.[16] For all states except Connecticut, the sample includes day and night messages; in Connecticut, day toll message data only are available. Though this introduces a variation, the difference appears minor.

The 50 per cent telephone isopleth describes an arc from western Massachusetts along the Connecticut boundary to eastern Connecticut and then coastwise, bisecting Nantucket and Martha's Vineyard (Fig. V). This line is similar to the news-

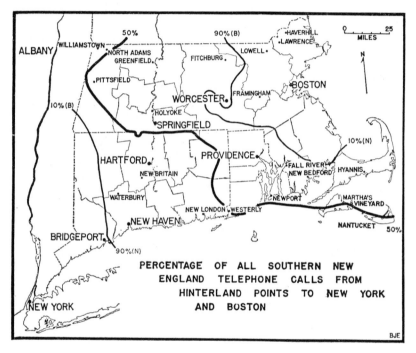

FIGURE V.

paper boundary although the distance between isopleths is greater than that described by newspaper circulation. The New York City 90 per cent isopleth encloses Connecticut west of Bridgeport, whereas Boston's 90 per cent isopleth pre-empts eastern Massachusetts.

[16] The New England Telephone and Telegraph Company serves all New England except Connecticut. The latter is served by the Southern New England Telephone Company.

Calls between Boston and Connecticut River Valley communities are greater than anticipated. One possible explanation: calls between Connecticut subsidiaries and Boston administrative offices. A number of government agencies, for instance, with regional headquarters in Boston, have branch offices in Hartford and Springfield with which frequent contact is necessary.

AGRICULTURE

In less mobile eras, urban centers developed because of the ability of the agricultural hinterland to produce surpluses. Southern New England reverses this theme; agriculture exists only in response to the demands of the great urban population.[17] The result is that the largest agricultural production in the area—dairy products, poultry, and eggs—fills immediate needs of the nearby communities and is not of significance for comparing the hinterland boundary between New York City and Boston.

In the economy of southern New England, agriculture utilizes only a small proportion of the total number of wage earners. For all of New England, including the more rural northern states, agriculture, forestry, and fishing combined, accounted for only 6 per cent of the employed workers in 1940.[18] In the main, New England is dependent upon other parts of the country for the greater part of its food.

Despite the attention given to milk production, southern New England is a deficit area which must import dairy products in order to satisfy its demands.[19] Practically the total production is consumed in local centers, almost none of it going either to New York City or Boston. Connecticut and Massachusetts combined provide less than 1 per cent of the milk received in New York City.[20] Most of this originates on farms in the extreme western

---

[17] "If the agriculture of New England had to be described in one sentence, that sentence would be that New England has the kind of agriculture that is commonly found near metropolitan centers." J. D. Black, *The Rural Economy of New England*, Cambridge, 1950, p. 228.

[18] Black, *op. cit.*, p. 87.

[19] For complete discussions of the dairy industry, see P. McComas: *The New England Dairy Industry*, unpublished Ph.D. thesis, Harvard University, 1947; W. H. Brown: *The Economics of Dairy Farming in Southern New England*, unpublished Ph.D. thesis, Harvard University, 1949; and Black, *op. cit.*, pp. 292-382.

[20] *Report of the New York Milkshed Price Committee.* Transmitted to the

portions of these states. Nearly all of Boston's milk is produced in northern New England, with just a small amount coming from the Massachusetts area northwest of Boston.

Poultry and egg production in New England has recently shown a notable increase, so that today it competes with dairying as a major source of income for farmers. The Connecticut supply of eggs and broilers finds its terminus largely in New York City. The rising production in New Hampshire and eastern Massachusetts is destined for the metropolitan Boston market.

Other crop and livestock production in southern New England represents only a small proportion of farm income, and supplies the metropolitan New York and Boston markets with a negligible amount of their total food supply. There is no sharp line of demarcation between the agricultural marketing areas of New York City and Boston. The intermediate urban centers consume a major portion of the agricultural supply within their own immediate vicinities.

RECREATION

Both New York City and Boston experience a summer exodus of vacationers into the hinterland. Not all metropolitan inhabitants spend their vacations within the hinterland; in an era of automobiles and airplanes, many travel farther for recreation. Nevertheless, many inhabitants take vacations within their metropolitan regions. A statistical study by the New England Council makes it possible to map the home state of vacationers.[21]

The home state data do not yield specific facts about the resorts patronized by New York City and Boston residents. The total population of New York and New Jersey, however, is about twice that of the New York City Standard Metropolitan Area; likewise, the Boston Standard Metropolitan Area contains about

---

Market Administrator, New York Metropolitan Milk Marketing Area, Feb. 1949, p. 166.

[21] By interviews and questionnaires, a large sample of resort proprietors were asked from what state the greatest number of their patrons come. For resorts located in Connecticut and Rhode Island, the propietors' answers were tallied for the state as a whole, whereas, in Massachusetts, the results were recorded by county in which the resort is located. See New England Council, *New England Vacation Business Inventory*, Part 1, *Overnight Accommodations for New England Vacation Visitors, A Statistical Summary*, Boston, 1947.

one-half of the inhabitants of Massachusetts. We assume in comparing home states that half of the Massachusetts vacationers are Bostonians and half those from New York and New Jersey are New Yorkers. This measure is rough but does suggest an answer.

The results depict a two-pronged movement of New York–New Jersey residents during vacation seasons: one advance is made northward into the interior hill-country of Connecticut and Massachusetts; the other (probably representing more people) along the Atlantic shoreline toward Cape Cod (Fig. VI).

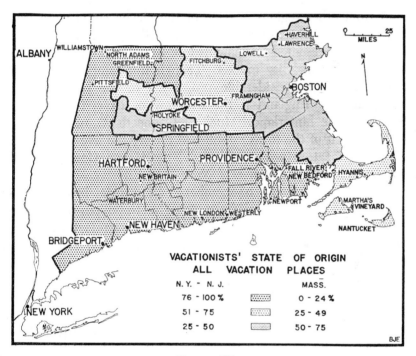

VACATIONISTS' STATE OF ORIGIN

ALL VACATION PLACES		
N. Y. - N. J.		MASS.
76 - 100 %		0 - 24 %
51 - 75		25 - 49
25 - 50		50 - 75

Figure VI.

Massachusetts residents exhibit a similar type of movement although in a different region. The coastal movements extend southward along the Massachusetts coast to Cape Cod and northward to the Maine–New Hampshire shoreline. A second thrust runs inland toward the hill and lake country of New Hampshire. In Massachusetts, the one exception, Hampden County, is probably due to the inclusion of urban hotels in Springfield.

MANUFACTURING

Southern New England is primarily an industrial community; manufacturing provided 47 per cent of all employment in 1947, a resultant income of 726 dollars for each person in New England. The region's metropolitan orientation is analyzed in two ways—in the relocation of new plants in southern New England and in the directorship of large plants already located in the area.

Twenty plant relocations in New England recently were studied in detail by Ellis; eleven represented shifts into New England from other regions.[22] Nine of the eleven shifts were from the New York City area, whereas the other two, from greater distances, represented movements into New England to be closer to the New York City market. Though this sample is small, it indicates that a considerable proportion of the relocations in southern New England is the overflow of New York-oriented firms into the hinterland. Much of Connecticut's new industry —62 per cent of the firms established during the five years 1945-1950—are located in Fairfield and New Haven Counties, both within commuting distance of New York City.[23]

The geographic ties of members of industrial boards of directors is a second way of determining metropolitan orientation. If the business addresses of directors (of all manufacturing firms employing more than 500 persons in southern New England) is either in New York City or Boston, we assume that the metropolis has a hand in directing the management of the firm.[24]

On the basis of this measure, nearly all of the three-state area is more closely linked to New York City than to Boston (Fig. VII). The limits of Boston's dominance are Fall River—New Bedford on the south and Worcester on the west. To the north, there is a minor extension of Boston influence westward along the northern border of the state—an area with few industrial firms.

[22] G. H. Ellis: *Postwar Industrial Location in New England*, unpublished Ph.D. thesis, Harvard University, 1949, pp. 160-175. See also his article "Why New Manufacturing Establishments Located in New England: August 1945 to June 1948," *Monthly Review*, Federal Reserve Bank of Boston, Vol. 31, No. 4, April 1949, pp. 1-12.

[23] *Connecticut Business Review*, Connecticut Development Commission, Hartford, 1950, p. 13.

[24] The basic source of information is *Poor's Register of Directors and Executives, United States and Canada*, New York, 1951.

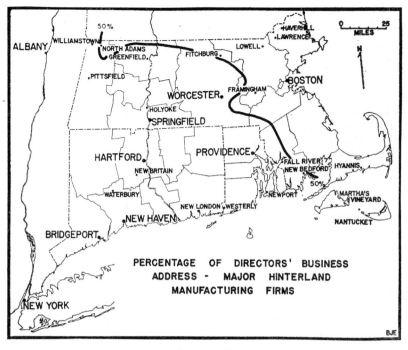

PERCENTAGE OF DIRECTORS' BUSINESS
ADDRESS - MAJOR HINTERLAND
MANUFACTURING FIRMS

FIGURE VII.

In Connecticut, major industrial hinterland centers have prac-tically no ties to Boston (Table 1). In only one firm out of 44 are there more Boston directors; 42 firms have more New York directors. In one, there is an equal number from New York and Boston. The Providence area in Rhode Island, though but 40 miles from Boston, has three firms with more New York directors to every one for Boston. In Massachusetts centers, Springfield maintains the three-to-one New York ratio seen in Providence, whereas the Worcester, Fall River–New Bedford, and Lawrence –Lowell areas are evenly divided between New York and Boston.

FINANCE

The development of financial dominance is a characteristic feature of the fully-developed metropolitan center. Regional financial functions today are largely embodied in Federal Reserve banks. Federal Reserve banks keep on deposit the legal reserves of member banks. This metropolitan concentration of funds al-

TABLE 1

HINTERLAND FIRMS

(500 or more employees)

Metropolitan Area *	Number	New York or Boston Directors	More New York Directors	More Boston Directors
CONNECTICUT				
Bridgeport	25	18	17	0
New Haven	14	10	10	0
Waterbury	14	9	9	0
New Britain—Bristol	16	3	2	1
Hartford	14	4	4	0
RHODE ISLAND				
Providence	46	32	24	8
MASSACHUSETTS				
Springfield	28	22	16	5
Worcester	9	6	3	3
Fall River—New Bedford.....	25	14	6	7
Lawrence—Lowell **	17	15	6	8

* Standard Metropolitan Area as defined in 1947 Census of Manufacturers.
** Standard Metropolitan Area as defined in 1950 Census of Population.

lows for quick movement of reserve money from the metropolis to hinterland cities if needed; powers are also available to drain money from hinterland cities, when it is in excess, into the metropolitan reserve. Machinery also exists for the inter-district movement of funds from one federal reserve metropolis to another. Thus, the present banking system in this country has established metropolitan financial functions in specific communities. Boston and New York are two such centers.

Two indicators shed light on this situation: (1) the votes by banks for choice of Federal Reserve City and subsequent adjustments, and (2) New York and Boston banks listed as correspondents of hinterland banks.

Federal Reserve Districts. In choosing sites for metropolitan regional Federal Reserve Banks in 1914, the Senate Committee charged with the responsibility polled future member banks on their three preferences of cities as Federal Reserve headquarters.[25] (Table 2). The results of the first-place votes are par-

[25] *Location of the Reserve Districts in the United States,* Senate Document 485, 63rd Congress, 2nd Session, 1914, pp. 352-355.

ticularly revealing: as early as 1914, only seven of 71 banks in Connecticut listed Boston as first choice. Even in Massachusetts, 17 of 154 banks thought New York a superior location. Among Rhode Island banks the 16 choices showed eleven banks favorable to Boston, four to New York; the other vote was cast for Providence.

TABLE 2

FIRST CHOICE VOTE FOR FEDERAL RESERVE BANK CITY

Member Bank State	Boston	New York City	Providence
Connecticut	7	64	0
Massachusetts	137	17	0
Rhode Island	11	4	1
Total	155	85	1

Despite this vote, the Boston district was set up to include Connecticut. By 1915, however, the complaints of Connecticut banks forced alteration of the boundary so that Fairfield County was transferred to the New York district. Why was Connecticut placed within the Boston district? Possibly because this addition gave Boston a sufficiently larger hinterland to equal in size most other reserve districts. The economy of the five remaining states could probably not offer sufficient reason to maintain a reserve bank in Boston.

Correspondent banks. The number of hinterland banks listing New York or Boston houses as correspondents is another measure of metropolitan orientation, although a rough gauge. The difficulty with this criterion is that a New York correspondent may get 99 per cent of the business and a Boston bank but one per cent, yet both would be listed as correspondents. As an example, Hartford banks listed more than twice as many New York as Boston correspondents; yet one bank shows more than seven times as many checks from New York at a total value 14 times greater than checks originating in Boston [26] (Table 3).

Nearly all Connecticut banks list a majority of New York correspondents (Fig. VIII). The sparsely settled eastern and northeastern parts of the state, closer to Boston, are less completely

[26] Brief prepared by Hartford Chamber of Commerce for Civil Aeronautics Board: *Statement of Facts Concerning Hartford, Conn.*, 1943, p. 10.

TABLE 3

CHECKS CLEARED BY ONE HARTFORD BANK, MARCH, 1943

Origin	Number of Checks	Value
Boston	993	$ 180,994
New York City	7,074	2,805,162

oriented to New York houses. In Massachusetts, the state borders are the boundary except for Williamstown in the extreme northwest and Springfield (where correspondents are equally divided between the metropolitan centers). Boston banks are dominant by at least two to one throughout the state, with several exceptions: Greenfield and Northampton in the Connecticut River Valley; Worcester; New Bedford; and possibly Cape Cod and southern Berkshire County (these two areas have few banks).

Rhode Island offers an interesting contrast. Whereas the southern half of the state appears in the boundary zone, and but

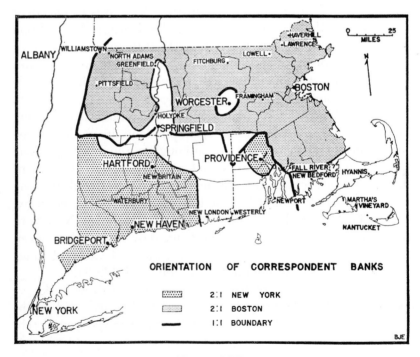

FIGURE VIII.

slightly weighted on the New York side, Providence is strongly linked with New York City.

There is a marked tendency for large hinterland cities to show stronger links with New York City than smaller communities in the same general area. Springfield is evenly divided, although Holyoke is definitely oriented to Boston. Worcester is less strongly linked with Boston than its location would indicate; similarly New Bedford. Providence, but 40 miles from Boston, is most completely tied to New York City. These facts, and discussions with bankers, indicate that major cities in the area look toward the financial capital of the country rather than to the regional center at Boston.

A second major factor in delimiting correspondent bank boundaries appears to be the importance of state borders. With few exceptions, Connecticut and Rhode Island could be placed within the New York sphere, Massachusetts within the Boston zone.

COMPOSITE BOUNDARY

Seven functional indicators presented in this paper can be synthesized to give a composite boundary. The indicators are: (1) railroad coach ticket purchases, (2) an estimate of truck freight movement to New York and Boston, (3) metropolitan newspaper circulation, (4) long-distance telephone calls, (5) metropolitan origin of vacationers, (6) business addresses of directors for major industrial firms, and (7) metropolitan correspondents for hinterland banks.

The median or middle boundary of the seven functional indicators measured stretches southwestward from the vicinity of North Adams to Pittsfield, then recurves in an arc, passing near Holyoke (Fig. IX). It arches northward from its southeasterly path to include Providence in the New York hinterland. Finally, this median boundary follows the Rhode Island–Massachusetts border to the sea.

Connecticut, with the minor exception of the extreme eastern section, is linked with New York by every measure. The northwestern tip of Berkshire County, Massachusetts, also shows a strong affinity for New York, as do southern coastal fringes of Rhode Island.

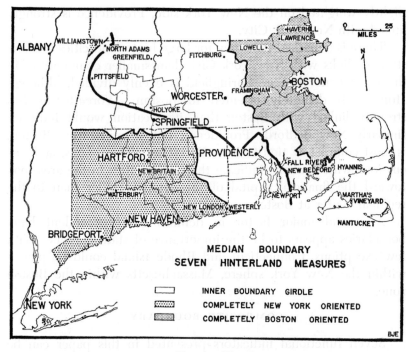

Figure IX.

Of the three-state area, eastern Massachusetts alone is tied closely to Boston. This strongly Boston-oriented section is bounded on the west by the eastern border of Worcester County and on the south by the farther limits of Plymouth County.

CONCLUSION

These results in part bear out the contention that Connecticut does not belong to the same region as Massachusetts. However, it is not just the proximity of Connecticut to New York City that is the reason for this realignment, as has been contended, but rather the close functional community of interest between the two. If the realignment of regions is to be based upon functional ties with metropolitan centers—nodal rather than homogeneous regions—then most of Rhode Island and southwestern Massachusetts must also be included within the New York City region.

New England remains a regional name, perhaps connoting an

area with a uniform historical development pattern prior to the era of suburban expansion, of the telephone, the automobile, the airplane, and the metropolitan centralization of management and finance.

DIFFERENTIATION IN METROPOLITAN AREAS *

LESLIE KISH

The metropolitan area is an increasingly important form of organization in modern industrial society. Due to the effect of motor transportation on spatial relations, and due to the structural demands of a highly integrated economy, there arises "a more open regional community composed of numerous territorially differentiated, yet interdependent, units of settlement." [1]

There have been numerous studies of the interdependence of the local communities in the metropolitan area surrounding the center.[2] The service areas of different institutions and of various specific functions have been mapped. It has been shown for some functions that the metropolitan area is organized from the dominant center into an axiate pattern of interdependent component units.

The methods of concentric circular zones have been applied fruitfully to the study of the metropolitan area to show "that the influence of a large city over surrounding settlement tends to wane with distance outward. This gradient pattern of a city's influence may be illustrated by many series of social statistics." [3] Circular zones taken at successively greater distances from the metropolitan center indicate that differentiation is present in the metropolitan area as a whole—that the metropolitan area is not homogeneous but structured toward the dominant center. These results are usually presented by comparing the averages of the

* Reprinted from the *American Sociological Review*, Vol. 19, No. 4 (August, 1954), pp. 388-398, with permission of author and publisher. The references in parentheses in this paper refer to pages in Leslie Kish, "On the Differentiation of Ecological Units," Ph.D. dissertation, University of Michigan, 1952, where more details of the results and of the methods may be found.

[1] R. D. McKenzie, *The Metropolitan Community*, New York: McGraw-Hill, 1933, p. 69.

[2] See A. H. Hawley, *Human Ecology*, New York: Ronald Press, 1950, Ch. 13.

[3] McKenzie, *op. cit.*, p. 113.

circular zones, and the trend line of these averages is sometimes called the "gradient." [4]

Studies of the trend of zonal averages reveal much about the structure of the metropolitan area. However, in yielding but a fraction of the total information, they may conceal much in the differences remaining hidden within each of the zones (pp. 8-12). "Obviously, the arbitrary concentric circle is useful only for purposes of comparison. It does not show the details of expansion, as growth is usually very uneven in different parts of the territory falling within a zone." [5] So stated McKenzie; and that: "It is well known that the suburbs of the very large city may differ greatly, one from another, in the make-up of their populations. Residential suburbs, particularly the most exclusive ones, tend to have a high proportion of women, a relatively low ratio of children, and a small proportion of foreign-born; while in most industrial suburbs the conditions are reversed." [6] Furthermore, this is no mere observed accident but a consequence of growth which has its place in social theory. "As the community grows, there is not merely a multiplication of houses and roads, but a process of differentiation and segregation takes place as well. Segregation is used here with reference to the concentration of population types within a community. Economic segregation is the most primary and general form." [7] Again: "One of the incidents of growth of the community is the social selection and segregation of the population, and the creation, on the one hand, of natural social groups, and, on the other, of natural social areas" (pp. 1-12). [8]

OBJECTIVES

This report presents a comparative study of the amount of differentiation shown by local communities *within* the concentric

---

[4] See, for example, Don J. Bogue, *The Structure of the Metropolitan Community*, Ann Arbor: University of Michigan, 1950.

[5] McKenzie, *op. cit.*, p. 175.

[6] *Ibid.*, p. 180.

[7] McKenzie, "The Ecological Approach to the Study of the Human Community," *Readings in Human Ecology*, ed. R. D. McKenzie, Ann Arbor: University of Michigan, 1934, p. 419.

[8] R. E. Park, "The Urban Community, A Spatial Pattern and a Moral Order," in *The Urban Community*, ed. E. W. Burgess, Chicago: University of Chicago, 1926, p. 3.

circular zones of the metropolitan area. Research has shown that the amount of interdependence (or organization) found in the concentric zones decreases outward, in conformity with the waning strength of the metropolitan influence from the center to the periphery. Now, the relation of organization to differentiation is fundamental in sociological and ecological theory: "Organization necessarily presupposes differentiation."[9] Hence, the amount of differentiation—as of organization—should vary directly with the strength of the influence of the metropolitan center. We should expect the amount of differentiation to be greater in the inner zones of the metropolitan area near the central city, and to be less in the outer zones near the periphery. The chief objective of the present paper is to demonstrate the existence of this difference in the amount of differentiation, and to devise methods for its measurement.

Four additional hypotheses were derived as effects of the strength of the metropolitan influence:

(1) There are consistent and distinct patterns of differentiation for different characteristics.

(2) The curve of decrease of differentiation is not a linear gradient. There is an inner metropolitan belt near the city with high values of differentiation; after a span of transition, at some distance from the city, a lower level of differentiation is reached. This lower *level* of non-metropolitan values prevails (with some fluctuation) in areas beyond the metropolitan influence.

(3) The larger the central city, the broader is the metropolitan belt around it.

(4) The larger the central city, the higher the values of differentiation in the metropolitan belt.

The results are in agreement with the first three of these minor hypotheses but not with the fourth.

In order to obtain a broad general test of the hypothesis, a great number of calculations were made separately in several areas and for several characteristics. But this was a one-person study of limited scope; it is frankly exploratory and neither universal in scope nor symmetrical in form. The writer hopes that the methods and results presented here will encourage future

---

[9] Hawley, *Human Ecology*, p. 41. This is a central theme with Durkheim, Spencer and others.

research projects designed to obtain more precise and systematic measurement.

UNITS OF MEASUREMENT

The data for the eight characteristics studied were taken from the 1940 U.S. Census volumes—with the addition of some data on voting taken from official state manuals. The characteristics were obtained originally as observations on individual persons or dwelling units. However, the Census published the data as aggregates for incorporated places with populations of 2500 or more for the personal characteristics, and for places with 1000 or more for the dwelling characteristics (pp. 25-28).[10]

The operational ecological unit for the measurement of differentiation in this study is the incorporated place, the suburban city or town. This in turn is also a group of its constituent elements, of persons or of dwellings. The ecological unit is a "communal" group of its elements; and, in turn, it appears also as a "corporate unit" in the larger community which is the metropolitan area.[11] The amount of variation among those units is used as the measure of differentiation. These measures of differentiation are obtained separately in successive zones of the metropolitan area. We shall show that the measures of differentiation are substantially greater in the inner zones of the metropolitan area than in the outer.

What are the boundaries of the metropolitan area? The extent of the influence of the metropolitan center varies with the nature of different specific functions. "It is possible to observe a series of concentric zones about a center which differ in the degree of attachment of their occupants to the center, in the frequency of movement to and from the center, and in the extent to which contacts with the center are direct, involving the movements of individuals, or indirect, involving a circulation of ideas and products rather than people. . . . The areas delimited by

---

[10] The characteristics may be noted as the results are presented separately later. If the reader is inclined to wonder whether the characteristics and units represent wise choices he is advised to search the 1940 census volumes for data available for a large number of suburbs. These data were taken from: U.S. Bureau of the Census, *Sixteenth Census of the United States: 1940.* Housing, Vol. I; Housing, Vol. II; Population, Vol. II. Washington: Government Printing Office.

[11] For definitions, see Hawley, *op. cit.,* pp. 206-233.

Galpin are what may be termed primary community areas; they are described by the radius of daily movement to and from a center. . . . A metropolis, though it may exercise influence over a wide hinterland, is nevertheless the center of a rather restricted *primary* area." [12] Hawley puts the boundary of this primary area at about 15 miles for some 1936 data on commuting to Detroit. He also distinguishes a "secondary communal area" going roughly to 50 miles, and beyond that a "tertiary communal area." The characteristics studied here pertain to the circulation of people rather than of ideas and products. Hence the "metropolitan area" investigated here includes roughly the primary and the secondary communal areas—in order to contrast the amount of differentiation in the inner primary zones with that in the outer secondary zones.

THE AREAS OF MEASUREMENT

From the 146 Standard Metropolitan Areas a probability sample of 24 areas was selected initially. However, only eleven of these contained a large enough number of communities to allow computations to be made separately for the area (pp. 132-133). The measurements presented for these eleven areas may be accepted as representing all those metropolitan areas in the U.S. which are large enough to sustain a separate analysis. In addition, all of the smaller metropolitan areas in Pennsylvania were combined and investigated jointly as one "area." A similar procedure investigation was made of the combined smaller metropolitan areas of the state of Michigan.

For four of the variables the analysis was carried through in each of those areas which had a sufficient number of suburbs. For another five variables arbitrary subselections were made among the areas in order to save work.

The suburbs of each of the metropolitan areas were classified into concentric circular zones; then within each zone they were sorted into five population classes (separated by the limits of 2500, 5000, 10,000 and 25,000 persons). The measure of differentiation (*rho*, as defined below) was calculated in each of these cells separately. This was done in order to separate from the

---

[12] Hawley, *op. cit.*, p. 255.

zonal differences the possible effects of the unequal presence in the different zones of suburbs of different sizes. Finally, from the five separate *rhos* a weighted average *rho* was calculated for the zone. It is these zonal average *rhos* that are presented in the tables (pp. 19-24).[13]

THE STATISTICAL MEASURE

What statistical device should be used to measure the amount of differentiation among ecological units? Let us think of a population made up of distinct ecological units. Each of the units is described by a characteristic which is the mean of the observations made on the individuals belonging (uniquely) to that unit. The extent to which the units are differentiated among themselves can be measured in terms of the variability among the units. The most generally used measure of variability is the variance, the mean square deviation. However, the calculation of the variance among the units of a population would not in itself fill our needs. Our aims lie in the *comparisons of the relative magnitudes* of these variances; we want to be able to compare these measures when derived for different populations, and for different characteristics. In order to do that it is best to eliminate the sources of confusion due to differences in the units of measurement, and also those due to differences in the level of the total variability of the individuals composing the population.[14]

---

[13] The location of a suburb within a zone was determined by its distance from the center of the central city. This information was taken from the material of the Metropolitan Decentralization Project, with the kind permission of Professor Hawley. Within each of the defined areas every place was included in the computations. To this rule there were five exceptions of small cities with large unusual populations: two resorts, one college town and two with very large institutions. In the cases of each of these three types of exceptions the functional relationship with the centers of population are not expressed in spatial terms. The hypotheses and analyses framed in spatial terms should exclude them, and in a more complete study it may be advisable to carry on a more thorough "purification."

[14] Let X_{ij} denote the value of the observation on the jth individual of the ith unit of the population. There are N_i elements in the ith unit and its mean is

$$\overline{X}_i = \frac{1}{N_i} \sum_{}^{N_i} X_{ij}$$

In the population there are M units and a total of

$$N = \sum_{}^{M} N_i$$

R. A. Fisher defined the coefficient of intraclass correlation as the *"fraction of the variance due to that cause which observations in the same family have in common."* [15] That is: the variance among the means of the units is taken as a proportion of the total variance among the individuals in the population. Thus we separate that proportion of the total diversity among the individuals of a population which is expressed in segregation among the separate units. This measure of the segregation of the individuals into units is proposed as a measure of the amount of differentiation among those units.

Let us define the coefficient of the intraclass correlation as:

---

individuals; hence an average of

$$\overline{N} = \frac{1}{M} \sum^{M} N_i$$

individuals per unit.
The mean observation per individual in the population is

$$\overline{X} = \frac{1}{N} \sum^{M} \sum^{N_i} X_{ij}$$

The total variance among all individuals in the population may be expressed as the sum of two terms: the variance among the unit means, plus the variance among the individuals around the means of the units to which they belong:

$$\frac{1}{N} \sum^{M} \sum^{N_i} (X_{ij} - \overline{X})^2 =$$

$$\frac{1}{N} \sum^{M} N_i (\overline{X}_i - \overline{X})^2 + \frac{1}{N} \sum^{M} \sum^{N_i} (X_{ij} - \overline{X}_i)^2$$

or briefly

$$\sigma^2 = \sigma_b^2 + \sigma_w^2$$

As an illustration let us take the differentiation of the proportion of professionals in the male labor force. The population consists of the N males in the labor force, who lived in 1940 in the M suburbs of a certain size class within a specific distance zone of a metropolitan area. The number of males in the labor force in the ith city is N_i. The proportion of professionals in the labor force of the city is $\overline{X}_i$, and in the whole population of M cities it is $\overline{X}$. The observation X_{ij} for the individual is given the value 1 if the person is designated as a professional, and 0 otherwise.

σ^2 is the variance among all persons in the labor force in the pooled population of the M suburbs. For proportions (binomial variables) this is equal to $\overline{X} (1 - \overline{X})$

Also
$$\sigma_b^2 = \frac{1}{N} \sum^{M} N_i (\overline{X}_i - \overline{X})^2 = \frac{1}{M} \sum^{M} \frac{N_i}{\overline{N}} (\overline{X}_i - \overline{X})^2$$

is the variance among the different proportions of professionals of the M suburbs, each weighted by its relative size.

[15] R. A. Fisher, *Statistical Methods for Research Workers*, 11th ed., New York: Hafner, 1950, Section 40, p. 224.

$$\text{rho} = \frac{\sigma_b{}^2}{\sigma^2} - \frac{1}{N-1}\frac{\sigma_w{}^2}{\sigma^2}$$

The first principal term is the ratio of the variance among the means of the units to the total variance among the individuals in the population. The second term merely serves to shift the expected value of *rho* to zero for the situation where the differences among unit means are due to the random sorting of individuals into units.

Under those conditions $\sigma_b{}^2$ has a positive value, but *rho* is brought to zero by means of the second term. When the units are perfectly alike $\sigma_b{}^2 = 0$ and the minimum value of *rho* $= -1/(\overline{N} - 1)$ is reached. (Note that this value is close to zero when the units are large.) The maximum value of *rho* $= +1$ is reached when all the individuals within each unit are alike; that is, when $\sigma_w{}^2 = 0$ (pp. 29-50 and 118-131).[16]

SUMMARY OF THE RESULTS

This study aims to demonstrate the existence of a greater amount of differentiation among the suburbs of the inner zones near the center of the metropolitan area than among the suburbs of the outer zones. The evidence on this point is positive and clear. In each of twelve areas tested (but not in the New York area) the differentiation among the incorporated suburbs was greater in the inner zones than in the outer zones. Furthermore, the effects were rather marked. The levels of differentiation in the zones of maximum differentiation were on the average roughly from two to six times as high as the levels of the outer

[16] This definition is somewhat different from Fisher's, which assumes infinite values for M and N_1; it can be found in W. E. Deming, *Some Theory of Sampling*, New York: Wiley, 1950, pp. 192-211. This *measure of homogeneity* within units has been useful in sample design; a somewhat different form is given in M. H. Hansen, Wm. N. Hurwitz and Wm. G. Madow, *Sample Survey Methods and Theory*, New York: Wiley, 1953, I, pp. 259-260.

As far as I know this measure has not been used in the literature of social science. However, the "mean-square contingency" has a close resemblance to the *rho* for a binomial variable (pp. 96-99 and 118-124). See Josephine J. Williams, "Another Commentary on So-Called Segregation Indexes," *American Sociological Review*, XIII (June, 1948), pp. 298-303.

The different measures of homogeneity mentioned here would all give very closely similar results for the present research.

zones. The effects are of a magnitude which is of statistical as well as sociological significance. Moreover, these higher levels of differentiation in the inner zones were found to exist in accord with the major hypothesis in tests on six characteristics.[17]

In accord with a further hypothesis we find *consistent* differences in the levels of differentiation shown by different characteristics (pp. 13-18 and 80-85). It is possible to recognize specific patterns in the value of the variations for different characteristics, and these will be pointed out.

The zones of the metropolitan influence were found in general to be wider for the larger central cities than for the smaller (as expected). The Chicago influence extends to 35 miles for most characteristics; the influence of two groups of somewhat smaller cities extended to about 25 and 15 miles respectively; and the joint tabulation of the small metropolitan areas of Pennsylvania and Michigan show their influence to be within five or ten miles.

This may explain why the New York area was the only one with negative results. New York is so hemmed in by other centers that it was suspected (and found) that the decrease in the metropolitan influence cannot manifest itself. The New York metropolitan area simply does not have an outer zone in terms of differentiation. Tests were made on four characteristics in the New York area; the results were weak and inconclusive. They are not included in the cross-area discussions of specific characteristics which follow.

The greater effect of the larger cities is manifested in a wider zone of influence, in a greater number of suburban places and even more of persons affected. But (for the variables tested) the maximum value of differentiation appears to be no higher in the areas of the larger central cities than in the areas of the smaller cities.

[17] The results obtained for individual metropolitan areas are quite variable and erratic, because they depend usually on effects created by the existence of only a few incorporated places with unusual characteristics among the rather limited numbers of suburbs in the zones of individual metropolitan areas. Future studies need be less exploratory and by combining information (as we did in Pennsylvania and Michigan) obtain greater stability and more detailed results. Some details are in the tables of the dissertation. In particular the results are presented in five-mile zones up to the 25 mile limit, and they are presented separately for suburbs with populations less than 10,000. Thus we see that the effects are not due to the unequal distribution of different sizes of suburbs in the various zones.

PROPORTION OF PROFESSIONALS IN THE
MALE LABOR FORCE

Clear and marked results were obtained, and are shown in condensed form in Chart I. The amount of differentiation in the

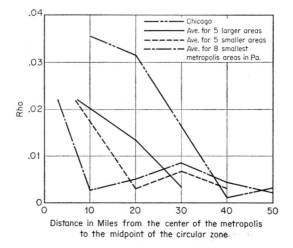

CHART I.   Differentiation of the Proportion of Professional Workers for Circular Distance Zones.*

* Data refer to the proportion of professional workers in the male labor force, for all urban suburbs. *U.S. Census of Population* (1940), Vol. II, Table 30.

inner zones is generally given by *rhos* between .015 and .040 for the individual areas; while in the outer zones the differentiation is at a much lower level of between .002 and .005. The lower level is reached in the 35-45 mile zone in the Chicago area, in the 15-25 mile zones in the areas of the other large cities, and within a distance of 15 miles in the metropolitan areas of the smaller cities (p. 89). There is a great deal of variability in the results for each city, based as they are on a rather small number of suburbs in each of the zones. Nevertheless, of the twelve areas, the only departure from the hypothesis is in the Detroit area, due solely to the university seat of Ann Arbor in the outer zones. (See Chart II.)

How variable are these characteristics?[18] As an illustration

[18] Are results which appear in the second position behind the decimal point worth bothering with? (a) It should be noted that *rho* gives directly the propor-

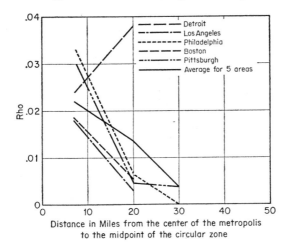

CHART II. Differentiation of the Percentage of Professional Workers for Circular Distance Zones in Five Metropolitan Areas.*

* Data refer to the proportion of professional workers in the male labor force, for all urban suburbs. *U.S. Census of Population* (1940), Vol. II, Table 30.

note the decrease of *rho* from about .030 in the inner zones of the Chicago area to about .005 in the outer zones—it denotes an interesting phenomenon. In the inner zones (up to 25 miles distance) the proportion of professionals is on the average about 9 per cent of the labor force. However, there are few suburbs near the average because the distribution of suburbs is widespread and bimodal. On the one hand there is a group of suburbs that have from 2 to 6 per cent professionals; on the other hand there is a distinct group for which the proportion is in the neighborhood of 15 per cent. The "average" suburb is conspicuous by its absence. However, the situation is quite different in the outer zones (past 35 miles). There the distribution is clearly unimodal with all the suburbs having proportions close to the zonal average of about 5 per cent. Again, in the inner zones the standard deviation of the suburbs is about 5 per cent, (around the mean of 9 per cent), whereas in the outer zones the sub-

tion of variance "accounted for"; whereas the ordinary correlation coefficient has to be squared to obtain that proportion. In these terms a *rho* of .030 is equivalent to an ordinary correlation coefficient of .173. (b) Again in terms of the variance "accounted for" in the data about professionals: the variation *within* the inner zones is six times as important as the marked difference between the averages of the inner versus the outer zones (5 per cent versus 9 per cent).

urbs are distributed with a standard deviation of only 1½ per cent (around a mean of 5 per cent).[19]

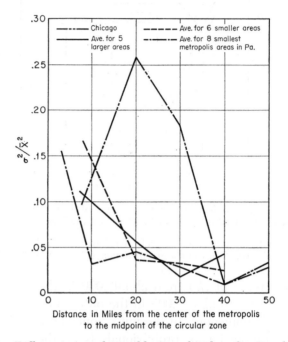

CHART III.   Differentiation of Monthly Rental Values for Circular Distance Zones.*

* Data refer to the average monthly rent (or rental values) of dwellings; for all incorporated places of 1000 or more population. *U.S. Census of Housing* (1940), Vol. I, Table 5.

AVERAGE MONTHLY RENTAL VALUE

OF DWELLING UNIT

In all of the twelve metropolitan areas we find the expected higher measures of differentiation in the inner zones rather than in the outer. Furthermore, the differences between the two levels of differentiation are marked. The higher levels of differentiation in the inner zones are between .08 and .30, and the lower levels

[19] Two remarks: (a) The bimodal distribution in the inner zones and the uni-modal distribution in the outer zones are also present when the several size classes and the ten mile wide zones are examined separately (p. 65). (b) The *clear* separation of the two types of suburbs in the inner zones may be of interest to those concerned with community typology.

in the outer zones are between .02 and .05 (Chart III).[20] The lower levels are reached generally within the same distance zones as we found in the results on the proportion of professionals. Again we find in the inner zones a bimodal distribution, with most of the suburbs far from the zonal average of 45 dollars; contrariwise, in the outer zones the distribution of the suburbs is unimodal and clustered close to the zonal average of 30 dollars (p. 88).

OPERATIVES AND KINDRED WORKERS IN THE MALE LABOR FORCE

The results on the proportion of "operatives and kindred workers" in the male labor force were mixed. Of eleven areas tested the hypothesis was confirmed in six with higher values of *rho* in the inner zones. But in five areas the hypothesis was not confirmed, three were inconclusive, and two went clearly against the hypothesis. Four of these five areas were in Pennsylvania, where in the outer zones a considerable proportion of the category of operatives consists of miners. The wide ring of the outer zones cuts through some regions with high proportions of miners and through others with low proportions, and the contrast of the two types results in high *rhos* in the outer zones. Perhaps the category of "operative and kindred workers" is not favorable to the testing of our hypothesis in those areas where miners form a considerable portion of the category.[21] (This may be an example of a negative empirical finding due to a lack of correspondence between the analytical formulation of the hypothesis and the

---

[20] The differentiation in rental value is not measured in terms of *rho* as are the other characteristics, but in terms of $\sigma_b{}^2/\overline{X}{}^2$, the square of the coefficient of variation of the unit means. This is because the data necessary for the calculation of σ^2 (hence of *rho*) for this variable, were not published by the Census; the other variables were binomial and for them $\sigma^2 = \overline{X}\,(1 - \overline{X})$ was calculated.

The measures $\sigma_b{}^2/\overline{X}{}^2$ were found to be roughly equal to 2 or 3 times larger values of *rho*. (pp. 42-43 and 129-131) Thus this characteristic is easily the most highly differentiated of all those presented here. In the inner zones (but not in the outer zones) as much as half of the total variability among the individual dwelling rental values is accounted for by its location within a particular suburb. This is considerably greater than the proportion of the variance accounted for by the marked differences among zonal averages, and it would take an ordinary correlation coefficient of $\sqrt{.5} = .7$ to do that much.

[21] This was suggested by Professor Ronald Freedman *before* the results were calculated.

operational definition of the available data.) However, of those seven tested areas which are *not* located in Pennsylvania, six support the hypothesis strongly, and only Detroit is inconclusive (p. 90).

PROPORTION OF NON-WHITE DWELLINGS

The calculations were carried out only in those six areas which contained more than a negligible proportion of non-whites (p. 99). Even in these six areas the proportions were small and the results irregular, although the level of differentiation is rather high (.07 to .16).[22] The differentiation is clearly higher in the inner zones on the average, and also specifically in four of the cities [23] (p. 99).

DWELLINGS IN NEED OF MAJOR REPAIRS

The results regarding the proportion of dwelling units in need of major repair or lacking private bath, although generally positive, are of least interest. This variable is reputed to be of low reliability, subject to a large error of response (p. 91). It is related to rental and other indexes of economic welfare; but the date of construction may be an important factor too. Of the eight places tested, seven have higher values on the average in the inner zones than in the outer zones. Boston's results alone are clearly against the hypothesis, due entirely to the very high figure for the town of Gloucester. The level of differentiation is relatively high, but very irregular, without a clear pattern.

[22] The percentage of non-whites in the suburban areas of the Northern cities is very low in general, often below one per cent. Only in the areas of a few of the largest cities does the proportion reach 2 or 3 per cent; and that small proportion is found unevenly distributed in a few of the larger suburbs. In the smaller suburban cities non-whites are either entirely or almost entirely absent, while one or two suburbs are composed largely of non-whites. It is the existence near the central city of one or two cities with high percentages of non-whites that gives the high values of *rho* to the inner zones.

[23] The results are confused in two cities; Philadelphia is one of these and Atlanta another. Around this Southern city the distribution of the large percentage of non-whites shows a pattern entirely different from our other areas which are all Northern.

THREE DEMOGRAPHIC VARIABLES

Very low levels of differentiation were found for the three variables here labeled as "demographic"—sex, age and labor force. These consisted of the proportions of males in the population, of those over 14 years of age among the males, and of members of the labor force among the males over 14. Eight calculations were made in three cities, and these, together with the brief examination of data for other cities, exhibit consistently low differentiation in all zones—the *rhos* were mostly between .0010 and .0040 [24] (p. 92).

The stability of these three characteristics is of some interest. It is in marked contrast with the unusual distribution possessed by many Census tracts *within* the limits of a large city—these often have grossly unequal sex compositions and irregular age distributions.[25] Now, in many respects the suburbs, like the tracts, are but neighborhoods of the enlarged city; thus we may be led to assume that grossly irregular age and sex compositions will be found in the suburbs too. Our negative findings (and further research) may eliminate that misleading assumption (pp. 109-110).

THE DEMOCRATIC VOTE

Calculations were made on the proportions of the Democratic vote in a presidential election in each of three cities, Philadelphia, Pittsburgh and Detroit. The three results were clearly in line with the hypothesis—the measures of differentiation *(rho)* were roughly .06 to .09 for the inner zones and .01 to .04 for the outer zones (p. 93).

TESTS OF STATISTICAL SIGNIFICANCE

Our interest lies chiefly in the regularity with which the principal hypothesis is confirmed in different metropolitan areas: the

[24] This means, for example, that for most suburbs the labor force will be within about four percent of the mean of about 80 per cent among the males over 14 years of age. However, that much variability may be important too, and one may suspect that interesting patterns of differentiation can be found by a study of sufficient size and proper design.

[25] See for example the "population pyramids" for Chicago tracts in figure 42 in Hawley, *Human Ecology*, p. 399.

hypothesis that the level of differentiation in the inner zones is higher than in the outer zones. A simple test is based on contrasting the average *rho* for the inner zones with the average *rho* for the outer zones for each of the metropolitan areas separately. We make a binomial test. According to the null hypothesis *rho* should be higher in the inner zones half of the time. On this null hypothesis the probabilities of obtaining the higher *rho* in the inner zones as often as we found, or oftener, are as follows: [26]

—monthly rent: P = .0017;

—proportion of professionals: P = .0032;

—proportion of operatives for places outside Pennsylvania: P = .0085;

—proportion of non-white dwellings in the North: P = .11 (excluding Atlanta, but including New York—without New York it is P = .03);

—dwellings in need of repair: P = .035;

—democratic vote: P = .12.

Not only is our hypothesis confirmed on the average, but the predicted difference in *rhos* appears in the large majority of individual metropolitan areas, and for several diverse characteristics.

THE CURVE OF DECREASING DIFFERENTIATION

We found the expected decrease in the amount of differentiation with distance from the center. The results of this study are not adequate to establish the nature of the curve of the decrease. However, the decrease does not appear to take place along a straight line (along a linear "gradient"). One may perceive of a narrow plateau of high differentiation in the inner metropolitan

---

[26] There are two other kinds of tests which may be desired on occasion. Both can be facilitated by two things: (a) because of the large number of individuals per unit, the variability of *rho* is due practically only to the variance of $\sigma_b{}^2$ in its denominator; (b) it is assumed that $\sigma_b{}^2$ is the variance of a normally distributed variable.

Now a chi-square test may be used to test whether any *rho* is significantly greater than zero. In the present instance this is trivial since it is rather obvious sociologically that people (and their characteristics) are not sorted into suburbs at random. Indeed with the large size of units we used, a *rho* as low as .001 (or lower) differs significantly from zero at the P = .05 level for five (or more) units. Two *rhos* may be compared by taking their ratio (with an easy minor adjustment) and applying Snedecor's F test. In this sense many of the observed sharp drops to the lower level of differentiation appear as statistically significant.

zones, a steep (but not vertical) descent, then a relatively flat lower level in the outer zones (an "S-shaped curve"). The "line" around the city where the descent takes place may be called perhaps the "influence boundary," and the inner zones inside that boundary may be thought to correspond to the "primary communal area." The distance of that boundary in any one area shows some consistency for different variables. Moreover, the size of the metropolis and the distance of the "boundary" are related directly to each other.[27]

SOME IMPLICATIONS

Let us focus our attention on some possible effects of the described phenomena on the increasingly large proportion of the nation's population organized into metropolitan communities. It seems that within the primary communal area people can choose to live in suburbs with little regard to specific location within that area; modern means of transportation will get them to and from their places of work. Whereas the productive activity requires usually the cooperation in one place of people from different layers of society, they can separate at the gates of the factory or office building as each goes home his own way. Thus a person can choose his neighbors; and his choices result in the homogeneous and highly differentiated "natural areas" within the metropolitan city. Moreover, now he can drive to a suburb of his choice, and again he chooses to have as neighbors people whose habits, income, occupation, and other characteristics, resemble his own. Whether by choice, influence or propensity, the charac-

---

[27] The imagination may picture then the high metropolitan values of differentiation as hills protruding from plains of approximately evenly low level of non-metropolitan values. In the countryside, away from the large cities, the cities and towns within the same region are not greatly differentiated. To this loose hypothesis we may enter immediately two exceptions. First, there are cities which, although spatially removed from the metropolitan centers, are in close specialized functional relationship with them (see footnote 13). Second, there may exist characteristics for which the cities and towns of a region are greatly differentiated quite apart of metropolitan influences. (See section on "operatives" in the male labor force.)

The nature of the curve of differentiation depends on the specific functional nature of the variables investigated. This study dealt with some residential characteristics of the suburbs. Other functions may exhibit a different curve of differentiation. For example, retail trade activities may well show a more gradual descent of the curve of differentiation.

teristics of people in each suburb tend to homogeneity. Thus we find some homogeneity of economic status, of occupation, and of attitudes; and they tend to reinforce each other. This may help to create a segmented society, to augment other tendencies toward stratification. The homogeneity and the integration among neighbors within the same residential suburb are increased, but at the expense of greater differences between the suburbs. These specific aspects of the problems of integration of our society may be of increasing interest because the metropolitan area is a rapidly growing segment of society.[28]

Previous studies of the gradient pattern of the averages for concentric circular zones revealed one aspect of the structure of the metropolitan area. This study of differentiation among the suburbs within each zone explores another aspect. There are many other aspects of the complex, indefinitely nucleated metropolitan structure which need to be studied; and the measurement of the intraclass correlation can become a useful tool in the analysis of the total variance into its components.

For example: (1) From more precise results on the values of the *rhos* the natures of the curves of differentiation of the metropolitan areas may be plotted. The necessary precision may be obtained through research on a larger scale, and by combining results from several areas. (2) The investigation of other types of ecological units may give equally interesting results. The analysis of the total variance into several components may be attempted (townships, Census tracts, enumeration districts, blocks). This would yield a picture of the total segregation of characteristics in the metropolitan community. (3) The increasing organization and differentiation of the metropolitan areas may be studied in time depth. (4) The spatial manifestation of differentiation depends on the underlying functional relationships. From studies on different types of characteristics the pat-

---

[28] Descriptions of the new "Suburbia" are given by William H. Whyte, Jr., in the July and November, 1953 issues of *Fortune Magazine*.

Incidentally, our empirical findings also have applicability to the design of multi-stage sample surveys. It is possible to delimit approximately the inner zones of metropolitan suburbs from the outer zones, and expect to find considerably greater differences between the suburbs of the inner than of the outer zones. This points to the use of smaller "clusters" in the suburbs of the inner than of the outer zones.

tern of the functional organization of the metropolitan area may emerge.

This method of measurement of variability, the intraclass correlation, has wide applicability in social research. It may be useful in any research problem where we want to know the fraction of the total variance due to causes which members of the same unit (or group) have in common. There is a common aspect of statistical measurement to the following three kinds of problems (e.g.) which seem distinct in sociological substance: (a) the differentiation among ecological units on the basis of observations made on component elements of those units (as in this study); (b) the segregation of individuals from social classes into separate social groups (as in "racial" segregation); (c) the homogeneity of individuals in social groups (as in the similarity of attitudes of members of primary groups).

SUMMARY

Research had shown that the degree of organization is greater in the inner zones near the metropolitan center than in the outer zones. According to sociological theory we should expect differentiation to be greater also in the inner zones. Tests were made of this hypothesis in eleven larger metropolitan areas, and in two state-wide combinations of smaller areas. The results gave clear and marked confirmation of the hypothesis.

The tests were based on eight characteristics from 1940 Census data and on voting behavior. Incorporated suburbs were sorted into distance zones. The coefficient of intraclass correlation was used to measure the differentiation among the suburbs of each zone. The expected increase of differentiation in the inner zones was found for six characteristics (in a consistent manner for three of these). Three demographic characteristics (sex, age, labor-force) showed no increase, but a rather marked stability and uniformly low differentiation. As expected, the amount of the differentiation and its metropolitan increase are rather consistent (though variable) for each characteristic, and vary with the characteristic. The pattern that seems to emerge is that of a primary communal area in which the suburban places are highly differentiated with regard to many population characteristics. This primary area is about twenty miles wide around the largest metropolitan cities, and only five miles wide for the smaller ones. Beyond those boundaries the degree of differentiation falls rapidly to a lower level.

The greater differentiation among the suburbs near the metropolis is an expression of its organizing influence. This segregation of the population into differentiated suburbs may represent a socially important trend, since the enlarged interdependent metropolitan community is a growing modern phenomenon.

The structure of the metropolitan area has been frequently studied in terms of gradients, i.e. averages for concentric circular zones. The addition of the measurement of variation among the suburbs which make up each zone enhances our knowledge of that structure. It is suggested that the same measure, the coefficient of intraclass correlation, can be used to study and compare the variability among other types of ecological units. Furthermore, as a measure of homogeneity among the individuals composing any kind of a social group, it should be of interest to social scientists in general.

Chapter 10

Urban Units as Functional Entities

THE MEASUREMENT OF THE ECONOMIC BASE
OF THE METROPOLITAN AREA *

JOHN M. MATTILA AND WILBUR R. THOMPSON

The current revival of interest in regional economic research has been quietly undergoing a subtle shift in areal orientation. Increasingly, emphasis has been diverted from the traditional national regional survey (e.g. the "mature New England economy," the "underdeveloped South," etc.) toward the spatially narrower, more intensive, *metropolitan area economic base study*.[1] The attractiveness of the "metropolitan area" as *the* appropriate unit of regional economic analysis stems primarily from the current rush of "regional economists" to recognize explicitly, albeit somewhat belatedly, differences in degree of spatial mobility between the various factors of production. The rapidity and easy accord with which the profession has practically unanimously characterized capital as possessing a much higher degree of interregional (as well as international) mobility than is characteristic of labor is so impressive and unusual as to be breath-taking.

* Reprinted from *Land Economics*, Vol. XXXI, No. 3 (August, 1955), pp. 215-228, with permission of authors and publisher.
[1] The "metropolitan area" in mind and statistically employed throughout this study is the census-defined "standard metropolitan area," generally composed of "a county or group of contiguous counties which contains at least one city of 50,000 inhabitants or more." Cf., Bureau of the Census, *U.S. Census of Population: 1950, Vol. 1, Number of Inhabitants*, Ch. 1 (U.S. Summary. Washington, D.C., U.S. Government Printing Office, 1952), p. xxxi.

Even though one might do well to distinguish between railroad freight cars and railroad rails on the one hand and apartment-dwelling bachelors and home-owning heads of families on the other hand, if this may be sloughed off for the present as quibbling, a distinctly new and highly intriguing areal focus has been brought to bear on the long-neglected field of regional economics. The substantive effect on regional economic analysis of emphasis on the spatial immobility of labor has been neatly and succinctly formulated by John V. Van Sickle in a recent observation.[2]

"Nonetheless, interregional labor movements are so sluggish compared to interregional capital movements that we are justified in basing our concept of economic regions on labor market areas.

"*What is a Region?* A region, from a strictly economic point of view is a consolidate area within which the resources (human, natural, and artificial) on which the population must depend—in the absence of outside aid—result in a pattern of factoral rewards which sets it off from adjacent areas. The persistence of a pattern is due, of course, to the fact that labor and entrepreneurship are not completely and perfectly mobile. . . . (The few, large) . . . . conventional regions of the United States are really expressions of historical, cultural, and sociological factors rather than strictly economic factors."

Thus, while the product market area of local industries may vary from a small fraction of the encompassing metropolitan area (e.g., various neighborhood retail trade and service activities) to the total national or even world economy (e.g., automobile and steel manufacturing), the labor market for most local industries is conceived as being roughly coincident with the metropolitan area. Accordingly, while human migration is entrusted to effect a secular tendency toward interarea income equalization, the spatial immobility of labor temporarily isolates the labor supply of the metropolitan area from the rest of the economy and closely identifies their economic welfare with the general prosperity of the metropolitan area within which they reside. Thus, the spatial

[2] John V. Van Sickle, "Regional Economic Adjustments: The Role of Geographical Wage Differentials," *Papers and Proceedings Sixty-sixth Annual Meeting of the American Economic Association*—December 28-30, 1953, May 1954, pp. 382-383. In contrast to Van Sickle, Seymour Harris is inclined to bracket "management" with capital with reference to spatial mobility, regarding them both as highly mobile intranationally. Seymour E. Harris, "Interregional Competition: With Particular Reference to North-South Competition," *ibid.*, p. 368.

immobility of labor provides the regional economist with a natural *spatial short run* which, for analytical purposes, is analogous to the classical economist's *functional short run* founded on the parallel functional immobility of capital. Carrying the analogy a step farther, the "metropolitan area" assumes a structural role comparable to the "industry" of partial equilibrium analysis fame.

Having selected the metropolitan area as the appropriate area of regional analysis, the common procedure is for the regional analyst to proceed directly to the task of identifying and segregating the area's economic base and, residually, the economic superstructure. Even as the welfare of the local labor force is tied to the prosperity of the metropolitan area, the metropolitan area's prosperity itself is tied to the vitality of a limited number of "basic" economic activities in which it has specialized. "Basic" activities are the areas' "breadwinners" in that they provide the export surplus which generates the net income stream upon which the economic well-being of the area's inhabitants is founded. Therefore, a fruitful investigation of the volume, level, stability and/or distribution of the income and employment of any regional area must perforce begin with the process of identifying and weighting (ranking) the area's basic (export) activities.

The current flood of *metropolitan area economic base studies* provides eloquent testimony on behalf of the theoretical attractiveness, empirical adaptability, and public policy relevance of the metropolitan area as the focal point of regional research.[3] The sole cause for any reservations concerning this current burst of regional research activity is the "clear and present danger" that only the most tentative, path-breaking, theoretical sorties have been launched into problems of methodology and measurement so as to ensure the harvesting of reasonably digestible fruits of research. At this point one must echo the remarks of a contemporary observer that, with the exception of a few chance theoretical insights, the urban base studies to date have been performed highly mechanically with undiscriminating recourse

[3] For an up-to-date bibliography of urban economic base studies see the list compiled by Katherine McNamara, Librarian, Department of City Planning and Architecture, Harvard University, reprinted in *Land Economics*, May 1954, pp. 186-91.

to the crudest tools of analysis in such a manner so as to be excused only by the relentless demands of the large scale pragmatic projects of which they were usually but a part.[4]

The purpose of this study is not nearly so ambitious as to attempt a *tour de force* of economic base identification and measurement techniques. Such legitimate avenues of investigation as individual firm and industry studies, questionnaire methods, and regional balance of payments analyses will be by-passed in order to concentrate on the much more limited and modest objective of reviewing various "aggregative" base identification techniques currently being employed by regional analysts. The *aggregate-comparative-inferential* methods of the day, lightly dubbed "macrocosmic" methods by Andrews, essentially rely on inferences drawn from a comparison of national and local patterns of economic activity.

Further, two simplifying steps will be taken of which the reader should be made aware. First, the "nation" will be considered as the framework of reference (and as such a "closed" economy), thereby ignoring the role of international trade. Second, a simple dichotomy of product market orientation of local industry has been constructed such that local products are either "exported" or locally consumed. No distinctions will be drawn between national and regional export markets of local industry, e.g., the national automobile market versus the southeastern Michigan regional wholesale trade market of Detroit. The effect of such a simple dichotomy is to understate a locality's export activity. Finally, a careful consideration of the numerous subtleties inherent in the choice of the data selected to represent economic activity will also be shrugged-off as outside of the scope of this study.[5] Thus, employment data has been selected not be-

---

[4] Richard B. Andrews, "Mechanics of the Urban Economic Base: General Problems of Base Identification," *Land Economics*, May 1954, pp. 171-72.

[5] However, in passing, it might be mentioned that the best theoretical alternatives to employment as indices of economic activity are empirically impracticable. Data on income generated, classified by industrial origin, is unattainable at less than the state level of areal subdivision. *Firm value added* data is available on a local basis but it generally measures the productive contribution of local labor and "foreign" capital, whereas, what is needed is a measure of *local value added*, i.e., the productive contribution of local labor and local capital, if any. Value of product data is useless for most economic research. The distortion created by equating local economic well-being to local employment (or even wage income) data rather than to a more sophisticated measure of economic

cause it is ideally suited to the problem at hand but, rather, because the data are easily available in a form suitable for use in illustrating the general "macrocosmic" statistical techniques currently being applied to various types of economic data.

AN INDEX OF LOCAL SPECIALIZATION

Unadjusted form. The index most commonly used to identify the urban economic base is a simple ratio of an industry's share of local employment relative to the industry's share of national employment or, alternatively, a locality's share of industry employment relative to the locality's share of national employment as shown below: [6]

$$\frac{\dfrac{e_i}{e_t}}{\dfrac{E_i}{E_t}} \quad \text{or} \quad \frac{\dfrac{e_i}{E_i}}{\dfrac{e_t}{E_t}} \qquad \text{where:}$$

e_i local industry employment

e_t local total employment

E_i national industry employment

E_t national total employment

In essence, this index indicates the importance of the industry to the locality *relative* to the importance of the industry to the nation.

The above index is commonly employed as an indicator of the product market orientation of a local industry (i.e. "basic" or "local service"), but, as will be highlighted below, this index must be interpreted with caution as a measure of the degree to which "basicness" is exhibited. The usual inference is that, when the value of the index is one, local production per capita is equal to the national production per capita and, therefore, local production is just sufficient to satisfy local consumption (demand) and the locality neither exports nor imports the good or service in question. Similarly, an index value greater than one presumably

---

well being such as *local disposable income* may well be questionable procedure in the economic analysis of small resort towns or "retirement communities." However, the use of employment data does not pose as serious a problem in the study of the large metropolitan area, where more refined techniques add so little to accuracy that the additional cost in time and money is usually unjustified.

[6] This index was first devised as a "location quotient" by P. Sargent Florence. Cf. Political and Economic Planning, *Report on the Location of Industry* (London: March 1939), p. 287; also, National Resources Planning Board, *Industrial Location and National Resources* (Washington: 1943), Ch. 5, p. 107.

indicates that the locality has "extra" workers, produces a "surplus" of the good or service, and "exports" this surplus.

To infer local specialization and exportation from an index value greater than one requires a special combination of interrelated assumptions. Specifically, a coefficient of greater than one indicates *per se* only that the locality's *labor force* is more heavily "specialized" in (allocated to) the industry in question than is true of the nation on the average. If average or greater productivity per worker is assumed for this locality, we may conclude that the locality's *production* is more heavily "specialized" in this good or service than is true of the nation on the average. The logical transition from local productive specialization to local exportation of this "surplus" production requires that the above assumption be supplemented by the further assumption that the locality's consumption per capita is equal to that of the nation on the average. Of course, the locality's per capita consumption of a good or service may deviate from the national average because of one or all of the following factors: local differences in taste patterns, income levels, or relative price patterns.[7]

In addition to the above, exceptional cases of local export industries are easily conceivable which exhibit coefficients of less than one due to high productivity per worker, or low consumption per capita relative to the national average. An instance of the latter case would be a *large tropical city* within commuting distance of a *small coal mine*. The general import of the preceding discussion is that, strictly interpreted, the index of *local specialization* is really a measure of labor force specialization *per se*, and only by successively more tenuous inferences may it be

[7] Surely, one could find numerous cases of industries for which the *index of local specialization* exhibits values of substantially greater or less than one when exportation or importation of the good or service seems, at least on the basis of *prima facie* evidence, a less reasonable inference than local variations in consumption per capita. For example, using census classifications and 1950 census data, an index value of 1.91 for "bowling alleys" of the Detroit Standard Metropolitan Area could probably be most easily "explained" by recourse to taste pattern peculiarities of the area. Similarly, an index value of 1.74 for "fuel and ice" of the Boston Standard Metropolitan Area as against a value of 0.30 for the San Francisco Standard Metropolitan Area also appears to be largely taste pattern phenomena (via climatic conditions). Again, "domestic service in private households," as a personal service industry, exhibits an index value of 1.48 for the Baltimore Standard Metropolitan Area, reflecting, at least partially, the much lower wage rates for domestic help in Baltimore than in the nation on the average (i.e., local differences in relative price patterns).

extended to the role of an index of product specialization and, ultimately, product-market orientation of local industry.

The adjusted form. A modified form of the *index of local specialization* deserves our attention at this juncture. The national ("benchmark") quantities are adjusted by subtracting the local economy from the national economy to eliminate the "overlap." [8] A later rationalization offered for this adjustment

$$\frac{\dfrac{e_i}{e_t}}{\dfrac{E_i - e_i}{E_t - e_t}}$$

was that "the subtraction was necessary to prevent a downward bias in the resulting quotients, particularly for specialized industries." [9] It will be noted that, when the unadjusted index is equal to one, the adjusted index will also equal one because the numerator and the denominator of the denominator of the index are each proportionately reduced. If the unadjusted index is greater than one, the adjusted index will be the larger because the numerator of the denominator will be reduced more (proportionately) than the denominator of the denominator of the index. Similarly, if the unadjusted index is less than one, the adjusted index will be the smaller. Thus, the effect of the adjustment is to spread out the values of the index about a value of one without changing the rank order. In essence, the adjustment eliminates the "averaging out" effect of including the locality in the benchmark economy. In light of the fact that the rank order of the indices remains unchanged, the usefulness of undertaking such a time-consuming adjustment seems dubious.

Further, and much more fundamental, the unadjusted *index of local specialization* has the added attraction of not only ranking industries according to degree of local specialization but, in addition, the unadjusted index serves as an indirect measure of "surplus" workers relative to total local industry employment. To

[8] George H. Hildebrand and Arthur Mace, Jr., "Employment Multiplier in an Expanding Industrial Market," *Review of Economics and Statistics,* August 1950, p. 245.

[9] Chester Rapkin, Louis Winnick and David Blank, *Housing Market Analysis, A Study of Theory and Methods* (Washington, D.C.: Housing and Home Finance Agency, December 1953), p. 50.

demonstrate this characteristic, let us consider the simple hypo-thetical example set forth below. Assume that e_i equals 12, e_t equals 120, E_i equals 30 and E_t equals 1,200 then the values of the unadjusted and adjusted index are as follows:

Unadjusted Index of Local Specialization

$$\frac{\dfrac{e_i}{e_t}}{\dfrac{E_i}{E_t}} = \frac{\dfrac{12}{120}}{\dfrac{30}{1,200}} = 4$$

Adjusted Index of Local Specialization

$$\frac{\dfrac{e_i}{e_t}}{\dfrac{E_i - e_i}{E_t - e_t}} = \frac{\dfrac{12}{120}}{\dfrac{30 - 12}{1,200 - 120}} = 6$$

The value of 4 for the unadjusted index indicates that the locality is 4 times as specialized in the industry as is the nation as a whole and by inference (employing the necessary assump-tions outlined above) has 4 times as many workers as are needed for the locality's own consumption of this good or service. Or, to rephrase, one-quarter of the locality's industry employment (3 workers) is required to satisfy domestic needs and the remain-ing three-quarters (9 workers) are "surplus" workers presumably producing for "export." This conclusion is confirmed by pro-rating to this locality a fraction of the total industry employment equal to its fraction (10%) of the labor force (population) or 3 workers. The remaining 9 workers in this locality may be identi-fied as "surplus" or, more inferentially, "export" workers.

Conversely, the adjusted *index of local specialization* exhibits a value of 6 and thereby overstates the multiple by which the local industry employment exceeds its pro-rata share. This is so because in the case of industries in which the locality has a greater than average specialization the use of the *remainder* of the economy as a base for determining the locality's pro-rata share of the industry understates the relative importance of the industry in the total economy (i.e. national consumption) and, by extension, understates the number of workers necessary to satisfy local requirements. In effect, the adjusted index measures the divergence between the locality and the outside world and becomes accordingly a measure of local *uniqueness*. For most purposes, an index that measures local *uniqueness* would seem to be less useful than an index which measures local specialization and, simultaneously, indirectly reflects the relative proportion of domestic and "surplus" workers.

AN INDEX OF SURPLUS WORKERS

Absolute form. Rather than relying on an index which only *implicitly* and *indirectly* measures "surplus" workers, an index may be constructed which *explicitly* and *directly* measures the absolute number of "surplus" workers by calculating the difference between actual local industry employment and the locality's pro-rata share of national industry employment as shown below: [10]

$$S = \frac{e_i - e_t}{E_t} E_i,$$ where S represents the absolute number of "surplus" workers in the industry "i"

The upper limit of this latter index approaches e_i asymptotically as the size of the locality under consideration becomes infinitely small relative to the benchmark economy (i.e. as $\dfrac{e_t}{E_t}$ approaches zero). This is equivalent to saying that the number of "surplus" workers in any local industry could never exceed or even equal that industry's total local employment. In passing, it may be noted that e_i itself, is limited by the value of E_i, or to phrase this more descriptively, the piccolo industry potentially could never play as basic a role in a given locality as the automobile industry. The lower limit of this index is:

$$\frac{e_t}{E_t} E_i,$$

i.e. the "deficit" of local industry workers could never exceed the

[10] An index based on the absolute number of "surplus" workers seems to have been constructed first by Homer Hoyt in a monograph prepared for the Regional Plan Association of New York, *Economic Status of the New York Metropolitan Region in 1944* (New York: 1944).

locality's pro-rata share of the national industry employment (assuming local per capita consumption equal to the national average), and even this value would be attained only if there were absolutely no local employment in the industry in question. These limits may be summarized as follows:

$$\frac{e_t}{E_t} \, E_i \leqslant \left[e_i - \frac{e_t}{E_t} \, E_i \right] < \; e_i \leqslant E_i$$

The distinction between the *index of local specialization* and the *index of surplus workers* as measures of the "basicness" of an industry in a locality's industrial structure is best demonstrated by recourse to the simply hypothetical example below.

	City "A"		"Nation"
e_i	20	E_i	50
e_j	40	E_j	200
e_t	100	E_t	1000

	Industry "i"	Industry "j"
Index of Local Specialization	$\dfrac{\frac{e_i}{e_t}}{\frac{E_i}{E_t}} = 4.0$	$\dfrac{\frac{e_j}{e_t}}{\frac{E_j}{E_t}} = 2.0$
Index of Surplus Workers	$e_i - \dfrac{e_t}{E_t} E_i = 15$	$e_j - \dfrac{e_t}{E_t} E_j = 20$

In the example above, even though City "A" appears to be more "specialized" in industry "i," industry "j" contributes a greater number of "surplus" workers to (i.e. accounts for a larger part of) its economic base. This is so because the larger size (locally) of industry "j" more than offsets industry "i"'s higher proportion of export activity to total activity. However, it will be noted that although industry "j" is twice as large as industry "i" locally, the former has less than twice as many "surplus" workers as the latter because industry "j" is four times as large as industry "i" nationally and, therefore, a greater *percentage* of industry "j"'s workers are locally "required" workers.

Now two distinct interpretations of the term "basicness" become apparent. Industry "i," with the greater *proportion* of "surplus" workers, exhibits the greater degree of "industry basicness," i.e. the degree to which the industry itself is a "basic" (export) industry. Industry "j," with the greater *number* of "surplus" workers exhibits the greater degree of "local basicness," i.e. the degree to which the industry is "basic" (vital) to its locality.

In essence, the primary distinction between the *index of local specialization* and the *index of surplus workers* is the dissimilarity of their respective weighting systems. The *index of local specialization* automatically accords to each local industry an equal weight, thereby implicitly assuming all local industries are equally "important" (i.e., afford equal employment opportunities) to the community.[11] Contrarily, the *index of surplus workers* automatically accords to each local industry a weight in direct proportion to its size (local employment). Since, almost without exception, in recent writing on the subject of the urban economic base, the concept of "basicness" of a local industry is treated as synonymous with capacity to generate net additions to local income from "foreign" sales, the relative size of local industries is clearly relevant. Since an absolute measure of the number of surplus workers automatically reflects relative industry size, the *index of surplus workers* is a better measure of the net income generating capacity of a local industry and therefore, it would seem that this index exhibits a clear advantage over the *index of local specialization* as a measure of the "basicness" *of an industry to its locality.* In that it is this latter concept of "basicness" that is usually at issue in the typical urban base study, investigators would do well to place primary reliance on the *index of surplus workers.*

Relative form. A further distinction between the two indices, in the form considered above, is that the *index of local specializa-*

---

[11] True, it is possible to modify the *index of local specialization* by explicitly introducing alternate weighting systems. For example, local-employment weighting may be accomplished by multiplying the index by local industry employment as a per cent of local total employment (e_i/e_t). However, this procedure is encumbered by the necessity of first identifying the export industries before applying the weighting system, otherwise, large non-export industries (i.e., local service industries which have unweighted indices of 1.0 or less but which account for a large share of local employment generally) may attain values (products) which exceed smaller export industries.

tion is expressed in terms of relatives and therefore is equally applicable to either inter- or intra-city industry comparisons, whereas, the above *index of surplus workers* is expressed in terms of absolutes and, therefore, is only appropriate for intra-city industry comparisons.[12] Fortunately, the *index of surplus workers* can be converted easily into a relative form for inter-city industry comparisons, where reference to relative size of city is desirable, by dividing the index either by total local employment or by total local surplus workers as shown below: [13]

$$\frac{e_i - \frac{e_t}{E_t}E_i}{e_t} \qquad\qquad \frac{e_i - \frac{e_t}{E_t}E_i}{\Sigma\left[e_i - \frac{e_t}{E_t}E_i\right]}$$

The relative forms of the *index of surplus workers* shown above produce identical rank orders of industries not only within cities but also between cities if the cities in question are equally self-sufficient, i.e., "surplus" workers as a percent of total local employment is the same for all the cities compared. However, in that there is no *a priori* reason for believing that all cities are equally self-sufficient and empirical evidence introduced below substantiates this doubt, the question is posed as to which of these two forms more accurately measures the "basicness" of an industry to its locality. Using the simple hypothetical data below, let us raise this fundamental question: Is industry "i" in city "A" or industry "j" in city "B" more "basic" to its respective locality?

[12] The *index of local specialization* may be used in interregional comparisons of a given industry, e.g., automobile manufacturing in Detroit versus Flint. However, since this index implicitly weights all industries equally, it is inappropriate for interregional comparisons of different industries, e.g., automobile manufacturing in Detroit versus steelmaking in Pittsburgh.

[13] The close relationship between the *index of local specialization* and the *index of surplus workers* is particularly striking when the latter is expressed in the relative form using total local employment as the common denominator.

$$\frac{e_i - \frac{e_t}{E_t}E_i}{e_t} = \frac{e_i}{e_t} - \frac{E_i}{E_t}\; ;\; \text{compare to:}\quad \frac{\frac{e_i}{e_t}}{\frac{E_i}{E_t}}$$

Or, in simple descriptive terms, the distinction between the *index of surplus workers*, expressed in the relative form above, and the *index of local specialization* is that the former measures the *difference* between local and national degree of specialization and the latter measures the *ratio* of local to national degree of specialization.

	City "A"	City "B"
"Surplus" workers in industry "i"	20	
"Surplus" workers in industry "j"		15
Total "surplus" workers	40	20
Total employment	100	100

Applying the two relative forms of the *index of surplus workers* to the above example, diametrically opposite results are obtained. The total-employment form shows an index value of 20 (or .20) for industry "i" which exceeds the corresponding index value of 15 for industry "j," whereas, the total-surplus-worker form shows an index value of 50 for industry "i" which is exceeded by the corresponding index value of 75 for industry "j."

To place this seeming paradox in more revealing perspective, consider the impact of a sudden disappearance or complete collapse of these two industries on their respective localities. Would city "A," which would lose a larger fraction of its total employment (20% to 15%), fare better or worse than city "B," which would lose a larger fraction of its export employment (75% to 50%)? If the industries in question are truly "basic" and *irreplaceable*, it seems clear that City "B" would fare the worse. The collapse of industry "j" would destroy three-quarters of the economic base and, presumably, three-quarters of the service-industry superstructure of City "B" as against a lesser collapse of only one-half the economy of City "A." To illustrate, an example of the disappearance of an irreplaceable, basic industry would be the depletion of the mineral upon which a mining town has been built.

Conversely, it could be argued that if these basic industries "i" and "j" are replaceable, the transition required of City "B" would be easier than that required of City "A" in that fewer workers would be involved in the industrial-occupational readjustment. This latter approach, however, is really not so much a consideration of the generally accepted concept of "basicness" with which we are concerned as it is a consideration of the functional adaptibility (or industrial mobility) of the cities involved.

Which, then, is the preferred index? In intra-city comparisons the rank orders and even the relative values of the two indices are identical; therefore, the preference would be for the total-employment form as it is statistically much the easier to construct. In inter-city comparisons, the preference probably would be for the statistically-more-complicated total-surplus-worker form which implicitly incorporates the breadth of the economic base (or, conversely, the degree of local self-sufficiency) into the measure.

AN EMPIRICAL APPLICATION OF THE INDICES

Certainly it is appropriate at this point to apply these indices to empirical data to illustrate their distinctiveness. In fact, there is almost a moral obligation to justify the aforegoing trial of the reader's patience by conclusively demonstrating that the careful distinctions drawn above embody more than mere mental exercise. In Tables 1 and 2 the five leading industries in each of six large metropolitan areas in the United States have been assembled and ranked according to the value of the indices employed above. Even the most cursory examination of the tables will confirm the above conclusion that, if the objective is to rank local industries according to the relative role they play in the economic base of their metropolitan area, strikingly different results would be obtained depending on the investigator's choice of indices.

Not only are the rank orders of the industries under the two indices highly dissimilar, but even the specific industries within the group change very noticeably. In three of the six metropolitan areas shown not one of the top five industries as identified by one index repeated its rank in the top industries as identified by the other index. In the remaining three areas (Detroit, New York, and Pittsburgh) only one industry "repeated." Of the full eleven large metropolitan areas studied, the average number of industries appearing in the top five ranks of both indices is slightly less than two out of five (21 "repeats" in 11 cases). The obvious explanation of this divergence is that industries with a high *index of local specialization* are often too small to be quantitatively significant in the economic base of their metropolitan areas.

In addition to illustrating the substantial dissimilarity of the rank order of local industries as determined by these two distinct

TABLE 1

THE FIVE LEADING INDUSTRIES IN SIX LARGE METROPOLITAN AREAS AS IDENTIFIED BY THE INDEX OF LOCAL SPECIALIZATION, 1950

Industry	$\dfrac{e_i}{E_i} \Big/ \dfrac{e_t}{E_t}$
Detroit	
Motor vehicles and motor vehicle equipment (mfg.)	18.22
Office and store machines and devices (mfg.)	2.98
Drugs and medicines (mfg.)	2.42
Advertising	2.04
Paints, varnishes, and related products (mfg.)	1.99
Pittsburgh	
Blast furnaces, steel works, and rolling mills (mfg.)	14.03
Glass and glass products (mfg.)	7.66
Miscellaneous petroleum and coal products (mfg.)	5.94
Railroad and misc. transportation equipment (mfg.)	4.86
Pottery and related product (mfg.)*	2.75
Cleveland	
Paints, varnishes and related products (mfg.)	6.50
Other primary iron and steel products (mfg.)	3.44
Primary nonferrous industries (mfg.)	3.37
Miscellaneous machinery, except electrical (mfg.)	3.27
Aircraft and parts (mfg.)	3.22
Philadelphia	
Ship and boat building and repairing (mfg.)	4.07
Railroad and misc. transportation equipment (mfg.)	3.84
Miscellaneous textile mill products (mfg.)	3.55
Leather: tanned, curried, and finished (mfg.)	3.47
Petroleum refining (mfg.)	3.29
New York	
Apparel and accessories (mfg.)	3.77
Security and commodity brokerage, and investment companies	3.52
Water transportation	3.24
Miscellaneous fabricated textile products (mfg.)	3.09
Drugs and medicine (mfg.)	3.03
San Francisco	
Ship and boat building and repairing (mfg.)	6.28
Water transportation	4.60
Air transportation	3.94
Petroleum refining (mfg.)	3.22
Canning and preserving fruits, vegetables, and sea foods (mfg.)	2.91

SOURCE: Based on data from *U.S. Census of Population: 1950, Detailed Characteristics*, Table 79.

* Supplants "Not specified food industries" which was considered to be too ambiguous to be comparable to the other industry classifications.

TABLE 2

THE FIVE LEADING INDUSTRIES IN SIX LARGE METROPOLITAN AREAS AS IDEN-
TIFIED BY THE ABSOLUTE, TOTAL EMPLOYMENT AND TOTAL SURPLUS
FORMS OF THE INDEX OF SURPLUS WORKERS, 1950

Industry	$e_i - \dfrac{e_t}{E_t} E_i$	$\dfrac{e_i - \dfrac{e_t}{E_t} E_i}{e_t}$	$\dfrac{e_i - \dfrac{e_t}{E_t} E_i}{\Sigma\left[e_i - \dfrac{e_t}{E_t} E_i \right]}$
Detroit			
Motor vehicles and motor vehicle equipment (mfg.)	317,339	26.62	84.01
Fabricated steel products (mfg.)	13,940	1.17	3.69
Office and store machines and devices (mfg.)	4,431	.37	1.17
Other primary iron and steel industries (mfg.)	3,261	.27	.86
Rubber products (mfg.)°	3,068	.26	.81
Pittsburgh			
Blast furnaces, steel works, and rolling mills (mfg.)	124,191	15.35	54.58
Electrical machinery, equipment and supplies (mfg.)	19,529	2.41	8.58
Glass and glass products (mfg.)	13,584	1.68	5.97
Railroads and railway express service	12,515	1.55	5.50
Fabricated steel products (mfg.)	8,238	1.02	3.62
Cleveland			
Miscellaneous machinery, except electrical (mfg.)	25,269	4.10	16.28
Fabricated steel products (mfg.)	16,880	2.74	10.88
Motor vehicles and motor vehicle equipment (mfg.)	16,811	2.73	10.83
Blast furnaces	13,862	2.25	8.93
Electrical machinery, equipment and supplies (mfg.)	11,387	1.85	7.34
Philadelphia			
Apparel and accessories (mfg.)	29,599	2.06	11.27
Electrical machinery, equipment and supplies (mfg.)	23,605	1.64	8.99
Petroleum refining (mfg.)	15,185	1.06	5.78
Ship and boat building and repairing (mfg.)	12,359	.86	4.71
Printing, publishing, and allied industries (mfg.)	12,240	.85	4.66
New York			
Apparel and accessories (mfg.)	256,853	4.83	18.91
Printing, publishing and allied industries (mfg.)	66,051	1.24	4.86
Real estate (incl. real estate-insurance-law-offices)	65,031	1.22	4.79
Food and related products (whlse)	63,848	1.20	4.70
Insurance	57,832	1.09	4.26
San Francisco			
Federal public administration	22,805	2.64	10.36
Ship and boat building and repairing (mfg.)	12,787	1.48	5.81
Water transportation	11,607	1.34	5.27
Insurance	11,317	1.31	5.14
Eating and drinking places	9,625	1.11	4.37

SOURCE: *ibid.,* Table 1.

° Supplants "Local public administration" because this latter activity appears, on the basis of subjective judgment, to be almost exclusively a local service activity.

indices, Table 2 offers some incidental but interesting by-products
on the nature of comparative urban economic bases. For example, Detroit and Pittsburgh provide excellent illustrations of
highly specialized manufacturing economies in which a single
industry (census-defined) accounts for an over-whelming majority (approximately 84% and 55% respectively) of its locality's "surplus," and presumably export, workers. Further,
again referring to Table 2, Cleveland and Philadelphia provide
excellent illustrations of more *diversified manufacturing* economies in which there is a broader economic base. Of the latter
two localities, Philadelphia exhibits the greater substantive and
functional diversification in that Cleveland's basic activities are
heavily concentrated in durable goods manufacturing, whereas,
Philadelphia's basic activities are rather evenly distributed between durable and non-durable goods manufacturing with a
slightly greater emphasis on non-durable goods. Finally, New
York and San Francisco provide excellent illustrations of more
generally diversified economies with economic bases which draw
more heavily on non-manufacturing industries. In fact, a random
set of five industries would probably be no more dissimilar than
those representing the economic base of San Francisco.

Earlier, in the theoretical section of this study, preference
was expressed for placing primary reliance on the *index of surplus
workers* in regional economic base studies. The reader is encouraged to compare the information presented in Tables 1 and 2
to satisfy himself that this index is the more useful measure.
However, it will be recalled that if interregional comparisons are
to be made it is necessary to convert the *index of surplus workers*
to a relative form by relating the absolute number of "surplus"
workers in a particular industry to either the locality's total employment or total "surplus" workers. Further, a distinction was
drawn between these two relative forms of the index on the basis
of an *a priori* judgment that cities (metropolitan areas) differed
markedly in their degree of self-sufficiency, i.e., their ratio of
"surplus" workers to total employment.

This *a priori* position is strikingly illustrated and the careful
distinction drawn between the two relative forms on the *index of
surplus workers* is fully justified by the evidence presented in the
third column of Table 3. The "proportion of surplus to service

workers," the usual form in which the degree of local self-sufficiency is expressed, varies from a low of 1: 1.99 in Chicago to a
high of 1: 4.47 in Philadelphia. To illustrate the application of
the *index of surplus workers* in its various forms, compare the
New York apparel industry with the Detroit automobile industry.
These two industries with 257,000 and 317,000 "surplus" workers,
respectively, are comparable in *absolute* size, however, since the
New York Metropolitan Area is almost five times as large as the
Detroit Metropolitan Area the Detroit automobile industry gains
five-fold in *relative* "basic" importance. This is reflected by the
values of 26.62 to 4.83 registered by the total-employment form
of *index of surplus workers* for the Detroit automobile industry
and the New York apparel industry, respectively.

TABLE 3

SURPLUS WORKERS AS A MEASURE OF THE CHARACTER OF THE ECONOMIC
BASE OF THE ELEVEN LARGEST METROPOLITAN AREAS IN THE
UNITED STATES, 1950

Metropolitan Area	Total Employment	Total Surplus Workers	Proportion of Surplus to Service Workers [*]	Surplus Workers in Top Five Industries	Surplus Workers in Top Five Industries as Per Cent of Total Surplus Workers
Chicago	2,361,782	790,119	1 : 1.99	295,413	37.39
Detroit	1,192,280	377,743	1 : 2.16	342,102	90.56
Pittsburgh ..	808,897	227,550	1 : 2.55	178,057	78.25
New York ..	5,314,028	1,358,318	1 : 2.91	510,335	37.57
San Francisco	864,976	220,228	1 : 2.93	68,141	30.94
Cleveland ..	615,723	155,179	1 : 2.97	84,209	54.27
Boston	914,953	220,146	1 : 3.16	82,610	37.53
Los Angeles .	1,690,395	404,704	1 : 3.18	138,569	34.24
Baltimore ...	527,911	121,356	1 : 3.35	48,180	39.70
St. Louis ...	676,881	138,469	1 : 3.89	44,645	32.24
Philadelphia	1,437,923	262,665	1 : 4.47	92,988	35.40

SOURCE: Based on data from *U.S. Census of Population: 1950, Detailed
Characteristics,* Table 79.

[*] "Service" workers are simply the difference between total employment and
"surplus" workers.

A further refinement in base measurement can be made by
considering the breadth of the economic bases of the two areas.
Now applying the total-surplus-worker form of the *index of sur-*

plus workers, the slightly greater degree of self-sufficiency characteristic of the New York Metropolitan Area (1: 2.91 as against 1: 2.16) is incorporated into the measure and, accordingly, the New York apparel industry gains slightly in basic importance relative to the Detroit automobile industry (values of 18.91 and 84.01, respectively) lessening the latter's dominance from approximately 5½ to 1 to 4½ to 1. That is to say, the total-surplus-worker form of *index of surplus workers* reveals that the automobile industry is about four times as basic to the Detroit economy as the apparel industry is to the New York economy.

The reader is cautioned that the "surplus" workers figures of Table 2 (as well as Table 3) are the product of the purely mechanical method of assigning all workers in a local industry beyond the locality's *pro rata* share of national employment of this industry to the category "surplus." To the extent that the local consumption pattern differs from the national consumption pattern due to differences in tastes, income or relative price structures, the number of "surplus" workers will differ from the actual number of export workers.[14]

The accuracy of the "surplus" workers figures is also affected by the breadth of the industry classification used. Generally, the broader the industry group (i.e., the fewer the number of industry subdivisions) the fewer the number of local "surplus" workers. This is so because aggregation tends to offset "deficit" (import) industries against "surplus" (export) industries. In that the industry subdivisions employed in this study are the narrowest (most detailed) employed in the 1950 Population Census,

[14] It often happens that an industry is characterized by a national market for its product and so the great majority of the workers in a local branch of this industry are producing goods which will be sold outside the local area, even though the locality may have only its *pro rata* share of national industry employment or less. This is a normal situation in markets characterized by a well developed "product differentiation." In a gross sense, the locality both exports and imports this product. Thus, the existence of "product differentiation," areal overlapping of firm product markets, and "cross-hauling" makes necessary the distinction between "gross" and "net" export workers. Obviously, it is "net" export workers which our index yields. Fortunately, it is "net" export workers which is the more useful figure. To illustrate, a national secular or cyclical slump of a particular industry will be shifted from the outside onto a locality to the degree that the locality exports the product in question and, in offsetting fashion, the slump will be shifted from the locality to the outside economy to the degree that the locality imports the product (i.e., exports the unemployment). The net impact of the slump on the locality is reflected in the measure "net" export workers.

the results of Table 3 may be defended at least on pragmatic grounds. Thus, with the deviations between local and national consumption patterns having an uncertain and perhaps random effect and our limited industry aggregation tending to slightly understate the number of "surplus" workers, the net effect is probably to slightly overstate the number of dependent service workers or, what amounts to the same thing, to overstate the degree of local self-sufficiency.

The last column of Table 3 indicates the degree of industrial concentration prevailing in the economic base of the eleven largest metropolitan areas. The per cent of the total "surplus" workers employed in the five most basic industries varies from a high of over 90% in Detroit to a low of only about 31% in San Francisco. Base concentration is conceptually equivalent to the community putting its export eggs "all in one basket."

While an analysis of local business cycle mechanics in general and the cycle sensitivity of these eleven metropolitan areas in particular is beyond the limited scope of this study, a measure of the degree of concentration in the economic base of a locality provides a possible point of departure for local business cycle analysis. It is true, of course, that base concentration may produce local stability or instability depending on the cycle patterns of the industries of local emphasis. Further, it is also true that random industrial diversification is not a panacea for local instability as "community boosters" too often seem to believe. Even so, local base concentration, other things equal, is probably at least moderately associated with local cycle instability. Consequently, a purely quantitative measure of base concentration would be useful in local cycle analysis if it were supplemented by a more qualitative consideration of the nature of the basic industries themselves (e.g., durable vs. nondurable).

CONCLUSION

After having led the reader along a rather labyrinthian way, it would be well to recapitulate the specific purpose and conclusions of this study of the urban economic base. Fundamentally, our purpose has been to devise a tool which when applied to the industry data of a local economy would enable the user to say: "This is the most basic industry in this local economy" and, more specifically, "it is x times as basic as this next most basic industry." In the course of the search for this ideal measure it became clear that, while many indices will serve to identify basic from local service industries, the relative weighting and ranking of these basic industries themselves requires care and discrimination in the choice of an appropriate index.

The *index of local specialization* indicates the importance of any industry to its locality relative to the importance of an industry to the nation. On the other hand, the *index of surplus workers*, which uniquely takes into consideration both the role (i.e., export versus local service) and the size of a local industry, indicates the importance of an industry to its locality relative to the importance of other industries to the same locality. Thus, the *index of local specialization* reflects the importance of the locality to the industry, considering the size of the locality; whereas the *index of surplus workers* reflects the importance of the industry to the locality, considering the size of the industry. It is a quantitative expression of this latter relationship that has been our objective from the beginning.

Further, by relating an *industry's surplus workers* to total surplus workers, a relative form of the *index of surplus workers* has been constructed which extends the analyst's power of comparison to the point where he can say: "The 'A' industry is x times as basic to the 'M' locality as the 'B' industry is to the 'N' locality." If used with care, the *index of surplus workers* in both its absolute and relative form should prove to be a highly useful tool in regional economic base studies.

THE FUNCTIONS OF NEW ZEALAND TOWNS *

L. L. POWNALL

New Zealand is young in length of European settlement. Although the sites of one or two towns are more than 100 years old, all urban development has taken place in less than a century. In

* Adapted from *Annals of the Association of American Geographers,* Vol. XLIII, No. 4 (December, 1953), pp. 332-350, with permission of author and publisher.

this short period the towns of these two islands have acquired a uniform and individually characterless appearance with their typical elongated business areas, checkerboard street patterns, and repetition of cream colored, frame houses with red galvanised iron roofs and neat front gardens.

To the superficial observer these urban areas appear to be simply market towns of varying size, but of similar mold, each serving a tributary farming community and each responding with increased commercial activity to the weekly and seasonal rhythms of its rural hinterland. Because of this apparent uniformity among New Zealand towns an analysis of the functions which they perform becomes of particular importance as a means of differentiating clearly among them. As a result this aspect of urban geography probably takes on an even greater significance in New Zealand than in most other countries. It is therefore of interest to distinguish the kinds of New Zealand towns on the basis of their functions and to classify the urban areas of this small country.

METHOD

The most practical method of classifying New Zealand towns according to the different functions which they perform consists of analysing the occupational structure of each town.[1] But to assign the greatest weight to the function which employs the largest number of people in a town and to classify urban areas on this basis is to overlook the fact that in all towns there is always a certain proportion of the population engaged in the manufacture and distribution of goods and in the provision of services. It is only where an "abnormal" percentage of the population of an urban area is engaged in any single function that that function becomes a distinguishing feature. These abnormalities may be recognized initially by the construction of national means and

---

[1] The calculation of the amount of surface area devoted to different uses is both impractical and theoretically imperfect as a measure of functional importance, and no statistics are available in New Zealand for comparing the incomes of employment groups in individual towns. C. D. Harris established the relative importance of different functions in towns by assigning higher percentages to some functions than to others on the basis of an analysis made of cities of well recognized types. See "A Functional Classification of Cities in the United States," *Geographical Review,* XXXIII No. 1 (1943): 86-99.

the measurement of deviations (or functional indices) from these means.

In the calculation of national means either of two bases could have been selected: means for employment groups for all urban areas with more than 1,000 population; or means for employment groups in towns of approximately the same size. To consider all urban areas together presupposes that approximately the same percentage of the population is engaged in identical functions in all New Zealand towns irrespective of their size. This is not so. It is more logical to construct national means for towns of approximately the same size rather than to group urban centers of 1,000 people with, say, metropolitan populations 200 to 300 times larger. This assumption has been taken as the basis of the present study.

In April and October of each year statistics are collected by the Department of Labour and Employment stating the number of workers gainfully employed in 69 different industrial codes, ranging from bush sawmilling through the manufacture of footwear to road transport and arts and sciences and religion. From the April, 1950 survey, means were calculated for some six different employment groups (combining the majority of the 69 industrial codes) in all towns of more than 1,000 population and of approximately the same size.[2]

The positive deviations from these national averages are taken here as criteria expressing the relative importance of six different functions: manufacturing, building and construction; primary industrial; transport and communications; distribution and financial; hotel and personal service; and administration and professional service. The seventh class, that of the residential function, is based on the national means calculated for the percentage of the total population gainfully employed in towns of approximately the same size. A positive deviation implies that the percentage of population in a town in actual employment is higher than normal; conversely, a negative deviation implies that fewer people are

[2] In 1950 one hundred towns in New Zealand had a population of more than 1,000, 67 per cent of this total being in the North Island and 33 per cent in the South Island. Of the total population of New Zealand 68 per cent is in the North Island and 32 per cent in the south. The absence of settlements between 12,000 and 19,000 and 53,000 and 91,000 population is a feature of the urban geography of New Zealand which has yet to be studied by New Zealand geographers.

employed than is to be expected in a town of that size, that is, the urban area in question is a residential center by national standards (Table 1).[3]

TABLE 1

MEANS FOR FUNCTIONAL GROUPS IN NEW ZEALAND TOWNS OF APPROXI-
MATELY THE SAME SIZE (APRIL 1950)

Size of towns (000's)	91-308	19-53	7-12	4-7	3-4	2-3	1-2
Number of towns	4	11	7	11	11	20	36

FUNCTIONS	NATIONAL MEANS Percentage of Total Population in Different Functions						
Residential	64.36	69.85	65.81	69.02	66.69	71.35	71.73
Manufacturing, Building and Construction	15.78	11.86	12.68	12.75	13.29	11.24	9.88
Primary Industrial.	0.09	0.13	0.37	0.08	1.29	0.17	2.55
Transport & Communications.	4.04	3.89	4.55	3.95	5.29	4.27	4.36
Distribution & Financial	8.06	6.57	7.19	7.53	6.45	6.02	4.84
Hotel & Personal Service	1.81	2.10	2.61	2.26	2.36	2.16	2.05
Administration & Professional Service	5.41	4.92	6.12	4.00	3.67	4.09	2.98
(Workers not included)	0.45	0.68	0.67	0.41	0.96	0.72	1.61

SOURCE: Location and Decentralization of Industry—District Office Returns, April, 1950; Dept. of Labour and Employment, N.Z.

CLASSIFICATION

An analysis of the occupational structure of New Zealand towns shows that all have at least one distinguishing function of national significance [4] (Table 2). For the purpose of this paper, however, it is most convenient to classify each town by individual

[3] For Papatoetoe only 8.86 per cent of the total population is actually employed within the town itself by comparison with the national average for towns of 4,000 to 7,000 population of 30.98 per cent, thus giving Papatoetoe a negative deviation of 22.12. In Table 1 the figures relating to the residential function are the complements of the national means for the gainfully employed population.

[4] It may be noted that there is no discernible relationship between the number of functions performed by an urban center and the range of deviations.

TABLE 2

Number of Significant Functions Performed by Different Classes of
New Zealand Towns Based on Positive Deviations from
National Means

(Negative deviations for residential function)

Functional Classes	Per Cent of N.Z. Towns in Different Classes	Per Cent in Class with One Function	Per Cent in Class with Two Functions	Per Cent in Class with Three or More Functions
Residential	52	17	41	42
Manufacturing, Building and Construction	44	6	32	62
Primary Industrial	17	6	18	76
Transport & Communications	42	2	7	91
Distribution & Financial	52	0	6	94
Hotel & Personal Service	37	0	14	86
Administration & Professional Service	44	0	14	86
All Towns		15	27	58

functions so that a town with four functions will be classified in four different sections irrespective of the fact that only one is predominant.[5] At the same time it should be noted that 85 per cent of New Zealand towns have more than one significant function by national standards and that to classify towns systematically in the above manner is "logical" rather than "realistic."

A SERVICE CLASSIFICATION OF AMERICAN CITIES *

HOWARD J. NELSON

Everyone is aware that modern cities are performing more and more of the services necessary to the functioning of society. There is an awareness, too, that these vital services are not performed in the same proportions by all cities. Almost every geographer would classify Detroit as a manufacturing city; Rochester,

[5] In practice the two leading functions of Pahiatua, those of distribution and finance, and administration and personal service, are of the same relative importance. For the remaining 99 towns, however, one function does predominate.
* Adapted from *Economic Geography*, Vol. 31, No. 3 (July, 1955), pp. 189-210, with permission of author and publisher.

Minnesota, as a professional town; and Hartford, Connecticut, as an insurance center; thereby indicating that one city does more than its share of the nation's manufacturing, another provides professional services in outstanding proportions, and the third specializes in serving the insurance needs of society.

But perhaps this classification is done more by faith or intuition than on the basis of exact knowledge. At what point does an economic activity become important enough in a city to be of special significance? Can criteria be devised that will determine which cities should be labeled insurance centers, or retail trade cities, or centers of public administration? It is the purpose of this article to present a method that will form a basis for such a classification.

PROCEDURE

The best practical source of recent statistical data for a study involving a large number of American cities is the 1950 Census of Population. Here is available raw material gathered from every settlement in the United States, broken down in generous detail for urban places with populations of 10,000 or more. As we are interested in "geographic" or "functional" cities rather than political entities, "Urbanized Areas," which take in the entire built-up area, are used whenever available—where the Central City had at least 50,000 persons in 1940. (For example, the Los Angeles Urbanized Area is considered as one functional unit, instead of using the 45 political entities within it: Los Angeles, Pasadena, Long Beach, and so on, as 45 separate cities.) "Urban Places," mainly political cities but occasionally isolated unincorporated concentrations of population, are used for the smaller centers. After the "Urban Places" within "Urbanized Areas" are excluded to eliminate duplication, some 897 individual urban concentrations of over 10,000 persons remain for consideration.

The proportion of the labor force of a city engaged in performing a service is perhaps the best means of measuring the distribution of that activity. It is one of the few measures that are easily comparable from activity to activity or from year to year. Furthermore, the proportion of the labor force actually employed in a service is of much more direct significance to the economy of the city than the value or volume of sales of goods or of services performed, or similar measures for the manufactured products in a city.

The Census of Population breaks down the services performed by the labor force of a city into 24 major industry groups. These are listed in the first column of Table 1. In considering the broad categories of services performed by urban areas for society, however, condensations and omissions seem called for. Agricultural workers, for example, who may simply reflect farm land within loosely drawn city limits, were omitted. So, arbitrarily, were the categories of utility and sanitary services, construction, and personal service in private households (though all other categories of personal service were included), on the grounds that these are not essentially services performed by urban areas for society as a whole. The following nine major categories of services were chosen for investigation in this study: Mining; Manufacturing; Transportation and Communication; Wholesale Trade; Retail Trade; Finance, Insurance and Real Estate; Personal Service; Professional Service; and Public Administration (see Table 1).

After the nine categories indicated by Table 1 had been decided upon, the percentages of the total labor force in each activity group for each of the 897 cities were calculated. Table 2 illustrates the procedure for several selected cities. However, as individual percentages are almost meaningless without some point of reference, the arithmetic averages for each activity group were computed. The final column of Table 2 indicates the average percentage of those gainfully employed in various activity groups for the total of 897 cities.

It is obvious from Table 2 that the average proportions of the labor force in each of the activity groups differ greatly. The performance of manufacturing service occupies the largest proportion of the labor force in the 897 American cities of 10,000 or more, 27.07 per cent. Another sizable fraction, nearly 20 per cent, is concerned with retail trade. Thus, over 45 out of every 100 workers in our cities are engaged in providing these two essential urban services—the fabrication of products and the distribution of goods at the retail level. The professional services necessary to society utilize about 11 per cent of the urban labor force—doctors, lawyers, teachers, engineers, and similar skills.

TABLE 1

Major Economic Activities

Census Classification by Industry Groups *	Service Classification
Agriculture, forestry, and fisheries	Omitted
Mining	Mining
Construction	Omitted
Manufacturing	Manufacturing
Railroads and railway express service Trucking service and warehousing .... Other transportation Telecommunications	Transportation and communication
Utilities and sanitary services	Omitted
Wholesale trade	Wholesale trade
Food and dairy produce stores, and milk retail Eating and drinking places .... Other retail trade	Retail trade
Finance, insurance and real estate	Finance, insurance and real estate
Business services Repair services	Omitted
Private households	Omitted
Hotels and lodging places Other personal service .... Entertainment and recreation	Personal service
Medical and other health services Educational services, government .... Educational services, private Other professional and related services	Professional service
Public administration	Public administration
Industry not reported	Omitted

* U.S. Census of Population, 1950, Vol. 2, Table 35—Economic Characteristics of the Population. . . .

The other six categories of urban services are performed by a relatively small fraction of urban workers. Transportation and communication account for 7.12 per cent; personal service, 6.2 per cent; public administration, 4.58 per cent; wholesale trade, 3.85 per cent; finance, insurance, and real estate, 3.19 per cent; and mining, 1.62 per cent.

Doubts might logically arise at this point—surely cities with variations in size of from 10,000 to 13,000,000 must vary considerably in the proportions of the labor force employed in the different services. How valid are averages taking in all of these differently sized cities? To shed some light on this question the

TABLE 2

PROPORTION OF LABOR FORCE IN SELECTED ACTIVITIES

Sample Cities

	New York		Detroit		Kearney, Neb.		Rochester, Minn.		Average of 897 Cities
	In 000's	Per Cent	In 000's	Per Cent	In 000's	Per Cent	In 000's	Per Cent	Per Cent
Population	12,296	—	2,659	—	12.11	—	29.88	—	—
Labor force	6,099	—	1,068	—	3.28	—	13.0	—	—
Manufacturing ..	1,573	25.8	501	46.9	0.27	8.3	0.81	6.1	27.07
Retail trade	822	13.5	164	15.3	1.18	36.2	2.72	20.7	19.09
Professional service	448	7.3	73	6.9	0.84	25.6	4.39	33.3	11.09
Transportation and comm. ...	475	7.8	71	6.7	0.32	9.7	0.73	6.3	7.12
Personal service ..	361	5.9	59	5.5	0.36	11.0	1.40	10.6	6.20
Public administration .	227	3.7	36	3.4	0.20	6.1	0.41	3.1	4.58
Wholesale trade..	274	4.5	33	3.1	0.22	6.6	0.42	3.1	3.85
Finance, insurance and real estate	353	5.8	36	3.4	0.13	3.9	0.39	2.9	3.19
Mining	3	0.05	0.3	0.01	0.005	0.15	0.01	0.09	1.62

SOURCE: Census of Population: 1950, Vol. II, Table 35.

897 cities were broken down into seven arbitrarily selected groups by size as shown in Table 3. This table indicates that though there is some correlation between size of city and the proportions of the labor force in each activity, no constant or regular change is in evidence. However, there is variation in some of the per-

TABLE 3

AVERAGE PERCENTAGE OF THOSE GAINFULLY EMPLOYED IN SELECTED
ACTIVITY GROUPS

	Manufacturing	Retail	Professional Service	Wholesale	Personal Service	Public Adm.	Trans. and Comm.	Finance, Insurance Real Estate	Mining	No. of Cities
In cities of from										
10,000 to 24,999.	26.65	19.66	11.34	3.72	5.79	4.39	7.03	2.96	2.11	550
25,000 to 49,999.	26.07	19.07	11.98	3.87	7.09	4.80	6.98	3.22	1.03	166
50,000 to 99,999.	29.31	18.56	9.76	4.24	6.47	4.79	7.75	3.39	0.48	59
100,000 to 249,999	29.77	18.07	9.50	4.21	6.61	5.22	7.14	3.74	0.71	71
250,000 to 499,999	28.10	17.81	9.22	4.40	6.86	6.40	7.58	4.38	1.24	25
500,000 to 999,999	27.21	18.16	9.17	5.10	6.72	4.96	8.83	5.06	0.41	14
1,000,000 and over	30.86	16.32	8.97	4.15	6.42	6.92	7.35	4.75	0.16	12
Average	27.07	19.23	11.09	3.85	6.20	4.58	7.12	3.19	1.62	897

centages and where they are small this may be quite significant. Generally speaking, the proportions of the labor force in retail trade, professional service, and mining vary inversely with city size, that is, the percentages decrease as the cities get larger. Most of the other activities seem to be performed in greater proportions in the larger cities. However, in almost every case the trend is marked by several exceptions.

FREQUENCY VARIATIONS

To portray graphically the distribution of economic services among American cities the frequency graphs shown in Figure I were constructed. These nine graphs show the frequency with which a given percentage of the labor force employed in an activity occurs in the 897 cities under consideration. In these graphs the vertical axis indicates the number of cities involved and the horizontal axis the percentage of the labor force in each service.

Striking variations in the distribution of the nine different services among our urban centers are apparent in Figure I. A unique type of distribution is illustrated by manufacturing service. Retail trade exemplifies a second, quite different type. The seven remaining services might be considered together as a third type, somewhat similar to type two.

The manufacturing services provided by American cities display a greater variation, in terms of percentage of labor force employed, than any other activity. Unlike the distribution of any other activities, manufacturing shows no sign of "peaking" or grouping around some "typical" percentages. No city is without some manufacturing, but a few cities get by with less than 5 per cent of the labor force in this service. On the other hand, some cities have more than 65 per cent of their employed persons in this activity, and 91 cities have over 50 per cent of their labor force in manufacturing. Obviously, less that is meaningful can be said about an average or "normal" amount of manufacturing in a city than about any other activity. How much manufacturing should a city have to consider itself "balanced," for example?

Retail trade, perhaps because of its general necessity wherever concentrations of population are found, presents a distribu-

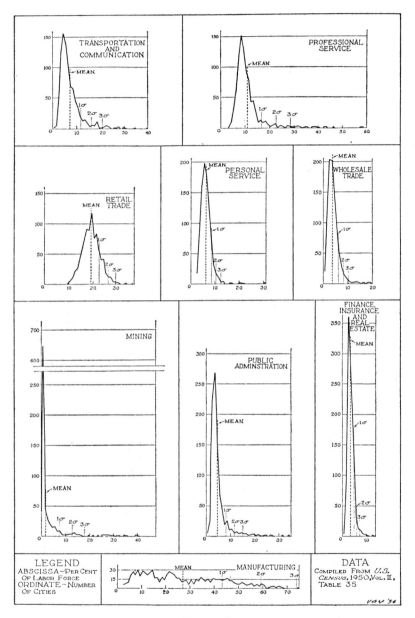

FIGURE I.

tion closer to a theoretical "normal curve" than any other service. In no city does less than 6 per cent of the working force serve the retail needs of the people. In some others 30 per cent and more, up to an extreme of 36.22 per cent, make their living providing this service. However, in about 120 cities the average is present, and there are almost the same number of cities with proportions below the average as there are with percentages above it.

The seven remaining activities fall into what may be considered a third general type of frequency distribution. Typically, most of the cities have a fairly common, rather low percentage of their labor force in a given activity. Then, in each case, there are a few cities in which the service is performed in outstanding amounts. Professional service, for example, commonly is supplied by from 6 to 12 per cent of the labor force. However, in a few cities these percentages rise many times above normal, with 30, 40, and, in several cases, nearly 60 per cent of the labor force employed in professional service. Generally speaking, transportation and communication, personal service, wholesale trade, finance, insurance, and real estate, and public administration follow a similar type of frequency distribution.

Mining perhaps warrants some special comments. This activity, which of course can exist only in the presence of minerals, is highly localized. This is the only activity which is not reported at all in a number of our cities. In 673 cities less than 1 per cent of the labor force is engaged in this activity. These, presumably, are workers in sand, gravel, and clay pits, limestone quarries, and the like. On the other hand, where minerals are present the percentage may go up appreciably. For example, 14 cities have more than 25 per cent of their workers in this activity, and the maximum is 41 per cent (in Shenandoah, Pennsylvania).

THE CLASSIFICATION PROBLEM

We now shift our focus from the services performed in cities to the cities themselves. From the appearance of the above frequency distribution curves, particularly of the services in which some cities have a far greater proportion than those at the peak, it would seem that it would be valid to attempt to separate those cities at the extreme from the general average. This is the second major problem: How large a percentage of the labor force must be employed in a particular service to make the performance of the service far enough above normal to warrant separate classification?

This particular question is one that has received considerable attention from geographers as well as from others interested in cities. The thinking has usually been to the effect that, if an activity is concentrated in a city in a certain amount, this activity dominates the city's economic life and becomes its major function. As a result, several functional classifications of cities have been attempted. However, most students of urban geography would probably agree that the problem of classification has never been satisfactorily solved.

Perhaps the most significant and influential of all functional classifications of cities was that worked out by Chauncy Harris in 1943.[1] It is one of the first in which stated criteria are used, and is based on material from the 1930 Census of Population and the 1935 Census of Business. In this classification the criteria for each class of cities were chosen as follows: "On the basis of an analysis of cities of well recognized types an empirical solution (to the problem of ruling out local service employment) has been evolved by assigning higher percentages to some functions than to others. . . ." [2] For example, the classification of manufacturing (M′) has for its principal criterion "Employment in manufacturing equals at least 74% of the total employment in manufacturing, retailing, and wholesaling," [3] plus a secondary criterion "Manufacturing and mechanical industries contain at least 45% of gainful workers." [4] In retail centers, "Employment in retailing is at least 50% of the total employment in manufacturing, wholesaling, and retailing and at least 2.2 times that in wholesaling alone." [5] Though the exact percentages are stated, we must have faith that the author has chosen cities of well recognized types—for they are not identified—and rely on his judg-

[1] Chauncy D. Harris: "A Functional Classification of Cities in the United States," *Geogr. Rev.*, Vol. 33, 1943, pp. 86-99.
[2] *Ibid.*, p. 87.
[3] *Ibid.*, p. 88.
[4] *Ibid.*
[5] *Ibid.*

ment as to the significance of the figures 74, 45, 50 and 2.2. Actually, the high reputation that this classification has maintained through the years attests to the general accuracy of the author's judgments.

A more up-to-date classification appears in a chapter by Victor Jones in the Municipal Year Book for 1953.[6] It is based on data from the 1948 Census of Manufacturing and the Census of Business of that same year. Jones' method is patterned after Harris', although his percentages are somewhat different. However, the same comments about faith must apply.

METHOD USED

It would seem to be a useful advance if a classification based on clearly stated statistical procedures could be devised in which each step could be checked and understood by other workers in the field. Once the data plotted on the distribution curves is prepared (Fig. I), a number of statistical procedures are available to provide an objective, uniform method of measuring variation from the average. Perhaps the most useful device for our purposes is the Standard Deviation (hereafter referred to as the SD). In the first place (regardless of the theoretical criticisms that may be leveled against it) the SD is the simplest and most widely understood of all statistical measures of variation. Secondly, the *degree* of variation can be compared by use of the SD even if in some cases we are dealing with large percentages (as in manufacturing) or with small numbers (as in wholesale trade). This would seem to be an advantage over the simple percentage deviation used by Pownall.[7]

Standard deviations from the mean were therefore calculated for each of the nine activity groups and are presented in Table 4. The SD's are also indicated on the frequency curves in Figure I by the letter σ. Three degrees of variation from the average were recognized, and the cities grouped in their appropriate categories. Cities that are over $+1$ SD from the average in manufacturing

[6] Victor Jones: "Economic Classification of Cities and Metropolitan Areas," *The Municipal Year Book,* 1953, pp. 49-54 and 69, and Table IV.
[7] L. L. Pownall, "Functions of New Zealand Towns," *Annals Assn. Amer. Geogrs.,* Vol. 43, 1953, pp. 332-350.

were given a Manufacturing 1 (or Mf1) rating, over 2 SD's an Mf2 rating, over 3 *or more* SD's an Mf3 rating. A similar procedure was followed for each activity group.

TABLE 4

AVERAGES AND STANDARD DEVIATIONS FOR SELECTED ACTIVITY GROUPS

	Manu-factur-ing	Retail Trade	Profes-sional Service	Trans-porta-tion and Commu-nication	Per-sonal Serv-ice	Public Admin-istra-tion	Whole-sale Trade	Fi-nance, Insur-ance and Real Estate	Min-ing
Average	27.07	19.23	11.09	7.12	6.20	4.58	3.85	3.19	1.62
S.D.	16.04	3.63	5.89	4.58	2.07	3.48	2.14	1.25	5.01
Average plus 1 S.D.	43.11	22.86	16.98	11.70	8.27	8.06	5.99	4.44	7.63
Average plus 2 S.D.	59.15	26.47	22.87	16.28	10.34	12.54	8.13	5.69	12.64
Average plus 3 S.D.	75.26	30.12	28.16	20.86	12.41	16.02	10.27	6.94	17.65

Inspection of Figure I indicated the point of the frequency curve at which the +1, 2, and 3 SD's occur. In a number of instances this point coincides fairly well with a "natural break" in the frequency curve. In other instances, as in the case of manufacturing, where a "natural break" would be difficult to determine, it provides a standard, objective division point. But, in any case, it is always clear where the divisions are made and why they are made at that point.

When applied to the 897 American cities chosen for this study, the method just described is not mutually exclusive, that is, a city may provide more than one type of service in outstanding proportions. This would seem to be an asset to the classification rather than a weakness, fitting observed reality.

Many cities high in professional service, for example, are also high in personal service. Thus Boulder, Colorado, is classified Pf3Ps2, indicating that the city is three or more SD's above the average in professional service and over two SD's above the average in personal service. Occasionally, a city may be far enough above the average to receive a rating in three, and even, rarely, in four categories.

Some cities do not rank high enough in any service to come under any of the nine categories. These are lumped together in a single Diversified group, although this is a somewhat misleading term. What is meant is that they are simply not unusually high in any service.

The final product of this research, a classification of 897 American cities, appears in the appendix to this article.[8]

APPENDIX

A Service Classification of American Cities

Key

	Plus 1SD	Plus 2SD	Plus 3SD
Manufacturing	Mf	Mf2	Mf3
Retail trade	R	R2	R3
Professional service	Pf	Pf2	Pf3
Transportation and communication	T	T2	T3
Personal service	Ps	Ps2	Ps3
Public administration	Pb	Pb2	Pb3
Wholesale trade	W	W2	W3
Finance, insurance and real estate	F	F2	F3
Mining	Mi	Mi2	Mi3
Diversified	D		

ALABAMA

Anniston	Pb
Auburn	Pf3Ps2
Birmingham	D
Decatur	D
Dothan	RW
Florence	D
Gadsden	Mf
Huntsville	RPbF
Mobile	Pb
Montgomery	PbF
Opelika	D
Phenix City	D
Selma	D
Sheffield	T
Talladega	D
Tuscaloosa	Pf

ARIZONA

Amphitheater	R
Phoenix	PsWF
Tucson	Ps2PfF

ARKANSAS

Blytheville	R2Ps
Camden	D
El Dorado	D
Fayetteville	Pf2Ps
Fort Smith	RW
Helena	D
Hot Springs	Ps3R
Jonesboro	RTW
Little Rock-North	
Little Rock	TWF
Pine Bluff	TW
Texarkana	Pb

CALIFORNIA

Alisal	W3
Anaheim	W
Antioch	Mf
Bakersfield	Ps
Brawley	W3
Chico	RWF
Corona	W3Ps

[8] A mimeographed table giving the SD values for all except the Diversified cities is available upon request from the author.

Costa Mesa	Mf	Greeley	RPfWF
El Centro	R3W3PsPbF	Pueblo	Pb
Eureka	D	Trinidad	RMi
Fresno	PsWF		
Fullerton	W	CONNECTICUT	
Hanford	R3	Ansonia	Mf2
Lodi	D	Bridgeport	Mf
Los Angeles	F	Danbury	Mf
Madera	R2	Derby	Mf2
Merced	R2Pb	Hartford	F3
Modesto	RWF	Meriden	Mf
Monterey	Ps2R	Middleton	D
Napa	D	New Britain-Bristol	Mf2
Newport Beach	F3R	New Haven	D
Oceanside	R2PsW	New London	Pb
Oildale	Mi2R	Norwich	D
Ontario	D	Shelton	Mf
Orange	Pf	Stamford-Norwalk	D
Oxnard	Pb3W2	Torrington	Mf
Petaluma	W2R	Wallingford	Mf2
Pittsburg	Mf	Waterbury	Mf
Pomona	W	Willimantic	Mf
Redding	R		
Riverside	PbWF	DISTRICT OF COLUMBIA	
Sacramento	Pb3	Washington	Pb3F
Salinas	W2RF		
San Bernardino	Pb	DELAWARE	
San Buenaventura	MiPb	Wilmington	D
San Diego	Pb2PsF		
San Francisco-		FLORIDA	
Oakland	F2	Bradenton	RPsF
San Jose	D	Brownsville-B.-G.	Pb3
San Luis Obispo	RPfT	Clearwater	Ps2F
Santa Ana	RPbF	Daytona Beach	Ps3F2R
Santa Barbara	Ps2F	Fort Lauderdale	F3Ps2R
Santa Cruz	Ps2RF	Fort Myers	R2Ps
Santa Maria	RPsW	Fort Pierce	W3RF
Santa Paula	W3Pb	Gainesville	Pf3Ps
Santa Rosa	R2WF	Hollywood	Ps3F3
Seaside	Ps2RPb	Jacksonville	TPsPbFW
Stockton	Pb	Key West	Pb3Ps
Tulare	R3W	Lakeland	F
Visalia	R	Lake Worth	R2F2Ps
Watsonville	W3R	Miami	Ps3RF
		Ocala	R2Ps
COLORADO		Orlando	Ps2F2W
Boulder	Pf3Ps2	Panama City	Pb
Colorado Springs	Ps2F	Pensacola	Pb2
Denver	WF	St. Augustine	Ps2T
Fort Collins	Pf2F	St. Petersburg	Ps2F2R
Grand Junction	TW	Sanford	W3

Sarasota	Ps3RF
Tallahassee	Pb2Pf
Tampa	PsW
Warrington	Pb3
West Palm Beach	Ps3RF

GEORGIA

Augusta	D
Albany	W
Americus	D
Athens	Pf
Atlanta	F2
Brunswick	Ps2
Columbus	D
Dalton	Mf
Decatur	F3W
Dublin	D
Gainesville	W
Griffin	D
La Grange	Mf
Macon	Pb
Marietta	F
Moultrie	D
Rome	D
Savannah	D
Thomasville	D
Valdosta	D
Waycross	T3

IDAHO

Boise City	F2PbW
Caldwell	RW
Coeur d'Alene	D
Idaho Falls	W2R
Lewiston	R
Moscow	Pf3Ps2
Nampa	T2
Pocatello	T3
Twin Falls	R2W2

ILLINOIS

Alton	D
Aurora	D
Bloomington	F3
Cairo	RW
Canton	D
Carbondale	PfT
Centralia	T3
Champaign	Pb3Ps
Chicago	F
Collinsville	D
Danville	D
Decatur	D
De Kalb	D
Dixon	D
Elgin	D
Freeport	F2
Galesburg	T2
Harrisburg	Mi3
Jacksonville	Pf3
Joliet	D
Kankakee	D
Kewanee	Mf
La Salle	Mf
Lincoln	Pf
Macomb	R
Marion	Mi2
Mattoon	T2
Monmouth	F3R
Mount Vernon	D
Ottawa	D
Pekin	D
Peoria	D
Quincy	D
Rockford	Mf
Springfield	PbF
Sterling	Mf
Streator	Mf
Urbana	Pf3
Waukegan	Pb
West Frankfort	Mi3
Wood River	Mf

INDIANA

Anderson	Mf
Bedford	D
Bloomington	Pf3
Columbus	Mf
Connersville	Mf
Crawfordsville	D
Elkhart	Mf
Elwood	Mf
Evansville	D
Fort Wayne	D
Frankfort	T3
Goshen	Mf
Huntington	D
Indianapolis	F
Kokomo	Mf
Lafayette	D
La Porte	Mf
Logansport	T2

Marion	D	Independence	D
Michigan City	D	Junction City	Pb3R2Ps
Muncie	Mf	Lawrence	Pf2Ps
New Castle	Mf	Leavenworth	Pb3
Peru	T3	Manhattan	Pf3PsPbF
Richmond	Mf	Newton	T3
Shelbyville	D	Ottawa	R
South Bend	Mf	Parsons	T3
Terre Haute	D	Pittsburg	T
Valparaiso	D	Salina	RWF
Vincennes	R	Topeka	TPbF
Wabash	Mf	Wichita	F
Washington	T3	Winfield	Pf
West Lafayette	Pf3Ps		

IOWA

KENTUCKY

		Bowling Green	D
Ames	Pf3Ps	Frankfort	Pb3
Boone	T3	Henderson	D
Burlington	W2	Hopkinsville	RPs
Cedar Rapids	R	Lexington	PfPs
Charles City	D	Louisville	D
Clinton	D	Madisonville	Mi3
Davenport, Ia.-Rock		Middlesborough	Mi2R
Island-Moline, Ill.	D	Owensboro	D
Des Moines	F3	Paducah	T2
Dubuque	D	Richmond	PfPb
Fort Dodge	R		
Fort Madison	T2		

LOUISIANA

Iowa City	Pf3	Alexandria	Ps
Keokuk	D	Bastrop	Mf
Marshalltown	D	Baton Rouge	D
Mason City	D	Bogalusa	D
Muscatine	D	Crowley	D
Newton	Mf	Houma	Mi3
Oskaloosa	R	Lafayette	D
Ottumwa	D	Lake Charles	D
Sioux City	W2	Monroe	PsW
Waterloo	D	New Iberia	MiW
		New Orleans	TWF
		Opelousas	R

KANSAS

		Ruston	Pf2
Arkansas City	T2	Shreveport	D
Atchison	D	West Monroe	RW
Chanute	T		
Coffeyville	D		
Dodge City	W2R2T		

MAINE

El Dorado	Mi	Auburn	Mf
Emporia	T2	Augusta	Pb2
Fort Scott	F3T	Bangor	W
Garden City	R2	Bath	D
Great Bend	Mi2	Biddeford	Mf2
Hutchinson	WR	Lewiston	Mf

Portland	WF
Saco	Mf
Sanford	Mf2
Waterville	D

MARYLAND

Annapolis	Pf3Pb2
Baltimore	D
Cambridge	D
Cumberland	T3
Frederick	Pb
Hagerstown	D
Salisbury	D

MASSACHUSETTS

Adams-Renfrew	Mf2
Boston	F
Brockton	Mf
Clinton	Mf
Fall River	Mf
Fitchburg	Mf
Gardner	Mf
Gloucester	W2
Greenfield	Ps
Haverhill	Mf
Leominster	Mf2
Lawrence	Mf
Lowell	Mf
Marlborough	Mf
Milford	Mf2
New Bedford	Mf
Newburyport	Mf
North Adams	Mf
Northampton	D
Plymouth	D
Southbridge	Mf2
Springfield-Holyoke	Mf
Taunton	Mf
Webster	Mf2
Worcester	D

MICHIGAN

Adrian	D
Albion	Mf
Alpena	D
Ann Arbor	Pf3
Battle Creek	D
Bay City	D
Benton Harbor	Mf
Cadillac	D

Detroit	Mf
Escanaba	T2
Flint	Mf
Grand Rapids	D
Holland	D
Ironwood	Mi3
Jackson	D
Kalamazoo	D
Lansing	D
Marquette	T2Pb
Menominee	Mf
Midland	Mf
Monroe	Mf
Mount Pleasant	PfMi
Muskegon	Mf
Niles	MfT
Owosso	D
Pontiac	Mf
Port Huron	D
Saginaw	Mf
St. Joseph	Mf
Sault Ste Marie	D
Springfield Place	Mf
Traverse City	Pf
Willow Run	Pf2
Ypsilanti	D

MINNESOTA

Albert Lea	D
Austin	Mf
Bemidji	R
Brainerd	T3
Duluth, Minn.-Superior, Wis.	T2W
Faribault	Pf2
Fergus Falls	RPf
Hibbing	Mi3
Mankato	W2R
Minneapolis-St Paul	F2W
Moorhead	W3R
Owatonna	F3
Red Wing	D
Rochester	Pf3Ps2
St. Cloud	Pf
Virginia	Mi3
Winona	D

MISSISSIPPI

Biloxi	Ps2Pb
Clarksdale	RPs
Columbus	D

Greenville	D	North Platte	T3
Greenwood	W2R	Omaha	F3W
Gulfport	Ps	Scottsbluff	R2W
Hattiesburg	D		
Jackson	PsF	**NEVADA**	
Laurel	Ps3	Las Vegas	Ps3
McComb	T3R	Reno	Ps2F
Meridian	D		
Natchez	D	**NEW HAMPSHIRE**	
Pascagoula	D	Berlin	Mf2
Tupelo	W2	Claremont	Mf
Vicksburg	D	Concord	PfPbF
MISSOURI		Dover	Mf
		Keene	F
Cape Girardeau	D	Laconia	D
Carthage	D	Manchester	Mf
Columbia	Pf3Ps	Nashua	Mf
Fulton	Pf3	Portsmouth	D
Hannibal	T	Rochester	Mf
Jefferson City	Pb3		
Joplin	W2R	**NEW JERSEY**	
Kansas City	F	Asbury Park	Ps3RPb
Kirksville	RPf	Atlantic City	Ps3R
Mexico	D	Bridgeton	Mf
Moberly	T3	Burlington	Mf
Poplar Bluff	RT	Long Branch	Pb3
St. Charles	Mf	Millville	Mf
St. Joseph	W	Phillipsburg	Mf
St. Louis	Ps	Princeton	Pf3
Sedalia	T2W	Red Bank	Pb2F
Sikeston	RW	Trenton	Pb
Springfield	TW		
Webster Groves	F3W	**NEW MEXICO**	
MONTANA		Albuquerque	Pb2PsF
		Carlsbad	Mi3
Anaconda	Mf	Clovis	T2Ps
Billings	W2RPsF	Hobbs	Mi3
Bozeman	Pf2RPs	Las Cruces	Pb2R
Butte	Mi3	Roswell	Ps2RPb
Great Fall	TF	Santa Fe	R2Pb2Ps
Helena	Pb3F3		
Missoula	PfT	**NEW YORK**	
NEBRASKA		Albany-Troy	Pb2
		Amsterdam	Mf2
Beatrice	D	Auburn	Mf
Fremont	RW	Batavia	D
Grand Island	TWF	Beacon	Pf2
Hastings	RW	Binghamton	R3Mf
Kearney	R3Pf2Ps2W	Buffalo	D
Lincoln	F2	Corning	Mf
Norfolk	R2W2		

Cortland	Mf
Dunkirk	Mf
Elmira	D
Fulton	Mf2
Geneva	D
Glens Falls	F3
Gloversville	Mf
Hornell	T3
Hudson	D
Ithaca	Pf3
Jamestown	Mf
Johnstown	Mf
Kingston	D
Lockport	Mf
Massena	Mf
Middletown	Pf
Newark	RPf
Newburgh	D
New York-North-eastern N. J.	F2
Niagara Falls	Mf
Ogdenburg	Pf
Olean	D
Oneida	Mf
Oneonta	T3
Oswego	D
Peekskill	T
Plattsburgh	Pf
Poughkeepsie	D
Rochester	Mf
Rome	Mf
Saratoga Springs	Ps2
Schenectady	Mf
Syracuse	D
Utica	D
Watertown	F

NORTH CAROLINA

Albemarle	Mf
Asheville	Ps
Burlington	Mf
Charlotte	WF
Concord	Mf
Durham	D
Elizabeth City	D
Fayetteville	Ps2R
Gastonia	Mf
Goldsboro	D
Greensboro	F
Greenville	Ps
Henderson	D

Hickory	D
High Point	Mf
Kannapolis	Mf2
Kingston	D
Lexington	Mf
Monroe	D
New Bern	Pb2
Raleigh	F2PfPbPs
Reidsville	Mf
Rocky Mount	T
Salisbury	T
Sanford	D
Shelby	D
Statesville	D
Thomasville	Mf2
Wilmington	T
Wilson	D
Winston-Salem	D

NORTH DAKOTA

Bismarck	Pb2WF
Fargo	W2F2R
Grand Forks	T
Jamestown	RTPf
Minot	RTW

OHIO

Akron	Mf
Alliance	Mf
Ashland	Mf
Ashtabula	T3
Athens	Pf2
Bellefontaine	T3
Bowling Green	Pf2R
Bucyrus	D
Cambridge	D
Canton	Mf
Chillicothe	D
Cincinnati	D
Cleveland	D
Columbus	F
Conneaut	T3
Coshocton	D
Dayton	Pb
Defiance	D
Delaware	Pf
East Liverpool	Mf
Findlay	D
Fostoria	Mf
Fremont	D
Hamilton	Mf

Kent	Pf
Lancaster	Mf
Lima	D
Lorain	Mf
Mansfield	Mf
Marietta	D
Marion	T
Mount Vernon	D
Newark	D
New Philadelphia	D
Painesville	Mf
Piqua	Mf
Portsmouth	T
Salem	Mf
Sandusky	Mf
Sidney	Mf
Springfield	D
Steubenville	Mf
Tiffin	D
Toledo	D
Troy	Mf
Van Wert	DF
Washington	R
Wooster	Pf
Xenia	Pb3
Youngstown	Mf
Zanesville	D

OKLAHOMA

Ada	RPs
Ardmore	RF
Bartlesville	Mi3
Chickasha	R
Duncan	Mi3
Durant	R2
El Reno	T3Pb
Enid	RW
Guthrie	Ps
Lawton	Ps2RPb
McAlester	Pb3R
Miami	D
Muskogee	D
Norman	Pf3Ps
Oklahoma City	Pb2F2
Okmulgee	D
Ponca City	D
Sapulpa	D
Seminole	Mi3
Shawnee	D
Stillwater	Pf3Ps
Tulsa	F

OREGON

Albany	R
Astoria	D
Bend	D
Corvallis	Pf3Ps2
Eugene	PfPsF
Klamath Falls	RT
Medford	RWF
Pendleton	D
Portland	WF
Salem	PbF
Springfield	D

PENNSYLVANIA

Allentown-Bethlehem	Mf
Altoona	T3
Berwick	Mf
Bloomsburg	D
Bradford	Mi
Bristol	Mf2
Butler	D
Cannonsburg	D
Carlisle	Pb2
Chambersburg	Pb3
Coatesville	Mf
Columbia	MfPb
Connellsville	T2
Conshohocken	Mf2
Donora	Mf2
Du Bois	T2
Easton	Mf
Ellwood City	Mf2
Erie	D
Farrell	Mf2
Franklin	D
Greensburg	F
Hanover	Mf
Harrisburg	Pb3T
Hazleton	Mi2
Indiana	Mi2Pf
Jeannette	Mf
Johnstown	D
Lancaster	Mf
Latrobe	Mf
Lebanon	Mf
Lewistown	D
Lock Haven	D
Mahanoy City	Mi3
Meadville	D

Monessen	Mf2
Mount Carmel	Mi3
New Castle	T
Norristown	Mf
Oil City	D
Philadelphia	F
Phoenixville	Mf
Pittsburgh	D
Pottstown	Mf
Pottsville	Mi
Reading	Mf
Scranton	Mi2
Shamokin	Mi2
Sharon	Mf
Shenandoah	Mi3
State College	Pf3Ps
Sunbury	T
Tamaqua	TMi3
Uniontown	R2Mi2
Warren	D
Washington	D
Waynesboro	Mf
West Chester	Pf
Williamsport	D
Wilkes-Barre	Mi3
York	D

RHODE ISLAND

Bristol	Mf2
Central Falls	Mf2
Newport	Pb3
Providence	Mf
Woonsocket	Mf2

SOUTH CAROLINA

Anderson	D
Brandon-Judson	Mf3
Charleston	D
Columbia	F
Florence	T
Greenwood	D
Greenville	F
Orangeburg	D
Rock Hill	Mf
Spartanburg	D
Sumter	E

SOUTH DAKOTA

Aberdeen	R2WF
Huron	RTW
Mitchell	R2W2

Rapid City	Ps2RPb
Sioux Falls	W2F
Watertown	R2W2

TENNESSEE

Bristol	D
Chattanooga	D
Clarksville	D
Cleveland	D
Columbia	D
Dyersburg	R
Elizabethton	D
Jackson	T
Johnson City	W
Kingsport	Mf
Knoxville	D
Memphis	W
Morristown	D
Murfreesboro	Pf
Nashville	F
Oak Ridge	MfPb

TEXAS

Abilene	PsWF
Alice	Mi2
Amarillo	W2TPs
Austin	PbF
Baytown	Mf
Beaumont	D
Big Spring	RT
Borger	Mi
Brownsville	D
Brownwood	RW
Bryan	Pf
Cleburne	T3
Corpus Christi	PsPb
Corsicana	D
Dallas	F3W
Del Rio	RTPs
Denison	T3
Denton	Pf2
Edinburg	W3R
El Paso	T
Fort Worth	D
Gainesville	RMi
Galveston	T2F2
Garland	WF
Greenville	R
Harlingen	RWF
Houston	F
Kingsville	T2

Lamesa	MiR	Danville	D
Laredo	R	Fredericksburg	D
Longview	D	Harrisonburg	RW
Lubbock	RWPsF	Hopewell	Mf
Lufkin	D	Lynchburg	D
McAllen	RWF	Martinsville	Mf
McKinney	Pf	Newport News	TPb
Marshall	T	Newsome Park	D
Mercedes	W3R	Norfolk-Portsmouth	Pb2
Midland	Mi3	Petersburg	D
Mission	R	Richmond	F2
Nacogdoches	D	Riverview	Pb3Ps
New Braunfels	Ps	Roanoke	T2
Odessa	Mi3	Staunton	D
Orange	D	Suffolk	W3
Palestine	T3	Waynesboro	Mf
Pampa	Mi2	Winchester	R
Paris	R		
Plainview	R2	WASHINGTON	
Port Arthur	Mf		
San Angelo	RPs	Aberdeen	D
San Antonio	Ps3Pb2F	Bellingham	D
San Benito	W3	Bremerton	D
Sherman	D	Everett	D
Snyder	Mi3	Hoquiam	Mf
Sweetwater	R	Kennewick	D
Temple	Pf	Longview	Mf
Terrell	Pf	Olympia	Pb3
Texarkana	Pb2	Pasco	T2
Texas City	D	Port Angeles	D
Tyler	RF	Pullman	Pf3Ps
Vernon	R2	Puyallup	D
Victoria	D	Richland	Mf2
Waco	W	Seattle	F2
Waxahachie	R	Spokane	F2W
Wichita Falls	RMiPs	Tacoma	PbF
UTAH		Walla Walla	D
		Wenatchee	RWF
Logan	Pf2R	Yakima	W2RF
Ogden	Pb3T2		
Provo	Pf	WEST VIRGINIA	
Salt Lake City	F		
		Beckley	Mi3
VERMONT		Bluefield	T2WF
		Charleston	D
Barre	F	Clarksburg	D
Burlington	Pf	Fairmont	Mi2
Rutland	T	Huntington, W. Va.-	
		Ashland, Ky.	T
VIRGINIA		Martinsburg	D
		Morgantown	PfMi
Bristol	D	Moundsville	Mf
Charlottesville	Pf		

Parkersburg	D	Marshfield	W
South Parkersburg	Mf	Menasha	Mf2
Weirton	Mf2	Milwaukee	D
Wheeling	D	Neenah	Mf
		Oshkosh	D
WISCONSIN		Racine	Mf
Appleton	D	Sheboygan	Mf
Ashland	T2	Stevens Point	F3
Beaver Dam	D	Two Rivers	Mf2
Beloit	Mf	Watertown	D
Chippewa Falls	D	Waukesha	D
Eau Claire	D	Wausau	F3
Fond du Lac	D	Wisconsin Rapids	Mf
Green Bay	TW		
Janesville	D	WYOMING	
Kenosha	Mf		
La Crosse	D	Casper	Mi
Madison	Pf2PbF	Cheyenne	T3Pb2
Manitowoc	Mf	Laramie	T2Pf2Pb2
Marinette	D	Rock Springs	T2
		Sheridan	D

ECONOMIC STRUCTURAL INTERRELATIONS OF METROPOLITAN REGIONS *

WALTER ISARD AND ROBERT KAVESH

The complex internal organization of any given metropolitan region is influenced by the delicately interwoven net of relationships that bind sets of city-regions into a unified whole. It is the purpose of this paper to study certain interurban connections. In setting forth hypotheses concerning spatial flows among metropolitan areas, we shall extend previously developd principles and illustrate with an abstract interdependence model.[1] In the first section a simplified model will be presented. In later sections this model will be qualified in an attempt to make it more realistic.

* Reprinted from *The American Journal of Sociology*, Vol. LX, No. 2 (September, 1954), pp. 152-162, with permission of authors and publisher. Copyright 1954 by the University of Chicago.
    [1] Elsewhere, a model depicting some of the structural interrelationships *within* a given metropolitan region has been sketched (W. Isard, R. A. Kavesh, and R. E. Kuenne, "The Economic Base and Structure of the Urban Metropolitan Region," *American Sociological Review*, XVIII (June, 1953), 317-321). Clearly, however, self-sufficiency is not characteristic of large city-regions.

I

Assume a large area is meaningfully divided into three regions. Each of the first two has a major focal point at which social and economic activity center, which is a major industrial city. These two are designated Metropolitan Region I and Metropolitan Region II. The third region, specializing in agricultural and extractive pursuits, lacks a single clear-cut focus and is designated Region III.

In addition to a delineation of regions, a classification of various economic and social activities is undertaken. Certain goods and services are marketed only in the region in which they are produced; in contrast, others are marketed not only in the region in which they are produced but also in the other regions, though to different degrees. The former are called "local" activities; the latter, "export."

To avoid cumbersome detail, the numerous economic functions are grouped into nine categories. These are recorded for each region in Table 1. The first for each region represents the characteristic export industry (heavy manufacturing for Metropolitan Region I, light manufacturing for Metropolitan Region II, and agriculture and extractive activity for Region III). The next eight are identical for each region: namely, power and communications; transportation; trade; insurance and rental activities; business and personal services; educational and other basic services; construction; and households.[2] Each of these eight activities is for the moment assumed to be local in nature. None of their output is shipped outside the region in which it is produced. Thus, by definition, it is through export activities alone that the simplified economies of the several regions are interrelated.

Classification of outputs represents only one phase of our problem. Another phase concerns input structures; more specifically, the inputs of each of several factors—raw materials, power, transportation, labor, equipment and other services—required to produce a unit of output. In actuality, much of the output of many industries such as basic steel is absorbed by other indus-

---

[2] The output of households roughly corresponds to the value of the services of labor and of capital and land owned by them.

TABLE 1

HYPOTHETICAL INTERMETROPOLITAN TRANSACTIONS TABLE, 19—— — CENTS WORTH OF INPUTS PER DOLLAR OF OUTPUT

Industry Purchasing

Industry Producing	Metropolitan Region I									Metropolitan Region II									Region III								
	(1) Heavy Manufacturing	(2) Power and Communication	(3) Transportation	(4) Trade	(5) Insurance and Rental	(6) Business and Pers. Serv.	(7) Educational and Other Serv.	(8) Construction	(9) Households	(10) Light Manufacturing	(11) Power and Communication	(12) Transportation	(13) Trade	(14) Insurance and Rental	(15) Business and Pers. Serv.	(16) Educational and Other Serv.	(17) Construction	(18) Households	(19) Agriculture and Extraction	(20) Power and Communication	(21) Transportation	(22) Trade	(23) Insurance and Rental	(24) Business and Pers. Serv.	(25) Educational and Other Serv.	(26) Construction	(27) Households
Metropolitan Region I:																											
1. Heavy manufacturing	33	1	3	1	—	9	1	18	3	2	1	3	1	—	9	1	18	3	1	1	3	1	—	9	1	18	3
2. Power and communication	1	11	5	2	8	4	2	—	1	—	—	—	—	—	—	—	—	—	—	—	—	—	—	—	—	—	—
3. Transportation	2	3	3	1	—	1	2	4	1	—	—	—	—	—	—	—	—	—	—	—	—	—	—	—	—	—	—
4. Trade	2	2	1	—	2	3	5	9	3	—	—	—	—	—	—	—	—	—	—	—	—	—	—	—	—	—	—
5. Insurance and rental activities	1	1	—	2	1	5	4	2	12	—	—	—	—	—	—	—	—	—	—	—	—	—	—	—	—	—	—
6. Business and personal services	1	1	3	5	2	—	2	4	12	—	—	—	—	—	—	—	—	—	—	—	—	—	—	—	—	—	—
7. Educational and other basic service	1	1	2	7	7	4	1	3	2	—	—	—	—	—	—	—	—	—	—	—	—	—	—	—	—	—	—
8. Construction	—	—	—	—	1	—	1	—	3	—	—	—	—	—	—	—	—	—	—	—	—	—	—	—	—	—	—
9. Households	34	58	58	63	53	46	50	40	10	—	—	—	—	—	—	—	—	—	—	—	—	—	—	—	—	—	—
Metropolitan Region II:																											
10. Light manufacturing	4	1	3	1	—	9	1	18	3	28	1	3	1	—	9	1	18	3	2	1	3	1	—	9	1	18	3
11. Power and communication	—	—	—	—	—	—	—	—	—	1	11	5	2	8	4	2	—	1	—	—	—	—	—	—	—	—	—
12. Transportation	—	—	—	—	—	—	—	—	—	2	3	3	1	—	1	2	4	1	—	—	—	—	—	—	—	—	—
13. Trade	—	—	—	—	—	—	—	—	—	2	2	1	—	2	3	5	9	3	—	—	—	—	—	—	—	—	—
14. Insurance and rental activities	—	—	—	—	—	—	—	—	—	1	1	—	2	1	5	4	2	12	—	—	—	—	—	—	—	—	—
15. Business and personal services	—	—	—	—	—	—	—	—	—	1	1	3	5	2	—	2	4	12	—	—	—	—	—	—	—	—	—
16. Educational and other basic services	—	—	—	—	—	—	—	—	—	1	1	2	7	7	4	1	3	2	—	—	—	—	—	—	—	—	—
17. Construction	—	—	—	—	—	—	—	—	—	—	—	—	—	1	—	1	—	3	—	—	—	—	—	—	—	—	—
18. Households	—	—	—	—	—	—	—	—	—	25	58	58	63	53	46	50	40	10	—	—	—	—	—	—	—	—	—
Region III:																											
19. Agriculture and extraction	6	1	3	1	—	9	1	18	3	28	1	3	1	—	9	1	18	3	28	1	3	1	—	9	1	18	3
20. Power and communication	—	—	—	—	—	—	—	—	—	—	—	—	—	—	—	—	—	—	1	11	5	2	8	4	2	—	1
21. Transportation	—	—	—	—	—	—	—	—	—	—	—	—	—	—	—	—	—	—	2	3	3	1	—	1	2	4	1
22. Trade	—	—	—	—	—	—	—	—	—	—	—	—	—	—	—	—	—	—	2	2	1	—	2	3	5	9	3
23. Insurance and rental activities	—	—	—	—	—	—	—	—	—	—	—	—	—	—	—	—	—	—	1	1	—	2	1	5	4	2	12
24. Business and personal services	—	—	—	—	—	—	—	—	—	—	—	—	—	—	—	—	—	—	1	1	3	5	2	—	2	4	12
25. Educational and other basic services	—	—	—	—	—	—	—	—	—	—	—	—	—	—	—	—	—	—	1	1	2	7	7	4	1	3	2
26. Construction	—	—	—	—	—	—	—	—	—	—	—	—	—	—	—	—	—	—	—	—	—	—	1	—	1	—	3
27. Households	—	—	—	—	—	—	—	—	—	—	—	—	—	—	—	—	—	—	40	58	58	63	53	46	50	40	1

tries as inputs rather than by households. Therefore, in order to
understand the economic base of metropolitan regions and to
anticipate changes within them, it is necessary to know the intermetropolitan input structures of industries. This requires a table
of intermetropolitan [3] interindustrial relations for a base year period, on the order of Table 1.[4]

In Table 1 any one column records the cents' worth of inputs
from each industrial category in each region per dollar's worth of
output of a given industrial category of a given region where
both the given industrial category and the region are specified by

[3] To avoid awkward phrases we use the term "intermetropolitan" as if Region
III were a metropolitan region.

[4] Most of the coefficients in Table 1 are based upon a consolidation of the
50 x 50 interindustry flow matrix developed by the Bureau of Labor Statistics
(W. D. Evans and M. Hoffenberg, "The Interindustry Relations Study for 1947,"
Review of Economics and Statistics, XXXIV (May, 1952), 97-142). In reducing the B.L.S. 50 industry classification to our three export and eight local industrial categories we crudely defined:

1. *Heavy manufacturing* as the aggregate of iron and steel, plumbing and
heating supplies, fabricated structural metal products, other fabricated metal
products, agricultural, mining, and construction machinery, metalworking machinery, other machinery (except electric), motors and generators, radios, other
electrical machinery, motor vehicles, other transportation equipment, professional
and scientific equipment, miscellaneous manufacturing, and scrap and miscellaneous industries.

2. *Light manufacturing* as the aggregate of food and kindred products, to-
bacco manufactures, textile mill products, apparel, furniture and fixtures, paper
and allied products, printing and publishing, chemicals, rubber products, and
leather and leather products.

3. *Agriculture and extraction* as the aggregate of agriculture and fisheries,
lumber and wood products, products of petroleum and coal, stone, clay, and glass
products, and nonferrous metal.

"Service Activities" were expressed in a less aggregative form in order to
present some detail on the internal structural processes of metropolitan regions
associated with these activities. The category, "Education and Other Basic Services" consists of the services of medical, educational and non-profit institutions,
amusement, and eating and drinking places.

Certain activities are omitted from the analysis because their levels of output
are not structurally related to the interindustrial matrix of coefficients. These
are: inventory change, foreign trade, government, capital formation, and unallocated. Households, generally included with this group, were introduced into
the structural matrix in order to catch the local multiplier effect of new basic
industry upon a community via the additional income generated.

The actual derivation of a coefficient involves the division of the total value
of inputs from a given sector into a second sector by the output of the second
sector. That is, if in 1947 the amount of chemicals used in steel production was
$99 million and the output of steel was $12.3 billion, the input coefficient representing the cents' worth of chemicals per dollar of steel would be 0.8049.

The data are rounded to the nearest whole figure. Inputs of less than one-
half cent per dollar output are not recorded.

the column heading. For example, reading down column 1 furnishes information on the cents' worth of various inputs from the several regions per dollar output of heavy manufacturing in Metropolitan Region I. Thirty-three cents' worth of heavy manufacturing in Metropolitan Region I is fed back as an input into the same activity in the same region for every dollar's worth of its output (such as Pittsburgh steel, which is fed back to Pittsburgh steelworks). Two cents of transportation services of Metropolitan Region I is absorbed per dollar's worth of heavy manufacturing of Metropolitan Region I. In addition to inputs from other service sectors and the household sector of Metropolitan Region I, the heavy manufacturers of Metropolitan Region I require inputs from the light-manufacturing industry of Metropolitan Region II and from agriculture and extractive activities of Region III. These latter, of course, entail interregional flows.

Consider another column, the fifteenth, which refers to "Business and Personal Services" in Metropolitan Region II. Per dollar of its output nine cents' worth of heavy-manufacturing products from Metropolitan Region I is required. None of the other sectors of Region I furnishes inputs, because these other sectors are defined as local and hence export nothing. Since the business and personal services sector of Metropolitan Region II does not consume any agricultural and extractive products, all its other inputs must come from Region II, as is depicted in Table 1.

Aside from their obvious descriptive value, of what significance are the data of Table 1? In general, input structures are not haphazard; rather they reflect to a large extent stable and meaningful relations. If the output of an efficient aluminum works is doubled, it is reasonable to expect that approximately twice as much power, alumina, carbon electrodes, and other inputs will be required. In short, subject to certain serious qualifications to be discussed later, the input of any service or good into a particular activity may be said within certain limits to vary appproximately in direct proportion with the output of that particular activity.

To illustrate the usefulness of input structure information, suppose a resource development program calls for an increase of one million dollars in the output of heavy manufacturing in Region I. How will this affect the output of each activity in each region?

In column 1 of Table 1 are listed coefficients which indicate the cents' worth of various inputs required per dollar output of heavy manufacturing. Multiplying these coefficients by one million gives us the direct inputs required to produce one million dollars' worth of heavy manufactures. These are called the first-round input requirements and are listed in column 1 of Table 2.

But to produce the first-round requirement of $330,000 of heavy manufacturing (item 1 in column 1, Table 2) likewise requires a whole series of inputs. These can be obtained by multiplying column 1 of Table 1 by 330,000. And to produce the $20,000 of transportation (item 3, column 1, Table 2) requires inputs which can be obtained by multiplying column 3 of Table 1 by 20,000. Similarly, the inputs required to produce each of the other items listed in column 1 of Table 2 can be derived. It should be noted that the $340,000, which is listed in the ninth cell of column 1, Table 2, represents an increment of income received by the households in Metropolitan Region I. This increment results in increases in effective demand for a series of products. On the arbitrary assumption that two-thirds of this new income is spent, these increases in effective demand can be obtained by multiplying column 9, Table 1 (which shows how a dollar spent by households is typically distributed among various products), by 226,667.

Adding together all these inputs (including the new effective demands of households) necessary for the production of the first round of requirements yields the second round of requirements which is recorded in column 2 of Table 2. In turn, the production of the second round of requirements necessitates a third round. This is computed in the same manner as was the second round. Furnishing a third round requires a fourth; a fourth round, a fifth; etc. Each of these rounds is recorded in Table 2. It should be noted that the totals of the rounds converge.[5] After a point it becomes feasible to stop the round-by-round computation and

[5] The convergence of rounds results from the assumption that only two-thirds of the income received by households in any given round is expenditure in the succeeding round and from the omission of the nonstructually related sectors of inventory change, foreign trade, government, capital formation and unallocated, as noted in n. 4.

TABLE 2

INPUT REQUIREMENTS (HYPOTHETICAL), BY ROUND, FOR $1 MILLION OUTPUT OF HEAVY MANUFACTURING IN METROPOLITAN REGION I

Industry Grouping	First-Round Input Requirements (1)	Second-Round Input Requirements (2)	Third-Round Input Requirements (3)	Fourth-Round Input Requirements (4)	Fifth-Round Input Requirements (5)	Sixth-Round Input Requirements (6)	Seventh-Round Input Requirements (7)	Sum of Rounds (8)
Metropolitan Region I:								
1. Heavy manufacturing	$330,000	$118,810	$47,793	$23,417	$13,407	$8,559	$5,884	$550,870
2. Power and communication	10,000	8,670	7,763	4,614	2,858	1,667	994	36,566
3. Transportation	20,000	14,910	7,417	4,508	2,516	1,475	871	51,697
4. Trade	10,000	31,440	15,687	11,021	6,042	3,573	2,060	79,823
5. Insurance and rental activities	10,000	32,940	18,965	12,612	7,135	4,155	2,430	88,237
6. Business and personal services	10,000	11,810	8,159	4,860	2,906	1,664	983	40,382
7. Educational and other basic services	—	22,700	10,077	7,463	3,945	2,359	1,344	47,888
8. Construction	—	2,600	4,759	2,731	1,789	1,031	622	13,532
9. Households	340,000	148,070	110,102	57,920	34,886	19,773	10,805	721,556
Metropolitan Region II:								
10. Light manufacturing	40,000	75,600	60,601	47,894	34,849	25,264	18,115	302,323
11. Power and communication	—	400	971	1,182	1,190	1,056	856	5,655
12. Transportation	—	800	1,781	1,821	1,601	1,309	1,016	8,328
13. Trade	—	800	2,364	3,044	2,858	2,470	1,963	13,499
14. Insurance and rental activities	—	400	1,696	2,689	2,706	2,490	1,972	11,953
15. Business and personal services	—	800	1,825	1,954	1,772	1,479	1,159	8,989
16. Educational and other basic services	—	—	670	1,387	1,394	1,275	1,033	5,759
17. Construction	—	—	104	325	446	455	391	1,721
18. Households	10,000	10,000	20,747	20,643	18,918	15,744	12,381	98,433
Region III:								
19. Agriculture and extraction	60,000	60,220	50,741	39,365	29,244	21,250	15,387	276,207
20. Power and communication	—	600	1,122	1,402	1,386	1,229	1,019	6,758
21. Transportation	—	1,800	2,430	2,360	2,085	1,673	1,310	11,658
22. Trade	—	1,200	3,226	3,541	3,481	2,922	2,385	16,755
23. Insurance and rental activities	—	2,400	4,646	4,962	4,701	3,917	3,156	23,782
24. Business and personal services	—	600	1,256	1,490	1,463	1,260	1,032	7,101
25. Educational and other basic services	—	—	1,600	1,876	1,969	1,680	1,397	8,522
26. Construction	—	—	372	664	719	682	581	3,018
27. Households	—	24,000	27,936	28,508	25,037	20,595	16,189	142,265
Total	$830,000	$571,570	$414,810	$284,253	$211,303	$151,006	$107,335	$2,583,277

to extrapolate the remaining requirements. However, we have not carried through any extrapolation; as a refinement it implies a degree of accuracy and stability in the data, which, as we shall see in the following section, does not exist in fact.

Thus, we have developed a round-by-round description of how an impulse acting upon one sector of a metropolitan region is transmitted to every sector in the same region and every other region. To derive the total effect, it is merely necessary to sum the rounds horizontally. The totals are recorded in column 8 of Table 2. These totals, of course, can be compared with other sets of totals which reflect impacts of other types of impulses.[6]

II

The simplified model presented above may now be qualified and fashioned somewhat more realistically.[7]

First, re-examine the problem of industrial classification. The categorization of an activity exclusively as local or export is, in many instances, unjustified. There is no provision for those industries, by far the majority, in which both local and export elements are coexistent. As an instance, most educational services are local in character; yet on the university level some are definitely national in that they perform services for persons whose permanent residences are in all parts of the country. As another example, the products of the cotton industry are for the most part export; yet the by-product cottonseed, which is typically consid-

---

[6] E.g., if instead of $1 million of new heavy manufacturing, an equivalent amount of new agricultural and extractive output is required, the impact will be more localized and confined to the region of initial expansion (Region III). For full details and other contrasts see R. Kavesh, "Interdependence and the Metropolitan Region" (unpublished doctoral dissertation, Harvard University, 1953), chap. iii.

[7] Because of limitation of space, we shall discuss only briefly the several important points which are raised. Full discussion of these points is contained in W. Leontief, *The Structure of the American Economy, 1919-1939* (New York: Oxford University Press, 1951); W. Leontief *et al., Studies in the Structure of the American Economy* (New York: Oxford University Press, 1953); W. Isard, "Inter-regional and Regional Input-Output Analysis: A Model of a Space-Economy," *Review of Economics and Statistics,* XXXIII (November, 1951), 318-328; W. Isard, "Regional Commodity Balances and Interregional Commodity Flows," *American Economic Review,* XLIII (May, 1953), 167-80; W. Isard, "Location Theory and Trade Theory; Short-Run Analysis," *Quarterly Journal of Economics,* LXVIII (May, 1954), 305-20; and various papers on input-output analysis at the Conference on Research in Income and Wealth, November, 1952.

ered as part of the cotton industry, is consumed almost entirely locally by various vegetable-oil-mills.[8]

In theory a fine enough classification of industries could be adopted so as to circumvent this shortcoming. In practice, however, such an industrial grouping would be infeasible in terms of the tremendous number of computations to be performed. Hence, whatever the classification finally chosen, some imperfection will exist which in turn will restrict the validity of the analysis.

Examination of the classification of Table 1 immediately discloses an oversimplification. In general, the exports of any metropolitan region do not fall into one category alone. Characteristically, exports consist of diverse outputs, ranging from agricultural and mining products to light and heavy manufactures. Therefore, the export sectors should be specified by component parts (subject to computational resources), particularly since disaggregation of any industrial category into finer parts is usually desirable where such is feasible.[9] On the other hand, one should not overlook the definite tendencies for metropolitan regions to assume definite specializations as implied by the oversimplified model.[10]

Second, reconsider the problem of stability of input coefficients—the assumption that from round to round the cents' worth of any input per unit of a given output remains constant, or the equivalent, namely, that the amount of any input supplied an industry varies proportionally with the output of that industry. As the output of an industrial activity expands, new combinations of the various inputs and new technical processes may become economically feasible. These new combinations and processes would require different percentage increases in the various inputs into the production process; this would be inconsistent with the basic

---

[8] The pattern of gasoline sales by metropolitan regions presents another interesting case of overlap. For the most part, gasoline is sold in neighborhood stations for local consumption. To this extent it is a local good. However, many service stations are situated along major intermetropolitan highways and sell gasoline for transient automobiles and trucks. In this sense, the consumption of gasoline takes place on a supraregional basis; thus there is a distortion of the local balance of production and consumption.

[9] See M. Holzman, "Problems of Classification and Aggregation," in W. Leontief *et al., op. cit.,* chap. ix. However, see qualifications below.

[10] See, e.g., Colin Clark, "The Economic Functions of Cities in Relation to Size," *Econometrica,* XIII (April, 1945), 97-113; and G. M. Kneedler, "Functional Types of Cities," *Public Management,* XXVII (July, 1945), 197-203.

assumption. For many industries such changes might involve minor substitutions of one type of input for another and hence not significantly bias the results. In other industries there may be major substitution effects.[11] However, to the extent that these effects can be anticipated, they can be incorporated into the model by the appropriate alteration of coefficients in the relevant rounds.

Associated with the above shortcoming are the restraints which limited resources impose. For example, as the demand for coal rises, veins of an inferior quality may need to be exploited. This in turn would lead to greater consumption of coal per unit of output of a coal-consuming industry. At the extreme, where there are fixed limits to a given resource (including human labor services), entirely new production techniques and/or locations may be dictated to realize increments of output.[12]

Again, to the extent that resource limitations and associated changes in production techniques can be anticipated, to the same extent the coefficients for the several rounds can be altered to incorporate into the analysis relevant information on these factors.

Still more critical a qualification stems from changes in consumption patterns incident to income changes.[13] Simple cents' worth of inputs per dollar of income, which are listed in columns

[11] See J. S. Duesenberry, "The Leontief Input-Output System" (Harvard Economic Research Project, Harvard University; Cambridge, Mass., 1950). (Mimeographed.)

[12] The data presented in the above tables are expressed in dollars and cents. Yet they can be easily translated into physical units. For example, consider the labor problem in a given market area (metropolitan region). It is possible to introduce new rows in Table 1, where each row corresponds to a particular type of labor (skilled, semiskilled, manual, etc.), the nature of the problem determining the particular breakdown of labor to be adopted. Reading down any column would denote the requirements of each type of labor (in terms of man-hours) to produce a unit of output corresponding to the industry and region listed at the head of the column. Thus, in studying the impact of any given resource development program, we can derive the additional requirements of various types of labor by regions; this in turn throws light not only on the short-run feasibility of a given resource development program but also upon the likely long-run interregional labor migrations (given information on reproduction rates and other population characteristics). In similar fashion, a conversion of the table into physical terms could supply insights on the adequacy of actual power facilities, housing, and transportation networks of various metropolitan regions.

[13] The socioeconomic data basic to Engel's law indicate this tendency. For discussion of this law see, among others, Carle C. Zimmerman, *Consumption and Standards of Living*, New York: D. Van Nostrand Co., 1936, and S. J. Prais, "Non-linear Estimates of the Engel Curves," *Review of Economic Studies*, XX, No. 2 (1952-53), 87-104.

9, 18, and 27 of Table 1, are misleading. Consumers' studies are required in which households are broken down by occupation, ethnic grouping, family size, rural-urban location, and other key indicators to reveal how expenditure patterns are related to changes in the level of income and associated occupational shifts. Once obtained, relevant information can be injected into the model to yield more valid results.

Another major set of qualifications is linked to the resource limitations already noted. As long as there is vacant housing in a metropolitan region, excess capacity in the transit and power systems, available space for expansion at the center, the calculated growth of the area can be effected. However, where vacant housing does not exist and where streets are congested and transit and power systems overloaded, additional capacity must be constructed to permit expansion in the various industries and service trades. Therefore, in addition to the inputs that are required to produce expanded outputs from existing and new facilities, a whole series of inputs is required to construct the new facilities.

Here, too, appropriate modification of the model can be made. For example, given a knowledge of the capacity of an existing housing complex (together with information on the doubling-up effect and other cultural adaptations to shortage known to be feasible, the nature of the demand for diverse types of housing, and the input structures of the several sectors of the housing industry), it is possible to allow for the phenomenon of housing expansion in our analytic framework. It should be borne in mind, however, that to the extent to which a particular resource in short supply is diverted from producing output on current account to building up plant equipment and other capacity to produce, then to a similar extent the expansion of the noncapacity-building activities are curtailed.[14]

In effect, the initial, highly simplified linear model—linear in the sense that each input varies in direct proportion to the output—has been molded into a less hypothetical, nonlinear model

---

[14] For a treatment of the problem underlying these assumptions see A. Grosse and J. S. Duesenberry, *Technological Change and Dynamic Models* (Conference on Research in Income and Wealth, November, 1952). To be published by the Princeton University Press, Princeton, N.J.

which does recognize important nonproportionalities in inter-activity relations.

III

In the previous section a number of considerations were introduced to lend more reality and validity to the simplified model of Section I. However, granted that data can be obtained to describe meaningfully nonlinear interrelations, to the extent that such a three-regional construct does not exist, the model remains hypothetical. Let us now re-examine this hypothetical characteristic.

It is a commonplace that social science has not yet reached the stage where it can explicitly consider every variable in a given problem. Those investigators who attempt to obtain results applicable to policy questions concentrate upon what they consider to be the relatively few important variables. Even though this procedure suffers from omission and oversimplification, it still may afford the most useful results for practice. This, too, must be our way of implementing the above model.

Let the problem be an attempt to project various economic magnitudes in the Greater San Juan Metropolitan Region, Puerto Rico. Immediately the problem of demarcating the boundaries of this region arises. Some sociologists might stress the rural-urban dichotomy and draw the line where the influences of the city proper become subordinate to those of the smaller settlements and rural communities. A strict economist might include only those contiguous areas trading extensively with San Juan. An ecologist might attempt to identify the dominant-subdominant-influent-subinfluent relationships of the core and the various sectors of the hinterlands.[15]

For our purposes, no single orientation suffices. If we imagine the Puerto Rican economy in 1975, we anticipate that improvements in transportation and communications will coordinate the entire island into one major region, with its focus at San Juan. This is not to deny that there will be major satellite

[15] Among others, see Stuart A. Queen and David B. Carpenter, *The American City* (New York: McGraw Hill Book Co., 1953) and Donald J. Bogue, *The Structure of the Metropolitan Community* (Ann Arbor: University of Michigan Press, 1949).

cities such as Ponce and Mayagüez; but the bonds of these cities to the San Juan area will be so strong and connections so closely interwoven that it will be feasible to recognize the whole of Puerto Rico as one "Greater" metropolitan region. Such a metropolitan region would be akin to the Greater New York Metropolitan Region, which includes such major satellite cities as Bridgeport, New Brunswick, and Norwalk.[16]

Consider the external relations of this Greater San Juan Metropolitan Region. Currently the major ties are with the metropolitan construct embracing the Greater New York-Philadelphia-Baltimore urban-industrial region. A lesser economic connection is with the Gulf Coast. Recognizing the difficulties of establishing new ties, and that institutional resistances and entrepreneurial inertia are among several forces tending to keep incremental economic activities within the framework of existing transportation and communication channels, one is inclined to anticipate that these two regions of the United States will continue to dominate the external relations of the Greater San Juan Metropolitan Region.

There is a second ground for such belief. From a transport-cost standpoint, Greater San Juan is closer to both the Gulf Coast and New York-Philadelphia-Baltimore urban-industrial region than to any other region of the United States. Even though in terms of physical distance the South Atlantic region is nearest Puerto Rico, at best the likelihood is small that a sufficient volume of commodity movement will be generated between the South Atlantic region and Puerto Rico to realize the economies of scale, both in handling costs and in use of transport facilities, which are achieved in the Gulf Coast and New York-Philadelphia-Baltimore trade. This signifies that from an economic standpoint the South Atlantic region is considerably more distant.

Moreover, Greater San Juan, as a growing economy, is likely to find that the sale of additional industrial output through displacing existing suppliers in a well-established market is more

---

[16] The 3,423 square miles of the Greater San Juan Metropolitan Region (the entire island) contrast with the 4,853 square miles included in the Census Los Angeles Metropolitan Area and with the 6,914 square miles included in the Greater New York Metropolitan Region as currently defined by the New York Regional Plan Association.

difficult than through capitalizing on new market demand. Because the Gulf Coast and the New York-Philadelphia-Baltimore areas will be among the most rapidly expanding regions of the United States, it does not appear unreasonable to expect that Puerto Rican businessmen will concentrate for the most part on these two regions for new sales outlets.

Hence, if the problem is to project the interrelations between Greater San Juan and the mainland and if we are given techniques of analysis which can treat only a relatively few variables, the Gulf Coast and New York-Philadelphia-Baltimore, urban-industrial complex may be considered the most significant external regions for our analysis. This lends a partial justification for our three-regional model.

The specific situation of Greater San Juan has still another point of contact with our model. As indicated above, in general no region specializes in one export product alone. Each usually produces a number of goods for export, although frequently with distinct specialization. For our particular problem, the Gulf Coast, with its extensive agricultural production as well as its emphasis on oil-refining, natural gas production, and other extractive industries, may be taken as Region III. This is specially relevant in the case of Puerto Rico, since her chief imports from the Gulf Coast are lumber, petroleum products, rice, wheat flour, and mixed dairy and poultry feeds.[17]

Furthermore, the presence of heavy manufacturing in the Greater New York-Philadelphia-Baltimore complex, with the corresponding shipments of finished goods to Puerto Rico, justifies treating this area as Metropolitan Region I. This judgment is reinforced by the major steel development program currently being undertaken in the Delaware River Valley. The heavy metal output of this area may by 1975 attain proportions comparable in magnitude to the present Pittsburgh complex.[18]

Finally, consider the human and natural endowment of Puerto Rico. Mineral and agricultural resources are of a very low or-

[17] S. E. Eastman and D. Marx, Jr., *Ships and Sugar: An Evaluation of Puerto Rican Offshore Shipping* (Rio Piedras: University of Puerto Rico Press, 1953).

[18] W. Isard and R. Kuenne, "The Impact of Steel upon the Greater New York-Philadelphia Urban-Industrial Region," *Review of Economics and Statistics*, XXXV (November 1953), 289-301.

der.[19] In contrast, population is excessive, which, together with the expectation of continued high reproduction rates, suggests the continuance of relatively depressed wage rates. Those industries migrating to Puerto Rico tend, therefore, to be both labor-oriented and of such a nature that the assembly of required raw materials and shipment of product incur relatively low transport costs. Textiles are a good example. Therefore, Greater San Juan may be taken to conform with our light-manufacturing economy, Metropolitan Region II.

IV

We have now converted a simplified model into one which though still hypothetical is of more practical significance. The initial 9-industry classification takes on added meaning when it is disaggregated into a 50-industry or even a 192-industry classification. This operation is currently feasible. Too, the recent input-output study of Puerto Rico permits a similar meaningful disaggregation for Metropolitan Region II (Greater San Juan).

At this point it is appropriate to re-examine the problem of substituting nonlinearities for linearities and nonproportionalities for proportionalities, with special reference to the input structures of the existing and potential industrial activities of Puerto Rico.

Consider the input structure of any particular industry of Puerto Rico. Since the area is still relatively underdeveloped, the stability of coefficients can be seriously questioned. It is quite likely that, as plants take root in Puerto Rico, new techniques will be used, especially since incipient industrialization has a significant effect on the attitudes of the working force, which in turn is reflected in labor productivity.[20] As a result, it is necessary to secure for such new plants the set of inputs which prospective management may expect to be required for current operation and/or to approximate from social science research studies the effects of the introduction of new industry upon labor productivity and in turn upon the set of inputs and techniques utilized.

---

[19] H. S. Perloff, *Puerto Rico's Economic Future* (Chicago: University of Chicago Press, 1950), chap. iv.
[20] See, e.g., W. E. Moore, *Industrialization and Labor* (Ithaca: Cornell University Press, 1951).

Obviously, where no adequate information is available, it becomes necessary to rely heavily upon individual judgment.

Another set of nonlinearities is introduced when we consider the problem of effective demand in underdeveloped countries such as Puerto Rico. In many cases the justification for erecting a plant in a given industry is lacking because the potential market is inadequate to absorb the output of a plant of a minimum technically feasible size. However, as development proceeds and effective demand mounts, a stage may be reached where demand does become adequate for a particular market-oriented operation, such as cement production. When effective demand does reach such a level, it becomes necessary to alter the entire set of technical coefficients relating the input of the given commodity, say, cement, from any given metropolitan region into each industrial activity of every metropolitan region. This and similar alterations can be effected in round-by-round computations if, beforehand, information relating to such potential shifts is available.

As indicated, another extremely important set of nonlinearities arises in attempting to anticipate consumption habits. Data are relatively sparse on how industrialization, increasing urbanization, rising incomes, and intensified contact with the mainland will influence cultural patterns of the island. Additionally, more research is required on how such institutional factors such as entrepreneurial vigor and savings schedules will be modified. Obviously in any attempt at a determination of the extensive ramifications of new industrial expansion, reliance upon the considered judgment of social scientists as well as local residents for pertinent information is necessary, the more so when relevant data are sharply limited.

v

To conclude, a model has been developed, which, it is hoped, will have some validity for purposes of projection, either in its present or in a less comprehensive form. The model has many shortcomings. Since they are fully discussed elsewhere, we have treated them here only cursorily. Further, there are serious problems arising from the inadequacies of the data, the unpredictability of changes in behavioral patterns and culture, and the uncertain direction and magnitude of technological development. Nevertheless, we feel that where decisions on metropolitan community development and regional welfare must be made *now* for planning for the future, this procedure is useful, especially as a complement to our existing set of analytical tools and techniques.

PART V

CHARACTERISTICS OF URBANIZATION

Introduction to Part V

Up to this point the analysis has been concerned with research methods as they apply to individual urban units. Part V is
a turning point as far as subject matter is concerned; it deals
with a topic that encompasses a new range of phenomena—the
characteristics of urbanization. These characteristics relate to
the urban units of a country (or national and world regions)
considered together rather than individually.

On the surface it might appear that the research methods
heretofore considered are adequate for the treatment of characteristics of urbanization on a national level. However, this is true
only if one considers these characteristics as representing nothing
more than the average of all of the individual urban units in a
country; but, as we shall see, this is decidedly not the case. Some
of them may have the quality of an average, but for the most part
they relate to a set of variables that have no counterpart on the
level of individual cities. Consequently, a general discussion of
the nature and importance of the characteristics of urbanization
is in order before we consider research methods for their treatment.

Of the various characteristics of urbanization, the one most
removed from an average of individual cities, and at the same
time perhaps the most important, is the *degree of urbanization,*
which is defined as the per cent of the total population of a country who reside in urban units (i.e., cities, urban areas, or metropolitan areas) above a specified minimum size. Far from being
an average, this variable is independent of the size of the urban
population, the number of urban units, and their average size.
To illustrate, if the number of city residents in a given country is
five million and the total population is ten million, then the degree of urbanization is 50 per cent; but if the total population
were one-hundred million, it would be only five per cent, even
though the number of city residents remains the same. Moreover,
in neither case would the degree of urbanization be contingent

on whether the people resided in one large city or several small ones.

Although the degree of urbanization is not a complex mathematical variable, its treatment in research poses several technical problems. This becomes apparent when one realizes that the per cent of the total population who reside in urban units is relative to the definitions employed and the methods utilized in delimitation. It is in this regard that the subject of Part I (The Boundaries of Urban Units) is just as relevant to the study of the characteristics of urbanization as it is to a consideration of individual cities. For the moment it will suffice to observe that measures of the degree of urbanization in different countries are not comparable unless based on the same type of urban unit (cities, urban areas, or metropolitan areas of a specified minimum size) and similar methods of delimitation. Questions concerning the types of urban units and delimitation methods that yield comparable and valid gauges of the degree of urbanization must await treatment of the subject in Chapter 11.

Despite the technical problems associated with its measurement, all research findings to date suggest that the degree of urbanization is by far the most important characteristic of urbanization in general. In fact, it is one of the fundamental traits of a society, as suggested by the fact that it appears to bear a close relation to other characteristics considered to be basic, such as technological efficiency, level of industrialization, mortality, fertility, literacy, and education.

It remains for future research to establish which is cause and which is effect in these relations, but the possibility that urbanization may have certain causal properties is immensely important. This is particularly true for the less industrialized countries. These parts of the world have yet to attain a low level of mortality, the control of fertility, technological efficiency, and a high degree of literacy; and this is a source of great concern in their attempts to solve the practical problems that confront them. Some of these countries are now undergoing an increase in the degree of urbanization; but it remains to be seen whether this increase will be associated with the appearance of the correlates mentioned above, as it did in Europe, North America, and

Oceania; and it also remains to be seen how long and how rapidly the process of urbanization will continue.

At the other extreme, in countries already highly urbanized, the possibility of an increase in the degree of urbanization is also of theoretical and practical importance. For one thing, it is conceivable that additional social, cultural, and economic transitions may occur if still higher levels of urbanization are reached. Also, the practical problems of highly urbanized nations—congestion, outmoded transportation systems, the need for governmental regulations, to mention a few—may be aggravated by additional urbanization.

Although of great theoretical and practical importance, the per cent of the total population residing in cities is only one characteristic of urbanization in a country. Some of the others that warrant recognition are:

(1) the number of people in the urban population,

(2) the total number of urban units,

(3) the number of people residing in urban units of a specified size (i.e., cities of between 50,000 and 100,000 inhabitants, metropolitan areas of over one million inhabitants, etc.), and

(4) the number of urban units in a specified size range.

Configurations of these and other characteristics may be said to form an urban structure, which varies in several respects from one country to another. Thus the degree of urbanization, which describes the size of the urban structure relative to the nation as a whole, currently varies from less than 15 to more than 70 per cent among the world's countries and territories. But, of two countries with roughly the same degree of urbanization, one may have a distribution of cities by size quite different from the other. Urban structures are also subject to change, with both the amount and type varying from one country to another.

Most of the characteristics that form a part of the urban structure have yet to be subjected to research in any systematic way, and the research methods for treating them are largely unstandardized. Most of them, like the degree of urbanization, are purely demographic in nature. But this does not mean that the characteristics of urbanization pertain only to demographic variables. On the contrary, as in the case of defining cities, the characteristics comprise widely diverse phenomena—cultural, political, economic, psychological—and particularly so when the traits of urban residents as individuals are considered. Up to now, however, formal treatment of the subject has been restricted on the whole to demographic and spatial variables, and this is continued in this volume.

The characteristics of urbanization considered up to this point treat the urban units in a nation on an aggregate basis; and as such, they do not reveal anything about the relations among the units. One consideration in this regard pertains to the relations of the size of one or more urban units to that of the others or, in more general terms, patterns in variations according to size. One such pattern is described in terms of the *rank-size rule,* according to which the largest city in a country has twice the population of the second largest, three times the population of the third largest, and so on. Where such a pattern exists it is possible to deduce the number of residents in a city from knowledge of the rank of its population size and the number of residents in the largest city. Thus, if the largest city has 1,000,000 inhabitants, then the city that ranks fifth in size will have 200,000 inhabitants, and the tenth largest will have 100,000.

While cities in the United States conform fairly closely to the rank-size rule, there is evidence to indicate that the situation in certain other countries is quite different. Moreover, it is evident that we know very little about the conditions that determine the extent of conformity to the rank-size rule.

Certain countries deviate from the rank-size rule in a particular way. We often find that the largest or primary city is not twice but many times the size of the second city. Paris, Bangkok, Mexico City, Buenos Aires, and Montevideo are outstanding examples. To the extent that the largest city exceeds the next few cities in size, it is considered to have a high degree of *primacy,* a term that applies to the country as a whole as well as to the largest city. Thus one of the characteristics of urbanization in France, Thailand, Mexico, Argentina, and Uruguay is high primacy. The United States, in contrast, has a low degree of primacy but marked conformity to the rank-size rule.

Another concern with the relations among the urban units of a country has to do with the patterns that appear in their spatial distribution. In some instances we find that cities are distributed in such a way that a fairly regular distance separates each one from its nearest neighbor. In other cases the pattern may be anything but uniform, with cities clustered at certain points but widely and unevenly spaced at others. Still another possibility is a correlation between the size of cities and their positions in the over-all spatial configuration. Although such a correlation may appear in various forms, one pattern is that of a direct relation between the size of a city and the distance between it and the nearest larger neighbor.

The various demographic and spatial relations among cities suggested above warrant consideration as characteristics of urbanization not because they are simply one more way in which countries may differ but because each one of them has considerable theoretical significance. In the introduction to Part IV we saw how cities are increasingly extending their influence beyond their immediate environs, so that the flow of goods and services has become inter-urban as well as rural-urban. Out of this inter-urban flow, which is facilitated by advances in transportation and communication, cities have become linked to each other to a degree far surpassing that in the early stages of urbanization. This linkage appears in the form of functional specialization, wherein cities process goods and provide services for parts of the nation that are outside either their service areas or metropolitan regions. Cities differ considerably in this respect. Some of them may render a few services for a few nearby smaller cities and surrounding rural territory, while others may offer a variety of highly specialized services to hundreds of cities and rural areas located throughout the country. These differences constitute a functional hierarchy, ranging from the village, which provides services only for farmers in the immediate vicinity, to the giant metropolises, such as London and New York, which provide services for cities scattered throughout the world.

Along with functional specialization and the development of functional hierarchies, some cities become completely dependent upon a particular service or services provided by others. Also involved is the centralization of the control of national or regional economic, cultural, and political activities in a few large cities. It is on the basis of the direction of dependence and the location of centers of control that we have come to speak of certain cities as occupying a *dominant* position or exercising *dominance* over one or more other cities.

The over-all consequence of the developments in urbanization described above is the integration of cities in a country to a point where a change in the characteristics of one city can influence the characteristics of the others, and in this sense they may be said to constitute a system. Because of the paucity of data relevant to the subject, this aspect of urbanization has not received extensive consideration; and the concept *system of cities* remains nebulous. However, whatever else may be entailed, there is general agreement that the factors which underlie any such *system* are probably reflected in one way or another in the demographic and spatial relations among cities. It is this general hypothesis that is the primary rationale for studying the relations.

Unlike the study of a particular city, where data may be obtained in the course of a field investigation, research on the characteristics of urbanization for all practical purposes depends on statistics provided by governmental agencies, typically those which conduct and report a national census of population. Given this situation, the availability and adequacy of official statistics on urbanization and the methods of their treatment pose critical research problems; and, as we shall see, this is all the more true when a study involves international comparisons.

For the purpose of furthering urban research, it is desirable that the newcomer to the field realize that international studies are much more feasible now than has heretofore been the case. For one thing, there has been a considerable increase in the number of countries and territories that conduct a census of population, the results of which, in one way or another, provide information on urbanization. Also, several organizations have assumed the responsibility of analyzing the results of these censuses and issuing reports on certain aspects of urbanization and the characteristics of individual cities. Two such organizations are International Urban Research, University of California, Berkeley (see its *The World's Metropolitan Areas*, Berkeley: University of California Press, 1959) and the International Statistical Institute, The Hague, Netherlands (see its *Demographic Statistics of Large Cities, 1946-51, Tables*, The Hague: 1954). Reports by these organizations serve not only as a source of information but also as guides to the solution of problems that are confronted in a world-wide study of urbanization.

The foremost source of data relating to urbanization has been the Statistical Office of the United Nations. This organization, in its *Demographic Yearbook*, gives statistics on the population of individual cities and agglomerations, the total rural and urban populations, and other urban topics, as these data are provided by governmental agencies in the different countries and territories.

Such official statistics are of great value, since they provide individual scholars with information that could not otherwise be obtained without considerable expenditure; but their use in research poses several problems. Statistics drawn from individual countries and territories, which are the basis for the United Nations reports, suffer from the fact that they are not based on the same definitions applied consistently from one case to the next. It is this quality of the statistics that creates doubts concerning their comparability. For example, while one country may report a higher percentage of its total population as "urban" than does another, the discrepancy may be largely due to the use of a different type of distinction between urban and rural in the two countries. There is also the problem of variation in the nature of the urban units; one country may report the size and additional demographic characteristics solely for its politically-defined cities, while another may report the same data either for urbanized areas or for metropolitan areas. In such a case the two sets of statistics are not comparable. Furthermore, even comparable statistics on urbanization in two or more countries may be inadequate. For instance, if reliable information on the populations of urbanized or metropolitan areas is sought, statistics on politically-demarcated cities cannot always be used, even if it is known that the cities are "overbounded" or "underbounded" to the same degree in each country.

The United Nations Statistical Office, as an official international body, cannot control the comparability or adequacy of the data that it reports. Of necessity it must generally accept the statistics provided by the individual countries or territories, although it can classify them by type (i.e., by the definition of "urban" used and the nature of the boundaries of the urban units) and by source of data. Consequently, persons who wish to make use of the information provided by the Statistical Office should become familiar with the practices followed by different nations in reporting statistics or urbanization and with the types of data suited for research as far as comparability and over-all adequacy are concerned.

Contents of the papers. Since the characteristics of urbanization relate to phenomena that have no counterpart among individual cities, their study requires a shift in orientation. The first paper in Chapter 11, "Some Demographic Characteristics of Urbanization," seeks to bridge the gap between the two levels of analysis. It does so by first linking the characteristics of urbanization to common experience. This is followed by a consideration of research methods for the treatment of a variety of demographic characteristics, each of which is illustrated in a comparison of urbanization in Australia and India. In the final section, the paper describes methods of studying urban change, with application to the growth of metropolitan centers and metropolitan population in the United States and India.

Despite the fact that the degree of urbanization has been studied more than any other characteristic, its treatment in urban research still poses a number of problems, all of which center on the definition of urban, the availability of data for international comparisons, and the adequacy of these data. As the beginning student will come to see, these problems are also basic to the study of virtually any aspect of urbanization. In recognition of this and the over-all importance of the degree of urbanization, the second paper in Chapter 11, "Conventional Versus Metropolitan Data in the International Study of Urbanization," undertakes an analysis of the research problems posed by international measures of urbanization. The findings, based on different measures for each of fifty countries, indicate the types of official statistics that offer the most comparable and valid gauges of urbanization.

As suggested earlier, for purposes of analysis, two types of characteristics of urbanization should be distinguished. On the one hand, all of the cities in a country can be treated in strictly aggregate terms, which enables us to compare countries according to the number of cities, the number of city residents, and the degree of urbanization, to mention a few characteristics. On the other hand, attention may focus on the spatial distribution of cities or on the structure of the city system according to the sizes of cities. The final paper in Part V (Chapter 12, "Some Measures of Demographic and Spatial Relationships Among Cities," by Harley L. Browning and Jack P. Gibbs) serves as an introduction to this second view of the characteristics of urbanization. It sets forth methods for describing demographic and spatial patterns in quantitative terms, and considers some of the patterns which prevail in Brazil, Canada, France, Italy, Mexico, and the Netherlands.

The papers deal with methods of describing and measuring urbanization or urban systems. They do not deal with the causes and consequences of international variation in these characteristics, but references to studies of causal factors are provided in the *Index to the Bibliography*—Section 31. Additional references to the characteristics of urbanization are provided in Section 32 of the *Index;* studies of urbanization in particular countries or regions are cited in Section 30; and analyses of demographic and spatial relations among cities are treated in Section 15.

Chapter 11

ON DEMOGRAPHIC ATTRIBUTES
OF URBANIZATION

SOME DEMOGRAPHIC CHARACTERISTICS
OF URBANIZATION *

JACK P. GIBBS **

Although urban research often deals with technical and abstract subjects, it is not so far removed from common experience as first impressions might suggest. The city, for example, either as a political entity or as a point of population concentration, is a concept familar to most persons. Moreover, when one speaks of all of the cities of a country considered together, the notion is not entirely alien to the layman. Virtually every person has some knowledge of cities in the vicinity of his residence. He may observe, for example, that there are only three cities in the region, that all three considered together do not contain more than 60,000 inhabitants, and that none of them has a population of over 30,000. On the basis of these observations alone he has achieved a conception of some of the characteristics of urbanization. Such a conception would perhaps be distorted and certainly limited, since it would encompass neither all of the cities in the country nor all of the types of observations that could be made; nevertheless, it enables one to grasp the idea of characteristics of urbanization on a national level and to understand how these characteristics may vary from one country to another. Thus, the

---

* Written especially for this volume.
** Member of the staff of International Urban Research.

ʼuld generalize from his immediate experiences and
ₐ country with a thousand cities containing 100,000,000
ᵢₐabitants, of which 10,000,000 are in the largest city. He
could also conceive of a sharply contrasting case—for example,
a country with only 400,000 people in its fifty cities, none of
which contains more than 25,000 inhabitants.

An appeal to common experience also makes highly abstract
characteristics of urbanization intelligible. One may observe that
of 80 persons known to him only 20, or 25 per cent of them, live
in cities. On this basis he can readily understand the meaning
of a technical term—the *degree of urbanization,* or, as commonly
defined, the per cent of the total population of a country residing
in territory considered to be urban.[1]

This paper has a very limited and specific purpose—to acquaint the beginning student with some uncomplicated methods
for the analysis of data on the demographic characteristics of
urbanization, characteristics which relate, in one way or another,
to the number of urban residents and the number of cities in a
country.[2] Space limitations preclude both a consideration of the
theoretical and practical significance of each characteristic and a
review of studies on the subject. This is most undesirable, of
course, since the beginning student must realize that the goal of
international urban research is not simply to describe urbanization in every part of the world. We want to know why the characteristics of urbanization in some countries are vastly different
from those in other countries, and we also want to establish the
consequences that stem from these differences.[3] For example,
the proportion of the urban population residing in large urban
areas (i.e., those of more than 100,000 inhabitants) is more than
twice as high in some countries as it is in others. Two questions
are posed by the contrast: first, why does such a difference exist?

[1] Political cities, urban areas, or metropolitan areas of some minimum size
(e.g., political cities of over 5,000 inhabitants, urban areas of over 10,000 inhabitants, etc.). Valid comparisons of countries with regard to the degree of urbanization can be made only when the same type of urban unit and the same minimum
size limit is used in each country.

[2] Demographic and spatial relations among individual cities (i.e., variations in
their size and patterns of location) as a feature of urbanization are treated in
Chapter 12.

[3] Comparisons among territorial units other than nations may also be made,
since the characteristics of urbanization to be considered apply to world regions,
intranational regions, territories, and colonies, as well as to autonomous countries.

and, second, in what ways is the difference reflected in the traits of the urban population and other features of the nations?

We will not undertake providing answers to these and similar questions; however, some insights into causes and consequences are suggested by the nature of the countries used to illustrate research methods. We shall first compare urbanization in Australia and India; and this is followed by a consideration of metropolitan growth in the United States and India. Two of these countries, Australia and the United States, have reached very high levels of economic and technological development, while India represents the opposite extreme. The contrasts noted in the analysis of the three countries thus indicate the nature of the relation between economic and technological development and characteristics of urbanization. However, differences in level of development only suggest in a general way the causes and consequences of variation in the characteristics of urbanization; [4] much remains to be known, and the beginning student is thrown back on his own imagination and a few existing studies as sources of hypotheses.[5]

IMPRESSIONS OF URBANIZATION VERSUS
SYSTEMATIC RESEARCH

The characteristics of urbanization are not far removed from common experience. Any observant person who travels in different parts of the world is likely to form some impression of the different ways in which urbanization varies from place to place. He may note, for example, that in some countries only a small number of persons live in cities, while in others a great number do so, or that in some regions cities are few and small, while in others there are numerous large cities. A formal study of urbanization concerns itself with much the same observations, but in a more systematic way.

[4] To date the degree of urbanization is the only characteristic that has received extensive consideration on an international basis, which is all the more reason for the beginning student to realize that explanation rather than description is the ultimate goal of urban research.
[5] See Sections 30-32 of the *Subject Index to the Bibliography.*

TABLE 1

DISTRIBUTION OF THE POPULATION OF AGGLOMERATIONS IN AUSTRALIA, 1947, AND INDIA, 1951, BY SIZE CLASSES OF AGGLOMERATIONS *

Col. 1 Size Classes of Agglomerations **	Col. 2 Population in Each Size Class	Col. 3	Col. 4 Population in Each Size Class and Over	Col. 5	Col. 6 Per Cent of Total National Population in Each Size Class ***	Col. 7	Col. 8 Per Cent of Total National Population in Each Size Class and Over	Col. 9
	Australia	India	Australia	India	Australia	India	Australia	India
2,000-4,999	588,514	59,108,973	5,620,801	134,454,465	7.8	16.6	74.2	37.7
5,000-9,999	360,527	20,753,736	5,032,287	75,345,492	4.8	5.8	66.4	21.1
10,000-19,999 ...	326,601	11,680,768	4,671,760	54,591,756	4.3	3.3	61.6	15.3
20,000-49,999 ...	374,062	11,804,047	4,345,159	42,910,988	4.9	3.3	57.3	12.0
50,000-99,999 ...	76,534	7,555,324	3,971,097	31,106,941	1.0	2.1	52.4	8.7
100,000 and over.	3,894,563	23,551,617	3,894,563	23,551,617	51.4	6.6	51.4	6.6
All size classes ...	5,620,801	134,454,465	—	—	74.2	37.7	—	—

* SOURCES: Australian data compiled from *Census of the Commonwealth of Australia, 30th June, 1947*, Vol. I, pp. 497-555, and data for India reported in *Demographic Yearbook, 1955*, p. 205.

** Population agglomerations (i.e., points of population concentration) without regard to fixed administrative boundaries.

*** Total national population figures: India—356,879,394; Australia—7,579,358.

IDENTIFICATION OF URBAN UNITS

An illustration is provided by a comparison of urbanization in Australia and India. A person who had traveled in both countries would doubtless report that the two differ remarkably in their urban picture. If reasonably observant, he would note that, among other things, India has a far greater number of cities and a much larger number of people residing in them. But he would also note that a smaller percentage of India's total population reside in cities. While such observations suggest a contrast between Australia and India, we are left in doubt on three points—what is considered to be a city, exactly how much Australia and India differ, and in what other ways the characteristics of urbanization are dissimilar. Systematic research attempts to answer queries on these points. This is accomplished, for purposes of illustration, in Tables 1-3, each of which describes a variety of characteristics of urbanization in Australia and India.

The word "city" does not appear in any of the three tables, because it is inadequate for describing the units that are the subject of the comparison. Cities may be thought of as political entities, economic units, or simply as points of population concentration; and as a consequence the term does not convey a specific meaning by itself. The word city is nothing more than a generic term which may be applied to any one of several types of *urban units*. In recognition of this, the "cities" of Australia and India are identified as "agglomerations" to indicate the types of units that are being compared. Agglomerations are points of population concentration (i.e., clusters of dwelling places and other buildings as they would appear in an aerial photograph) without regard either to fixed administrative boundaries or to the occupations of the residents.[6] We may call these agglomerations

---

[6] The fact that the units are identified as "agglomerations" does not allay all doubts as to what is being compared. The source of the statistics on India (see Table 1) indicates that the data pertain to "agglomerations without regard to fixed administrative boundaries," but India's census report (see *Census of India, 1951*, Vol. I, Part II-A, p. 2) reveals that the population figures refer partly to administrative divisions known as "villages." These villages, despite their name, may include considerable open land surrounding the inhabited area. In a few cases administrative boundaries separate contiguous towns that would otherwise be considered parts of one agglomeration. However, the settlement pattern in India is

"cities" and refer to their inhabitants as "urban populations," but the units are not necessarily either "political cities" or "concentrations of predominantly nonagricultural populations."[7] In neither India nor Australia do all of the agglomerations conform to administrative boundaries and some of them, particularly the smaller ones, are not centers for governmental activities. The populations of practically all of Australia's agglomerations of over 2,000 inhabitants are doubtless predominantly nonagricultural; but it is equally probable that a large number of the Indian agglomerations, particularly those of between 2,000 and 5,000 inhabitants, are simply agricultural villages.

Consequently, if our comparison called for us to define cities as nonagricultural populations, some means of excluding agglomerations that do not qualify would have to be employed. One way of accomplishing this would be to consider only agglomerations of over 10,000 inhabitants, since most places of this size are much more likely to meet the nonagricultural criterion (e.g., more than 65 per cent of the workers in nonagricultural occupations) than are those of less than 10,000 residents.[8]

In the final analysis, the type of unit used in international comparisons of urbanization is guided by the availability of data and the particular definition of cities employed in the study. However, the same type of definition should be applied in all countries, whenever possible, and it should be noted that the results of any particular comparison are always relative to the type of urban unit considered. Thus, one should not use political cities

---

such that the population of a village tends to be concentrated in a single cluster of houses, and the data have been used as though they referred to agglomerations.

The Australian data have been derived from census figures on "localities." These localities correspond fairly closely to agglomerations, although it appears that municipal boundaries have been used to demarcate those in the medium size range. Thus, the data for both countries relate to populations that in some instances only approximate agglomerations. We have here an illustration of why it is always desirable to identify the units being compared beyond simply referring to them as political cities, urban areas, metropolitan areas, etc.

[7] Agglomerations are often described in terms that apply also to "urban areas." However, in so far as urban areas are defined and delimited in terms of a nonagricultural criterion, the two terms are not interchangeable.

[8] This would mean of course that places with less than 10,000 inhabitants and more than 65 per cent nonagricultural workers would be excluded. The only alternative is to apply both a size and nonagricultural rule to each individual agglomeration. See "The Influence of the Definition of the Urban Place on the Size of the Urban Population" by Miloš Macura, which appears as the first paper in Chapter 1 of this volume.

in one case, concentrations of predominantly nonagricultural populations in another, and simply agglomerations in still another.[9]

Also involved in the identification of the type of urban unit used in comparisons is the notion of population size. Most definitions of cities suggest, in one way or another, that a certain minimal number of people residing in close proximity to each other is at least one of their features, but there is little agreement as to what should be taken as the minimum number. Any rule in this regard, just as one establishing either a nonagricultural or density criterion, is bound to be an arbitrary one. It can only be said that whatever minimum size limit is adopted, it should be applied uniformly in each country.

As the first column in Tables 1-3 shows, the minimum size rule applied in the comparison of Australia and India is 2,000 inhabitants, with any agglomeration below that number excluded from consideration. This limit was selected not because it is best suited for this particular comparison,[10] but rather because it is the smallest population size that is ordinarily considered as indicative of urban status and because it provides a basis for a broad range of comparisons.

PARTICULAR CHARACTERISTICS OF URBANIZATION

Having identified the type of territorial unit we shall consider urban, we may now turn to a comparison of the features of urbanization in the two countries, with frequent references to Tables 1-3.

Size of the urban population. The bottom figures in columns two and three of Table 1 reflect one of the outstanding contrasts in the features of urbanization in Australia and India—the absolute size of their urban populations. In 1951 India had approximately 129 million more inhabitants of agglomerations of 2,000 or more residents than did Australia in 1947, or a ratio of about 24 to one. As the other figures in the two columns show, India

[9] For a discussion of the types of data available for international studies of urbanization and the relative adequacy of each type see Jack P. Gibbs and Kingsley Davis, "Conventional Versus Metropolitan Data in the International Study of Urbanization," the following paper in this chapter.

[10] A minimum size of 10,000 would be much better if our concern were with cities as concentrations of nonagricultural populations rather than agglomerations *per se.* For other observations on the minimum size limit see Gibbs and Davis, *op. cit.*

also had a larger number of residents in each of the six agglomeration size classes.[11] However, as the size classes become larger, there is a tendency for the difference between the two countries to become less and less. Accordingly, the contrast between the size of the urban population in Australia and India is largely a question of the minimum size rule employed in the definition of urban. This is shown in columns four and five of Table 1.[12] The ratio of India's total urban population to that of Australia is, as we have seen, about 24 to one; but for agglomerations over 5,000 the corresponding ratio is 15 to one; and, for all above 10,000, only twelve to one. This ratio continues to decrease until in the largest size class, 100,000 and over, it is only six to one.

Per cent of the total national population in urban units. Since the urban population can never exceed the total national population, the number of urban residents in Australia in 1947 could not have exceeded seven and a half million. In contrast, the urban population of India could have been as large as 356 million in 1951, had every person resided in an agglomeration of over 2,000 inhabitants.[13] For many purposes, however, it is the proportion rather than the absolute number that is of interest. The bottom figures in columns six and seven of Table 1 show that 74.2 per cent of Australia's total national population resided in agglomerations of 2,000 or more, while the corresponding per cent for India was 37.7. These figures represent the *degree of urbanization* in the two countries.[14] This characteristic is defined as the per cent of the total national population residing in cities, but the meaning of such a per cent depends upon the type of territorial unit that is treated as a city. In this case the units are agglomerations of 2,000 or more inhabitants.

[11] The size classes employed in Tables 1-3 conform to those commonly used by national and international agencies that report statistics on urban populations; however, the choice of one set of size classes as over against another depends on the purpose of the study and the availability of data. In making comparisons among countries the same set of size classes should be applied in each case, and, ordinarily, it is desirable to employ classes of 100,000-499,999; 500,000-999,999; and 1,000,000 and over, rather than 100,000 and over.

[12] That is, each size class and all larger ones.

[13] Kashmir-Jammu and tribal areas of Assam are not included in any of the figures on India reported in this paper.

[14] The degree of urbanization in a country is determined neither by the number of cities nor the size of the urban population. See Kingsley Davis and Hilda Hertz Golden, "Urbanization and the Development of Pre-Industrial Areas," *Economic Development and Cultural Change,* Vol. 3 (October, 1954), pp. 6-8.

Other figures in columns six and seven relate to the per cent of the total national population residing in agglomerations of a particular size range. In certain instances we find here a sharp contrast between Australia and India, and these contrasts tend to conform to a pattern. The per cent of the national population residing in small agglomerations (i.e., 2,000-4,999) in India is over twice the per cent in Australia; but at the other end of the size scale, agglomerations of over 100,000 inhabitants, the reverse is true: 51.4 for Australia and 6.6 for India. Thus, not only is the degree of urbanization higher in Australia than in India, but also a far greater proportion of Australia's total population resides in large cities.

That the degree of urbanization is relative to the minimum population size employed in the definition of urban (or "city") is illustrated by the figures in columns eight and nine of Table 1, which represent the per cent of the national population of Australia and India in each size class of agglomerations and all larger size classes. If the degree of urbanization is reckoned in terms of all agglomerations of 2,000 or more inhabitants, it is twice as high in Australia as in India; but it is over three times as high if we consider agglomerations of 5,000 or more inhabitants; and it is four times as high for the size range 10,000 and over. The difference between the two countries increases steadily with the size of the agglomerations up to the maximum size class, 100,000 or more, at which point the per cent of the total national population residing in agglomerations is about eight times as high in Australia as in India.[15]

[15] The degree of urbanization in a country is relative to both the minimum population size rule *and* the type of urban unit considered. Had we considered political cities in the case of Australia and towns or town groups (which are described as having a "definite urban character") in the case of India, the comparisons would have yielded quite different results. This becomes evident when population figures on these units (shown below) are compared with those in Table 1.

	Size Class					
	2,000-4,999	5,000-9,999	10,000-19,999	20,000-49,999	50,000-99,999	100,000+
Australia*	653,011	564,777	874,793	2,023,884	1,078,458	228,069
India**	2,015,405	8,369,405	9,034,551	10,350,605	6,268,116	25,829,027

* SOURCE: *Census of the Commonwealth of Australia, 30th June, 1947*, Vol. I, pp. 497-555.
** SOURCE: *Census of India, 1951*, Vol. I, Part II-A, pp. 61-97.

Distribution of the urban population by class of urban units.
The size-class structure is independent of the absolute or relative
size of the urban population. Theoretically, the urban residents
might be concentrated in a few giant metropolises or exclusively
in small cities.[16]

Rarely do we find a contrast more striking than in the case of
Australia and India, as shown in Table 2. Nearly one-half of In-

TABLE 2

PERCENTAGE DISTRIBUTION OF THE AGGLOMERATION POPULATION IN
AUSTRALIA, 1947, AND INDIA, 1951, BY SIZE CLASSES OF
AGGLOMERATIONS [*]

Col. 1	Col. 2	Col. 3	Col. 4	Col. 5
	Per Cent of Agglommeration Population in Each Size Class		Per Cent of Agglomeration Population in Each Size Class and Over	
Size Classes of Agglomerations	Australia	India	Australia	India
2,000-4,999	10.5	44.0	100.0	100.0
5,000-9,999	6.4	15.4	89.5	56.0
10,000-19,999 ..	5.8	8.7	83.1	40.6
20,000-49,999 ..	6.6	8.8	77.3	31.9
50,000-99,999 ..	1.4	5.6	70.7	23.1
100,000 and over	69.3	17.5	69.3	17.5
All size classes ..	100.0	100.0	—	—

[*] See Table 1 for data used in computations, sources of data, and explanatory
notes.

dia's urban population is concentrated in agglomerations of
between 2,000 and 4,999 inhabitants, but more than one-half of
Australia's urban residents are found in agglomerations of 100,000
or more inhabitants. Viewed another way, 89.5 per cent of Australia's urban population reside in agglomerations of 5,000 or
more inhabitants, while this is the case for only 56.0 per cent of
India's urban population. The social or economic significance of
such differences may be great. If, for example, a particular type of
urban influence is not operative in cities of less than 20,000 inhabitants, then only 31.9 per cent of India's urban population is
exposed to it, while the corresponding per cent is 77.3 in Australia.

[16] This is only a logical possibility, of course, and in actual practice we find
that a high degree of urbanization tends to be closely associated with the concentration of the urban population in large cities.

Number of urban units. For every urban resident in Australia there are twenty-four in India. This difference in the size of the urban population is more than matched by the contrast between the two countries with regard to the number of agglomerations. As shown by the bottom figures in the second and third columns of Table 3, there were only 284 agglomerations in Australia, while

TABLE 3

DISTRIBUTION OF AGGLOMERATIONS IN AUSTRALIA, 1947, AND INDIA, 1951, BY SIZE CLASSES *

Col. 1	*Col. 2* *Col. 3* Number of Agglomerations		*Col. 4* *Col. 5* Number of Agglomerations in Each Size Class and Over		*Col. 6* *Col. 7* Per Cent of Agglomerations in Each Size Class		*Col. 8* *Col. 9* Per Cent of Agglomerations in Each Size Class and Over	
Size Classes of Agglomerations	*Australia*	*India*	*Australia*	*India*	*Australia*	*India*	*Australia*	*India*
2,000-4,999 ...	190	20,508	284	25,050	66.9	81.9	100.0	100.0
5,000-9,999 ...	53	3,101	94	4,542	18.7	12.4	33.1	18.1
10,000-19,999 .	23	856	41	1,441	8.1	3.4	14.4	5.7
20,000-49,999 .	11	401	18	585	3.9	1.6	6.3	2.3
50,000-99,999 .	1	111	7	184	0.3	0.4	2.4	0.7
100,000 and over	6	73	6	73	2.1	0.3	2.1	0.3
All size classes..	284	25,050	—	—	100.0	100.0	—	—

* See Table 1 for sources of data and explanatory notes.

there were more than 25,000 in India, or about 88 times the Australian number. If we consider the other figures in columns two and three it is readily apparent that the difference holds true in each size class, but its magnitude tends to decrease as the agglomerations become larger. This is perhaps even more evident in columns four and five, where the figures show the accumulative number of agglomerations. At the lower size range (all agglomerations of over 2,000) the ratio of India's agglomerations to those of Australia is 88 to one, as we have seen, but at the upper size range, places of 100,000 or more inhabitants, the ratio is only about 12 to one.

When we turn from numbers of agglomerations to their percentage distribution in each size-class, as shown in the last four columns of Table 3, the over-all picture is one of a greater similarity between Australia and India than has heretofore been the case. In common with all other countries, the vast majority of agglomerations in India and Australia are very small places. Size-class 2,000-4,999 accounts for 66.9 per cent of Australia's agglomerations and 81.9 per cent of India's. Only 2.4 per cent of Australia's agglomerations have 50,000 or more inhabitants and less than 0.7 per cent of India's do so. In other words, small agglomerations predominate in both countries, but less in Australia than in India.

CHANGE IN THE CHARACTERISTICS OF URBANIZATION

There have been only a small number of truly international studies of change in the characteristics of urbanization, and these are limited mainly to the growth of urban populations and shifts in the degree of urbanization.[17] These topics are basic, but the process of urbanization involves changes in other aspects as well.

A change in the size of the urban population or the number of cities is merely a matter of an absolute numerical increase or decrease; but change in either the degree of urbanization or the per cent of the total population residing in cities of a particular size class is determined by the growth of the urban population *relative* to that of the national total.[18]

Methods of expressing changes in such relative attributes are illustrated by their application to Metropolitan Areas over a ten year period in the United States (1940-1950) and India (1941-1951). Each Metropolitan Area (or M.A.) contains a population of at least 100,000 residing in territory that comprises a political city, or urban area, and all contiguous civil divisions with not less than 65 per cent of the labor force engaged in nonagricultural industries.[19]

Size of metropolitan population. Table 4 reveals that the number of metropolitan residents in the United States increased

[17] A few studies have considered other aspects of change in urbanization, such as growth among cities in different size classes. See, for example, Kingsley Davis and Ana Casis, "Urbanization in Latin America," *Milbank Memorial Fund Quarterly*, Vol. 24 (April, 1946), pp. 186-297; Leo F. Schnore and Gene B. Petersen, "Urban and Metropolitan Development in the United States and Canada," *The Annals of the American Academy of Political and Social Science*, Vol. 316 (March, 1958), pp. 60-68.

[18] It is thus possible for the degree of urbanization to increase even when the absolute number of urban residents decreases, provided that the total population decreases at a greater rate than the urban population.

[19] For a more complete description of the M.A.'s see Gibbs and Davis, *op. cit.*, and International Urban Research, *The World's Metropolitan Areas* (Berkley and Los Angeles: University of California Press, 1959).

TABLE 4

CHANGE IN THE CHARACTERISTICS OF URBANIZATION IN THE UNITED STATES, 1940-50, AND INDIA, 1941-51, IN THE FORM OF THE GROWTH OF METROPOLITAN AREAS AND THEIR POPULATIONS [*]

Characteristics of Urbanization	Start of Period [**]		End of Period [***]		Average Annual Per Cent Growth	
	U.S., 1940	India, 1941	U.S., 1950	India, 1951	U.S.	India
Population of M.A.'s [****] by size classes						
100,000-199,999	7,927,201	3,952,666	8,083,654	5,504,326	0.2	3.3
200,000-499,999	16,026,462	3,877,696	16,787,482	6,117,951	0.5	4.5
500,000-999,999	8,852,168	2,306,972	14,479,435	3,160,991	4.8	3.1
1,000,000+	34,962,884	7,011,964	44,946,386	13,143,670	2.5	6.1
All sizes	67,768,715	17,149,298	84,296,957	27,926,938	2.2	4.8
Number of M.A.'s by size classes						
100,000-199,999	56	28	56	41	0.0	3.8
200,000-499,999	50	12	54	21	0.8	5.5
500,000-999,999	13	3	23	4	5.6	2.9
1,000,000+	11	3	14	5	2.4	5.0
All sizes	130	46	147	71	1.2	4.3
Per cent of total national population in M.A.'s by size classes						
100,000-199,999	6.0	1.3	5.4	1.5	−1.1	1.4
200,000-499,999	12.2	1.2	11.1	1.7	−0.9	3.4
500,000-999,999	6.7	0.7	9.6	0.9	3.6	2.5
1,000,000+	26.6	2.2	29.8	3.7	1.1	5.1
All sizes	51.5	5.4	55.9	7.8	0.8	3.6

[*] Sources of data: 1950 and 1951—International Urban Research, *The World's Metropolitan Areas;* United States, 1940—Donald J. Bogue, *Population Growth in Standard Metropolitan Areas, 1900-1950;* India, 1941—Statistics compiled from census reports.

[**] Places that did not meet the population size requirement (100,000) until after the start of the growth period are excluded.

[***] Includes places that reached 100,000 and thereby qualified as Metropolitan Areas during the growth period.

[****] Metropolitan Areas.

by more than sixteen million over the ten year period, 1940-1950, while the corresponding increase in India was about eleven million between 1941 and 1951. Expressed in the last two columns of Table 4 as average annual per cent growth,[20] the growth of

[20] This measure of change, which can be applied to any demographic characteristic of urbanization, is derived from the average arithmetical formula: $Cr = 200(C_2 - C_1)/t(C_2 + C_1)$, where Cr is the average annual per cent change, C_1 is the value of a characteristic at a given date, C_2 is the value at a later point in time, and t is the number of years in the intervening period. This formula is only one of several ways by which the amount of change can be expressed. The amount, for any characteristics of urbanization, can also be considered in absolute terms (e.g.,

India's metropolitan population was over twice that of the U.S. (4.8 as compared to 2.2 per cent per year).

Table 4 also enables us to compare India and the United States as to increase in the number of metropolitan residents in different M.A. size classes. Using the *class method* (comparing the number of people in a given size class of cities at two points in time, ignoring shifts of individual cities from one class to another during the period [21]), we find that in only the size class 500,000-999,999 did the average annual increase of metropolitan residents in the U.S. exceed the corresponding increase for India. However, the difference is much greater for particular size classes than it is for all Metropolitan Areas. For example, in India the number of residents in M.A.'s of between 200,000 and 500,000 increased at a rate nine times that of the United States, while the corresponding ratio for all M.A.'s is less than three to one.[22]

The number of Metropolitan Areas. Urbanization as a process usually takes place in two ways—the expansion of the size of existing urban units and the appearance of new units.[23] With regard to the latter, this means that some localities in a country may

---

the metropolitan population of the U.S. increased 16,528,242 between 1940 and 1950). However, when comparing absolute changes in the characteristics of urbanization in two countries over a different number of years (e.g., a period of ten years in one case but five in the other), the amount of increase or decrease should be expressed in units of time. Thus the metropolitan population of the U.S. increased 1,652,824 per year between 1940 and 1950. This figure does not represent the amount of growth that took place in each of the ten years, but rather the average annual increase (the arithmetic mean of the increases during each year). Change in population size can also be expressed in simple percentage terms (e.g., the metropolitan population of the U.S. increased 24.4 per cent between 1940 and 1950), but to express this change in units of time (e.g., on an average annual basis) the above average arithmetical formula should be used rather than dividing the per cent by the number of years in the period.

[21] See Davis and Casis, *op. cit.*, pp. 196-199.

[22] An alternative means of expressing growth in a particular size class is to relate the amount of change to that of all urban units. Thus, in the U.S. the size class 500,000-999,999 accounted for 34.0 per cent of the total increase in metropolitan residents, and its average annual per cent growth was 2.6 higher than that of all size classes (4.8 minus 2.2), or about 2.2 times as high. Still another way of expressing an increase in the total urban population and the residents in a particular size class is to relate it to the growth of the national population. The addition of 10,777,640 persons to India's metropolitan population between 1941 and 1951 represents 25.6 per cent of the total national growth during the period, and the average annual per cent growth of the metropolitan population was 3.5 points higher than that of the national total (4.8 minus 1.3), or 3.7 times as high.

[23] See Hope Tisdale, "The Process of Urbanization," *Social Forces*, Vol. 20 (March, 1942), pp. 311-316.

qualify as urban between the start and the end of a given period.

The increase in the size of the metropolitan populations in the United States and India over the decade was associated with the appearance of several new M.A.'s in both countries. According to Table 4, India had 46 M.A.'s at the beginning of the decade and 71 at the end, an increase of 25, while the number in the U.S. changed from 130 to 147, an increase of 17.[24] The per cent growth was much higher for India than the United States for all M.A.'s and in all size classes other than 500,000-999,999.[25]

Per cent of the total national population in M.A.'s. One of several possible measures of the degree of urbanization is the per cent of the total population in Metropolitan Areas. As shown in the bottom row of Table 4, this per cent was 51.5 in the United States as of 1940, but it was only 5.4 for India in 1941. During the following ten years it increased in both countries, but whether the amount of increase in the one case was larger than in the other is altogether a matter of method used to expressed change.[26] In percentage points the rise was greater in the U.S. than in India (from 51.5 to 55.9 as compared with 5.4 to 7.8).[27] However, the proportional increase in the percentage was greater for India than the U.S. (3.6 as compared to 0.8 per cent per year).

The change in the proportion of the total population residing in M.A.'s varied considerably from one size class to the next in both countries, particularly in the United States. Despite an increase in the number of people in M.A.'s of less than 500,000 in-

[24] The difference between the number of urban units at the start of the period and the number at the end of the period ordinarily indicates how many new units have been added. Actually, however, the number of new urban units may be larger than the difference suggests, since some localities that qualified as urban at the start of the period may not qualify as such at the end of the period. This rarely happens, but an accurate count of new urban units would consider only localities that qualified as urban between the start and end of the growth period. The difference between the number at the start and end of the period thus reflects the *net change* of urban units.

[25] In considering individual size classes it is particularly important to note that the figures reflect a net change in the number of M.A.'s and not the number of new M.A.'s. Each size class may lose as many M.A.'s, through shifts to a different size class, as it gains.

[26] This may apply, of course, to any characteristic of urbanization.

[27] Absolute increases need not be reduced to an average annual basis in this comparison, since the growth period was ten years for both the United States and India.

habitants, the per cent of the total population residing in such places decreased over the decade.[28]

Change as expressed by the "city method." Table 4 shows that the increase in metropolitan residents tends to vary from one M.A. size class to the next, with the per cent growth of residents in M.A.'s of 100,000-199,999 being much less than that in any other size class. This might suggest that very little population increase took place in small Metropolitan Areas, but such a conclusion does not make allowance for shifts of individual M.A.'s from one size class to another during the decade.

If the goal is to determine the amount of population increase in M.A.'s of a particular size at the start of the growth period, the *city method* must be used rather than the class method.[29] This method considers particular cities (i.e., in this case, those in a given size class) at the start of the period and traces their subsequent growth to the end of the period, without concern for the fact that some of them may have shifted to another size class during the intervening time. This method may yield a picture quite different from that produced by the class method. For instance, in Table 5 we see that the United States M.A.'s in the size class 100,000-199,999 had, at the start of the growth period, a total population of 7,927,201. Ten years later these same M.A.'s had reached 10,276,600. The average annual growth in this case

---

[28] The data in Table 4 do not cover all of the changes in the characteristics of urbanization that are related to Metropolitan Areas. However, the methods for expressing change considered in this section can be applied to virtually any characteristic that can be described in quantitative terms.

[29] See Davis and Casis, *op. cit.*, pp. 196-199.

TABLE 5

GROWTH OF THE POPULATIONS OF METROPOLITAN AREAS ACCORDING TO THE SIZE CLASS OF THE METROPOLITAN AREAS AT THE START OF GROWTH PERIOD, UNITED STATES, 1940-50, AND INDIA, 1941-51 *

Size Classes of M.A.'s ** at Start of Period	Population of M.A.'s at Start of Period		Population of M.A.'s at End of Period		Average Annual Per Cent Growth	
	U.S., 1940	India, 1941	U.S., 1950	India, 1951	U.S.	India
100,000-199,999	7,927,201	3,952,666	10,276,600	5,321,286	2.6	3.0
200,000-499,999	16,026,462	3,877,696	19,669,059	5,524,102	2.0	3.5
500,000-999,999	8,852,168	2,306,972	11,089,574	3,781,854	2.2	4.8
1,000,000+	34,962,884	7,011,964	41,276,558	10,283,876	1.7	3.8

* See Table 4 for sources of data.
** Metropolitan Areas.

is 2.6 per cent, a rate higher than that of any other size class. Exactly the opposite is true when growth is traced by the class method, which yields an average annual per cent growth for this class of 0.2, which is lower than that of any other size class.

An inspection of the last two columns of Table 5 reveals that the amount of variation in the per cent growth figures from one size class to the next is, in both India and the U.S., far less than the corresponding variation in Table 4. This indicates that a great deal of difference among the size classes is due to the shifting of M.A.'s from one class to another.

Two sources of urban growth. Between 1940 and 1950, 16,-528,242 people were added to the metropolitan population of the U.S., and in India, 10,777,640 were added. The expansion in each case can be traced to two sources shown in Table 6: first, the

TABLE 6

GROWTH OF POPULATIONS IN SPECIAL CLASSES OF METROPOLITAN AREAS, UNITED STATES, 1940-50, AND INDIA, 1941-51 *

Classes of M.A.'s **	Population at Start of Period		Population at End of Period		Average Annual Per Cent Growth	
	U.S., 1940	India, 1941	U.S., 1950	India, 1951	U.S.	India
M.A.'s of 100,000 or more at end of period	69,209,827	19,163,626	84,296,957	27,926,938	2.0	3.7
M.A.'s of 100,000 or more at start of period	67,768,715	17,149,298	82,311,791	24,911,118	1.9	3.7
Places that reached 100,000 and qualified as M.A.'s during period ***	1,441,112	2,014,328	1,985,166	3,015,820	3.2	4.0

* For sources of data see Table 4.
** Metropolitan Areas.
*** 25 places in India and 17 in the United States.

growth of those places which were Metropolitan Areas at the start of the period, with population increases of 14,543,076 in the U.S. and 7,761,820 in India; and, second, the population at the end of the period of those places that became Metropolitan Areas during the period—about two million in the United States and about three million in India.[30]

[30] Under ideal conditions a study of urban growth would be based on the application of the same urban definition to all of the localities in a country at the start and at the end of the growth period, and it would also involve the delimita-

Thus, the metropolitan populations of the two countries expanded in two ways—the growth of existing M.A.'s and the addition of new ones during the decade—and this makes it necessary to distinguish between two types of growth rates. One of them— the *gross rate* of growth—appears in Table 4. There it can be seen that the total metropolitan population of the U.S. jumped from 67,768,715 to 84,296,957 over the ten years, and in India from 17,149,298 to 27,926,938. Since the places which qualified as M.A.'s during the decade do not enter into the numbers at the start of the period, the percentage growth represented by these figures is a *gross rate*—2.2 and 4.8 per cent respectively.

Taking instead the population increase in all places that were M.A.'s at the *end* of the growth period (the first row of Table 6), we find that the average annual per cent growth of the metropolitan population was 2.0 for the U.S. and 3.7 for India. These two figures are *net growth rates,* and there is a substantial difference between them and the gross rates, particularly in the case of India. To the extent that the gross rate exceeds the net rate, the multiplication of urban units (i.e., the appearance of new ones) has played an important role in the over-all increase of urbanization. The rates noted above make it evident that the appearance of new M.A.'s during the growth period played a more important role in urbanization in India than in the United States. An alternative means of comparing the two in this regard is to consider the per cent of over-all metropolitan growth that can be attributed to the appearance of new M.A.'s. The three million people added to India's metropolitan population by the appearance of 25 new M.A.'s represents 28 per cent of the over-all metropolitan increase, while the appearance of 17 new M.A.'s in the U.S. accounts for only 12 percent of the increase.

---

tion of the boundaries of each locality at these two points in time. The Metropolitan Areas of India and the United States have not been treated in exactly this way. For one thing, their boundaries were established at the end of the growth period and retrojected to the earlier date (i.e., the area was held constant over the decade). Whether a locality qualified as a M.A. at the start of the growth period was determined on the basis of population size alone, with only those having 100,000 or more inhabitants considered as Metropolitan Areas. Had the nonagricultural criterion been applied at both the start and the end of the growth period some of the smaller places (those just over 100,000) might not have qualified as M.A.'s at the beginning of the decade.

CONVENTIONAL VERSUS METROPOLITAN DATA IN THE INTERNATIONAL STUDY OF URBANIZATION *

JACK P. GIBBS AND KINGSLEY DAVIS

Most of urban sociology rests upon observations made in countries representing a small and biased sample of the world as a whole. Any attempt, however, to remove this narrow restraint—that is, any attempt to extend comparative urban analysis to include all parts of the earth—runs into the complex problem of comparability. In the present paper we have no solution to offer for this problem as it affects all aspects of urban sociology, but we do have some information bearing upon the validity of one type of international comparison—namely, the degree of urbanization as between one country and another. This is perhaps the type of urban statistic most frequently used in comparing countries. The proportion of people living in urban places or in cities of a given size is considered a fundamental trait of any society. The data required for computing such proportions are, for many countries at least, readily obtainable and hence widely used.

In view of the importance and wide use of data on the degree of urbanization in countries and regions, it is essential that such data be at least approximately comparable from one area to another. There must be assurance that persons included as city residents in one country are not excluded in other countries, and vice versa. The researcher who makes comparisons of the extent of urbanization must normally, however, rely on the statistics that governmental agencies provide on cities. He therefore has control neither over the type of data reported nor over the demarcation of towns and cities as statistical units. Since, as is well known, different governments follow different procedures in delimiting their urban units, there is great danger that apparent differences among countries in the proportion of the population living in towns or cities may be in part the result of contrasting definitions and statistical practices. Even within the same coun-

* Reprinted from *American Sociological Review*, Vol. 23, No. 5 (October, 1958), pp. 504-514, with permission of authors and publisher.

try there may be little uniformity from one province or state to another or from one city to another in drawing the urban boundaries.

The lack of comparability stems, of course, from the fact that the so-called "city" is often a political or administrative unit. As such, its boundaries may or may not approximate the actual limits of the demographic or ecological "city." Some cities, as defined by the government concerned, are "underbounded" in the sense that their territory embraces only a part of the total area that makes up the ecological city and their population includes only a part of the total urban aggregate; others are "overbounded" in the sense that their limits extend far beyond the city as a continuous urban area, embracing land that is rural by virtually any standard.[1]

This situation obviously poses a dilemma for the student of urban phenomena. On the one hand, he must of necessity often work with data on administratively defined cities; yet on the other hand he knows that the data are not strictly comparable. One way to resolve this dilemma would be to provide the student of international urbanization with an idea of the actual degree of comparability or incomparability of official data on urban proportions in the world's nations. This could best be done, of course, if by some magic we had information on the populations of the actual demographic cities of the earth, for then we could compare the official data with the correct data. Since we do not generally have this information, the next best procedure is to compare the official statistics with the data on metropolitan areas delimited throughout the world according to a roughly comparable standard. Such a task is now possible because the International Urban Research office has just finished a world-wide delimitation of Metropolitan Areas of 100,000 or more inhabitants. The present paper therefore attempts to assess the validity of international comparisons of degree of urbanization based on

[1] In most industrial countries, the "cities" are underbounded. In the United States in 1950, for example, the central cities held only 70 per cent of the residents and only 49 per cent of the land encompassed in the Urbanized Areas. In the case of the Philippines, on the other hand, some of the "Chartered Cities" are overbounded to an extreme degree, for they embrace great stretches of purely rural and sometimes uninhabited land. A fuller treatment of the question of urban delimitation will be found in International Urban Research, *The World's Metropolitan Areas,* to be published in 1959 by the University of California Press.

official statistics by checking such comparisons against those made with our data on Metropolitan Areas. The question is not only whether or not *any* comparison of national urbanization based on official statistics is valid, but also which kinds of official statistics on urbanization are *most* valid.

TREATMENT OF DATA AND SOURCES

Since the procedures employed in our world-wide delimitation of Metropolitan Areas are set forth at length in another publication,[2] we shall describe them only briefly. We began with a list of all administratively defined cities or continuous urban areas of 50,000 or more, designating them as principal cities. Then the administrative or territorial units around these cities were examined to determine the percentage of their labor force engaged in agriculture and their distance from the principal city. To be included in a Metropolitan Area, an administrative unit had to (1) touch upon the principal city or an administrative area already included in the M.A.; (2) have at least 65 per cent of its labor force engaged in non-agricultural occupations; (3) be located close enough to the principal city to make commuting feasible. In some cases the lack of data made it necessary to substitute a density criterion for the non-agricultural criterion, in which case any unit included in the M.A. had to have a density either equal to half or more of the density of the principal city (or the next inner ring) or twice that of the next outer ring. If the boundary of the area established by these criteria failed to include at least 100,000 people, we dropped it from the list.

This procedure for delimiting metropolitan areas, crude as it may be, is sufficiently standardized to guarantee a high degree of comparability. Furthermore, it can be applied to most of the world's countries and particularly to those containing numerous cities. It therefore furnishes a yardstick for assessing the validity of comparisons made on the basis of officially reported urban statistics.

The present analysis is made with reference to the 50 independent countries shown in Table 1, representing approximately half of the world's population and 42 per cent of its inhabited

[2] International Urban Research, *op. cit.*

TABLE 1

PER CENT OF TOTAL POPULATION URBAN AND PER CENT IN METROPOLITAN AREAS AND LOCALITIES OF SIX SIZE RANGES BY COUNTRIES, *Circa* 1950

Countries by Type of Locality [*]	Per Cent of Total Population in Localities by Size Ranges [**]						Per Cent Urban [**]	Per Cent in Metropolitan Areas [***]
	2,000+	5,000+	10,000+	20,000+	50,000+	100,000+		
Type A								
Argentina, 1947	62.5	56.9	52.7	48.3	42.1	37.2	62.5	43.8
Australia, 1947	74.2[1]	66.4[1]	61.6[1]	57.3[1]	52.4[1]	51.4[1]	68.9	55.4
Cuba, 1953	50.9[1]	45.0[1]	40.9[1]	36.5[1]	28.5[1]	21.9[1]	57.0[1]	26.0
Denmark, 1950 [a]	58.8	55.7	51.4	44.8	36.7	33.5	67.3	45.5
France, 1954	50.2[1]	42.4[1]	36.8[1]	29.8[1]	21.2[1]	15.0[1]	55.9	34.4
India, 1951	37.7	21.1	15.3	12.0	8.7	6.6	17.3	7.8
Ireland, 1951	40.5	35.5	32.2	28.3	23.7	17.6	41.5	23.4
Israel, 1949 [b]	73.6[1]	66.2[1]	61.9[1]	51.3[1]	45.6[1]	45.6[1]	71.3[1]	55.9[c]
Italy, 1951	56.5[1]	45.4[1]	37.5[1]	30.3[1]	21.9[1]	17.0[1]	40.9[1]	27.3
Netherlands, 1947	72.6	63.6	56.1	49.8	41.3	32.7	54.6	45.6
Norway, 1950	44.1	40.3	38.4	32.7	26.0	19.8	32.2	21.8
Pakistan, 1951	10.2[1]	10.0[1]	9.1[1]	8.0[1]	5.9[1]	5.1[1]	11.4	5.1
Portugal, 1950	31.2	24.6	19.4	16.4	12.7	12.7	31.2	19.6
Sweden, 1950	51.9	45.4	40.3	33.0	25.5	19.4	47.5	31.8
United States, 1950 [d]	65.1[1]	60.3[1]	56.2[e]	52.0[e]	46.8[1]	43.9[1]	64.0	55.9
Type B								
Australia, 1947	71.5[1]	62.9[1]	55.4[1]	43.9[1]	17.2[1]	3.0[1]	68.9	55.4
Brazil, 1950	30.8	26.8	23.4	20.2	16.3	13.2	36.2	17.6
Canada, 1951	50.7	45.3	40.2	35.1	27.5	23.3	61.6	45.5
Ceylon, 1946	15.2	14.8	14.0	11.4	8.7	5.4	15.4	9.5

Colombia, 1951	34.7[1]	29.1[1]	25.5[1]	22.4[1]	18.2[1]	14.7[1]	36.3	18.6
Costa Rica, 1950	28.6	23.7	18.8	10.9	10.9	0.0	33.5	19.9
Dominican Republic, 1950	21.5	18.5	16.0	11.1	11.1	8.5	23.8	11.2
Ecuador, 1950	27.7	24.0	21.3	17.8	14.6	14.6	28.5	14.9
El Salvador, 1950	27.6	21.7	17.3	12.9	11.5	8.7	36.5	11.9
Finland, 1950	35.1	31.6	28.2	22.2	14.2	14.2	32.3	17.0
Greece, 1951	49.7[1]	38.3[1]	33.9[1]	26.8[1]	16.0[1]	12.7[1]	36.8	22.0
Guatemala, 1950	23.9	16.8	12.5	11.2	10.2	10.2	25.0	10.6
Haiti, 1950	10.0	8.2	6.3	5.1	4.3	4.3	12.2	6.0
Honduras, 1950	17.2	11.8	9.8	6.8	5.3	0.0	31.0	7.3
India, 1951	17.3[1]	16.7[1]	14.4[1]	11.9[1]	9.0[1]	7.2[1]	17.3	7.8
Japan, 1950	59.6[1]	58.0[1]	50.7[1]	42.1[1]	33.2[1]	25.6[1]	37.5	36.3
Malaya, 1947	24.3	21.2	19.0	17.1	10.2	7.4	26.5	12.7
Mexico, 1950	45.5[1]	34.6[1]	28.9[1]	24.0[1]	18.7[1]	15.1[1]	42.6[1]	20.3
New Zealand, 1951	65.7	60.2	57.0	54.2	41.6	32.8	61.3	43.6
Nicaragua, 1950	28.0	21.7	19.0	15.2	10.3	10.3	34.9	13.3
Panama, 1950	42.5	33.8	27.8	22.4	22.4	15.9	36.0	23.9
Paraguay, 1950	28.1	20.2	18.4	15.2	15.2	15.2	34.6	15.6
Peru, 1940	25.5[1]	20.4[1]	17.5[1]	13.9[1]	10.5[1]	8.4[1]	36.1[1]	10.4
Philippines, 1948	21.0[1]	13.8[1]	8.9[1]	6.3[1]	4.1[1]	3.4[1]	24.1[1]	10.3
Thailand, 1947	9.9[1]	9.8[1]	8.9[1]	6.7[1]	4.5[1]	4.5[1]	9.9	6.8
Turkey, 1950	28.7	22.4	18.7	14.5	10.1	8.2	21.9	14.0
Union of South Africa, 1951	39.8	36.2	33.2	30.7	28.2	24.0	42.6	31.5
United Kingdom, 1951	79.7[1]	77.6[1]	74.0[1]	66.9[1]	50.8[1]	36.1[1]	80.3[1]	77.0
United States, 1950	59.8[1]	54.4[1]	49.0[e]	43.0[e]	35.3[1]	29.4[1]	64.0[1]	55.9
Venezuela, 1950	49.7[1]	42.4[1]	36.8[1]	32.2[1]	24.7[1]	20.6[1]	53.8	26.2
Type C								
Austria, 1951	65.7	49.3	43.1	39.8	35.2	32.9	49.2	38.9
Belgium, 1947	82.3	62.7	46.6	32.0	17.9	10.5	62.7	41.4

TABLE 1—Continued

Per Cent of Total Population Urban and Per Cent in Metropolitan Areas and Localities of Six Size Ranges by Countries, *Circa* 1950

Countries by Type of Locality [*]	Per Cent of Total Population in Localities by Size Ranges [**]						Per Cent Urban [**]	Per Cent in Metropolitan Areas [***]
	2,000+	5,000+	10,000+	20,000+	50,000+	100,000+		
Egypt, 1947	90.9	64.1	40.3	29.1	22.7	19.3	30.1	19.6
France, 1954	62.6	49.8	41.5	33.3	23.1	16.8	55.9	34.4
Germany, East, 1950 [f]	70.1[e]	57.2[e]	47.7[1]	39.2[1]	25.6[1]	20.8[1]	67.6[1]	37.9
Germany, West, 1950 [g]	72.5	59.5	50.9	44.1	35.7	30.3	72.4[1]	51.2
Greece, 1951	55.4	42.0	36.3	28.1	16.2	12.7	36.8	22.0
Iraq, 1947	99.9	99.5	94.7	76.9	34.9	16.6	33.8	17.5
Italy, 1951	93.1	73.9	55.4	41.2	28.0	20.4	40.9[1]	27.3
Japan, 1950	98.0	75.1	53.9	42.4	33.2	25.6	37.5	36.3
Philippines, 1948	99.4	97.2	85.7	55.5	17.5	9.3	24.1	10.3
Spain, 1950 [h]	83.2	66.3	51.8	39.8	30.3	24.1	37.0	24.2
Switzerland, 1950	68.1	48.1	36.4	29.1	24.7	20.6	36.5	41.2
Thailand, 1947	100.0	99.9	99.4	95.2	57.4	13.3	9.9	6.8

[*] See text for a description of the three types of localities.

[**] Unless designated otherwise the percentages shown in these columns are based on figures reported in the *Demographic Yearbook, 1955*, Tables 7 and 8.

[***] Based on provisional figures prepared by International Urban Research.

[a] Excluding the Faeroe Islands; [b] Per cent urban for the year 1952; [c] 1951; [d] Urbanized Areas and incorporated or unincorporated places outside of Urbanized Areas treated as localities; [e] Estimate made by International Urban Research; [f] Including East Berlin; [g] Including West Berlin; [h] Including Canary Islands; [1] Census reports or official yearbooks used as source.

land area. For each country, as explained above, we utilize two kinds of data: our M.A. delimitations derived from the last census prior to 1954;[3] and the officially reported data on localities. Localities for which populations are officially reported fall into different classes according to how the areas are delimited by the government concerned; and this fact in part accounts for the scepticism of many people concerning the comparability of urban data from one country to another. The United Nations, in its latest report on the population of localities by countries,[4] distinguishes three classes, as follows: Type A—agglomerations or clusters of population without regard to official boundaries or administrative functions; Type B—localities having fixed boundaries and an administratively recognized "town" status, usually characterized by some form of local government operating under a charter or terms of incorporation, and normally called by some such term as "city," "borough," "urban district," or "municipality"; Type C—minor civil divisions (often the smallest of the administrative divisions) which have fixed boundaries and which together comprise the entire territory of the country.[5] Our analysis in this paper undertakes to deal with each of these classes separately. For officially reported populations of localities in each class we have drawn upon the valuable data provided by the United Nations Statistical Office in the *Demographic Yearbook* (cited above), where the localities are grouped by ten size-classes. It has proved necessary, however, to go beyond the Statistical Office's data, either by including additional countries or data on one of the types of locality not provided for a particular country.[6]

For each of the 50 countries the reader will find in Table 1 the percentage of the nation's total population residing in localities of six open-ended size-classes. The countries are grouped in this

[3] This dating was violated in two cases: France, where the census was taken *in* rather than *prior* to 1954, and Ceylon, where the census of 1946 was used instead of that of 1953 (which was unavailable).

[4] United Nations, *Demographic Yearbook,* 1955, New York: 1955, Table 8, pp. 198-215.

[5] *Ibid.,* p. 17.

[6] In the case of France, for example, the localities reported by the United Nations are minor civil divisions (Type C). We have made use of these figures in our analysis, but have also obtained data from French census reports on agglomerations (Type A).

TABLE 2

COEFFICIENTS OF CORRELATION (r) BETWEEN PER CENT IN METROPOLITAN AREAS AND SEVEN INDICES OF URBANIZATION BY COUNTRIES, *Circa* 1950

Countries by Type of Locality	Per Cent in Localities by Size Range						Per Cent Urban *
	2,000+	5,000+	10,000+	20,000+	50,000+	100,000+	
15 Countries with Type A Localities (urban aggregates or clusters)	+.91	+.96	+.96	+.96	+.96	+.95	+.94
30 Countries with Type B Localities (administratively demarcated "towns" and "cities")	+.92[a]	+.94[a]	+.95[a]	+.95[a]	+.95[a]	+.90[a]	+.92
14 Countries with Type C Localities (minor civil divisions)	−.56	−.68	−.68	−.59	−.19	+.59	+.86
Countries with Types A or B Localities	+.92[b]	+.95[b]	+.96[b]	+.95[b]	+.95[b]	+.91[b]	+.92[c]

* Per cent urban as administratively defined. These figures have no necessary connection with the types of localities as defined in the stub, but simply characterize the countries in question.

[a] Excluding Australia, N = 29. If Australia is included as a Type B country (N = 30), the correlations for each size-class, from left to right, are as follows: .93, .95, .95, .95, .89, and .74.

[b] Excluding Australia as a Type B country, N = 44. With Australia included as a Type B country (N = 45) the corresponding correlations, from left to right, are: .93, .95, .96, .95, .91, and .82.

[c] Excluding all Type B countries which are also included as a Type A, N = 42.

table according to the type of locality used as a reporting unit—Types A, B, and C. Some countries appear twice in the table because for them two types of localities are reported. To be sure, questions concerning the proper classification of countries by type of locality used as a reporting unit present a problem. In several cases it is difficult to ascertain the exact status of the localities, and in other cases it appears that the localities constitute a mixture of Types A and B. The seriousness of this problem is lessened, however, by our results, as will be seen presently.

Having, on the one hand, the percentage of the population living in M.A.s of 100,000 or over based on our own delimitations [7] and, on the other hand, the officially reported data for percentage "urban" and percentage in six size-classes of locality (grouped into three definition-classes), we proceeded to run correlations as a test of the validity of the officially reported information.

ANALYSIS OF FINDINGS

The results, shown in Table 2, strikingly belie the hypothesis that officially reported statistics on either urban agglomerations (Type A) or administratively defined cities and town (Type B) are grossly non-comparable as between countries. The product-moment coefficients of correlation(r) between the percentage in any size-class of urban agglomerations or clusters (Type A) and the percentage in M.A.s is .91 or above. As could be expected, the correlations are generally lower between the percentages in cities and towns defined administratively (Type B) and the proportion in M.A.s; but the difference between this and the Type A case is amazingly small.

Special interest attaches to the last column of Table 2. The proportion of the population said to be "urban" presumably varies from one country to the next in part because the dividing line between "rural" and "urban" is arbitrary and unstandardized. The United Nations *Demographic Yearbook* for 1955 (p. 16) lists several reasons for noncomparability in this respect, and Table 7 in this issue, showing the proportion urban by countries, is careful to include in each case the definition of "urban." [8] As the

---

[7] The M.A. percentages given in Table 1 must be considered provisional.

[8] The *Demographic Yearbook* for 1952 followed the same procedure in giving

last column of our Table 2 shows, however, the defects in the official distinction between "rural" and "urban," although real and admittedly undesirable, do not render meaningless the reported figures on the percentage urban. In fact, so long as the countries are using definitions that relate to Type A or Type B localities, regardless of the exact rural-urban dividing line they prescribe, the proportion urban constitutes an index of national urbanization that can be used with some degree of confidence.

Because the boundaries of Type A and Type B localities are drawn on a different basis, one might infer that an index of urbanization based on the one is not comparable with an index based on the other. Although this is true in the sense that there is an obvious danger in mixing the two, especially if individual countries are being compared, the fact remains that both classes are highly correlated with the proportion in M.A.s. Furthermore, when the two groups are combined, as in the last line of Table 2, the correspondence with the proportion in 100,000-plus M.A.s remains very high. We can thus conclude that in comparing groups of countries with reference to urbanization, those that define localities in Type A terms can be compared to those that define localities in Type B terms with relative safety.

Our results, however, are by no means uniformly positive. We shall have occasion below to sound a warning about the use of official data on urban places *in general.* For the moment, let us cite the results referring specifically to countries that publish data on localities defined in Type C terms. It will be recalled that these are minor civil divisions (usually the smallest in the country) which, taken together, comprise the entire national area. In other words, they are territorial divisions like "counties" in the United States, "taluks" or "thanas" in India, or "municipios" in Latin America. As shown by line 3 in Table 2, the proportion of the population in such localities by size-class varies inversely with the proportion of the population in Metropolitan Areas. The only exception involves the minor civil divisions having a population of 100,000 or more; for when they become this

---

data by countries for the proportion urban. It also included a discussion of the validity of the data, concluding (on pp. 9-10) that international comparisons of the percentage urban should be avoided "except in the most general way." However, it was found (p. 11) that the percentage urban correlates with the percentage in cities of 100,000 or more to the extent of 0.84.

large they apparently are in many cases urban and there is a correlation, albeit not a strong one, with the percentage in M.A.s. It seems clear that the proportion of the population in Type C localities, regardless of size-class, cannot be used with any security for purposes of international comparison.

A GENERAL WARNING

In addition to noting the unacceptability of Type C data for urban comparisons, it must be stressed that no international statistics on towns and cities should be used without critical examination. The point can be illustrated by reference to two cases, Australia and Thailand. Australia follows the extremely unusual practice of cutting up its urban agglomerations into very small politically-defined "cities." Therefore, if the figures for these "cities" (which are Type B units) are utilized uncritically as they stand, one winds up by reporting what is actually one of the world's most urbanized countries as having only 3 per cent of its population living in "cities" of 100,000 or more! When Australia is included in Table 2 as one of the countries in the Type B category, the correlations drop markedly, as shown in the table's footnotes. Fortunately, Australian census reports cover actual aggregates as well as politically defined places, and, as shown in Table 1, we need not depend on the Type B data for an index of urbanization in that country. But it is clear that uncritical use of Australian statistics for political localities might easily produce erroneous conclusions.

The case of Thailand shows the error of the uncritical use of the percentage urban as administratively defined. In this country the communes of more than 2,500 inhabitants are evidently designated in official reports as urban.[9] Since the commune is a minor civil division, this practice is tantamount to according urban

---

[9] *Statistical Yearbook of Thailand*, 1952, Bangkok: Central Statistical Office, 1953, Table 15, p. 42. Interestingly, the United Nations, in its *Demographic Yearbook*, 1955, p. 193, does not utilize the figures given in the Thai yearbook, but instead gives a much more realistic figure for the percentage urban—9.9. This is the figure we have used in Table 1. How this percentage was obtained is not known, but in another table, p. 207, the *Demographic Yearbook* places the Thai localities into Type C and gives figures showing 99.9 per cent of the population as living in localities of more than 5,000 inhabitants.

status to all counties in the United States having a population of, say, 10,000 or more.

When the percentage urban in Thailand as reported in the Thai Yearbook (90.85) is used rather than the figure provided by the U.N.'s Statistical Office, the correlation between the percentage urban and the percentage in M.A.s is +.69 among Type B countries, +.22 for Type C countries, and +.76 when Types A and B countries are combined. The discrepancy between these correlations and the corresponding ones in Table 2 indicates that the percentage urban as administratively defined may in certain isolated cases bear no relationship whatever to the true extent of urbanization in a country. This is particularly the case when, as in Thailand, the urban-rural distinction is based on the population size of minor civil divisions (Type C localities).

THE CUTTING POINT FOR THE RURAL-URBAN DISTINCTION

One reason, of course, why the correlations in Table 2 show so little variation is that the size-classes are open at the top and therefore cumulative. In other words, the size-class 5,000 and over behaves statistically much like the class 10,000 and over because it is made up principally by the latter class. In the United States, for example, the 10,000-plus class of places includes 90.1 per cent of the population of all places of 5,000-plus.

To what extent, then, will the size-classes correlate with the metropolitan percentage when they are defined as mutually exclusive classes? The expectation, of course, is that on the whole the correlations will be reduced—and this is what happens, as Table 3 shows. But the variations are interesting. In Column 1, for example, it appears that the percentage of the population in places of 2,000 to 5,000 bears no relation to the percentage in metropolitan areas of 100,000 or more. The explanation is doubtless the following: The proportion of people who live in places of this size is not a function primarily of economic development or per capita wealth, but a function of the pattern and the density of rural settlement. In a country such as India, for instance, the proportion in places of this size would be comparatively high, not because India is highly urbanized but because the Indian countryside is very densely settled and its rural people follow the custom of congregating in villages rather than living in isolated farmsteads. In the United States a lesser proportion can be expected to be in such places, because the farmers tend to live on farmsteads and the business people tend to live in places larger than 5,000. Inspection of the actual proportions shows the expectations to hold true, as follows:

POPULATION IN PLACES OF 2,000-4,999

	Number	As Per Cent of Total Population	As Per Cent of Population in All Places 2,000+
India, 1951, Type A	59,108,973	16.6	44.0
U.S.A., 1950, Type A	7,290,205	4.8	7.4

We know that the United States is far more urban than India. The fact that it has a lesser proportion in towns of 2,000 to 5,000 inhabitants has nothing to do with the degree of urbanization in the two countries but a great deal to do with the average density and the residential agglutination in rural areas.

The data of Table 3 suggest that the cutting point between rural and urban should not be assumed, as most governments so do, to be somewhere between 2,000 and 5,000. This may be the appropriate range for a cutting point in some countries but not in others. An arbitrary boundary applied to all countries within this range would thus lead to distortion rather than to comparability. Actually, the best cutting point probably does not lie even in the 5,000 to 10,000 range. If a lower limit to the size of places to be called urban is to be adopted for international comparison, we believe that it would best be set at nothing less than 10,000 population. This may seem unorthodox, but the fact is that at best we are always using an *index* of urbanization; there is no absolute measure. An index based on the proportion of the population in places of 10,000 and over will correlate highly with the proportion in Metropolitan Areas of 100,000 or over. Putting the floor at this level not only has the advantage that data are easier to secure, but the virtue that the distortion introduced by the "standard" definition as between one type of country and another is minimized.

TABLE 3

Coefficients of Correlation (r) between Per Cent in Metropolitan
Areas and Four Component Indices of Urbanization by
Countries, *Circa* 1950

Countries by Type of Locality	Per Cent in Localities by Size Range of Locality			
	2,000-4,999	5,000-9,999	10,000-19,999	20,000-49,999
Countries with Type A Localities N = 15	−.08	+.26	+.55	+.40
Countries with Type B Localities * N = 29	+.01	+.43	+.54	+.75
Countries with Types A or B Localities * N = 44	+.07	+.43	+.58	+.67

* Australia excluded as a Type B country.

THE DEVIANT CASES AND URBAN ANALYSIS

In all studies of statistical association, special interest attaches
to the deviant instances. In the present case, we may view the
marked divergence of any country from the regression line as an
invitation to investigate either the validity of the Metropolitan
Areas delimited for it or the validity of its reporting for Type A
or Type B localties.

In Figure I, which shows a scatter diagram involving countries that supply data on Type B localities, the United States
appears to be quite deviant, having a higher proportion in metropolitan areas than the percentage in cities and towns of 20,000
or more would seem to justify. Since the Standard Metropolitan
Areas delimited by the Census Bureau were used for the United
States, does this deviation from the trend line mean that the
S.M.A.s are larger than they should be, as many critics have
alleged; or does it mean that localities of over 20,000 are not fully
representative of the degree of urbanization because, by the Type
B definition, many places that are parts of big urban agglomerations are necessarily omitted? On the basis of Figure I alone, we
would have no way of settling this issue, but the solution is sug-

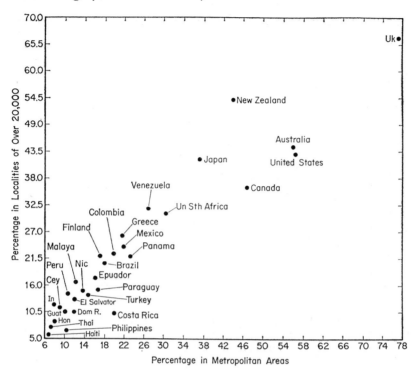

FIGURE I. The Relationship by Countries Between the Percentage of the Population in Type B Localities of Over 20,000 and the Percentage in Metropolitan Areas, *Circa* 1950.

gested by Figure II. There it is seen that when Type A units are used—that is, actual urban aggregations, in this case Urbanized Areas delimited by the Census Bureau—the proportion in M.A.s in the United States is much nearer the line of best fit. In other words, it looks as if the deviation of the United States in Figure I is the fault of the "cities of 20,000 and over" rather than the fault of the "Standard Metropolitan Areas."

A situation similar to that in the United States is found in the case of Australia. Whereas it deviates from the trend line in Figure I, it is very close to the line in Figure II. Thus, as suggested earlier, the Type A localities provide the most valid gauge of urbanization in Australia.

We cannot pursue this line of analysis in the present paper, but Figure I suggests that Canada, the United States, Australia,

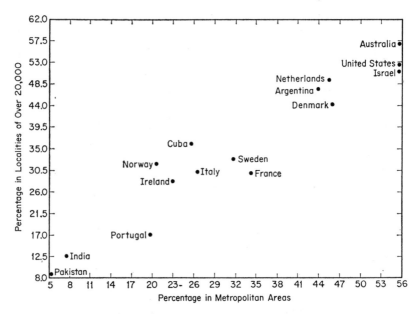

FIGURE II. The Relationship by Countries Between the Percentage of the Population in Type A Localities of Over 20,000 and the Percentage in Metropolitan Areas, *Circa* 1950.

and the United Kingdom all fail more than most countries to include the whole urban population in their administrative "cities" and "towns." In such countries there is particular reason to develop data of both the type called "metropolitan areas" and the type called "urbanized areas." Further analysis of this situation would greatly contribute to a clarification of the weaknesses and strengths of existing types of urban statistics.

CONCLUSION

Since official statistics on urbanization have been and will continue to be used for international comparisons, their validity should be assessed as carefully as possible. Although no absolute yardstick exists by which the accuracy of the official data can be judged, we have utilized as a means of assessment an index of urbanization that is more standardized than any other available —namely, the proportion in Metropolitan Areas of 100,000 or more inhabitants, areas we delimited according to common criteria.

The correlations between this index and indices of urbanization based on official statistics run so high as to justify the conclusion that the latter, when carefully selected and critically used, possess a high degree of validity for comparative research purposes. Since the individual researcher lacks the resources necessary to construct measures of urbanization that go beyond official statistics, this conclusion should encourage scholars to make full though careful use of officially published urban statistics for comparative research.

Of course, the results of our analysis do not prove that the boundaries of all cities are comparable. The findings indicate only that selected current official statistics on urban aggregates or administratively defined cities and towns (Type A and B localities) contain no bias so serious as to yield an unrealistic index of urbanization. The question of the comparability of the official boundaries of individual cities is a matter not dealt with here.

A further consequence of our investigation is the conclusion that the size-classes of places from 2,000 to 10,000 are of little use in constructing an index of the degree of urbanization. The frequency of towns of this range in a population is so much a matter of the particular circumstances of the country concerned that a standard definition of "urban" in terms of a cutting point within this range (for example, 2,500 inhabitants) would introduce distortion rather than standardization into comparative analysis. If a cutting point is desired, it seems better to take 10,000 as the floor of the "urban" class than anything smaller.

Finally, it is worth noting that the relationship between proportions urban according to reported urban statistics and the proportions urban according to M.A. data offers means of finding countries with weak types of statistics on either side. By developing estimating equations from the regression lines, the expected proportion of the population in "urban" or in "metropolitan" areas can be derived for any particular country. If the expected differs sharply from that actually found, this is a signal to investigate carefully the data making up the actual fractions on both sides of the equation.

Chapter 12

Systems of Cities

SOME MEASURES OF DEMOGRAPHIC AND SPATIAL RELATIONSHIPS AMONG CITIES *

HARLEY L. BROWNING AND JACK P. GIBBS **

This paper is devoted to an explication of methods for describing national and regional patterns in the size of cities and their location. We have undertaken this explication for two reasons. First, while methods for the study of individual cities and urbanization (in which all of the cities in a country or region are considered together in aggregate terms) are fairly well established, the same cannot be said for demographic and spatial relations among cities. And, secondly, as subsequent observations will indicate, there are grounds for believing that these relations are of considerable theoretical and practical importance.

We should first note that differences among countries and regions with regard to inter-urban demographic and spatial relations are often pronounced. For example, in certain cases we find that one city in a country is several times as large as any other city, while in other countries the first two cities are about the same size. Contrasts in spatial patterns are equally apparent, with cities highly concentrated in some countries but more or less evenly distributed in others.

These differences are interesting in themselves and call for explanation. But demographic-spatial relations do not exist in isolation; they are linked to other considerations. For one thing,

* Written especially for this volume.
** Members of the staff of International Urban Research.

there are reasons to believe that they partially reflect and condition functional relations [1] among cities. This is only a working hypothesis, of course, and it is not our intention to offer explanations of the various patterns that appear in demographic-spatial relations. In short, our concern is not with the causes and consequences of these patterns. We shall restrict our attention almost entirely to methods for describing the patterns in objective and standardized terms, since the formulation of such methods is a necessary first step in explaining national or regional differences in demographic-spatial relations among cities, and in determining their theoretical and practical significance.

We have selected methods on the basis of two guiding principles: 1) that they be uncomplicated and applicable to a variety of data, and 2) that they yield measures which make possible comparisons among countries and regions.

BOUNDING THE SYSTEM OF CITIES

Geographical limits. One notion underlying research on demographic-spatial relations is that the cities under consideration somehow constitute a "system" in the sense that the cities are related to each other in some orderly way.[2] Whether this is the case depends, at least in part, on the criteria for including or excluding cities; that is, of identifying the boundaries of the "system." One of the first concerns is, of course, the geographical limits. At present there can be no set rules in this regard, but the investigator should at least be aware of the consequences of his choice of boundaries.

In this paper, although the methods considered are applicable

---

[1] Functional relations, as opposed to those which are demographic or spatial, refer to the flow of goods and services among cities.

[2] The terminology in this field has not been standardized. A variety of terms with varying shades of meaning on an implicit rather than explicit basis are current: "network," "pattern," "spacing," "complex," "hierarchy," and "system," among others. We will not attempt here to make formal definitions of these terms except to note that "system" offers the most comprehensive means of characterizing the structure of relations among cities. By a system of cities we mean a configuration of urban centers interdependent to the point at which a change in one brings about a change in all others. Each system has a "vertical" dimension which appears in the order of cities according to their population size, amount of functions, and the size of their service areas. This order constitutes an urban hierarchy.

to any type of territory, nations will serve as the units of analysis.[3] National units offer two distinct advantages: 1) most countries, especially those with a long history, are viable economic, social, and cultural entities; and 2) national statistics are more readily available and standardized than is the case for international regions.

Population size limits. Once the geographical limits of the system of cities have been established there remains the decision as to the lower size limit of urban places. This decision will often be influenced by practical considerations, for even a moderate-sized country will have thousands of points of population concentration. It will also depend on whether a macroscopic or microscopic approach is to be used; if it is to be a comparative study involving a large number of countries this will impose limits on the amount of attention that can be devoted to each country.[4]

As in the case of geographical limits, most of the techniques in this paper can be readily adapted to a large or small number of cities; it is simply a matter of more or less work. The examples in this paper will be limited to the upper end of the urban hierarchy; nothing smaller than Metropolitan Areas [5] will be considered.

THE PRIMARY CITY AND VARIATIONS IN PRIMACY

Urbanization is never an even process. Some cities grow at a more rapid rate than others, and this differential growth is a source of concern for planners and for persons interested in eco-

[3] For certain purposes subnational systems may be established. For a study on this level see the article by Rupert B. Vance and Sara Smith on the hierarchy of major urban centers in the American South, "Metropolitan Dominance and Integration," in Rupert B. Vance and Nicholas T. Demerath (eds.), *The Urban South* (Chapel Hill: The University of North Carolina Press, 1954), Chapter 6.

[4] There can be no substitute for the painstaking and detailed investigation of individual countries, and studies of this kind are to be encouraged. Comparative research ideally should be able to draw upon the results of many thorough individual studies of countries in formulating general conclusions.

[5] A Metropolitan Area (or M.A.) is a territorial unit which contains either a city or continuous urban area of 50,000 or more inhabitants and all continuous civil divisions with not less than 65 per cent of the labor force engaged in nonagricultural industries. The minimum population size of a Metropolitan Area is set at 100,000 inhabitants. For a more complete description see International Urban Research, *The World's Metropolitan Areas* (Berkeley and Los Angles: University of California Press, 1959).

nomic development on the national level. It is often remarked, especially in underdeveloped countries, that the largest city, or "primary city" as we shall call it, is "disproportionately" large. These judgments, as a rule, are not made on the basis of objective standards. It is our purpose here to set forth methods which provide an objective description of the demographic position of the primary city within its national context.

Take six rather heterogeneous countries: France, Mexico, United Kingdom, United States, Brazil, and Italy. All have large total populations and numerous metropolitan centers, and their primary cities (really bounded as Metropolitan Areas, but for the sake of convenience we shall call them cities) all contain well over a million inhabitants. Let us first consider these primary cities with respect to their share of both the total population and the population in Metropolitan Areas.

Country	Primary City	Census Date	Population of Primary City	Per Cent Primary City is of National Population	Per Cent Primary City is of M.A. Population
France	Paris	1954	6,737,836	15.7	45.3
Mexico	Mexico City	1950	2,960,120	11.5	55.8
U.K.	London	1951	10,282,928	20.5	28.7
U.S.A.	New York City	1950	12,911,994	8.6	15.3
Brazil	Rio de Janeiro	1950	3,052,012	5.9	33.6
Italy	Milan	1951	1,972,980	4.2	16.5

SOURCE: The population figures for the primary city and the other Metropolitan Areas is taken from International Urban Research, *The World's Metropolitan Areas* (Berkeley and Los Angeles: The University of California Press, 1959).

Several points are of interest in this comparison. There is a considerable variation in the size of the primary cities and it is not closely correlated wth the size of the national population. As shown by the table, the primary city in a number of countries represents an important share of the total national population, and an even greater share of the total metropolitan population. On this basis alone the primary city is certain to have an important influence on any urban size hierarchy.

We have yet to consider the primary city in relation to units other than aggregate ones, such as total population or total metropolitan population. If we are to determine whether a given primary city is "disproportionate" in size, we must consider the relation of its population to that of the other major cities within the country; those cities which are likely "competitors" with the primary city.

For this purpose we need an index of the "primacy" of the first city. The simplest index is the ratio of the population of the first city to that of the second city: $I = \dfrac{P_1}{P_2}$, where "I" is the index of primacy, "P_1" is the population of the first city, and "P_2" is the population of the second city. This index can be computed for countries and for subnational or international systems of cities. Other indices, similarly constructed but using a larger number of cities, may be derived. Along with the "Two-City Index" just described let us also construct a "Four-City Index" ($I = \dfrac{P_1}{P_2 + P_3 + P_4}$) for each of the six countries.

	France	*Mexico*	*U.K.*	*U.S.A.*	*Brazil*	*Italy*
Two-City Index ...	7.49	7.15	4.08	2.35	1.25	1.12
Four-City Index ...	2.68	2.87	1.48	.95	.85	.49

The relations which now appear could not have been entirely predicted from the earlier table. In France, Paris is seven and one-half times larger than the second Metropolitan Area, the Lille-Roubaix-Tourcoing complex. At the other extreme the Milan Metropolitan Area of Italy is not much larger than that of Rome. The United States occupies a middle position, with New York more than twice as large as Chicago. The Four-City Index presents roughly the same relations as the Two-City Index, although inspection reveals that the effect of the third and fourth cities on the index varies appreciably from country to country.

These indices provide an objective basis for the ranking of countries according to high or low primacy, and thereby offer a way of assessing whether a primary city is "disproportionately" large. Beyond this, the primacy indices enable one to undertake studies of countries in order to determine what social and economic features are related to primacy variation.

THE RANK-SIZE RULE AND THE URBAN-SIZE
HIERARCHY

Research relating to an urban-size hierarchy is faced with
three questions:

Is the hierarchy different from what might be expected?;
Is the size of any particular city within the hierarchy more or less
what might be expected?;
How much does the hierarchy differ from that of other countries?

An answer to such questions presupposes the existence of some
standard to which the hierarchy may be compared. Measures of
the extent to which hierarchies deviate from the standard reveal
differences, if any, among the hierarchies themselves. On the
other hand, if the standard is to provide a basis for expecting a
city to have a certain size or for expecting a particular feature in
a size hierarchy, it must bear some correspondence to reality.
Our consideration of the use of a standard in constructing measures which describe urban size hierarchies may thus begin with
a question: Is there any basis for expecting a discernible pattern
in the size distribution of cities in a county? Certain observations
made over the last several decades would suggest an affirmative
reply to this question. These observations, most commonly associated with the name of George K. Zipf, have produced the idea
of the "rank-size rule." [6] Stated in its simplest form the rule depicts a harmonic progression of cities within the urban hierarchy,
such that if the population of the largest city is known the populations of all other cities can be derived from the rank of their
size. Thus, if the largest city has 1,000,000 inhabitants, the tenth
city will have one-tenth as many, or 100,000, and the hundredth
city will have one-hundredth as many, or 10,000.[7]

[6] Attesting to the fascination of the problem, a substantial literature continues
to be built up around this topic. For recent surveys see Brian J. L. Berry and
William L. Garrison, "Alternative Explanations of Urban Rank-Size Relationships," *Annals of the Association of American Geographers,* Vol. 48 (March,
1958), pp. 83-91; Otis Dudley Duncan, "The Measurement of Population Distribution," *Population Studies,* Vol. XI (July, 1957), pp. 27-45; and Charles T.
Stewart, Jr., "The Size and Spacing of Cities," *Geographical Review,* Vol. XLVIII
(April, 1958), pp. 222-245.

[7] This relationship can be expressed as: $Pi = \dfrac{Lc}{Ri}$, where Pi is the population
of a given city, Ri is the rank of the size of the city, and Lc the population of

TABLE 1

APPLICATION OF THE RANK-SIZE RULE TO THE METROPOLITAN AREAS OF MEXICO, 1950 *

Col. 1 Metropolitan Areas	Col. 2 Rank of Population Size	Col. 3 Reciprocal of Rank	Col. 4 Actual Population Size	Col. 5 Expected Population Size	Col. 6 Difference Between Expected and Actual Size	Col. 7 Difference as Per Cent of Actual Size	Col. 8 Difference as Per Cent of Expected Size
Mexico City	1	1.00000	2,960,120	1,668,603	1,291,517	43.6	77.4
Guadalajara	2	.50000	413,629	834,302	420,673	101.7	50.4
Monterrey	3	.33333	367,663	556,201	188,538	51.3	33.9
Puebla	4	.25000	250,961	417,151	166,190	66.2	39.8
Torreón–Gómez Palacio	5	.20000	231,673	333,721	102,048	44.0	30.6
Mérida	6	.16667	159,410	278,101	118,691	74.5	42.7
León	7	.14286	157,343	238,372	81,029	51.5	34.0
San Luis Potosí	8	.12500	155,238	208,575	53,337	34.4	25.6
Tampico	9	.11111	137,685	185,400	47,715	34.7	25.7
Ciudad Juárez	10	.10000	131,308	166,860	35,552	27.1	21.3
Aguascalientes	11	.09091	118,434	151,691	33,257	28.1	21.9
Chihuahua	12	.08333	112,466	139,050	26,584	23.6	19.1
Veracruz	13	.07692	110,443	128,354	17,911	16.2	14.0
ΣX	—	3.18013	5,306,373	5,306,381	2,583,042	596.9	436.4
ΣX/N**	—	—	408,183	408,183	198,696	45.9	33.6

* SOURCE OF DATA: International Urban Research, *The World's Metropolitan Areas* (Berkeley and Los Angeles: University of California Press, 1959).

** N = 13

Our use of the simplified rank-size rule should not be taken to suggest that we believe it provides an adequate description of all urban hierarchies. We shall merely use it as a standard for constructing measures which reflect differences among hierarchies and as a basis for deriving an expected population size for each city in any given hierarchy.

There are a number of ways to express the rank-size relation and deviations from it. One is to plot rank by size of place on a logarithmic-scale graph. Another way is to calculate both the number of places and the populations which would be anticipated for various size classes and to compare these figures with the actual distribution.[8] Our procedure will be to apply the simplified rank-size model to a limited number of urban places at the upper end of the size hierarchy—Metropolitan Areas—and derive the expected populations for each of the M.A.'s. The detailed steps in deriving the rank-size expected populations of Metropolitan Areas are as follows:

1) Arrange the Metropolitan Areas according to their population size and assign a rank to each. 2) Determine the reciprocal of each rank-number. 3) Sum the reciprocals. 4) Sum the populations of all of the M.A.'s. 5) Divide the total M.A. population by the sum of the reciprocals; the resulting figure is the expected size of the first and largest M.A. 6) Divide the expected population of the first M.A. by two to get the expected population of the second M.A., by three to get the expected population of the third M.A., and so on, until expected populations for all M.A.'s are derived. 7) Sum the expected populations of all of the M.A.'s. As a check this total should very closely approximate the sum of the actual populations.[9]

Table 1 illustrates each of the above steps as applied to the Metropolitan Areas of Mexico, with expected populations shown in column 5. The figures in the column are, of course, purely hypothetical, since they represent what the size of each Metro-

---

the largest city. In practice the population of the largest city is often modified by a constant to provide a better fit to the distribution.

[8] For these methods applied to the United States of 1950 see Otis Dudley Duncan and Albert J. Reiss, Jr., *Social Characteristics of Urban and Rural Communities, 1950* (New York: John Wiley & Sons, 1956), pp. 26-27.

[9] While the units considered here are Metropolitan Areas, the procedures described are applicable to all types of urban places (cities, urban areas, etc.).

politan Area would be if all of them conformed to the rank-size rule.[10] A comparison of columns 4 and 5 will reveal that the expected and the actual size distribution are by no means the same. To express the degree of correspondence between the actual and expected distributions in terms of an over-all index of deviation from the rank-size rule we sum the absolute differences in column 6 and divide the total by two. The resulting quotient is then expressed as a per cent of the total metropolitan population. This represents the per cent of metropolitan residents who would have to move from one M.A. to another one to bring about a perfect correspondence between the urban hierarchy and the rank-size rule. The per cent for Mexico is 24.3.

The index described above is a good over-all measure of the lack of conformity to the rank-size rule (the greater the per cent, the less the conformity), but it suffers from the fact that it may be influenced a great deal by only one or two of the large urban centers. Mexico City, for example, accounts for about one-half of the total amount of deviation for all M.A.'s.

To establish the average discrepancy between the actual and expected size of individual places independent of their size, we utilize the figures in column 7 of Table 1. These represent the difference between the actual and expected size of each M.A. as a per cent of the actual size. The number in each case represents the per cent that the population of the M.A. would have to increase or decrease,[11] to bring about a correspondence between actual and expected size. When the sum of these figures is divided by the number of M.A.'s, the resulting quotient is the average amount that the M.A.'s would have to increase or decrease (in percentage terms) to fit the rank-size rule. As shown at

---

[10] We do not say that the expected populations of the Metropolitan Areas are based on the assumption that the entire urban hierarchy conforms to the rank-size rule. This goes back to our earlier remarks about the bounding systems of cities by population size limits. Our system of units is not the entire urban hierarchy but only a part of it—all Metropolitan Areas. If we were to take, as Duncan and Reiss do for the United States, all places of 1,000 or more in arriving at a rank-size formula, we would come out with different expected populations than are reported here. We are only concerned with the way in which Metropolitan Areas are related to each other. Other selections are possible, of course; one may compare for example the distributional patterns of the first 10 or 20 cities of a number of countries.

[11] The question of the direction of the deviation (i.e., whether the M.A. is too large or too small) will be considered in a later section.

the bottom of column 7, this summary figure is 45.9 for Mexico ($596.9/13 = 45.9$).

Another means of describing the correspondence between the urban hierarchy and the rank-size rule is provided by the figures in column 8, where the difference between the actual and expected size of each M.A. is expressed as a per cent of the expected population. These figures show the per cent error in predicting the population of a M.A. on the basis of the rank-size rule. Thus, as shown at the bottom of column 8, the expected population of an M.A. in Mexico is, on the average, 33.6 per cent above or below the actual size of the M.A.

Each of the above measures indicates that Mexico's metropolitan hierarchy deviates considerably from that anticipated on the basis of the rank-size rule. However, as can be seen in Table 2, not all countries deviate from the rule as much as Mexico. There is in fact considerable variation among the countries, which suggests that the measure is sensitive to differences in size hierarchies. And, as the last two columns of the table indicate, the measure is independent of both the number of M.A.'s and the size of the total metropolitan population.

Patterns in deviation. The measures shown in Table 2 indicate only the amount of deviation from the rank-size rule and not the pattern of deviation among the individual Metropolitan Areas. Certain types of patterns do appear and, as we shall see, they vary in character from one country to another. The possible patterns with regard to the size of Metropolitan Areas are:

(A) The larger the M.A. the greater the discrepancy between its actual and expected size.

(B) The smaller the M.A. the greater the discrepancy between its actual and expected size.

(C) No discernible connection between the size of an M.A. and the extent of the discrepancy between its actual and expected size.

(D) The larger the M.A. the more its expected size exceeds its actual size.

(E) The smaller the M.A. the more its expected size exceeds its actual size.[12]

---

[12] Patterns A and B refer only to the extent of deviation, while D and E take into account both the extent and direction of deviation.

TABLE 2

SUMMARY MEASURES OF THE DEVIATION OF METROPOLITAN AREAS FROM
THE RANK-SIZE RULE: SIX COUNTRIES

Col. 1	*Col. 2*	*Col. 3*	*Col. 4*	*Col. 5*	*Col. 6*
		Average Deviation of Metropolitan Areas			
		Difference Between Actual and Expected Size as Per Cent of Actual Size °°	*Difference Between Actual and Expected Size as Per Cent of Expected Size* °°°		
Countries and Year	*Over-all Deviation from Rank-Size Rule* °			*Metropolitan Population*	*Number of M.A.'s*
Brazil, 1950	16.1	45.1	33.4	9,094,368	16
Canada, 1956 ...	9.3	11.5	12.2	7,181,775	13
France, 1954	20.2	26.0	20.4	14,877,774	30
Italy, 1951	9.3	8.8	9.2	11,926,676	28
Mexico, 1950 ...	24.3	45.9	33.6	5,306,373	13
Netherlands, 1947	10.5	12.0	12.8	4,381,346	14

° Per cent of metropolitan residents who would have to move out of one M.A. and into another to bring about a perfect correspondence between the rank-size rule and the metropolitan size hierarchy.

°° Figures indicate the average per cent that each M.A. would have to increase or decrease to conform to the rank-size rule.

°°° Average per cent error in predicting the actual size of a M.A. from its expected size.

(F) No discernible connection between the size of an M.A. and the direction of its deviation from the rank-size rule.[13]

The discrepancy between actual and expected size for Mexico's Metropolitan Areas is expressed as a per cent of the actual size in column 2 of Table 3 and as a per cent of the expected size in column 5.[14]

[13] As subsequent measures of the relation between size and deviation from the rank-size rule will show, the presence or absence of each of the six patterns (A–F) in a country is a matter of degree. Patterns A and B form a continuum, with pattern C representing the midpoint. Patterns D and E form a second continuum, with F at the midpoint.

[14] It is necessary to express the difference between actual and expected size in percentage terms, because the discrepancy can be much greater for large M.A.'s than for small ones.

A minus sign before a number in the second column indicates the M.A.'s size would have to decrease to conform to the rank-size expectation, while a positive sign indicates that an increase would be required. Mexico City, for example, would have to decrease its population 43.6 per cent, but Guadalajara would have to increase 101.7 per cent.

A minus sign before a number in column 5 indicates that the actual ex-

The rank of the numbers shown in column 2 are given in column 3, with the signs ignored (i.e., only the amount that the M.A. would have to increase or decrease is considered). If pattern A holds in Mexico, we should find that the ranks in column 3 agree closely with the ranks of population size in column 8, but if pattern B holds there should be an inverse relation between the ranks. The rank-order coefficient of correlation *(rho)*[15] is +.80, which reveals that pattern A prevails in Mexico and to a very high degree. In short, the larger the population size of an M.A., the greater is the discrepancy between its actual and its expected size. Pattern A also prevails when the discrepancy is expressed as a per cent of the expected rather than the actual size. *Rho* between the ranks in columns six and eight is +.92.

The presence of pattern A in a country indicates only that as the M.A.'s increase in size, the more do they deviate from the rank-size rule; it does not indicate whether pattern D or pattern E prevails (i.e., whether size is correlated directly or inversely with the excess of the expected size over the actual size).

To establish the presence or absence of patterns D and E, the signs of the number in column 2 must be taken into account. This is done in column 4, where the M.A. with the greatest excess of expected over actual size is assigned the rank of 1 (Guadalajara) and the M.A. with the least excess (Mexico City, where the actual size exceeds the expected size) is assigned a rank of 13. *Rho* between the ranks shown in columns 4 and 8 is +.49, which indicates that as the size of the M.A.'s increases the more the expected population exceeds the actual population. Thus, pattern D prevails in Mexico, and also it prevails when the excess of the expected over the actual is considered as a per cent of the expected (see column 5). *Rho* between the ranks in columns 7 and 8 is again +.49.

Two features of the patterns in Mexico's metropolitan size hierarchy should be noted. First, it is of significance that there is some discernible association between the size of M.A.'s and the

---

ceeds the expected size, while a positive sign indicates that the reverse is true. Thus, the expected size of Mexico City is 77.4 per cent too low, and the expected size of Guadalajara is 50.4 per cent too high.

[15] $Rho = 1 - 6\Sigma d^2/N(N^2 - 1)$ where d is the difference between each pair of ranks and N is the number of cases (thirteen M.A.'s in this instance).

TABLE 3

DIFFERENCE BETWEEN THE ACTUAL SIZE OF METROPOLITAN AREAS IN MEXICO AND THEIR EXPECTED SIZE ACCORDING TO THE RANK-SIZE RULE, 1950 *

Col. 1 Metropolitan Areas	Col. 2 Expected Size Minus Actual Size As Per Cent of Actual Size **	Col. 3 Rank of Col. 2, Ignoring Signs	Col. 4 Rank of Col. 2, Considering Signs	Col. 5 Expected Size Minus Actual Size as Per Cent of Expected Size ***	Col. 6 Rank of Col. 5, Ignoring Signs	Col. 7 Rank of Col. 5, Considering Signs	Col. 8 Rank of Actual Population Size
Mexico City	−43.6	7	13	−77.4	1	13	1
Guadalajara	+101.7	1	1	+50.4	2	1	2
Monterrey	+51.3	5	5	+33.9	6	5	3
Puebla	+66.2	3	3	+39.8	4	3	4
Torreón—Gómez Palacio	+44.0	6	6	+30.6	7	6	5
Mérida	+74.5	2	2	+42.7	3	2	6
León	+51.5	4	4	+34.0	5	4	7
San Luis Potosí	+34.4	9	8	+25.6	9	8	8
Tampico	+34.7	8	7	+25.7	8	7	9
Ciudad Juárez	+27.1	11	10	+21.3	11	10	10
Aguascalientes	+28.1	10	9	+21.9	10	9	11
Chihuahua	+23.6	12	11	+19.1	12	11	12
Veracruz	+16.2	13	12	+14.0	13	12	13

* Data drawn from Table 1.

** Per cent figures indicate how much each Metropolitan Area would have to increase (plus sign) or decrease (minus sign) to conform to the rank-size rule.

*** Per cent figures indicate amount of error in predicting actual from expected size, with a plus sign indicating an over-estimate and a minus sign indicating an underestimate.

extent to which they deviate from the rank-size rule. Second, size is correlated far more closely with the extent of deviation than with the direction of the deviation.

While the procedures described above provide standardized measures of certain patterns in the deviation of urban places from the rank-size rule, they are useful only insofar as these patterns actually appear in different countries. If Mexico were the only country in which there is some order in deviation, or if approximately the same pattern appeared in all countries, the measures would be of little value in comparative research.

Any doubts on the matter should be allayed by the findings reported in Table 4. There is actually a variety of patterns which are present in the different countries. The correlation between the size of Metropolitan Areas and deviation from the rank-size rule varies, depending on the country and the measure considered, from —.77 to +.92. Thus, pattern A is found in France and Mexico, but in contrast, pattern B is remarkably strong in Brazil. Further, a mixture of patterns C, D, E, and F is found among the six countries.

TABLE 4

CORRELATIONS (*Rho's*) BETWEEN THE SIZE OF METROPOLITAN AREAS AND VARIOUS MEASURES OF THE DISCREPANCY BETWEEN THEIR ACTUAL POPULATION AND THAT EXPECTED ON THE BASIS OF THE RANK-SIZE RULE WITHIN SIX COUNTIES

| | Correlation of the Size of Metropolitan Areas with: | | | |
| | Difference Between Actual and Expected Size | | Expected Size Minus Actual Size | |
Countries and Year [*]	As Per Cent of Actual Size [**]	As Per Cent of Expected Size [**]	As Per Cent of Actual Size [***]	As Per Cent of Expected Size [***]
Brazil, 1950	—.70	—.47	—.77	—.77
Canada, 1956 ...	+.29	+.24	+.49	+.49
France, 1954 ...	+.63	+.64	+.44	+.44
Italy, 1951	+.47	+.46	—.18	—.18
Mexico, 1950 ...	+.80	+.92	+.49	+.49
Netherlands, 1947	+.36	+.35	+.23	+.23

[*] Number of Metropolitan Areas: Brazil, 16; Canada, 13; France, 30; Italy, 28; Mexico, 13; Netherlands, 14.

[**] Positive coefficients indicate that size varies directly with the magnitude of the discrepancy between actual and expected size.

[***] Positive coefficients indicate that size varies directly with the amount that the expected size exceeds the actual size.

THE STABILITY OF THE URBAN SIZE HIERARCHY

Up to this point our comparisons and illustrations have been restricted to one point in time. All of the methods we have presented, however, can be used as readily for comparisons of the same country at different times, and such comparisons reveal the extent to which the urban size hierarchy has remained stable over the period. There are two ways of treating a system of cities with regard to stability. One method, the "class" method, considers all of the cities in a country above a given minimum size limit at one point in time and all cities of this size at a later point in time, ignoring the fact that cities may have been added or dropped during the period. The other method, the "city" method, considers the same cities at both the start and end of the period, which is the procedure followed here.

Our first concern is with stability in the characteristics of the entire size distribution, ignoring the fact that individual cities may have increased their population at a rate substantially more or less than other cities. One measure of this aspect of stability is a change in the conformity of the urban size hierarchy to the rank-size rule.

In the preceding section an index of over-all deviation from the rank-size rule (the per cent of people who would have to move from one M.A. to another one to bring about complete conformity to the rank-size rule) was computed for a number of countries. Now let us compare conformity to the rank-size rule for the same countries for census dates twenty to thirty-five years earlier than the ones already presented. The results are presented below: *

	Brazil 10 Cities (1920; 1950)	Canada 13 M.A.'s (1921; 1956)	France 30 M.A.'s (1926; 1954)	Italy 28 Cities (1921; 1951)	Mexico 13 Cities (1930; 1950)	Netherlands 14 Cities (1920; 1947)
Earlier date..	8.2	9.0	19.5	13.3	18.1	11.1
Later date ..	13.2	9.3	20.2	9.0	21.5	10.4

* City limits have been used for those countries where it was not feasible to retroject the boundaries of M.A.'s.

We will not attempt to analyze these findings except to note that 1) the two countries indicating little change, Canada and

France, had quite different metropolitan and national growth rates during their time periods, and 2) it is the two most underdeveloped countries, Brazil and Mexico, that show the greatest movement away from conformity to the rank-size rule.

Another aspect of change in the urban-size hierarchy is the movement of individual cities within the hierarchy. If the rates of growth for all cities during a period are the same, there is no change in their ranks within the hierarchy. Thus a comparison of the size ranks of cities at one point in time with that at a later time reveals how much movement has taken place during the period. A summary measure in this case is provided by a rank-order coefficient of correlation between the size ranks of cities at two points in time.[16]

If we take the same countries, the same urban units, and the same time periods reported in the above table, the rank-order correlations, *rho*'s, are as follows: Brazil, +.81; Canada, +.87; France, +.97; Italy, +.97; Mexico, +.88; Netherlands, +.82. It is to be expected that France, which did not have much urban growth during the interval, would not change as much as the rapidly growing M.A.'s of Brazil. We need not go into the implications of stability or instability of city ranking except to say that instability suggests uneven economic development of different regions within a country. The major exception to this generalization is functionally specialized cities, such as manufacturing centers, which do not rely on the prosperity of the surrounding region.[17]

SPATIAL RELATIONSHIPS AMONG CITIES

If it were possible to view a country, or any other large area, from an immense height we would be able to see the arrange-

[16] Such a measure is applicable, of course, only when the "city" method is used.

[17] Not very much work has been done with this method. It is described and given preliminary testing in A. J. Jaffe, "The Stability of Cities; Some Considerations and Calculations," mimeographed report, Bureau of Applied Social Research, Columbia University, 1951. Kingsley Davis discusses the changes in the ranks of the largest cities of pre-partition India in his *Population of India and Pakistan* (Princeton: Princeton University Press, 1951), pp. 131-132. Carl Madden has used more complicated procedures in "Some Temporal Aspects of the Growth of Cities in the United States," *Economic Development and Cultural Change*, Vol. VI (Jan., 1958), pp. 143-169.

ment of urban centers as they are distributed over the land and to note the concentration or dispersion of these cities. As in the case of the population size ranking of cities, the question arises as to whether there is any identifiable pattern in the spatial distribution of urban centers. This problem has interested a number of scholars, for it has long been assumed that the locational patterns in some way reflect and condition functional relations among cities. Various models and explanations of these patterns have been put forward,[18] but there has been insufficient work in establishing the patterns for various countries in comparable terms. This information is, of course, needed for the evaluation of the adequacy of existing theories and the formulation of new ones.

The importance of spatial relations among cities is obvious, even though the different patterns cannot be fully explained. For example, the distance separating cities sets limits, relative to the mode of transportation and communication, on the flow of goods and services between them. This suggests the possibility that, modes of transportation and communication being the same, functional specialization is more likely to occur among cities which are located in close proximity to each other, and if the distance separating a particular city from other centers is markedly different from the national pattern, it could conceivably make the city atypical as far as economic characteristics are concerned. However, whether the subject is a particular city or all of the cities in a country, some method must be used to describe national patterns in the spatial distribution of urban centers.

If it were simply a matter of representing our bird's eye view of the spatial distribution of urban centers, some form of cartographic representation would be satisfactory. Concern with a comparative mode of investigation makes it necessary, however, to employ a standardized measure which can be applied to any

[18] See Edward Ullman, "A Theory of Location for Cities," *American Journal of Sociology*, Vol. 46 (May, 1941), pp. 853-864, for a review of the literature on the subject. Since Ullman's paper, three books that bear directly on the subject have been published: Walter Isard, *Location and Space Economy* (New York: John Wiley and Sons, Inc., 1956); Edgar M. Hoover, *The Location of Economic Activity* (New York: McGraw-Hill Book Company, Inc., 1948); August Lösch, *Economics of Location* (New Haven, Connecticut: Yale University Press, 1953).

number of areas and the results easily compared. To this end we shall present a few uncomplicated methods for describing some of the less complex spatial relations among the Metropolitan Areas of a country.

We know from experience that in some countries the major urban centers tend to be concentrated in certain regions, while in other countries they are more evenly dispersed throughout the land. How can these differences be expressed in quantitative terms? If the number of urban centers and the area of a country are known, we can determine what the approximate distance between each center and its nearest neighbor would be under conditions of an even spatial distribution. This hypothetical distance can be computed on the basis of a simple formula:

$$\mathrm{Hd} = 1.11\sqrt{\frac{A}{N}}$$

where *Hd* is the hypothetical distance, *A* is the area of the country (in square miles or kilometers), and *N* is the number of centers.[19]

The above formula has been applied to the Metropolitan Areas of six countries, with the results shown in column 5 of Table

[19] See James A. Barnes and Arthur H. Robinson, "A New Method for the Representation of Dispersed Rural Population," *Geographical Review,* Vol. 30 (January, 1940), pp. 134-137, for a discussion of the mathematical basis of this formula.

TABLE 5

ACTUAL AND HYPOTHETICAL MEAN DISTANCE BETWEEN METROPOLITAN AREAS AND NEAREST METROPOLITAN AREA: SIX COUNTRIES

Col. 1	Col. 2	Col. 3	Col. 4	Col. 5 Hypothetical	Col. 6
Country and Year	Number of M.A.'s	Area in Square Miles	Actual Mean Distance Between M.A.'s and Nearest M.A.°	Mean Distance Under Con- ditions of an Even Spatial Distribution of M.A.'s °	Actual Mean Distance as Per Cent of Hypo- thetical
Brazil, 1950	16	3,287,195	154	502	30.7
Canada, 1956	13	3,851,106	171	604	28.3
France, 1954	30	212,821	59	93	63.4
Italy, 1951	28	116,303	43	71	60.6
Mexico, 1950	13	760,335	160	269	59.5
Netherlands, 1947	14	12,529	22	33	66.7

° Direct line distance in statute miles.

TABLE 6

DISTANCE BETWEEN EACH METROPOLITAN AREA IN MEXICO AND ITS NEAREST NEIGHBOR AND NEAREST LARGER NEIGHBOR, 1950

Col. 1 Metropolitan Areas	Col. 2 Distance Between Each M.A. and Its Nearest Neighbor*	Col. 3 Deviation of Distance of Each M.A. from National Mean	Col. 4 Rank of Distance Between M.A. and Its Nearest Neighbor	Col. 5 Rank of Population Size	Col. 6 Size Rank Ignoring Mexico City	Col. 7 Rank of Distance Between M.A. and Nearest Larger M.A.	Col. 8 Distance Between M.A. and Nearest Larger M.A.*
Mexico City	70	90	10.5	1	—	—	—
Guadalajara	110	50	8	2	1	4	285
Monterrey	200	40	5	3	2	3	390
Puebla	70	90	10.5	4	3	11	70
Torreón—Gómez Palacio	200	40	5	5	4	6.5	200
Mérida	435	275	1	6	5	1	565
León	65	95	12.5	7	6	9	110
San Luis Potosí	87	73	9	8	7	10	87
Tampico	200	40	5	9	8	6.5	200
Ciudad Juárez	220	60	2.5	10	9	2	460
Aguascalientes	65	95	12.5	11	10	12	65
Chihuahua	220	60	2.5	12	11	5	220
Veracruz	135	25	7	13	12	8	135
ΣX	2,077	1,033	—	—	—	—	2,787
ΣX/N	160[a]	79[b]	—	—	—	—	232[a]

* Direct line distance in statute miles.
[a] National mean distance.
[b] Average deviation of Metropolitan Areas from national mean.

5. The figures given there indicate what the mean (average) distance between M.A.'s and their nearest neighbors would be under a condition of an even spatial distribution of M.A.'s throughout the country.[20] Comparisons of the actual and the hypothetical mean distance figures reveal that the latter exceed the former in all six countries. If the actual distance equalled the hypothetical, there would be no concentration of M.A.'s; accordingly, when the actual distance is expressed as a per cent of the hypothetical (column 6), the resulting figure is a measure of the extent to which the M.A.'s are dispersed rather than concentrated, with values approaching 0.0 indicating minimum dispersion and values approaching 100.0 indicating maximum dispersion. The results reported in column 6 of Table 5 conform to our general knowledge of the countries. Brazil and Canada are very different from the other countries and their low values are not just a reflection of huge land areas but of large virtually uninhabited regions. Similarly, Netherlands has the highest value not because of a small land area but because virtually all of its land area is inhabited.

Another feature of the spatial distribution of urban centers in a country is the regularity in the distance between M.A.'s and their nearest neighbors. If a regularity exists, the distance separating each M.A. from its nearest neighbor would be close to the mean distance for all of the M.A.'s in the country. Accordingly, the average deviation of the M.A.'s from the national mean provides an indication of regularity in the distance separating M.A.'s and their nearest neighbors.

The procedure for determining the average deviation of the distance between M.A.'s and their nearest neighbor is stated below, with each step illustrated by Table 6.

(1) Determine the distance between each M.A. and its nearest neighbor and the mean of these distances (column 2). (2) Determine the deviation of each M.A. from the national mean (column 3). (3) Sum the differences between each M.A. and the national mean (second figure from bottom of column 3). (4) Divide this sum by the number of urban centers (figure at bottom of column 3), and

---

[20] Only Metropolitan Areas are considered in this study, and the "nearest neighbor" is always another M.A.

the resulting quotient indicates how much each center differs on the average from the national mean.

The average deviation of the distances between M.A.'s and their nearest neighbors from the national mean (all M.A.'s) is shown in column 3 of Table 7. These numbers should not be

TABLE 7

MEAN DISTANCE BETWEEN METROPOLITAN AREAS AND THEIR NEAREST
NEIGHBORS: SIX COUNTRIES

Col. 1 Country and Year	Col. 2 Mean Distance Between M.A.'s and Nearest M.A.'s °	Col. 3 Average Deviation of M.A.'s from Mean Distance	Col. 4 Average Deviation as Per Cent of Mean
Brazil, 1950	154	99	64.3
Canada, 1956	171	124	72.5
France, 1954	59	25	42.4
Italy, 1951	43	28	65.1
Mexico, 1950	160	79	49.4
Netherlands, 1947....	22	14	63.6

° Direct line distance in statute miles.

compared without taking the size of the country into account, since the greater the mean distance between M.A.'s and their nearest neighbors the more it is possible for individual M.A.'s to deviate from the pattern. This factor is taken into account in column 4 by expressing the average deviation as a per cent of the mean distance, with each percentage figure providing a gauge of the irregularity in the spacing of Metropolitan Areas: the lower the per cent the more regular is the spacing. Thus, of the six countries, the M.A.'s of France are the most regularly spaced, while a high degree of irregularity characterizes the spatial distribution of M.A.'s in Canada.

Size of urban centers as a factor in the spatial patterns. Heretofore we have considered urban centers simply as points in space, without regard to any of their other characteristics. It so happens, however, that all observations on patterns in the location of urban centers suggest some connection between the non-spatial characteristics of urban centers and inter-urban distance.

Two characteristics of urban centers have received a great deal of attention in considerations of locational patterns: (1)

the nature and amount of the services which they provide for surrounding territory and other centers, and (2) their population size. Of the two we shall concern ourselves here with population size.

Size is considered not only because the focus is on demographic relations among cities, but also because it is one of the major variables in Christaller's theory of locational patterns [21]—a theory which has influenced much subsequent work.

Christaller's scheme depicts cities as performing "central" functions (i.e., services) for the surrounding territory. This territory, the service area, has an areal extent in direct proportion to the size of the urban center. The service areas of some urban centers overlap, with parts of the area of a smaller center being contained in the area of the closest larger center, but the areas of centers of approximately the same size do not overlap.

This arrangement produces a particular type of spatial pattern, the essential features of which are:

(1) A somewhat regular distance between each urban center and its nearest neighbor.

(2) The greater the size of the urban center the greater the distance between it and the nearest larger center.

We are not here concerned with the assumptions underlying Christaller's scheme, nor with the causes and consequences of deviation from the pattern.[22] We are concerned only with the formulation of methods for measuring the relationship between size and locational factors. If Christaller's scheme applies to the locational pattern of Metropolitan Areas, we should expect to find that the size of a M.A. bears little relation to the distance between it and its nearest neighbor. This calls for a standardized measure of the relation between the size of M.A.'s and the distance between them and their nearest neighbors. An uncomplicated measure is provided by a rank-order coefficient of correlation (*rho*). We may illustrate the procedure followed in computing *rho* with data from Table 6. In column 4 we find the ranks of the distance between each M.A. and its nearest neighbor,[23] and

[21] Walter Christaller, *Die zentralen Orte in Süddeutschland* (Jena: 1935).

[22] See Ullman, *op. cit.*, for a summary of criticisms of Christaller's scheme.

[23] Our measure of distance is in statute miles. Undoubtedly a more meaningful measure would be one in terms of time-cost units along transportation routes.

in column 5 we find the rank of each M.A.'s population size. The application of the *rho* formula to these two sets of ranks results in a coefficient of —.18, which indicates in Mexico the distance between a M.A. and its nearest neighbor is not closely related to the size of the M.A. This feature of the locational pattern shows some consistency with Christaller's scheme.

The second demographic-spatial connection suggested by Christaller's scheme is that of a direct relationship between the size of an M.A. and the distance separating it from the nearest larger M.A. Once again a simple measure of the relation is provided by *rho*. Its computation in the case of Mexico is based on the ranks of the population size of the M.A.'s (see column 6 of Table 6) and the ranks of the distance between each M.A. and the nearest larger M.A. (see column 7).[24] The *rho* coefficient in this case is +.23. The direction of the correlation is as anticipated by Christaller's scheme (the larger the M.A. the greater the distance to its nearest larger neighbor), but the magnitude of the coefficient indicates that size is not a crucial factor in this feature of the locational pattern in Mexico.[25]

The correlations reported for Mexico should not be interpreted to mean that the relationship between the size of M.A.'s

[24] The largest urban center, Mexico City in this case, must be excluded in computing *rho* because the distance measure in question does not apply to it.

[25] The distance relations considered in this paper by no means exhaust all of the possibilities. One of the other measures which could be considered is distance to all centers.

TABLE 8

CORRELATIONS (*Rho*) WITHIN COUNTRIES BETWEEN SIZE OF METROPOLITAN AREAS AND DISTANCE TO OTHER METROPOLITAN AREAS

Country and Year	Correlation of Size of Metropolitan Areas with:	
	Distance to Nearest Metropolitan Area	Distance to Nearest Larger Metropolitan Area *
Brazil, 1950	+.01	+.62
Canada, 1956	—.32	+.32
France, 1954	—.34	+.29
Italy, 1951	+.37	+.72
Mexico, 1950	—.18	+.23
Netherlands, 1947	+.13	+.39

* Largest M.A. in country not included.

and their distance from other M.A.'s is negligible in all countries. On the contrary, Table 8 shows that both the strength and direction of the relation vary considerably from one country to another. In Italy, for example, there is some tendency for large M.A.'s to be located at a considerable distance from other M.A.'s, but the reverse is true for Canada and France. Variability in the relation between the size of M.A.'s and distance to the nearest larger M.A. is equally striking, with *rho* for Brazil and Italy ($+.62$ and $+.72$) being well above that of the other countries.

SUMMARY AND CONCLUSIONS

We have considered a number of methods for treating demographic and spatial relationships among the cities of a country or region. These methods provide standardized measures of:

1) the relation of the size of the largest or primary city to that of other major cities,
2) the conformity of the urban size hierarchy to a set standard (the simplified rank-size rule),
3) the patterns among cities with regard to deviation from the standard,
4) the stability of the urban size hierarchy over time,
5) the degree to which the cities are spatially concentrated,
6) the regularity in the distance separating cities from the nearest city, and
7) the relationship between the size of a city and the distance separating it from other cities.

For purposes of illustration, the above measures were applied to the Metropolitan Areas of Brazil, Canada, France, Italy, Mexico, and the Netherlands. The results show that certain distinct patterns exist in the demographic-spatial relations among Metropolitan Areas and that the patterns in some countries are quite different from those in others.

These methods of course do not provide explanations of the various patterns in urban size hierarchies and in the spatial distribution of cities. However, they do provide a basis for systematic comparative studies, which are essential in formulating and testing theories on demographic and spatial relations among cities.

Part VI

RURAL-URBAN DIFFERENCES

Introduction to Part VI

As with most stereotypes, there is probably an element of truth in the commonly held picture of the rural person and the urbanite. We tend to see the rural person as a religious creature, interacting with only those he has known since boyhood, a family man, profoundly ignorant of world affairs, and the servant of tradition. In contrast, the urbanite often appears to us as having dismissed the gods, a stranger to all, a creature with little care for matrimony and even less for progeny, all-knowing in his own way, and contemptuous of anything that happened earlier than yesterday.

Turning to census data and research findings on the characteristics of urban and rural populations, it is not difficult to see why these stereotypes persist. In any given country we may find that in comparison to the rural population a far greater proportion of the urban residents are atheists, living alone, unmarried, without children, literate, and well-educated. We may go beyond the stereotypes and note that the urban population is often either more masculine or more feminine than the rural population. Its age composition is typically also different, with a greater proportion of the population in the productive years of life. And, consistent with some aspects of the stereotype, the urbanite is typically far more migratory and less likely to remain in the social class of his father.

Although cities and their inhabitants can be studied without reference to rural populations, it is such stereotypes and observations as the above that suggest the full impact of urbanization on man and his culture. With the exception of an apparent lull in urbanization during the period between 3,000 and 1,000 B.C. and its decline in Europe during the Dark Ages, the global growth of cities has been continuous, faster in recent times than ever before. This prompts one to ask: In what manner have the sociocultural aspects of man's existence changed with the course of urbanization? Unlike some other inquiries concerning evolution-

462

ary phenomena, this question can be subjected to research. The differences between rural and urban populations represent contrasts between the old and the new, and in a sense they provide us with some insights into the character of man's social and cultural life prior to urbanization. However, only in a very limited sense do the dissimilarities between the two indicate the course of man's development since the dawn of history. This becomes evident when it is realized that the nature of the contrasts between the two divisions varies not only from one society to another but from one period to the next. For example, it appears that in virtually all countries the fertility of urban dwellers is lower than that of the rural population, but the magnitude of this difference is by no means the same from one country to another.

Variation in rural-urban differences cannot be wholly attributed to the fact that urbanization has gone further in some cases than in others, for the characteristics of rural populations change just as do those of city inhabitants. A modern farmer hardly resembles his Neolithic ancestor, and a resident of New York City would doubtless find life in the rural parts of a highly urbanized society more comprehensible than that in ancient Babylon. Rural-urban differences are a function of a greater change in the cities than in the rural sectors, and the nature of the differences between the two varies from society to society and from one historical epoch to the next. It is this variation that forms the core of a broad set of problems for urban research.

We first want to know what forms of rural-urban differences are universal. Beyond this we want to know why the two divisions may be dissimilar in some respects but not in others, and also why dissimilarities vary from place to place and time to time. For example, granted that urbanites may differ from their rural cousins in that they have lower fertility, participate more in voluntary associations, and lead a more anonymous form of life, to mention a few contrasts, why is it that the language of one does not always become unintelligible to the other? Or why is it that monogamy may prevail in both parts of a society? Moreover, granted that literacy is generally more widespread among city dwellers than among agriculturists, why is the difference between the two in this respect small in some cases but large in others?

A similar question may be posed regarding virtually any difference between the two.

It has been suggested that rural-urban differences historically tend to bear a close relation to the degree of urbanization. The random observations made to date suggest a fairly uniform pattern. In the early stages of urbanization, when a small per cent of the total population resides in cities, the differences are at a minimum; but as time passes and urbanization increases, rural-urban contrasts rapidly become more and more prominent. This process does not continue indefinitely, however, for as the degree of urbanization reaches higher levels, differences between the two become less pronounced. Far from being an explanation, this pattern presents some major theoretical questions and research problems. In the first place, we do not know whether this pattern holds among countries as well as through time. One should expect to find that rural-urban differences are at a minimum in countries with either an extremely high or an extremely low degree of urbanization, but the paucity of comparable international data has made it impossible to ascertain the nature of the pattern through systematic research.

Even if the pattern should appear as anticipated, we would still face the task of accounting for it. It may well be that minimal differences at the two extremes of urbanization are due to different factors. This consideration prompts us to take into account additional characteristics of urbanization and some of the mechanisms that possibly give rise to rural-urban differences. In recognition of the relation between the population size of urban centers and certain socio-cultural patterns, one possibility is that rural-urban differences are never great unless the urban population is concentrated in large cities. Also, the amount of difference between the two is in part a function of changes in the rural sector which originated in cities. Where there is an exchange of goods, services, and migrants between cities and agricultural areas, rather than only the political subjugation and economic exploitation of the latter by the former, there is likely to be a greater diffusion of urban innovations and a greater resemblance between city dwellers and the rural population. This would appear to be the case as nations achieve a high degree of urbanization.

It is not realistic to expect every aspect of rural-urban contrast to bear the same relation to the degree of urbanization. Where exceptions occur, theory and research should take into account, in addition to other characteristics of urbanization and rural-urban interrelations, the prevailing conditions in rural areas. For example, where a high level of agricultural production is possible without the mechanization of farming (hand cultivation or "hoe-culture"), the rural population is likely to be less dependent upon cities; and this probably influences the nature of rural-urban differences. Other characteristics of rural populations—such as their density, economic well-being, and location relative to cities—may also be of importance in determining how much and in what way they will differ from city dwellers.

Research on the subject must consider the possibility that a series of rural-urban differences stem from or are influenced by one primary or basic dissimilarity. For example, the fact that the urban population typically has a greater proportion of persons in the most productive years of life tends to affect rural-urban differentials regarding mortality, fertility, and marital statuses. Accordingly, a causal analysis of rural-urban differences must be able to control statistically the influence of particular variables.

A final consideration is the possibility that certain developments on the national level, particularly in the technological sphere, may have the effect of reducing rural-urban contrasts. An example of this is provided by the rapid advances in preventive medicine, which in certain countries has undoubtedly brought about a greater correspondence between rural and urban mortality by reducing death rates in both populations to a very low level.

The observations offered above suggest the immense scope of research problems in the study of rural-urban differences either internationally or domestically. Some related considerations will be taken up in Part VII, which is devoted to the topic of rural-urban interrelations.

Turning now from theoretical and speculative considerations to empirical studies, we find two major questions confronting research on rural-urban differences. First, what definition should be employed to distinguish between rural and urban? And, second, what is the nature of available data for national and international studies on the subject?

The first question is virtually identical to that considered in Part I (The Boundaries of Urban Units). If the urban population is equated with the residents of all of the cities in a country, as is often the practice, its size and characteristics are largely a matter of the way in which cities are defined and delimited. The arguments on this point considered in Part I will not be repeated here. It will suffice to note that however the urban population be defined and delimited, the definition and methods utilized must be made explicit in a report of research. This guards against regarding as scientific discoveries things that are true by definition. Without this distinction we are tempted to "discover," for example, that the urban population is more heterogeneous than the rural, when in reality this may be true by the very definition used to distinguish them.

Furthermore, international comparisons of rural-urban differences must take into account the absence of a common distinction between rural and urban. One country may ascribe urban status to minor civil divisions, while another considers only points of population concentration; some may take into account the legal status of a locality and/or its administrative functions, while others ignore any kind of political consideration; and the minimum population size rule employed in one country may be quite different from that employed by others.

There are two ways to adjust for variation in national practices. One is to group countries and territories by type of definition, and treat each group separately from the others in the course of research. Unfortunately, however, a common definition does not mean that it has been applied in the same way. The alternative is to consider all countries and territories together and attempt to determine how much the differences in definitions may have influenced the results of a particular comparison. For example, suppose we are concerned with the relation between the degree of a country's urbanization and the difference between urban and rural fertility. Let us further suppose we find that as the degree of urbanization increases the rural-urban fertility differential decreases. Such a finding would pose a question: to what extent is the relation due to variations in the definitions of urban from one country to the next? One possibility is immediately suggested. Defining very small concentrations of people as urban artificially increases the proportion of the population reported as urban, and at the same time may reduce the difference between rural and urban fertility. A test can be made by grouping the countries and territories according to the minimum population-size limit for urban localities. If the previous finding does not hold for each group, it must be subjected to reinterpretation, for it is partly a function of variation in the definition of urban. Variations in the definition of urban may influence one type of rural-urban difference more than others, and each comparison should be treated as though it is a special case.

So far we have treated the urban and rural worlds as dichotomous. However, there is a growing tendency in contemporary research to think in terms of a continuum rather than a dichotomous distinction. Under this conception a given locality is treated as neither completely rural nor completely urban, but rather as occupying a position somewhere between two extremes.

The continuum notion by no means eliminates the problem of defining urban, for it is not possible to speak of a locality as being "more urban" than another without first deciding what the attributes of "urbanness" are. Moreover, even if we should agree that a locality is "more urban" to the extent that it has a larger population, a higher population density, and a larger percentage of its labor force in non-agricultural occupations, there remains the question of delimitation. Whether a locality has the characteristics mentioned above is contingent on the way in which its boundaries are demarcated. Thus, the rural-urban continuum is meaningful only when the localities have been delimited according to some criteria as to what is urban and what is rural. Once their boundaries are determined, the localities can be arranged in the order of their population size, density, and/or the per cent of the labor force in non-agricultural occupations. Comparisons based on a rural-urban continuum rest on the assumption that each of the localities has been delimited in approximately the same way. Also, when comparisons are made among countries, it is essential that the same type of rural-urban continuum be employed in each case. Thus, if the localities are arranged according to population-size classes in one case, they should be treated similarly in all other countries.

Gradation in rural-urban differences may occur. In the United

States there is a decrease in the per cent of females 14 years old
and over who are married as one goes from the rural to the urban
end of the scale (see Table 4 of Otis Dudley Duncan's "Community Size and the Rural-Urban Continuum" in Chapter 13). This
pattern is possibly present in all countries, but less so in some than
in others. Furthermore, the range may vary from one country,
or from one trait, to another. In the United States, 73.7 per cent
of the females 14 years old or over in the nonvillage rural farm
population were married in 1950, while the corresponding per
cent was only 61.4 for urbanized areas of over 3,000,000 inhabitants. Thus the maximum rural-urban difference in this case is
12.3 percentage points, with the rural exceeding the urban, but
the range and/or the direction of the difference may vary from
country to country.

Until recently considerations of rural-urban differences were
for the most part based on random observations limited to a few
of the world's more advanced countries. This necessarily was the
case since systematic research and comparisons among countries
are virtually out of the question without access to a large number
of national census reports that distinguish between rural and
urban populations. As more and more countries have initiated
censuses, the possibilities for truly international research on the
subject have increased immensely.

The major characteristics tabulated for the populations of
urban and rural areas in some of the recent national censuses are:
sex, age, marital status, place of birth, legal nationality, language,
literacy, educational attainment, occupations, industry groups,
number of households, size of households, number of children,
religion, income, migration status, physical or mental defects,
and types of housing. This list suggests an abundance of information on rural-urban differences, although it by no means includes
all we might wish to know for a particular problem.

Moreover, only a small number of countries may report a particular characteristic for both rural and urban populations; for
example, it appears that less than 15 per cent of recent national
census reports tabulate urban and rural income. No country tabu-
lates *all* of the characteristics listed above in its census reports,
and those that report a particular rural-urban characteristic often
constitute a biased global sample, the more advanced countries

being typically overrepresented. Finally, two countries reporting data on the *same* trait may not report them in comparable form. For example, one country may report rural-vs.-urban occupational composition in terms of categories that are different from those employed in another country.

Two United Nations publications should prove of value in international research on rural-urban differences. One of them, *Data on Urban and Rural Population in Recent Censuses* (Population Studies, No. 8), provides a report on census practices in 49 countries. This report deals in most cases with the next to the last census (*circa* 1940) rather than the most recent one; nevertheless, it does indicate the types of data that are available for use in international study. While it covers national practices with regard to the definition of "urban," it does not consider problems of international comparability in census definitions of population characteristics. These problems are dealt with in another United Nations publication, *Population Census Methods* (Population Studies, No. 4).

Contents of the papers. As the above observations suggest, the definition of rural and urban is a major research problem in the study of differences between the two. In recognition of this two papers that bear directly on the problem are presented in Chapter 13.

The first paper, "On the Distinction Between Urban and Rural: National Practices and Recommendations," considers the definitions of "urban" as applied in the censuses of various countries, and how variation in definitions may influence the comparability of international data. In addition to providing a survey of national practices, the paper reports certain recommendations for distinguishing between urban and rural areas.

Virtually all of the countries that distinguish between urban and rural for census purposes do so by treating them as dichotomies. A different approach is offered in the second paper in Chapter 13, "Community Size and the Rural-Urban Continuum," by Otis Dudley Duncan. This paper considers the idea that communities and their populations are neither completely rural nor completely urban, with each being only more or less urban than others. The research method associated with the notion of a rural-urban continuum is illustrated by its application to localities in the United States.

Since Duncan does not undertake a comparison of countries, certain observations on the use of his method in international research are in order. Although Duncan arranges communities in the United States according to population—size classes, there are several other possibilities, such as the per cent in non-agricultural occupations and population density, or a combination of these two with size. The only requirement in international comparisons is that the rural-urban continuum be constructed in approximately the same way in each country. Thus, if one seeks to replicate Duncan's study in another country, the same population size classes must be used and the nonvillage residents treated in a similar way. It would also be necessary to consider only population characteristics that correspond to those employed in Duncan's study.

Of the three papers in Chapter 14 two were written not as illustrations of a method of analysis but as reports of substantive research. The first, "Traits of the Urban and Rural Populations of Latin America," reports a study of rural-urban contrasts that is truly international in scope and systematic in technique. In addition to describing some major patterns in rural-urban differences among Latin American countries, the treatment provides examples of research problems that arise in such an analysis and suggests ways of handling them.

International comparisons are of course only one aspect of the study of rural-urban differences. Of equal importance is a consideration of variation in these differences over time in a single country. This is the subject of the second paper in Chapter 14, "Trends in Rural and Urban Fertility." In addition to dealing with differential fertility, the paper considers several problems in establishing and interpreting trends in rural-urban differences.

The final paper in Chapter 14, "Regional Comparisons Standardized for Urbanization," considers one of the consequences of rural-urban differences. Some regions of a country may become heavily urbanized long before others. Under such a condition, given a somewhat uniform rural-urban difference throughout the nation, the characteristics of the highly urbanized regions will be much unlike those of the other regions. To determine how much inter-regional differences are due to factors other than urbanization, it is necessary to treat the regions as though they all have the same urban structure. The method considered by Duncan for achieving such a standardization is applicable to countries as well as regions, provided that requisite data are available.

Studies that relate to rural-urban differences are included in Section 23 of the *Index to the Bibliography,* and sources of data on such differences in Section 22.

Chapter 13

ON THE DISTINCTION BETWEEN
RURAL AND URBAN

ON THE DISTINCTION BETWEEN URBAN AND
    RURAL: NATIONAL PRACTICES AND
    RECOMMENDATIONS *

UNITED NATIONS

Census statistics of the urban and rural population have a variety of important uses. The process of urbanization has long been recognized as a concomitant of social and economic development, but the precise inter-relations have never been thoroughly understood and the demographic implications have not been fully analysed. It is desirable, therefore, to follow the process of urbanization in the various countries and to relate it with (1) economic indices that reflect the progress of industrial development in terms of increases in production, trade, national income, etc., (2) indices of social and political change in such fields as education, health, standards of living, political participation and governmental organization, and (3) demographic trends as indicated by rates of population growth, family characteristics, mobility of the population, age structure, size and composition of the economically active population, and the like. The results of such studies should be valuable guides to planning economic and

* Adapted from United Nations, *Data on Urban and Rural Population in Recent Censuses*, Population Studies, No. 8, Lake Success, N. Y., July 1950 (United Nations Publications, Sales No.: 1950 • XIII • 4), with the permission of the publisher. This study covers the most recent censuses on which reports were published prior to 1950.

social development on an international as well as a national scale.

A second large area of application of these data is in the comparison of the conditions and characteristics of urban and rural people with respect to patterns of fertility, mortality, age and sex composition, housing, sanitation, levels of living, etc. Such studies are helpful in determining the particular problems of urban and rural areas and, beyond these, in understanding the role or function of cities in society and in exploring the possibilities of controlling their growth and planning their development.

Another use of the data is in connexion with the implementation of specific projects or programmes such as those undertaken by the United Nations and the specialized agencies. For example, the Food and Agriculture Organization of the United Nations is especially concerned with the problems and welfare of rural people. Census statistics on the rural population are essential to the furtherance of this work.

In order for analyses of the types just described to be most conclusive in their findings, it is essential that census statistics of urban and rural population be as closely comparable as possible. This point is less important for the purpose of comparing the urban and rural components of the population than for comparing degrees or levels of urbanization in various countries or regions, or for comparing urban or rural characteristics in one area with those in another. The reason for this is that urban-rural comparisons, no matter how "urban" and "rural" are defined, are likely to be heavily weighted with the highly concentrated, clearly urban population on the one hand, and with the village, or dispersed and clearly rural population on the other hand, with the result that differences between urban characteristics and rural characteristics are bound to be reflected if not precisely measured in the statistics. However, when the urban or rural population is expressed as a proportion of the total population, differences in definition may have a rather profound effect.

The basic meaning of the terms "urban" and "rural" is fairly clear, the former referring to the city and the latter to the country or to areas outside the city. But actual patterns of settlement are much less clear-cut than the basic concepts imply. Furthermore, the terms themselves have taken on overtones and added meanings whereby they have come to refer to ways of life, cultural patterns, attitudes, value systems, etc. In this process of ideological transformation, the intangible aspects have tended to supersede the tangible as criteria of urban or rural attributes. The intangible aspects are of course quite real, but they are difficult to pin down in a census frame of reference, especially in view of the fact that all kinds of people live in both rural and urban areas.

It would seem advisable, therefore, to use a relatively objective criterion for identifying urban and rural areas in the census and to retain as nearly as may be the original meaning of "city" and "country." A proper unit of classification from this point of view is the agglomeration or cluster of population.

With any concept of urban and rural, there is no definite point, in the continuum from scattered dwellings or small clusters to the great metropolitan agglomerations, where the rural ends and the urban begins. The concepts are clear only as they apply to the two extremes of the continuum, i.e., to the most urban and the most rural. The distribution is not really a two-fold one in which one part of the population is wholly rural and the other wholly urban, but a graduated distribution along a continuum from the least urban to the most urban or from the most rural to the least rural. Consequently, the line that is drawn between urban and rural for statistical or census purposes is necessarily arbitrary.

These considerations do not invalidate the urban-rural classification, but rather point to the need for a more systematic classification in accordance with a definite criterion such as size of agglomeration (preferably a classification that allows for several size groups rather than only two) on the basis of which trends and differences of an urban-versus-rural character may be more carefully studied and more thoroughly understood.

The problem of international comparability. Although the problem of differentiating between urban and rural population is theoretically a demographic one, concerned with the classification of *people* with respect to the size of the agglomerations in which they live, it has generally become (and necessarily perhaps) a matter of the classification of the areas in which people live rather than of the people themselves. The two ideas are not, of course, unrelated since agglomerations occur in space and have to be identified in some kind of geographic terms. But as a result of a natural tendency to apply the classification as urban or rural to the territorial or administrative organization already in existence, practices with respect to urban and rural definition or classification are closely bound up with national, historical and political considerations, and a particular scheme of classification, once established, tends to become fixed and resistant to change. The population, on the other hand, changes constantly; agglomerations grow in size and multiply in number without much regard to traditional boundary lines.

There is, then, a wide variation among countries in the type of territorial and administrative organization that has developed, in the point in time at which an urban-rural classification was adopted, and in the rate at which urbanization has proceeded. In consequence, there is also a wide variation both in the definition of urban and rural population and in the degree to which the application of the official or generally accepted definition conforms to the original intention of distinguishing city people from rural people—or city areas from rural areas.

RECOMMENDATIONS OF INTERNATIONAL AGENCIES

The truly formidable difficulties in the way of developing standard methods of urban and rural classification have long been recognized, but because of the importance of these data, international organizations have concerned themselves with the problem.

The International Statistical Institute. In 1938, the Congress of the International Statistical Institute adopted proposals for standard urban and rural classifications, in response to the request of the Health Section of the League of Nations. The main purpose of these proposals was to obtain data for use in computing internationally comparable vital rates for rural areas. The proposals submitted were as follows:

"(1) The rural population is the total population of all the *communes* (or smallest administrative districts) designated as rural.

"(2) The *communes* (or smallest administrative districts) should be divided, if possible, into categories according to the proportion of the total population of the *commune* that is agricultural population (i.e., all persons actively engaged in agricultural occupations and family members directly dependent upon them).

"*Communes* should be divided into at least three categories:

"Rural *communes*, more than 60 per cent;

"Mixed *communes*, 40 to 60 per cent;

"Urban *communes*, less than 40 per cent.

"The total population in each of these three categories should be obtainable. If more than three categories are distinguished, their limits should be such as to permit combination into the three categories indicated above.

"(3) In countries where this classification cannot be made, *communes* should be classified according to the size of the principal nucleus (the most populous centre) of the *commune* and divided into two categories;

"(a) *Communes* whose principal nuclei contain no more than 2,000 inhabitants;

"(b) *Communes* whose principal nuclei contain more than 2,000 inhabitants." [1]

These proposals were adopted after deletion of the words "rural," "mixed" and "urban" in paragraph 2.

It will be noted that the Congress endorsed an occupational approach to the problem of urban-rural classification. Adoption of this approach would involve an abandonment of the attempt to obtain a direct measure of the patterns and degrees of population agglomeration and dispersion.

Subsequent actions taken by international organizations have indicated a disposition to separate the concept "agricultural" from the concept "rural," at least in so far as census operations are concerned, and to follow the principle of measuring the urban population directly in terms of the unit of urbanization, namely the city or the agglomeration. This does not mean that the relating of occupational data to urban-rural data is not an important type of analysis. Rather, it furnishes an independent source of information which can make the study of inter-relations more fruitful.

The alternative proposal of the Congress—the classification of administrative divisions according to the size of the largest popu-

[1] Original text in French. See: Bunle, Henri. "Rapport de la Commission pour la Définition de la Population Rurale," *Bulletin de l'Institut International de Statistique* 30 (2): 158-163. 1938 (The Hague).

lated centre in the division—presents rather serious problems of comparability. These are related primarily to variations in the size of the area, the organization, and the function of the smallest administrative divisions of the various countries. The *commune* in France, for example, is quite different from the minor civil division in the United States, the latter being, in many parts of the country, little more than a convenient device for keeping land and tax records and bearing no such consistent relation to community organization or patterns of settlement as appears to be the case in France and in many other countries.

United Nations Population Commission. At its fourth session, in April 1949, the United Nations Population Commission made the following recommendations concerning urban-rural classification in censuses of population to be taken in or around 1950:

"Urban and rural population

"Because of the diversity of conditions affecting the classification of areas as urban and rural in various countries, it is not practicable at present to establish uniform definitions of urban and rural population for international use. It is desirable, however, that in each census provision be made for obtaining the aggregate population of all identifiable agglomerations or clusters of population, classified by size and other characteristics so that the results may be used as far as possible to improve the international comparability of existing data on this subject.

"It is therefore suggested that, for purpose of international comparisons, the following classification of the population by size of the agglomeration or cluster be tabulated, in addition to the tabulations normally made for urban and rural populations as defined in each country:

"(a) Population in places of 500,000 or more inhabitants;
"(b) Population in places of 100,000 to 500,000 inhabitants;
"(c) Population in places of 25,000 to 100,000 inhabitants;
"(d) Population in places of 10,000 to 25,000 inhabitants;
"(e) Population in places of 5,000 to 10,000 inhabitants;
"(f) Population in places of 2,000 to 5,000 inhabitants;
"(g) Population in places of 1,000 to 2,000 inhabitants;
"(h) Population in places of 500 to 1,000 inhabitants;

"(i) Population in places of less than 500 inhabitants;

"(j) Population not in identifiable agglomerations or clusters (if the whole population is not included in the above categories).

"It is also desirable that the number of places of each size group be tabulated.

"Since this distribution involved more classes than the usual urban-rural classification, the problem of tabulation by other characteristics is somewhat enlarged. In view of this fact, it may not be feasible to make extensive cross-tabulations. It is desirable, however, that the population in places of various size classes be tabulated for each sex, at least by age groups listed in paragraph 17. (Under 5 years, 10-year groups from 5 to 64 years, 65 years and over.) In this cross-tabulation, some of the categories in the above classification by size of place may have to be combined. In that case, however, it is desirable that at least the distinction between places of 10,000 or more and those with less than 10,000 inhabitants be maintained." [2]

At its fifth session, in May 1950, the Commission reconsidered its recommendations in regard to the size group of agglomerations or clusters of population to be used in summary cross-tabulations in those cases in which an extensive classification by size of place would not be feasible. It proposed, in place of the originally suggested distinction between places of 10,000 or more and those with less than 10,000 inhabitants:

"(a) that population censuses include summary tabulations of the population classified as a minimum by sex and age (under 5, 10-year groups from 5 to 64 years, and 65 and over) for agglomerations or clusters of population living in built-up contiguous areas which, according to the definition adopted in each country, are considered as single localities or population centres. These summary tabulations would be made for such population agglomerations grouped by size, as follows:

"Under 2,000, together with the population not in identifiable agglomerations or clusters,

"2,000 and under 10,000,

"10,000 and over;

[2] *Report of the fourth session of the Population Commission.* United Nations document E/1313. Lake Success, 21 April 1949. Pages 38-39.

"(b) that the categories presented in such tabulations not be termed 'urban' or 'rural' for purposes of international comparability . . ."

In addition, the Commission called attention to the fact that the World Health Organization Regulations, no. 1, article 6, calls for the classification of mortality for certain urban-rural aggregates by sex and by age in the following groups as a minimum: under 1 year; 1-4 years; 5-14 years; 15-24 years; 25-44 years; 45-64 years; 65-74 years; 75 years and over.

It was suggested by the Commission that if population tabulations by age are to be used in conjunction with these mortality tabulations, the age group 65 and over in the former should be divided into 65-74 years and 75 years and over.[3]

The Committee on the 1950 Census of the Americas. At its third session, in January 1950, this Committee made the following recommendations:

"Urban and rural population

"(a) *Topic*
"It is recommended that in each census, in addition to the information on urban and rural population needed for national purposes, measures be taken to obtain data on the population of all places or agglomerations of population which are identifiable by quantative, socio-economic, and other objective criteria, whether or not such places would be urban according to the definitions of the particular country.

"(b) *Tabulations*
"It is recommended as a minimum tabulation that the population be presented according to size (number of inhabitants) of agglomeration.

"The population should be classified according to the size (number of inhabitants) of the agglomeration in at least the following categories: 500,000 or more inhabitants, 100,000-500,000, 25,000-100,000, 10,000-25,000, 5,000-10,000, 2,000-5,000, 1,000-2,000, 500-1,000, less than 500 inhabitants. If the entire population is not included in these categories, data should be presented

[3] *Report of the Population Commission (fifth session).* United Nations document E/1711. Lake Success, 2 June 1950. Pages 13-14.

also for the population not classified in agglomerations or identifiable settlements.

"The tabulations should show at least the number of places of each size and their population, classified by (1) sex, and (2) whether urban or rural according to the country's own definition. The definitions of urban and rural adopted in the census of each country should be stated in the census publications." [4]

It will be noted that the recommendations of both the Commission and the Committee refrain from attempting to establish a definitive or final dichotomy between urban and rural, but provide for the classification of agglomerations or clusters of population into a series of size groups which represent breaks along the continuum from scattered dwellings and small villages to large concentrations. This type of classification not only ensures comparability of the results, but is in keeping with the realities of the situation, which preclude a two-fold mutually exclusive division. The comparability obtained is, to be sure, strictly in terms of the unit being classified, namely, the agglomeration. If size of agglomeration shows a closer correspondence in some countries than in others to characteristics that are commonly regarded as "urban," this is the result of cultural differences and is itself an appropriate subject of inquiry, but not one for which the other systems of classification described in this report could readily furnish the materials—unless they were made in combination with the one proposed by the Commission. Such a combination is in fact proposed by the Committee on the 1950 Census of the Americas.

DEFINITIONS AND CLASSIFICATIONS IN
RECENT CENSUSES

Some distinction between urban and rural population is made in the statistics of practically all censuses. The categories shown may not bear the labels "urban" and "rural"; the country may not even have an official definition of urban and rural population; but almost without exception, the census data can be made to yield

---

[4] *Resolutions and motions of the third session of the Committee on the 1950 Census of the Americas,* Bogotá, January 9-21, 1950. Document 1950 a — (COTA) — 2/1/50 — 400. Page 14.

information for purposes of urban-rural comparison. The distinction between urban and rural may be in the form of statistics for individual important cities which, taken together, furnish data on urban characteristics that may be compared with data for the country as a whole, or for the remainder of the country. Again, the distinction may be in the form of statistics for small geographic divisions, which, when classified into population size groups, usually bear a positive relation to the degree of urbanization and may therefore form a basis for urban-rural comparisons of a simple type.

Of the fifty-three countries for which one or more censuses were examined for this study, fifty-one give statistics which may be regarded as urban-rural classifications. The two exceptions are Costa Rica (1927) and Thailand (1947) which specifically disclaim such a classification, but which do give statistics for minor geographic divisions that can be combined into size groups. In a few other cases there is not an official designation of these data as urban or rural, and perhaps no official definition of urban or rural population, but the authorization to regard the data as approximating an urban-rural classification is nevertheless given. In the 1930 census of the Netherlands, for example, statistics are shown for *communes* by size classes, but it is pointed out that, while *communes* of 20,000 or more inhabitants may be regarded as urban, there are several *communes* in this class that are partially or entirely rural and a number of smaller *communes* that should be considered as urban. Again, in connexion with the Belgian census of 1930, it is stated that *communes* having 5,000 or more inhabitants are "generally considered as urban."

The methods used in the various censuses for classifying the population as urban or rural represent two general approaches. The first is the classification of administrative divisions (usually the relatively small or smallest geographic units into which the country is divided for administrative purposes) in which the whole population of the *commune,* municipality, township or other minor civil division is classified as either urban or rural on the basis of chosen criteria. In this method, the unit of classification is the administrative division rather than the agglomeration.

A variation of this approach, which perhaps represents a third approach (and which will be treated separately in the discussion that follows) is the method in which the administrative centres of all minor divisions are classified as urban and the remainders of the divisions are classified as rural.

The other general approach is the classification of agglomerations or population clusters, in which the urban population is identified as the inhabitants of closely settled "localities," "places," or "centres" above a given size, or with other specified characteristics. In this method, the unit of classification is the agglomeration, and official boundary lines of administrative divisions are ignored unless they happen to furnish convenient units for combination to form the larger agglomerations.

Classifications of administrative divisions. The smallest administrative divisions in the different countries vary in area, organization and function. They often contain some concentrated population and some dispersed population, some population engaged in typically urban occupations and some in typically rural pursuits. Any classification in which the whole population of the administrative divisions is treated as a unit therefore yields somewhat heterogeneous categories. However, such a classification has the advantage of producing census statistics for areas that have relatively stable and generally recognized boundaries. Usually, comparable classifications can readily be made in other statistics, such as vital statistics, that are compiled only for administrative areas. The possibility of combination with statistics from other sources is much more limited when special areas that do not conform to established geographic boundaries are delineated by the census for the purposes of urban-rural classification.

The classification of administrative divisions is effected in a number of different ways and in accordance with various criteria. They are of three general types: (a) based on the kind of local government, (b) based on the total number of inhabitants, and (c) based on characteristics that do not apply to the whole area (e.g., the size of the principal cluster or the percentage of the population engaged in agriculture).

(a) Classifications by type of local government. The most common basis for classifying administrative divisions into urban and rural categories is the type of local government or administration. By this method, centres of population that have what is regarded as a city or urban form of government are classified as

urban and all other areas are classified as rural. Somewhat less than half the censuses included in this review used this criterion in one form or another in distinguishing the urban from the rural population.

In many countries, it is the practice to set up special forms of local government, involving considerable autonomy in matters of taxation, police protection, sanitation, etc., in areas of significant concentration of population. The establishment of these city or urban forms of government may be through incorporation, issuance of charters, or some other official action. This type of procedure furnishes a very convenient basis for identifying urban areas. Among the countries which are covered in this study, the following have defined the urban population, for census purposes, as residents of such areas (or have presented separate statistics for such areas):

Australia	Romania
Bulgaria	Union of South Africa
Canada	USSR
Ceylon	United Kingdom
Finland	England and Wales
Hungary	Northern Ireland
Ireland	Scotland
Japan	United States
New Zealand	Yugoslavia
Poland	

In addition, Denmark, Norway and Sweden have published statistics in accordance with this definition as well as in accordance with a more comprehensive definition that includes in the urban classification, suburban concentrations and population clusters of a non-administrative type.

Because practices differ, both within and among the countries, with respect to the granting of "urban" status in the administrative or governmental sense, there is considerable variation in the size and characteristics of the population units that were classified as urban in the censuses. Thus, the smallest urban places in Canada had less than 200 inhabitants while the smallest in Japan had more than 20,000. Again, the boundaries of the incorporated places in the United States, while usually enclosing only thickly settled territory, often excluded suburban concentrations that might well be classified as urban; whereas the incorporated municipality of Japan often included more than one cluster of population as well as considerable territory of a definitely rural character.

Certain of the countries listed above have restricted the urban classification, for census purposes, to those areas with urban status that have more than a given number of inhabitants. Scotland has adopted a minimum of 1,000, Ireland of 1,500 and the United States of 2,500. In the statistics of Canada, the urban is often taken as incorporated places of 1,000 or more, although the official definition includes incorporated places of all sizes.

Further, Australia, New Zealand, Ireland and the United States have departed from the basic definition by delineating certain additional population clusters, and classifying them as urban even though they have not been formally established as such.

It should be noted again here that some of the countries which give statistics separately for areas with urban status and for other areas do not have "official" definitions. Moreover, it should be remembered that some countries may not have very close equivalents of the terms "urban" and "rural" in their languages or at least in their census terminology. For example, in the statistics of Japan, the term *shi* (referring to the incorporated municipality) is usually translated as "city" and the term *gun* as "rural county." The terms *machi* and *mura* (referring to the two types of area that comprise the *gun*) are often translated as "towns" and "villages." Actually these areas, like the *shi*, generally contain one or more clusters of population and some dispersed population and open country. On the whole, the *machi* contains larger clusters than the *mura*. For many purposes, the division between urban and rural is made by taking each *shi, machi* and *mura* above a given population size as urban and the remainder as rural.

(b) Classifications by total number of inhabitants. In some censuses, the basis of the urban-rural classification is the total number of inhabitants of the minor administrative divisions. The minimum number that has been set for qualifying an area as urban varies considerably. The seven countries using this type of definition in their censuses had the following minimum requirements:

Austria	2,000
Belgium	5,000
Czechoslovakia	2,000
Germany	2,000
Netherlands	20,000
Spain	10,000
Switzerland	10,000

The Netherlands and Spain also show statistics for an intermediate size class, the Netherlands for *communes* of 5,000 to 20,000, and Spain for *municipios* of 2,000 to 10,000 inhabitants.

(c) *Classifications based on characteristics not applicable to the entire population of minor administrative divisions.* In four censuses, the entire division was classified as rural or urban on the basis of characteristics of part of the population. In the censuses of France and Luxembourg, *communes* containing an administrative centre (or *chef-lieu*) of 2,000 or more inhabitants were classified as urban, all other *communes* as rural. In the 1940 census of Greece, *communes* or municipalities whose largest agglomeration exceeded 5,000 inhabitants were classified as urban, all others as rural. In the 1936 census of Italy, *communes* with less than 50 per cent of the economically active population engaged in agriculture were classified as urban, all others as rural.

Classifications based on administrative functions. In some censuses, the population cluster that serves as a seat of administration for the minor administrative division is classified as urban and the remainder of the division as rural. Such seats of administration of course include national capitals and the capitals of major or intermediate divisions. In general, the capital of a major division is also the administrative centre of the intermediate or minor division in which it is located. Countries which have used this type of classification in their censuses are: Egypt, Brazil, Colombia, the Dominican Republic, El Salvador, Honduras, Guatemala, Peru, and Turkey.[5] In these countries, some urban places may be very small, in some cases less than 100 inhabitants.

Turkey has added to the urban classification all other towns

[5] The definition used by Nicaragua in 1940 has not been determined, but inspection of the census data for geographic areas suggests that this type of classification was made in that census.

with a population of more than 2,000, but there were in the census of 1945, eight places of less than 500 inhabitants which qualified as urban through being the chief centres of minor divisions. Similarly, Peru has added to the urban classification all non-administrative clusters with a population that exceeds the national average for administrative centres. Colombia, on the other hand, has limited the urban classification to capitals and administrative centres of over 1,500 inhabitants.

Classifications of agglomerations or clusters of population. In nine of the countries, census statistics of the urban and rural population have been based on a classification of agglomerations or clusters of population. In one case (Cuba, 1943) all nuclei of population were included in the urban total, the smallest places containing less than fifty inhabitants. However, rather extensive tabulations were given for places of 5,000 or more inhabitants, so the latter might be regarded as the effective definition. The other nine countries have adopted minimum size designations, as follows:

Argentina	2,000
Chile	1,000
Denmark	250
Iceland	300
India	5,000
Mexico	2,500
Panama	1,500
Portugal	2,000
Venezuela	2,500

The statistics for Denmark are generally shown by the following divisions:

1. The Capital;
2. Suburbs of the Capital;
3. Provincial cities;
4. Suburbs of provincial cities;
5. Agglomerations in rural *communes;*
6. Strictly rural areas.

The first five items represent sub-divisions of the urban population. This list indicates how an administrative or governmental definition of urban, which included items 1 and 3, has been revised to approximate an "agglomeration" type of definition. For most purposes, the inclusion of agglomerations as small as 250 may seem to stretch the concept of urban areas too far, but the collection of data of this type furnishes the basis for a graduated distribution that can be classified into successive size groups and be used in accordance with various definitions of urban.

Norway and Sweden have adopted similar classification schemes which offer the possibility of expanding the urban category to include suburbs of cities and agglomerations of a nonadministrative character, but for most of their tabulations they retain the local-government type of definition.

India and Panama made certain exceptions to the established minimum and included some places of smaller size that had definite urban characteristics. Chile included centres of less than the minimum (1,000 inhabitants) that were administrative centres of *communes*.

Some fifteen additional countries identified all "inhabited places" designated variously as "localities," "populated centres," "populated places" or "villages," for purposes of the census but most of them did not use these data for purposes of urban-rural classification. It has already been indicated that Peru, Ireland, and Australia made certain adaptations of the basic administrative definition to add suburbs or agglomerations to the urban classification. New Zealand and the United States have also delineated areas for special purposes which include with a central city the thickly settled outlying areas ordinarily classified as rural for general census purposes. These are the "urban areas" in New Zealand and the "metropolitan districts" in the United States.

For the 1950 census, the United States has made plans for identifying the "urban fringe" around all incorporated places of 50,000 or more inhabitants and for identifying all agglomerations in unincorporated territory that have 2,500 or more inhabitants. These areas will be included in the urban classification.

The chief problem involved in implementing a classification by agglomerations is the identification of the agglomerations or clusters of population in the census. Comparability depends in some measure on the use of relatively uniform rules for delimiting the cluster. The object is to count together all the inhabitants

of a continuous, thickly settled area that functions as an integrated social unit. Cities and towns with official status and fixed
boundaries furnish a convenient starting point. Separate data for
such places are usually required in any case for various administrative or fiscal purposes. It is the delimitation of suburban
fringes and of agglomerations that do not have official status that
creates some difficulty.

Various methods have been used to delimit such areas. As
indicated earlier, approximately half the countries included in
this report have obtained separate population counts either for all
inhabited places or for those above a stated minimum. In some
cases, the census instructions provided for the preliminary determination by local authorities of the places that were to be
counted as separate units. In others, enumerators were instructed
to count together the inhabitants of all places with names and to
specify the category to which each place belonged, as town, village, settlement, farm, ranch, station, camp, etc. In still others,
enumerators were instructed to classify as urban and count together the inhabitants of any group of structures that had a place
name and was laid out in streets with names and house numbers.

The classification of areas on the basis of population density is
a possible method, but one that involves complications connected
with the size and constitution of the geographic units for which
the density is to be computed. For the purpose of distinguishing
agglomerations from unagglomerated population, this method
rather begs the question, since the density of an agglomeration
cannot be computed until its limits have been set. A density criterion does have some value, however, in the delimiting of suburbs or urban fringes, providing data are obtainable on the area
and population of small geographic units. The United States has
used such a criterion in delineating "metropolitan districts,"
adding to the central incorporated city all the adjacent and contiguous minor civil divisions with a density above a predetermined level.

Another kind of criterion that has been suggested, and appears to have been used to a limited extent, is the presence or
absence of certain institutionalized services that are usual concomitants of urban life. Among these are: systems of local public
transportation; telephone service; availability of running water,

electricity and gas; door-to-door mail delivery; presence of churches, schools, market places, or other symbols of localized community life. The difficulty here is that in some regions, some or all such services have been extended far into farm and rural areas. In other regions, many of these services are lacking even in rather important centres of population. Thus, they represent characteristics that are not necessarily confined to or typical of the city in the spatial or physical sense, but are associated with urbanism in the cultural sense. It would seem, therefore, that any use of criteria of this type would necessarily be, at most, of a supplementary nature only, their application confined to cases where other conditions more closely related to agglomerations *per se* have already been met.

The applicability or relevance of the methods described above varies in accordance with the conditions existing in the several countries. It would be impossible to construct a set of specific rules for the identification and delimitation of population clusters that would be susceptible of international adoption at this juncture. Probably, the comparability of statistics would not be seriously affected by considerable variation in the methods whereby the limits of the cluster are determined. The greatest potential contribution to comparability is already achieved when agreement is reached on the general principle of classifying the population by size of agglomeration and when a standard set of size classes has been adopted.

Whatever particular method is adopted, a preliminary listing and mapping of all clusters that are to be identified and counted in the census is desirable, since this ensures relatively uniform and objective standards of classification, at least at the national level. Where it is not practicable to undertake listing and subsequently enumerating all the numerous very small clusters of population that exist in almost every country, a careful guess at the size of small clusters could be made during the preliminary listing, and places below a given size eliminated from the list. This "given size" should be well below any minimum that is contemplated for presentation in census results, so as to provide for a full count of clusters at the minimum level.

COMMUNITY SIZE AND THE RURAL-URBAN CONTINUUM *

OTIS DUDLEY DUNCAN

Despite the ubiquity and convenience of the dichotomous classification, urban *vs.* rural, most students of urbanism have long agreed that it is but a crude device at best. Thus, alongside well-known efforts to typify "the city" or "the rural world," one finds such cautions as the following: "In reality the transition from a purely rural community to an urban one . . . is not abrupt but gradual. . . . There is no absolute boundary line which would show a clearly cut cleavage between the rural and the urban community." [1] Or the following: "The city and the country may be regarded as two poles in reference to one or the other of which all human settlements tend to arrange themselves." [2]

Actually, no competent sociologist, for at least a generation, has maintained that the distinction between urban and rural is a sharp one. Even the standard Census Bureau classification, employed in much sociological research, involves three categories—urban, rural nonfarm, and rural farm—and is supplemented by such concepts as that of the "metropolitan district." Yet, in recent years writers on rural-urban sociology seem to have found it necessary to rediscover the inadequacy of the "rural-urban dichotomy," [3] and a new label for an old idea has crept into the literature: the "rural-urban continuum."

This paper suggests that students take a careful look at the new terminology before admitting it permanently to the professional argot. Nothing is gained by replacing an objectionable concept with one having equally misleading, if somewhat different,

* Reprinted from Paul K. Hatt and Albert J. Riess, Jr. (eds.), *Cities and Society* (Glencoe, Illinois: The Free Press, 1957), pp. 35-45, with permission of author and publisher.

[1] Pitirim Sorokin and Carle C. Zimmerman, *Principles of Rural-Urban Sociology* (New York: Henry Holt and Co., 1929), p. 14.

[2] Louis Wirth, "Urbanism as a Way of Life," *American Journal of Sociology,* XLIV (July, 1938), p. 3.

[3] For example, Neal Gross, "Sociological Variation in Contemporary Rural Life," *Rural Sociology,* 13 (September, 1948), 256-269; Irving A. Spaulding, "Serendipity and the Rural-Urban Continuum," *Rural Sociology,* 16 (March, 1951), 29-36.

connotations. The approach of the paper is empirical, as well as critical; and an incidental objective is to set forth some recent data on one type of intercommunity differentiation. These data have descriptive value independent of the paper's argument.

It is convenient to take as a point of departure a succinct formulation of the "hypothesis of the rural-urban continuum." A current text asserts that "there is a continuous gradation in the United States from rural to urban rather than a simple rural-urban dichotomy and . . . as human communities are arrayed along this rural-urban continuum, consistent variations occur in patterns of behavior." [4] Insofar as this statement is a substantive proposition, and not a mere definition or terminological convention, it is subject to acceptance or rejection on adequate empirical grounds. To accept the hypothesis, one would require essentially unequivocal confirmation by a large body of evidence, even if the proposition is left in the form of a statement in the present tense about a single country, and not extended to cover other places or time periods. On the other hand, even a small number of significant negative instances—cases where the proposition is incorrect or intolerably imprecise—would require its outright rejection or substantial modification. Thus, although this paper perhaps exhibits more "pro" than "con" instances, the latter are the more important as a test of the proposition's cogency.

Before turning to the data it is necessary to consider briefly two key terms in the foregoing statement of the "continuum" hypothesis: "continuous gradations" and "consistent variations." Even if a "continuum" exists, it can be analyzed only by using discrete categories. The range of the variable must, perforce, be broken down into intervals. In this paper eleven such intervals are used. This is a much larger number than is ordinarily employed in rural-urban comparisons, and should afford ample basis for a practical judgment as to whether "continuous gradation" is in evidence. The meaning of "consistent variations" in the present context is not entirely clear. But the term seems to imply

---

[4] Stuart A. Queen and David B. Carpenter, *The American City* (New York: McGraw-Hill Book Co., 1953), p. 38. There is no intention here to single out these authors for criticism. Their statement, rather than some other one, is cited only because it states the "continuum" hypothesis concisely. For a similar point of view, see, for example, James A. Quinn, *Urban Sociology* (New York: American Book Co., 1955), pp. 24-27.

that as one moves from the rural to the urban pole of the "continuum" any variable related to urbanism should increase (or decrease) in magnitude monotonically, or any attribute related to urbanism should increase (or decrease) in relative frequency monotonically. Minor irregularities aside, then, one would count as evidence against the hypothesis a case in which a dependent variable has a low value at the rural pole, a high value at some intermediate point, and a low value again at the urban pole. From the standpoint of "continuous gradation," another negative case for the hypothesis would be one in which a dependent variable is practically constant over a considerable part of the range of the "rural-urban continuum" and then increases abruptly with the next interval. Inasmuch as the paper sets forth the data on which its conclusions rest, the reader may form an independent judgment of the acceptability of those conclusions.

Data and Procedure. A key assumption of this paper is that the most natural way to approach the construction of a "rural-urban continuum" is to classify communities by size. Almost all writers on rural-urban differences stress the significance of community size. And while most of them agree that "characterization of a community as urban on the basis of size alone is obviously arbitrary," [5] no one has suggested a practical basis for including other variables among the criteria of urbanism to be applied to all communities in standard fashion. The acceptability of this assumption is discussed further below.

The community size classification, then, stands for the "rural-urban continuum" as an independent variable. Several dependent variables are related to the independent variable, and their regressions on community size are examined for evidence of "continuous gradation" and "consistent variation." Both the community size classification and the population characteristics studied as dependent variables are drawn from a 1950 Census Report, *Characteristics by Size of Place.*[6]

---

[5] Wirth, *op. cit.,* p. 4.

[6] Special Report, P-E No. 5 A (Washington: Government Printing Office, 1953). The data in this report are based on a 3⅓ per cent sample of the returns of the 1950 Census enumeration. Summary figures based on these data are, therefore, subject to sampling variability. It is doubtful, however, that the amount of sampling variability is large enough to affect this paper's conclusions materially.

Table 1 presents the community size classification, together with the distribution of the population by community size groups. The first four size categories include the 157 urbanized areas recognized in 1950. The concept of "urbanized area" was first introduced in the 1950 Census, and it has some important ad-

TABLE 1

DISTRIBUTION OF POPULATION BY SIZE OF COMMUNITY, FOR THE
UNITED STATES: 1950

Size of Community	Number of Places	Per Cent of Total Population
Total	17,217*	100.0
Urbanized areas		
3,000,000 or more	3	14.0
1,000,000 to 3,000,000	9	11.1
250,000 to 1,000,000	37	11.6
50,000 to 250,000	108	9.3
Places outside urbanized areas		
25,000 or more	193	4.7
10,000 to 25,000	547	5.5
2,500 to 10,000	2,513	7.9
1,000 to 2,500	4,158	4.3
Under 1,000 (incorporated)	9,649*	2.7
Nonvillage rural †		
Nonfarm	—	13.9
Farm	—	15.0

* Does not include unincorporated places of under 1,000 population.
† Includes population of unincorporated places of under 1,000 population.

vantages for a study of the present type. In general, an urbanized area consists of a "central city" of at least 50,000 population plus its adjacent or nearby incorporated "suburbs," and, in addition, such unincorporated territory as is contiguous, or nearly so, to any other part of the area and has a closely spaced street pattern with at least 500 dwelling units per square mile, or which is the site of commercial or industrial activities functioning in close relation to the central city. Several urbanized areas contain more than one central city; for example, Minneapolis-St. Paul and San Francisco-Oakland. The important point is that the entire agglomeration is treated as a single unit, and its size classification is determined by the aggregate population. Hence, in the community size classification, a suburban municipality of, say, 10,000 population is regarded simply as part of a large "city," and not as comparable with an independent town of 10,000 population.

The next five size classes include progressively smaller places outside urbanized areas. Not only incorporated places, but also some 1,430 unincorporated places of 1,000 population or more, are included in these categories.

The two final categories include that part of the "rural" population (population outside places of 2,500 inhabitants or more) not included in places of 1,000 to 2,500 or in incorporated places of less than 1,000. The distinction between the nonfarm and farm parts of this rural residual is not, strictly speaking, based on community size. Nonetheless, on an *a priori basis* it seems reasonable to regard the farm category as "more rural" on the whole than nonfarm. It should be noted that in most Census tabulations all population in the last four categories is classified as "rural," with the bulk of the population in villages of 1,000 to 2,500 and under 1,000 inhabitants falling into the "rural nonfarm" category. The separation of villages from the other rural categories is one of the virtues of the community size classification.

Some difficulties with the community size classification must be recognized. The delineation of urbanized areas was not carried out for central cities of less than 50,000 population. But smaller cities, as well, have "suburbs" and "fringe" populations. A more thoroughgoing classification would doubtlessly result in shifting some of the present "rural" and small town population into higher size groups.[7] Another source of error is the heterogeneity of the rural nonfarm (RNF) category. Perhaps one-sixth, or more, of the population in this category resides in unincorporated villages of less than 1,000 and properly belongs with the incorporated places of this size. Another substantial segment, no doubt, consists of residents of the "fringe" around small cities and towns and of the "satellite" territory of larger places. The RNF category also includes disproportionate numbers of persons

[7] Moreover, because the Census Bureau had to delineate the urbanized areas in advance of the 1950 enumeration, there are 21 places of 50,000 or more which attained that size for the first time in 1950 and were not included in urbanized areas, but in places outside urbanized areas of 25,000 or more. This overlap between the size class 50,000 to 250,000 and the size class 25,000 or more is probably a minor source of error for the purposes of this paper, however.

in the Armed Forces, living on military posts outside cities and towns, and persons living in institutions (prisons, sanatoria, and the like). In addition to these disparate population elements, persons residing in the open country but not on farms are classified as rural nonfarm residents. Evidently, any summary of the characteristics of the RNF category must be interpreted with caution.

In relating dependent variables to community size, one must realize that there is considerable variability in the characteristics of communities in the same size group. With communities aggregated into size classes the most that can be done is to determine *average relationships* of dependent variables to community size. It is beyond the scope of this paper to consider the relative importance of other factors in intercommunity differentiation in comparison to community size.

Definition of Urbanism. In accepting the community size classification as an operational counterpart to the hypothetical "rural-urban continuum," one violates the premise of many authorities that urbanism must be defined in terms of several characteristics. One should inquire, therefore, how community size is related to other criteria of urbanism. Wirth's definition of a "city" specified as minimal elements size, density, and "social heterogeneity." [8] Sorokin and Zimmerman, in their "compound definition," included these elements, and several others, among which they emphasized the importance of agricultural occupations as a criterion of rurality.[9]

Table 2 shows the relation to community size of population density, the frequency of farm occupations, and as the only available indicator of "heterogeneity," the proportions of the population classified as nonwhite and foreign-born white.

Density figures are not available for villages, and it is perhaps doubtful whether a meaningful density could be computed for the RNF category. But over the first seven size categories density declines regularly with decreasing community size. The density of the entire rural population (village and nonvillage rural) is undoubtedly well below that of any of the urban categories. On

---

[8] Wirth, *op. cit.*, p. 8.
[9] Sorokin and Zimmerman, *op. cit.*, Chapter II.

the average, then, classifying communities by size yields an ordering in terms of density as well.

As community size increases, there is a decline in the proportion of the working force engaged in farm occupations (farmers and farm managers, and farm laborers and foremen). The "consistent variation" of farm pursuits with community size is disturbed only by the somewhat lower figure for the RNF category than for the smaller villages. It is noteworthy that even the "most rural" category has scarcely more than three-fourths of its employed males engaged in farm occupations, and even in moderately large towns and small cities there is a significant number of farm workers. The criterion of farm occupation, like density, is generally consistent with that of community size.

It is not so easy to measure "social heterogeneity," a characteristic which is usually discussed somewhat diffusely.[10] But one frequently mentioned aspect of heterogeneity is ethnic diversity. There is a theoretical basis for expecting ethnic diversity to vary with other criteria of urbanism. Large communities are supposed to recruit their populations through immigration from a more extended territory than that on which smaller places draw. The data in Table 2 do reveal a tendency for the proportions of nonwhites and foreign-born whites to vary directly with community size. But there are several exceptions to this relation at the rural end of the community size scale. In fact the highest proportion of nonwhites occurs in the rural-farm (RF) category for communities in the South. Even with the South removed, the nonwhite proportion is higher in the RF category than in villages in the remainder of the country. The RNF category has higher proportions of both nonwhites and foreign-born whites than would be expected from its position on the community-size scale. In fact, the least ethnic heterogeneity is observed in the case of the small villages (under 1,000). To explain the deviations from a regular relationship one has only to refer to the historical concentrations of Negroes on southern farms and the segregation of American Indians in rural parts of the West. However, unless one takes the position that these historical facts "explain away" the deviations, the data on ethnic diversity raise a doubt as to the

[10] See Sorokin and Zimmerman, *op. cit.*, pp. 23-28, and Wirth, *op. cit.*, pp. 16-18.

TABLE 2

CHARACTERISTICS DEFINING "URBANISM"

Size of Community	Population Per Square Mile	Per Cent of Employed Males in Farm Occupations	PER CENT NONWHITE		PER CENT FOREIGN-BORN WHITE	
			North and West	South	North and West	South
Urbanized areas						
3,000,000 or more	7,679	0.5	8.9	—§	16.4	—§
1,000,000 to 3,000,000.	6,776	0.3	10.7	22.4	11.7	4.8
250,000 to 1,000,000 ..	4,468	0.5	5.7	21.5	8.2	2.7
50,000 to 250,000	3,869	0.8	3.7	22.7	8.6	2.5
Places outside urbanized areas						
25,000 or more	3,339°	1.3	3.0	21.7	6.6	2.0
10,000 to 25,000	2,721°	2.3	2.6	21.0	5.9	1.6
2,500 to 10,000	1,992°	3.9	1.6	19.8	5.6	1.3
1,000 to 2,500	—†	6.3	1.3	18.1	5.4	1.0
Under 1,000 (incorporated)	—†	12.6	0.7	16.5	4.0	0.6
Nonvillage rural						
Nonfarm	—†	11.2	3.0	18.9	5.5	1.0
Farm	13‡	76.8	1.6	26.6	4.2	0.6

° Based on incorporated places only. Land areas are for 1940 or are roughly estimated for 12 per cent of the incorporated places of 10,000 to 25,000 and 9 per cent of the incorporated places of 2,500 to 10,000. The corresponding density figures are probably slightly too high.

† Not available.

‡ Total farm population divided by total land in farms.

§ No community of this size in the South.

unidimensionality of a "rural-urban continuum" compounded of variables of size, density, farm occupations, and heterogeneity.

Demographic Characteristics. One of the most familiar rural-urban differences is the high proportion of males in rural areas as compared to cities. On the hypothesis of the "rural-urban continuum," then, one would expect the proportion of males in the population to increase with decreasing community size. Instead, as is shown in Table 3, the masculinity of the population is virtually constant over the first nine community size categories, then increases abruptly for the RNF and RF categories. The contrast is all the more striking in that females outnumber males in each of the urban and village categories, whereas the reverse is true of the nonvillage rural population. If one drew a line between "rural" and "urban" between the RNF category and the small villages, instead of between places of 2,500 or more and places under 2,500 (the Census classification), he would certainly note an "abrupt

TABLE 3

DEMOGRAPHIC AND SOCIO-ECONOMIC CHARACTERISTICS

Size of Community	Per Cent Male	Per Cent 65 Years Old and Over	Intra-County Mobility Rate °	Per Cent High-School Graduates †	White-Collar Workers as Per Cent of All Nonfarm Workers ‡	Median Income § (Dollars)
Urbanized areas						
3,000,000 or more	48.5	7.8	9.5	39.4	43.8	2,492
1,000,000 to 3,000,000	48.5	7.6	10.5	39.9	39.8	2,443
250,000 to 1,000,000	48.4	7.8	14.3	39.9	39.9	2,160
50,000 to 250,000	48.3	8.0	13.7	38.3	37.9	2,057
Places outside urbanized areas						
25,000 or more	48.4	8.4	14.4	38.9	38.3	1,899
10,000 to 25,000	48.2	8.8	14.2	37.9	37.0	1,822
2,500 to 10,000	48.2	9.3	13.5	35.4	35.6	1,700
1,000 to 2,500	48.5	10.3	12.0	33.0	33.7	1,634
Under 1,000 (incorporated)	48.4	13.5	11.0	30.3	35.9	1,368
Nonvillage rural						
Nonfarm	51.4	7.3	14.3	27.3	26.0	1,605
Farm	52.3	7.5	9.6	19.0	21.7	1,111

° Per cent of all persons one year old and over living in the same county in 1950 as in 1949 who lived in a different house in 1949.

† Persons 25 years old and over.

‡ Employed males 14 years old and over.

§ For persons 14 years old and over with income in 1949.

transition" from rural to urban rather than a "continuous gradation."

Table 3 shows a rather "continuous gradation" in one aspect of age distribution, the percentage of the population 65 years old and over. However, the gradient extends only over the urban and village size groups and is abruptly broken when the RNF and RF categories are reached. The latter are actually more similar to the largest cities in their proportions of old persons than to any of the intervening size groups.

A third demographic variable exhibits still a different type of departure from expectations based on the "continuum" hypothesis. An approximation to the amount of local residential mobility is given by expressing the number of persons living in a different house within the same county as a percentage of all those living in the same county in 1950 as in 1949. This calculation disregards persons who moved from one county to another over the one-year period. The figures in Table 3 show that the intracounty mobility rate is lowest for the largest urbanized areas and for the nonvillage rural-farm population, and rises to a peak toward the middle of the community size scale. The high RNF value is an exception to this relationship. In this case, then, the extremes of the "continuum" resemble each other more closely than either resembles the median points.

Socio-Economic Characteristics. On the whole, measures of socio-economic status fall into the regular gradient pattern expected on the "continuum hypothesis." As Table 3 shows, educational attainment, the percentage of white-collar workers in the nonfarm labor force, and the median cash income of persons with income are highest at the upper end of the community size scale and lowest at the rural pole. There are some minor fluctuations from one size category to the next, but perhaps the only serious disturbance of the pattern is the comparatively high median income for the RNF category.

One remark should be made, however. In the case of each of the three socio-economic series, the index value for the largest urbanized areas is about twice as large as that for the RF category. In the case of median income the middle size category (places of 10,000 to 25,000) is about half-way between the two extreme categories. But for the percentages of high-school graduates and white-collar workers, places of 10,000 to 25,000 are much closer to the largest cities than to the RF category. This finding means that one must expect to discover different types of community size gradients, even within the class of those relationships which are generally consistent with the "continuum hypothesis."

Family Characteristics. Many authorities believe that one of the most basic differences between rural and urban communities lies in the greater strength of familistic values in the former. On the "continuum hypothesis" one would expect various measures of family organization and functioning to exhibit a regular gradient pattern by size of community. The data in Table 4 provide general support for this expectation, but reveal some significant exceptions.

If allowance is made for variations in age distribution, the percentage of married females increases regularly from a low point in the largest communities to a maximum in RF areas.

The extreme difference of 12 percentage points in the age-standardized proportion married and the stepwise progression of the proportions yield a pattern as closely in line with the "continuum hypothesis" as one might hope to find. The finding for the males is not quite so neat: The differences are smaller and less regular; and after reaching a maximum for the two groups of villages, the proportions drop rather sharply for the RNF and RF categories. A major part of the explanation for this drop undoubtedly lies in the excess of males over females in RNF and RF areas; i.e., males in these areas have less opportunity for marriage.

Labor force participation of females belongs in a discussion of family characteristics, because gainful employment of women outside the home represents a departure from traditional familistic patterns. As Table 4 shows, there is a marked rural-urban contrast in the proportion of women in the labor force. However, a community size gradient is observed only for places under 25,-000, and the labor force participation rate is practically constant among the five categories of places larger than 25,000. This finding is a bit surprising in view of the variation in proportion married and in marital fertility among the larger community size groups. Since employment competes with marriage and childbearing, one would expect labor force participation to be highest where the proportion married and the index of fertility are lowest. Perhaps if the labor force participation rates were standardized for marital status and number of children, one would actually find lower rates in the largest communities than in those of intermediate size.

Table 4 reveals a regular gradient pattern in the fertility ratio, here defined as the number of children under the age of five per 100 married women aged 14 to 44. The RF fertility ratio is nearly 50 per cent larger than that of the largest communities.

In view of the finding on fertility, one might expect a gradient in size of family. The statistics in Table 4 are for primary families, which means families comprised of a household head and all of his or her relatives by blood or marriage living in the same household (household heads living alone, or with nonrelatives only, are not included). There is, indeed, a pronounced rural-urban contrast, i.e., a substantial difference between the RNF and RF categories and all other community size categories, in the

TABLE 4

Family Characteristics

Size of Community	Per Cent Married (Standardized for Age) *		Per Cent of Females in the Labor Force †	Fertility Ratio ‡	Average Size of Primary Families
	Male	Female			
Urbanized areas					
3,000,000 or more	65.2	61.4	34.0	56	3.41
1,000,000 to 3,000,000	65.2	61.5	33.0	61	3.53
250,000 to 1,000,00 ..	68.0	62.9	33.9	62	3.44
50,000 to 250,000	68.4	63.5	34.1	63	3.47
Places outside urbanized areas					
25,000 or more	68.2	63.6	33.9	64	3.44
10,000 to 25,000	69.3	64.6	32.6	63	3.45
2,500 to 10,000	70.0	66.4	30.4	66	3.53
1,000 to 2,500	70.4	68.5	27.2	69	3.59
Under 1,000 (incorporated)	70.2	70.4	23.4	70	3.53
Nonvillage rural					
Nonfarm	67.7	71.2	21.1	78	3.91
Farm	67.8	73.7	16.0	83	4.14

* Persons 14 years old and over. Standardized by the indirect method, on the basis of age-specific percentages married for the entire population of the United States.
† Females 14 years old and over.
‡ Children under five years old per 100 married women 14 to 44 years old.

mean number of persons per family. But over the nine categories of urban and village communities there is relatively little variation in family size. The finding on average family size provides a negative case for the "continuum hypothesis" similar to that on the proportion of males.

Conclusions. The empirical materials of this paper reveal several "negative instances" for the "hypothesis of the rural-urban continuum," i.e., relationships between community size and dependent variables which do not fall into the pattern one would expect if the hypothesis had high descriptive validity. It appears that there are two important ways in which the hypothesis may prove misleading. (1) Suppose that an investigator working with a simple rural-urban dichotomy has observed a substantial difference between rural and urban areas on some important characteristic. He might then reason from the "continuum hypothesis" that if he established a scale of several intervals along a rural-urban dimension, an index of the characteristic in question would change gradually from one step on the scale to the next. Such an expectation would be in error for characteristics like the masculinity of the population or the size of families. The point is not wholly academic, for it is a common misconception that large cities have higher proportions of females, on the average, than do small cities and towns. (2) Suppose that an investigator has observed a consistent relationship between some dependent variable and community size over part of the range of community sizes. He might then reason from the premise of the "rural-urban continuum" that the relationship would hold over the entire range. Such an extrapolation, as has been shown, would lead to erroneous results for variables like the proportion of persons 65 years old and over, the intracounty mobility rate, the proportion of nonwhites in the population, or the female labor force participation rate.

The results of the study certainly support what might be called the "weak form" of the "continuum hypothesis," i.e., the merely negative assertion that there is no unique, sharp breaking point between rural and urban. In particular, the Census Bureau's practice of designating as "urban" communities of 2,500 population or more is justified solely on grounds of convenience. In dealing with characteristics like those studied here one finds as often as not that villages resemble small towns (in the "urban" category) more closely than they do the nonvillage rural areas. Clearly, the data presented above demonstrate the value of working with a classification of communities more detailed than the rural-urban dichotomy or the trichotomy of rural farm, rural nonfarm, and urban residence.

On the other hand, the "strong form" of the "continuum hypothesis" does not withstand careful examination, for even the few series of statistics examined here contain several instances where either "continuous gradation" or "consistent variation" is not to be found. To accord this conclusion the emphasis it deserves, these supporting points are offered: (1) While this study is limited to an analysis of census data, it touches on a number of characteristics usually thought to be fundamental in a consideration of rural-urban differences or regarded as basic correlates of urbanization.[11] It is doubtful that equally clear-cut results, for or against the hypothesis, could be obtained for characteristics inferred from a smaller quantity of data or less precise data than those of the census. (2) The results of the study depend, but only in part, on the use of a community size classification as the operational counterpart to the hypothetical "rural-urban continuum." It is doubtful that the outcome would be different in net effect, if communities were scaled according to population density or the proportion engaged in agriculture, rather than according to size. In view of the conceded significance of community size as an indicator of urbanism, it would be difficult to accept as valid an empirical scaling of the "continuum" which disregarded community size. In any case, the results of the study place on the proponent of the "continuum hypothesis" the burden of *exhibiting* a measuring instrument which performs in the hypothesized manner. One may note that it is rather easier to posit a hypothetical "continuum" than to demonstrate the empirical relationships which it suggests. (3) There are defects in the community size classification, especially the ambiguity of the RNF category. But although the characteristics of this category are perhaps more frequently out of line with the "continuum hypothesis" than those of any other single category, none of the paper's conclusions rests on this fact alone. Even if one disregards the data on RNF category, there remain several cases in which the hypothesis does not withstand scrutiny.

The writer's general position is that careful inductive classifications of communities are of greater scientific value than hypothetical constructs like the "rural-urban continuum." The latter perhaps has some heuristic value in suggesting one kind of intercommunity variation. But it is highly doubtful that the unidimensional continuum, in any rigorous, mathematical sense, is a sufficiently realistic model for research on intercommunity variation. Realistic classifications will almost necessarily be multidimensional ones. Moreover, the precision of measurement along the various dimensions will doubtlessly be much less than is

---

[11] For an analysis of a number of other census characteristics and a fuller treatment of those discussed in this paper, see the monograph by the writer and Albert J. Reiss, Jr., *Social Characteristics of Urban and Rural Communities, 1950* (New York: John Wiley and Sons, 1956), Part I.

suggested by the idea of a continuum in mathematics. If this is true, then does not the social scientist reveal more pretentiousness than insight in insisting on a term like "continuum"? Finally, although it does not provide a "rural-urban continuum" in a definitive sense, the community size classification employed here— or, better, a refinement thereof—will no doubt prove to be a useful tool in research.

Chapter 14

RESEARCH ON SOME
RURAL-URBAN CONTRASTS

TRAITS OF THE URBAN AND RURAL
POPULATIONS OF LATIN AMERICA *

ANA CASIS AND KINGSLEY DAVIS

If, as has been shown, the cities of Latin America already embrace a substantial portion of the population, and if (under the impact of industrialization) they are destined to embrace a still larger portion,[1] the next question is this: What are the leading characteristics of the city populations as contrasted with the rural? What is the nature and extent of the gulf that separates the two? The answer to this question will help explain the process of urbanization in the region. It will also throw light on the future of Latin America, because, with the further diffusion of urbanism, the city characteristics of today will become tomorrow those of the whole country.

Statistics on rural-urban characteristics in the Latin American region are scarce and fragmentary. The data are not always broken down according to the rural-urban difference or according to size of city. For some countries, however, the existing statistics are either satisfactory or can serve as a basis of reasonable estimates. It is thus possible to assemble considerable information

* Adapted from *The Milbank Memorial Fund Quarterly*, Vol. XXIV, No. 3 (July, 1946), pp. 292-314, with permission of authors and publisher.
[1] See Davis, Kingsley and Casis, Ana: Urbanization in Latin America. *The Milbank Memorial Fund Quarterly*, 24, April 1946, pp. 186-207.

on the vital rates, the age distribution, the sex ratio, the marital status, the place of birth, and the literacy of the city and non-city populations. Since the countries for which data exist are scattered and varied, the basic facts about rural-urban differences within these countries seem applicable in a general way to the region as a whole.

We shall try to show that the cities are dependent on the countryside for their people, the countryside dependent on the cities for its cultural advance. First we shall deal with the supply of people, i.e., with the vital statistics—births, deaths, and migration; then we shall deal with their biological characteristics, such as sex and age, and finally with their cultural traits. We shall find that these topics are all interrelated, and that the facts help to clarify not only the evolution of Latin American cities but also the evolution of Latin America itself.

VITAL RATES

Fertility. There can be no doubt that the urban dwellers of Latin America, like those in the rest of the world,[2] have fewer offspring than the rural dwellers. Proof can be found in two independent lines of evidence: First, in the few countries having fairly reliable birth registration, the reported birth rates of the cities are lower than those of the country. Second, in all countries having censuses the urban child-woman ratio is lower than the rural. Both kinds of evidence are subject to error, but the biases would seemingly tend to minimize rather than exaggerate the rural-urban differential. Consequently, the existence of differential fertility may be accepted without cavil.

Reported birth rates for four countries are depicted in Figure I, the top row of diagrams. In each case, despite some tendency for outlying inhabitants to hospitalize their births and thus report them in the city, and despite better registration in the cities, the urban rates are lower than the rural. Only in Chile in 1941-1943 was the relationship reversed. In general the differential is apparently not so great as in the United States, but this result

---

[2] Jaffe A. J.: Urbanization and Fertility. *American Journal of Sociology*, 48, July 1942, pp. 48-60. Davis, Kingsley: Human Fertility in India. *American Journal of Sociology*, 52, November 1946, pp. 243-254.

may be due as much to error as to a real situation; exact comparisons between countries as to rural-urban fertility differences are extremely hard to make. Since Latin America is in an early stage of industrial development, we should expect that the differential between city and country fertility has not yet reached its greatest width. If births were fully reported and were allocated to place of mother's residence, the trend in the differential could be accurately gauged.

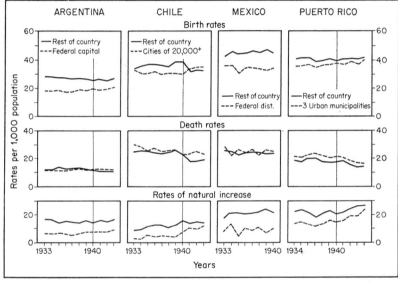

Office of Population Research, Princeton University

Figure I.   Vital Rates for Cities and Rural Areas in Four Countries.

The evidence furnished by child-woman ratios is as impressive as that furnished by registered births. Figure II gives, for seven countries, the number of children 0-4 per 1,000 women 15-49 in two sizes of cities and in rural areas. In every case the urban ratios are substantially lower than the rural, and in general they are lowest in the larger cities. The cities of 100,000 and over have a ratio, on the average, only half as high as do the places under 10,000. Below are given, for the seven countries combined, the average ratio found in each kind of place.[3] It can

[3] The censuses from which the figures were derived did not all occur in the

Children 0-4 per 1,000 Women 15-49

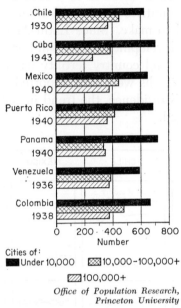

Cities of :
■ Under 10,000   ⬚ 10,000-100,000+
▨ 100,000+

Office of Population Research,
Princeton University

FIGURE II.   Child-Woman Ratios in Cities by Size Class and in Rest of
Country. Selected Countries.

be seen not only that the larger cities have the lowest ratio, but
also that the difference between them and the smaller cities is
far less than the difference between cities in general and the rest

	Children 0-4 per 1,000 Women 15-49 (Seven Countries)
Cities 100,000 plus	352
Cities 10,000-100,000	412
Places under 10,000	659

of the country. In other words, the gulf between cities of different size is less, in this respect at least, than the gulf between city
and country.

same year in these countries. The dates are given in Figure II. The disparity of
dates, not great in any case, is not fatal for this kind of average.
    The age structure of women 15-49 is not sufficiently dissimilar in the cities
and rural areas to justify a refinement of the child-woman ratio on this basis.
The large bias lies in the differential underenumeration and mortality of children
under 5, not in the distortion of female age distributions within the 15-49 range.

One would like to know how long these differentials have prevailed, and whether they have grown or declined. But in addition to the incompleteness of registration and the infrequency of censuses, changes in the habits of hospitalization, of registration, of enumeration, and of presenting the data all frustrate an attempt to get valid statistical series. Historical analysis of rural-urban fertility differentials therefore seems impossible for the present.

Even without the historical data on rural-urban fertility, however, one can rely on the current differential and two other known trends to furnish a prediction that fertility in Latin America will decline in the fairly near future. The two trends are (a) the faster growth of population in urban than in rural areas,[4] and (b) the spread of urban patterns to the rural population. Given the existing differential fertility, these twin processes—urban growth and urban diffusion—will in time lower the birth rate substantially. But there may be still a third factor at work—namely, a secular decline in urban fertility itself. It is this third factor that cannot be proved for Latin America on the basis of present statistics.

The influence of urbanization in lowering fertility seems observable from the figures presented in Table 1. Here the countries are listed according to their urbanization index, and then their reported or estimated birth rates and their child-woman ratios are given. It can be seen that there is a fairly good negative correlation between a country's degree of urbanization and its general fertility. In fact the correlation is surprisingly good in view of the ragged nature of the data. The growth of cities and the diffusion of their reproductive habits is already, it appears, having a depressive effect on national birth rates.

Mortality. If the data on fertility are poor, those on mortality are even worse. To judge by reported rates there is no marked or consistent difference between city and country. If anything, as shown in the second row of diagrams in Figure I, the cities tend to have a higher mortality, but this conclusion must be accepted with care. Obviously the possible advantages run both ways: the cities have better sanitation and more medical service, but they are also more crowded and possibly offer poorer diets. Probably

---

[4] See Davis and Casis, *op. cit.*, pp. 196-199.

TABLE 1

BIRTH RATES, CHILD-WOMAN RATIOS, AND URBANIZATION INDEX FOR
SELECTED COUNTRIES

Country	Date [a]	Urbanization Index [1]	Average Birth Rate	Children 0-4 per 1,000 Women 15-49 [1]
Argentina ...	1943	43.1[b]	25.2[c2]	425[d3]
Chile	1940	35.8	33.4[e2]	528[f]
Cuba	1943	30.5	37.8[g4]	535
Panama	1940	23.4	44.8[h4]	594
Mexico	1940	19.1	43.8[e2]	580
Puerto Rico ..	1940	17.8	40.0[e2]	606
Venezuela ...	1941	17.4	43.2[i4]	593
Colombia ...	1938	13.3	45.6[j4]	628
Peru	1940	13.1	44.3[h4]	654

[a] The date in this column refers to columns (2) and (4).
[b] Derived from estimated populations.
[c] 1940-1943 average.
[d] 1938.
[e] 1940-1944 average.
[f] 1930.
[g] 1933-1943 average.
[h] 1930-1940 average.
[i] 1931-1941 average.
[j] 1928-1938 average.
[1] Computed from census returns.
[2] Averages computed from official reports.
[3] Alejandro E. Bunge, *Una Nueva Argentine.* Buenos Aires: Guillermo Kraft, Ltda., 1940, p. 116.
[4] Birth rates estimated by using survival rates, ages 0-9, from roughly applicable Latin American life table to trace the age group 0-9 back to the births that presumably gave rise to them. Since the census age distributions have not been smoothed, the estimates are probably lower than reality.

the registration of deaths is much better in the city, and the death rate is artificially increased by deaths of rural people in urban hospitals. Unfortunately there is no measure of rural-urban mortality independent of the reported figures—nothing comparable, that is, to the child-woman ratio. Until further evidence is in, it seems safe to say that the rural-urban difference in mortality is less than the difference in fertility, and possibly has an opposite direction.

Natural increase. If the cities manifest a birth rate lower than, and a death rate equal to or higher than the country, their natural increase will fall considerably below that of the rural areas. This seems to be the case with the four countries presented in Figure

I (bottom row). Here the natural increase in the urban areas has ordinarily been between a third and four-fifths of the rural figure. It should be borne in mind that the "urban" population, for the purpose of this chart, is represented only by the Federal District in Argentina and Mexico, only by the three major cities in Puerto Rico, and only by the cities 20,000 and over in Chile. Nevertheless, the magnitude of the differential suggests that in general the rural population enjoys a rate of natural increase far superior to that of the urban population.

RURAL-URBAN MIGRATION

Granting the correctness of these results concerning vital rates, we reach the conclusion that the faster growth of urban than rural population in Latin America has been due primarily to rural-urban migration, and not to a higher natural increase in urban zones. This conclusion is buttressed by a study of those population characteristics that reflect migration.

In Chile it is possible to compare the natural increase of the population in places of 20,000 and over and in the rest of the country with the actual population growth in each of these zones. Theoretically, the figures should run as follows:

Cities 20,000 and Over
  Population Growth less Natural Increase = in-migration
Rest of Country
  Natural Increase minus Population Growth = out-migration

The in-migration to the cities and the out-migration from the country should approximately equal each other. Actually, because of great under-registration, much late registration, and some foreign immigration, this is not the case. The data are sufficient, however, to permit estimates to be made for the 1930-1940 decade, and from these it appears that more than 50 per cent of the growth of the population in cities 20,000 and over is due to rural-urban migration. The rest of the country apparently lost about 17 per cent of its natural increase to the cities. Since the decade in question was a period of severe depression for Chile, we may assume that this rural-urban movement was not exceptional.

In Puerto Rico there are three centers of urban concentration
—San Juan-Rio Piedras, Ponce, and Mayaguez. By computing
natural increase and population increase for the four municipalities containing these centers,[5] it is possible, as in the case of
Chile, to form an estimate of the migration into these centers,
which can be checked by forming an estimate of the migration

[5] The only one of the four municipalities that is not mainly urban is Rio
Piedras, but it has a density of 1,240 per square mile (1940) and is the main
area of expansion from San Juan, which is entirely urban.

TABLE 2

PER CENT OF TOTAL POPULATION AND PER CENT OF FOREIGN-BORN IN
SPECIFIED URBAN AREAS [1]

Country and Urban Areas	Census Date	Per Cent of Total Population in Urban Area	Per Cent of Foreign-Born in Urban Area
Argentina	1914		
Capital Federal		19.8	32.5
Places 1,000 Plus		57.4	68.3
Chile	1930		
Santiago and Valparaiso.		21.5	55.9
Cities 10,000 Plus		34.7	77.9
Colombia	1938		
Urban Municipios [a]		10.5	47.5
Cuba	1943		
City of Havana		13.8	30.8
Cities 10,000 Plus		35.7	50.1
Jamaica	1943		
Kingston-Port Royal, and St. Andrew Parishes ..		19.3	56.0
Mexico	1940		
Federal District		14.6	28.6
Panama	1940		
Panama City and Colon.		24.8	72.5
Peru	1940		
Lima and Callao		14.7	62.6
Puerto Rico	1940		
City of San Juan		9.1	44.0
Places of 2,500 Plus		30.3	76.2

[a] Includes only those municipios having 70 per cent of their population in
cities of 10,000 and over.
[1] Computed from census returns.

out of the other municipalities. The results indicate that no less than 61.5 per cent of the population gain in the four municipalities was due to in-migration, while the rest of the island lost approximately 29 per cent of its natural increase. These findings are roughly similar to those for Chile. It seems correct to say that throughout Latin America the rapid growth of cities is due in large part to rural-urban migration.

Not only does internal migration contribute heavily to city growth, but in some areas foreign immigration does the same. In this region, as elsewhere, immigrants have tended to settle in the cities rather than in the country.[6] Evidence of this is presented in Table 2. In all the countries examined the immigrants are concentrated in the urban parts and particularly in the larger cities.

AGE DISTRIBUTION

The age structure of the cities reflects both their lower fertility and their greater attraction to migrants. As compared with the country, the cities have a deficiency of children and an excess of adults. In Table 3, for example, there are six countries for which the proportion in broad age-sex groups is given as a percentage of the proportion found in the general population. (*See* also Figure III.) It will be noticed that in both small and large cities there is, in addition to a low percentage of children, a heavy concentration of males and females in the age class 15-49. The concentration is somewhat greater in the larger cities, but as between males and females it is approximately equal. In the age group 50 and over, however, the concentration is greater for small cities than for large, and much greater for women than for men. Apparently, then, there is a tendency for the cities to attract both men and women in the vigorous period of life, and the larger cities exert a greater pull than the smaller ones. In the later adult ages the pull is not so great for males, especially in the larger cities; but it is just about as great for females. In the older ages there is a

---

[6] For the Brazilian situation, see Smith, T. Lynn: *Brazil: People and Institutions.* Baton Rouge, Louisiana State University Press, 1946, pp. 199-200. For the world situation see Forsyth, W. D.: *The Myth of the Open Spaces.* Melbourne, Melbourne University Press, 1942, Chs. 3 & 6. The case of Buenos Aires and other Latin American cities is described in Davis and Casis, *op. cit.,* pp. 199-200.

heavy concentration of females, greater than is found in Canadian cities. This concentration of elderly women in Latin American cities is possibly due to greater employment opportunities there, especially in domestic and other service occupations. It may also reflect a tendency to live with urban rather than rural relatives when both are available.

TABLE 3

PER CENT WHICH CITY AGE DISTRIBUTIONS FORM OF THE TOTAL COUNTRY
(Proportion of Total Country in Each Age Group = 100)

Size of City and Country	Date of Census	Under 15 Both Sexes	15-49		50 and Over	
			Males	Females	Males	Females
Cities 10,000 to 100,000						
Chile	1930	92.5	106.6	106.5	92.2	97.2
Colombia ..	1938	87.3	110.7	110.9	92.3	108.7
Mexico	1940	90.1	104.5	106.7	106.3	115.4
Panama	1940	63.6	123.0	122.0	137.0	116.8
Puerto Rico	1940	83.5	108.7	112.1	104.3	123.6
Venezuela ..	1936	82.3	112.9	109.9	100.4	125.0
Average— 6 Countries		*83.2*	*111.1*	*111.4*	*105.4*	*114.4*
Canada ª ...	1941	79.2	109.5	110.4	101.8	104.0
Cities 100,000 Plus						
Chile		83.7	111.6	113.1	87.4	104.5
Colombia ..		79.7	116.2	118.2	86.8	112.2
Mexico		82.8	113.8	114.4	88.1	110.2
Panama		73.0	120.4	118.7	103.1	111.6
Puerto Rico		78.8	116.0	116.6	95.9	113.5
Venezuela ..		81.8	114.8	108.4	100.6	129.1
Average— 6 Countries		*80.0*	*115.5*	*114.9*	*93.6*	*113.5*
Canada		81.9	106.2	108.7	103.4	108.0

ª Cities 20,000 to 100,000.

Professor T. Lynn Smith, who has noted similar age phenomena in Brazil, has this to say: "In general . . . the age profiles of Brazilian cities are of the type that arises where rural-urban migration is a one-way process. There is little evidence to indicate that persons who have moved to the cities in early life, later seek a home on the land in which to spend their declining years, as is prevalent in the United States and some of the European countries."[7]

SEX RATIO

The concentration of women in the cities occurs not only at elderly ages, but at all ages above 15. In Table 3 and Figure III,

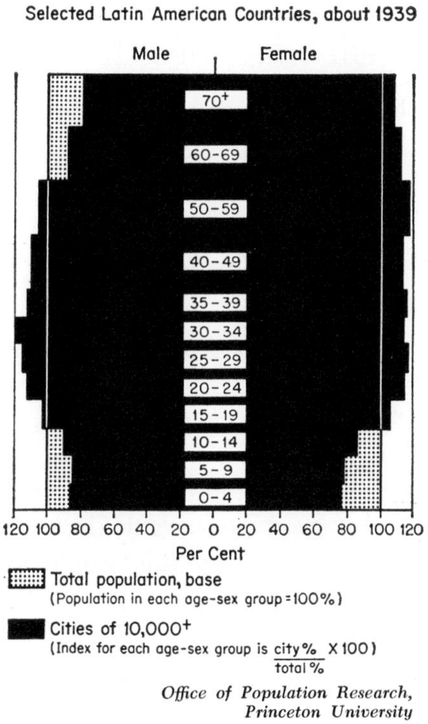

Selected Latin American Countries, about 1939

FIGURE III. City Age Distribution Compared with Total Population.

however, the sex ratio cannot be determined, because each percentage relates to a given sex, not to the other sex. In Table 4, on the other hand, the sex ratio is given for the population above age 15. In all of the six countries except Panama (which is in a peculiar situation) the rural sex ratio is substantially more masculine than the urban, and in every case except Puerto Rico and

[7] *Op. cit.*, pp. 210-211.

TABLE 4

Males Per 100 Females in Population Aged 15 and Over, for Cities
by Size Class and Rest of Country

Country and Census	Census Date	Places Less Than 10,000	Cities 10,000 to 100,000	Cities 100,000 and Over
Chile [a]	1930	104	91	80
Colombia [a]	1938	98	86	76
Mexico [b]	1940	98	81	77
Panama	1940	107	119	100
Puerto Rico	1940	106	82	84
Venezuela [a]	1936	93	80	86
Canada	1941	110[c]	98[d]	96

[a] In Chile, Colombia, and Venezuela the characteristics of the population of cities are not given. Instead, the population characteristics are given for the comunas, municipios, or distritos. We took those units that had 70 per cent or more in the city and assumed that their characteristics were practically the same as those of the city that each contained.
[b] Includes only 22 out of the total of 32 states.
[c] Places less than 20,000.
[d] Cities 20,000 to 100,000.

Venezuela, the small city ratio is more masculine than the large city ratio.[8]

The accumulation of women above age 15 is exactly what one would expect. In an area where urban growth is based on light industry, commerce, political centralization, and leisure-class interest, and where the rural areas sadly lack civilized conveniences, short-run rural-urban migration would normally tend to be feminine in character. This is not the case in India, where a different kind of culture has produced cities that are dominantly masculine, but it is the case in Western lands. In this matter the Latin American countries resemble the United States and Northwestern Europe, except that there appears to be less variation from city to city in the Latin American region. In the United States the sex ratio of the cities varies markedly according to the type of industry,[9] but on the whole the cities of Latin America are

[8] Smith, *op. cit.*, pp. 215-216, finds that the capital of each state in Brazil had, on the average, a lower sex ratio than the rest of the state, according to the 1920 census.
[9] U.S. Bureau of the Census, Sixteenth Census of the United States, *Population*, Vol. II, Characteristics of the Population, Part I, p. 116. For regional differences see Vance, Rupert B.: *All These People.* Chapel Hill, University of North Carolina Press, 1946, Ch. 4.

not yet so occupationally specialized. The main disturbances to the sex ratio appear to come as a result of foreign immigration.

Usually in the city, as compared to the country, people marry later and less frequently. Certain peculiarities of Latin American culture, however, appear to reverse this pattern (Table 5). In a country such as Venezuela, for example, a greater percentage of persons aged 15 and over in the city are married than in the country. But the key to this situation lies in the term "married." The Venezuelan census does not give figures on the number of consensual unions—i.e., unions entered into without a formal marriage and capable of being broken without a formal separation or divorce.[10] Presumably it classifies people in such unions as "single," although probably some of them slip into the "married" column. If, on the other hand, we take a country that does give figures on consensual unions, we find that the proportion of persons living together, whether in wedlock or in consensual union, is greater for the rural areas than for the city. In Panama, for instance, the figures are as follows:

| | Per Cent Living in Marriage or in Consensual Union | | | |
| | Males | | Females | |
	15-49	50+	15-49	50+
Cities of Panama and Colon	42.0	59.1	47.4	33.3
Rest of Country	46.1	62.4	56.7	35.4

Thus the apparent reversal of the urban tendency toward late and infrequent marriage is not a real reversal. This fact must be

[10] The Cuban census of 1943, pp. 767-68, in accordance with the 1940 Constitution, did not inquire into the legality of the union, but the census authorities believe that most persons living in consensual union were listed as "single" and in the comparative tables of this Census they were so treated. In Chile, where also no inquiry was made, it is thought, on the other hand, that most of those in consensual unions recorded themselves as "married" (Census of 1930, Vol. II, p. ix). Colombia also made no attempt to get data on consensual unions, and hazards no guess as to how they were returned (Census of 1938, Vol. VII, p. xi). For a treatment of the institution of concubinage in Latin America, see Davis, Kingsley: "Contemporary Modes of Marriage" in Becker, Howard and Hill, Reuben: *Marriage and the Family.* New York, Heath, 1941, pp. 100-06.

TABLE 5

Per Cent in Each Marital Status, by Age and Sex, Urban Areas and
Rest of Country, Selected Countries [1]*

	Males		Females	
	15-49	*50+*	*15-49*	*50+*
Argentina 1914 [a]				
Federal Capital				
Single	50.3		38.6	
Married	46.6		50.2	
Widowed	3.1		11.2	
Rest of Country				
Single	55.2		43.1	
Married	40.9		47.2	
Widowed	3.9		9.7	
Chile 1930				
Cities 100,000+				
Single	52.8	12.6	47.9	18.9
Married	45.2	70.2	45.8	31.7
Widowed	2.0	17.2	6.3	49.4
Rest of Country				
Single	59.2	16.5	49.6	17.1
Married	38.8	66.2	46.1	43.3
Widowed	2.0	17.3	4.2	39.6
Colombia 1938				
Cities 100,000+				
Single	64.1	19.7	62.3	34.4
Married	34.7	67.6	32.9	27.4
Widowed	1.2	12.7	4.8	38.3
Rest of Country				
Single	65.2	22.2	58.1	30.7
Married	33.2	65.1	37.7	35.5
Widowed	1.6	12.7	4.2	33.8
Cuba 1943 [b]				
Province of Havana				
Single [c]	64.3	26.5	53.0	22.7
Married	34.0	60.6	42.3	41.8
Widowed	.9	11.8	2.9	33.9
Divorced	.8	1.2	1.8	1.6
Rest of Country				
Single [c]	74.9	33.6	65.2	27.7
Married	24.0	55.2	32.3	43.6
Widowed	.8	10.6	2.0	28.1
Divorced	.3	.5	.6	.6
Jamaica 1943				
Kingston, Port Royal				
and St. Andrew				
Single	53.0	20.0	56.7	34.6
Married	25.3	58.0	23.5	30.6
Consensual	21.1	12.6	17.4	2.9
Widowed	.4	9.1	2.2	31.6
Divorced [d]	.2	.4	.2	.3
Rest of Country				
Single	58.9	20.7	52.4	32.6

TABLE 5—*Continued*

	Males		Females	
	15-49	*50+*	*15-49*	*50+*
Married	20.2	57.5	24.0	36.5
Consensual	20.4	12.8	21.9	4.6
Widowed [e]	.5	9.0	1.7	26.3
Mexico 1930 [f]				
Federal District				
Single	43.6	9.9	42.1	16.1
Married	40.8	50.6	32.3	12.7
Consensual	13.1	7.3	10.8	2.2
Widowed	2.4	23.0	14.4	68.7
Divorced	.2	.2	.4	.3
Rest of Country				
Single	34.3	6.0	31.7	11.9
Married	47.4	60.3	44.2	23.8
Consensual	14.8	11.1	13.8	4.8
Widowed	3.2	21.9	9.8	58.8
Divorced	.4	.7	.5	.6
Panama 1940				
Panama City				
Single	57.4	28.8	50.2	33.6
Married	23.0	44.4	24.6	24.0
Consensual	18.5	17.3	21.2	7.1
Widowed	.7	8.7	3.4	34.4
Divorced	.4	.8	.6	.9
Rest of Country				
Single	53.4	30.1	41.1	37.0
Married	16.3	32.0	20.1	21.0
Consensual	29.3	29.3	35.9	15.2
Widowed	.8	8.3	2.6	26.3
Divorced	.1	.3	.3	.5
Venezuela 1936				
Cities 100,000+				
Single	70.4	29.8	64.8	44.3
Married	26.4	56.0	28.7	20.0
Widowed	1.7	13.3	5.6	35.2
Divorced	.5	.8	.9	.5
Rest of Country				
Single	79.0	41.6	73.9	54.2
Married	18.9	45.0	21.9	19.3
Widowed	1.8	13.0	3.9	26.2
Divorced	.2	.4	.2	.2

[*] Argentina, Chile, and Colombia do give any data on divorce.
[a] Argentina gives data only for "15 years and over" combined.
[b] The breakdown below age 50 for Cuba is 14-49.
[c] Includes single, consensual union, and unknown.
[d] Includes divorced and "not specified."
[e] Includes widowed, divorced, and "not specified."
[f] The breakdown by age for Mexico for Males is 16-59 and 60+; for Females, 14-59 and 60+.
[1] Computed from census data of the given date.

borne in mind in interpreting Table 5. But the fact that a larger proportion of people living together in the city are officially married indicates once more that the city is ahead of the country in cultural advance. It is the backward and out-of-way areas that have the highest proportion of consensual union. As the influence of the city spreads, the amount of consensual mating will probably decline. At the same time, the formation of effective reproductive partnerships of all kinds, legal or non-legal, may also decline.

As might be expected, the proportion of persons widowed and divorced is also greater for the city. The tendency of widows to concentrate in the city is very apparent, although there is no such tendency for widowers.

LEGITIMACY

If more of the city people are "married" in comparison to the country, it follows that more of the city births will be "legitimate." This actually turns out to be the case in the few countries for which the data could be found (Table 6). Most of the so-called illegitimate children are of course merely the offspring of consensual unions. What the proportion is, and what the rural-urban differences are with respect to offspring of promiscuous relations, nobody knows. It is possible that such promiscuous illegitimacy is more frequent in the city than in the country. As for recorded illegitimates, the rural-urban difference appearing in the statistics is probably a minimum, because the registration may be poorer for illegitimate births in general, and for those in the country in particular.

LITERACY

Another evidence that the cities are in the van of cultural change in Latin America is the fact that the urban populations show a considerably higher literacy than the rural (Table 7). In some cases (e.g., Mexico and Panama) the literacy in places of more than 10,000 is twice that of the rest of the country. In others (e.g., Chile and Puerto Rico) the difference is much less. Apparently the Latin American countries are in an intermediate

TABLE 6

PER CENT OF REGISTERED BIRTHS THAT ARE ILLEGITIMATE, BY CITIES AND
REST OF COUNTRY [1]

Country and Area	Per Cent Births Illegitimate
Chile 1940-1943	
Cities 100,000+ [a]	20.1
Rest of Country	25.5
Mexico 1937-1939	
Federal District	30.9
Rest of Country	37.9
Venezuela 1940-1944	
Federal District	48.6
Rest of Country	61.9
Cities 100,000+ 1939-1940	46.8
Cities 10,000+ 1939-1940 [b]	52.9
Peru, July, 1941-June, 1943	
Lima and Callao [c]	43.4
Rest of Country	45.7

[a] Includes Santiago, Valparaiso, and Viña del Mar.

[b] Includes only eleven out of the sixteen cities listed by the 1936 census in this size class. The cities included, however, represent 84.7 per cent of all cities 10,000+ in 1936.

[c] Includes the entire province of Callao and the entire department of Lima. Data for cities are not available.

[1] Data taken from official reports.

stage so far as literacy is concerned. The cities are not completely literate as yet, but they are beginning to approach that condition. In the meantime, the countryside lags behind and promises to catch up only after the lapse of some years.

Literacy does not necessarily increase with size of city. As Table 7 shows, the cities below 50,000 generally manifest a lesser literacy than those above 50,000, but once this point is passed an increase in size of city does not consistently mean a higher literacy. Perhaps the largest cities have the heaviest rural-urban migration and therefore draw a larger proportion of their citizens from the relatively illiterate countryside.

A question important for estimating future social development can now be raised: Is literacy increasing faster in the cities or in the country? If it is slower in the country, we may expect future improvements in general literacy to take painfully long.

TABLE 7

PER CENT LITERATE AGE 10 AND OVER, FOR CITIES BY SIZE CLASS AND
REST OF COUNTRY [1]

Country	Total Population	Above and Below 10,000		Cities Over 10,000		
		−10	10+	10-50	50-100	100+
Chile 1930 [a]	73	65	87	84	89	88
Colombia 1938 [a] ...	56	53	80	69	84	82
Mexico 1940 [b]	46	35	77	72	76	79
Panama 1940	65	50	94	94	—	93
Puerto Rico 1940...	68	65	80	76	77	83
Venezuela 1936	36	29 [c]	73 [d]	[e]	[e]	79 [f]

[a] Classified as literate: those able to read. For the other four countries the classification includes only those able to read and write.

[b] The percentage for total population is based on data from twenty-six states. Other percentages are based on data from twenty-one states.

[c] Computed by subtracting from the total population the urban districts of Girardot, Maracaibo, Heres, Puerto Cabello, and the Federal District.

[d] Includes the above mentioned districts.

[e] Not available.

[f] Includes Caracas and the whole district of Maracaibo.

[1] Computed from data in census volumes.

One commonly hears, indeed, that education for rural peons means little, because they cannot use it in their elementary pursuits. Such opinions might lead us to expect progress in the country to be slower than in the cities. But according to the results given in Table 8, this is apparently not the case. In four out of five countries having available data, the non-urban parts manifest a higher ratio between literacy age 10-19 and the age 20-plus than do the cities. The only exception, Venezuela, involves merely an insignificant difference between the two ratios. The higher ratio of childhood to adult literacy in rural parts means that, as against the cities, these parts will gain in the future. It *could* mean simply that rural youth, having learned to read and write in school, later forget this skill more often than urban inhabitants, or that the city draws by migration the more literate individuals from the rural areas. On the other hand, it seems logistically plausible that as the cities approach fairly complete literacy, their percentage increase in literacy will decline, whereas the rural rate of increase will remain high. There is at least one place, Puerto Rico, where recently the rural literacy is known to have grown faster than the urban. Here between 1910 and 1940 rural literacy increased by 145 per cent, urban literacy by only 31 per cent. For various reasons, then, the hypothesis that the rural areas are gaining faster in literacy seems acceptable. This means that the citizens of Latin America are becoming more homogeneous with reference to cultural development, and that the old gulf between hinterland and metropolis is being bridged.

TABLE 8

RATIO OF PER CENT LITERATE AGE 10-19 TO PER CENT LITERATE AGE 20 PLUS, FOR CITIES 10,000 AND OVER AND FOR REST OF COUNTRY [1]

		Per Cent Literate		
	Date	Age 10-19	Age 20 Plus	Ratio
Cities 10,000 Plus				
Chile [a]	1930	91.9	84.8	1.08
Mexico [b]	1940	75.1	77.3	0.97
Panama	1940	97.5	92.4	1.06
Puerto Rico [c]	1935	88.8	71.1	1.25
Venezuela	1936	70.3	74.6	0.94
Rest of Country				
Chile [a]		72.5	61.9	1.17
Mexico [b]		39.9	34.1	1.17
Panama		63.9	43.9	1.46
Puerto Rico [c]		78.6	48.4	1.62
Venezuela		27.0	30.0	0.90

[a] Literates include also those able to read but not write.

[b] Estimate required to get this age breakdown. Ratio of literates 15-19 to those 15-39 in Mexico was assumed to be the same in Panama.

[c] Urban population defined as that living in cities and towns, rural population as that living out of cities and towns. "Cities and towns" includes some places of less than 2,500. See *Census of Puerto Rico, 1935*, Bulletin 2, p. 1.

[1] Data taken from relevant census volumes.

LANGUAGE

One of the reasons for the country-city gap in literacy, at least in Western South America and Central America, is the concentration of Indians in rural sections. Generally if a person speaks an Indian language as his native tongue he is not literate, because Indian languages have not usually been made a medium for popular written communication. Also such a person is generally in a rural section, because it is in the outlying parts that Indian culture has persisted. Consequently, the greater the proportion of a nation's inhabitants speaking an Indian language, the larger the gap between rural and urban literacy. In Table 8, for example, the largest gap is found in Mexico where there are many Indians, and the smallest in Puerto Rico where there are none. In countries having large Indian populations (e.g., Mexico, Guatemala, and Peru) there is, by departments or states, a strong correlation between the percentage speaking an Indian language and both the percentage illiterate and the percentage rural.

The census publications do not give much attention to language, and when they do include it, they do not always break down the data on the basis of rural and urban categories. But it seems safe, on the basis of available information, to say that the Indian-European dichotomy is one of the factors helping to create a gulf between country and city in Latin America.

CONCLUSION

Founded by Europeans and serving as links with the outer world, the cities of Latin America have grown rapidly. They have grown, not because of heavy industrialization as in most other regions, but because of water-borne foreign commerce, political centralization, and large-scale land ownership. They have reflected foreign influence to a high degree, and consequently have been separated from their own hinterlands by a wide cultural gulf. The extent of this gulf is revealed clearly by the characteristics of the urban and rural populations. In every way (with the possible exception of risk of death) the city traits are closer to those associated with modern industrial civilization, even though heavy industry is still largely absent.

The urban population has a markedly lower fertility and a lower natural increase. Its more rapid growth, therefore, is due to a heavy rural-urban migration. This migration does not take away all of the natural increase of the agricultural areas, but it undoubtedly helps to postpone pressure in these areas; and it apparently contributes 50 per cent or more of the city growth. As a result of the low birth rate and the heavy intake of migrants, the cities have a concentration of persons in the productive ages. Also, because the cities perform primarily commercial, political, and cultural rather than industrial functions, their adult sex ratios are predominantly feminine. The migrants, especially the female migrants, tend to stay in the city rather than return to the country in old age.

In apparent contradiction to other Western experience, the Latin American cities show a higher proportion of married persons than do the rural sections. When, however, the consensual unions are taken into account, the proportion of mated persons is lower. "Illegitimacy" is definitely lower in the cities, but again this largely arises from the lower proportion of consensual unions.

The cities are much more literate, in some cases twice as literate. The reasons lie in everything that has served to emphasize the city as against the country, including the concentration of Indians in rural regions, the preference for urban expenditure, and the tendency of immigrants to settle in the cities. It appears from age data and historical analysis, however, that rural literacy will increase faster than urban in the future, and that the gap will thus be reduced.

All told the rural-urban differences are such as one might expect in a region basically Western in culture but still in the industrial revolution.[11] Such peculiarities as are found arise from the transplantation of Iberian social institutions to the particular geographical and cultural environment of South and Central America. These peculiarities are likely to be temporary, being modified as the process of industrialization accelerates. It is significant that the trend toward urbanization shows no slackening as yet, and that the gap between country and city seems to be narrowing. With further industrialization it seems likely that the cultural characteristics of the cities will soon become those of the rural population, and that the gulf between city and country will eventually become no greater than in the United States today. If in the meantime the Latin American nations can profit by the experience of more developed lands, to hasten and guide the process of industrial advance and urban diffusion, so much the better.

[11] For an analysis of the demographic stage in which Latin America finds itself today, see Davis, Kingsley: Population Trends and Policies in Latin America, *Proceedings of Conference on Economic Aspects of Post-War Inter-American Relations.* Austin, Institute of Latin-American Studies, University of Texas, 1946.

TRENDS IN RURAL AND URBAN FERTILITY RATES *

T. J. WOOFTER, JR.

The relative trend of indigenous fertility on the farm and in the city is of basic importance in any future planning which involves the potential size and distribution of the labor force and the rate of growth of cities. It is, of course, well understood that farm fertility is much higher than that in urban areas and that rural non-farm rates are in an intermediate position. It is also known that the birth rates in all of these areas were declining rapidly up to the late 1930's. Any effort to project these trends into the future, however, soon involves the question as to whether the relative rate of decline is bringing the level of fertility on the farm nearer to that in the city or whether the gap between the two is growing wider.

The term "indigenous fertility," as used in this article, refers to the basic family pattern of a group rather than the acquired pattern which may be the result of previous births which occurred when the women were living in some other group or which may be the result of family customs acquired from another group. Illustrations of acquired urban fertility would be the effect on the urban child-woman ratios of the presence of an appreciable number of couples who lived on the farm during their early life, had two or three children, and then moved to the city; or of an appreciable number of couples who acquired their ideas as to optimum family size on the farm and, as a consequence, had larger than the average families after moving to the city. The rise in the crude birth rate in California from 1935 to 1940 was more rapid than that in the rest of the country. This was probably the result of fertility acquired by reason of the migration of large numbers of farm families from the Plains States. On the other hand, indigenous fertility would define the behavior of couples who were reared either in the city or on the farm and who, subsequently, spent their married life in the same environment. Since indigenous fertility, by definition, is not affected by

*Reprinted from *Rural Sociology*, Vol. 13, No. 1 (March, 1948), pp. 3-9, with permission of author and publisher.

migration, it is that concept which is basic in determining the true relationship between fertility trends.

Definitive studies on this point are lacking. Some allusions are to be found in the literature of the 1930's which indicate the belief that the differential between urban and rural fertility is narrowing and will continue to do so. An illustration of this is the data quoted by Warren Thompson in his *Population Problems* (page 138) which make the crude comparison between States classified as industrial with those classified as agricultural. This table shows a slight narrowing of the differential between these groups of States. Again, Frank Lorimer in *Problems of a Changing Population* (page 127) shows by the percentage change in fertility, by nativity and race in communities of different sizes, that from 1910 to 1930 the ratios of native white children to women declined more rapidly on the farm than in the rural non-farm or urban areas, but that foreign-born white fertility declined most rapidly in rural non-farm areas, next in cities, and least on the farms. Negro groups showed a mixed trend which was confused by migration. As we shall see later, the trends of the native white group as shown by this measure could also largely be accounted for by migration. Lorimer concludes:

> The more rapid decline of the birth rate among native white women in rural areas, which first made greatest headway in cities, is now spreading rapidly throughout the rural population. How much this will reduce the present large differential between urban and rural women cannot be foretold at the present time.

This author set out to see what verification could be obtained for the hypothesis that the gap was narrowing. The apparent conclusion from the data as they stand is so at odds with preconceived ideas that this study turned into an analysis of the characteristics of the measures used. These measures are shown in Tables 1 and 2 for 30- and 40-year periods. Table 1 is based on the children under 5 years of age per 1,000 women, age 15 to 49. This measure records conditions which prevailed for 5-year periods prior to the various Census enumerations and is based on the women who were living on the farm or in the city at the time of the enumeration, regardless of how long they had resided there. Table 2 shows the completed generation fertility or the total number of children ever born to women who had passed age 40. The residence of these women was also that in which they were located on the date of the enumeration without regard to how long they had lived there. The children reported were born over a previous period of 30 years; hence the incidence in Table 2 is earlier than in Table 1. Both of these tables indicate a slight widening of the gap between farm and urban fertility from 1910 to 1940. Table 1 indicates a ratio of farm to urban fertility of 1.64 in 1910 as against 1.80 in 1940. Table 2 indicates similar change from 1.54 to 1.70 in 30 years and from 1.37 to 1.54 in the preceding 10 years. Closer examination of these measures raises serious doubt as to whether the gap in intrinsic fertility is really widening, is stationary, or perhaps even narrowing slightly. The reason for this uncertainty is that these measures are obviously affected by factors other than changes in intrinsic fertility, notably by the virtual elimination of foreign-born women from the childbearing ages and particularly by the changes in these ratios which are attributable to farm-to-city migration rather than to any changes in indigenous fertility. Since the cities had a higher percentage of foreign-born and since the decrease in foreign-born was more rapid in cities, this would be an influential factor in the more rapid decrease in total white urban fertility.

Since the total size of cities has been constantly increasing, with the result that the *proportion* of recently arrived farm mi-

TABLE 1

CHILDREN UNDER 5 YEARS OLD PER 1,000 WOMEN, 15-49 YEARS OLD FROM
U. S. CENSUS [a]

	Urban	Rural-Farm	Ratio of Rural-Farm to Urban
1910	336	551	1.64
1930	296	487	1.65
1940	221	397	1.80
Per Cent Decrease 1910-30	12	12	
Per Cent Decrease 1930-40	25	18	

[a] U.S. Census of 1940—*Population—Differential Fertility 1940 and 1910—Fertility for States and Large Cities*, pp. 21 and 22.

grants in the urban population is becoming smaller, the effect of the farm-to-city movement is evidently diminishing in importance. Without the bolstering effects of a continuously large proportion of newcomers from the farm, it would be expected that urban child-woman ratios would decline more rapidly.

Ideally, a study of the relative trends of fertility on farm and in cities would be based on populations which were comparable in race and nativity composition and which had resided continuously either on the farm or in the city during their entire adult life. No such populations are, however, available for comparison without elaborate field study of selected samples. One method for such a study in selected areas would be to compare the number of children born to mothers and to their daughters who had completed the childbearing period where both generations had lived continuously in the city or on the farm. Lacking such data, the effects of migration must be discontinued as much as possible by deductive logic.

TABLE 2

GENERATION GROSS REPRODUCTION RATES ESTIMATED FROM NUMBER OF CHILDREN EVER BORN [a]

Age of Women When Enumerated	Generation Span	Urban	Rural- Farm	Ratio of Rural- Farm to Urban
50-54 in 1910	1875-1905	208	285	1.37
40-44 in 1910	1885-1915	161	249	1.54
50-54 in 1940	1905-1935	128	206	1.66
40-44 in 1940	1915-1945	106	176	1.70
Per cent Decrease 1905-15		23	13	
Per cent Decrease 1915-35		20	17	
Per cent Decrease 1935-45		18	15	

[a] U.S. Census of 1940—*Population—Differential Fertility 1940 and 1910—Fertility for States and Large Cities*, pp. 13-17. Estimate allows for under-reporting of children and differential mortality. Cf. T. J. Woofter, "Completed Generation Reproduction Rates," *Human Biology* (September, 1947).

On the basis of deductive logic, Table 3 has been compiled to indicate qualitatively the probable effect of migration on ratios of children to women, which may be quite independent of changes in intrinsic fertility. In general, it would appear from this table that the effect of migration on farm fertility ratios is probably slight, except as a result of the disproportionate number

of young people who moved off the farm in the young marriage-
able ages; whereas the presence or absence of farm-city movement may have a marked effect on urban ratios. Such migration,
resulting in age bias, would obviously lower the farm ratio of
children under 5 years of age and increase the urban, but
would not disturb the "generation" or completed fertility rate in
Table 2 since this is an age-specific rate. Besides the biased age
structure, the most important effect of migration on urban birth
rates is the addition to urban populations of considerable numbers of young people who, because they were reared on the
farm, have had their ideas as to an optimum family based on the
farm family pattern. These couples, probably even for some
years after their movement to the city, continue to have a higher
birth rate than that of the city-born population. As mentioned
above, the constant growth of cities which results in the decrease
in the proportion of farm-born, of course has no effect on farm
child-woman ratios, but tends to lower urban ratios by diminishing the bolstering effects of a large farm-born group. This factor
becomes even more important in periods when there is a back-to-
the-farm movement or a cessation of farm-to-city movement.
Obviously, under these conditions, the proportion of newcomers
from the farm who are to be found in the city is even more rapidly reduced. The question as to whether migration selects from
the farm population those young people who already have
adopted the urban family pattern as their ideal and, hence, are

TABLE 3

EFFECTS OF MIGRATION ON RATIOS OF CHILDREN TO WOMEN

Factor	Farm Effect	Urban Effect
1. Farm-to-city movement:		
(a) Bias in age structure	Lowers	Increases
(b) Transfer of rural fertility pattern	None	Increases
(c) Growth of cities resulting in smaller proportion of farm born	None	Lowers
(d) Possible selection of couples wanting fewer children	Slightly increases	Little effect
2. Back-to-farm movement	Reverses factors 1(a) to (d) incl.	
3. Cessation of foreign immigration	Lowers slightly	Lowers sharply
4. Suburbanization	No effect	Lowers

predetermined to have a smaller number of children is prob-lematical. To the extent to which such selection does take place, farm fertility is slightly increased without much effect on urban fertility. The cessation of foreign immigration has been discussed above. The last factor mentioned in this table (suburbanization) has practically no effect on the farm population and will be dis-cussed in connection with the effects on the rural non-farm areas.

The relative importance of these factors varies from region to region and from time to time, but, as stated above, statistics are lacking from which their quantitative relationships can be measured.

Table 1, however, indicates somewhat more rapid widening of the gap between farm and urban rates from 1930 to 1940 than in the previous 20 years. It is probable that this is largely due to virtual cessation of farm-to-city migration during the depres-sion and the continuation of the suburban movement. The pro-portion of foreign-born women in the childbearing population in 1930 was already so small that its decrease had little effect in the following decade. On the other hand, in 1930 the cities contained a substantial proportion of young couples recently from the farm who by the year 1940 had aged beyond the young childbearing years and who not been replaced by fresh tides of new farm-born young people.

The conclusions of the previous paragraph are based on the period before 1940 when the birth rates of all segments of the population were falling and when the effects of farm-to-city mi-gration were diminishing in importance. From 1940 to 1946, however, birth rates were rising sharply. Likewise, farm-to-city migration had been resumed on a large scale. The question then arises as to whether the relative trends in differentials between farm and urban fertility ratios would be reversed in the decade of 1940 to 1950. Population was in such a state of flux during the war years and residence so ephemeral that data from which to generalize fertility trends in the early 1940's are at best sketchy. However, some fragmentary evidence is available from the Sam-ple Surveys made by the Bureau of the Census.[1] The net repro-duction rates for both races calculated from these data in com-

---

[1] These results are described in *Population—Special Reports, Recent Trends in Population Replacement*, Series P. 47, No. 2, U.S. Bureau of the Census.

parison with those of 1940 indicate an increase from 1940 to 1946 for both races of 34 per cent in the urban ratio and 18 per cent in the rural-farm ratio, indicating that the urban rates rose more rapidly in the 1940's and narrowed the gap; whereas, in the previous 30 years they had fallen more rapidly and widened the gap. Again, it is not possible to segregate the influence of migration from the differential farm and urban response to better economic conditions.

Much of what has been said about the difficulty of measuring relative farm and urban trends applies also to comparisons of rural-farm with rural-nonfarm areas. Just as the urban increase is largely dependent upon immigration, so, to some extent, is the increase in rural non-farm areas. In a recent article by George W. Hill and Douglas G. Marshall [2] the belief is indicated that the differential between farm and rural is narrowing, although the extent of approach shown is too small to be convincing. In fact, in the State of New York the differential shown became wider. In spite of the inconclusive nature of the data, these authors state: "The data show *clearly* that the differences in behavior of farm families and rural families, so far as their fertility index reveals, are *rapidly* disappearing." [3] One peculiarity of the method used by these authors should, however, be especially noted. They did not make a direct comparison between rural-farm and rural-nonfarm rates, but between "rural" and "farm." Obviously, since the total rural includes the farm population, they were comparing a total with one of its parts. Under these circumstances, arithmetic can be deceptive. It is possible for the birth rate of each of the parts to remain constant, but for the total rate to change if the relative importance of the two parts changes. Something of this nature happened within the rural population from 1910 to 1940. In 1910 only 43 per cent of the rural women, 15 to 49 years of age, were in nonfarm areas; whereas in 1940 the nonfarm women constituted 52 per cent of all rural women. Since nonfarm birth rates were lower to begin with, this increase in the *proportion* of nonfarm in the total would, by arithmetic, lower the total rate even if no change had occurred either in the

[2] "Reproduction and Replacement of Farm Population and Agricultural Policy," *Journal of Farm Economics*, (May, 1947).
[3] The italics are ours.

farm or the nonfarm rates. Actually, from 1910 to 1940 in the total United States white population the ratio of children under 5 years of age to women of childbearing age decreased by 28 per cent in the rural-farm group and by 30.4 per cent in the rural-non-farm group, with a total rural decrease of 29.8 per cent. Thus, while the ratio of the farm to the total rural appears practically unchanged, the ratio of the farm to the rural-non-farm became slightly larger. As in the case of the farm-urban comparisons, this change may also be attributed to factors associated with migration rather than to any changes in indigenous fertility.

An additional disturbance of rural-nonfarm rates arises from suburbanization. It is not known whether the couples who move from the central city in order to rear children in the suburbs tend to have families which are larger than those of the people already living in non-farm areas or not, but it is possible that suburbanization tends to bolster the rural-nonfarm birth rate to a slight extent. Also, the growth of industrial villages in rural-nonfarm areas would tend to have the same effect on the birth rate in these villages as the farm-to-city movement has on the urban rates.

Comparisons of fertility rates between States which have had different migration histories are subject to the same criticism.

The annual reproduction rates (net and gross reproduction rates) are less influenced by past migration, since these are age-specific rates and biases in the age structure are eliminated. Unfortunately, however, these measures are not available for long-time farm-urban comparisons, because it is only recently that the vital statistics have re-allocated births to the residence of the mother.

To recapitulate: The available measures of fertility rates from 1910 to 1940 indicate some widening of the gap between birth rates on the farm and in the city and also a slight widening between those in rural-farm and rural-nonfarm areas. The effect of migration on these measures is, however, such that it is problematical whether the change indicated by these measures is a change in indigenous fertility or merely a series of changes in the composition of the population which have been caused by migration. This seems to be a problem which is worthy of further intensive study.

REGIONAL COMPARISONS STANDARDIZED
FOR URBANIZATION *

OTIS DUDLEY DUNCAN

Rural-urban differences within regions are frequently of greater magnitude than inter-regional differences, when the latter are measured by a gross ratio or average pertaining to the region as a whole.[1] Furthermore, in the case of many variables used as indices of the cultural status of regions, there are significantly large variations by size of city. Hence, in citing a summary figure for an entire region, one runs the risk of indicating merely its relative degree of urbanization. A more justifiable procedure would be to present comparisons among regions only for sectors of the regions' populations which are at comparable levels of urbanization. This is cumbersome, however, particularly where it is desirable to use a breakdown of three or more size categories in preference to the usual rural-urban classification.

For certain purposes, it is possible to compute by the technique of "standardization" a summary figure for regional comparisons which partially overcomes these difficulties. By way of illustration, standardized ratios of physicians in active practice per 10,000 population in 1930 are worked out for the nine census geographic divisions,[2] using a breakdown of five size groups of cities. The population in unincorporated places is allocated among the size groups in each region in proportion to the number of cities in each group. (Some such arbitrary expedient is unavoidable, lacking exact knowledge of the proportions of tributary populations dependent on various sized cities for medical services. The procedure seems fairly satisfactory, except in the case of New England, for special reasons noted below.)

* Reprinted from *Social Forces*, Vol. 26, No. 4 (May, 1948), pp. 430-433, with permission of author and publisher.

[1] Cf. William F. Ogburn, "Regions," *Social Forces*, 15 (October 1936), pp. 6-11.

[2] The data on numbers of physicians and the estimates of population base figures by size groups are taken from R. G. Leland, *Distribution of Physicians in the United States*, rev. ed. (Chicago: Bureau of Medical Economics, American Medical Association, 1936). For a map showing the supply of physicians per 10,000 population, by states, for 1930, see Howard W. Odum, *Southern Regions of the United States* (Chapel Hill: University of North Carolina Press, 1936), p. 370.

The requisite computations are outlined for two regions in Table 1, following the form for calculating standardized vital rates set forth in statistics textbooks.[3] The standardized ratio obtained by the "direct method" is simply a weighted mean of the ratios for the individual size groups, where the weights are the proportions in those size groups in some standard population (in this case, the 1930 total population of the United States). The "indirect method" of standardization depends on the application of "size-group-specific" ratios observed in the standard population to the actual distribution of population by size groups in

[3] See, e.g., Margaret J. Hagood, *Statistics for Sociologists* (New York: Reynal and Hitchcock, 1941), pp. 836-847; G. Udny Yule and M. G. Kendall, *An Introduction to the Theory of Statistics*, 13th ed. (London: Charles Griffin and Company, 1944), pp. 305-306.

TABLE 1

CALCULATION OF STANDARDIZED RATIOS OF PHYSICIANS PER 10,000 POPULATION, 1930, FOR THE EAST NORTH CENTRAL AND SOUTH ATLANTIC DIVISIONS, USING THE TOTAL POPULATION OF THE UNITED STATES AS THE STANDARD POPULATION

Size Group (1)	Standard Population (Per Cent of Total) (2)	Physicians per 10,000 Population			Population (Per Cent)	
		East North Central (3)	South Atlantic (4)	In Standard Population (5)	East North Central (6)	South Atlantic (7)
Under 5,000 ..	43.0	7.75	5.96	7.43	34.2	62.8
5,000-10,000 .	6.9	11.31	12.14	10.52	6.4	5.9
10,000-25,000	9.0	11.43	13.12	12.22	8.0	6.0
25,000-100,000	11.3	13.21	16.67	13.83	14.1	10.4
100,000 & over	29.8	17.15	23.31	19.01	37.3	14.9
All groups ...	100.0	12.55	10.45	12.24	100.0	100.0

Computations

	East North Central	South Atlantic
Direct Method:		
Standardized ratio	Σ (2) $\times$ (3)/100 = 11.8	Σ (2) $\times$ (4)/100 = 13.4
Indirect Method:		
Preliminary ratio	Σ (5) $\times$ (6)/100 = 13.23	Σ (5) $\times$ (7)/100 = 10.29
Adjustment factor (= ratio in standard population ÷ preliminary ratio for region)	12.24/13.23 = 0.9252	12.24/10.29 = 1.1895
Standardized ratio (= crude ratio $\times$ adjustment factor)	12.55 $\times$ 0.9252 = 11.6	10.45 $\times$ 1.1895 = 12.4

(Note: Figures for "all groups" are not used in product-sums.)
SOURCE: Leland, *op. cit.*, Tables 16, 19, and 21.

the several regions; the supplementary steps necessary to obtain the final result are indicated in notes to Table 1.

Table 2 gives the observed or "crude" ratios and the ratios standardized by the two methods for each region, together with the ranking of the regions on each of the three series. It is immediately apparent that the standardized ratios order the regions quite differently from the crude ratios, with every region shifting two or more places in rank order. An especially interesting case is the improvement of two ranks of the East South Central division; this region is frequently at the bottom in regional comparisons. Such shifts are expected when (a) the regions vary markedly—as they do—in the composition of their populations by urban size groups, and (b) the index under examination shows important differences by level of urbanization.

TABLE 2

NUMBER OF PHYSICIANS IN ACTIVE PRACTICE PER 10,000 POPULATION, BY
GEOGRAPHIC DIVISIONS, 1930: CRUDE AND STANARDIZED RATIOS, AND
RANKS BASED ON RATIOS

| | Physicians per 10,000 Population | | | Ranks Based on Ratios * | | |
| | | Standardized Ratios | | | | |
Geographic Division	Crude Ratio	Direct Method	Indirect Method	Crude	Direct	Indirect
New England	13.6	16.3	11.8	3	1	7
Middle Atlantic ...	13.9	12.0	11.7	2 (2)	8 (7)	8 (7)
East North Central.	12.6	11.8	11.6	4 (3)	9 (8)	9 (8)
West North Central	12.3	14.3	14.1	5 (4)	3 (2)	1 (1)
South Atlantic	10.5	13.4	12.4	7 (6)	4 (3)	4 (4) **
East South Central.	9.4	12.3	11.8	9 (8)	7 (6)	6 (6)
West South Central	10.3	12.6	12.4	8 (7)	6 (5)	5 (5) **
Mountain	11.5	15.2	14.0	6 (5)	2 (1)	2 (2)
Pacific	14.9	13.3	13.3	1 (1)	5 (4)	3 (3)
United States	12.2					

* Figures in parantheses are the ranks, omitting New England.
** The South Atlantic is higher than the West South Central by a fraction lost in rounding.
SOURCE: Leland, *op. cit.,* Tables 16-25.

To examine in detail an instance of shift in rank and reversal of the relative positions of two regions, we may refer back to Table 1, which shows the number of physicians per 10,000 population for each of the five size groups in the East North Central and South Atlantic divisions, together with the crude and standardized ratios for the two regions as a whole. Although the crude ratio for the East North Central division is twenty per cent greater than that of the South Atlantic, only for the size group "under 5,000" is its specific ratio of physicians to population actually the higher. Since over three-fifths the population of the South Atlantic division is found in this size group, as against only one-third the East North Central population, the discrepancy between the two regions in this one size group is disproportionately weighted in the gross comparison afforded by the crude ratio. When all size groups are weighted in the same manner for the two divisions, the superiority of the South Atlantic division in the remaining four size categories is reflected in the relative improvement of its standardized ratios.

The assumptions which must hold for the indirect method to yield ratios closely approximating those given by the direct method [4] do not necessarily obtain for the distribution of cultural phenomena by population size groups. Nevertheless, in the present illustration the over-all patterns yielded by the two methods are similar. With the exception of New England, both methods modify the observed crude ratios in the same direction; and with the same exception, the differences between the direct and indirect standardized ratios are less than the differences between either of them and the crude ratio. The rank patterns produced by the two methods are closely comparable. However, there are sufficient discrepancies to warrant hesitation in the application of the indirect method except in instances where the data do not permit the computation of a ratio standardized by the direct method; and then only where the variations of specific ratios by size groups are considerable, and there is some basis for assuming that the size-group-specific ratios for the regions are approximately proportional to those of the standard population.

The case of the New England standardized ratios emphasizes one of the specific hazards of the standardization technique, with the population base data currently available. Relatively few New England towns below 5,000 population are incorporated. Hence, in apportioning unincorporated population among the size groups

[4] See Yule and Kendall, *loc. cit.*

of incorporated places, a spuriously small population base for this size group is obtained, and the resulting ratio of physicians to population is spuriously high—twice that of any other region for the given size group. The error is greatest under the direct method, where this inflated ratio is given a relatively large weight (43 per cent of the standard population is in the size group, "under 5,000"). While the other regions also vary somewhat in the extent to which small places are incorporated, these variations are probably not serious in comparisons of the standardized ratios.[5]

A further limitation,[6] of a general nature, on the use of standardized ratios should be noted. The standardized ratio is a statistical artifact. It cannot be presumed, for example, that the ratio obtained for a region of the South, by attributing to it a greater degree of urbanization than it actually has attained, is representative of the actual crude ratio it would have if there were a greater growth of cities and a decline in the rural population. Such a profound population movement could not occur without equally profound changes in social and economic organization, which would undoubtedly be reflected in most cultural indices. Thus, although the discrepancy between observed and standardized indices may be hypothetically conceived as due to the effect of urbanization, it is important not to interpret the magnitude of the difference in a literal sense. Furthermore, as a measure of the gross incidence of a given phenomenon, the crude ratio requires no modification. It is only when it is desired to clarify the components of a summary figure that meaningful resort may be had to the standardized figure.[7] As a matter of practice, therefore, standardized indices should be presented only

---

[5] See Paul H. Landis, "The Number of Unincorporated Places in the United States and Their Estimated Population," *Research Studies of the State College of Washington*, 6 (December 1938), pp. 160-188. In the size group 1,000-2,500, 7.7 per cent of New England villages are incorporated, as against 70.1 per cent in the United States as a whole (Table 9, p. 175). Landis' figures do not cover the size group 2,500-5,000; however, a substantial portion of the New England population probably resides in unincorporated places of this size.

[6] There are, of course, various technical cautions to be observed in the use of any statistical device for holding factors constant. Cf. Ernest R. Groves and William F. Ogburn, *American Marriage and Family Relationships* (New York: Henry Holt and Company, 1928), p. 162, fn. 4.

[7] For example, the crude ratio would have the greater interest for the medical economist as indicating the total need for medical care; whereas the standardized ratio will be of use to regional sociologists for making more valid comparisons of the cultural levels of regions.

in conjunction with the corresponding crude indices. In many cases, it is perhaps the comparison of the two, rather than the absolute value of either, which will prove more enlightening.

Despite the necessity of careful interpretation, cultural indices standardized for urbanization provide an important perspective in interregional comparisons. A great number of indices commonly used for regional comparisons would probably show interesting shifts if examined by means of the standardization technique; for example: professional students per 100,000 population, persons in *Who's Who* per 100,000 population, per capita library circulation, criminal offenses per 100,000 population, newspaper circulation per 1,000 population.[8] The principal hindrance to the more widespread use of standardized indices is the lack of data classified by population size groups. It is strongly urged that, in the compilation of primary data for publication, greater attention be given this important type of classification.

---

[8] These items are chosen more or less haphazardly from the variables cited by Odum, *Southern Regions, op. cit.*

PART VII

RURAL-URBAN INTERRELATIONS

Introduction to Part VII

However great the differences between the rural and urban sectors of a society, neither constitutes a world isolated from the other. The influence that each exerts on the other varies from country to country and from one epoch to the next, but in all cases there is some type of interrelation.

The most fundamental relation is suggested by the very definition of a city. Since cities are concentrations of people who do not grow their own food, they depend upon the farmer for sustenance, and he depends on them for his market. The necessity of the relation is readily apparent, but there are certain ramifications which warrant consideration. Disregarding the role of international trade for the moment, it is evident that the productivity of the farmer sets certain limits on the degree of urbanization. For example, if the surplus food of nine farm families is on the average sufficient to support only one urban family, the per cent of the total population residing in cities is fixed at around ten per cent.

The limitations imposed on the degree of urbanization by the per capita productivity of the agriculturalists is nowhere seen more clearly than in ancient times. In all probability cities did not come into existence until after the Neolithic revolution, the principal feature of which was an increase in agricultural productivity through the domestication of plants. We may also note that since the Neolithic revolution certain surges in urbanization appear to have been closely associated with technological improvements in agriculture, culminating in the almost complete mechanization of farming in the most urbanized countries.

So far we have considered only the dependence of city dwellers on the rural population. In the early stages of urbanization cities were probably "parasitical" to an extreme degree, meaning that they depended on farmers for support but offered little economically in return. Under such a condition the rural population was more subject to exploitation by the city than dependent on it. However, such is not the case at present, at least in highly urbanized countries. In these countries the very fact that the urban population is the primary market for agricultural products makes rural inhabitants dependent on city dwellers. The tastes of the urban population, its size, its location relative to areas under cultivation, and the degree to which it is concentrated in large cities all operate to determine what the farmer will produce, how much he will produce, and his access to the major markets. Furthermore, the technological improvements in agriculture noted previously could not have taken place without the existence of an urban population. Mechanization of farming on a grand scale requires industrialization and the associated processes of mass production in manufacturing, conditions that are realized only through the concentration of a large proportion of the total population in cities.

Rural-urban interdependence neither appears in the same form among all societies nor remains the same from one epoch to the next. In the first place, an increase in agricultural productivity, although a necessary condition for the expansion of urbanization without international trade, may result in a larger rural population or at least a better nourished one, rather than a growth of cities. Even today some parts of the world doubtless have an agricultural surplus that would support a much larger number of city dwellers. The extent to which an agricultural surplus produces a growth in cities and the reasons for such a result constitute two of the major problems for research and theory. Another problem worthy of consideration relates to variation from one country to another in the degree to which urban residents depend on the rural population. This variation has been brought about by international trade, but it remains to be determined how much urban-rural dependence has been reduced by such trade in each of the different countries. It also remains to be determined how much and in what way international trade influences each of the various characteristics of urbanization.

Cities in highly urbanized societies have stimulated agricultural productivity through the mechanization of farming, the development of transportation lines and centers, and the creation of efficient systems for marketing farm products. However, this does not mean that all of the world's cities have stimulated agri-

cultural productivity to the same extent. It is not unlikely that
some cities, particularly those in unindustrialized countries, are
as parasitic as those of ancient times. We have grown accustomed
to the belief that a small urban population goes hand in hand
with backward peasants who are incapable of high per capita
productivity. This overlooks the possibility that a low degree of
urbanization in a country is as much a product of the nature of
its cities as it is a consequence of the rural sector.

There is general agreement that most social and economic
innovations originate in cities. Thus, while city-dwellers are dependent on the agriculturalists for sustenance, the latter looks
to the former for innovations, and it appears that cases in which
socio-cultural change has taken entirely different directions in the
rural and urban divisions of a society are rare if not altogether
unknown.

While certain aspects of the over-all picture are clear, there
remain several questions concerning rural-urban relations in the
process of change. It appears that a lag exists between the onset
of socio-cultural transition in the two divisions, with its duration
varying from one country to another and from one epoch to the
next. However, even when an allowance is made for the lag, the
over-all amount of change is likely to be less in the rural than in
the urban sectors. This points to selectivity on the part of rural
residents, much like that which occurs in the diffusion of cultural
traits when a preliterate society comes into contact with Europeans. Thus, even though all major changes in the rural sector
may have originated in cities, not all of the urban innovations are
automatically accepted by the agriculturalists.

In Part VI we saw how the demographic characteristics of
urban and rural populations often differ considerably. Although
the difference may vary from one country to another, we find as
a rule a divergence between the two populations as to rates of
growth, age composition, and the sex ratio. These differences are
largely due to a type of rural-urban relation which is here designated as demographic interaction. This form of interaction appears in the flow of migrants between rural and urban areas.

Certain consequences of demographic interaction are immediately obvious. Rates of population growth are higher for urban
than rural populations because cities draw more migrants from

farms than they lose to them. The importance of rural-urban migration is fully realized when one considers that an excess of deaths over births has often prevailed in cities, and particularly those in highly urbanized countries since the early part of the 19th century. Thus, in certain cases, the movement of people from rural areas not only determines how rapidly cities will grow but also in some cases whether they will grow at all.

An increase in the urban population is only one of several consequences of demographic interaction. Although its nature may vary in several ways, there is almost always a selective aspect in rural-urban migration, a factor that creates differences in the composition of urban and rural populations. For one thing, there is a tendency for rural-urban migrants to concentrate in the more productive years of life (14-45), leaving the rural population with a deficit of persons in this age group. Although a less uniform pattern, there is also a tendency for one sex to move to cities more than the other. The imbalance varies both as to amount and as to whether males or females are predominant. For example, rural-urban migration in the United States is apparently less selective of one sex than it is in either Middle America, South America, Asia, or Africa. Currently it appears that females are predominant among migrants to cities in the Americas, but males are predominant in Africa and Asia.

Selectivity in rural-urban migration occurs also with respect to intelligence, education, social class and other traits. However, it should be noted that in some cases there is no obvious pattern in selectivity with respect to these characteristics, and also that there is no reason to believe that selectivity operates in the same way under all conditions.

Data on the characteristics of rural and urban populations by countries are particularly limited in scope for studying interrelations between the two. However, it is possible to suggest, at least in general terms, certain kinds of information relevant to the subject. With regard to sustenance interrelations the volume of agricultural products exported and imported by a country is indicative of the extent to which its farmers look to urban countrymen as consumers, and the extent to which the latter is dependent upon domestic agriculture. Statistics on the mode of agricultural production, the degree of mechanization in particular, provide some indication of the services rendered by cities in exchange for farm products; and this also is true for data that describe the industry composition of the urban labor force (i.e., the per cent in manufacturing, commerce, government, etc.).

With regard to socio-cultural factors, concern with rural-urban interrelations focuses on comparisons of the two populations as to the prevalence of socio-cultural traits (material and nonmaterial) that originated in cities. Depending on the availability of data and the purpose of the study, such comparisons may encompass a wide variety of traits—literacy; school attendance; subscriptions to newspapers; dietary habits; the use of particular articles of clothing; voting in local or national elections; membership in voluntary associations; the presence of radios, telephones, and television sets in homes; and the ownership of automobiles; to name a few possibilities. Comparisons of this sort indicate the extent to which urban traits have been accepted by rural residents, and change in the prevalence of these traits in the two populations reflect a lag in the diffusion of urban innovations.

Research on the demographic interaction between the rural and urban divisions of a country has a somewhat narrower range of problems than is the case for either sustenance or socio-cultural interrelations. The major task is to establish, for each of a large number of countries, the amount of rural-urban movement and the characteristics of the migrants versus the nonmigrants, with the latter comparison indicating the nature and degree of selectivity.

Up to this point we have viewed rural-urban interrelations as they are manifested in the characteristics of the rural and urban populations and differences between the two. Still another approach considers the influence which the position of rural areas relative to cities has on the characteristics of the areas. The influence of an urban center on surrounding territory is manifested in a gradient, which appears in the tendency of the characteristics of rural populations to resemble those of the urban population in a direct ratio to the proximity of the two populations. Although proximity may be judged in terms of linear distance, it should be gauged in terms of transportation time and cost.

A gradient may appear in a variety of characteristics—sustenance (the size of farms, their productivity, their type of product, and mode of agriculture), socio-culture traits (literacy, education, the use of urban technological devices, etc.), and demographic interaction (the amount of movement to cities and the selectivity of migration)—and the point at which a given characteristic ceases to change with distance from the city marks the territorial extent of perceptible urban influence.

Rural-urban gradients can be analyzed in a variety of ways, with each of their properties suggesting something about the nature of urban influence in the country. For one thing, as mentioned earlier, it can be used to determine the territorial extent of the influence exerted by a particular city, or the average of all cities in a country. Another consideration is the degree to which the urban population and rural populations adjacent to cities resemble each other, which is indicative of the maximum influence of cities; while a similar comparison involving rural populations most removed from cities yields results that suggest the minimum degree of urban influence. Still another consideration is the difference between rural populations located adjacent to cities and those most removed from cities, with the amount of difference indicating how much the strength of urban influence is conditioned by distance. Also to be noted is the possibility that the gradient for one particular characteristic may be quite different from that of another, with such differences suggesting the spheres where urban influence is most pronounced. Finally, rural-urban gradients can be examined in relation to the size of cities to determine how much size conditions the amount of urban influence exerted on surrounding rural territory.

Whatever the research methods employed, the study of rural-urban interrelations has two ultimate goals. The first is to arrive at an adequate explanation of variation in the character of rural-urban interrelations from country to country and from one epoch to the next. The second goal is that of making use of knowledge of these interrelations to account for variation in rural-urban differences, in traits of rural populations, and in the characteristics of urbanization.

Contents of the papers. To date there are no systematic international comparisons of rural-urban interrelations which could be used as models for future investigations. However, there have been a few intranational studies on the subject. Two papers in Chapter 15, "Gradients of Urban Influence on the Rural Population" and "Note on Farm Tenancy and Urbanization" by Otis Dudley Duncan, report investigations illustrative of this type of research. Both studies employed the method of grouping rural units by the size of the major city in their vicinity. Such an arrangement does not directly take distance into account, but it does reveal the extent to which the influence of cities on rural sectors is contingent on the size of the cities.

While Duncan's findings are for the United States only, his method can be applied in any country without substantial modification. The major problem is the selection of a territorial unit to represent the rural environs of cities. Metropolitan regions, or service areas, would be ideal, but the labor of delimiting them makes their use unfeasible. The alternative is to select some census division that encompasses, as a rule, the city and surrounding rural territory. This was accomplished in Duncan's research by treating the largest city and the rural parts of either Standard Metropolitan Areas or counties as one unit. In nations other than the United States, the United Kingdom, Canada, and New Zealand, where counties are part of the administrative structure, it would be necessary to use census divisions that are generally larger than cities (communes, municipios, districts, etc.) and groups of divisions that include parts of or touch on cities not contained within one census division. It would also be necessary to use urban areas where there is no counterpart to a U.S. political city, or where the cities are "underbounded" to an appreciable degree.

The final paper, "On the Estimation of Rural-Urban Migration" (Chapter 16) has been written to acquaint the beginning student with methods for determining the net movement of population from the rural parts of a country to its urban units over a given period. Since the nature of statistics relating to internal migration varies from country to country, several methods are presented. The investigator can select the method best suited to the circumstances of his study.

Section 22 of the *Index to the Bibliography* provides references to sources of data on rural-urban interrelations; Section 24 gives references to a small number of studies and observations on the subject either within a particular country or among different countries; and Sections 9 and 25 pertain to studies of migration.

Chapter 15

URBAN INFLUENCE
ON RURAL AREAS

GRADIENTS OF URBAN INFLUENCE ON THE RURAL POPULATION *

OTIS DUDLEY DUNCAN

The general hypothesis of this study is that the rural population in areas under the immediate influence of urban centers differs systematically from the rural population in areas somewhat remote from these centers. This hypothesis was tested by (1) classifying the counties of the United States according to presumed degree of urban influence, and (2) analyzing demographic differences among the categories of this classification scheme.

Counties were classified as "metropolitan" if they were wholly or partly within Standard Metropolitan Areas, and as "non-metropolitan" if they were wholly outside S.M.A.'s. Metropolitan counties were divided into those in which the central urbanized areas exceeded a quarter of a million population, and those with a smaller center. Non-metropolitan counties were divided into those in which the largest place in the county exceeded 25,000 population, and those with no place as large as 25,000. Published census data on the rural-farm and rural-nonfarm populations for 1950 were aggregated into these four groups. The analysis was

* Reprinted from *The Midwest Sociologist*, Vol. XVIII, No. 1 (Winter, 1956), pp. 27-30, with permission of author and publisher.

carried out individually for the nine census geographic divisions, to provide a check on the consistency of the results.

The major results of the study appear in the accompanying table. This brief paper will not consider characteristics for which results were inconsistent among the several geographic divisions, although these are not without interest.

I.

The first thing to notice is the extent to which the rural population is concentrated in counties near large urban centers. The metropolitan counties of the United States cover only six per cent of the country's land area, but they contain nearly 12 per cent of the rural-farm population, and no less than 29 per cent of the rural-nonfarm population. Thus, there are about twice as many rural-farm inhabitants in metropolitan counties as would be expected on an area basis, and five times as many rural-nonfarm inhabitants. This implies, of course, that the density of rural population is substantially greater within metropolitan counties than outside them, a finding confirmed in Bogue's *The Structure of the Metropolitan Community.*

A second point on population distribution: the more urban the county, the higher is the ratio of rural-nonfarm to rural-farm population. In fact, if the ratio of rural-nonfarm to rural-farm population in the first three groups of counties were the same as in counties with no urban center as large as 25,000, the total rural-nonfarm population would be only about 25 million in place of 31 million. The discrepancy of six million may perhaps be accepted as a minimum estimate of the number of persons now classified as rural-nonfarm, who might be grouped more accurately with the unincorporated urban population on the peripheries of large cities in a "rural-urban fringe" category.

II.

A study of population pyramids not shown here reveals that the age-sex structure of both the rural-nonfarm and rural-farm population responds to urban influence. In most urban counties the rural-nonfarm pyramid strongly resembles that of the suburban population, whereas in the least urban counties it is more like that of the village population, with its relatively high proportion of older people, and low proportion of young adults. The rural-farm pyramid near large centers has relatively high proportions of older adults, and low proportions of children and youth, when compared with the pyramid for the rural-farm population in the least urban counties. Apparently the classic query, "How are you going to keep them down on the farm?" applies with greatest force when the farms are located fairly near to the lights of the city.

SUMMARY TABLE

SELECTED CHARACTERISTICS OF THE RURAL NON-FARM AND RURAL-FARM POPULATION, BY TYPE OF COUNTY, FOR THE UNITED STATES: 1950

Characteristic and Residence	All Counties	Metropolitan Counties, by Size of Largest Place in S.M.A.		Nonmetropolitan Counties, by Size of Largest Place in County	
		250,000 or More	Under 250,000	25,000 or More	Under 25,000
Per cent of total population					
Rural nonfarm	100.0	16.7	12.5	9.6	61.2
Rural farm	100.0	4.9	6.7	6.9	81.5
Fertility ratio					
Rural nonfarm	681	618	670	671	704
Rural farm	762	613	700	741	778
Per cent aged 65 and over					
Rural nonfarm	8.6	7.3	7.0	7.8	9.5
Rural farm	7.6	9.2	7.9	7.6	7.5
Median school years completed					
Rural nonfarm	8.8	10.0	9.0	8.9	8.7
Rural farm	8.4	8.8	8.6	8.5	8.3
Per cent in the labor force, females					
Rural nonfarm	22.7	23.5	23.3	23.9	22.2
Rural farm	15.7	20.0	18.8	17.6	15.0
Per cent white-collar workers					
Rural nonfarm, males	26.2	30.4	25.8	25.7	25.1
Rural nonfarm, females	47.0	52.0	45.7	45.1	46.1
Rural farm, males	5.3	13.1	8.4	6.2	4.6
Rural farm, females	26.8	42.0	32.3	28.3	24.7
Per cent of rural farm males in nonfarm occupations	24.6	47.1	37.9	29.3	21.7
Per cent of farm operators working off their farms 100 days or more, 1949	23.3	39.7	34.5	28.0	21.0
Per cent of farms with nonfarm family income exceeding farm income, 1949	21.1	41.9	37.9	31.9	27.3

Both rural-nonfarm and rural-farm fertility ratios grade upward, moving from the most urban to the least urban counties, but the effect is more pronounced for the rural-farm fertility ratio. In the most urban countries there is little difference between rural-nonfarm and rural-farm fertility, the slight difference being in favor of the former. In the least urban counties rural-farm fertility is more than ten per cent higher than rural-nonfarm fertility.

Differentials in educational attainment by type of county may reflect both the superior educational opportunities of rural areas near cities and the stimulation to accept these opportunities provided by contact with the urban way of life. The rural-nonfarm median in the most urban counties differs very little from the median for the entire urban population (10.0 versus 10.2); but there is a difference of 1.3 years in the median number of school years completed, as between the rural-nonfarm population in the most urban counties and those in the least urban counties. Although the difference is smaller for the rural-farm population, even here it amounts to a full half-year, despite the fact that age differences operate to mask the effect.

Participation of females in the labor force is recognized as an urban characteristic. But this aspect of urbanism clearly extends into rural areas near cities. In the most urban counties 20 per cent of the rural-farm females are in the labor force, as compared with only 15 per cent in the least urban counties. Furthermore, near large cities, far fewer of the employed rural-farm females are unpaid family workers than in the least urban counties. There is, however, no particular urbanization effect on the rates of labor force participation for rural-nonfarm females.

Although urbanization does not greatly modify the labor force participation rates of the rural-nonfarm population, it does influence the kinds of occupation pursued. For both males and females, the proportion employed in white-collar occupations is substantially higher in metropolitan counties with large centers than in the other groups of counties.

The urbanization gradient for occupations is much more marked for the rural-farm than for the rural non-farm labor force. The proportion of rural-farm employed males in white-collar occupations is over two-and-one-half times as great in the most

urban as in the least urban counties. Over two-fifths of the rural-
farm employed females are in white-collar occupations in the
most urban counties, but no more than one-fourth in the least
urban counties.

Still other indexes show the extent of urban influence on
the economic activities of the farm population. Nearly half of the
rural-farm employed males work in nonfarm occupations in the
most urban counties, as compared with just over one-fifth of those
in the least urban counties. The gradient between these extremes
makes it clear that the closer the contacts of the farm population
with the urban population, the more it follows urban types of
pursuits. There is no way to tell how much of this effect is due
to people employed in cities shifting their residences to farms.
Although this undoubtedly occurs, the writer's opinion is that it
explains only a fraction of the difference observed. The Census
of Agriculture provides relevant data. These pertain to farm operators, rather than persons who merely reside on farms. One
finds the proportion of farm operators working off their farms
100 days or more to be nearly twice as great in the most urban
counties as in the least urban counties. A difference of the same
sort, though not quite so marked, appears for the proportion of
farms for which the family income from nonfarm sources exceeded the farm income in 1949.

III.

Although the Census provides only a limited range of data for
counties by rural and urban residence, there are enough statistics,
when analyzed by the methods of this study, to demonstrate that
residence near cities profoundly affects the economic activities,
family organization and functions, and demographic structure of
the rural population. There are two further observations about
these effects, though the data to support them cannot be set forth
here. First, it appears that in many respects, though not all, the
gradient of urban influence is more pronounced for the rural-
farm than for the rural-nonfarm. This may merely mean, as was
suggested already, that a large segment of the rural-nonfarm
population is "rural" only in a formal or nominal sense, and

would appear under some other category in a more refined classification scheme. Second, in many cases, though not all, the gradient of urban influence is steeper in those geographic divisions which are on the whole less urbanized (e.g., those in the South) than in the more urbanized divisions (e.g., in the Northeast).

Both these observations suggest that the effects of urbanization on the rural population will appear less pronounced, the more urbanized the national economy becomes. The distinction between rural and urban, though important, is blurred. Galpin, among others, saw this, when he proposed the neologism, "rurban community." The cross-sectional analysis here, together with a variety of supporting trend data, presents a prospect of still further blurring. Sorokin and Zimmerman, twenty-five years ago, concluded that in highly urbanized countries the magnitude of rural-urban differences had reached a peak and was due to diminish.[1] Recently, Kingsley Davis has outlined a notation of a "grand cycle of urbanization," whose outcome would, of course, be the same.[2]

The paper closes, as it began, on a methodological note: statisticians must make valiant efforts to keep their categories abreast of the realities of social changes. Despite the important advances of the 1950 Census in delineating urbanized areas and unincorporated urban places, the figures for the urban population still understate the extent of urbanization. One can think of further refinements to improve the situation. Perhaps the so-called rural-nonfarm population should be classified in terms of type of economic activity, or even in terms of the location of places of work, rather than residential location, because substantial numbers of rural-nonfarm residents near large cities actually work in those cities and their suburbs. But without taking so drastic a step, it would be feasible to present census statistics on characteristics of the population by residence, not only in terms of the present rural-farm, rural-nonfarm, and urban trichotomy, but also by a

[1] P. A. Sorokin and C. C. Zimmerman, *Principles of Rural-Urban Sociology* (New York: Henry Holt, 1929), Ch. 27.

[2] K. Davis and H. H. Golden, "Urbanization and the Development of Pre-Industrial Areas," *Economic Development and Cultural Change,* III (October, 1954), pp. 6-26.

metropolitan-nonmetropolitan dichotomy.[3] This would increase the number of residence categories from three to six. But the cost should be measured against the important gain in the realism with which social research could depict one of the most important trends of our times, the movement of the entire economy toward virtually complete urbanization.

NOTE ON FARM TENANCY AND URBANIZATION *

OTIS DUDLEY DUNCAN

Previous research has shown that rural people living in the vicinity of large cities differ systematically from the more isolated rural population in a number of significant demographic and socio-economic characteristics. For example, in terms of the classification employed in this paper, 47 per cent of the rural-farm employed males in the most urbanized counties of the United States were engaged in nonfarm occupations in 1950, as compared with only 22 per cent in the least urbanized counties.[1]

Observations like this have suggested three major hypotheses concerning rural-urban relationships that bear on the economics of agriculture:

(1) Rural areas near cities undergo "suburbanization" or "fringe development" when urban people take up rural residences on the periphery of the urban community.[2] This population movement may be prompted by industrial decentralization, or it may be a strictly residential shift. In either case, a segment of the population which is nominally rural by residence, and which may even engage in some agricultural production, remains city-

---

[3] The metropolitan-nonmetropolitan dichotomy is already being used by the National Office of Vital Statistics.

* Reprinted from *Journal of Farm Economics,* Vol. XXXVIII, No. 4 (November, 1956), pp. 1043-1047, with permission of author and publisher.

[1] Otis Dudley Duncan and Albert J. Reiss, Jr., *Social Characteristics of Urban and Rural Communities, 1950* (New York: John Wiley and Sons, 1956), Chapter 13; see also Otis Dudley Duncan, "Gradients of Urban Influence on the Rural Population," *Midwest Sociologist,* 18 (Winter 1956), 27-30.

[2] See Interregional Land Tenure Research Committee, *Agricultural Land Tenure Research* (Chicago: Farm Foundation, 1955), pp. 29-30.

oriented in terms of primary economic activity and social relations.

(2) With improvements in communication and transportation and a rising rural level of living, the social and economic opportunities of the city become more accessible to rural residents in the immediate hinterland, supplementing those based on agricultural activity and focused in the rural community. Thus there ensues a "rurbanization" of the rural population.

(3) As some agricultural economists believe, the agricultural sector of the economy operates more efficiently in locations accessible to the foci of economic development;[3] or, as Lösch put it, ". . . in a dynamic economy Thünen rings must be formed."[4] Human ecologists have subsumed this hypothesis under "metropolitan dominance."[5]

The purpose of this note is not to resolve the differences among these hypotheses or to assess their relative importance. Instead, it calls attention to some empirical relationships considered worthy of further study under any of them.

Table 1 summarizes cross-sectional relationships between certain characteristics of farms, including tenancy, and the degree of urbanization of the counties in which they are located. Counties were classified as metropolitan if they were wholly—or in New England partly—inside standard metropolitan areas (S.M.A.'s). Metropolitan counties were dichotomized according to the size of the largest urbanized area in the S.M.A., and nonmetropolitan counties according to the size of the largest urban place in the county. These classifications produced four groups of counties, assumed to vary from high to low in urbanization. Not quite one-fifth of the farms fell in the three groups of counties considered moderately to highly urbanized (Table 1, panel 1). County data on farm characteristics in 1950 were aggregated to secure summary figures for the four groups of counties, the computations being carried out for the• country as a whole and for each of the nine census geographic divisions.

[3] Theodore W. Schultz, *The Economic Organization of Agriculture* (New York: McGraw-Hill, 1953), p. 147.

[4] August Lösch, *The Economics of Location* (New Haven: Yale University Press, 1954), p. 57.

[5] Donald J. Bogue, *The Structure of the Metropolitan Community* (Ann Arbor: University of Michigan, 1949).

TABLE 1

SELECTED CHARACTERISTICS OF FARMS, BY TYPE OF COUNTY, FOR THE
UNITED STATES: 1950

Characteristic	All Counties	Metropolitan Counties, by Size of Largest Place in S.M.A.		Nonmetropolitan Counties, by Size of Largest Place in County	
		250,000 or More	Under 250,000	25,000 or More	Under 25,000
1. Per cent distribution of farms					
United States	100.0	5.2	6.5	6.8	81.5
2. Per cent of farms operated by tenants					
United States	26.8	13.4	19.0	23.3	28.6
Weighted mean of divisions					
Observed	26.8	18.4	23.1	26.3	27.3
Standardized for economic class	26.8	20.8	25.2	26.6	27.1
3. Per cent of tenant farms operated by cash tenants					
United States	14.7	37.6	21.6	16.8	13.5
Weighted mean of divisions	14.7	30.4	20.8	16.3	13.9
South, omitting croppers	21.5	37.3	28.3	22.7	20.8
4. Full owners as per cent of all owners and managers					
United States	78.5	84.5	83.2	81.1	77.3
Weighted mean of divisions	78.5	83.5	82.0	80.4	77.9
5. Per cent of operators working off farms 100 days or more in 1949					
United States	23.3	39.7	34.5	28.0	21.0
Weighted mean of divisions	23.3	40.1	33.8	26.9	21.7
6. Per cent of farms with nonfarm family income exceeding farm income in 1949					
United States	29.1	41.9	37.9	31.9	27.3
Weighted mean of divisions	29.1	43.2	38.6	31.5	27.8
7. Commercial farms as per cent of all farms					
United States	68.8	57.6	60.9	67.2	70.3
Weighted mean of divisions	68.8	53.8	58.5	66.5	70.2
8. Per cent of commercial farms in economic classes I and II					
United States	13.3	22.2	19.4	16.0	12.2
Weighted mean of divisions	13.3	18.7	17.6	14.4	12.8

SOURCE: *1950 Census of Agriculture.*

The data reveal significant urbanization gradients for the incidence of farm tenancy, the form of tenure, and farm characteristics related to tenancy. The proportion of farms operated by

tenants was more than twice as great in the least urban counties as in the most urban counties (panel 2). The relative frequency of cash tenants among all tenants was nearly three times as great in the most urban as in the least urban counties (panel 3). Similarly, the proportion of full owners among all owners and managers was directly related to urbanization (panel 4).

Before commenting on these results, one should examine certain obvious factors affecting their interpretation. It might be suspected that the urbanization gradient in incidence of tenancy merely reflects geographic differentials in both tenancy and urbanization. Inspection of the divisional data (not shown here) reveals, however, that in each of the seven divisions outside the Northeast, the tenancy proportion was higher in the least urban than in the most urban counties. The second line of panel 2 reports averages of the divisional percentage computed so as to eliminate variation in the divisional distribution of the type-of-county groups; i.e., divisional percentages were averaged with a constant set of weights, the percentage distribution of all farms by division. These averages still exhibit an urbanization gradient, but one that is less steep than that shown by the unadjusted figures. It should be observed that the divisional averages understate the urbanization effect, inasmuch as there is a between-division relation of tenancy to urbanization, in addition to the relation within divisions, as may be seen from the following tabulation:

Division	Per Cent of Farms in Least Urban Counties	Per Cent of Farms Operated by Tenants
Pacific	51.1	10.6
Middle Atlantic	51.7	7.9
New England	54.6	3.7
East North Central	74.3	19.8
South Atlantic	84.6	32.1
Mountain	85.3	16.0
West North Central	89.3	28.2
West South Central	89.4	33.7
East South Central	90.8	36.6

Tenancy proportions by division, therefore, reflect an interaction between geographic and urbanization effects; an allocation of some fraction of the interaction to urbanization would result in an urbanization gradient intermediate between those of the first two lines of panel 2. (Similar comments apply, in varying degree, for the other farm characteristics covered in Table 1.)

Aside from geographic differentials, the incidence of tenancy also varies considerably according to economic class of farm, which, in turn, exhibits an urbanization gradient. Panels 5 and 6 show that the relative importance of off-farm employment and nonfarm income varies directly with degree of urbanization. Since these factors are involved in the classification of farms as commercial and noncommercial, the proportion of commercial farms varies inversely with urbanization (panel 7). But within the category of commercial farms, there is a distinct tendency for the proportion of larger farms (in terms of economic size) to vary directly with urbanization. The proportion of commercial farms in economic classes I and II (value of products $10,000 or more) was nearly twice as high in the most urban as in the least urban counties in 1950 (panel 8).

Evidently, tenancy differentials by degree of urbanization may reflect variations in the relative frequency of noncommercial (part-time, residential, and abnormal) farms and the average economic size of farms. For the United States as a whole, in 1950, the tenancy proportion for noncommercial farms was only slightly more than one-half as great as that for commercial farms; and tenancy was inversely related to economic class, within the category of commercial farms, though this was not the case in all geographic divisions. To hold constant the effects of these factors, the tenancy proportion in each type-of-county group in each division was standardized, by the indirect method, for economic class, making use of tenancy proportions specific for division and economic class. (There are seven classes altogether, six classes of commercial farms according to value of products, and the seventh class of noncommercial farms.) The weighted averages of the standardized divisional figures appear in the third line of panel 2. These results make it clear that part of the urbanization gradient in tenancy can be explained by the covariation of economic class of farms and urbanization. Nonetheless, a distinct inverse relation of tenancy to urbanization remains after statistical elimination of the economic class effect. The net relation shown, is, for the reasons already indicated, a minimum statement of the urbanization effect.

In qualification of the foregoing results, it must be acknowledged that the within-division urbanization gradients in tenancy were not all as regular as those shown for the United States. Rather, there was a general tendency for the urbanization gradient to be most pronounced in those divisions with comparatively high over-all tenancy proportions and low average urbanization.[6] The disproportionate share of the country's farms concentrated in these divisions weights the national results heavily.

Additional qualifications pertain to any cross-sectional analysis of the effects of urbanization. The decline in tenancy proportions since the 1930's is consistent with the urbanization trend, but the increase in tenancy from 1880 to 1930 is not. It is perhaps significant, however, that the decline in tenancy began first in the most urbanized region of the United States, the Northeast. Only historical comparisons of changes in tenancy and urbanization could distinguish the longitudinal effects of urban expansion on agricultural land tenure from the cross-sectional relationships between these variables.

A final comment on the study concerns the relatively crude units and classifications employed. More refined techniques will obviously be required to reach an explanation of the empirical relationship demonstrated here. The writer believes that further manipulation of county-unit data may clarify aspects of the problem, particularly if the analysis combines a cross-sectional with a time-series approach. But it will be possible to formulate an adequate description of the impact of rural-urban relationships on farm tenure only on the basis of carefully conducted field investigations.

[6] Space limitations preclude publication of the divisional figures, but the author will supply a set of tables for divisions, paralleling Table 1, upon request.

Chapter 16

RURAL-URBAN MIGRATION

ON THE ESTIMATION OF RURAL-URBAN MIGRATION *

JACK P. GIBBS **

Although the volume of movement from farms to cities varies from place to place and time to time, the importance of rural-urban migration in the process of urbanization is well documented and appears to be a universal phenomenon.[1] Moreover, while the rural populations of highly urbanized countries no longer support a rapid growth of cities, rural-urban movement seems destined to be one of the central features of urbanization in unindustrialized countries.

On the surface the measurement of rural-urban migration may seem a simple matter, but it presents difficulties of both a practical and theoretical nature. Our treatment is limited to *net rural-urban migration*—the balance between the number of people who move from rural to urban territory and the number who move in the opposite direction.[2] Thus, to use a hypothetical example,

---

* Written especially for this volume.

** Member of the staff of International Urban Research.

[1] See Conrad Taeuber, "Rural-Urban Migration," *Agricultural History*, Vol. 15 (July, 1941), pp. 151-160; and Pitirim A. Sorokin, Carle C. Zimmerman, and Charles J. Galpin (eds.), *A Systematic Source Book in Rural Sociology*, Vol. 3 (Minneapolis: The University of Minnesota Press, 1932), Ch. 12.

[2] Such movements are considered as involving a change in either the usual or legal place of residence. Both types of changes may be defined in a variety of ways, and investigations must accept whatever definition is used by the statistical agency which provides data on migration. It is not known how much influence the various definitions of place of residence have on migration statistics, but it is imperative, for the purpose of assessing comparability, that the definition employed in the collection of data be clearly described in a research report.

if during a given period 10,000,000 persons move from rural areas to cities and 500,000 move in the other direction, net rural-urban migration is 9,500,000. While this is only one aspect of rural-urban migration,[3] it is a most important aspect because it determines the growth of the urban population beyond the excess of births over deaths and foreign immigration.[4]

METHODS FOR ESTIMATING THE AMOUNT OF NET RURAL-URBAN MIGRATION

In estimating the amount of rural-urban migration for a country, all of the urban units, however defined, are considered together as comprising the urban territory. This is necessarily different from determining the net migration for an individual city, since in the latter case neither the source of the migrants (rural, urban, or foreign) nor the destination of persons leaving the city needs to be considered.

At the outset it should be recognized that investigations of rural-urban migration rarely possess resources sufficient to conduct a nation-wide research survey on the subject. Consequently, they must rely on published or otherwise readily available data as the basis for estimates. The nature of such data varies from place to place, and the methods which can be employed in some countries often cannot be used in others.

For example, the techniques utilized in the classic studies of Moore [5] and Thomas [6] on migration in Sweden can be applied in only a few countries. This is the case for any method that relies

---

[3] In particular net migration should not be confused with either *volume of migration* or *mobility rates*. See Rudolph Heberle, "Migratory Mobility: Theoretical Aspects and Problems of Measurement," *Proceedings of the World Population Conference, 1954,* Vol. 2, pp. 527-542 for a discussion of these and other aspects of migration.

[4] The amount that net migration actually contributes to the growth of a population over an intercensal period is of course contingent on rates of mortality and fertility among the migrants. If all of the immigrants die before the end of the period, net migration, regardless of the amount, is not a source of growth during the period. None of the procedures considered here can be used to determine the number of migrants who have survived to the end of the period, nor can they be used to gauge the influence of the fertility of migrants on population growth.

[5] Jane Moore, *Cityward Migration* (Chicago: University of Chicago Press, 1938).

[6] Dorothy Swaine Thomas, *Social and Economic Aspects of Swedish Population Movements, 1750-1933* (New York: The Macmillan Company, 1941).

on a system of population registration, census data on place of birth, or census data on place of prior residence.[7] Such methods will not be considered here, not only because they call for certain types of information which are only rarely available but also because they are complicated, laborious to apply, and, at least in the case of census data on place of birth and prior residence, not necessarily free of some rather serious defects.

Considering that the nature of readily available data on migration varies from place to place, and with an international audience in mind, this discussion will center on uncomplicated methods that can be applied in the greatest number of countries.

Assuming that the urban areas of a country have fixed territorial limits, the amount of increase in the urban population attributable to net migration can be estimated on the basis of the formula:

(1) $Nm = Pu_2 - Pu_1 - Bu + Du$

where Nm is net rural-urban migration, Pu_1 and Pu_2 represent the size of the urban population at the start and the end of the period, and Bu and Du represent the number of births and deaths occurring in the urban population during the period.[8]

If births and deaths are recorded by place of occurrence (i.e., deaths of non-residents and births of children to non-resident parents are not distinguished from those of residents), *formula 1* and all similar formulas yield the balance between the number of people who enter and leave the urban territory during the period, but they do not necessarily reflect rural-urban movement involving a change in the place of residence. *Formula 1* yields a reliable estimate of net rural-urban residential changes only when:

(a) births and deaths are allocated to urban and rural territory by place of residence, or

[7] Even where such data are available they are not useful in the study of rural-urban migration unless the territorial units employed in reporting them can be distinguished as to being urban or rural. This is not the case where the registration system, place of birth, or place of prior residence is based on *major* civil divisions (states, provinces, etc.).

[8] This is a derivation of the formula which expresses change in population size: $P_2 = P_1 + (B - D) + (I - O)$, with I and O representing the number of persons who enter and leave the territory occupied by the population. See Kingsley Davis, *Human Society* (New York: The Macmillan Co., 1949), pp. 551-52.

(b) the discrepancy between the number of births and deaths by place of residence and place of occurrence is small, or

(c) the number of deaths of non-residents in the urban territory equals the number of births of children to non-resident parents.[9]

While *formula 1* usually provides a fairly reliable estimate of the amount of net migration, gains or losses in the urban population cannot be attributed solely to rural-urban movement when a large number of foreign immigrants settle in the urban territory during the period, or when a large number of urban residents emigrate to another country.

An overestimation stemming from foreign immigration can be avoided if urban residents are tabulated in census reports by country of birth. Where such data are available the appropriate formula for arriving at net rural-urban migration is:

(2) $\text{Nm} = \text{Pu}_2 - \text{Pu}_1 - \text{Bu} + \text{Du} - \text{Puf}_2 + \text{Puf}_1$

where Puf_1 is the number of foreign-born persons in the urban territory at the start of the period and Puf_2 the number of foreign-born in the urban territory at the end of the period.

Another means of taking international migration into account is made possible by data which can be used to determine the number of immigrants arriving in the country during the period and their destination in terms of rural or urban.[10] Such information is the basis for the formula:

(3) $\text{Nm} = \text{Pu}_2 - \text{Pu}_1 - \text{Bu} + \text{Du} - \text{Fiu}$

where *Fiu* is the number of immigrants destined to settle in urban territory.

In the event that only the number of immigrants during the period can be determined (i.e., not their destination in terms of rural or urban) the appropriate formula is:

(4) $\text{Nm} = \text{Pu}_2 - \text{Pu}_1 - \text{Bu} + \text{Du} - \text{Fi}\,(\text{Pu}_1/\text{P}_1)$

[9] All formulas similar to 1 should be regarded as providing nothing more than a rather rough estimate, if only because the recording of births and deaths by place of residence (or place of occurrence for that matter) and the enumeration of population at the start and end of the period are never entirely accurate. Some degree of error is inevitable, and particularly if births and deaths are allocated to place of residence but the population is enumerated in terms of the location of people at a given time (a *de facto* census) rather than their usual place of residence. For a discussion of the reliability of census and vital statistics see Hugh H. Wolfenden, *Population Statistics and Their Compilation* (Chicago: University of Chicago Press, 1954), pp. 32-67.

[10] For a discussion of information on immigration see United Nations, *Problems of Migration Statistics* (New York: November, 1949).

where *Fi* is the number of foreign immigrants, and P_1 represents
the total population of the country at the start of the period. The
application of the formula involves the assumption that immigrants are distributed among the urban and rural populations in
proportion to the size of the two populations at the start of the
period. The extent to which this assumption is warranted varies,
of course, from place to place and time to time.[11]

If the nativity of the urban residents can be established only
at the start of the period, one means for adjusting for immigration
is:

(5) $\mathrm{Nm} = \mathrm{Pu_2} - \mathrm{Pu_1} - \mathrm{Bu} + \mathrm{Du} - \mathrm{Fi}\,(\mathrm{Puf_1/P_1})$

This formula assumes that foreign immigrants who arrive during
the period settle in urban and rural territory in much the same
proportion as those who arrived before the period. This assumption is subject to question in certain cases, but on the whole it is
doubtless more valid than the assumption involved in *formula 4.*

There is a defect in *formulas 2, 3,* and *4* which tends to produce an underestimation. This defect stems from the fact that
the urban residents who have emigrated to another country during the period are treated as though they have moved to rural
territory. Where records of overseas departures are such that the
origin (rural or urban) of emigrants can be determined,[12] a reliable estimate of net rural-urban migration is produced by one
of these formulas:

(6) $\mathrm{Nm} = \mathrm{Pu_2} - \mathrm{Pu_1} - \mathrm{Bu} + \mathrm{Du} - \mathrm{Puf_2} + \mathrm{Puf_1} + \mathrm{Ue}$

(7) $\mathrm{Nm} = \mathrm{Pu_2} - \mathrm{Pu_1} - \mathrm{Bu} + \mathrm{Du} - \mathrm{Fiu} + \mathrm{Ue}$

(8) $\mathrm{Nm} = \mathrm{Pu_2} - \mathrm{Pu_1} - \mathrm{Bu} + \mathrm{Du} - \mathrm{Fi}\,(\mathrm{Pu_1/P_1}) + \mathrm{Ue}$

(9) $\mathrm{Nm} = \mathrm{Pu_2} - \mathrm{Pu_1} - \mathrm{Bu} + \mathrm{Du} - \mathrm{Fi}\,(\mathrm{Puf_1/P_1}) + \mathrm{Ue}$

with *Ue* representing the number of urban residents who have
emigrated during the period.

We have noted that a failure to take into account *Fiu* leads to
an overestimation of net rural-urban migration, but the reverse
is true when *Ue* is ignored. Thus errors in estimation can be substantially reduced if the balance between the two, *Fiu* and *Ue*,
can be determined. Where the two numbers are not known the

[11] The chief advantages of *formulas 3* and *4* are that they do not require a
census tabulation of the population by country of birth or the registration of
deaths by nativity.

[12] See *Ibid.* for a discussion of information on emigrants.

balance can be estimated indirectly. This is accomplished by first determining the balance between immigrants and emigrants for the nation as a whole (i.e., regardless of their origin or destination) during the period on the basis of the formula:

(10) $Ie = P_2 - P_1 - B + D$

where *Ie* is the excess of immigrants over emigrants and other letters relate to the nation as a whole.

Given *Ie* the appropriate formula for estimating net rural-urban migration is:

(11) $Nm = Pu_2 - Pu_1 - Bu + Du - Ie\,(Pu_1/P_1)$

The assumption underlying the use of the formula is that net loss or gain of population through international migration is shared by the rural and urban components in proportion to their size at the start of the period.

All of the formulas so far given depend upon knowledge of the number of births and deaths in the urban population. Where vital statistics cannot be used, it is necessary to employ cruder estimating procedures. One such procedure begins with the assumption that the rural and urban populations had the same rates of natural increase during the period. This enables one to estimate what the size of the urban population would have been at the end of the period *had there been no net rural-urban migration* by applying the rate of growth of the total population to the urban component. The difference between this estimated size (which is purely hypothetical) and the actual size of the urban population is an estimate of the amount of net rural-urban migration:

$$(12)\ Nm = Pu_2 - Pu_1\left(\frac{P_2 - P_1}{P_1}\right) - Pu_1$$

Since virtually all evidence points to higher rates of fertility for rural than urban populations,[13] *formula 12* cannot be regarded as producing other than an estimate of the minimum amount of net rural-urban migration.[14]

Even without vital statistics, some adjustment for differential

---

[13] A. J. Jaffe, "Urbanization and Fertility," *American Journal of Sociology,* Vol. 48 (July, 1942), pp. 48-60; and United Nations, *Demographic Yearbook, 1952* (New York: 1952), pp. 15-17.

[14] Whenever possible, the various ways of taking international migration into account should be used in conjunction with *formula 12.*

fertility can be made, provided that the ages of the urban population are tabulated in census reports. One adjustment is accomplished in *formula 13*.

$$(13) \quad Nm = Pu_2 - Pu_1 \left[\frac{P_2 - P_1}{P_1} - \left(\frac{Tc}{P_1} - \frac{Uc}{Pu_1} \right) \right] - Pu_1$$

Tc and *Uc* represent the number of children in the total population and the urban population at the end of the period who, as
judged by their reported ages, were born during the period. This
formula, and others of a similar nature, rests on two assumptions:
that there is no major rural-urban difference between the mortality of children or for any other age groups, and that there is
no net rural-urban migration of families with children in these
age groups.

A more conventional gauge of fertility can be used in attempting to adjust for rural-urban differentials when age by sex is
tabulated in census reports at the beginning and end of the period:

$$(14) \quad Nm = Pu_2 - Pu_1 \left[\frac{P_2 - P_1}{P_2} - \left(\frac{Tc_1 + Tc_2}{Tw_1 + Tw_2} - \right. \right.$$
$$\left. \left. \frac{Uc_1 + Uc_2}{Uw_1 + Uw_2} \right) \right] - Pu_1$$

In *formula 14 c* is the number of children 0-4 and *w* is the number of women 15-49.[15] This formula is subject to all of the assumptions that apply to *formula 13*. It should also be noted that
the age group 0-4 is one of the most unreliable as far as accuracy
of census enumeration is concerned, but this is compensated for
in cases where the same enumeration bias applies to both the
urban and total populations.[16] Where age and sex are tabulated
for the population only at the start of the period, or only at the
end of the period, it is necessary to consider the child-woman
ratio at one point in time. In such a case trends in fertility during
the period cannot be taken into account, and a rural-urban trend
differential will produce an error in estimation.

[15] Other age groups—0-6 and 14-44, for example—can be used. It is necessary, of course, that the age groups be the same for the urban and total populations.

[16] See George W. Barclay, *Techniques of Population Analysis* (New York:
John Wiley and Sons, Inc., 1958), pp. 24-25 and 172, for other observations on
the use of the child-woman ratio.

In addition to the assumptions involved in attempting to adjust for rural-urban fertility differentials, it should also be noted that *formulas 13* and *14* do not take mortality and international migration into account. Both of them assume that mortality is more or less the same in the urban and rural population.[17] Higher rates of mortality in the urban population would tend to produce an underestimation of net migration. Net migration tends to be overestimated, however, when the urban population claims a disproportionate share of a gain in population through international migration.[18]

We have considered some thirteen possible approaches to estimating net rural-urban migration. Some of the formulas produce nothing more than the crudest kind of estimate, and they should be used only where available data do not provide alternatives. The most reliable estimates are produced, of course, by formulas based on a count of births, deaths, immigrants, and emigrants; and, in general, the greater the number of assumptions involved, the more the estimate is subject to question. Accordingly, it is imperative that all reports of net rural-urban migration provide a description of the estimating procedure followed. This description should include a listing of the assumptions underlying the estimates and a judgment as to whether the assumptions have produced an overestimation or an underestimation. It is also desirable, where the availability of data permit, to utilize several different methods and derive as many estimates as possible, with the procedure and assumptions specified in each case. This range of estimates provides a more concrete basis for judgments as to the probable true amount of net migration.

THE PROBLEM OF URBAN BOUNDARIES

Each of the above formulas is applicable only to populations who occupy a territory with fixed limits. If the territorial limits expand during the period, the result is likely to be an addition of persons who have not actually changed their place of residence;

---

[17] This assumption appears to be far more valid than is the corresponding assumption concerning rural-urban fertility differentials.

[18] *Formulas 2-11* provide several means of taking international migration into account, each of which can be used in conjunction with *formulas 13* and *14*.

and, since none of the formulas take this source of growth into account, the persons are erroneously treated as migrants. The consequence is an overestimation of net migration, and this is especially true when the formulas are applied to cities, urban areas, or metropolitan areas, as these units are often characterized by expanding boundaries.

The most feasible solution to the problem is, as we shall see, to establish fixed boundaries that encompass, at both the start and end of the period, all of the urban population and a minimum of rural territory.[19]

The situation is further complicated by the fact that certain types of information on the urban and total population must be obtained to apply the estimational formulas. Most of the formulas require knowledge of the number of births and deaths in the urban territory, as well as the size of the urban population at the beginning and end of the period. Such information can often be secured from census and vital statistics reports, but this is true only if the urban boundaries correspond to the territorial units employed in the enumeration of population and the recording of births and deaths. Thus, to summarize, urban boundaries must be constant, realistic (i.e., distinguish rural from urban territory), and such that information on the population contained within them is readily available.

The problem of urban boundaries will be considered here in the context of estimating net migration from the rural territory of a country to its urban areas.[20] It should be recognized at the outset that urban areas are rarely treated as territorial units in both census enumerations and the recording of vital events, if only because of the administrative problems imposed by the absence of fixed boundaries. Cities, in a political sense, on the other hand, are often so used. Consequently, since the boundaries of political cities may at times correspond fairly closely to

[19] Such a consideration necessarily involves the problem of distinguishing between rural and urban. However, as subsequent observation indicates, the solution is dictated more by practical concerns than theoretical reasons. For a discussion of rural-urban distinctions see Parts I and VI of this volume.

[20] This is not the only way of viewing rural-urban migration. In certain cases it may be necessary, or desirable for a particular purpose, to focus on movement to either political cities or metropolitan areas. The problems are much the same regardless of the type of urban unit, but estimates of net migration are always relative to the type of unit considered as making up the urban territory.

those of the urban areas, an investigation of migration can best begin with a consideration of the conditions under which city limits may be used in demarcating urban territory.

Figure I depicts five hypothetical urban areas at two points in time, along with the boundaries of associated political cities and civil divisions. The first set of urban areas (A-1 and A-2) illustrate the *underbounded* city—one in which the political limits encompass only a part of the urban territory. In countries where underbounded cities prevail, political limits are of little use in the study of rural-urban migration, even though they may be constant and provide access to census data and vital statistics, because persons who move from rural territory to the periphery of the urban areas will not be counted as migrants.

The second set of urban areas, B-1 and B-2, demonstrate the need to consider the relationship of political limits to urban areas at both the start and end of the period. The relationship in this case is one of a close correspondence at the beginning of the period (B-1), but at the end of the period (B-2) the city is overbounded, meaning that its limits extend far beyond the urban territory. Were one of the formulas applied to such a case, it would probably yield a gross overestimation, because the population added to the city by an expanding boundary would be counted as migrants.

At a first glance it might appear that the city boundaries in the case of C-1 and C-2 are ideal for the study of rural-urban migration, since they correspond closely to the urban area at both points in time. The situation is indeed better than depicted in the cases of A and B, but it is still far from perfect. As the boundary is shifted people are added to the population, and the sources of these additions (i.e., migrants or non-migrants) cannot be differentiated by any of the formulas.[21] It could be argued, of

[21] It is possible to arrive at an estimate of the population added to a city by an expansion of its boundary ("annexation"), but there is a great deal of labor involved in making such estimates for all of the cities in a country. Moreover, the results are often neither satisfactory nor useful, since the estimates do not distinguish between migrants and non-migrants. Two examples of research on the subject are: Albert G. Ballert, "The Rises and Declines of American Urban Centers During the 1940's," *Land Economics*, Vol. 28 (August, 1952), pp. 203-211; and Donald J. Bogue and Emerson Seim, "Components of Population Change in Suburban and Central City Populations of Standard Metropolitan Areas: 1940 to 1950," *Rural Sociology*, Vol. 21 (September-December, 1956), pp. 267-275. The second paper appears in Chapter 5 of this volume.

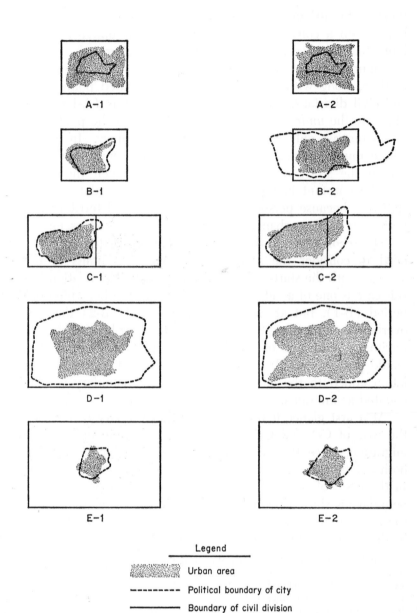

FIGURE I.   Boundaries of Urban Areas, Political Cities, and Civil Divisions
at Two Points in Time: Hypothetical Cases.

course, that the expansion of the boundary must be due either to the peripheral movement of the city residents or to the peripheral location of migrants. This is true, but it overlooks one important point—as the boundary is expanded it encompasses persons who were residing outside of the limits at the start of the period, and these persons are erroneously treated as migrants on the basis of the estimational formulas. Furthermore, unless the change in the political limits and the recording of births and deaths are closely synchronized with shifts in the urban area, additions due to the natural increase of the population on the periphery will be attributed to net migration.

The best units for the study of rural-urban migration are cities with a constant boundary which extends beyond the urban area at both the beginning and end of the period (i.e., overbounded cities at both points in time). Such is the case for D-1 and D-2 in Figure I, where the city limits encompass the expansion of the urban area, even though remaining fixed during the period.

There are two sources of error in the use of overbounded cities as territorial units. Persons who settle in the rural territory within the city limits are counted as urban migrants, which leads to an overestimation of the actual amount of net rural-urban migration. On the other hand, residents of rural territory within the city limits who move to the urban areas are not counted as migrants, which contributes to an underestimation. These errors may cancel each other, and they are likely to be serious only when the city limits include a large amount of rural territory (see B-2 in Figure I) and contain a large number of rural residents.

Given the need for constant boundaries that encompass the urban territory, the most feasible solution, in cases where city limits cannot be used, is to utilize the smallest civil divisions that are employed in census enumerations and the recording of vital statistics.[22] The divisions shown in Figure I are larger than the urban areas, and in the case of A, B, and C provide a better basis

[22] Civil divisions are administrative units which together comprise all of the country. These divisions vary in size and shape from place to place and, as a rule, only those that are typically larger than cities (counties, communes, etc.) are used to record and report vital events. The smallest type of civil division should be used whenever possible, so as to insure a close correspondence between administrative limits and urban territory. For observations on the demarcation of urban areas in terms of administrative boundaries, see Chapter 3 of this volume.

for estimating net rural-urban migration than do the city limits.[23] In some cases, such as C in Figure I, it is necessary to use two or more civil divisions, even though the urban area may be contained within only one of them at the beginning of the period, but it is not desirable to include civil divisions which contain only a small part of the urban area (see C-2 in Figure I), since they would probably add more rural than urban residents to the population.

In establishing urban boundaries, it is neither necessary nor desirable to use civil divisions in each instance. For example, as we have seen, city limits rather than civil division boundaries should be used in cases that resemble D-1 and D-2 in Figure I, since the limits are constant and contain less rural territory than do the civil division boundaries. The political limits of the city should also be used in cases which resemble E-1 and E-2, where the civil divisions are much larger than the urban area, even though they may not correspond closely to the urban territory and even though they may not remain fixed over the period. In such cases it is simply a matter of less chance of error in the one case than in the other.[24]

It often happens that an investigation of rural-urban migration is unable to exercise any choice on the matter of boundaries. When this is the case, however, it is still necessary to consider how the character of the territorial units may have influenced the estimates of net migration and qualify all interpretations of the estimates accordingly.

INTERNATIONAL COMPARISONS OF NET RURAL-URBAN MIGRATION

Deriving estimates of the amount of net rural-urban migration is only the starting point in undertaking international compari-

---

[23] The use of civil division boundaries which extend beyond the urban area involves the same source of error as does the utilization of overbounded cities (see D-1 and D-2 in Figure I).

[24] Where the civil divisions are uniformly large, it may be necessary to restrict the study to large cities, so as to reduce the size of the rural population in the civil divisions (i.e., to bring about a close correspondence between the urban areas and the civil division boundaries that contain them). This means, however, that the net migration is not strictly rural-urban, since small urban centers are merged with the rural territory.

sons. Given the tendency for the amount of net migration to vary directly with the size of the urban and rural populations and also with the number of years in the period, these factors should be controlled before differences among countries are subjected to interpretation. It is also desirable to consider how much migration contributes to urban expansion in comparison to other sources of growth, and this calls for a special type of measure.

The amount of net migration in relation to the urban population can best be expressed as the average annual number of net migrants per 1,000 urban residents. The formula for computing this *net urban migration rate* is set forth in Table 1, which shows several different measures of net migration for four hypothetical countries. In each of the four cases the net rural-urban movement is 2,000,000, but when this amount is expressed in such a way as to control for differences in population size and the number of years in the period, some sharp differences appear. For example the *average annual urban net migration* rate is 9.1 for country "B" but only 6.4 for "A," [25] but when the amount of net migration is considered relative to the size of the rural population the situation is reversed.

As a final consideration, we should note that the role of rural-urban movement in urban growth is not completely revealed by rates of net migration. In some countries the amount of movement may be large, yet only constitute a small proportion of total urban growth, while in other countries urban growth may be almost entirely a function of migration. This can be demonstrated through a comparison of country "A" with countries "B," "C" and "D." It has the lowest rate of net urban migration, but, as shown in the last row of figures in the table, rural-urban movement accounts for a greater proportion of urban growth in the case of "A" than it does for any of the other three countries. This distinction between sources of growth takes on added significance when one considers that the causes and consequences of an increase through net migration are probably different in many respects from those related to natural increase and foreign immigration.

[25] Note that the amount of net migration is expressed in terms of the mean or average population over the years rather than the population at the start of the period.

TABLE 1

A Comparison of Different Measures of Net Rural-Urban
Migration in Hypothetical Countries

Population Data and Measures of Net Rural-Urban Migration	Countries and Growth Period			
	"A" 1950-60 y = 10 °	"B" 1950-60 y = 10	"C" 1950-60 y = 10	"D" 1955-60 y = 5
Urban population (P₁)**	30,000,000	20,000,000	25,000,000	25,000,000
Urban population (P₂)***	32,500,000	24,000,000	28,000,000	28,000,000
Rural population (Rp₁)**	25,000,000	50,000,000	30,000,000	30,000,000
Rural population (Rp₂)***	25,500,000	54,000,000	31,000,000	31,000,000
Net rural-urban migration (Nm).	2,000,000	2,000,000	2,000,000	2,000,000
Average annual net urban migration rate: 2,000Nm/y(P₂+P₁)	6.4	9.1	7.5	15.1
Average annual net rural migration rate: 2,000Nm/y(Rp₂+Rp₁)	−7.9	−3.8	−6.6	−13.1
Percent urban growth due to net migration:	80.0	50.0	66.7	66.7

* Number of years in growth period.
** Population size at start of growth period.
*** Population size at end of period.

Subject Index to the Bibliography

SECTION 1—Age and Sex Structure

10; 102; 296; 331; 391; 526; 657; 715; 760

SECTION 2—Cities and Urbanization: General Considerations

45; 61; 75; 94; 122; 126; 127; 177; 201; 224; 234; 277; 287; 288; 313; 329; 338; 344; 352; 353; 362; 370; 371; 434; 448; 450; 475; 478; 499; 510; 512; 513; 532; 538; 541-543; 564; 566; 568-570; 572; 573; 599; 637; 646; 662; 663; 694; 704; 706; 767; 785-788; 809; 812

SECTION 3—Cities and Urbanization: Governmental-Administrative
Aspects

29; 70-73; 93; 266; 268; 286; 346; 356; 471; 478, chp. 22; 522; 580; 712; 768

SECTION 4—Cities and Urbanization: Historical Aspects

75; 83; 113-115; 122; 160; 171; 174; 176; 218; 238; 362; 440; 549; 550; 574; 579; 609; 757, chps. 1-2; 766

SECTION 5—Cities: Intra-Urban Population Mobility

4; 31; 59; 81; 97; 103; 104; 109; 136; 143; 155; 157; 191; 196; 197; 204; 208; 241; 242; 244-246; 279; 280; 334; 392; 402; 439; 459; 592; 608; 623; 628; 692; 693; 701; 765; 775

SECTION 6—Cities: Political Boundaries

69; 70; 73; 266; 292; 478, chp. XIV; 522

SECTION 7—Cities: Population Density

120; 135; 303; 695; 782

SECTION 8—Cities: Population Growth

28; 51; 59; 62; 66; 88; 123; 138; 145; 150; 152; 181; 213; 216; 264; 303; 341; 399; 404; 442; 452; 527; 589; 610; 716

SECTION 9—Cities: Population Migration

11; 12; 56; 60; 66; 68; 101; 107; 109; 185; 250; 251-253; 279; 280; 284; 315; 334; 402; 459; 504; 505; 533; 535; 559; 560; 608; 645; 710; 711; 731; 757, chp. 4; 773; 810; 811

SECTION 10—Cities: Population Size

118; 119; 200; 203; 296; 351; 394; 395; 457; 520; 532; 578; 612; 634; 695; 721

SECTION 11—Cities: Shape

52; 151; 359; 360; 380; 452; 467; 534; 556

SECTION 12—Cities: Studies of Particular Cities

15; 48; 49; 77; 98; 99; 144; 145; 172; 192; 237; 256; 270; 275; 316; 317; 324; 339; 340; 385; 386; 394; 395; 399; 408; 415; 437; 438; 452; 472; 501; 506; 552; 607; 638; 639; 677; 696; 700; 709; 770; 779; 780; 783; 805; 806

SECTION 13—Cities: Functional Types

6; 7; 16-24; 53; 54; 89; 108; 118; 119; 148; 156; 164; 173; 174; 178; 179; 187; 188; 200; 217; 218; 221; 225; 236; 239; 240; 269; 271; 290-293; 310; 311; 325; 326; 333; 343; 351; 363; 377; 381; 384; 400; 411; 414; 417; 430; 435; 438; 465; 508; 523; 548; 554; 555; 557; 574; 595; 602; 604; 612; 629; 638; 673; 709; 713; 721; 755, chp. 1; 770; 805

SECTION 14—Cities: Urban Sub-Areas, Spatial Structure, and Spatial Distribution

1; 14; 15; 31; 33; 35; 41-44; 46; 48-52; 59; 77; 78; 95; 98-100; 104; 111; 121; 128; 139; 144; 145; 149; 151; 153; 154; 157; 158; 169; 170; 173; 183; 184; 187; 190; 192; 195; 198; 199; 202; 205-211; 228; 231-233; 241; 243; 247; 248; 256; 257; 263; 270; 272-275; 289; 294; 295; 297-302; 317; 326; 332; 336; 337; 339; 340; 345; 349; 354; 355; 358; 372; 373; 379; 380; 382; 385-388; 392; 405; 406; 408; 411; 415; 417; 418; 427; 437; 445-447; 449; 451; 472; 474; 476; 477; 478, chps. 15-20; 494; 502; 506; 514; 516-518; 530; 540; 543, chp. II; 545; 547; 548; 556; 557; 562; 563; 567; 571; 575-577; 590; 594; 600; 603; 606; 613; 622; 628-632; 639; 648; 649; 651; 670; 677; 702; 705; 728; 754; 755, chp. 5; 771; 772; 774; 783; 784; 789; 799; 806; 811; 813

SECTION 15—Demographic and Spatial Relations Among Cities

8; 9; 11; 32; 38; 47; 86; 89; 90; 106; 107; 119; 121; 132; 142; 164; 165; 174; 195; 202; 257; 271; 328; 372-375; 397; 398; 401; 410; 418; 449; 465; 466; 477; 479-481; 496; 520; 548; 554; 600; 660; 665-668; 687; 689-691; 697; 725; 732; 759; 764; 797; 798; 809-812

SECTION 16—Fertility and Mortality Rates

26; 30, chps. 4-6; 66; 79; 80; 123; 194; 394; 436; 486; 641; 715; 735; 790; 802

SECTION 17—Functional Relations Among Cities

13; 89-91; 108; 119; 148; 156; 165; 173; 178; 179; 187; 225; 271; 290-293; 310; 311; 328; 374; 375; 396-398; 401; 465; 478, Part III; 537; 548; 665-667; 681; 691; 726; 757, chp. 6

SECTION 18—Metropolitan Areas

31; 73; 76; 92; 109; 130; 131; 135; 149; 180; 182; 183; 187; 191; 285; 290-293; 324; 326; 395; 417; 429; 445; 446; 453; 456; 489; 548; 591; 592; 605; 628-632; 652; 665-667; 695; 701; 703; 719; 746; 765

SECTION 19—Metropolitan Regions

31; 55; 76; 105; 108; 109; 130; 134; 147; 165; 172; 175; 178; 179; 255; 288; 290-293; 305; 324; 400; 413; 423; 478; 539; 546; 548; 553; 555; 557; 593; 598; 665-667; 703; 708; 755, chp. 2

SECTION 20—Population Projections and Estimates

57; 85; 140; 146; 186; 219; 222; 309; 312; 350; 368; 461; 519; 615-621; 623-627; 650; 654; 655; 658; 674; 749; 776; 777; 791

SECTION 21—Research Surveys

6; 112; 124; 137; 166; 167; 194; 220; 230; 281; 282; 306; 318-323; 330; 342; 367; 389; 390; 407; 425; 426; 438; 482; 484; 507; 528; 544; 635; 636; 644; 647; 664; 682-686; 707; 729; 734; 747; 792; 795; 801; 803

SECTION 22—Rural and Urban Data: Sources and References to National Censuses

531; 597; 672; 723; 733; 736; 737-745; 748; 750-753

SECTION 23—Rural-Urban Differences

5; 26; 39; 40; 49; 96; 116; 117; 159; 168, chp. III; 212; 223; 304; 403; 421; 424; 458; 483; 485; 500; 521; 529; 581-587; 671; 676; 678; 688; 722; 736; 737; 739; 744; 763; 778

SECTION 24—Rural-Urban Interrelations

2; 13; 14; 25; 27; 37; 55; 64; 65; 74; 87, chp. V; 93; 229; 254; 258; 259; 274; 278; 364; 369; 416; 419; 421; 431; 432, pp. 261-280; 433; 441; 443; 462; 463, chp. 7; 464; 473; 485; 489; 492; 497; 498; 515; 561; 565; 581-588; 596; 603; 653; 680; 714; 717; 730; 769; 796; 807

SECTION 25—Rural-Urban Migration

101; 249; 261; 262; 276; 314; 315; 361; 412; 428; 444, pp. 174-221; 469; 470; 493; 505; 524, chp. 7; 596; 676, Vol. III, chp. 12; 698; 699; 710; 711; 808

SECTION 26—Statistical Techniques

36; 67; 189; 235; 283; 307; 308; 366; 558; 643; 656; 679; 762; 804

SECTION 27—Urban Areas

14; 62; 78; 215; 226; 228; 267; 285; 365; 388; 551; 601; 642; 669; 675; 719; 727; 758; 769; 789; 800

SECTION 28—Urban Planning

1; 27; 33; 78; 82; 111; 170; 232; 255; 260; 297-299; 502; 511; 614; 761; 768; 789; 793; 794; 799

SECTION 29—Urban Service Areas

31; 49; 72; 73; 89; 91; 108; 130; 147; 169; 174; 236; 258; 273; 290-293; 324; 335; 365; 369; 392; 417; 419; 422; 431; 433; 441; 443; 451; 460, chp. 9; 463, chp. 6; 473; 489; 492; 498; 525; 536; 546; 548; 555; 561; 565; 593; 598; 603; 611; 661; 665-667; 701; 708; 755, chp. 2; 769; 807

SECTION 30—Urbanization and Urban Populations: Studies of Particular Countries or Regions

3; 34; 58; 62; 63; 84; 86; 90; 110; 125; 129; 133; 141; 161; 193; 213; 214; 226-228; 264; 327; 350; 357; 394; 395; 409; 455; 468; 479-481; 487; 488; 491; 495; 509; 633; 716; 718; 726; 757; 781

SECTION 31—Urbanization: Causes and Consequences

141; 160-163; 193; 265; 346-348; 350; 361; 376; 378; 393; 403; 450; 454; 490; 495; 596; 640; 646; 659; 672; 680; 712; 756; 781

SECTION 32—Urbanization: Characteristics

63; 86; 141; 160-163; 347; 495; 633; 720

BIBLIOGRAPHY

(Compiled in 1959)

1 ABERCROMBIE, PATRICK, *Greater London Plan, 1944.* London: H.M.S.O., 1945.

2 ACHARYA, HEMALATA, "Urbanizing Role of a One-Lakh City," *Sociological Bulletin,* 5 (September, 1956), 89-101.

3 AHMAND, KAZI S., "Urban Population in Pakistan," *Pakistan Geographical Review,* 10 (No. 1, 1955), 1-16.

4 ALBIG, WILLIAM, "A Comparison of Methods of Recording Urban Residential Mobility," *Sociology and Social Research,* 21 (January-February, 1937), 226-233.

5 ALEXANDER, FRANK D., "The Problems of Locality-Group Classification," *Rural Sociology,* 17 (September, 1952), 236-244.

6 ALEXANDER, JOHN W., "An Economic Base Study of Madison, Wisconsin," *Wisconsin Commerce Papers,* 1 (June, 1953), 1-98.

7 —— "The Basic-Nonbasic Concept of Urban Economic Functions," *Economic Geography,* 30 (July, 1954), 246-261.

8 —— "Location of Manufacturing: Methods of Measurement," *Annals of the Association of American Geographers,* 48 (March, 1958), 20-26.

9 ALLEN, G. R., "The 'Courbe des Populations': A Further Analysis," *Bulletin of the Oxford University Institute of Statistics,* 16 (May-June, 1954), 179-189.

10 ANDERSON, ODIN W., "A Suggested Single Index for a Measure of Changing Age Distributions in General Populations," *Social Forces,* 33 (October, 1954), 86-87.

11 ANDERSON, THEODORE R., "Intermetropolitan Migration: A Comparison of the Hypotheses of Zipf and Stouffer," *American Sociological Review,* 20 (June, 1955), 287-291.

12 —— "Intermetropolitan Migration: A Correlation Analysis," *American Journal of Sociology,* 61 (March, 1956), 459-462.

13 —— and JANE COLLIER, "Metropolitan Dominance and the Rural Hinterland," *Rural Sociology,* 21 (June, 1956), 152-157.

14 ANDREWS, RICHARD B., "Elements in the Urban-Fringe Pattern," *Journal of Land and Public Utility Economics,* 18 (May, 1942), 169-183.

15   —— "Urban Fringe Studies of Two Wisconsin Cities," *Journal of Land and Public Utility Economics*, 21 (November, 1945), 375-382.

16   —— "Mechanics of the Urban Economic Base: Historical Development of the Base Concept," *Land Economics*, 29 (May, 1953), 161-167.

17   —— "Mechanics of the Urban Economic Base: The Problem of Terminology," *Land Economics*, 29 (August, 1953), 263-268.

18   —— "Mechanics of the Urban Economic Base: A Classification of Base Types," *Land Economics*, 29 (November, 1953), 343-350.

19   —— "Mechanics of the Urban Economic Base: The Problem of Base Measurement," *Land Economics*, 30 (February, 1954), 52-60.

20   —— "Mechanics of the Urban Economic Base: The Concept of Base Ratios," *Land Economics*, 31 (February, 1955), 47-53.

21   —— "Mechanics of the Urban Economic Base: Causes and Effects of Change in the Base Ratios and the Ratio Elements (I)," *Land Economics*, 31 (May, 1955), 144-155.

22   —— "Mechanics of the Urban Economic Base: Causes and Effects of Change in the Base Ratios and the Ratio Elements (II)," *Land Economics*, 31 (August, 1955), 245-256.

23   —— "Mechanics of the Urban Economic Base: Causes and Effects of Changes in the Base Ratios and the Ratio Elements (III)," *Land Economics*, 31 (November, 1955), 361-371.

24   —— "Mechanics of the Urban Economic Base: The Base Concept and the Planning Process," *Land Economics*, 32 (February, 1956), 69-84.

25   ASHBY, A. W., "The Effects of Urban Growth on the Countryside," *Sociological Review*, 31 (October, 1939), 345-369.

26   BADENHORST, L. T., "Territorial Differentials in Fertility in the Union of South Africa—1911-1936," *Population Studies*, 6 (November, 1952), 135-162.

27   BALK, H. H., "Rurbanization of Worcester's Environs," *Economic Geography*, 21 (April, 1945), 84-116.

28   BALLERT, ALBERT G., "The Rises and Declines of American Urban Centers During the 1940's," *Land Economics*, 28 (August, 1952), 203-211.

29   BALTZELL, E. DIGBY, "Urbanization and Governmental Administration in Lower Bucks County," *Social Problems*, 2 (July, 1954), 38-46.

30   BARCLAY, GEORGE W., *Techniques of Population Analysis*. New York: John Wiley and Sons, 1958.

31   BARKLEY, ROBERT E., *Origin-Destination Surveys and Traffic Volume Studies*. Washington: U.S. Highway Research Board, Bibliography No. 11, 1951.

32   BARNES, JAMES A. and ARTHUR H. ROBINSON, "A New Method for the Representation of Dispersed Rural Population," *Geographical Review*, 30 (January, 1940), 134-137.

33   BARTHOLOMEW, HARLAND, *Land Uses in American Cities*. Cambridge: Harvard University Press, 1955.

34   BASCOM, WILLIAM, "Urbanization Among the Yoruba," *American Journal of Sociology*, 60 (March, 1955), 446-454.

35   BATSCHELET, C. E., "General Principles of Tract Delimitation," *Jour-*

nal of the American Statistical Association, 37 (June, 1942), 245-246.

36 BAUR, EDWARD JACKSON, "Statistical Indexes of the Social Aspects of Communities," *Social Forces,* 33 (October, 1954), 64-75.

37 BEALS, RALPH L., "Urbanism, Urbanization and Acculturation," *American Anthropologist,* 53 (January-March, 1951), 1-10.

38 BECKMANN, MARTIN J., "City Hierarchies and the Distribution of City Size," *Economic Development and Cultural Change,* 6 (April, 1958), 243-248.

39 BEEGLE, J. ALLAN, "Characteristics of Michigan's Fringe Population," *Rural Sociology,* 12 (September, 1947), 254-263.

40 BEERS, HOWARD W., "Rural-Urban Differences: Some Evidence From Public Opinion Polls," *Rural Sociology,* 18 (March, 1953), 1-11.

41 BELL, WENDELL, "The Social Areas of the San Francisco Bay Region," *American Sociological Review,* 18 (February, 1953), 39-47.

42 —— "A Probability Model for the Measurement of Ecological Segregation," *Social Forces,* 32 (May, 1954), 357-364.

43 —— and MARION D. BOAT, "Urban Neighborhoods and Informal Social Relations," *American Journal of Sociology,* 62 (January, 1957), 391-398.

44 —— and MARYANNE T. FORCE, "Urban Neighborhood Types and Participation in Formal Associations," *American Sociological Review,* 21 (February, 1956), 25-34.

45 BERGEL, EGON E., *Urban Sociology.* New York: McGraw-Hill Book Company, Inc., 1955.

46 BERKMAN, HERMAN G., "Decentralization and Blighted Vacant Land," *Land Economics,* 32 (August, 1956), 270-280.

47 BERRY, BRIAN J. L. and WILLIAM L. GARRISON, "Alternate Explanations of Urban Rank-Size Relationships," *Annals of the Association of American Geographers,* 48 (March, 1958), 83-91.

48 BEYNON, ERDMANN DOANE, "Budapest: An Ecological Study," *Geographical Review,* 33 (April, 1943), 256-275.

49 BLIZZARD, SAMUEL W., "Research on the Rural-Urban Fringe: A Case Study," *Sociology and Social Research,* 38 (January-February, 1954), 143-149.

50 BLUMENFELD, HANS, "On the Concentric-Circle Theory of Urban Growth," *Land Economics,* 25 (May, 1949), 209-212.

51 —— "On the Growth of Metropolitan Areas," *Social Forces,* 28 (October, 1949), 59-64.

52 —— "Theory of City Form, Past and Present," *Journal of the Society of Architectural Historians,* 8 (July-December, 1949), 7-16.

53 —— "The Economic Base of the Metropolis," *Journal of the American Institute of Planners,* 21 (Fall, 1955), 114-132.

54 BOATENG, E. A., "The Study of Human Settlements," *Universitas* (Accra), 1 (June, 1954), 16-18.

55 BOGUE, DONALD J., *The Structure of the Metropolitan Community: A Study of Dominance and Subdominance.* Ann Arbor: The University of Michigan, 1949.

56 —— *An Exploratory Study of Migration and Labor Mobility Using Social Security Data.* Oxford, Ohio: Scripps Foundation, 1950.

57 —— "A Technique for Making Extensive Population Estimates," *Jour-*

nal of the American Statistical Association, 45 (June, 1950), 149-163.

58 —— "Changes in Population Distribution since 1940," *American Journal of Sociology,* 56 (July, 1950), 43-57.

59 —— *Metropolitan Decentralization: A Study of Differential Growth.* Oxford, Ohio: Scripps Foundation, 1950.

60 —— *A Methodological Study of Migration and Labor Mobility in Michigan and Ohio in 1947.* Oxford, Ohio: Scripps Foundation, 1952.

61 —— *Needed Urban and Metropolitan Research.* Oxford, Ohio: Scripps Foundation, 1953.

62 —— *Population Growth in Standard Metropolitan Areas, 1900-1950, With An Explanatory Analysis of Urbanized Areas.* Washington: U.S. Housing and Home Finance Agency, 1953.

63 —— "Urbanism in the United States, 1950," *American Journal of Sociology,* 60 (March, 1955), 471-486.

64 —— *Metropolitan Growth and the Conversion of Land to Nonagricultural Uses.* Oxford, Ohio: Scripps Foundation, 1956.

65 —— "The Spread of Cities," *American Economic Review,* 46 (May, 1956), 284-292.

66 —— *Components of Population Change, 1940-50: Estimates of Net Migration and Natural Increase for Each Standard Metropolitan Area and State Economic Area.* Oxford, Ohio: Scripps Foundation, 1957.

67 —— and DOROTHY L. HARRIS, *Comparative Population and Urban Research Via Multiple Regression and Covariance Analysis.* Oxford, Ohio: Scripps Foundation, 1954.

68 —— and WARREN S. THOMPSON, "Migration and Distance," *American Sociological Review,* 14 (April, 1949), 236-244.

69 BOLLENS, JOHN C., "Changes in City Areas," *The Municipal Year Book, 1949.* Chicago: International City Managers' Association, 1949, 92-101.

70 —— "Annexations in 1950," *The Municipal Year Book, 1951.* Chicago: International City Managers' Association, 1951, 94-103.

71 —— "Relating City Areas to Functions: The California Experience," *Journal of the American Institute of Planners,* 17 (Winter, 1951), 13-22.

72 —— "Controls and Services in Unincorporated Urban Fringes," *The Municipal Year Book, 1954.* Chicago: International City Managers' Association, 1954, 53-61.

73 —— "Metropolitan Special Districts," *The Municipal Year Book, 1956.* Chicago: International City Managers' Association, 1956, 47-55.

74 BOPEGAMAGE, A., "Village Within a Metropolitan Aura," *Sociological Bulletin,* 5 (September, 1956), 102-110.

75 BOTERO, GIOVANNI, *The Reason of State and The Greatness of Cities.* London: Routledge & Kegan Paul, 1956.

76 BOWDEN, WILLIAM K. and RALPH CASSADY, JR., "Decentralization of Retail Trade in the Metropolitan Market Area," *Journal of Marketing,* 5 (January, 1941), 270-275.

77 BOWERS, RAYMOND V., "Ecological Patterning of Rochester, New York," *American Sociological Review,* 4 (April, 1939), 180-189.

78 BRANCH, MELVILLE C., JR., *Aerial Photography in Urban Planning and Research.* Cambridge: Harvard University Press, 1948.

79 BRASS, W., "The Derivation of Fertility and Reproduction Rates from Restricted Data on Reproductive Histories," *Population Studies*, 7 (November, 1953), 137-166.

80 —— "The Estimation of Fertility Rates From Ratios of Total to First Births," *Population Studies*, 8 (July, 1954), 74-87.

81 BREESE, GERALD W., *The Daytime Population of the Central Business District of Chicago.* Chicago: University of Chicago Press, 1949.

82 —— and DOROTHY E. WHITEMAN (eds.), *An Approach to Urban Planning.* Princeton: Princeton University Press, 1953.

83 BRIDENBAUGH, CARL, *Cities in the Wilderness: The First Century of Urban Life in America, 1625-1742.* New York: The Ronald Press Company, 1938.

84 BROOKFIELD, H. C., "Urbanization Among the South African White Population," *Geography*, 42 (January, 1957), 63-64.

85 BROWN, HUGH H., "Technique for Estimating the Population of Counties," *Journal of the American Statistical Association*, 50 (June, 1955), 323-343.

86 BROWNING, HARLEY L., "Recent Trends in Latin American Urbanization," *The Annals of the American Academy of Political and Social Science*, 316 (March, 1958), 111-120.

87 BRUNNER, EDMUND DE S. and J. H. KOLB, *Rural Social Trends.* New York: McGraw-Hill Book Company, Inc., 1933.

88 —— and T. LYNN SMITH, "Village Growth and Decline, 1930-1940," *Rural Sociology*, 9 (June, 1944), 103-115.

89 BRUSH, JOHN E., "The Hierarchy of Central Places in Southwestern Wisconsin," *Geographical Review*, 43 (July, 1953), 380-402.

90 —— "The Urban Hierarchy in Europe," *Geographical Review*, 43 (July, 1953), 414-416.

91 —— and HOWARD E. BRACEY, "Rural Service Centers in Southwestern Wisconsin and Southern England," *Geographical Review*, 45 (October, 1955), 559-569.

92 BUNTING, ROBERT L., "Commuting and Wage Relatedness," *Southern Economic Journal*, 22 (January, 1956), 370-372.

93 BURCHFIELD, LAVERNE, *Our Rural Communities: A Guidebook to Published Materials on Rural Problems.* Chicago: Public Administration Service, 1947.

94 BURGESS, ERNEST W. (ed.), *The Urban Community.* Chicago: The University of Chicago Press, 1926.

95 —— "The Determination of Gradients in the Growth of the City," *Proceedings of the American Sociological Society*, 21 (1927), 178-184.

96 BURNIGHT, ROBERT G., NATHAN L. WHETTEN, and BRUCE D. WAXMAN, "Differential Rural-Urban Fertility in Mexico," *American Sociological Review*, 21 (February, 1956), 3-8.

97 CAPLOW, THEODORE, "Incidence and Direction of Residential Mobility in a Minneapolis Sample," *Social Forces*, 27 (May, 1949), 413-417.

98 —— "The Social Ecology of Guatemala City," *Social Forces*, 28 (December, 1949), 113-133.

99   —— "Urban Structure in France," *American Sociological Review,* 17 (October, 1952), 544-549.

100 CARLS, NORMAN, *How to Read Aerial Photographs for Census Work.* Washington: U.S. Bureau of the Census, 1947.

101 CARPENTER, NILES, "Migration Between City and Country in the Buffalo Metropolitan Area" in Norman E. Himes (ed.), *Economics, Sociology and the Modern World: Essays in Honor of T. N. Carver.* Cambridge, Massachusetts: Harvard University Press, 1935, 269-291.

102 CARRIER, N. H., and A. M. FARRAG, "The Reduction of Errors in Census Populations for Statistically Underdeveloped Countries," *Population Studies,* 12 (March, 1959), 240-285.

103 CARROLL, J. DOUGLAS, JR., "Some Aspects of the Home-Work Relationships of Industrial Workers," *Land Economics,* 25 (November, 1949), 414-422.

104 —— "The Relation of Homes to Work Places and the Spatial Pattern of Cities," *Social Forces,* 30 (March, 1952), 271-282.

105 —— "Defining Urban Trade Areas," *Traffic Quarterly,* 9 (April, 1955), 149-161.

106 CARROLL, JOHN B., "Zipf's 'Law of Urban Concentration,'" *Science,* 94 (December 26, 1941), 609.

107 CARROTHERS, G., "An Historical Review of the Gravity and Potential Concepts of Human Interactions," *Journal of the American Institute of Planners,* 22 (Spring, 1956), 94-102.

108 CARRUTHERS, IAN, "A Classification of Service Centers in England and Wales," *Geographical Journal,* 123 (September, 1957), 371-385.

109 CASEY, HARRY J., JR., "The Law of Retail Gravitation Applied to Traffic Engineering," *Traffic Quarterly,* 9 (July, 1955), 313-321.

110 CASTO, E. RAY and OSCAR W. DOTSON, "Urban Population of Palestine," *Economic Geography,* 14 (January, 1938), 68-72.

111 CHAPIN, F. STUART, JR., *Urban Land Use Planning.* New York: Harper and Brothers, 1957.

112 CHEVRY, GABRIEL, "Control of a General Census by Means of an Area Sampling Method," *Journal of American Statistical Association,* 44 (September, 1949), 373-379.

113 CHILDE, V. GORDON, *What Happened in History.* Harmondsworth, England: Penguin Books, 1943.

114 —— *Archaeological Ages as Technological Stages.* London: Royal Anthropological Institute of Great Britain and Ireland, 1944.

115 —— *Man Makes Himself.* London: Watts and Co., 1948.

116 CHRISTENSEN, HAROLD T., "Rural-Urban Differences in the Time Interval Between the Marriage of Parents and the Birth of Their First Child, Utah County, Utah," *Rural Sociology,* 3 (June, 1938), 172-176.

117 —— "Rural-Urban Differences in the Spacing of the First Birth From Marriage: A Repeat Study," *Rural Sociology,* 18 (March, 1953), 60.

118 CLARK, COLIN, "The Economic Functions of a City in Relation to Its Size," *Econometrica,* 13 (April, 1945), 97-113.

119 —— "The Distribution of Labor Between Industries and Between Locations," *Land Economics,* 26 (May, 1950), 136-144.

120 —— "Urban Population Densities," *Journal of the Royal Statistical Society,* 114 (1951), 490-496.

121 CLARK, PHILIP J. and FRANCIS C. EVANS, "Distance to Nearest Neighbor as a Measure of Spatial Relationship in Populations," *Ecology,* 35 (October, 1954), 445-453.

122 CLERGET, PIERRE, "Urbanism: A Historic, Geographic, and Economic Study," *Annual Report of the Board of Regents of the Smithsonian Institution, 1912.* Washington: Government Printing Office, 1913, 653-667.

123 COALE, ANSLEY J., "A New Method for Calculating Lotka's *r*—The Intrinsic Rate of Growth in a Stable Population," *Population Studies,* 11 (July, 1957), 92-94.

124 COCHRAN, W. G., "Sampling Theory When the Sampling-Units Are of Unequal Size," *Journal of the American Statistical Association,* 37 (June, 1942), 199-212.

125 COLE, WILLIAM E., "Urban Development in the Tennessee Valley," *Social Forces,* 26 (October, 1947), 67-75.

126 —— *Dynamic Urban Sociology.* Harrisburg, Pa.: The Stackpole Co., 1954.

127 —— *Urban Society.* Boston: Houghton Mifflin Company, 1958.

128 COMHAIRE, J. L. L., "Urban Segregation and Racial Legislation in Africa," *American Sociological Review,* 15 (June, 1950), 392-396.

129 —— "Some Aspects of Urbanization in the Belgian Congo," *American Journal of Sociology,* 62 (July, 1956), 8-13.

130 CONVERSE, P. D., "New Laws of Retail Gravitation," *Journal of Marketing,* 14 (October, 1949), 379-384.

131 —— and ROBERT V. MITCHELL, "The Movement of Retail Trade Within a Metropolitan Area," *Journal of Marketing,* 2 (July, 1937), 61-67.

132 COOLEY, CHARLES H., "The Theory of Transportation," *Publications of the American Economic Association,* 9 (May, 1894), 1-148.

133 COOPER, EUNICE, "Urbanization in Malaya," *Population Studies,* 5 (November, 1951), 117-131.

134 COPLAND, B. D., "A Practical Application of the Theory of Hinterlands," *Journal of Geography,* 120 (December, 1954), 476-482.

135 COPP, G. FREDERIC, "Metropolitan Districts: Their Areal Relationships," *Land Economics,* 25 (May, 1949), 213-215.

136 CORBALLY, JOHN E., "Measures of Intra-Urban Mobility," *Sociology and Social Research,* 14 (July-August, 1930), 547-552.

137 CORNFIELD, JEROME, "On Certain Biases in Samples of Human Populations," *Journal of the American Statistical Association,* 37 (March, 1942), 63-68.

138 COWGILL, DONALD OLEN, "The Theory of Population Growth Cycles," *American Journal of Sociology,* 55 (September, 1949), 163-170.

139 —— "Trends in Residential Segregation of Nonwhites in American Cities, 1940-1950," *American Sociological Review,* 21 (February, 1956), 43-47.

140 COX, PETER R., "Estimating the Future Population," *Applied Statistics,* 1 (June, 1952), 82-94.

141 CRANE, ROBERT I., "Urbanism in India," *American Journal of Sociology,* 60 (March, 1955), 463-470.

142   CREAMER, DANIEL B., *Is Industry Decentralizing? A Statistical Analysis of Locational Changes in Manufacturing Employment, 1899-1933.* Philadelphia: University of Pennsylvania Press, 1935.

143   CRESSEY, PAUL, "Population Succession in Chicago: 1898-1930," *American Journal of Sociology,* 44 (July, 1938), 59-69.

144   —— "The Ecological Organization of Rangoon, Burma," *Sociology and Social Research,* 40 (January-February, 1956), 166-169.

145   CRONE, G. R., "The Site and Growth of Paris," *Geographical Journal,* 98 (July, 1941), 35-47.

146   CROSETTI, ALBERT and ROBERT C. SCHMITT, "A Method of Estimating the Intercensal Population of Counties," *Journal of the American Statistical Association,* 51 (December, 1956), 587-590.

147   CUBER, JOHN F., "City and Country Services Utilized by Farm Families," *Sociology and Social Research,* 23 (November-December, 1938), 157-161.

148   CUMBERLAND, JOHN H., "Interindustry Analysis, New Tool in Economics," *Scientific Monthly,* 83 (October, 1956), 189-197.

149   CUZZORT, RAYMOND P., *Suburbanization of Service Industries Within Standard Metropolitan Areas.* Oxford, Ohio: Scripps Foundation, 1955.

150   DALE, ALFRED G., "What Supports a City's Growth?," *Texas Business Review,* 28 (January, 1954), 11-13.

151   DAVIE, MAURICE, "The Pattern of Urban Growth," in George Peter Murdock (ed.), *Studies in the Science of Society.* New Haven, Conn.: Yale University Press, 1937, 133-161.

152   DAVIES, ARTHUR, "Logarithmic Analysis and Population Studies," *Geography,* 33 (June, 1948), 53-60.

153   DAVIS, BEVERLY, *Centralization of Industry, Chicago, 1947.* Chicago: University of Chicago, Population Research and Training Center, Urban Analysis Report No. 2, November, 1951.

154   —— *Spatial Distribution of Occupational Groups: Chicago, 1940.* Chicago: University of Chicago, Population Research and Training Center, Urban Analysis Report No. 4, February, 1952.

155   —— *Degree of Work-Residence Separation for Wage and Salary Workers: Chicago, 1950-51.* Chicago: University of Chicago, Population Research and Training Center, Urban Analysis Report No. 17, April, 1953.

156   —— and OTIS DUDLEY DUNCAN, *Inter-Industry Linkage: Chicago, 1947.* Chicago: University of Chicago, Population Research and Training Center, Urban Analysis Report No. 6, February, 1952.

157   —— and OTIS DUDLEY DUNCAN, *Spatial Patterns of Labor Force Industry Groups in Chicago, by Place of Work, 1947, and Place of Residence, 1940.* Chicago: University of Chicago, Population Research and Training Center, Urban Analysis Report No. 5, May, 1952.

158   —— and OTIS DUDLEY DUNCAN, *Residential Rental Value as a Factor in the Ecological Organization of the City.* Chicago: University of Chicago, Population Research and Training Center, Urban Analysis Report No. 9, July, 1952.

159 DAVIS, KINGSLEY, "Human Fertility in India," *American Journal of Sociology*, 52 (November, 1946), 243-254.

160 —— "The Origin and Growth of Urbanization in the World," *American Journal of Sociology*, 60 (March, 1955), 429-437.

161 —— and ANA CASIS, "Urbanization in Latin America," *Milbank Memorial Fund Quarterly*, 24 (April, 1946), 186-207.

162 —— and HILDA HERTZ GOLDEN, "Urbanization and the Development of Pre-Industrial Areas," *Economic Development and Cultural Change*, 3 (October, 1954), 6-26.

163 —— and HILDA HERTZ, "The World Distribution of Urbanization," *Bulletin of the International Statistical Institute*, 33, Part 4, 227-242, Proceedings of the International Statistical Conferences, New Delhi and Calcutta, 1951.

164 DEFFONTAINES, PIERRE, "The Origin and Growth of the Brazilian Network of Towns," *Geographical Review*, 28 (July, 1938), 379-399.

165 DeFLEUR, MELVIN L., and JOHN CROSBY, "Analysing Metropolitan Dominance," *Social Forces*, 35 (October, 1956), 68-75.

166 DEMING, W. EDWARDS, "On Simplifications of Sampling Design Through Replication With Equal Probabilities and Without Stages," *Journal of the American Statistical Association*, 51 (March, 1956), 24-53.

167 —— and FREDERICK F. STEPHAN, "On the Interpretation of Censuses as Samples," *Journal of the American Statistical Association*, 36 (March, 1941), 45-49.

168 DESAI, AKSHAYA R., *Introduction to Rural Sociology in India*. Bombay: Indian Society of Agricultural Economics, 1953.

169 DEWEY, RICHARD, "Peripheral Expansion in Milwaukee County," *American Journal of Sociology*, 54 (September, 1948), 118-125.

170 —— "The Neighborhood, Urban Ecology, and City Planners," *American Sociological Review*, 15 (August, 1950), 502-507.

171 DIAMOND, WILLIAM, "On the Dangers of an Urban Interpretation of History," in Eric F. Goldman (ed.), *Historiography and Urbanization*. Baltimore: The Johns Hopkins Press, 1941, Chp. IV.

172 DICKEN, SAMUEL N., "Monterrey and Northeastern Mexico," *Annals of the Association of American Geographers*, 29 (June, 1939), 127-158.

173 DICKINSON, ROBERT E., "The Commercial Functions of the Nuclei of the English Conurbations," *Sociological Review*, 21 (January, 1929), 38-49.

174 —— "The Distribution and Functions of the Smaller Urban Settlements of East Anglia," *Geography*, 17 (March, 1932), 19-31.

175 —— "The Metropolitan Regions of the United States," *Geographical Review*, 24 (April, 1934), 278-291.

176 —— "The Development and Distribution of the Medieval German Town," *Geography*, 27 (March and June, 1942).

177 —— "The Scope and Status of Urban Geography: An Assessment," *Land Economics*, 24 (August, 1948), 221-238.

178 —— *The West European City: A Geographical Interpretation*. London: Routledge and Kegan Paul, Ltd., 1951.

179   —— *City Region and Regionalism*. London: Routledge and Kegan
        Paul, 1956.
180   —— "The Geography of Commuting: The Netherlands and Belgium,"
        Geographical Review, 47 (October, 1957), 521-538.
181   Diehl, Larry F., "Major Aspects of Urbanization in the Philadelphia
        Metropolitan Area," *Journal of Land and Public Utility Eco-
        nomics*, 19 (August, 1943), 316-328.
182   Dobriner, William, *The Suburban Community*. New York: G. P.
        Putnam's Sons, 1958.
183   Doherty, Richard P., "The Movement and Concentration of Trade
        in Metropolitan Areas," *Journal of Marketing*, 5 (April, 1941),
        395-401.
184   —— "Decentralization of Retail Trade in Boston," *Journal of Market-
        ing*, 6 (January, 1942), 281-286.
185   Dorn, Harold F., "Migration and the Growth of Cities," *Social
        Forces*, 16 (March, 1938), 328-337.
186   —— "Pitfalls in Population Forecasts and Projections," *Journal of
        the American Statistical Association*, 45 (September, 1950), 311-
        334.
187   Dornbusch, Sanford M., *A Typology of Suburban Communities:
        Chicago Metropolitan District, 1940*. Chicago: University of Chi-
        cago, Population Research and Training Center, Urban Analysis
        Report No. 10, May, 1952.
188   —— *Manufacturing Cities in the United States: 1940*. Chicago: Uni-
        versity of Chicago, Population Research and Training Center,
        Urban Analysis Report No. 12, May, 1952.
189   —— and Calvin F. Schmid, *A Primer of Social Statistics*. New York:
        McGraw-Hill Book Company, Inc., 1955.
190   —— and Elijah L. White, *Segregation of Churches, Chicago, 1950:
        The Cost-Utility Approach Applied to the Spatial Patterns of
        Social Institutions*. Chicago: University of Chicago, Population
        Research and Training Center, Urban Analysis Report No. 7,
        February, 1952.
191   —— and Elijah L. White, *Commutation Movement and Urbanism*.
        Chicago: University of Chicago, Population Research and Train-
        ing Center, Urban Analysis Report No. 11, September, 1952.
192   Dotson, Floyd, and Lillian Ota Dotson, "Ecological Trends in the
        City of Guadalajara, Mexico," *Social Forces*, 32 (May, 1954),
        367-374.
193   —— and Lillian Ota Dotson, "Urban Centralization and Decentrali-
        zation in Mexico," *Rural Sociology*, 21 (March, 1956), 41-49.
194   Downes, Jean, "The Accuracy of the Recorded Birth Statistics in
        Urban and Rural Areas," *Journal of the American Statistical Asso-
        ciation*, 24 (March, 1929), 15-27.
195   Driver, Harold E., "The Measurement of Geographical Distribu-
        tion Form," *American Anthropology*, 41 (October-December,
        1939), 583-588.
196   Duncan, Beverly, "Factors in Work-Residence Separation: Wage
        and Salary Workers, Chicago, 1951," *American Sociological Re-
        view*, 21 (February, 1956), 48-56.
197   —— "Intra-Urban Population Movement," in Paul K. Hatt and Albert

J. Reiss, Jr., (eds.), *Cities and Society,* 2nd ed. Glencoe, Illinois: The Free Press, 1957, 297-309.

198 DUNCAN, OTIS DUDLEY, *Centralization of Retail Trade in Chicago, 1935: A Pilot Study in Cost-Utility Analysis.* Chicago: University of Chicago, Population Research and Training Center, Urban Analysis Report No. 1, November, 1951.

199 —— *Cost-Utility Framework for Measurement of Locational Patterns: Definition and Illustrative Applications.* Chicago: University of Chicago, Population Research and Training Center, Urban Analysis Report No. 3, January, 1952.

200 —— "Urbanization and Retail Specialization," *Social Forces,* 30 (March, 1952), 267-271.

201 —— "Research on Metropolitan Population: Evaluation of Data," *Journal of the American Statistical Association,* 51 (December, 1956), 591-596.

202 —— "The Measurement of Population Distribution," *Population Studies,* 11 (July, 1957), 27-45.

203 —— "Optimum Size of Cities," in Paul K. Hatt and Albert J. Reiss, Jr., (eds.), *Cities and Society,* 2nd ed. Glencoe, Illinois: The Free Press, 1957, 759-772.

204 —— and BEVERLY DAVIS, *Inter-Industry Variations in Work-Residence Relationships of the Chicago Labor Force.* Chicago: University of Chicago, Population Research and Training Center, Urban Analysis Report No. 13, October, 1952.

205 —— and BEVERLY DAVIS, *Contributions to the Theory of Segregation Indexes.* Chicago: University of Chicago, Population Research and Training Center, Urban Analysis Report No. 14, February, 1953.

206 —— and BEVERLY DAVIS, *A New Type of "Matter-Most" Map.* Chicago: University of Chicago, Population Research and Training Center, Urban Analysis Report No. 15, March, 1953.

207 —— and BEVERLY DAVIS, *Measures of Population Distribution in an Urban Area.* Chicago: University of Chicago, Population Research and Training Center, Urban Analysis Report No. 16, April, 1953.

208 —— and BEVERLY DAVIS, *Ecological Aspects of the Labor Force in the Chicago Metropolitan Area.* Chicago: University of Chicago, Population Research and Training Center, Urban Analysis Report No. 20, May, 1953.

209 —— and BEVERLY DAVIS, *The Chicago Urban Analysis Project: A Summary Report.* Chicago: University of Chicago, Population Research and Training Center, November, 1953.

210 —— and BEVERLY DUNCAN, "Residential Distribution and Occupational Stratification," *American Journal of Sociology,* 60 (March, 1955), 493-503.

211 —— and BEVERLY DUNCAN, "A Methodological Analysis of Segregation Indexes," *American Sociological Review,* 20 (April, 1955), 210-217.

212 —— and ALBERT J. REISS, JR., *Social Characteristics of Urban and Rural Communities: 1950.* New York: John Wiley & Sons, Inc., 1956.

213 DYER, DONALD R., "Urban Growth in Florida: Exemplified by Lakeland," *Journal of Geography,* 55 (September, 1956), 278-286.

214 —— "Urbanism in Cuba," *Geographical Review,* 47 (April, 1957), 224-233.

215 EARDLEY, A. J., *Aerial Photographs: Their Use and Interpretation.* New York: Harper and Brothers, 1942.

216 *Eastern Economist,* "Growth of Industrial Towns in India," 28 (January, 1957), 52-54.

217 EBERHARD, WOLFRAM, "Types of Settlement in Southeast-Turkey," *Sociologus,* 3 (1953), 49-63.

218 —— "Data on the Structure of the Chinese City in the Pre-Industrial Period," *Economic Development and Cultural Change,* 4 (April, 1956), 253-268.

219 EBERLE, GEORGE J., "Population Estimates of Local Communities and Economic Planning," *Journal of the American Statistical Association,* 33 (December, 1938), 694-704.

220 ECKLER, A. ROSS, and LEON PRITZKER, "Measuring the Accuracy of Enumerative Surveys," *Bulletin of the International Statistical Institute,* 33 (December, 1951), 7-23.

221 EDWARDS, ALBA M., "Occupation and Industry Statistics," *Journal of American Statistical Association,* 36 (September, 1941), 387-392.

222 ELDRIDGE, HOPE TISDALE, "Problems and Methods of Estimating Postcensal Population," *Social Forces,* 24 (October, 1945), 41-46.

223 EMMETT, W. G., "The Intelligence of Urban and Rural Children," *Population Studies,* 7 (March, 1954), 207-221.

224 ERICKSEN, E. GORDON, *Urban Behavior.* New York: The Macmillan Company, 1954.

225 EVANS, W. DUANE and MARVIN HOFFENBERG, "The Interindustry Relations Study for 1947," *The Review of Economics and Statistics,* 34 (May, 1952), 97-142.

226 FAWCETT, C. B., "British Conurbation in 1921," *Sociological Review,* 14 (April, 1922), 111-122.

227 —— "Distribution of the Urban Population in Great Britain, 1931," *Geographical Journal,* 79 (February, 1932), 100-112.

228 FEERY, L. M., "Conurbations in England and Wales," *Proceedings of the World Population Conference,* 4 (1954). New York: United Nations, 1955, 615-624.

229 FEI, HSIAO-TUNG, *China's Gentry: Essays in Rural Urban Relations.* Chicago: University of Chicago Press, 1953.

230 FESTINGER, LEON and DANIEL KATZ (eds.), *Research Methods in the Behavioral Sciences.* New York: The Dryden Press, 1953.

231 FIREY, WALTER, "Sentiment and Symbolism as Ecological Variables," *American Sociological Review,* 10 (April, 1945), 140-148.

232 —— "Ecological Considerations in Planning Rurban Fringes," *American Sociological Review,* 11 (August, 1946), 411-421.

233 —— *Land Use in Central Boston.* Cambridge, Massachusetts: Harvard University Press, 1947.

234 FISHER, ROBERT MOORE, (ed.), *The Metropolis in Modern Life.* Garden City, N.Y.: Doubleday and Company, Inc., 1955.

235 FISHER, R. A., *Statistical Methods for Research Workers,* 12th ed. New York: Hafner Publishing Company, Inc., 1955.

236 FLEMING, J. B., "An Analysis of Shops and Service Trades in Scottish Towns," *Scottish Geographical Magazine*, 70 (No. 3, 1954), 97-106.

237 FLETCHER, MERNA IRENE, "Rochester: A Professional Town," *Economic Geography*, 23 (April, 1947), 143-151.

238 FLEURE, H. J., "The Historic City in Western and Central Europe," *Bulletin of the John Rylands Library, Manchester*, 20 (July-August, 1936), 312-331.

239 FLORENCE, P. S., W. G. FRITZ, and R. C. GILLES, "Measures of Industrial Distribution," in National Resources Planning Board, *Industrial Location and National Resources*. Washington: Government Printing Office, 1943, 105-124.

240 FOGG, WALTER, "Villages, Tribal Markets and Towns: Some Considerations Concerning Urban Development in the Spanish and International Zones of Morocco," *Sociological Review*, 32 (January-April, 1940), 85-107.

241 FOLEY, DONALD L., "Urban Facility Use and Transportation: A Case Study in St. Louis," *Journal of the American Institute of Planners*, 16 (Fall, 1950), 179-185.

242 —— "The Daily Movement of Population into Central Business Districts," *American Sociological Review*, 17 (October, 1952), 538-543.

243 —— "Census Tracts and Urban Research," *Journal of the American Statistical Association*, 48 (December, 1953), 733-742.

244 —— "Urban Daytime Populations: A Field for Demographic-Ecological Analysis," *Social Forces*, 32 (May, 1954), 323-330.

245 —— and GERALD BREESE, "The Standardization of Data Showing Daily Population Movement into Central Business Districts," *Land Economics*, 27 (November, 1951), 348-353.

246 FORD, RICHARD G., "Population Succession in Chicago," *American Journal of Sociology*, 56 (September, 1950), 156-160.

247 FORM, WILLIAM H., "The Place of Social Structure in the Determination of Land Use: Some Implications for a Theory of Urban Ecology," *Social Forces*, 32 (May, 1954), 317-323.

248 FRAZIER, E. FRANKLIN, "Negro Harlem: An Ecological Study," *American Journal of Sociology*, 43 (July, 1937), 72-88.

249 FREEDMAN, RONALD, "Health Differentials for Rural-Urban Migration," *American Sociological Review*, 12 (October, 1947), 536-541.

250 —— "Distribution of Migrant Populations in Chicago," *American Sociological Review*, 13 (June, 1948), 304-309.

251 —— *Recent Migration to Chicago*. Chicago: University of Chicago Press, 1950.

252 —— and AMOS H. HAWLEY, "Unemployment and Migration in the Depression (1930-35)," *Journal of the American Statistical Association*, 44 (June, 1949), 260-272.

253 —— and AMOS H. HAWLEY, "Migration and Occupational Mobility in the Depression," *American Journal of Sociology*, 55 (September, 1959), 171-177.

254 FRIEDL, ERNESTINE, "The Role of Kinship in the Transmission of Na-

tional Culture to Rural Villages in Mainland Greece," *American Anthropologist,* 61 (February, 1959), 30-38.

255 FRIEDMANN, JOHN R. P., "The Concept of a Planning Region," *Land Economics,* 32 (February, 1956), 1-13.

256 FRYER, D. W., "The 'Million City' in Southeast Asia," *Geographical Review,* 43 (October, 1953), 474-494.

257 FURFEY, PAUL HANLY, "A Note on Lefever's 'Standard Deviational Ellipse,'" *American Journal of Sociology,* 33 (July, 1927), 94-98.

258 GALPIN, C. J., *The Social Anatomy of An Agricultural Community.* Madison: University of Wisconsin Agricultural Experiment Station, Research Bulletin No. 34, May, 1915.

259 GARIQUE, PHILIP, "French Canadian Kinship and Urban Life," *American Anthropologist,* 58 (December, 1956), 1090-1101.

260 GEDDES, PATRICK, *Cities in Evolution,* new and rev. ed. New York: Oxford University Press, 1950.

261 GEE, WILSON, "A Qualitative Study of Rural Depopulation in a Single Township: 1900-1930," *American Journal of Sociology,* 39 (September, 1933), 210-221.

262 —— and DEWEES RUNK, "Qualitative Selection in Cityward Migration," *American Journal of Sociology,* 37, (September, 1931), 254-265.

263 GEORGE, PIERRE, "La Notion de Quartier Urbain: Son Application a la Recherche Demographique et Statistique," *Proceedings of the World Population Conference,* 4 (1954). New York: United Nations, 1955, 673-681.

264 GHURYE, G. S., "Cities of India," *Sociological Bulletin,* 2 (March, 1953), 47-80.

265 GIBBS, JACK P., and WALTER T. MARTIN, "Urbanization and Natural Resources: A Study in Organizational Ecology," *American Sociological Review,* 23 (June, 1958), 266-277.

266 GILBERT, E. W., "The Boundaries of Local Government Areas," *Geographical Journal,* 111 (September, 1948), 172-198.

267 —— "English Conurbations in the 1951 Census," *Geographical Journal,* 118 (March, 1952), 64-68.

268 GILL, NORMAN N., and MARY S. BENSON, "Classes and Forms of Municipal Government," *The Municipal Year Book, 1945.* Chicago: International City Managers' Association, 1945, 90-123.

269 GILLIES, JAMES and WILLIAM GRIGSBY, "Classification Errors in Base-Ratio Analysis," *Journal of the American Institute of Planners,* 22 (Winter, 1956), 17-23.

270 GILMORE, H. W., "The Old New Orleans and the New: A Case for Ecology," *American Sociological Review,* 9 (August, 1944), 385-394.

271 —— *Transportation and the Growth of Cities.* Glencoe, Illinois: The Free Press, 1953.

272 GIST, NOEL P., "Developing Patterns of Urban Decentralization," *Social Forces,* 30 (March, 1952), 257-267.

273 —— "The New Urban Fringe," *Sociology and Social Research,* 36 (May-June, 1952), 297-302.

274 —— "Ecological Decentralization and Rural-Urban Relationships," *Rural Sociology,* 17 (December, 1952), 328-335.

275 —— "The Ecology of Bangalore, India: An East-West Comparison," *Social Forces,* 35 (May, 1957), 356-365.

276 —— and CARROLL D. CLARK, "Intelligence as a Selective Factor in Rural-Urban Migrations," *American Journal of Sociology,* 44 (July, 1938), 36-58.

277 —— and L. A. HALBERT, *Urban Society.* New York: Thomas Y. Crowell Co., 1956.

278 GOLDBERG, DAVID, "The Fertility of Two-Generation Urbanites," *Population Studies,* 12 (March, 1959), 214-222.

279 GOLDSTEIN, SIDNEY, "City Directories as Sources of Migration Data," *American Journal of Sociology,* 60 (September, 1954), 169-176.

280 —— "Repeated Migration as a Factor in High Mobility Rates," *American Sociological Review,* 19 (October, 1954), 536-541.

281 GOLDTHORPE, J. E., "Attitudes to the Census and Vital Registration in East Africa," *Population Studies,* 6 (November, 1952), 163-171.

282 GOODE, WILLIAM J. and PAUL K. HATT, *Methods in Social Research.* New York: McGraw-Hill Book Company, 1952.

283 GOODMAN, LEO A., "On Urbanization Indices," *Social Forces,* 31 (May, 1953), 360-362.

284 GOODRICH, CARTER, *et al., Migration and Economic Opportunity.* Philadelphia: University of Pennsylvania Press, 1936.

285 GOTTMANN, JEAN, "Megalopolis or the Urbanization of the Northeastern Seaboard," *Economic Geography,* 33 (July, 1957), 189-200.

286 Government Affairs Foundation, Inc., *Metropolitan Communities: A Bibliography.* Chicago: Public Administration Service, 1956.

287 GRAS, N. S. B., *An Introduction to Economic History.* New York: Harper and Brothers, 1922.

288 —— "The Rise of the Metropolitan Community," in Ernest W. Burgess (ed.), *The Urban Community. Selected Papers from the Proceedings of the American Sociological Society, 1925.* Chicago: University of Chicago Press, 1926, 183-191.

289 GREBLER, LEO, "Measuring the Suburbanization of Manufacture," *Land Economics,* 32 (November, 1956), 380-381.

290 GREEN, F. H. W., "Bus Services as an Index to Changing Urban Hinterlands," *Town Planning Review,* 22 (January, 1952), 345-356.

291 —— "Community of Interest Areas in Western Europe," *Economic Geography,* 29 (October, 1953), 283-298.

292 —— "Community of Interest and Local Government Areas," *Public Administration,* (Spring, 1956), 39-49.

293 —— "Community of Interest Areas," *Economic Geography,* 34 (July, 1958), 210-226.

294 GREEN, HOWARD W., "Cultural Areas in the City of Cleveland," *American Journal of Sociology,* 38 (November, 1932), 356-367.

295 GREEN, NORMAN E., "Scale Analysis of Urban Structures: A Study of Birmingham, Alabama," *American Sociological Review,* 21 (February, 1956), 8-13.

296 GREENBERG, JOSEPH H., "City Size and Sex Distribution," *American Sociological Review,* 14 (February, 1949), 42-44.

297 GREENE, WALTER L., "Neighborhood and Other Social-Economic

Units," *Journal of Real Estate Management,* 2 (November, 1936), 259-268.

298 —— "Internal Physical Structure of Urban Communities," *Journal of Real Estate Management,* 2 (February, 1937), 311-322.

299 —— "Internal Social-Economic Structure of Urban Communities," *Journal of Real Estate Management,* 3 (May, 1937), 77-87.

300 GREER, SCOTT, "Urbanism Reconsidered: A Comparative Study of Local Areas in a Metropolis," *American Sociological Review,* 21 (February, 1956), 19-25.

301 GRIFFIN, F. L., "The Center of Population for Various Continuous Distributions of Population Over Areas of Various Shapes," *Metron,* 11 (June, 1933), 11-16.

302 GRODZINS, MORTON, "Metropolitan Segregation," *Scientific American,* 197 (October, 1957), 33-41.

303 GROSS, EDWARD, "The Role of Density As A Factor in Metropolitan Growth in the United States of America," *Population Studies,* 8 (November, 1954), 113-120.

304 HAER, JOHN L., "Conservatism-Radicalism and the Rural-Urban Continuum," *Rural Sociology,* 17 (December, 1952), 343-347.

305 HAGOOD, MARGARET JARMAN, "Statistical Methods for Delineation of Regions Applied to Data on Agriculture and Population," *Social Forces,* 21 (March, 1943), 287-297.

306 —— and ELEANOR H. BERNERT, "Component Indexes as a Basis for Stratification in Sampling," *Journal of the American Statistical Association,* 40 (September, 1945), 330-341.

307 —— NADIA DANILEVSKY, and CORLIN O. BEUM, "An Examination of the Use of Factor Analysis in the Problem of Subregional Delineation," *Rural Sociology,* 6 (September, 1941), 216-233.

308 —— and DANIEL O. PRICE, *Statistics for Sociologists,* rev. ed. New York: Henry Holt and Company, 1952.

309 —— and JACOB S. SIEGEL, "Population Projections for Sales Forecasting," *Journal of the American Statistical Association,* 47 (September, 1952), 524-540.

310 HAIG, ROBERT MURRAY, "Toward an Understanding of the Metropolis: I. Some Speculations Regarding the Economic Basis of Urban Concentration," *Quarterly Journal of Economics,* 40 (February, 1926), 179-208.

311 —— "Toward An Understanding of the Metropolis: II. The Assignment of Activities to Areas in Urban Regions," *Quarterly Journal of Economics,* 40 (May, 1926), 402-434.

312 HAJNAL, JOHN, "The Prospects for Population Forecasts," *Journal of the American Statistical Association,* 50 (June, 1955), 309-322.

313 HALLENBECK, WILBUR C., *American Urban Communities.* New York: Harper and Brothers, 1951.

314 HAMILTON, C. HORACE, "Population Pressure and Other Factors Affecting Net Rural-Urban Migration," *Social Forces,* 30 (December, 1951), 209-215.

315 —— and F. M. HENDERSON, "Use of the Survival Rate Method in Measuring Net Migration," *Journal of the American Statistical Association,* 39 (June, 1944), 197-206.

316 HANCE, WILLIAM A., and IRENE S. VAN DONGEN, "The Port of

Lobito and the Benguela Railway," *Geographical Review,* 46 (October, 1956), 460-487.

317 HANSEN, ASAEL T., "The Ecology of A Latin American City," in E. B. Reuter, (ed.), *Race and Culture Contacts.* New York: McGraw-Hill Book Company, Inc., 1934, 124-142.

318 HANSEN, MORRIS H., and PHILIP M. HAUSER, "Area Sampling—Some Principles of Sample Design," *Public Opinion Quarterly,* 9 (Summer, 1945), 183-193.

319 —— and WILLIAM N. HURWITZ, "Relative Efficiencies of Various Sampling Units in Population Inquiries," *Journal of the American Statistical Association,* 37 (March, 1942), 89-94.

320 —— and WILLIAM N. HURWITZ, "On the Theory of Sampling from Finite Populations," *Annals of Mathematical Statistics,* 14 (Decemmer, 1943), 333-362.

321 —— WILLIAM N. HURWITZ, and MARGARET GURNEY, "Problems and Methods of the Sample Survey of Business," *Journal of the American Statistical Association,* 41 (June, 1946), 173-189.

322 —— WILLIAM N. HURWITZ, and WILLIAM G. MADOW, *Sample Survey Methods and Theory* (2 volumes). New York: Wiley and Sons, Inc., 1953.

323 —— and WILLIAM N. HURWITZ, and LEON PRITZKER, "The Accuracy of Census Results," *American Sociological Review,* 18 (August, 1953), 416-423.

324 HARRIS, CHAUNCY D., *Salt Lake City: A Regional Capital.* Chicago: University of Chicago Press, 1940.

325 —— "A Functional Classification of Cities in the United States," *Geographical Review,* 33 (January, 1943), 86-99.

326 —— "Suburbs," *American Journal of Sociology,* 49 (July, 1943), 1-13.

327 —— "The Cities of the Soviet Union," *Geographical Review,* 35 (January, 1945), 107-121.

328 —— "The Market as a Factor in the Localization of Industry in the United States," *Annals of the Association of American Geographers,* 44 (December, 1954), 315-348.

329 —— and EDWARD L. ULLMAN, "The Nature of Cities," *Annals of the American Academy of Political and Social Science,* 242 (November, 1945), 7-17.

330 HARRIS, MARILYN, D. G. HORVITZ, and A. M. MOOD, "On the Determination of Sample Sizes in Designing Experiments," *Journal of the American Statistical Association,* 43 (September, 1948), 391-402.

331 HART, JOHN FRASER, "Age Pyramids for Indiana's Counties and Larger Cities," *Indiana Academy of Science,* 67 (1953), 187-193.

332 —— "Central Tendency in Areal Distributions," *Economic Geography,* 30 (January, 1954), 48-59.

333 —— "Functions and Occupational Structures of Cities of the American South," *Annals of the Association of American Geographers,* 45 (September, 1955), 269-286.

334 HARTSHORNE, E. Y., "Metabolism Indices and the Annexation of Austria: A Note on Method," *American Journal of Sociology,* 45 (May, 1940), 899-917.

335 HASSINGER, EDWARD and ROBERT L. McNAMARA, "The Pattern of

Medical Services for Incorporated Places of 500-or-more Population in Missouri, 1950," *Rural Sociology,* 21 (June, 1956), 175-177.

336 HATT, PAUL, "Spatial Patterns in a Polyethnic Area," *American Sociological Review,* 10 (June, 1945), 352-356.

337 —— "The Concept of Natural Area," *American Sociological Review,* 11 (August, 1946), 423-427.

338 —— and ALBERT J. REISS, JR. (eds.), *Cities and Society,* 2nd ed. Glencoe, Illinois: The Free Press, 1957.

339 HAUGHTON, JOSEPH P., "The Social Geography of Dublin," *Geographical Review,* 39 (April, 1949), 257-277.

340 HAUSER, FRANCIS L., "The Ecological Pattern of Four European Cities and Two Theories of Urban Expansion," *Journal of the American Institute of Planners,* 17 (Summer, 1951), 111-129.

341 HAUSER, PHILIP M., "How Declining Urban Growth Affects City Activities," *Public Management,* 22 (December, 1940), 355-358.

342 —— "The Use of Sampling in the Census," *Journal of the American Statistical Association,* 36 (September, 1941), 369-375.

343 —— "The Labor Force and Gainful Workers—Concept, Measurement, and Comparability," *American Journal of Sociology,* 54 (January, 1949), 338-355.

344 —— "Ecological Aspects of Urban Research," in Leonard D. White (ed.), *The State of the Social Sciences.* Chicago: The University of Chicago Press, 1956, 229-254.

345 —— "The Changing Population Pattern of the Modern City," in Paul K. Hatt and Albert J. Reiss, Jr. (eds.), *Cities and Society,* 2nd ed. Glencoe, Illinois: The Free Press, 1957, 157-174.

346 —— "Some Political Influences of Urbanization," in Paul K. Hatt and Albert J. Reiss, Jr. (eds.), *Cities and Society,* 2nd ed. Glencoe, Illinois: The Free Press, 1957, 527-536.

347 —— (ed.), *Urbanization in Asia and the Far East,* Proceedings of the Joint UN/UNESCO Seminar (in cooperation with the International Labor Office) on Urbanization in the ESCAFE Region, Bangkok 8-18 August, 1956. New York: Columbia University Press, 1958.

348 —— "Demographic Indicators of Economic Development," *Economic Development and Cultural Change,* 7 (January, 1959), 98-116.

349 —— OTIS DUDLEY DUNCAN, and BEVERLY DAVIS DUNCAN, *Methods of Urban Analysis: A Summary Report.* San Antonio, Texas: U.S. Air Force Personnel and Training Research Center, Serial No. AFPTRC-TN-56-1 (January, 1956).

350 —— and HOPE T. ELDRIDGE, "Projection of Urban Growth and Migration to Cities in the United States," *Milbank Memorial Fund Quarterly,* 25 (July, 1947), 293-307.

351 HAWLEY, AMOS H., "An Ecological Study of Urban Service Institutions," *American Sociological Review,* 6 (October, 1941), 629-639.

352 —— "Ecology and Human Ecology," *Social Forces,* 22 (May, 1944), 398-405.

353 —— *Human Ecology: A Theory of Community Structure.* New York: The Ronald Press Company, 1950.

354 — "Land Value Patterns in Okayama, Japan, 1940 and 1952," *American Journal of Sociology*, 60 (March, 1955), 487-492.

355 — *The Changing Shape of Metropolitan America: Deconcentration Since 1920.* Glencoe, Illinois: The Free Press, 1956.

356 — "Metropolitan Population and Municipal Government Expenditures in Central Cities," in Paul K. Hatt and Albert J. Reiss, Jr. (eds.), *Cities and Society*, 2nd ed. Glencoe, Illinois: The Free Press, 1957, 773-782.

357 — and DONALD J. BOGUE, "Recent Shifts in Population: The Drift Toward the Metropolitan District, 1930-40," *Review of Economic Statistics*, 24 (August, 1942), 143-148.

358 — and OTIS DUDLEY DUNCAN, "Social Area Analysis: A Critical Appraisal," *Land Economics*, 33 (November, 1957), 337-345.

359 HAWTHORN, HARRY B., and AUDREY E., "The Shape of a City: Some Observations on Sucre, Bolivia," *Sociology and Social Research*, 33 (November-December, 1948), 87-91.

360 HAYNER, NORMAN S., "Mexico City: Its Growth and Configuration," *American Journal of Sociology*, 50 (January, 1945), 295-304.

361 HEBERLE, RUDOLPH, "The Causes of Rural-Urban Migration: A Survey of German Theories," *American Journal of Sociology*, 43 (May, 1938), 932-950.

362 HILBERSEIMER, LUDWIG, *The Nature of Cities.* Chicago: Paul Theobald and Co., 1955.

363 HILDEBRAND, GEORGE H., and ARTHUR MACE, JR., "The Employment Multiplier in an Expanding Industrial Market: Los Angeles County, 1940-47," *Review of Economics and Statistics*, 32 (August, 1940), 241-249.

364 HILLER, E. T., "Extension of Urban Characteristics into Rural Areas," *Rural Sociology*, 6 (September, 1941), 242-257.

365 HILLERY, GEORGE A., JR., "Definitions of Community: Areas of Agreement," *Rural Sociology*, 20 (June, 1955), 111-123.

366 HIRSCH, WERNER Z., *Introduction to Modern Statistics.* New York: The Macmillan Company, 1957.

367 HOCHSTIM, JOSEPH R., and DILMAN M. K. SMITH, "Area Sampling or Quota Control?—Three Sampling Experiments," *Public Opinion Quarterly*, 12 (Spring, 1948), 73-80.

368 HOEL, PAUL G., "On the Choice of Forecasting Formulas," *Journal of the American Statistical Association*, 42 (December, 1947), 605-611.

369 HOFFER, CHARLES R., "A Study of Town-Country Relationships," East Lansing: Michigan State College, Agricultural Experiment Station, Special Bulletin No. 181, October, 1928.

370 HOLLINGSHEAD, AUGUST B., "A Re-Examination of Ecological Theory," *Sociology and Social Research*, 31 (January-February, 1947), 194-204.

371 — "Community Research: Development and Present Condition," *American Sociological Review*, 13 (April, 1948), 136-146.

372 HOOVER, EDGAR M., "The Measurement of Industrial Localization," *The Review of Economic Statistics*, 18 (November, 1936), 162-171.

373 —— "Interstate Redistribution of Population, 1850-1940," *Journal of Economic History*, 1 (November, 1941), 199-205.

374 —— *The Location of Economic Activity*. New York: McGraw-Hill Book Company, 1948.

375 —— "The Concept of a System of Cities: A Comment on Rutledge Vining's Paper," *Economic Development and Cultural Change*, 3 (January, 1955), 196-198.

376 HOSELITZ, BERT F., "The Role of Cities in the Economic Growth of Underdeveloped Countries," *Journal of Political Economy*, 61 (June, 1953), 195-208.

377 —— "Generative and Parasitic Cities," *Economic Development and Cultural Change*, 3 (April, 1955), 278-294.

378 —— "Urbanization and Economic Growth in Asia," *Economic Development and Cultural Change*, 6 (October, 1957), 42-54.

379 HOYT, HOMER, *One Hundred Years of Land Values in Chicago*. Chicago: The University of Chicago Press, 1933.

380 —— *The Structure and Growth of Residential Neighborhoods in American Cities*. Washington, D.C.: Federal Housing Administration, 1939.

381 —— "Economic Background of Cities," *The Journal of Land and Public Utility Economics*, 17 (May, 1941), 188-195.

382 —— "Forces of Urban Centralization and Decentralization," *American Journal of Sociology*, 46 (May, 1941), 843-852.

383 —— "Is City Growth Controlled by Mathematics or Physical Laws," *Land Economics*, 27 (August, 1951), 259-262.

384 —— "On the Development of Economic Base Concept," *Land Economics*, 30 (May, 1954), 182-191.

385 HUDGINS, BERT, "Evolution of Metropolitan Detroit," *Economic Geography*, 21 (July, 1945), 206-220.

386 HUGHES, R. H., "Hong Kong: An Urban Study," *Geographical Journal*, 117 (March, 1951), 1-23.

387 HURD, RICHARD M., *Principles of City Land Values*. New York: The Record and Guide, 1903.

388 HUYBENS, RENE A., *La Photographie Aérienne et l'Urbanisme*. Linkebeek: Imprimerie A. Pinkers, 1955.

389 HYMAN, HERBERT H., *et al.*, *Interviewing in Social Research*. Chicago: University of Chicago Press, 1954.

390 —— *Survey Design and Analysis: Principles, Cases, and Procedures*. Glencoe, Illinois: The Free Press, 1955.

391 HYRENIUS, HANNES, "Summary Indices of the Age Distribution of a Population," *Population Studies*, 2 (March, 1949), 454-460.

392 IKLÉ, FRED CHARLES, "Sociological Relationship of Traffic to Population and Distance," *Traffic Quarterly*, 8 (April, 1954), 123-136.

393 INTERNATIONAL AFRICAN INSTITUTE, *Social Implications of Industrialization and Urbanization in Africa South of the Sahara*. Paris: UNESCO, 1956.

394 INTERNATIONAL STATISTICAL INSTITUTE, *Demographic Statistics of Large Cities, 1946-1951: Tables*. The Hague: 1954.

395 INTERNATIONAL URBAN RESEARCH, *The World's Metropolitan Areas*. Berkeley and Los Angeles: University of California Press, 1959.

396 ISARD, WALTER, "Interregional and Regional Input-Output Analysis:

A Model of a Space-Economy," *The Review of Economics and Statistics*, 33 (November, 1951), 318-328.

397 —— "A General Location Principle of an Optimum Space-Economy," *Econometrica*, 20 (July, 1952), 406-430.

398 —— *Location and Space Economy.* New York: John Wiley and Sons, Inc., 1956.

399 —— and CAROLINE ISARD, "The Transport-Building Cycle in Urban Development: Chicago," *The Review of Economic Statistics*, 25 (November, 1943), 224-226.

400 —— ROBERT A. KAVESH, and ROBERT E. KUENNE, "The Economic Base and Structure of the Urban-Metropolitan Region," *American Sociological Review*, 18 (June, 1953), 317-321.

401 —— and VINCENT WHITNEY, "Metropolitan Site Selection," *Social Forces*, 27 (March, 1949), 263-269.

402 ISBELL, ELEANOR COLLINS, "Internal Migration in Sweden and Intervening Opportunities," *American Sociological Review*, 9 (December, 1944), 627-639.

403 JAFFE, A. J., "Urbanization and Fertility," *American Journal of Sociology*, 48 (July, 1942), 48-60.

404 —— "Population Trends and City Growth," *The Annals of the American Academy of Political and Social Science*, 242 (November, 1945), 18-24.

405 JAHN, JULIUS A., "The Measurement of Ecological Segregation: Derivation of an Index Based on the Criterion of Reproducibility," *American Sociological Review*, 15 (February, 1950), 100-104.

406 —— CALVIN, F. SCHMID, and CLARENCE SCHRAG, "The Measurement of Ecological Segregation," *American Sociological Review*, 12 (June, 1947), 293-303.

407 JAHODA, MARIE, MORTON DEUTSCH, and STUART W. COOK, *Research Methods in Social Relations.* New York: The Dryden Press, 1951.

408 JARRETT, H. REGINALD, "Some Aspects of the Urban Geography of Freetown, Sierra Leone," *Geographical Review*, 46 (July, 1956), 334-354.

409 JEFFERSON, MARK, "Distribution of the World's City Folks: A Study in Comparative Civilization," *Geographical Review*, 21 (July, 1931), 446-465.

410 —— "The Law of the Primate City," *Geographical Review*, 29 (April, 1939), 226-232.

411 JOHNSON, EARL S., "The Function of the Central Business District in the Metropolitan Community," in Paul K. Hatt and Albert J. Reiss, Jr. (eds.), *Cities and Society*, 2nd ed. Glencoe, Illinois: The Free Press, 1957, 245-259.

412 JOHNSON, ELMER H., "Methodological Note on Measuring Selection in Differential Migration," *Social Forces*, 33 (March, 1955), 289-292.

413 JONES, LEWIS W., "The Hinterland Reconsidered," *American Sociological Review*, 20 (February, 1955), 40-44.

414 JONES, VICTOR, "Economic Classification of Cities and Metropolitan Areas," *The Municipal Year Book, 1953.* Chicago: International City Managers' Association, 1953, 49-57.

415 Joshi, R. V., "Urban Structure in Western India: Poona, A Sample Study," *Geographical Review of India*, 14 (March, 1952), 7-19.

416 Kapadia, K. M., "Rural Family Patterns: A Study in Urban-Rural Relations," *Sociological Bulletin*, 5 (September, 1956), 111-126.

417 Kelley, Eugene J., "Retail Structure of Urban Economy," *Traffic Quarterly*, 9 (July, 1955), 411-430.

418 Kelly, Burnham, "The Necessity for Dispersion," *Journal of the American Institute of Planners*, 19 (Winter, 1953), 20-25.

419 Kensler, Gladys and Bruce L. Melvin, "A Partial Sociological Study of Dryden, New York," Ithaca, N.Y.: Cornell University Agricultural Experiment Station, Bulletin No. 504, May, 1930.

420 Keyes, Fenton, "Urbanism and Population Distribution in China," *American Journal of Sociology*, 56 (May, 1951), 519-527.

421 Keyfitz, N., "Differential Fertility in Ontario. An Application of Factorial Design to a Demographic Problem," *Population Studies*, 6 (November, 1952), 123-134.

422 Kinneman, John A., "Urbanization as Measured by Hospitalization," *American Sociological Review*, 5 (October, 1940), 723-730.

423 —— "Newspaper Circulation from Small Metropolitan Centers," *American Sociological Review*, 11 (April, 1946), 150-154.

424 Kinsey, Alfred C., Wardell B. Pomeroy, and Clyde E. Martin, "Rural-Urban Background and Sexual Outlet," in Paul K. Hatt and Albert J. Reiss, Jr. (eds.) *Cities and Society*, 2nd ed. Glencoe, Illinois: The Free Press, 1957, 500-504.

425 Kiser, Clyde V., "Pitfalls in Sampling for Population Study," *Journal of the American Statistical Association*, 29 (September, 1934), 250-256.

426 Kish, Leslie, "A Two-Stage Sample of A City," *American Sociological Review*, 17 (December, 1952), 761-769.

427 Kitagawa, Evelyn M. and Donald J. Bogue, *Suburbanization of Manufacturing Activity Within Standard Metropolitan Areas*. Oxford, Ohio: Scripps Foundation, 1955.

428 Klineberg, Otto, "The Intelligence of Migrants," *American Sociological Review*, 3 (April, 1938), 218-224.

429 Klove, Robert C., "The Definition of Standard Metropolitan Areas," *Economic Geography*, 28 (April, 1952), 95-104.

430 Kneedler, Grace M., "Economic Classification of Cities," *Municipal Year Book, 1945*. Chicago: International City Managers' Association, 1945, 30-38.

431 Kolb, John H., "Service Institutions of Town and Country." Madison: University of Wisconsin, Agricultural Experiment Station, Research Bulletin No. 66, December, 1925.

432 —— and Edmund de S. Brunner, *A Study of Rural Sociology*, 4th ed. Boston: Houghton Mifflin Company, 1952.

433 —— and R. A. Polson, "Trends in Town-Country Relations." Madison: University of Wisconsin, Agricultural Experiment Station, Research Bulletin No. 117, September, 1933.

434 Kolb, William L., "The Social Structure and Functions of Cities," *Economic Development and Cultural Change*, 3 (October, 1954), 30-46.

435 Kolesnikoff, Vladimir S., "Standard Classification of Industries in

the United States," *Journal of the American Statistical Association*, 35 (March, 1940), 65-73.

436 KOOP, J. C., "Notes on the Estimation of Gross and Net Reproduction Rates by Methods of Statistical Sampling," *Biometrics*, 7 (June, 1951), 155-166.

437 KUPER, LEO, HILSTAN WATTS, and DONALD DAVIES, *Durban: A Study in Racial Ecology*. New York: Columbia University Press, 1958.

438 KURTZ, MAXINE, "Denver Economic Survey," *Journal of the American Institute of Planners*, 19 (Spring, 1953), 62-77.

439 LAMBERT, RICHARD D., "Method of Measuring Intra-Urban Population Movements," *Social Forces*, 27 (March, 1959), 269-271.

440 LAMPARD, ERIC E., "The History of Cities in the Economically Advanced Areas," *Economic Development and Cultural Change*, 3 (January, 1955), 81-136.

441 LANDIS, PAUL H., "South Dakota Town-Country Trade Relations, 1901-1931," Brookings, South Dakota: South Dakota State College, Agricultural Experiment Station Bulletin, No. 274, September, 1932.

442 —— "The Growth and Decline of South Dakota Trade Centers, 1901-1933." Brookings, South Dakota: South Dakota State College, Agricultural Experiment Station, Bulletin No. 279, April, 1933.

443 —— "Washington Farm Trade Centers, 1900-1935." Pullman: State College of Washington Agricultural Experiment Station, Bulletin No. 360, July, 1938.

444 —— *Rural Life in Process*. New York: McGraw-Hill Book Company, Inc., 1948.

445 LANGDON, GEORGE, "Delimiting the Main Line District of Philadelphia," *Economic Geography*, 28 (January, 1952), 57-65.

446 —— "Evolution of a Transportational Route as the Core of a Suburban Region," *Scientific Monthly*, 76 (June, 1953), 325-334.

447 LEE, ROSE HUM, "The Decline of Chinatowns in the United States," *American Journal of Sociology*, 54 (March, 1949), 422-432.

448 —— *The City: Urbanism and Urbanization in Major World Regions*. Philadelphia: J. B. Lippincott Co., 1955.

449 LEFEVER, D. WELTY, "Measuring Geographic Concentration by Means of the Standard Deviational Ellipse," *American Journal of Sociology*, 32 (July, 1926), 88-94.

450 LEIBENSTEIN, HARVEY, *Economic Backwardness and Economic Growth*. New York: John Wiley and Sons, Inc., 1957.

451 LEIFFER, MURRAY H., "A Method for Determining Local Urban Community Boundaries," *Publications of the American Sociological Society*, 26, 137-143.

452 LEONARD, OLEN E., "La Paz, Bolivia: Its Population and Growth," *American Sociological Review*, 13 (August, 1948), 448-454.

453 LEPAWSKY, ALBERT, "Redefining the Metropolitan Area," *National Municipal Review*, 25 (July, 1936), 417-422.

454 LEWIS, OSCAR, "Urbanization Without Breakdown: A Case Study," *Scientific Monthly*, 75 (July, 1952), 31-41.

455 LEYBURN, JAMES G., "Urban Natives in South Africa," *American Sociological Review*, 9 (October, 1944), 495-502.

456 LIEPMANN, KATE K., *The Journey to Work: Its Significance for In-*

dustrial and Community Life. New York: Oxford University Press, 1944.

457 LILLIBRIDGE, ROBERT M., "Urban Size: An Assessment," *Land Economics,* 28 (November, 1952), 341-352.

458 LILLYWHITE, JOHN D., "Rural-Urban Differentials in Divorce," *Rural Sociology,* 17 (December, 1952), 348-355.

459 LIND, ANDREW W., "A Study of Mobility of Population in Seattle," *University of Washington Publications in the Social Sciences,* 3 (October, 1925), 1-63.

460 LINDSTROM, DAVID E., *American Rural Life: A Textbook in Sociology.* New York: The Ronald Press Company, 1948.

461 LOOMER, HARLIN G., "Accuracy of the Ratio Method for Forecasting City Population: A Reply," *Land Economics,* 28 (May, 1952), 180-183.

462 LOOMIS, CHARLES P., *Studies of Rural Social Organization in the United States, Latin America and Germany.* East Lansing, Michigan: State College Book Store, 1945.

463 —— and J. ALLAN BEEGLE, *Rural Social Systems: A Textbook in Rural Sociology and Anthropology.* New York: Prentice-Hall, Inc., 1950.

464 —— and J. ALLAN BEEGLE, *Rural Sociology, The Strategy of Change.* Englewood Cliffs, N.J.: Prentice-Hall, Inc., 1957.

465 LÖSCH, AUGUST, *Economics of Location.* New Haven, Connecticut: Yale University Press, 1954.

466 LOTKA, ALFRED J., "The Law of Urban Concentration," *Science,* 94 (August 15, 1941), 164.

467 LYNCH, KEVIN, "The Form of Cities," *Scientific American,* 190 (April, 1954), 54-63.

468 McCALL, DANIEL F., "Dynamics of Urbanization in Africa," *Annals of the American Academy of Political and Social Science,* 298 (March, 1955), 151-160.

469 McCORMICK, THOMAS C., "Urban Migration and Educational Selection—Arkansas Data," *American Journal of Sociology,* 39 (November, 1933), 355-359.

470 —— "An Approach to the Measurement of Farm Population Pressure in Wisconsin," *Journal of the American Statistical Association,* 38 (June, 1943), 165-177.

471 McDOUGAL, MYRES S., "The Impact of the Metropolis Upon Land Law," in Robert M. Fisher (ed.), *The Metropolis in Modern Life.* New York: Doubleday & Company, Inc., 1955, Chp. 10.

472 McINTYRE, WALLACE E., "The Retail Pattern of Manila," *Geographical Review,* 45 (January, 1955), 66-80.

473 McKAIN, WALTER C., JR., and ROBERT G. BURNIGHT, "The Sociological Significance of the Rural-Urban Fringe from the Rural Point of View," *Rural Sociology,* 18 (June, 1953), 108-114.

474 McKENZIE, RODERICK DUNCAN, *The Neighborhood: A Study of Local Life in the City of Columbus, Ohio.* Chicago: The University of Chicago Press, 1923.

475 —— "The Ecological Approach to the Study of the Human Community," *American Journal of Sociology,* 30 (November, 1924), 287-301.

476 —— "Spatial Distance and Community Organization Pattern," *Social Forces*, 5 (June, 1927), 623-627.

477 —— "Spatial Distance," *Sociology and Social Research*, 13 (July-August, 1929), 536-544.

478 —— *The Metropolitan Community*. New York: McGraw-Hill Book Company, Inc., 1933.

479 MADDEN, CARL H., "On Some Indications of Stability in the Growth of Cities in The United States," *Economic Development and Cultural Change*, 4 (April, 1956), 236-252.

480 —— "Some Spatial Aspects of Urban Growth in the United States," *Economic Development and Cultural Change*, 4 (July, 1956), 371-387.

481 —— "Some Temporal Aspects of the Growth of Cities in the United States," *Economic Development and Cultural Change*, 6 (January, 1958), 143-170.

482 MADOW, LILLIAN H., "Systematic Sampling and Its Relation to Other Sampling Designs," *Journal of the American Statistical Assocation*, 41 (June, 1946), 204-217.

483 MANGUS, A. R., "Personality Adjustment of Rural and Urban Children," *American Sociological Review*, 13 (October, 1948), 566-575.

484 MARKS, ELI S., W. PARKER MAULDIN, and HAROLD NISSELSON, "The Post-Enumeration Survey of the 1950 Census: A Case History in Survey Design," *Journal of the American Statistical Association*, 48 (June, 1953), 220-243.

485 MARSHALL, D. G., "Hamlets and Villages in the United States: Their Place in the American Way of Life," *American Sociological Review*, 11 (April, 1946), 159-165.

486 MARTIN, C. J., "Note on the Use of Statistics of Total Fertility to Provide Estimates of Crude Birth Rates," *Population Studies*, 8 (July, 1954), 88-91.

487 MARTIN, WALTER T., "The Growth of Metropolitan Regions on the Pacific Coast, 1900-1950," *Research Studies of the State College of Washington*, 23 (June, 1955), 102-109.

488 —— "Continuing Urbanization on the Pacific Coast," *American Journal of Sociology*, 62 (November, 1956), 320-328.

489 —— "Ecological Change in Satellite Rural Areas," *American Sociological Review*, 22 (April, 1957), 173-183.

490 MASUOKA, JITSUICHI, "Urbanization and the Family in Japan," *Sociology and Social Research*, 32 (September-October, 1948), 535-539.

491 MATHERLY, WALTER J., "The Emergence of the Metropolitan Community in the South," *Social Forces*, 14 (March, 1936), 311-325.

492 MATHER, W. G., T. H. TOWNSEND, and DWIGHT SANDERSON, "A Study of Rural Community Development in Waterville, New York," Ithaca, New York: Cornell University Agricultural Experiment Station, Bulletin No. 608, 1934.

493 MAULDIN, W. PARKER, "Selective Migration from Small Towns," *American Sociological Review*, 5 (October, 1940), 748-758.

494 MAYER, HAROLD M., "Patterns and Recent Trends of Chicago's Out-

lying Business Centers," *The Journal of Land and Public Utility Economics,* 18 (February, 1942), 4-17.

495 MAYO, SELZ C., "Two Factors in Urban Population Growth," *Social Forces,* 22 (October, 1943), 80-81.

496 MELAMID, ALEXANDER, "The Geographical Distribution of Communities in Cyprus," *Geographical Review,* 46 (July, 1956), 355-374.

497 MELVIN, BRUCE, "Rural Population of New York, 1855-1925," Ithaca, New York: Cornell University Agricultural Experiment Station, Memoir No. 116, June, 1928.

498 —— "Village Service Agencies, New York, 1925," Ithaca, New York: Cornell University Agricultural Experiment Station, Bulletin No. 493, August, 1929.

499 MERRIAM, CHARLES E., "Urbanism," *American Journal of Sociology,* 45 (March, 1940), 720-730.

500 MINER, HORACE, "The Folk-Urban Continuum," *American Sociological Review,* 17 (October, 1952), 529-537.

501 —— *The Primitive City of Timbuctoo.* Princeton, New Jersey: Princeton University Press, 1953.

502 MITCHELL, ROBERT B., and CHESTER RAPKIN, *Urban Traffic: A Function of Land Use.* New York: Columbia University Press, 1954.

503 MONKHOUSE, FRANCIS J., and H. R. WILKINSON, *Maps and Diagrams: Their Compilation and Construction.* New York: E. P. Dutton & Co., Inc., 1952.

504 MOORE, ELON H., "Methods of Isolating the Mobility Factor in Population Change," *Sociology and Social Research,* 24 (November-December, 1939), 124-139.

505 MOORE, JANE, *Cityward Migration: Swedish Data.* Chicago: The University of Chicago Press, 1938.

506 MOSCHELES, JULIE, "The Demographic, Social and Economic Regions of Greater Prague," *Geographical Review,* 27 (July, 1937), 414-429.

507 MOSER, CLAUS, *Survey Methods in Social Investigation.* New York: The Macmillan Company, 1958.

508 MUKERJEE, RADHAKAMAL and F. K. GIRLING, "Economic Structure in Two Breton Villages," *Rural Sociology,* 14 (December, 1949), 295-305.

509 MUKHERJEE, S., "Urbanization in Burdwan Division," *Calcutta Statistical Association Bulletin,* 6 (March, 1955), 1-16.

510 MUMFORD, LEWIS, *The Culture of Cities.* New York: Harcourt, Brace and Company, 1938.

511 —— *City Development: Studies in Disintegration and Renewal.* New York: Harcourt, Brace and Company, 1945.

512 MUNTZ, EARL E., *Urban Sociology.* New York: The Macmillan Company, 1938.

513 MURDOCK, GEORGE P., "Feasibility and Implementation of Comparative Community Research," *American Sociological Review,* 15 (December, 1950), 713-720.

514 MURPHEY, RHOADS, "Boston's Chinatown," *Economic Geography,* 28 (July, 1952), 244-255.

515 —— "The City As a Center of Change: Western Europe and China,"

Annals of the Association of American Geographers, 44 (March, 1954), 349-362.

516 MURPHY, RAYMOND E. and J. E. VANCE, JR., "A Comparative Study of Nine Central Business Districts," *Economic Geography,* 30 (October, 1954), 301-336.

517 —— J. E. VANCE, JR., and BART J. EPSTEIN, "Internal Structure of the CBD," *Economic Geography,* 31 (January, 1955), 21-46.

518 MYERS, JEROME K., "Note on the Homogeneity of Census Tracts: A Methodological Problem in Urban Ecological Research," *Social Forces,* 32 (May, 1954), 364-366.

519 MYKLEBOST, HALLSTEIN, "Population Forecasts by Simple Methodology," *Land Economics,* 26 (August, 1950), 308-311.

520 NEALE, E. P., "The Size of Towns," *Economic Record,* 28 (May, 1952), 81-88.

521 NELSON, CHARLES W., "Testing the Influence of Rural and Urban Environment in A. C. E. Intelligence Test Scores," *American Sociological Review,* 7 (December, 1942), 743-751.

522 NELSON, HOWARD J., "The Vernon Area—A Study of the Political Factor in Urban Geography," *Annals of the Association of the American Geographers,* 42 (June, 1952), 177-191.

523 —— "Some Characteristics of the Population of Cities in Similar Service Classifications," *Economic Geography,* 33 (April, 1957), 95-108.

524 NELSON, LOWRY, *Rural Sociology,* 2nd ed. New York: American Book Co., 1955.

525 NEW, PETER KONG-MING, "Use of Birth Data in Delineation of Medical Service Areas," *Rural Sociology,* 20 (September-December, 1955), 272-281.

526 NEWCOMB, CHARLES, "Graphic Presentation of Age and Sex Distribution of Population in the City," in Paul K. Hatt and Albert J. Reiss, Jr. (eds.), *Cities and Society,* 2nd ed. Glencoe, Illinois: The Free Press, 1957, 382-392.

527 NEWMAN, DOROTHY K., "Metropolitan Area Structure and Growth as Shown by Building-Permit Statistics," *Business Topics,* 4 (November, 1956), 1-7.

528 NEYMAN, JERZY, "On the Two Different Aspects of the Representative Method: The Method of Stratified Sampling and the Method of Purposive Selection," *Journal of the Royal Statistical Society,* 97 (Part 4, 1934), 558-625.

529 NICHOLS, CHARLES K., "A Suggested Technique for Determining Whether A Community Can Be Classified As Rural or Urban," *Rural Sociology,* 5 (December, 1940), 454-460.

530 O'BRIEN, ROBERT W., "Beale Street, A Study in Ecological Succession," *Sociology and Social Research,* 26 (May-June, 1942), 430-436.

531 Office of Population Research, Princeton University, Princeton, New Jersey, *Population Index.* (published quarterly)

532 OGBURN, WILLIAM F., *Social Characteristics of Cities.* Chicago: International City Managers' Association, 1937.

533 —— "Size of Community as a Factor in Migration," *Sociology and Social Research,* 28 (March-April, 1944), 255-261.

534 — "Inventions of Local Transportation and the Patterns of Cities,"
     Social Forces, 24 (May, 1946), 373-379.
535 OSBORNE, E., "This Changing World: Inter-County Migration in
     South-eastern England," *Geography,* 40 (January, 1955), 47-48.
536 PAINTER, NORMAN W., "Procedure and Problems of Delineating
     Locality Groups in Latin America," *Rural Sociology,* 19 (June,
     1954), 181-183.
537 PAPPENFORT, DONNELL M., *Industrial Control in the Metropolitan
     Community: A Study in Metropolitan Dominance.* Chicago: Uni-
     versity of Chicago, Population Research and Training Center,
     Urban Analysis Report No. 19, May, 1953.
538 PARK, ROBERT E., "The City: Suggestions for the Investigation of
     Human Behavior in the City Environment," *American Journal of
     Sociology,* 20 (March, 1915), 577-612.
539 — "Urbanization As Measured by Newspaper Circulation," *Ameri-
     can Journal of Sociology,* 35 (July, 1929), 60-79.
540 — "Succession, an Ecological Concept," *American Sociological Re-
     view,* 1 (April, 1936), 171-179.
541 — "Human Ecology," *American Journal of Sociology,* 42 (July,
     1936), 1-15.
542 — *Human Communities: The City and Human Ecology.* Glencoe,
     Illinois: The Free Press, 1952.
543 — ERNEST W. BURGESS, and RODERICK D. McKENZIE, *The City.*
     Chicago: The University of Chicago Press, 1925.
544 PARTEN, MILDRED B., *Surveys, Polls, and Samples: Practical Proce-
     dures.* New York: Harper, 1950.
545 PATTISON, WILLIAM D., "The Cemeteries of Chicago: A Phase of
     Land Utilization," *Annals of the Association of American Geog-
     raphers,* 45 (September, 1955), 245-257.
546 PAVER, JOHN, and MILLER McCLINTOCK, *Traffic and Trade.* New
     York: McGraw-Hill Book Company, Inc., 1935.
547 PETERS, WILLIAM S., "A Method of Deriving Geographic Patterns of
     Associated Demographic Characteristics Within Urban Areas,"
     Social Forces, 35 (October, 1956), 62-68.
548 PHILBRICK, ALLEN K., "Principles of Areal Functional Organization
     in Regional Human Geography," *Economic Geography,* 33 (Oc-
     tober, 1957), 299-336.
549 PIGGOTT, STUART, *Prehistoric India.* Harmondsworth, England: Pen-
     guin Books, 1950.
550 PIRENNE, HENRI, *Medieval Cities: Their Origins and the Revival of
     Trade.* Princeton, New Jersey: Princeton University Press, 1925.
551 PORTE, J., "Introduction d'un Code des Agglomerations dans la Sta-
     tistique Demographique Francaise," *Proceedings of the World
     Population Conference, 1954,* 4 (1955), 835-841.
552 POWNALL, L. L., "Metropolitan Auckland, 1740-1945: The Historical
     Geography of a New Zealand City," *New Zealand Geographer,*
     6 (October, 1950), 107-124.
553 — "Town and Region: A Comparison of Palmerston North, Wan-
     ganui, and New Plymouth," *New Zealand Geographer,* 9 (April,
     1953), 1-16.

554 —— "The Origins of Towns in New Zealand," *New Zealand Geographer*, 12 (October, 1956), 173-188.

555 —— "The Retail Potential of Some Representative New Zealand Towns," *Economic Geography*, 33 (April, 1957), 163-170.

556 —— "Surface Growth of New Zealand Towns," *New Zealand Geographer*, 13 (October, 1957), 99-116.

557 PRATT, SAMUEL, "Metropolitan Community Development and Change in Sub-center Economic Functions," *American Sociological Review*, 22 (August, 1957), 434-440.

558 PRICE, DANIEL O., "Factor Analysis in the Study of Metropolitan Centers," *Social Forces*, 20 (May, 1942), 449-455.

559 —— "Nonwhite Migrants to and from Selected Cities," *American Journal of Sociology*, 54 (November, 1948), 196-201.

560 —— "Examination of Two Sources of Error in the Estimation of Net Internal Migration," *Journal of the American Statistical Association*, 50 (September, 1955), 689-700.

561 PRICE, H. BRUCE, and C. R. HOFFER, "Services of Rural Trade Centers in Distribution of Farm Supplies." St. Paul: University of Minnesota Agricultural Experiment Station, Bulletin No. 249, October, 1928.

562 PROUDFOOT, MALCOM J., "City Retail Structure," *Economic Geography*, 13 (October, 1937), 425-428.

563 —— "The Selection of a Business Site," *Journal of Land and Public Utility Economics*, 14 (November, 1938), 370-381.

564 QUEEN, STUART A., and DAVID B. CARPENTER, *The American City*. New York: McGraw-Hill Book Company, Inc., 1953.

565 —— and DAVID B. CARPENTER, "The Rural-Urban Fringe From the Urban Point of View," *Rural Sociology*, 18 (June, 1953), 102-108.

566 QUINN, JAMES A., "The Nature of Human Ecology: Reexamination and Redefinition," *Social Forces*, 18 (December, 1939), 161-168.

567 —— "The Burgess Zonal Hypothesis and Its Critics," *American Sociological Review*, 5 (April, 1940), 210-218.

568 —— "Topical Summary of Current Literature on Human Ecology," *American Journal of Sociology*, 46 (September, 1940), 191-226.

569 —— "Human Ecology and Interactional Ecology," *American Sociological Review*, 5 (October, 1940), 713-722.

570 —— "Culture and Ecological Phenomena," *Sociology and Social Research*, 25 (March-April, 1941), 313-320.

571 —— "The Hypothesis of Median Location," *American Sociological Review*, 8 (April, 1943), 148-156.

572 —— *Human Ecology*. New York: Prentice-Hall, Inc., 1950.

573 —— *Urban Sociology*. New York: American Book Company, 1955.

574 RAISTRICK, A., "A Fourteenth Century Regional Survey," *Sociological Review*, 21 (July, 1929), 241-249.

575 RAPHAEL, EDNA, *Calculation of Population Potential for an Urban Area*. Chicago: University of Chicago, Population Research and Training Center, Urban Analysis Report No. 18, May, 1953.

576 RATCLIFFE, RICHARD U., "The Problem of Retail Site Selection," *Michigan Business Studies*, 9 (1939), 1-93.

577 —— *Urban Land Economics*. New York: McGraw-Hill Book Company, Inc., 1949.

578 RATCLIFFE, S. C., "Size As a Factor in Population Changes of Incorporated Hamlets and Villages, 1930-1940," *Rural Sociology,* 7 (September, 1942), 318-328.

579 RAZA, MOONIS, "Urbanization in Prehistoric India," *The Geographer,* 4 (May, 1951), 15-29.

580 REDFIELD, CHARLES E., *et al.* "The Impact of Levittown on Local Government," *Journal of the American Institute of Planners,* 17 (Summer, 1951), 130-141.

581 REDFIELD, ROBERT, "The Folk Society and Culture," *American Journal of Sociology,* 45 (March, 1940), 731-742.

582 —— *The Folk Culture of Yucatan.* Chicago: University of Chicago Press, 1941.

583 —— *Tepoztlan, A Mexican Village: A Study of Folk Life.* Chicago: University of Chicago Press, 1946.

584 —— "The Folk Society," *American Journal of Sociology,* 52 (January, 1947), 293-308.

585 —— "The Natural History of the Folk Society," *Social Forces,* 31 (March, 1953), 224-228.

586 —— *The Little Community: Viewpoints for the Study of a Human Whole.* Chicago: University of Chicago Press, 1955.

587 —— *Peasant Society and Culture: An Anthropological Approach to Civilization.* Chicago: University of Chicago Press, 1956.

588 —— and MILTON B. SINGER, "The Cultural Role of Cities," *Economic Development and Cultural Change,* 3 (October, 1954), 53-73.

589 REDICK, RICHARD W., "Population Growth and Distribution in Central Cities, 1940-1950," *American Sociological Review,* 21 (February, 1956), 38-43.

590 REEDER, LEO G., "The Central Area of Chicago—A Re-examination of the Process of Decentralization," *Land Economics,* 28 (November, 1952), 369-373.

591 —— "Industrial Deconcentration As A Factor in Rural-Urban Fringe Development" *Land Economics,* 31 (August, 1955), 275-280.

592 —— "Social Differentials in Mode of Travel, Time and Cost in the Journey to Work," *American Sociological Review,* 21 (February, 1956), 56-63.

593 REILLY, WILLIAM J., "Methods for the Study of Retail Relationships," *University of Texas Bulletin,* No. 2944 (November, 1929), 1-50.

594 REISS, ALBERT J., JR., "Research Problems in Metropolitan Population Redistribution," *American Sociological Review,* 21 (October, 1956), 571-577.

595 —— "Functional Specialization of Cities," in Paul K. Hatt and Albert J. Reiss, Jr. (eds.), *Cities and Society,* 2nd ed. Glencoe, Illinois: The Free Press, 1957, pp. 555-575.

596 Research Centre on the Social Implications of Industrialization in Southern Asia, *The Social Implications of Industrialization and Urbanization: Five Studies of Urban Populations of Recent Rural Origin in Cities of Southern Asia.* Calcutta: UNESCO, 1956.

597 —— "Social Science Projects in Southern Asia," *Research Information Bulletin,* No. 1. Calcutta: UNESCO, December, 1956.

598 REYNOLDS, ROBERT B., "A Test of the Law of Retail Gravitation," *Journal of Marketing,* 17 (January, 1953), 273-277.

599 RIEMER, SVEND, *The Modern City.* New York: Prentice-Hall, Inc., 1952.

600 ROBINSON, ARTHUR H., and RIED A. BRYSON, "A Method for Describing Quantitatively The Correspondence of Geographical Distributions," *Annals of the Association of American Geographers,* 47 (December, 1957), 379-391.

601 ROBINSON, G. W. S., "British Conurbations in 1951: Some Corrections," *Sociological Review,* 4 (July, 1956), 91-97.

602 ROCHEFORT, MICHAEL, "La Structure Professionelle des Villes Alsaciennes et les Effets de la Centralisation Economique sur son Evolution Recante," *Proceedings of the World Population Conference, 1954,* 4, 845-854.

603 RODEHAVER, MYLES W., "Fringe Settlement as a Two Directional Movement," *Rural Sociology,* 12 (March, 1947), 49-57.

604 RODGERS, ALLAN, "Some Aspects of Industrial Diversification in the United States," *Economic Geography,* 33 (January, 1957), 1-30.

605 ROHRER, WAYNE C., and ROBERT HIRZEL, "A Methodological Note on Demographic Analyses of the Rural-Urban Fringe," *Rural Sociology,* 22 (March, 1957), 71-73.

606 ROLPH, INEZ K., "The Population Pattern in Relation to Retail Buying, as Exemplified in Baltimore," *American Journal of Sociology,* 38 (November, 1932), 368-376.

607 ROPER-POWER, E. R., "The Social Structure of an English County Town," *Sociological Review,* 29 (October, 1937), 391-413.

608 ROSSI, PETER H., *Why Families Move: A Study in the Social Psychology of Urban Residential Mobility.* Glencoe, Illinois: The Free Press, 1955.

609 ROSTOVTZEFF, MICHAEL I., "Cities in the Ancient World," *Urban Land Economics.* The Institute for Research in Land Economics, Ann Arbor: Edwards Brothers, Publishers, 1922, 17-58.

610 ROTERUS, VICTOR, "Effects of Population Growth and Non-Growth on the Well-Being of Cities," *American Sociological Review,* 11 (February, 1946), 90-97.

611 SAUNDERS, J. V. D., "Delineation of a Florida County-Seat Community," *Rural Sociology,* 21 (June, 1956), 180-181.

612 SCHETTLER, CLARENCE, "Relation of City-Size to Economic Services," *American Sociological Review,* 8 (February, 1943), 60-62.

613 SCHMID, CALVIN F., "Generalizations Concerning the Ecology of the American City," *American Sociological Review,* 15 (April, 1950), 264-281.

614 SCHMITT, ROBERT C., "Demography and City Planning," *Social Forces,* 30 (March, 1952), 300-304.

615 —— "Short-cut Methods of Estimating County Population," *Journal of the American Statistical Association,* 47 (June, 1952), 232-238.

616 —— "Estimating Current Populations of Census Tracts," *Sociology and Social Research,* 37 (September-October, 1952), 12-15.

617 —— "Differential Migration and City Population Estimates," *Sociology and Social Research,* 37 (May-June, 1953), 327-328.

618 —— "A New Method for Forecasting City Population," *Journal of the American Institute of Planners,* 19 (Winter, 1953), 40-42.

619   —— "Short-Cut Methods of Forecasting the Population of Census Tracts," *Journal of Marketing*, 18 (January, 1954), 266-270.

620   —— "Correlation of Time Series in Population Forecasting," *Sociology and Social Research*, 38 (January-February, 1954), 159-161.

621   —— "A Method of Estimating the Population of Cities," *American Journal of Public Health*, 44 (November, 1954), 1426-1427.

622   —— "Suburbanization: Statistical Fallacy," *Land Economics*, 32 (February, 1956), 85-87.

623   —— "Estimating Daytime Populations," *Journal of the American Institute of Planners*, 22 (Spring, 1956), 83-85.

624   —— "Methods of Estimating the Postcensal Population of Census Tracts," *Land Economics*, 32 (November, 1956), 376-379.

625   —— and ALBERT H. CROSETTI, "Accuracy of the Ratio Methods for Forecasting City Population," *Land Economics*, 27 (November, 1951), 346-348.

626   —— and ALBERT H. CROSETTI, "Short-Cut Methods of Forecasting City Population," *Journal of Marketing*, 17 (April, 1953), 417-424.

627   SCHNEIDER, J. R. L., "Note on the Accuracy of Local Population Estimates," *Population Studies*, 8 (November, 1954), 148-150.

628   SCHNORE, LEO F., "The Separation of Home and Work: A Problem for Human Ecology," *Social Forces*, 32 (May, 1954), 336-343.

629   —— "The Functions of Metropolitan Suburbs," *American Journal of Sociology*, 61 (March, 1956), 453-458.

630   —— "The Growth of Metropolitan Suburbs," *American Sociological Review*, 22 (April, 1957), 165-173.

631   —— "Metropolitan Growth and Decentralization," *American Journal of Sociology*, 63 (September, 1957), 171-180.

632   —— "Satellites and Suburbs," *Social Forces*, 36 (December, 1957), 121-127.

633   —— and GENE B. PETERSEN, "Urban and Metropolitan Development in the United States and Canada," *Annals of the American Academy of Political and Social Science*, 316 (March, 1958), 60-68.

634   —— and DAVID W. VARLEY, "Some Concomitants of Metropolitan Size," *American Sociological Review*, 20 (August, 1955), 408-414.

635   SCHOENBERG, ERIKA H. and MILDRED PARTEN, "Methods and Problems of Sampling Presented by the Urban Study of Consumer Purchases," *Journal of the American Statistical Association*, 32 (June, 1937), 311-322.

636   SCHWAB, WILLIAM B., "An Experiment in Methodology in a West African Urban Community," *Human Organization*, 13 (Spring, 1954), 13-19.

637   *Scientific Monthly*, "Symposium on Viewpoints, Problems, and Methods of Research in Urban Areas," 73 (July, 1951), 37-50.

638   SCOTT, PETER, "Some Functional Aspects of Cape Town," *Economic Geography*, 30 (October, 1954), 347-363.

639   —— "Cape Town: A Multi-Racial City," *Geographical Journal*, 121 (June, 1955), 149-157.

640   SEGOE, L., "Urban Population and Industrial Trends," *Public Management*, 17 (June, 1935), 163-170.

641   SEKAR, C. CHANDRA and W. EDWARDS DEMING, "On a Method of

Estimating Birth and Death Rates and the Extent of Registration," *Journal of the American Statistical Association,* 44 (March, 1949), 101-115.

642 SEMON, THOMAS T., "The Case for a Broader 'Urbanized-Area' Concept," *Journal of Marketing,* 19 (October, 1954), 162-163.

643 SENDERS, VIRGINIA L., *Measurement and Statistics.* New York: Oxford University Press, 1958.

644 SENG, YOU POH, "Practical Problems in Sampling for Social and Demographic Inquiries in Underdeveloped Countries," *Population Studies,* 3 (September, 1949), 170-191.

645 SHANNON, H. A., "Migration and the Growth of London, 1841-1891," *Economic History Review,* 5 (April, 1935), 79-86.

646 SHANNON, LYLE W., *Underdeveloped Areas.* New York: Harper and Brothers, 1957.

647 SHAUL, J. R. H., "Sampling Surveys in Central Africa," *Journal of the American Statistical Association,* 47 (June, 1952), 239-254.

648 SHEVKY, ESHREF and WENDELL BELL, *Social Area Analysis.* Stanford, California: Stanford University Press, 1955.

649 —— and MARILYN WILLIAMS, *The Social Areas of Los Angeles, Analysis and Typology.* Berkeley: University of California Press, 1949.

650 SHRYOCK, HENRY S., "The Current Status of State and Local Population Estimates in the Census Bureau," *Journal of the American Statistical Association,* 44 (June, 1949), 157-173.

651 —— "Population Redistribution within Metropolitan Areas: Evaluation of Research," *Social Forces,* 35 (December, 1956), 154-159.

652 —— "The Natural History of Standard Metropolitan Areas," *American Journal of Sociology,* 63 (September, 1957), 163-170.

653 SIEGEL, BERNARD J., "The Role of Perception in Urban-Rural Change: A Brazilian Case Study," *Economic Development and Cultural Change,* 5 (April, 1957), 244-256.

654 SIEGEL, JACOB S., "Forecasting the Population of Small Areas," *Land Economics,* 29 (February, 1953), 72-88.

655 —— HENRY S. SHRYOCK, JR., and BENJAMIN GREENBERG, "Accuracy of Postcensal Estimates of Population for States and Cities," *American Sociological Review,* 19 (August, 1954), 440-446.

656 SIEGEL, SIDNEY, *Nonparametric Statistics for the Behavioral Sciences.* New York: McGraw-Hill Book Company, Inc., 1956.

657 SILCOCK, H., "Estimating by Sample the Size and Age-Sex Structure of a Population," *Population Studies,* 6 (July, 1952), 55-68.

658 —— "Precision in Population Estimates," *Population Studies,* 8 (November, 1954), 140-147.

659 SIMON, HERBERT A., "Effects of Increased Productivity Upon the Ratio of Urban to Rural Population," *Econometrica,* 15 (January, 1947), 31-42.

660 SINGER, H. W., "The 'Courbe des Populations': A Parallel to Pareto's Law," *Economic Journal,* 46 (June, 1936), 254-263.

661 SISCO, PAUL H., "Geographic Training and Method Applied to Trade Area Analysis of Local Shopping Centers," *Journal of Geography,* 56 (May, 1957), 201-212.

662 SJOBERG, GIDEON, "Urban Community Theory and Research: A Partial

Evaluation," *American Journal of Economics and Sociology,* 14 (January, 1955), 199-206.

663 —— "The Preindustrial City," *American Journal of Sociology,* 60 (March, 1955), 438-445.

664 SLONIM, MORRIS J., "Sampling in a Nutshell," *Journal of the American Statistical Association,* 52 (June, 1957), 143-161.

665 SMAILES, A. E., "The Urban Hierarchy in England and Wales," *Geography,* 29 (June, 1944), 41-51.

666 —— "The Urban Mesh of England and Wales," *Transactions of the Institute of British Geographers,* 11 (1946), 84-101.

667 —— "The Analysis and Delimitation of Urban Fields," *Geography,* 32 (December, 1947), 151-161.

668 SMITH, GEORGE C., JR., "Lorenz Curve Analysis of Industrial Decentralization," *Journal of the American Statistical Association,* 42 (December, 1947), 591-596.

669 SMITH, H. T. U., *Aerial Photographs and Their Applications.* New York: D. Appleton-Century Co., 1943.

670 SMITH, JOEL, "A Method for the Classification of Areas on the Basis of Demographically Homogeneous Populations," *American Sociological Review,* 19 (April, 1954), 201-207.

671 SMITH, MAPHEUS, "An Urban-Rural Intellectual Gradient," *Sociology and Social Research,* 27 (March-April, 1943), 307-315.

672 SMITH, MARIAN W., *Technological Change and Social Disorganization: Bibliography on Asia and the Pacific.* Paris: Conseil International des Sciences Sociales, Bureau International de Recherche sur les Implications Sociales du Progrès Technique, 1955.

673 SMITH, T. LYNN, "The Locality Group Structure of Brazil," *American Sociological Review,* 9 (February, 1944), 41-49.

674 SNOW, E. C., "The Application of the Method of Multiple Correlation to the Estimation of Post-Censal Population," *Journal of the Royal Statistical Society,* 74 (May, 1911), 575-620.

675 SOKOLOVA, N. A., *Aerofotosyemka Gorodov v Masshtabakh 1:2000 i 1:5000.* Moskva: Gosoodarstvyennoye Izdatyelstvo, 1952.

676 SOROKIN, PITIRIM A., CARLE C. ZIMMERMAN, CHARLES J. GALPIN, (eds.), *A Systematic Source Book in Rural Sociology* (3 vols.). Minneapolis: The University of Minnesota Press, 1930-1932.

677 SPATE, O. H. K. and L. W. TRUEBLOOD, "Rangoon: A Study in Urban Geography," *Geographical Review,* 32 (January, 1942), 56-73.

678 SPAULDING, IRVING A., "Serendipity and the Rural-Urban Continuum," *Rural Sociology,* 16 (March, 1951), 29-36.

679 SPROWLS, R. C., *Elementary Statistics for Students of Social Science and Business.* New York: McGraw-Hill Book Company, Inc., 1955.

680 SRINIVAS, M. N., "The Industrialization and Urbanization of Rural Areas," *Sociological Bulletin,* 5 (September, 1956), 79-88.

681 STEINER, ROBERT L., "Urban and Inter-Urban Economic Equilibrium," *Land Economics,* 32 (May, 1956), 167-174.

682 STEPHAN, FREDERICK F., "Practical Problems of Sampling Procedure," *American Sociological Review,* 1 (August, 1936), 569-580.

683 —— "Stratification in Representative Sampling," *Journal of Marketing,* 6 (July, 1941), 38-46.

684 —— "History of the Uses of Modern Sampling Procedures," *Journal of the American Statistical Association,* 43 (March, 1948), 12-39.

685 —— EDWARDS DEMING, and MORRIS H. HANSEN, "The Sampling Procedure of the 1940 Population Census," *Journal of the American Statistical Association,* 35 (December, 1940), 615-630.

686 —— and PHILIP J. McCARTHY, *Sampling Opinions: An Analysis of Survey Procedure.* New York: John Wiley and Sons, 1958.

687 STEWART, CHARLES T., JR., "The Size and Spacing of Cities," *Geographical Review,* 48 (April, 1958), 222-245.

688 —— "The Urban-Rural Dichotomy: Concepts and Uses," *American Journal of Sociology,* 64 (September, 1958), 152-158.

689 STEWART, JOHN Q., "Empirical Mathematical Rules Concerning the Distribution and Equilibrium of Population," *Geographical Review,* 37 (July, 1947), 461-485.

690 —— "The Development of Social Physics," *American Journal of Physics,* 18 (May, 1950), 239-253.

691 STOLPER, WOLFGANG, "Spatial Order and the Economic Growth of Cities: A Comment on Eric Lampard's Paper," *Economic Development and Cultural Change,* 3 (January, 1955), 137-146.

692 STOUFFER, SAMUEL A., "Intervening Opportunities: A Theory Relating Mobility and Distance," *American Sociological Review,* 5 (December, 1940), 845-867.

693 SULLENGER, T. EARL, "The Social Significance of Mobility: An Omaha Study," *American Journal of Sociology,* 55 (May, 1950), 559-564.

694 —— *Sociology of Urbanization: A Study in Rurban Society.* Ann Arbor, Michigan: Bran-Brumfield, Inc., 1956.

695 SWEETSER, FRANK L., JR., "Population, Area, and Density of Comparable Metropolitan Districts and Standard Metropolitan Areas," *American Sociological Review,* 20 (August, 1955), 414-419.

696 SYLVESTER, DOROTHY, "Durham City," *Sociological Review,* 36 (January-October, 1944), 67-75.

697 TAAFFE, EDWARD J., "Air Transportation and United States Urban Distribution," *Geographical Review,* 46 (April, 1956), 219-238.

698 TAEUBER, CONRAD, "Rural-Urban Migration," *Agricultural History,* 15 (July, 1941), 151-160.

699 —— "Recent Trends of Rural-Urban Migration in the United States," *Milbank Memorial Fund Quarterly,* 25 (April, 1947), 203-213.

700 TALBERT, ROBERT H., *Cowtown Metropolis: Case Study of a City's Growth Structure.* Fort Worth, Texas: Leo Potishman Foundation, 1956.

701 TANNER, JOHN C., "The Sampling of Road Traffic," *Applied Statistics,* 6 (November, 1957), 161-170.

702 TARVER, JAMES D., "Suburbanization of Retail Trade in the Standard Metropolitan Areas of the United States, 1948-54," *American Sociological Review,* 22 (August, 1957), 427-433.

703 TAYLOR, GRAHAM ROMEYN, *Satellite Cities: A Study of Industrial Suburbs.* New York: D. Appleton and Company, 1915.

704 TAYLOR, GRIFFITH, "Environment, Village, and City—A Genetic Approach to Urban Geography, with Some Reference to Possibilism," *Annals of the Association of American Geographers,* 32 (March, 1942), 1-67.

705 —— "The Seven Ages of Towns," *Economic Geography,* 21 (July, 1945), 157-160.

706 —— *Urban Geography.* London: Methuen and Company, Ltd., 1949.

707 TEPPING, BENJAMIN J., WILLIAM HURWITZ, and W. E. DEMING, "On the Efficiency of Deep Stratification in Block Sampling," *Journal of the American Statistical Association,* 38 (March, 1943), 93-100.

708 THADEN, J. F., "The Lansing Region and Its Tributary Town-Country Communities." East Lansing: Michigan State College Agricultural Experiment Station, Special Bulletin, No. 302, March, 1940.

709 THOMAN, RICHARD S., "Portland Maine: An Economic-Urban Appraisal," *Economic Geography,* 27 (October, 1951), 348-367.

710 THOMAS, DOROTHY S., *Research Memorandum on Migration Differentials.* New York: Social Science Research Council, Bulletin No. 43, 1938.

711 —— *Social and Economic Aspects of Swedish Population Movements, 1750-1933.* New York: The Macmillan Company, 1941.

712 THOMPSON, JOHN GIFFEN, *Urbanization, Its Effects on Government and Society.* New York: E. P. Dutton and Company, 1927.

713 THOMPSON, JOHN H., "A New Method for Measuring Manufacturing," *Annals of the Association of American Geographers,* 45 (December, 1955), 416-436.

714 —— "Urban Agriculture in Southern Japan," *Economic Geography,* 33 (July, 1957), 224-237.

715 THOMPSON, WARREN S., "Some Factors Influencing the Ratios of Children to Women in American Cities, 1930," *American Journal of Sociology,* 45 (September, 1939), 183-199.

716 —— *The Growth of Metropolitan Districts in the U.S., 1900-1940.* Washington: U.S. Bureau of the Census, 1947.

717 —— and NELLE E. JACKSON, "Fertility in Rural Areas in Relation to Their Distance From Cities, 1930," *Rural Sociology,* 5 (June, 1940), 143-162.

718 —— and P. K. WHELPTON, "Changes in Regional and Urban Patterns of Population Growth," *American Sociological Review,* 5 (December, 1940), 921-929.

719 THROOP, VINCENT M., *The Suburban Zone of Metropolitan Portland, Oregon.* Chicago: University of Chicago Press, 1948.

720 TISDALE, HOPE, "The Process of Urbanization," *Social Forces,* 20 (March, 1942), 311-316.

721 TOBKIN, LEONARD and EDGAR Z. PALMER, *Types of Business in Nebraska Towns,* Lincoln, Nebraska: University of Nebraska Publication, No. 186, Business Research Bulletin No. 57, 1954.

722 TRUESDELL, LEON E., "The Development of the Urban-Rural Classification in the United States, 1874 to 1949," *Current Population Reports,* Series P-23, Washington: U.S. Bureau of the Census, 1949.

723 TREWARTHA, GLENN T., "The Unincorporated Hamlet: An Analysis of Data Sources," *Rural Sociology,* 6 (March, 1941), 35-42.

724 —— "The Unincorporated Hamlet: One Element of the American Settlement Fabric," *Annals of the Association of American Geographers,* 33 (March, 1943), 32-81.

725 —— "Chinese Cities: Numbers and Distribution," *Annals of the Association of American Geographers*, 41 (December, 1951), 331-347.

726 —— "Chinese Cities: Origins and Functions," *Annals of the Association of American Geographers*, 42 (March, 1952), 69-93.

727 TROREY, LYLE G., *Handbook of Aerial Mapping and Photogrammetry.* Cambridge, England: University Press, 1950.

728 TRYON, ROBERT C., *Identification of Social Areas by Cluster Analysis: A General Method with an Application to the San Francisco Bay Area.* Berkeley: University of California Press, 1955.

729 TUKEY, JOHN W., "Some Sampling Simplified," *Journal of the American Statistical Association*, 45 (December, 1950), 501-519.

730 TURNER, RALPH E., "The Industrial City: Center of Cultural Change," in Caroline F. Ware (ed.), *The Cultural Approach to History.* New York: Columbia University Press, 1940, 228-242.

731 TURNER, RALPH H., "Migration to a Medium-Sized American City: Attitudes, Motives, and Personal Characteristics Revealed by Open-End Interview Methodology," *Journal of Social Psychology*, 30 (November, 1949), 229-249.

732 ULLMAN, EDWARD, "A Theory of Location for Cities," *American Journal of Sociology*, 46 (May, 1941), 853-864.

733 UNITED NATIONS, *Demographic Yearbook, 1948.* New York: United Nations Publication, Sales No.: 1949.XIII.1, 1949.

734 —— *Population Census Methods.* New York: United Nations Publication, Sales No.: 1949.XII.4, 1949.

735 —— *Methods of Using Census Statistics for the Calculation of Life Tables and Other Demographic Measures—With Application to the Population of Brazil.* New York: United Nations Publication, Sales No.: 1950.XIII.3, 1949.

736 —— *Data on Urban and Rural Population in Recent Censuses.* New York: United Nations Publication, Sales No.: 1950.XIII.4, 1950.

737 —— *Demographic Yearbook, 1949-50.* New York: United Nations Publication, Sales No.: 1951.XIII.1, 1950.

738 —— *Fertility Data in Population Censuses.* New York: United Nations Publication, Sales No.: 1950.XIII.2, 1950.

739 —— *Demographic Yearbook, 1952.* New York: United Nations Publication, Sales No.: 1953.XIII.1, 1952.

740 —— *Bibliography of Recent Official Demographic Statistics.* New York: United Nations Publication, Sales No.: 1953.XIII.14, 1954.

741 —— *Demographic Yearbook, 1954.* New York: United Nations Publication, Sales No.: 1954.XIII.5, 1954.

742 —— *Demographic Yearbook, 1955.* New York: United Nations Publication, Sales No.: 1955.XIII.6, 1955.

743 —— *Demographic Yearbook, 1957.* New York: United Nations Publication, Sales No.: 1957.XIII.1, 1957.

744 —— *Report on the World Social Situation.* New York: United Nations Publication, Sales No.: 1957.IV.3, 1957.

745 —— *Population and Vital Statistics Report* (Statistical Papers, Series A, issued quarterly since January, 1953).

746 U.S. BUREAU OF THE BUDGET, *Standard Metropolitan Area Definitions.* Washington: June 5, 1950.

747   U.S. BUREAU OF THE CENSUS, *A Chapter in Population Sampling.*
      Washington: Government Printing Office, 1947.
748   —— *Foreign Statistical Publications,* Washington, issued quarterly.
749   U.S. DEPARTMENT OF COMMERCE, *Better Population Forecasting for
      Areas and Communities* by Van Beuren Stanberry. Domestic
      Commerce Series No. 32. Washington: Government Printing
      Office, September, 1952.
750   U.S. LIBRARY OF CONGRESS, CENSUS LIBRARY PROJECT, *General
      Censuses and Vital Statistics in the Americas.* Washington: Gov-
      ernment Printing Office, 1943.
751   —— *National Censuses and Vital Statistics in Europe, 1918-1939: An
      Annotated Bibliography.* Washington: Government Printing Of-
      fice, 1948.
752   —— *National Censuses and Vital Statistics in Europe, 1940-1948 Sup-
      plement: An Annotated Bibliography.* Washington: Government
      Printing Office, 1948.
753   —— *Population Censuses and Other Official Demographic Statistics of
      British Africa: An Annotated Bibliography.* Washington: Govern-
      ment Printing Office, 1950.
754   VAN ARSDOL, MAURICE D., JR., SANTO F. CAMILLERI, and CALVIN F.
      SCHMID, "The Generality of Urban Social Area Indexes," *American
      Sociological Review,* 23 (June, 1958), 277-284.
755   VAN CLEEF, EUGENE, *Trade Centers and Trade Routes.* New York:
      D. Appleton-Century Co., 1937.
756   VAN PAASSEN, CHARLES, "Stedelijke Overbevolking, Verwaarloosd
      Aspect van de Theorie der Overbevolking" (Urban Overpopula-
      tion: A Neglected Aspect of the Theory of Overpopulation),
      Tijdschrift Voor Economische en Sociale Geographie (Rotterdam),
      46 (December, 1955), 265-276.
757   VANCE, RUPERT B. and NICHOLAS J. DEMERATH (eds.), *The Urban
      South.* Chapel Hill: The University of North Carolina Press, 1954.
758   VEREŠÍK, JÁN, "K Metódam Vymedzovania Hraníc Miest" (Methods
      of Delimiting the Boundaries of Cities), *Geograficky Časopis,* 7
      (1955), 5-14.
759   VINING, RUTLEDGE, "A Description of Certain Spatial Aspects of an
      Economic System," *Economic Development and Cultural Change,*
      3 (January, 1955), 147-195.
760   VON HENTIG, HANS, "The Sex Ratio: A Brief Discussion Based on
      U.S. Census Figures," *Social Forces,* 30 (May, 1952), 443-449.
761   WALKER, MABEL L., *et al.,* *Urban Blight and Slums: Economic and
      Legal Factors in Their Origin, Reclamation, and Prevention.*
      Cambridge, Massachusetts: Harvard University Press, 1938.
762   WALLIS, W. ALLAN and HARRY V. ROBERTS, *Statistics: A New Ap-
      proach.* Glencoe, Illinois: The Free Press, 1956.
763   WARKENTIN, DONALD L., ORRY C. WALZ, and E. JACKSON BAUR,
      "An Index of Urbanism for the West North Central Region,"
      Midwest Sociologist, 19 (May, 1957), 71-78.
764   WARNTZ, WILLIAM, "Measuring Spatial Association With Special
      Consideration of the Case of Market Orientation of Production,"
      Journal of the American Statistical Association, 51 (December,
      1956), 597-604.

765 WATSON, JOHN E., "Travelling Time to Work: Some Notes From the New Zealand Census of 1945," *Social Forces,* 30 (March, 1952), 283-292.

766 WEBER, A. F., *The Growth of Cities in the Nineteenth Century: A Study in Statistics.* New York: The Macmillan Company, 1899.

767 WEBER, MAX, *The City.* Glencoe, Illinois: The Free Press, 1958.

768 WEBSTER, DONALD H., *Urban Planning and Municipal Public Policy.* New York: Harper and Brothers, 1958.

769 WEHRWEIN, GEORGE S., "The Rural-Urban Fringe," *Economic Geography,* 18 (July, 1942), 217-228.

770 WEIGEND, GUIDO G., "Bordeaux: An Example of Changing Port Functions," *Geographical Review,* 45 (April, 1955), 217-243.

771 WEIMER, ARTHUR M., and HOMER HOYT, *Principles of Urban Real Estate.* New York: The Ronald Press Company, 1946.

772 WENDT, PAUL F., "Theory of Urban Land Values," *Land Economics,* 33 (August, 1947), 228-240.

773 WHETTEN, N. L. and DON MITCHELL, "Migration From a Connecticut Suburban Town, 1930-1937," *American Sociological Review,* 4 (April, 1939), 173-179.

774 WHITE, ELIJAH L., and SANFORD M. DORNBUSCH, *Centralization of Churches, Chicago, 1950: The Cost-Utility Approach Applied to the Spatial Patterns of Social Institutions.* Chicago: University of Chicago, Population Research and Training Center, Urban Analysis Report No. 8, March, 1952.

775 WHITING, ROBERT F., "Home-to-Work Relationships of Workers Living in Public Housing Projects in Chicago," *Land Economics,* 28 (August, 1952), 283-290.

776 WHITNEY, VINCENT H., "Notes on the Reliability of Atlasses for Estimating The Populations of Unincorporated Places," *Rural Sociology,* 10 (December, 1945), 387-393.

777 —— "The Estimation of Populations for Unincorporated Places," *American Sociological Review,* 11 (February, 1946), 98-103.

778 —— "Rural-Urban People," *American Journal of Sociology,* 54 (July, 1948), 48-54.

779 WHITTLESEY, DERWENT, "Kano: A Sudanese Metropolis," *Geographical Review,* 27 (April, 1937), 177-199.

780 —— "Dakar and the Other Cape Verde Settlements," *Geographical Review,* 31 (October, 1941), 609-638.

781 WILKINSON, THOMAS O., "The Pattern of Korean Urban Growth," *Rural Sociology,* 19 (March, 1954), 32-38.

782 WILLCOX, WALTER F., "A Redefinition of 'City' in Terms of Density of Population," in Ernest W. Burgess (ed.), *The Urban Community: Selected Papers from the Proceedings of the American Sociological Society, 1925.* Chicago: University of Chicago Press, 1926, 115-121.

783 WILLIAM-OLSSON, W., "Stockholm: Its Structure and Development," *Geographical Review,* 30 (July, 1940), 420-438.

784 WIRTH, LOUIS, *The Ghetto.* Chicago: University of Chicago Press, 1928.

785 —— "Urbanism As A Way of Life," *American Journal of Sociology,* 44 (July, 1938), 1-24.

786 —— "The Urban Society and Civilization," *American Journal of Sociology,* 45 (March, 1940), 743-755.
787 —— "Urban Communities," *American Journal of Sociology,* 47 (May, 1942), 829-840.
788 —— "Human Ecology," *American Journal of Sociology,* 50 (May, 1945), 483-488.
789 WITENSTEIN, MATTHEW M., "Uses and Limitations of Aerial Photography in Urban Analysis and Planning," *Photogrammetric Engineering,* 21 (September, 1955), 566-572.
790 WOLFENDEN, HUGH H., *Population Statistics and Their Compilation,* rev. ed. Chicago: University of Chicago Press, 1954.
791 WOLFF, REINHOLD D., "The Forecasting of Population by Census Tracts in an Urban Area," *Land Economics,* 28 (November, 1952), 379-383.
792 WOOD, WALTER F., "Use of Stratified Random Samples in a Land Use Study," *Annals of the Association of American Geographers,* 45 (December, 1955), 350-367.
793 WOODBURY, COLEMAN, *Urban Redevelopment: Problems and Practices.* Chicago: University of Chicago Press, 1953.
794 —— (ed.), *The Future of Cities and Redevelopment.* Chicago: The University of Chicago Press, 1953.
795 WOOLSEY, THEODORE D., *Sampling Methods for a Small Household Survey.* Washington: U.S. Department of Health, Education and Welfare, 1956.
796 WOOTEN, H. H., *Major Uses of Land in the United States.* Washington: U.S. Department of Agriculture, Technical Bulletin No. 1082, October, 1953.
797 WRIGHT, ALFRED, "Ohio Town Patterns," *Geographical Review,* 27 (October, 1937), 615-624.
798 WRIGHT, JOHN K., "Some Measures of Distributions," *Annals of the Association of American Geographers,* 27 (December, 1937), 177-211.
799 WRIGLEY, ROBERT, JR., "The Sanborn Map as A Source of Land Use Information for City Planning," *Land Economics,* 25 (May, 1949), 216-219.
800 —— "Urbanized Areas and the 1950 Decennial Census," *Journal of the American Institute of Planners,* 16 (Spring, 1950), 66-70.
801 YANG, HSIN-PAO, *Fact-finding With Rural People: A Guide to Effective Social Survey.* Rome: Food and Agricultural Organization of the United Nations, 1957.
802 YERACARIS, CONSTANTINE A., "Differential Mortality, General and Cause Specific in Buffalo, 1939-41," *Journal of the American Statistical Association,* 50 (December, 1955), 1235-1247.
803 YOUNG, PAULINE V., *Scientific Social Surveys and Research,* 2nd ed. New York: Prentice-Hall, Inc., 1949.
804 YULE, G. UDNY and M. G. KENDALL, *An Introduction to the Theory of Statistics,* 14th ed. London: C. Griffin and Company, Ltd., 1950.
805 ZIERER, CLIFFORD M., "Melbourne As A Functional Center," *Annals of the Association of American Geographers,* 31 (December, 1941), 251-288.

806 —— "Land Use Differentiation in Sydney, Australia," *Annals of the Association of American Geographers,* 32 (September, 1942), 255-308.

807 ZIMMERMAN, CARLE C., "Farm Trade Centers in Minnesota, 1905-29: A Study in Rural Social Organization." St. Paul, Minnesota: Agricultural Experiment Station, Bulletin No. 269, September, 1930.

808 —— and LYNN SMITH, "Migration to Towns and Cities," *American Journal of Sociology,* 36 (July, 1930), 41-45.

809 ZIPF, GEORGE K., *National Unity and Disunity: The Nation as a Bio-Social Organism.* Bloomington, Indiana: The Principia Press, Inc., 1941.

810 —— "The $\frac{P_1 P_2}{D}$ Hypothesis: On The Intercity Movement of Persons," *American Sociological Review,* 11 (December, 1946), 677-686.

811 —— "The Hypothesis of the 'Minimum Equation' As A Unifying Social Principle: with Attempted Synthesis," *American Sociological Review,* 12 (December, 1947), 627-650.

812 —— *Human Behavior and the Principle of Least Effort: An Introduction to Human Ecology.* Cambridge, Massachusetts: Addison-Wesley Press, Inc., 1949.

813 ZORBAUGH, HARVEY W., *The Gold Coast and the Slum: A Sociological Study of Chicago's Near North Side.* Chicago: University of Chicago Press, 1929.

Subject Index

Aerial photographs: 59-60, 64-65, 198, 218
Age composition: 84-85, 128-139, 513-515, 577
Age groups: 134, 477-479
Age-sex pyramid: 132-133
Agglomerations: 25, 31-44, 48, 405-412, 425, 474, 486-488
Aging index: 135-136
Agricultural and non-agricultural: 14, 27-30, 33, 42-44, 50, 53-55, 57, 61, 66-72, 74, 255, 273-274, 299-300, 350, 355-356, 406-407, 421, 464-465, 475-476, 485, 496, 542-544, 547, 550-561
Annexation: 38-39, 114-129
Arterial urbanization: 52, 61-62
Australia: 403-412, 429, 433-434

Basic and exchange services: 254-255, 259, 329-349
Bibliography: 7, 11, 581-621
Blocks: 144-145, 148-166, 211-213
Boston: 286-309, 322
Built-up land: 34, 38-39, 52, 60-61
Bus services: 263-268

Census tracts: 145, 148-150, 166-175
Census units, territorial: 62-76, 145
Central business district: 142-143, 146, 187-219
Centralization: 236, 243-246
Coefficient of intraclass correlation: 314-316
Commuting: 42-44, 54-55
Comparative research: 1-3, 11, 42, 77, 129-130

Concentration: 236-239
Concentric zones: 105, 250, 309-328
Conurbations: 20, 42, 45, 47-53

Decentralization: 236, 246
Deconcentration: 236, 239-243
Dependency ratio: 135-136

Economic activities: 24, 26-33, 42-44, 54-55, 66-76, 130, 197, 261-262, 290-307, 329-349, 352-360, 374-390, 405-407, 421, 467, 495-497, 556-561
Economic base studies: 331-332
England and Wales: 47-53, 263-285

Fertility: 10-11, 19, 39-40, 84-85, 130, 506-509, 526-533, 579
Functional types: 255-261, 349-374, 578

Germany: 41-45
Governmental-administrative functions: 10-11, 29-31, 482-486, 577
Gradients: 309-328, 550-561

Hinterlands: 254-328
Horizontal growth: 108-114

Index of local specialization: 333-336, 342-349
Index of surplus workers: 337-349
India: 403-418, 430
Inter-city relations: 260-262, 374-390, 395-397, 436-459, 579

Land use: 61, 202-205
Land values: 199-202

623

Maps: 34-35, 43, 58, 62, 100, 117, 151, 159-160, 174-175, 191-219
Metropolitan areas: 17-18, 42, 62, 73-76, 87, 309-331, 412-418, 421-425, 438-459, 579
Metropolitan regions: 255-258, 286-309, 374-390, 579
Migration: 114-129, 139, 511-513, 544-548, 562-576, 578, 580
Mortality: 10-11, 19, 39-40, 49, 84-85, 130, 507-510, 579

Natural increase: 114-129, 510-511
New York: 286-309, 317
New Zealand: 349-353

Pedestrian counts: 197-198
Planning: 10-11, 580
Political boundaries: 21-31, 34-39, 41, 45-48, 50-51, 57-59, 419-421, 425-429, 475-476, 481-484, 577
Population density: 22-23, 25, 42, 45-47, 54-55, 66-72, 80-99, 108, 195-197, 495-496, 577
Population estimates: 5, 11, 579
Population growth: 18-19, 83-84, 107-130, 412-418, 578
Population projections: 5, 11, 579
Population pyramid: 132-133
Population size: 17-18, 21-31, 45-47, 53-56, 80-85, 351-352, 356-358, 467, 484-486, 492-494, 578
Primacy: 395, 438-440
Puerto Rico: 385-389

Quantification: 4, 100

Rank-size rule: 395, 441-449
Rural farm: 490-504, 532, 550-556
Rural non-farm: 490-504, 532, 550-556
Rural population: 469, 473, 475-480
Rural territory: 25-26, 61, 472-489
Rural-urban continuum: 234, 467-470, 474, 490-504
Rural-urban data: 465, 468-469, 579
Rural-urban differences: 234, 462-539, 579

Rural-urban distinction: 41, 429-431, 435, 466, 469, 472-489, 579
Rural-urban interrelations: 542-549, 550-561, 580

Serbia: 21-31
Service areas: 255-258, 263-285, 580
Sex composition: 84-85, 129-139, 513-517
Shapes of urban units: 80-83, 99-106, 578
Spatial association: 203, 208, 246-249, 578
Spatial distribution of cities: 397, 399-400, 451-459, 578
Spatial structure: 142-147, 176-187, 249-250, 258-259, 309-328, 578
Standard Metropolitan Areas: 51, 114-129, 432-434, 550-552, 557-558
Standard Metropolitan Statistical Areas: 46-47, 53-56
Subject Index to the Bibliography: 11, 20, 85, 147, 262, 400, 471, 549, 577-580
Suburbs: 18, 23, 39, 42, 114-128, 309-328
Surveys: 10-11, 579
System of cities: 397, 436-438

Territorial differentiation: 248, 309-328
Theory: 8-9, 11
Traffic flow: 197-198

Unindustrialized countries: 2, 5, 7, 11, 67, 71, 393, 403, 430
United States: 45-47, 53-56, 114-128, 353-374, 412-418, 431-434, 490-504, 526-533, 534-539, 550-561
Urban areas: 41-44, 57-74, 87, 111-114, 580
Urban data: 10, 26, 42, 50-51, 53, 62, 131-132, 148-165, 419-427, 570
Urban facilities: 29-31, 488-489
Urban facilities, use of: 146-147, 220-234, 269-270

Urban functions: 29-31, 254-255, 269-270

Urban hierarchies: 264, 396-397

Urban influence: 542-561

Urban place: 22-26

Urban population: 21-31, 41, 394, 407-408, 466, 469, 473, 475-480, 580

Urban structure: 23-31, 394

Urban sub-areas: 142-147, 176-187, 220-224, 578

Urban sub-areas, demographic: 178-180, 184-187

Urban sub-areas, ecological: 177-178, 184-187

Urban sub-areas, social: 180-187

Urban territory: 21-31, 34-39, 41-44, 61, 88-89, 466, 570-574

Urban units, boundaries of: 16-20, 21-26, 34-39, 41, 57-77, 103-104, 108-114, 569-574

Urban units, definitions of: 3, 14-16, 19, 21-31, 34, 41, 405-407

Urbanism: 9-10, 394-395, 473-474

Urbanization: 392-435, 462-465, 534-539, 542-543, 580

Urbanization, degree of: 392-394, 408-409, 419-435

Urbanized Areas: 45-47, 60, 66, 433-434, 493-494

Urban-size hierarchy: 394-395, 410-412, 441-451

Vertical growth: 108-114

Zoning regulations: 86-99

DATE DUE

2. 07. '85	

BRODART, INC

Cat. No. 23-221